The Evolution of Love

The Evolution of Love

Theology and Morality in Ancient Judaism

Sheldon W. Liebman

WIPF & STOCK · Eugene, Oregon

THE EVOLUTION OF LOVE
Theology and Morality in Ancient Judaism

Copyright © 2021 Sheldon W. Liebman. All rights reserved. Except for brief quotations in critical publications or reviews, no part of this book may be reproduced in any manner without prior written permission from the publisher. Write: Permissions, Wipf and Stock Publishers, 199 W. 8th Ave., Suite 3, Eugene, OR 97401.

Wipf & Stock
An Imprint of Wipf and Stock Publishers
199 W. 8th Ave., Suite 3
Eugene, OR 97401

www.wipfandstock.com

PAPERBACK ISBN: 978-1-7252-7471-6
HARDCOVER ISBN: 978-1-7252-7472-3
EBOOK ISBN: 978-1-7252-7473-0

04/05/21

Contents

Acknowledgements | vii

Introduction | 1

Chapter One: The Traditional View of Judaism | 22
    The Jews in the New Testament | 26
    Deicide, Legalism, and Pharisaism | 39
    Judaism and Quid pro Quo | 51

Chapter Two: The Contemporary View of Judaism | 63
    The Pharisees Revisited | 68
    Retrojection | 76
    Who Killed Jesus? | 92

Chapter Three: The Pentateuch | 104
    In the Beginning | 109
    The Exodus | 126
    In the Wilderness | 142

Chapter Four: The Covenant | 159
    The Pentateuch Revisited | 164
    The Prophets | 178
    Repentance | 195

Chapter Five: A Crisis of Faith | 210
    The Old View in the Psalms and Proverbs | 212
    The New View | 227
    Disillusionment | 244

Chapter Six: Apocalypse | 264
    Intertestamental | 269
    The Essenes at Qumran | 287
    The Christian Jews | 297

Chapter Seven: Covenant, Community, and Compassion | 308
    Doing the Will of God | 310
    Perfectionism | 324
    Love | 335

Chapter Eight: The Hidden Revolution | 350
    The Disappearance of God | 352
    The Restoration of God | 369
    The New Covenant | 388

Endnotes | 403

Bibliography | 497

Acknowledgements

For Sheldon Liebman, *The Evolution of Love* was his deep expression of love for the origin and tenets of Judaism. It was also his final scholarly achievement. Sheldon died September 15, 2020, with the manuscript in the editing process. As his loving partner, my role quickly switched from caregiver to next-steps-taker. And so, let me first extend my deepest appreciation to the team at Wipf & Stock Publishers—particularly Caleb Shupe, Zechariah Mickel, and Emily Callihan—for their kind words of comfort and their professional expertise in assisting me, an untested novice, to understand and continue moving the pre-publication process forward.

Although battling a raging cancer, revising and perfecting the manuscript for *The Evolution of Love* in the spring of 2020 was Sheldon's purpose and focus, and brought him great joy. And while he could no longer join in the lively discussions over drinks and supper in little cafes with colleagues from Wilbur Wright College, their outpouring of affection, respect, and support helped sustain him.

Among those colleagues, I extend my most heartfelt gratitude and indebtedness to Adrian Guiu, PhD, who, in addition to his own rigorous academic schedule, offered to step in after Sheldon's death to assist in the completion of the editing process. He did so with enthusiasm and an abundant knowledge of Sheldon's ideas and beliefs, and the query phase of editing was completed November 17, 2020, on what would have been Sheldon's eightieth birthday.

As Sheldon's health declined, his voice and our conversations waned to literal whispers of our former passionate discussions, arguments, agreements. But the early Judaic principles he embraced through decades of religious study remained constant in both frequency and consistency: Love your neighbor. Welcome the stranger. Take care of everyone.

Gail Fiske Crantz
La Grange Park, Illinois
November 22, 2020

Introduction

What I have found has been in many ways surprising to me, and though not surprising to experts in the field, may be surprising to readers of [my] book.
—ROBERT N. BELLAH, *RELIGION IN HUMAN EVOLUTION*

THIS BOOK IS AN examination of Judaism as it evolved over a period of approximately 1,500 years, from the middle of the second millennium BC to the early first millennium AD. It is not a history of the Jews from the time of Abraham onward. Rather, it is an analysis of the Hebrew Bible and other ancient Jewish writings, with special emphasis on the two most important concepts in the study of religion: theology and morality.

My objective is to show how the faith of the Israelites developed from a fairly typical "primitive" religion into something entirely new: a religion that was in many ways significantly different from most of the established faiths of the ancient world. As Alan F. Segal says, "Judaism underwent radical religious changes in response to important historical crises."[1] More specifically, Judaism began as a set of beliefs that were in many ways indistinguishable—and to some degree derived—from those of other societies in the Near East.[2] And these beliefs developed, eventually, into a religion that embraced many of the main features that characterized the major religions of the Axial Age: Taoism, Buddhism, Zoroastrianism, and Platonism.

As different from each other as these religions may be, they share the common assumption that the universe is not ruled by amoral and impersonal gods that must be appeased by sacrifice or controlled by magic. Unlike the Egyptians and many other residents of the Near East, who worshiped many gods and understood them to be morally imperfect,[3] they collectively affirmed the idea that the relationship between humanity and the Other—whether it is called God or Nature or Spirit—is not based on fear and sustained by the performance of rituals. On the contrary, it is honored and supported by human beings who conduct their lives according to such principles as virtue, compassion, and justice. To be sure, according to two of the religions that emerged in the first millennium BC—Judaism and Zoroastrianism—the universe is ruled by a force whose capacity to inflict pain and provide pleasure far surpasses the offensive and defensive capabilities of mankind. Instead of being cowed and controlled by the kind of superior power that a mighty king might use against his subjects, however, members of both of these faiths, as well as Taoists, Buddhists, and Platonists are invited to participate freely in a world order that requires moral probity, not abject submission and blind obedience.

According to Segal, "Dislocation, war, and foreign rule forced every variety of Jewish community to rebuild its ancient national culture into something almost unprecedented, a religion of personal and communal piety."[4] Speaking of the book in which this spiritual metamorphosis appears most clearly, Robin Lane Fox says that Deuteronomy is "a text of commands and warnings which struck a new and alarming note in the entire history of Hebrew texts." Focused on "God's orders for human behavior," the book is "not so much a code of ceremony and ritual as a book of conduct and commandments."

On the one hand, Fox continues, Deuteronomy covers a broad range of subjects, describing as it does "the proper attitudes of the Israelites in worship, their justified aggression toward their heathen neighbors, their respect for the poor and the defenceless, their festivals, some of their rules of law and the right behavior of their kings." On the other hand, however, it is the theological and moral formulation "of a single, jealous God who required total love from his chosen people" and thereby "distinguished Israel from her Gentile neighbors." Indeed, even in its discussion of "some of the great festivals and ceremonies," Fox adds, the book "emphasizes the scope for inner piety and charity on these occasions."[5]

What is different about the faith of the Jews, however—that is, what separates it from the four religions mentioned above—is that Judaism did not suddenly break away from existing religious traditions, at least in the same way that Taoism, Buddhism, Zoroastrianism, and Platonism turned their backs on the ancient religions of China, India, Persia, and Greece. Nor was Judaism founded by one man (or the followers of one man), as were the religions established by Lao-Tse, the Buddha, Zoroaster, and Plato. This means that Judaism is not represented by the ideas of a single person and is not understandable by reading a single brief book—such as the *Tao-te-Ching*, the *Gathas*, the *Sayings of the Compassionate Buddha*, or the *Phaedo*—composed by either the religious founder or his disciples. Rather, Judaism developed over a very long period of time, its principles are expressed in a very large book written by many different writers, and its dominant ideas and practices are often inconsistent and contradictory. For these reasons, the Hebrew Bible—and, consequently, ancient Judaism itself—has long been regarded as extremely difficult to explain—which is, again, the main objective of this book. There are several obstacles.[6]

Change. According to Alfred Gottschalk, "Revolutions within religious thought, reformations of its beliefs and practices, 'updating' and adjustments to the times, are not new to the thoughtful student of the history of religion."[7] Thus, as I said, the religion of the Jews changed over time, particularly in relation to its view of God and its

Introduction

definition of morality. Stephen A. Geller asks, "Can one summarize biblical religion in a way that will organize its disparate traditions?" He answers, "The Bible is the most unsystematic of sacred texts, representing 1,000 years of textual development from different areas and social and religious groups."[8] As Meek explains: "[T]he Hebrew Torah is not one consistent whole, the creation of a single legislator, Moses, or anyone else. Law does not originate in that way. It comes into existence slowly to meet the ever-changing needs of the time, and this is more evident in the Hebrew Torah than in any of the other codes, because we have here not one book but several, separated by many centuries of time."[9]

On the subject of God, Robert Wright says, "If you read the Hebrew Bible carefully, it tells the story of a god in evolution, a god whose character changes radically from beginning to end."[10] Thus, according to John Barton, although Christians (and no doubt others) read the Jewish Bible "to learn about God," they "are soon disappointed. They find that the God it shows them is, at best, something of a mixed blessing. Although at times he is loving, gentle and trustworthy, at others he seems capricious, harsh and unfeeling."[11] Mark S. Smith comments: "The historical reconstruction of Israel's religion that notes the variegated roles of state and popular religion, the mixture of indigenous and imported religious features, and the complex features of convergence and differentiation undermines some of the main scholarly views about Israelite religion in general and Israelite monotheism in particular."[12]

On the subject of morality, Barton comments: "Any historical study of ethical conduct, norms and systems in ancient Israel is bound to be highly complex, for the OT provides material from which to reconstruct the life and thought of a whole nation over a period of about a thousand years; and we could hardly expect that everything would have remained the same throughout this period."[13] James L. Kugel reminds us that "[t]he Hebrew Bible is actually not one book, but an anthology." Some parts of this collection "go back very far, at least to some time in the tenth century BCE—or considerably earlier," while "[i]ts latest chapters . . . belong to the early second century BCE." Because it was "written over the course of a thousand years, the texts themselves were likely to "disagree with one another on the most fundamental matters."[14] Indeed, Barton says elsewhere that "the huge *variety* of ethical commitments and points of view" in ancient Israel means that "[a]nyone who wants to treat the biblical text as an absolute authority will have problems in deciding which line of thought is to be followed in this matter."[15] In short, as Jon D. Levenson has said, "this notion that all the literature of the Hebrew Bible, which was composed over a millennium, has one message presents grave historical problems."[16]

As we shall see, if the student of ancient Judaism begins with the book of Genesis, he or she will encounter a deity who is first described in highly anthropomorphic terms. This God is referred to as having body parts (hands and feet), a voice, and a volatile temperament, which allows him to pass through a wide range of emotions, including satisfaction, disappointment, and anger.[17] Yet he is consistently friendly to

3

and supportive of all of the patriarchs, to whom he offers advice and assurances of his goodwill, speaks intimately and warmly, and—except for his condemnation of Adam and Eve, their son Cain, Noah's contemporaries, the builders of the Tower of Babel, and the residents of Sodom and Gomorrah—seldom provides negative criticism, at least to the patriarchs and their wives. Like some other gods of the ancient world, he is simply called El, which means "god." And he offers no moral code. He uses words such as *righteous* and *blameless*, but he never bothers to explain what these words mean. Indeed, he seems far more interested in cultic matters—such as circumcision and the construction of altars—than in morality.

In this regard, according to Frankfort, speaking especially of Egypt, Israel at the time was very much like its neighbors, who, finding no correlation between "man's dependence upon God and God's concern for man"—which is, after all, the main theme of both the Old and New Testaments, absent though it may be from Genesis—offered "no specific divine commands which gave man directives for the shaping of his actions." The Egyptian gods "require[d], in a general way, that man respect Maat," the principle of justice and order, but otherwise they "remain[ed] aloof." As a result, the Egyptians "were without divine guidance in their daily lives.[18] According to J. E. Manchip White, the Egyptian gods had no basis for making moral demands since they "were not categorized as good or bad."[19]

However, the God who first appears in Genesis is, through the centuries, transformed into a more powerful and transcendent deity, who is often not only angry with his people, the Israelites, but quite punitive; jealous of their worship of other gods; and impatient with their ongoing failure to believe in his promises, unlike the patriarchs, their ancestors. To be sure, God tells the Israelites his name, Yahweh; provides them with a large body of both ceremonial and moral laws—all of this in spectacular fashion at Mt. Sinai; and spells out precisely the terms of their relationship. Unlike El in Genesis, however, who asks for little in return for his promises of security and prosperity, Yahweh in the middle books of the Pentateuch requires obedience to his commandments in exchange for his many gifts. He is no longer a friend, as he was in Genesis (except to Moses, of course), but a king, who not only rules through the threat of violence—indeed the complete destruction of the Hebrew people—but also engages in the mass murder of the native population of Canaan, not because these people are sinful, but merely because they occupy the land that he has promised to the Israelites.

By the middle of the first millennium, with the writing of Deuteronomy, the Psalms, and the works of the prophets, Judaism had embraced the idea that God is a compassionate father; that his relationship with his people is based on love rather than fear; that his response to their commission of sins is based on the assumption that they are capable of repentance and worthy of forgiveness; and that, rather than the threat of murder, he can use chastisement to bring them back to faith and obedience. In other words, the Covenant, which was first established as an almost unconditional promise

Introduction

in the book of Genesis and became a treaty-based *quid pro quo* agreement in the books of Exodus and Numbers, finally became a document in which love—mutually shared and equally proffered—emerged as the foundational principle of Judaism.[20]

It is also clear that the story of the liberation of the Israelites from oppression in Egypt eventually became a basis in the literature of the ancient Jews for the view of God as the Redeemer and Savior whose act of salvation was an expression of his grace and mercy, as well as love, that could only be responded to with gratitude—that is, matching love. The prophets and psalmists, in particular, as well as the intertestamental writers, returned again and again to this event and understood it in the same way and with the same fervor that Moses recalled it in Deuteronomy.[21]

Discontinuity. What muddies the water, however, is the fact that this transition across a thousand years was not a linear development. As Robert Wright explains: "You can't just start reading the first chapter of Genesis and plow forward... The first chapter of Genesis was almost certainly written later than the second chapter of Genesis, by a different author. The Hebrew Bible took shape slowly, over many centuries, and the order in which it was written is not the order in which it appears."[22] The God of love, who makes his strongest appearance in Deuteronomy, is first introduced much earlier, in Exodus—briefly in 20:6 and more emphatically in 34:6–7. The idea that the Covenant is a *quid pro quo* agreement, which dominates the books of Exodus and Numbers, persists in many psalms and proverbs, especially the latter. The portrayal of Yahweh as a God of War, who emerges first in Exodus, reappears not only in Deuteronomy, but also in the books of Joshua and Judges, as well as many of the psalms. The concept of forgiveness, which is important to the prophets, is introduced by Joseph in the final pages of Genesis. And the command that human beings should love each other makes its first appearance in Leviticus 19:18, as part of the Holiness Code.

Furthermore, Judaism retained its earliest legends, such as the stories in Genesis and Exodus, which remained inspirational not only in the remaining books of the Pentateuch, but also in the works of the prophets and psalmists, including God's covenant with Abraham and the Israelites' disobedience at Sinai, as well as the liberation from Egypt. As Bernhard W. Anderson explains: "The most distinctive feature of the Jewish people is their sense of history." Indeed, "Judaism is the religion of a people who have a unique memory that reaches back through the centuries to the stirring events of their Bible, events that formed them as a people with a sense of identity and vocation. Whenever the Passover is celebrated, whenever the law is celebrated in the synagogue, whenever a parent instructs his child in the tradition, this memory is kept alive."[23] According to Robert N. Bellah, whereas the Egyptians and Mesopotamians "elided ... from [their] cultural memory" any evidence of their "premonarchical development," the Jews retained their memory of that experience, which, of course, plays "a prominent role in the Hebrew Bible."[24]

Yehezkel Kaufmann says that, in refusing to ignore the past, the ancient Jews also distinguished themselves from the Greeks and Indians: "In marked contrast to the repudiation of Greek popular religion by the higher religion of Greece's philosophers, or Buddhism's independence of and aloofness toward the religion of the masses, biblical religion neither disdains nor detaches itself from the popular legends."[25] Meek makes the same point about Jewish laws, which not only arose to meet new needs, but remained, as did the laws of other Near Eastern countries, a veritable hodge-podge of precedents with no discernible order or clarity: "New and old material is found in all of them, even the latest, so that the Torah, as we have it, is the accumulation of centuries, a legislative snowball that has rolled down the avenues of time, gathering more and more material from various sources the further it rolled and taking on new forms with every change in the course."[26] Thus, says Michael E. Stone, "when we make statements about 'developments' or 'innovations' or the like, we cannot mean that with the emergence of each new stage all vestiges of the past vanish and no intimations of the still unborn future can yet be discerned."[27] That is simply not the way the Bible was composed.

In other words, it is not as if, in the so-called Axial Age of the first millennium BC, one Judaism replaced another, as Greek philosophy supplanted the religion of Zeus and his associates or Buddhism turned its back on Vedic Hinduism. Rather, at different times and in different places, Yahweh was worshiped as a God of mercy as well as a God of vengeance, faithfulness was expressed in ceremonial activities as well as moral actions, and morality itself was understood to be a matter of obedience as well as love. Unlike Christianity, with its Nicene Creed and Westminster Confession, there was no point at which Judaism was understood to embrace a particular view of God, a particular statement of faith, or a particular body of practices. As Raymond E. Brown explains, "The need to give expression to the centrality of Jesus in the new covenant made Christianity a creedal religion in a manner dissimilar to Judaism."[28]

Diversity. In short—and this is the third major obstacle to understanding Judaism—the Jewish faith remained a religion without a creed, meaning that it is and always has been diverse in belief and practice, with many quite varied ideas and actions competing for legitimacy as expressions of the one true faith. On the one hand, some scholars argue that there *is* an essential Judaism that, despite the disagreements, is shared by all Jews. Donald H. Akenson says that there are four basic principles of Judaism, pertaining to the divinity of Yahweh, the legal authority of the Pentateuch, the special status of the Jews, and the importance of the Temple.[29] W. H. Davies names three main ideas in the Jewish faith: (1) "The One God . . . [who] was Holy in his will, and asked of man to love mercy and to do justly"; (2) "The One People . . . with] a special relation between the One God and the One people'; and (3) "The One Law . . . [in which] the God of Israel had revealed his will."[30] Patrick D. Miller argues that Israelite religion culminated in a faith that could be called "orthodox and normative." It was "probably best represented in the words of the prophets, the history as told by the Deuteronomists and the religious system by which they measured it, and the cultic establishment of the priestly elements and writers of exilic and postexilic Judah."[31]

Introduction

On the other hand, however, most scholars emphasize the diversity of Judaism. George F. Moore, for example, suggests that although there is no way to summarize or explain the essence of Judaism, it "survived because it succeeded in achieving a unity of belief and observance among Jews in all their wide dispersion then and since." However, "this unity and universality . . . was not based upon orthodoxy in theology, but upon uniformity of observance."[32] Referring to the many biblical stories that Jews had to interpret, James D. Tabor says: "[T]here was no systematic treatment of these and a hundred other subjects related to the core beliefs of Judaism. What characterized Jewish life . . . was this endless ongoing discussion and debate of the meaning and interpretation of the stories, commandments, and teachings of the Torah and the Prophets."[33] Speaking of the pre-exilic period, Miller says: "Any effort to describe the religion of ancient Israel comes up against clear indications that, as in most religious communities, there was not a single understanding or expression of what that religion was. Both biblical and extrabiblical evidence suggest a certain degree of pluralism, of multiformity rather than uniformity."[34]

Ekkehard W. and Wolfgang Stegemann argue that "the postexilic situation in the land of Israel was shaped by 'multicentrism, heterogeneity, and socio-religious multiplicity.'"[35] Furthermore, according to L. Michael White, after the sixth century BC, "the Judean state and Jewish religion were in constant flux due to the external political forces. The responses were as much religious as political, and in the process new religious ideas, groups, and practices resulted within the broad spectrum of what we may call 'formative Judaism.'"[36] Thus, says Paul Joyce, "it is in any case always risky to speak about typical 'Israelite Thought' as something that may be precisely described (largely because Israel and its literature contain such an enormous variety of ways of thinking)." And this, in turn, is "because Israel was such a diverse entity, extending through many centuries, increasingly spread out in many lands, and producing a great variety of religious literature."[37] Segal attributes this diversity in belief partly to the spread of Judaism to the Roman-controlled Diaspora: Hellenization, the dominant cultural tendency of the Empire, brought about a "wider diversity of opinion" and individualism.[38]

Speaking of the intertestamental period, from 200 BC to AD 100, D. S. Russell comments: "The Judaism of the period . . . was a most complex system, containing within itself many different parties and groups and sects whose names and distinctive beliefs have not always been recorded in history. To quote the words of R. H. Pfeiffer, 'Judaism in the period under consideration was so alive, so progressive, so agitated by controversies, that under its spacious roof the most contrasting views could be held.'"[39] All of this was particularly true in the first century AD, when Jesus—like the leaders of the Essenes, the Pharisees, and other Jewish groups—offered yet another interpretation of Judaism to his fellow Jews.

According to John P. Meier, "Judaism around the time of Jesus was a rich tapestry of many different religious tendencies."[40] James Charlesworth says of this period,

"Most scholars have come to discard the concept of 'normative Judaism' for pre-70 phenomena." Jews "shared a common confession: the Shema"—the famous Jewish prayer that announces the oneness of God and his requirement to love him with heart, soul, and might (Num 6:4–9). However, they embraced different ways of obeying this commandment. As Charlesworth puts it: "Suffice to say for the present that Early Judaism was not anarchistic and totally torn apart. Neither was it so unified and systematic as scholars have tended to portray it. We should not think about Judaism as a uniform 'religion'; rather, we should think about *Judaisms* and the various dimensions and freedom of expression and reflection before 70."[41]

Multiple sources. Of course, if Judaism had flourished in a homogeneous society, it might have had a chance to develop a single theology and a single morality. As it happened, however, "the Jews have always been diverse," says Anderson, not only in theology and culture, but "even in racial characteristics."[42] Kaufmann notes that the Israelites were, from the very beginning, made up of a variety of ethnicities: "Israel is thus depicted as an ethnic mixture of Hebrew, Aramaic, Canaanite, and Egyptian elements."[43] We think of the Israelites as made up exclusively of twelve *Hebrew* tribes, but, according to Meek, this was not the case. The tribes who settled in the north "were more native than Hebrew and became Hebrew only as they were drawn into the Hebrew confederacy by a common peril." And the southern tribes, led by Judah, Simeon, and Levi, were joined by "Kenites, Calebites, Kenizzites, and Jerahmeelites."[44]

Meek also mentions the fact that—no doubt, partly because of its geographical location and ethnic diversity—Israel borrowed freely and extensively from its neighbors, thus "adding the attainments of others to [its] own," but also significantly diversifying the pool of ideas from which it drew.[45] After all, as Bellah argues, "Israel was not . . . an isolated society or one surrounded only by tribal peoples. It was, rather, one of several 'frontier societies' with highly differentiated religious systems. Probably in premonarchical and certainly in early monarchical Israel something of archaic polytheism was present."[46] Merrill C. Tenney says: "As long as the people lived in Palestine, surrounded by prosperous and powerful heathen neighbors and subjected to their influence, they were tempted to experiment with alien worship and to desert"—at least for a time—"the God of their fathers. The prophets protested in vain against this tendency which had appeared during the wilderness wanderings of the people (Num. 25:13), and which had persisted into the period of the captivity and exile" (Ezek 14:1–5; Jer 7:16–20).[47]

Thus, Geller argues that "biblical religion is not a unity but rather a congeries of differing and often competing opinions and traditions." Of "the three major forms of biblical religion in the Bible"—Deuteronomic, Priestly, and Wisdom—all are derived, to some degree, from foreign sources. As revolutionary as Deuteronomic religion may be, its covenantal formula comes from Hittite sources. Judaism's so-called Priestly religion, which dominates the book of Leviticus, comes from the cultic traditions that constitute the common heritage of the Near East (and, indeed, the rest of the world). And

Introduction

Wisdom religion, which appears in the book of Proverbs, is easily traceable to both Egypt and Mesopotamia.⁴⁸ William A. Irwin says, "It has long been recognized that a considerable portion of the Old Testament legal system, notably the social legislation in Exod. 21–23, was originally Canaanite but received Israel's characteristic stamp."⁴⁹ In short, according to James Muilenburg, "It is obvious that the literary materials [of the Hebrew Bible] are of great complexity, that various sources have gone to their making, and that the point of view of the compilers has left it stamp upon their compilations."⁵⁰

Gerhard von Rad argues that, unlike Greek thinking, which "seeks a 'uniform natural principle' of the cosmos, . . . Hebrew thinking is thinking in historical traditions." The result is a mixture of "acts of revelation" and other events "without a centre": "The most varied traditions are superimposed upon one another, and even interwoven. Thus, a fragment of archaic uninterpreted legend can without the least difficulty be brought into conjunction with a text which has been subjected to thorough theological reflection." Especially in the case of the earliest books of the Bible, "a number of old, detached tribal or local traditions, previously quite unrestricted in in range and currency, were incorporated in the Hexateuch or the Deuteronomic history; but now they are all related to 'Israel.' In the process the old disassociated traditions have been given a reference and interpretation which in most cases was foreign to their original meaning."⁵¹

However, even if Israel had not been a multi-ethnic society and had borrowed nothing at all from its neighbors, the Jewish Bible would still have been a complicated text for the simple reason that it was not composed by a single writer. Although every book of the Bible might have been inspired by God, each book was written by a different person (or persons), some living in the northern kingdom, some in the southern, some living in exile, and all living at different times, from the eighth through second centuries BC. The situation is further muddled by the fact that the answer to Richard Elliott Friedman's titular question, "Who wrote the Bible?" is "We really don't know" because *all* of the books of the canonical Hebrew Bible are anonymous. As Fox explains, speaking of a work included in the Apocrypha, "Not until c. 200 BC is a Hebrew author known to us by name in a surviving text: Jesus ben Sirach, author of our Bibles' Ecclesiasticus." Even the Jewish books written after Ecclesiasticus but before the writing of the New Testament, with the exception of the works of Philo and Josephus, were anonymous compositions.⁵²

Furthermore, scholars as early as the eighteenth century speculated that the frequency of "doublets" in the Pentateuch, particularly in Genesis and Exodus,⁵³ meant that some stories had been written by two different writers, who came to be known as J and E, based on whether they called God *Jahweh* (the German spelling of Yahweh) or *Elohim*. Eventually, four different writers were identified, including, in addition to J and E, the Priestly writer (who was largely responsible for the end of Exodus, all of Leviticus, and the beginning of Numbers) and the Deuteronomist (who was responsible for Deuteronomy and the history books that follow it, from Joshua to 2 Kings).⁵⁴

Thus, Karen Armstrong says, "[w]hen the editors fixed the canons of both the Jewish and Christian testaments, they included competing visions and placed them, without comment, side by side." Furthermore, "biblical authors felt free to revise the texts they had inherited and give them entirely new meanings."[55]

William M. Ramsay says that "the book of Exodus in the form we now have it used different versions of the same stories, traditions that had been passed down orally by different tribes in different places before being written down for different purposes." Ramsay also notes that other books of the Bible are similarly compromised by multiple authorship, including the prophecy of Isaiah, which is now understood to have been composed by three different writers, before, during, and after the exile.[56] I use the word *compromised* because the problem presented by these twice-told tales is twofold. First, in some instances, such as the two versions of Joseph's betrayal by his brothers, there is no way of knowing which story is true. Did the resolution of the conflict come from Reuben or Judah? Was Joseph sold to strangers or put into a pit? And who were his new captors, Ishmaelites or Midianites?[57]

More significantly, as Friedman says, the different writers of these stories, often presented side by side, offer different views of God, morality, and religious practice. Friedman says: "The combination of sources did more than just affect individual Bible stories. It had an impact on the biblical conception of God. J, E, and D pictured God in very personal ways: moving around on the earth, taking visible forms, engaging in discussion and even debate with humans. P's conception was more of a cosmic, transcendent deity." Furthermore, Friedman adds, "[i]n the P text"—meaning the entire body of P's work in the middle books of the Pentateuch—"there is not a single reference to God as *merciful*." Indeed, "[t]he very words 'mercy,' 'grace,' 'faithfulness,' and 'repent' never occur."[58] Ramsay observes that, faced with multiple views of the important issues, among other daunting problems, "people are known to begin reading the Bible, full of high expectations for finding inspiration and guidance, only to give up the study after a few pages out of confusion—even boredom."[59]

Summarizing these issues, Cuthbert A. Simpson says that between the sixteenth and eighteenth centuries scholars identified three problems related to the composition of the Pentateuch: "(a) the occurrences of two or more versions of what appeared to be the same incident, (b) the inconsistencies in the narrative, and (c) its recurring chronological difficulties."[60] Anthony J. Saldarini states that such problems as these may have resulted, in part, from the fact that the books of the Bible were copied and redacted by "copyists and unsystematic interpreters" who "made comments and interpretations at various points in the text, some of which have been incorporated into the text as we have it." Furthermore, we have no way of identifying the "various groups" who participated in this process, many of whom, because of "[c]onflicts within society," inevitably "produced competing interpretations." Saldarini concludes, "All the Biblical materials have been passed on in such a complex way that the activity of

Introduction

learned interpreters and tradents must be postulated for all of Israel's history from the monarchic period on."[61]

Several other problems have been identified by Mark Smith. First, some Bible passages refer to "mythic images," such as Leviathan and other "cosmic foes" of God, without including the "mythic narratives" from which these figures derive, giving the reader "only a glimpse of the larger understanding" that the original narrative would provide. Second, many biblical texts "have been written so much after the fact or have undergone such long redactional histories" that "[t]he work [of interpretation" necessarily "remains highly inferential." Third, despite the availability of archeological and iconographic evidence, the lack of "aid from roughly contemporary textual sources" makes it difficult to be confident about the reliability of many textual accounts. Furthermore, "biblical material"—that is, the resources that make interpretation possible—are "unevenly . . . distributed over the history of ancient Israel." Consequently, Smith adds, "much more is known about the late monarchy," for example, "than either the period of the judges or the first half of the monarchy."[62]

Subjectivism. Another obstacle to an objective understanding of Judaism is the fact that *all* acts of interpretation are made difficult by two elements: the ambiguity of the texts and the subjectivity of the interpreters. Both issues have been thoroughly explored by Bible scholars and theologians. Speaking of all writing, Robert Wright says that, because "words can have more than one meaning," the act of reading "involves making choices"—that is, inevitably *arbitrary* decisions.[63] Speaking of all sacred texts, Robert M. Grant says that the essential problem in the interpretation of any religion is that "the primary documents are not self-explanatory."[64] And speaking of the Hebrew Bible, Jon D. Levenson notes that the meaning of a particular passage changes as we read other passages and that the meaning of the whole text can change as we read other related texts. That is, "just as each piece on a chess board changes the meaning and value of every other piece, so does each text in the Bible change our readings of all the others." Levenson adds, "Just as text has more than one context, and biblical studies more than one method, so scripture has more than one sense."[65]

Segal says that ancient Judaism was characterized by "the proliferation of competing sects and interpretations of Scripture" for "two reasons": "First, the text itself is refractory. What the Torah means to say is not always clear. Second, and more important (as I mentioned earlier), Hellenization of the country made a greater variety of responses to the ancient document both possible and necessary, in order to comprehend the wider diversity of opinion and individualism encouraged by Hellenistic society."[66] To the first point, Shaye Cohen says that, to both "modern literary critics" and "ancient Jewish exegetes," the ancient texts were "multivalent, that is, they convey numerous meanings." Thus, "no single interpretation could accurately reflect all meanings imparted by the text."[67]

To the second point, Wright argues that, just as people from different cultures inevitably interpret texts from different perspectives, so do people from different

11

time periods: "When the context of the original composition is very different from the reader's context—long ago or far away, or both—the choices made may steer the text away from the author's intent."[68] Abraham Heschel comments: "All language is relative, adapted to the ideas and associations cherished in a particular age and capable of evoking them. But so is our understanding relative, attuned to the ideas and associations cherished in our age. In reading ancient words, it is difficult to ascertain the ideas which they represented and the thoughts which they sought to evoke in their contemporaries."[69]

Another consequence of reading a text from a great distance in time and space is that it may appear to be so strange and alien as to be forbidding, as well as incomprehensible. As Bellah says, "From the point of view of a modern historical approach, the data concerning ancient Israel, and the scholarly interpretations of the data, are very nearly baffling."[70] Indeed, in the view of many scholars and even general readers, the Bible seems to be unapproachably removed from either understanding or appreciation. According to John Barton, part of the problem is that "the book which to Christians . . . seems a comfort and an inspiration strikes others as thoroughly barbaric and alien; it seems to come from a world so remote from our own that it can have nothing to say to us." The Jewish Bible, in particular, Barton adds, is problematic because of "the Old Testament's rootedness in a culture which is not ours, its internal contradictions, and its use of categories of thought which are alien to modern thinking about morality."[71] Muilenburg says that, for such reasons, "the Old Testament is unintelligible outside of Israel, the living historical community which passes through varying vicissitudes and through deep chasms of crisis and destruction."[72] And John J. Collins adds, "To understand the Bible in its historical context is first of all to appreciate what an alien book it is."[73] Thus, E. P. Sanders argues, "The act of historical understanding requires that this alienation be overcome and that the ancient religion be seen as it really is."[74]

These spatial and temporal limitations on our ability to understand a text as the original author intended it to be understood contribute to the second problem, the subjectivity of the interpreter. Indeed, in Wright's words, they "combine to give believers"—i.e., readers or interpreters—"great influence on the meaning of their religion." Indeed, "people can look at their holy texts and see what they want to see—see what meets their psychological, social, political needs."[75] This is because interpretation depends on the context of the Interpreter as well as the context of the work in question. Tim Gorringe explains: "The sociology of knowledge"—an area of study developed by Karl Mannheim—"establishes that what we write, as authors, or what we understand, as readers, is profoundly influenced by the society in which we live and our place in it. Exegesis which takes account of these factors will ask of the text, of the commentary and of the reader questions about the type of society they come from, their class allegiance and where they stand in relation to the conflicts of their society." In short, "the reader always brings a 'pre-understanding' to the text,"[76] and the pre-understanding may be religious as easily as it may be political.[77]

Introduction

Thus, Mark Smith comments, concerning interpretations of ancient Judaism, "like the ancient historians of Israel, modern historians investigating ancient history often have a personal, theological interest in the subject, even if they attempt to maintain a critical distance from the subject. Indeed, the research of modern scholars is dictated in large measure by both the concern with historical accuracy and scholars' religious interest in the biblical record."[78] Barton points out that the distortion that concerns Smith and many other contemporary scholars is not necessarily a product of conscious anti-Semitism, but merely a consequence of reading the Bible from a religious perspective: "The vast majority of biblical interpreters until very recently have been religious believers. Many have worked in ecclesiastically supported colleges and faculties, and most have been intensely interested in the religious relevance of their exegetical work. E. P. Sanders's trenchant criticisms of most scholars who have written on Jesus and Paul show that their reconstructions have normally been heavily influenced by their religious beliefs: by the need to show the uniqueness of Jesus, or the essentially Lutheran character of Paul's teaching."[79]

Depending on where and when we are engaged in the interpretive act—specifically, what we have learned, what we believe, and what we value—we bring our own biases to the act of interpretation, so that not only "whatever is written is written from some point of view," as John P. Meier has said, but also whatever is observed is observed from some point of view. That is, everyone "writes from some ideological vantage point; no critic is exempt."[80] Segal says that every Jewish sect in the ancient world—and the point applies to every religious sect, past or present—"quite naturally read the Torah *as if it uniquely prophesied their position.*"[81] Many scholars have noted that this naïve kind of interpretation began to be challenged in the eighteenth century. According to John Rogerson, for example, "Before 1750, critical scholarship was ultimately a defence of whatever type of orthodoxy a scholar accepted . . . After 1750, critical scholars were more prepared to let their biblical scholarship challenge their own orthodoxy."[82]

Nevertheless, Meier says that "the legion of scholars"—no doubt, including some scholars in the modern period"—"peered narcissistically into the pool of the historical Jesus only to see themselves."[83] Thus, Kugel argues, despite the currently almost universal awareness (at least, among scholars) that because bias is inherent in *all* faiths it must be confronted, analyzed, and (as much as possible) minimized, if not expunged, the task is evidently harder than it appears to be. Committed to the scientific principles of modern literary criticism and quite willing to dispense with the "ancient interpretive methods" that were maintained by the Christian church until the last century, modern scholars nevertheless suffer from the need to defend or protect their own religious beliefs while they simultaneously honor the standards of scientific criticism. The result is an unsatisfactory effort to occupy the middle ground between the old and the new: "In fact, so much of what liberal theologians and commentators have to say is typically not all that modern scholarship has brought to light, but rather represents an attempt to find a compromise between that scholarship and what the commentators themselves would still like the Bible to be . . . At times, their interpretations are scarcely less forced than those of ancient midrashists [i.e., interpreters] and usually far less clever."[84]

Misrepresentation. The biggest obstacle to our understanding of ancient Judaism, however, is the fact that this kind of subjectivity is not only a danger to any contemporary student of the Bible. It was also a very serious problem for the many writers in the ancient world who left us with a rather large body of writings that have for many centuries served as a principal source of our knowledge about the Jews and their religion. Among Jewish writers, for example, Josephus, the first-century historian, wrote from the point of view of a sympathizer with the Imperial Roman government as well as a defender of Judaism. Philo wrote as a Hellenized Jew who defended Judaism against the criticism of his Greek-speaking contemporaries in Alexandria. And the Jews who wrote the Hebrew Bible were patriots—defenders of the faith—who were obviously committed to presenting their co-religionists in the best possible light.[85] In short, subjectivity, including some degree of misrepresentation, has been a longstanding feature of the very sources with which any student of the Jewish religion must deal and on which any conclusions about that subject necessarily depend.

The problem facing twenty-first-century students of ancient Judaism, however, is not the inevitable bias of Jews writing about Jews, which is predictable and therefore both understandable and discountable. Rather, the problem is now understood to be the extraordinary bias of *non-Jews* writing about Jews. It goes without saying that the Romans were sometimes contemptuous of Judaism, although their hostility did not ordinarily result in gratuitous acts of discrimination and violence. As Alan F. Segal explains, "Anti-Semitism was known during the Hellenistic period. But it was not especially prevalent. More often than not the anti-Jewish writings of Greeks and Romans turn out to express a general dislike of foreigners rather than a specific anti-Semitism."[86]

However, the other non-Jewish sources of information about the ancient Jews and their religion were written by Christians. And *their* hostility to their religious opponents, unlike that of the pagan Romans, was often virulent, destructive, and unremitting. At the very least, as Jay Parini says, "the evangelists each had a subjective view, an intended audience, with ideological assumptions that would have shaded their reflections."[87] But historical circumstances made those personal points of view far more negative than they would have been otherwise. Shortly after the Revolt of AD 66, when Jews began to expel Christian proselytizers from their synagogues, and Christians were struggling for their survival—conflict became increasingly hostile, which deeply affected the evangelists, who at that very time were composing their accounts of Jesus' interactions with his fellow Jews. Thus, John P. Meier says, "The Gospels reflect the struggle between nascent Christianity and nascent rabbinic Judaism."[88]

Introduction

According to Karen Armstrong, "A thread of hatred runs through the New Testament. It is inaccurate to call the Christian scriptures anti-Semitic, as the authors were themselves Jewish, but many of them had become disenchanted with Jewish religion." By the time John wrote his Gospel, in Armstrong's words, the "bias" against the Jews, represented by the Pharisees, turned into "vitriolic hatred."[89] This means, of course, that many of the available sources of information on the ancient Jews, including accounts written by Matthew and Luke, were undermined by distortions, exaggerations, and outright misrepresentations.

The idea that Christians mischaracterized the Jews and portrayed their religion unsympathetically and therefore negatively is a commonplace among contemporary scholars. John Shelby Spong, for example, argues that "a wretched spirit of anti-Jewish hatred was . . . pervasive" among Christians from the Gospel writers onward. And later Christians continued to believe that "the Gospels were the word of God, were objectively true, that they described events of literal history, and that all that was contained therein did in fact happen just as it was written." They read the Gospels "with a deeply prejudiced anti-Jewish bias that distorted their understanding." And "this bias was challenged less and less as the years rolled by, until this attitude became viewed, not as a prejudiced distortion, but as an unchallenged kind of orthodoxy." Spong continues, "It was, furthermore, on the basis of these gentile interpretations that the creeds, theological systems, and ecclesiastical superstructures of the Church were erected."[90]

This means that even the most objective student of Judaism is unable to achieve a true understanding of or come to reliable conclusions about ancient Judaism insofar as they are based—uncritically—on this collection of judgments and interpretations. The problem is compounded by the fact that, although the New Testament picture of the Jews has been seriously challenged by Bible scholars, historians, and theologians in recent years, this challenge has had little impact on the thinking of contemporary Christians, who have always suffered from the same lack of knowledge that, as Meier says, inspired "the rabid anti-Jewish polemic of many patristic writers," such as St. John Chrysostom and St. Jerome.[91]

To be sure, for the past millennium and a half, almost nobody (except scholars) has read the writings of anti-Semitic Romans. Unfortunately, however, most Christians have read at least parts of the New Testament without understanding its limitations as an objective record of Christian-Jewish relations. This is partly why the other source of Christian hostility to Judaism is Christian scholarship—more specifically, the work of *many* scholars over most of the past two millennia who either wittingly or unwittingly looked at Judaism through the distorting lenses of anti-Judaism and anti-Semitism, particularly those who relied on the New Testament for their information. This is an issue that has been systematically ignored for centuries, but it has been brought to the attention of the scholarly community (as well as the reading public, to some degree) in the past half century, particularly as a consequence of the intense and comprehensive study of the Jewish background of Jesus, taken up in the last few decades by both Jewish and Christian students of the Bible and the history of early Christianity. Thus, as Mark Smith says, "[i]n rendering a picture of ancient Israel, modern historians customarily avoid the heavily theological interpretations of events that lace biblical historiography."[92]

Since I intend to examine this subject in some detail in the first two chapters of this book, I will defer further commentary until then. Suffice it to say that references to both biblical and scholarly anti-Judaism and anti-Semitism can be found in Paula Fredriksen, *From Jesus to Christ*, xxvi–xxvii; Martin Hengel, *The Four Gospels and the One Gospel of Jesus Christ*, 31–33; Donald H. Akenson, *Saint Saul*, 52–53; Charles Guignebert, *The Jewish World in the Time of Jesus*, 71; Marcus Borg and John Dominic Crossan, *The Last Week*, xi, 127–28; James Carroll, *Constantine's Sword*, 73, 85, 103; and Amy-Jill Levine, *The Misunderstood Jew*, 119,124–25, 158–59. The most important book-length studies of the subject are Rosemary R. Ruether's *Faith and Fratricide*, John G. Gager's *The Origins of Anti-Semitism*, James W. Parkes's *The Conflict of the Church and the Synagogue: A Study of the Origins of Antisemitism*, and Charlotte Klein's *Anti-Judaism in Christian Theology*.

The Contemporary View of Judaism. After I examine the subject of misrepresentation in my first two chapters, I will turn to a study of ancient Judaism from the perspective of modern biblical scholarship. From this point of view, Judaism emerges as an ongoing attempt to answer two fundamental questions, as the title of this book suggests. The first is the theological question, Who is God? The second is the ethical question, What does he want us to do? As I discussed above, the answers to these questions are complicated because the religion of the ancient Jews came from many different sources, was influenced by many different cultures and their religions, and changed over time in what can best be described as fits and starts.

Indeed, the answers are further complicated by the fact that the Jewish Bible can be said to preserve many of these different sources and influences and to represent, therefore, a multiplicity of views. Speaking only of the evolution of the concept of theophany but making a point that applies to all aspects of ancient Judaism, James L. Kugel comments: "The history of divine encounters as reported in the Bible is not one step forward and then the next, but includes lateral jumps, idiosyncratic depictions that become traditional for a time, followed by later imitations and slight modifications, then fresh starts and various subsequent resumptions and reiterations."[93]

Despite these problems, however, it is possible to demonstrate that ancient Judaism began as a more or less generic faith, similar in terms of theology and morality to other so-called primitive religions of the second millennium BC. As I said earlier, it is equally possible to show that the Jewish faith developed over the ensuing centuries into a religion very similar to those that arose in the mid-first millennium in China, India, Persia, and Greece: namely, Taoism, Buddhism, Zoroastrianism, and Platonism. This change first began in Israel under the prophets of the eighth through

Introduction

sixth centuries and continued under the psalmists in the exilic and post-exilic periods and under the Deuteronomist sometime in the middle of the first millennium. Ancient Judaism reached what most scholars consider to be its final stage of development under the Pharisees and the Rabbis in the early centuries of the Common Era, when it became the foundation of modern Judaism.

Again, despite the haphazard way in which the Jewish Bible was composed—especially its mixture of legend and history—it is widely assumed that the earliest phases of ancient Judaism can be seen in the first four books of the Pentateuch, which are believed to lead from the origins of Judaism through several phases of its development. In Genesis, God's primary goal is to be obeyed. He tells Adam not to eat "of the tree of the knowledge of good and evil," and he orders Noah not to commit murder and not to "eat flesh with its life, that is, its blood." Although he neglects to tell them in advance, God evidently wants the patriarchs not to engage in forbidden sexual acts or to construct high towers, but, as he does tell them, to be righteous, to build shrines dedicated to him, and even to sacrifice their children if he requests it. More explicitly, they must perform circumcisions, clearly an act that has no purpose other than to honor God by fulfilling the patriarchs' part of the Covenant. Notably, the word "righteousness," which God attributes to both Noah (6:9, 7:1) and Abraham (15:6) is never defined in Genesis, and God's interest in morality—except for prohibitions against murder, sodomy, and onanism—is minimal.

Aside from his banishment of Adam, Eve, Cain, and the builders of the Tower of Babel, as well as his destruction of all of humanity (except for Noah and his family) and the residents of Sodom and Gemorrah (except for Lot and his daughters), God is a friendly advisor in Genesis, who has been described by scholars as a personal god, usually identified with and accessible to tribal chieftains, and therefore known among ancient Jews as the God of Abraham, Isaac, and Jacob, who are heads of clans or tribes. As James Muilenburg explains: "With each of the patriarchs there is associated a special theophany in which the deity reveals himself in a highly personal way ... These were family or clan gods with family names and associations."[94] Thus, God occasionally appears to people one-on-one—as he does with the patriarchs, especially but not exclusively (12:7, 17:1, 18:1, 26:2, 35:9), at which times the recipients of God's visit sometimes either fall on their faces in astonishment or bow "to the earth" as an expression of worship. Except for these few incidents, as well as God's or his angel's encounter with Jacob in Haran (28:12–15), God ordinarily speaks to people invisibly; his speech is unaccompanied by any pyrotechnics; and he delivers his helpful and more or less unambiguous message in a measured, unemotional manner.

In Exodus, despite his self-description as a God of mercy, graciousness, love, faithfulness, and forgiveness (34:6–7), God seems to be interested in promoting his reputation *as God*—to the Egyptians as well as the Israelites (7:4–5; 8:10; 9:14–16, 29; 10:1–2; 11:9; 14:4, 17–18; 15:1–18)—and discouraging the worship of other gods. Moses is able to persuade God not to kill all of the Israelites for their idolatry by reminding him of his Covenant with the patriarchs *and his concern for his reputation among the Egyptians*: "Why should the Egyptians [be able to] say," Moses says to God, "'With evil intent did he bring them forth, to slay them in the mountains, and to consume them from the face of the earth'? Turn from thy fierce wrath, and repent of this evil against thy people" (32:12).

Although much of Exodus is devoted to spelling out in great detail what God means by "righteousness," one-fourth of the book is devoted to directions for building "a sanctuary" (including a tabernacle, a tent of meeting, and an ark for the Covenant) and establishing a priesthood. Nevertheless, God offers the Israelites a long list of commandments and makes it perfectly clear what he expects from them as part of his Covenant with them. Besides announcing himself to Moses as Yahweh, God has evidently turned into a God of War. He performs both small and large miracles, including the rescue of the Israelites from Egypt, the destruction of the Egyptian army, and the care and feeding of his people in the desert. On Mt. Sinai, his actions are carried out in an atmosphere that can only be described as spectacular—including, as it does, thunder, lightning, an earthquake, and "a very loud trumpet blast." God speaks understandably only to Moses, but his voice is loud enough to be heard by the hundreds of thousands of people in attendance, whose reaction is, of course, a mixture of terror, confusion, and awe.

In Leviticus, entirely composed by the so-called Priestly writer, God is associated with "mercy" only in reference to the "mercy seat," which the editors of *The Oxford Annotated Bible* define as "the cover of the ark," which serves as "the footstool of the Lord's throne" in the tabernacle (99–100). The word "love" occurs, importantly and famously, in what might be called the capstone verses of the Holiness Code, God's command to love both "neighbor" and "stranger" (19:18, 34), but nowhere else. As the editors of the *Oxford Bible* also mention, outside of the Holiness Code (chs. 17–26), the God of Leviticus focuses on directions for the worship of God—including laws of sacrifice, priestly consecration, purity laws, the Day of Atonement, and religious vows. Except for chapter 19, the Code is largely devoted to issues pertaining to cultic matters.

In the first ten chapters of Numbers, also written by the Priestly writer, God continues to focus on aspects of worship. After this, when the story of the exodus journey is resumed, the fierce God of Exodus reappears and deals again with the disobedience of his people, this time, however, far more harshly and unforgivingly than he does in Exodus. Here, instead of responding sympathetically to the Israelites' "murmurings," God interprets them as hostile acts and, once again, threatens to kill everyone: "How long will this people despise me?" (14:11, 28, 35; 17:10). He responds favorably to Moses' passionate request to relent because *Moses, once again, tells God that his act will stain his reputation*, not just among the Egyptians, but to "the nations who have heard thy fame" (14:13–16).

In the earlier books, God does not merely want to be obeyed; he also wants to be worshiped—indeed, as he is in some psalms, praised and lauded for his power,

Introduction

majesty, and righteousness. Not until Exodus does he show any interest in morality. And, even then, his commandments are (1) a mixed bag of moral and ceremonial laws; (2) presented as a test of his people's loyalty, violations of which result not only in the loss of God's rewards but also in the loss of life; and (3), at least in Numbers, violations of which are not merely treated as sins but as personal insults to God. God responds to these offenses by imposing no fewer than five plagues on his people, resulting in thousands of deaths (11:33, 14:37, 17:47, 25:8–9, 31:16). Again, as far as God is concerned, the Israelites' expressions of regret (about leaving Egypt in the first place), frustration (regarding difficult living conditions in the Sinai desert), and uncertainty (concerning their destiny and God's intentions) are nothing more than spiteful and mean-spirited reactions to his extraordinary devotion and beneficence.

As a glance at the major Jewish works of the mid-first millennium (including Deuteronomy) demonstrates, a different view of God developed—and one that led directly to the God of the Pharisees and Rabbis. It is especially in the work of the prophets and the psalmists that a radically new picture of God emerges. Here, he is a father rather than a king, asking for love rather than fear, and responding to wickedness or disobedience not just in anger, but in a wide variety of ways, including sorrowfully, compassionately, graciously, mercifully, forgivingly, patiently, and helpfully. His options are no longer limited either to ignoring humanity's' failures or to punishing "the wicked" severely, even irrevocably, but to pity, chasten, discipline, and especially *teach* them, as the individual cases required.

In several psalms, either God expresses his *intention to teach* his laws to the Israelites (32:8, 34:11, 132:12), or the Israelites express their *desire to be taught* (25:4, 27:11, 51:6, 86:11, 90:12, 94:12, 143:10). Psalm 119, for example, is a long poem in which the psalmist repeatedly states his wish to learn and asks God to teach him his commandments. In Deuteronomy, Moses explains to the Israelites that he has been ordered by God "to teach [them] statutes and ordinances (4:1, 9, 14; 5:31; 6:1, 18:20) and that they must in turn teach the laws to their children (6:7, 11:19).

Having heard the cries of the psalmists, God presumably understood that his people were not always—indeed, perhaps very seldom—disobeying out of contempt or indifference, as the God of the book of Numbers continually charges, but because of uncontrolled desires, manifesting themselves in acts of greed, covetousness, lust, and selfishness; as well as other kinds of shortcomings, such as weakness, lack of understanding, forgetfulness, or negligence. And it was evidently, as he saw it, part of his covenantal obligation to caution them, strengthen them, educate them, remind them, and chasten them as an expression of his undying love. Some people were "hapless"— that is, unfortunate—the psalmist says (10:8, 10, 14), because they were victimized, exploited, or oppressed—and God is therefore appealed to throughout the psalms because he offers such people a "refuge." And he helps them not because they have earned a reward but because he pities them.

Furthermore, if the Israelites had actually acted contemptuously or indifferently, God was also, again, as a consequence of his covenantal relationship with them, ready to forgive them as long as they were willing to admit their wrongdoing and change their ways—that is, repent. Anyone might be beset by obstacles, but everyone, no matter what limitations he or she was living under, was capable of understanding an admonition, rebuke, or chastisement and responding to it in the prescribed manner—that is, by feeling contrite, asking for forgiveness, and promising to reform. Even in Exodus, God provides Moses with "the tables of stone," which he has "written *for their instruction*" (24:12; my emphasis). And, in Deuteronomy, God's secret is that, during the exodus from Egypt, he was *teaching* the Israelites, although they were unaware of his motives (8:2–3): "Know then in your heart that, as a man disciplines his son, the Lord your God disciplines you" (8:5). In Psalm 89, God promises to punish those who "forsake [his] law" by "punish[ing] their transgression with the rod and their iniquity with scourges," but he "will not remove [them] from [his] steadfast love" (vv. 30–34).

The intertestamental literature is particularly emphatic about God's desire to subject every individual to a spiritual test, as Judith acknowledges: "[L]et us give thanks to the Lord God, who is putting us to the test as he did our ancestors" (8:25). Sirach says: God "rebukes and trains and teaches, and turns them back, as a shepherd his flock. He has compassion on those who accept his discipline and who are eager for his precepts" (18:13–14). And the result was, of course, forgiveness, as Tobit explains: "If you turn to him with all your heart and with all your soul, to do what is true before him, then he will turn to you and will no longer hide his face from you" (13:6).[95] The result of the "test" was not, as it had been in the past, a kind of trial that people would either pass or fail, but an opportunity for them to learn and change.

What God teaches, of course, is the Covenant Code, presented in three books of the Pentateuch, which provides not so much guidelines for individuals—even though it offers specific laws obviously intended to mandate justice in every sphere of life—but *principles* of social, economic, and political organization that lay the groundwork for establishing a society based on and driven by God's most important attribute—compassion. In conformity with these values, the prophets speak eloquently and persistently in opposition to any and all violations of the Covenant ideals and make it clear that oppression and exploitation, the enemies of social order, are unacceptable whether they are practiced by kings, landowners, merchants, priests, tradesmen, or peasants. To be sure, the prophets indicate, they are the everyday crimes of the rich and powerful, but they are particularly dangerous because they contaminate every level of human society. And they are expungable only if every individual repents—that is, not merely acknowledges his or her sin and asks for forgiveness but undergoes a profound transformation that enables everyone to embrace the covenantal ideals sincerely and completely.

Although the earliest psalms merely reiterate the idea of God as the administrator of a cosmic system of rewards and punishments, the later psalms underscore

Introduction

the ideals of the prophets, condemning as they do the kinds of social and economic crimes that characterized all urban agricultural societies in the ancient world. Here, however, it is not the voice of angry prophets speaking for God that we hear, but the voice of suffering humanity, who raise the kinds of questions about God's justice and mercy expressed more directly in Ecclesiastes and the book of Job. The pathetic cry of "How long, O Lord?" however, remains unanswered, as it is by Job and Koheleth. And it clearly expresses a pervasive question that also remained unanswered throughout much of the postbiblical period. For many scholars, the time between the destruction of the First Temple in the sixth century BC and the destruction of the Second Temple in the first century AD was a time of growing disappointment and disillusionment, particularly regarding God's moral program of *quid pro quo*, which appears in Deuteronomy and some earlier Jewish writings.

In the context of centuries of foreign occupation, ongoing conflict between the haves and the have-nots, and the persistent maldistribution of rewards and punishments, many ancient Jews turned to messianism, apocalypticism, and political rebellion in an effort to preserve their hopes for freedom and justice. Indeed, Jewish sects of the intertestamental age—most obviously, the Essenes, Christians, and Pharisees—rededicated themselves to the laws of the Covenant in an effort to change the situation they found themselves in and practiced their respective versions of Judaism in *imitatio Dei*—that is, perfectly, in imitation of God. To be sure, the rebellions invariably failed, the hope for God's transformation of the world faded, and, under the leadership of the Pharisees (and later the Rabbis), most Jews turned to a democratized, personalized, and individualized version of their faith, with special emphasis on the study of the Torah and the other books of the Jewish Bible.

In the final stage of the development of ancient Judaism—that is, extending from the mid-first millennium BC to the first and second centuries AD—we can see something roughly definable and understandable emerging as yet another refinement of this body of beliefs. Particularly, if we focus on what most modern scholars regard as the foundational writings of ancient Judaism—that is, the many iterations of the Covenant—we can identify a core body of theological ideas and moral principles that can be said to constitute the religion of the Jews. Specifically, what came out of that long evolution of faith was a religious and social vision based on the love of God and the love of humanity. That vision was understood to require not only faith but the enactment of the will of God—specifically, the establishment of a community based on political, economic, and social laws that enforce the principles of justice and mercy. And that process came to be seen as inevitably and necessarily dependent on human agency—the need for human beings to fulfill God's commandments. In Judaism, loving neighbors (and strangers) came to be understood as the principal—and, for many Jews, the *only*—way of loving God.

Chapter One

The Traditional View of Judaism

THE PICTURE OF JUDAISM that has dominated New Testament scholarship for most of the past two millennia is based primarily on the description of the Jews and their religion in the four Gospels and Acts of the Apostles. From the perspective of these works, Judaism was a failed religion, rejected by Jesus and superseded by Christianity. For their part, the Jews not only rejected Jesus, but also killed him for what they considered to be the sin of blasphemy. As Paula Fredriksen explains, "Most New Testament scholars, taking their cue from the controversy stories" in the Gospels, have claimed that Jesus' death was arranged "by Jews whom he had offended religiously." His offense was his announcement "in his person and ministry that the authority of the [Jewish] Law had come to an end" and that "[h]enceforth salvation would be accorded to whoever responded in faith to him." In this way, "Jesus at least implicitly proclaimed also the end of Judaism as a religion . . . Jews hearing such a message, Jesus knew, would naturally kill the messenger; and that, through the agency of Rome, is what they did."[96]

The faith that Jesus passed on to his disciples thus replaced Judaism as the New Israel. And this religion won the day because it was based on universalism (an appeal to all people) rather than particularism (an appeal to Jews only), salvation through grace rather than works, and the idea of God as a father rather than a king, demanding love rather than obedience. Indeed, owing to the inability of the Jews to follow the religion they inherited from Moses—that is, their inability or unwillingness to obey God's laws and live up to the standards that God established in the Jewish Bible—God himself rejected the Jews and established a New Covenant with the followers of Jesus. Fredriksen comments: "The [Jewish] religion had so lost its way that it no longer understood the very concepts that stood at the heart of its own scriptures, namely, ethical monotheism and the mission to the Gentiles. Small wonder that, with the arrival of a religious movement that was true to these principles, spiritually desiccated [Judaism] ceased to be a viable religion."[97]

James Carroll reminds his readers that, by the time the New Testament was written, the "new Christians" used the words "the Jews" to refer to a group to which Jesus'

The Traditional View of Judaism

followers no longer belonged. "It is at this point that something unprecedented and truly dangerous began to happen. 'Jews' became the embodiment of the other. Because the conflict was cast as one between good and evil, . . . 'the Jews' now became identified in the minds of Christians with the devil. An ethos of fulfillment became an ethos of demonization."[98] Even as recently as 2011, N. T. Wright said of Jesus' fate in the first century, "Rome and rebel Israel are the unwitting tools of Satan."[99] In the absence of any doctrinal, theological, or scholarly tradition in which the Romans are vilified as demonic forces, this kind of statement can only sustain the ongoing myth of Jewish service to the Devil.[100]

This view of Judaism has persisted for two reasons. First, throughout most of the past two thousand years, the Bible has been read as if it were the word of God. Since it is divinely inspired, it is, by definition, assumed to be inerrant—that is, true in every word. Thus, since Jews and their religion are negatively portrayed in the New Testament, many Christians have unquestioningly accepted (and perpetuated) this view.[101] This idea was not challenged until the eighteenth century, the Age of Reason, when new theories of knowledge enabled some philosophers and historians to question not only the validity of all revealed religions (that is, religions based on revelation), but also the accuracy and authenticity of all sacred texts associated with them.

In the course of the ensuing reassessment of Christianity and both testaments of the Bible, the traditional picture of Jesus and Judaism came under scrutiny, especially by students of a new discipline called theology.[102] Jaroslav Pelikan says, "During the . . . Enlightenment of the seventeenth and eighteenth centuries, the orthodox Christian image of Jesus Christ came in for severe attack and drastic revision."[103] Some theologians also questioned the idea that first-century Judaism was so reprehensible as to be unacceptable and therefore inevitably supplanted by Christianity.

The second reason for the endurance of the traditional view of Judaism arose in the nineteenth century, when other theologians developed a concept of Judaism that gave the traditional, Bible-based theory the respectability it had begun to lose in the Age of Reason. Specifically, in the face of the reexamination of the Bible initiated by the rationalists and Deists of the eighteenth century, Julius Wellhausen and others presented a new theory of the historical development of Judaism that supported the New Testament view. Briefly, Wellhausen argued that Judaism reached its moral peak in the writings of the prophets but fell to its nadir under the influence of the so-called Priestly writings, particularly the books of Leviticus and Numbers.

The message of the prophets, which Jesus heard loudly and clearly, first appeared in the eighth, seventh, and sixth centuries BC. The laws concerning food, purity, and ritual appeared in the post-exilic period and reshaped Judaism between the fourth century BC and the lifetime of Jesus. To Wellhausen, according to S. David Sperling, the change in Judaism was "accompanied by an increasing formalism and legalism."[104] Thus, what Jesus encountered, particularly in the words and actions of the Pharisees, is a religion that had (1) severed its connection to its own spiritual foundations, (2) foundered because it had turned from the religion of the prophets to the religion of the priests; and (3) abandoned its sacred duties, namely those defined by the moral pronouncements of Isaiah and others.

Jon Levenson calls attention to the fact that, in Wellhausen's view, the religion of the Jews was simply dead. The problem, specifically, was not merely the book of Leviticus, which is mostly given over to cultic issues, but the entire Torah—the Pentateuch. That is, in Wellhausen's words, "what distinguishes Judaism," the depraved and departed form of the Jewish religion, "from ancient Israel," represented by the writings of the prophets, "is the written Torah." Indeed, the oral Torah was put into written form at the very moment that it was in the throes of death, and it represents "the ghost of ancient Israel." Levenson continues: "The ultimate apparition of this ghost, according to Wellhausen, was the Pharisees of Jesus' day who were 'nothing more than the Jews in the superlative'—narrow, legalistic, exclusivistic, obsessive, compulsive, and hypocritical."

The only thing to be thankful for is that Wellhausen did not embrace *all* the ideas of his mentor, G. W. F. Hegel, which included the claim that the Jews could not accept Christianity because the divine "cannot make its home in excrement."[105] Levenson adds, "The use of death language to describe Judaism was hardly unique to Wellhausen among Christians in Germany in the last century [i.e., the nineteenth]. Schleiermacher [in 1799] described Judaism as 'a dead religion . . . whose practitioners sit lamenting in the presence of their 'imperishable mummy,'"[106] an accusation that, according to Hans W. Frei, expressed "the animus which many Rationalist, Romantic, and Idealistic thinkers bore toward" what many of them considered to be "Jewish particularism."[107]

The relevance of the Wellhausen hypothesis to the first-century relationship between Judaism and Christianity is clear in the following summary by Joseph Blenkinsopp: "[T]he historical development" of Judaism, "after reaching its apex in prophecy, ended in spiritual failure and *prepared for the advent of Christianity*."[108] According to Blenkinsopp, this theory "seems to imply in the first place that post-biblical Judaism . . . is a different entity from the [religion of the] Old Testament and represents, in effect, a disintegration . . . Coming as it does between the Old Testament and early Christianity, it can providentially serve to illustrate the problem to which the New Testament provides the answer or, alternatively, the failure of a way of life (works, observances) which highlights by contrast the Christian dispensation (grace)."[109] In other words, Judaism was the problem, and Christianity was the solution. As N. T. Wright puts it, the question was (and still is) whether the promise of Judaism "is anything more than a dream." To this theological query, Wright responds: "The whole New Testament is written to answer that question. And the answers all focus, of course, on Jesus of Nazareth."[110]

Wellhausen explains the decline of Second Temple Judaism explicitly in his article on Judaism in the *Encyclopedia Britannica*: "The Creator of heaven and earth becomes the manager of a petty scheme of salvation; the living God descends from his throne to make way for the law. The law thrusts itself in everywhere; it commands and blocks up the access to heaven; it regulates and sets limits to the understanding of the divine working on earth. As far as it can, it takes the soul out of religion and spoils morality." Says Blenkinsopp, summarizing Wellhausen, Judaism ends "in *Erstarrung* [rigidity, ossification], the dead hand of ritualism, heteronomy, and institutional control." How does Christianity fit into this scheme? Wellhausen answers by distinguishing between "Old Testament" religion, which is the prophetic (and authentic) version of the Jewish faith, and "Judaism," which is its priestly (and legalistic) bastardization: "Judaism is a mere empty chasm over which one springs from the Old Testament to the New."[111] "Jewish legalism," says Sperling, "was contrasted by Wellhausen with the person of Jesus for whom 'love is the means, and the community of love the end.'"[112]

Equally important is the fact, in Blenkinsopp's words, that Wellhausen's idea "dominate[d] Old Testament theology down to the very recent past." It was "enormously influential."[113] "In fact," Levenson says, "few scholarly models have been more enduring in any field than the degenerative model of ancient Israelite history in biblical studies, with its ideal early period being progressively corrupted by Jewish priests and legists."[114] This thesis was repeated, with some variations, by several Old Testament scholars, such as Hermann Schultz, Eduard Konig, and Walther Eichrodt, and endured well into the twentieth century. For example, in a work first published in 1980, John Riches restates the Wellhausen hypothesis. Speaking of "the major authoritative literary corpus of the second Temple period, namely the Pentateuch," Riches says that its "singular achievement . . . was to have created a system of divine laws centred on the worship of the Temple and administered by a hereditary priesthood, the Aaronides. In so doing they set very firm limits on the prophets and subordinated Israel, not to the living word of Yahweh, spoken through his prophets, but to the codified Law given once to his servant Moses and now administered by a central authority, the High Priests and the Great Council."[115]

Charlotte Klein devotes an entire chapter to this subject, entitled "'Late Judaism' and 'Jewish Religious Community,'" in which she discusses the work of more than twenty European (mostly German) scholars. "What is common to the authors cited here," Klein says, "is their view of Jewish religion after the Exile. They see it as a break with the true Yahweh-faith of ancient Israel. Something new emerged, a kind of ethical world-view which can scarcely be called religion any longer. The former religion, founded on trust and love for the God who had rescued the Israelites from bondage and made them his covenant-people was forgotten, and a progressive decline set in, leading away from Israel to Judaism." Klein adds later: The Jewish faith—as described by such famous and influential scholars as Emil Schurer, Martin Dibelius, Gunther Bornkamm, Georg Fohrer, and Martin Noth—went through a period of "decadence," at the end of which Judaism had become "externalized and rigid." In addition, "God had become a distant God and the prophetic message was forgotten."[116]

Wellhausen acknowledged that he had synthesized the ideas of several predecessors, which means that he was the major figure in a scholarly tradition that extended from Immanuel Kant, who believed that Judaism underwent a "levitical corruption" in the post-exilic period,[117] to Eichrodt, who made the same point: "The essence of the Jewish religion of the Law may therefore be seen as a regulation of the God-Man relationship which exhausts itself in endless casuistry, and leaves the heart empty . . . The fact that Jesus and his apostles had recourse to the Old Testament in their description of the right attitude toward God witnesses plainly to the fact that in them the inner schizophrenia of Jewish piety . . . had been overcome, and that the liberation of Man for willing surrender to God had once more emerged into the light of day."[118] Of course, this concept of the relationship between Judaism and Christianity is nothing more than a particular expression of a long-standing general theory. According to Daniel C. Maguire, "Christians have disparaged the genius of Judaism and their filial debts to it partly to aggrandize Jesus and Christianity. Discontinuity was valued over continuity, so that Jesus could be seen as the fulfillment of that which was faintly presaged in Israel."[119]

The Jews in the New Testament

It is impossible to read any of the Gospels without seeing that Jesus' encounters with his fellow Jews were basically unsuccessful. From the perspective of the evangelists, Jesus was offering salvation. However, the reaction he almost invariably received was not gratitude but hostility. He was questioned, contradicted, and spurned by Jews who found his words and actions offensive and contemptible. In the synoptic Gospels, Jesus is challenged again and again not by Zealots or Sadducees (except, by the latter, in Matt 12:18, Mark 22:23, Luke 20:27), but by Pharisees,[120] who appear to be offended by his violations of Jewish law and, as a result, dedicated to having him arrested and punished. Jesus and/or his disciples are criticized by one or more Pharisees for dining with sinners, refusing to fast, declining to wash their hands before eating, and healing or plucking grain on the Sabbath.

In addition, the Pharisees demand a sign that validates Jesus' authority, and (except in the Gospel of Luke) they question him on the subjects of divorce and paying taxes to Caesar. In Luke, the Pharisees refuse to be baptized and, later, accuse Jesus of allowing a sinner to wash his feet. Sometimes, the Pharisees are paired with the scribes (legal experts associated with the Temple). And, in some instances, Jesus is challenged by non-Pharisees. In Mark and Matthew, respectively, Jesus is questioned on the subject of fasting by "people" (Mark 2:18) and by the disciples of John the Baptist (Matt 9:14). Jesus is asked which is the "first of all" commandments by a scribe in Mark (12:28), although the question is asked by the Pharisees in Matthew (22: 36).

To be sure, as Fredriksen says, "Jesus' ministry almost immediately occasions crisis and conflict." Nevertheless, the challenges raised by the Pharisees and other Jews

The Traditional View of Judaism

appear at first to be nothing more than expressions of opposition to Jesus' behavior. "The Pharisees protest his violation of the Sabbath and the laws of purity and criticize his consorting with sinners, whether Jewish or Gentile."[121] And in every instance, Jesus' response is neither hostile nor defensive. He answers the Pharisees as if he is merely *interpreting* the Jewish law, not *violating* it. Indeed, Jesus does not merely dismiss his opponents' objections, but in many instances justifies his actions by quoting a passage from the Jewish Bible.

Thus, Jesus dines with sinners because, according to Ezekiel, it is important to help the weak, the sick, the crippled, the strayed, and the lost (34:4, 16). Indeed, in Matthew, Jesus explicitly quotes Hosea 6:6: "Go and learn what this means, 'I desire mercy, and not sacrifice'" (Matt 9:13). He and his disciples do not fast because "the bridegroom rejoices over the bride" (Isa 62:5), a concept which, according to William Barclay, "goes back to a whole circle of ideas that are part of Old Testament thought."[122] Jesus justifies his disciples' plucking of grain on the Sabbath by summarizing two Old Testament passages, the first referring to David, in 1 Samuel 21:1-6, and the second referring to Temple priests, in Numbers 28:9-10 (Matt 12:3-5; the second reference does not appear in Mark and Luke). The Pharisaic defense of hand washing evokes from Jesus a quotation of Isaiah 29:13: "[T]his people draw near with their lips, while their hearts are far from me" (Matt 15:8-9). Finally, Jesus supports his view of divorce by citing three passages from Genesis (1:27, 2:24, and 5:2).

Before long, however, the shocked and exasperated Pharisees turn vicious. They are no longer interested in challenging Jesus' departures from their particular interpretations of purity and Sabbath laws. In fact, they not only scoff at him (Luke 16:14). They even accuse him of being empowered by "the prince of demons" (Matt 10:34), that is, Beelzebul (12:24). And they also conspire to trap him into saying something blasphemous or doing something contrary to Jewish law, with the goal of having him arrested and, ultimately, executed. In all of the synoptic Gospels, the Pharisees "watched to see whether he would heal on the Sabbath, so that they might accuse him" (Mark 3:2; Matt 12:10; Luke 6:7). After Jesus heals the man whose right hand has withered, "the scribes and the Pharisees . . . were filled with fury and discussed with one another what they might do to Jesus" (Luke 6:7, 11; Mark 3:6; Matt 12:14).

By the time the Pharisees get around to asking Jesus for a sign, inquiring about his view of divorce, and determining whether he supports paying taxes to Rome, they are clearly more interested in "testing" him than in understanding him: "The Pharisees came and began to argue with him, seeking a sign from heaven, to test him. And he sighed deeply in his spirit" (Mark 8:11-12, 10:2; Matt 12:38, 16:1, 19:3). In Matthew, when the Pharisees and Herodians ask Jesus about paying taxes to Caesar, he is aware of their "malice," as if he knows that they previously "took counsel how to entangle him in his talk" (22:15-18). Based on these encounters, C. F. D. Moule says that "all through the ministry, the genuinely religious leaders of Judaism—the Pharisees and especially their rabbis and scribes—did recognize the threat to their system presented

The Evolution of Love

by this revolutionary and subversive teacher." Indeed, "for the most part, they are the real antagonists."[123] Eventually, of course, Jesus' sigh turns into a direct verbal assault on the Pharisees. Early in Mark, he looks at them "with anger, grieved at their hardness of heart" (3:5). In Matthew, Jesus calls them "hypocrites" and "blind guides" (15:7, 14; 22:18; Mark 12:13). And in Luke he says to the Pharisees, "[Y]ou are full of extortion and wickedness. You fools!" (11:39–40). Later, he accuses the Pharisees of being "lovers of money" (16:14).

At this point in the Gospels of Matthew and Luke, Jesus launches into two kinds of attack. One is a curse on the Pharisees and scribes, after the fashion of the great Jewish prophets—Isaiah, Jeremiah, and Ezekiel—who curse their fellow Jews for their moral failures:[124] "But woe to you Pharisees! For you tithe mint and rue and every herb, and neglect justice and the love of God . . . Woe to you Pharisees! For you love the best seat in the synagogues and salutations in the market places. Woe to you! For you are like graves which are not seen, and men walk over them without knowing it" (Luke 12:42–44; Matt 23:23–24; Mark 12:38–40). The last point means that the Pharisees themselves are the source of the uncleanliness they so abhor. Matthew's Jesus also curses both Pharisees and scribes for failing to practice what they preach, imposing too many petty laws on the people, and publicly displaying their piety (23:1–10). Furthermore, they are "full of extortion and rapacity" and "full of hypocrisy and iniquity" (23:25, 28).

In Matthew, these curses culminate in the other kind of attack: the prediction that the Pharisees will be condemned for eternity: "You serpents. You brood of vipers, how are you to escape being sentenced to hell?" (23:33). Elsewhere in the Gospels, this warning is addressed not only to the Pharisees, but to the entire generation of Jews whom Jesus has failed to persuade to follow him, "upon [whom] may come all the righteous blood shed on earth" (23:35), and which, in Matthew, they accept for themselves forever, during Jesus' trial before Pontius Pilate: "His blood be upon us and on our children!" (27:25). In Mark, Jesus says: "Why does this generation seek a sign? Truly, I say to you, no sign shall be given to this generation" (8:12). This generation is "adulterous and sinful" (8:38; Matt 12:39, 16:4; Luke 9:41, 11:29), so Jesus asks them, "[H]ow long am I to be with you?" (Mark 9: 19; Matt 17:17).[125] All of this echoes John the Baptist's criticism of the Pharisees and the Sadducees early in Matthew and Luke—"You brood of vipers!"—whom John warns that, short of their "repentance," they will be punished as "chaff" and "will burn with unquenchable fire" (Matt 3:7, 12; Luke 3:7, 9).

Most of Jesus' accusations against the Pharisees in the synoptic Gospels are quite general, as when he calls them wicked, hard-hearted, and blind. However, his dominant criticism is quite specific: They are hypocrites. That is, they pretend to be pious, but they are actually interested in prestige, power, and money. Furthermore, some of Jesus' criticisms of the Pharisees are theological, as I suggested earlier, based on disagreements about Sabbath restrictions and other Jewish laws. On this point, like the prophets, Jesus argues that morality is always more important than piety, as his reference to Hosea 6:6 suggests: "I desire mercy, and not sacrifice," meaning that loving humanity is a more profound way of loving God than performing rituals. Specifically, Jesus says, it is allowable to heal on the Sabbath, to work on that day in order to satisfy one's hunger, and to dine with the lost sheep in order to bring them back to the fold. Also, it is more important to be concerned about what we say and do than about what foods we eat.

Jesus is especially critical of the Pharisees' embrace of what they call the Oral Tradition, an expansion of the written commandments, which was intended to both update the laws and to protect Jews from even accidentally sinning. That is, these additional laws, which are addressed to a wide range of specific situations, in the words of the Rabbis, "put a fence around the Torah": They prevent Jews from even unintentionally violating the Law. On this basis, Jesus dismisses the Pharisees' emphasis on some purity laws, like hand washing before dining, and some rules of separation, like not interacting too intimately with sinners. To Jesus, these are "traditions" (i.e., man-made laws) whose enforcement interferes with the written laws (i.e., God-made laws), which mandate kindness and compassion. Thus, he says to the Pharisees in Mark, "You leave the commandment of God, and hold fast the tradition of men" (7:8; Matt 15:3).

E. P. Sanders, in particular, notes that the "kind of meticulous activity" notoriously engaged in by the Pharisees was seen "in the first century"—i.e., in the Gospels—as "casuistic, nitpicking and trivial." There and in subsequent Christian writings, it was believed to be "undertaken to limit one's response to God, allowing followers to feel self-righteous while in fact they followed such trivial pursuits instead of attending to weightier ones." Sanders continues: "Throughout the early chapters of the synoptic gospels the Pharisees (and scribes) are depicted as harrassing Jesus over what we now regard as trivia, such as allowing his disciples to pluck grain on the sabbath (Mark 3:24). Another way of putting this sort of accusation was to say that the Pharisees observed only the externals of the law, such as washing cups, while being spiritually dead within; that is, they were hypocrites (Matt. 23.25)." Worse yet, the New Testament portrait of the Pharisees, based particularly on their purity laws, have led "Christian scholars . . . to draw an extremely denigrating view of the Pharisees as self-righteous exlusivists, who avoided contact with non-Pharisees." Furthermore, their claim to possess "special knowledge" allowed them "to despise the common people."[126]

One of the surprising features of the synoptic Gospels is the nearly complete absence of any ethnic identification of Jesus, his disciples, members of his family, his audience in general, Pontius Pilate, or the other Romans, although it seems likely that "soldiers" and "centurions" would automatically have been understood to be Romans. Aside from many references to Jesus as "the King of the Jews," the word "Jews" appears only four times in the first three Gospels (Matt 28:15; Mark 7:3; Luke 7:3, 23:51), and, although the word "Israel" appears several times in Matthew and Luke, it appears in the Gospel of Mark only as part of the Shema, which is quoted in 12:29.[127] The word "Romans" appears only once. The Greek woman whom Jesus encounters in "the region of Tyre and Sidon," also identified as Syrophoenician, is an exception (Mark 7:26; the woman is called Canaanite in Matt 15:22), as are the Samaritans in the Gospel of Luke: first, those who refuse to welcome Jesus on his way to Jerusalem (9:52); second, the main figure in the Parable of the Good Samaritan (10:33); and, third, the Samaritan leper who returns to thank Jesus for healing him (17:16).

The result of the ethnic cleansing of these Gospels is incalculable. First, at the very least, it guarantees that Jesus will in no way be understood to have been born a Jew, to have been educated as a Jew, and to have lived as a Jew—a point made by a large majority of contemporary scholars and a subject I will discuss at length in chapter 2. To be sure, Luke indicates that Jesus was circumcised, that his parents presented him at the Temple in Jerusalem, and that they both performed the appropriate rituals, including purification. However, many countries in the ancient Near East practiced circumcision, and most ancient religions required their members to perform rituals celebrating such major events as births, marriages, and deaths. Second, the absence of ethnic identities in the Gospels also makes it impossible to understand that almost everyone whom Jesus encountered, except for Roman officials, was Jewish, *including his followers as well as his enemies.*

Indeed, throughout the synoptic Gospels, although Jesus is vilified by some Jews, he is often enthusiastically greeted by others, including not only his disciples, but also "the crowds" of Jews who, according to Matthew, enthusiastically welcome him to Jerusalem by spreading their garments and tree branches on the road, shouting "Hosanna to the Son of David!" and whose large numbers and obvious devotion make it necessary for those who want to arrest him to do so "by stealth"—"lest there be a tumult among the people" (i.e., the Jews; 21:8–9, 26:4–5; Mark 11:8–9). Luke comments, "And the chief priests and the scribes were seeking how to put him to death; for they feared the people" (i.e., the Jews). And when Jesus is finally arrested, he says to "the captains of the temple" and others, "But this is your hour, and the power of darkness" (22:2, 53)—that is, the cover of night.

Third, besides their de-Judaization, the Gospels are generally devoid of any kind of contextualization that would allow their readers to understand events from a broad social or historical perspective. This is particularly true in relation to the activities of Jesus. That is, what Jesus says and does is seldom if ever compared to or contrasted with the activities of other Jews, past or present, the result of which is that his words and actions appear to be unique as well as unprecedented. Most conspicuously, there is no indication that, because disease and disability were assumed to be the result of demon-possession or divine punishment in ancient times, exorcism and healing were common practices, not only all over the world but especially among the Jews. As Howard Clark Kee notes, "Jesus [was] one among other charismatic healers and exorcists of the time" and also solidly in the tradition of miracle workers who appeared

The Traditional View of Judaism

in the Old Testament.[128] Furthermore, first-century Israel was awash in prophets and self-appointed messiahs (three of whom—Judas the Galilean, Theudas, and the Egyptian—are referred to in Acts of the Apostles), who attracted large numbers of followers and, like Jesus, incurred the wrath of the Jewish elite. The age was characterized by apocalypticism and messianism, both of which were represented by Jesus in his role as prophet of the coming Kingdom of God and as divine messenger. According to Bart D. Ehrman, Albert Schweitzer was right to claim "that Jesus is to be situated in the context of first-century Palestinian Judaism and that he was himself an apocalyptist."[129]

Of course, it is not too difficult to believe that many gentiles who read the Gospels in the first few centuries AD, especially those who either lived far from Jerusalem or were unacquainted with Jews or Christians, were unable to identify the main characters in the Gospels either ethnically or religiously. In other words, they had no idea that, aside from telling the story of Jesus' missionary activities and his arrest and execution, these narratives focus on two principal subjects: (1) the conflict between Jesus and the Jews and (2) the responsibility of the Jews for Jesus' death, as well as the innocence of Pontius Pilate and the Romans generally.[130] However, it is hard to imagine that any contemporary Christian, Jew, or Muslim could be unaware of the national origins and/or the religious affiliations of the people in these New Testament books. Indeed, it is likely that anyone who has the opportunity to read these accounts understands the main theme: that the Pharisees represent the Jews, and that they, not the Romans, were Jesus' principal enemies. The capstone of this account in each of the synoptic Gospels is, of course, the execution of Jesus, which Ruether describes as a complete misrepresentation: "[T]he account . . . defies all records of the actual power relations between these two authorities." Furthermore, it shifts the blame not only to the Jews, but also on to religious grounds, i.e., blasphemy."[131]

In the Gospel of John, the Pharisees reappear in exactly the same role they have in the synoptic Gospels—that is, as Jesus' opponents. Thus, the Pharisees send provocateurs to ask John the Baptist why he is baptizing, since he is not the Messiah or Elijah or a prophet (1:24–25). After his first visit to Jerusalem for Passover, Jesus leaves Judea when he finds out that the Pharisees have been told that his followers are "baptizing more disciples than John" (4:1–2). The chief priests and Pharisees, aware of Jesus' growing popularity, "sent officers to arrest him" (7:32). And, when the officers return without Jesus, the priests and Pharisees wonder if the officers have been taken in by Jesus—clearly, to them, a *false* prophet, since "no prophet is to rise from Galilee" (7:52). When he returns to Jerusalem for another festival, Jesus is pursued by the chief priests and Pharisees, who, because they heard "the crowd muttering about him"—evidently quite favorably—try to arrest him (8:32).

Later, knowing that Jesus has raised Lazarus from the dead, the chief priests and Pharisees call a meeting of "the council" and discuss whether they should kill him. They are persuaded by the chief priest Caiaphas that Jesus must die, at which point "Jesus therefore no longer went about openly among the Jews" (11:46–57). Witnessing

The Evolution of Love

Jesus being welcomed by "a great crowd" and greeted as "the King of Israel" upon his entrance into Jerusalem for another Passover celebration, the Pharisees say to each other, "You see that you can do nothing; look, the world has gone after him" (12:12–19). Finally, with Judas' help, "a band of soldiers and some officers from the chief priests and the Pharisees . . . seized Jesus and bound him" (18:3, 12).

What is particularly interesting in this Gospel is John's failure to acknowledge the fact that the "great crowd" of people who enthusiastically welcome Jesus to Jerusalem are ethnically indistinguishable from "the Jews" among whom Jesus refuses to go "openly among." Both groups are Jews. Ernst Bammel might attribute the oversight to what he calls "the blunt anti-Jewish polemic on so many pages of the Gospel."[132] And that is precisely what Judith Lieu does. Of the Gospel of John, she says, "[T]he different groupings—crowds, Pharisees, scribes, elders, Sadducees—of the earlier tradition are becoming absorbed into the undifferentiated and alienating terminology of 'the Jews', leaving a sense that neither Jesus nor his true disciples are counted among 'the Jews.'"[133]

The only difference between the Gospel of John and the other Gospels on the subject of the Pharisees is that, in John, the Pharisees actually participate in the arrest of Jesus.[134] That is, as the synoptic Gospels get closer and closer to the final days of Jesus, the Pharisees fade out of the picture. They are replaced by the chief priests, who, unlike the Pharisees, actually have an official position in the government: "And the chief priests and the scribes . . . sought a way to destroy him; because they feared him, because all the multitude was astonished at his teaching" (Mark 11:18; Luke 20:19; Matt 21:45). Before the Crucifixion, the Pharisees appear for the last time in Matthew in chapter 23 (except for their return in 27:62, after the Crucifixion); in Luke, in chapter 19; and, in Mark, in chapter 12. That is, in the official acts of arresting and trying Jesus, the chief priests are in charge: "Then the chief priests and the elders of the people gathered in the palace of the high priest, who was Caiaphas, and took counsel together in order to arrest Jesus by stealth and kill him" (Matt 26:3–4; Mark 14:1; Luke 22:2). Later, "a great crowd with swords and clubs, from the chief priests and the elders of the people" actually arrest Jesus (Matt 26:47; Mark14:43; Luke 22:52) and pass him on to Caiaphas. "Now the chief priests and the whole council sought false testimony against Jesus that they might put him to death" (Matt 26:59; Mark 14:55; Luke 22:66).

What is particularly surprising in the Gospel of John is a series of rather bizarre conversations between Jesus and the Pharisees, in which Jesus explains his theology—often in a language heavily influenced by Platonic ideas, which his auditors, notoriously anti-Hellenist, find incomprehensible. The first exchange occurs between Jesus and Nicodemus, who appears later as a defender of Jesus against his fellow Pharisees (7:50–51) and, in the end, helps Joseph of Arimathea carry Jesus' body to its resting place (19:39–40). After Nicodemus politely addresses Jesus—"Rabbi, we know that you are a teacher come from God ; for no one can do these signs that you do, unless God is with him"—Jesus explains that in order to enter the kingdom of God, one must be "born anew," "born of water and Spirit," since only "that which is born of the

The Traditional View of Judaism

Spirit is spirit." Furthermore, only those who have descended from heaven can return there; and only those who believe in the Son of man "may have eternal life" (3:1–15). Nicodemus, rather helplessly, it appears, responds: "How can a man be born when he is old?" And when Jesus says, "The wind blows where it wills, and you hear the sound of it, but you do not know whence it comes or whither it goes; so it is with every one who is born of the Spirit," Nicodemus asks, "How can this be?"[135]

Jesus' subsequent encounters are less friendly on the part of his interlocutors, but no less confusing to them, as well as to non-Christian readers of the Gospel. When Jesus says, "I am the light of the world," the Pharisees complain that he is making a claim that is not verified by others: He is merely "bearing self-witness." Jesus responds, "Even if I do bear witness to myself, my testimony is true, for I know whence I have come and whither I am going." The Pharisees, however, have no idea where Jesus came from or where he is going, for the simple reason that he does not tell them. When Jesus says that his witness is "the Father who sent me," they ask, "[W]here is your Father?" When Jesus says, "[W]here I am going, you cannot come," they think he means that he intends to "kill himself." And when he says, "You are from below, I am from above," they respond, "Who are you?" (8:1–25).

Later, Jesus launches once more into a highly figurative explanation, this time referring to himself as "the good shepherd": "I know my own and my own know me, as the Father knows me and I know the Father; and I lay down my life for the sheep." The response to this claim is mixed, some auditors saying, "He has a demon, and he is mad." Finally, at "the feast of the Dedication," or Hanukkah, Jesus extends the metaphor. The people at the Temple ask, "How long will you keep us in suspense? If you are the Christ, tell us plainly." To this request, Jesus does not say, "I *am* the Christ." He says, "My sheep hear my voice, and I know them, and they follow me; and I give them eternal life." He concludes this brief speech with the announcement "I and the Father are one," as a result of which his listeners pick up stones, with the intention of killing him (10:14–30). John says of Jesus' reference to himself as a shepherd, "[T]hey did not understand what he was saying to them" (10:6). *They did not understand.*

Unlike the writers of the synoptic Gospels, however, John does not attribute hostility toward Jesus only to the Pharisees. That is, he does not hesitate to call the Jews the Jews. Whereas Mark, Matthew, and Luke, refer to the Jews of Palestine as "they" or "them" or "people," a word which is used by Luke more than fifty times, John simply refers to them as "Jews," which he does, according to Anthony J. Saldarini, "about seventy times."[136] Thus, his readers have no need to speculate about the identity of the members of Jesus' audience, who, like the Pharisees, never understand Jesus' words, always misinterpret his actions, grow increasingly hostile toward him, and celebrate his death on the Cross. Written sometime between AD 90 and 100—that is, later than the other Gospels—and perhaps composed for a more Hellenized community, populated by gentiles rather than Jews, the Gospel of John is unconditionally not only

33

anti-Judaic (that is, critical of Judaism as a religion), but also anti-Semitic (that is, critical of the Jews as a race).

John's direct assault on the Jews begins after Jesus "cleanses" the Temple by driving out the sellers of oxen, sheep, and pigeons and by "pour[ing] out the coins of the money-changers: "The Jews then said to him, 'What sign have you to show us for doing this,'" by which they mean, Why should we recognize your authority to render this judgment against the Temple? But Jesus answers them with as much relevance and specificity and clarity as he answers the Pharisees: "Destroy this temple, and in three days I will raise it up" (2:15–19). At the synagogue at Capernaum, Jesus claims to be "the bread which came down from heaven," in response to which the Jews in the congregation say: "Is not this Jesus, the son of Joseph, whose father and mother we know? How does he now say, 'I have come down from heaven?'" (6:41–42). After Jesus continues, "[I]f any one eats of this bread, he will live for ever," the Jews "disputed among themselves, saying, 'How can this man give us his flesh to eat?'" (6:51–52. At this point, even Jesus' disciples reply, "This is a hard saying; who can listen to it?" And then, apparently befuddled by Jesus' strange words, "many of his disciples drew back and no longer went about with him" (6:60, 66).

Teaching at the Temple during the feast of Tabernacles, Jesus is again the subject of dispute among the Jews, some (but evidently not all) of whom say that "he is leading the people astray" and question how he acquired his learning since "he has never studied" (7:12, 15). Furthermore, because these Jews recognize Jesus and know his origins, they conclude that he cannot be the Messiah: "[W]hen the Christ appears, no one will know where he comes from" (7:26–27). When Jesus explains that he will soon "go to him who sent me," where they "cannot come," they ask, "Does he intend to go to the Dispersion [i.e., the Jewish Diaspora] among the Greeks and teach the Greeks?" (7:33–36). His figurative language remains elusive and therefore beyond anyone's capacity to understand it.

Still in the Temple, Jesus says "to the Jews who had believed in him" that, if they continue as his disciples, they "will know the truth," and "the truth will make [them] free." They answer, "We are the descendants of Abraham, and have never been in bondage to anyone." When he accuses them of being slaves to sin, they claim that they are innocent since God is their Father, to which Jesus responds, "You are of your father the devil, and your will is to do your father's desires." The Jews, in turn, accuse Jesus of having a demon (8:31–34, 42–52). Finally, after Jesus leaves the Temple and restores the sight of a man who was born blind, "[t]he Jews did not believe that he had been blind"; his parents, interviewed by these doubters, pretend not to know who healed their son "because they feared the Jews"; and, when the man identifies Jesus as a prophet, "they cast him out" of the synagogue (9:18, 22, 34).

The Jews whom Jesus encounters in the small towns of Galilee as well as in Jerusalem not only misunderstand him. Like the Pharisees, they also make many attempts to kill him, though not by official means. The Pharisees threaten execution; the other

The Traditional View of Judaism

Jews threaten stoning. At yet another feast in Jerusalem, Jesus heals a lame man on the Sabbath, which is "why the Jews persecuted Jesus." Indeed, they wanted "to kill him, because he not only broke the Sabbath but also called God his Father, making himself one with God" (5:8–9, 16–18). After he announces that his followers must eat his flesh and drink his blood, Jesus "would not go about in Judea, because the Jews sought to kill him" (7:1). Furthermore, "for fear of the Jews, no one spoke openly of him" (7:13). In his argument with Jews in which he accuses them of being slaves to sin, he says to them, "I know you are descendants of Abraham; yet you seek to kill me, because my word finds no place in you" (8:31). At the feast of the Dedication, "[t]he Jews took up stones again to stone him." They say, "We stone you for no good work but for blasphemy; because you, being a man, make yourself God" (10:31–33). After Jesus' trial before Pilate, the Jews prefer to save Barabbas rather than Jesus; cry out to Pilate, "If you release this man" meaning Jesus, "you are not Caesar's friend"; and cry out again, "Crucify him!" (18:38–40; 19:12, 15).

Although Luke uses the word "Jews" only twice in his Gospel and twice in the first eight chapters of Acts of the Apostles, the word appears almost sixty times in chapters 9–28 of Acts. The shift occurs at the moment when Luke's attention turns from the story of Peter to the story of Paul, which is dominated by Paul's always hostile and frequently violent encounters with Jews, mostly in the Diaspora, but also in Jerusalem. Ruether comments: "Here the 'Jews' appear as constantly 'plotting' against the lives of Peter and Paul, even though they don't succeed in killing either. The actual arrest of Paul in Jerusalem and his transfer to a prison in Caesarea is elaborately excused to make the Jews look responsible, while the Romans who constantly recognize Paul's innocence and want to release him, appear as innocent victims of Jewish malice."[137]

The conflict between Christians and Jews in Acts begins in the second chapter, with Peter's speech to the "Men of Judea" after the Pentecostal experience of Jesus' followers. The speech is important because it introduces the themes that will be repeated again and again by Peter as well as Stephen and Paul: (1) that Jesus was sent by God as the Savior of all of humanity, (2) that this fact was predicted by the writers of the Old Testament, (3) that Jesus demanded repentance in exchange for forgiveness, (4) that he was killed by the Jews, and (5) that he was resurrected.[138] Peter says: "Jesus of Nazareth, a man attested to you by God with mighty works and wonders and signs which God did through him in your midst, as you yourselves know—this Jesus, delivered up according to the definite plan and foreknowledge of God, you crucified and killed by the hands of lawless men. But God raised him up" (2:22–24). "Let all the house of Israel therefore know assuredly that God has made him both Lord and Christ, this Jesus whom you crucified" (2:36). When the members of "the house of Israel" (who are not, however, identified as Jews) ask,[139] because "they were cut to the heart" by Peter's accusation, "Brethren, what shall we do?" Peter says, "Repent, and be baptized every one of you in the name of Jesus Christ for the forgiveness of your sins." (2:37–38).

One can readily assume that the Jews were "cut to the heart" particularly by Peter's accusation that they killed Jesus. Peter repeats the charge in Acts 3:12–15; 4:10–12, 27; 5:27–30; and 10:38–39. In response, Jewish officials arrest Peter and other disciples, first because they are "annoyed" (4:1–3) and second because they are "jealous" (5:17–18, 26). Indeed, after Peter's third reiteration of the same charges, in violation of the Jewish "council's" request that he and his fellow Christians not "speak or teach at all in the name of Jesus" (4:17), the Jews want to punish Peter and his companions more severely: "When they heard this they were enraged and wanted to kill them" (5:33).

Stephen carries these charges further by stating quite clearly that the Jewish murder of Jesus was nothing more than a culmination of two ongoing manifestations of Jewish corruption: the unrelenting failure of the Jews to obey God's laws, which began after their liberation from Egypt, and their habitual murder of prophets sent by God. Stephen emphasizes the Jews' disobedience to Moses (7:39),[140] and he calls them "stiff-necked people" because they killed the prophets (7:51–53). In response, the Jews in Stephen's audience are, like Peter's auditors, "enraged." However, being ordinary people who lack the authority to arrest Stephen and subject him to some kind of formal judicial procedure of the kind that results in Peter's arrest and release (or miraculous escape), they simply stone him to death (7:58).

The next stage in this saga of Jewish hostility to Christianity occurs in chapter 8 of Acts, with the Jewish persecution of Christians, first witnessed by Paul and later perhaps directed by him.[141] Somewhat obliquely, we are told that Saul (later Paul) "was consenting" to Stephen's death. We do not know the significance of Paul's approval because we have no idea what position Paul had at the time. It seems, however, that he was at least a supporter of the Jews who stoned Stephen rather than an innocent bystander. What matters is that subsequently he became a leading player in what is described as a massive assault on the Christian community in Jerusalem: "And on that day a great persecution arose against the church in Jerusalem . . ." (8:1). As a Jew, "Saul laid waste the church" by searching for Christians in "house after house," and "he dragged off men and women and committed them to prison" (8:3). "[S]till breathing threats and murder against the disciples of the Lord, [he] went to the high priest and asked him for letters to the synagogues at Damascus" (9:1–2). Paul later boasts that he "persecuted this Way [i.e., Jesus' followers] to the death, binding and delivering to prison both men and women" (22:4). To Jesus, in a vision, he says that "in every synagogue I imprisoned and beat those who believed in thee" (22:19).

After his conversion, Paul becomes the victim instead of the perpetrator of violence. The reason is that he carries Stephen's accusatory message not directly to the gentiles, but to the synagogues of the Diaspora, where he encounters a relatively small number of welcoming Jews and (presumably) a larger number of welcoming Jewish proselytes and gentile God-fearers. The latter are like Cornelius, the centurion who is converted by Peter and who is described as "a devout man who feared God with all his household, gave alms liberally to the people, and prayed constantly to God" (10:1–2)—that is, they are synagogue attendees who follow most Jewish laws but remain uncircumcised. In almost every instance of his visit to a city with a large enough Jewish population to sustain a synagogue, Paul has a modest amount of success, but he also stirs up the anger of some of the Jews who find his appeal both insulting and threatening.

Indeed, because of Paul's decision to spend the rest of his life almost exclusively visiting synagogues and therefore addressing Jews, Jewish proselytes, and God-fearers, he is in constant conflict with the Jewish leaders in cities from the Near East to Rome. Paul delivers his first public address at a synagogue in Damascus, where he spends "many days" explaining to the Jews of the city "that Jesus was the Christ." It seems likely that he included in his remarks the accusation that the Jews in his audience were guilty of murdering Jesus since the Jews of the city "plotted to kill him." In fact, so intent are they to capture him that they watch "the gates day and night," and his only means of escape is to be let down over the city wall "in a basket" (9:19–25). Fleeing Damascus, Paul returns to Jerusalem, where he tries to convince his fellow Christians that he has undergone a spiritual transformation. In addition, following in Stephen's footsteps (6:8–10), "he spoke and disputed against the Hellenists," who, like Stephen's Diasporan auditors, were so outraged by his words that they "were seeking to kill him" (9:29). Once more, Paul is saved by "the brethren," who help him get back to his hometown, Tarsus (9:30).

On orders from the Holy Spirit, Paul and Barnabas travel to Cyprus, where, beginning with Salamis, "they proclaimed the word of God in the synagogues of the Jews" throughout "the whole island." In Paphos, Paul confronts "a Jewish false prophet" named Bar-Jesus, whom he calls a "son of the devil," an "enemy of all righteousness, full of deceit and villainy." Because the prophet is "seeking to turn the proconsul [Sergius Paulus] from the faith," Paul accuses him of "making crooked the straight paths of the Lord." Under the influence of the Holy Spirit, Paul blinds him temporarily (13:6–11). After a trip to Perga and a brief return to Jerusalem, "Paul and his company" go to a synagogue in Pisidian Antioch, where the visitors are invited by "the rulers of the synagogue" to address the congregation. Since Paul speaks in synagogue after synagogue, wherever he goes, it is possible that he is always invited to do so, and often he stays for weeks and even months—and in Ephesus for two years. As Morton Scott Enslin explains: "Any qualified man might be invited to read, translate, or speak [at a synagogue]. Scholars who were either members of the particular congregation or present as visitors might be invited; they had no special rights."[142]

In Antioch, Paul gives a summary of God's gifts to the Jews since their departure from Egypt, a series of saving acts that culminate in the appearance of Jesus. After Paul goes through the usual litany of claims, including the charge that the Jews "asked Pilate to have [Jesus] killed" (13:16–41), his audience "begged" him to return on "the next Sabbath." Indeed, "many Jews and devout converts to Judaism followed Paul and Barnabas, who spoke to them and urged them to continue in the grace of God."

However, because on the following Sabbath "almost the whole city gathered together to hear the word of God," two important events occur. First, "when the Jews"—evidently those other than the ones who were initially impressed by Paul's preaching—"saw the multitudes, they were filled with jealousy, and contradicted what was spoken by Paul, and reviled him." Second, Paul and Barnabas respond by saying that, although they were obliged to address the Jews first, they will now take their mission to the gentiles: "Since you thrust it from you," he says to the Jews, "and judge yourselves unworthy of eternal life, behold, we turn to the Gentiles" (13:42–46).[143] The gentiles cheer, and the mission "spread[s] throughout all the region." However, the leading citizens of Antioch "stirred up persecution against Paul and Barnabas, and drove them out of their district" (13:48–51).

Having stated assertively and unequivocally that they are now initiating the gentile mission, Paul and Barnabas next find themselves at the Jewish synagogue in Iconium, where the same series of events occurs. The missionaries speak to Jews and gentiles, "unbelieving Jews" stir up the crowd, the city is divided between supporters of the Christians and their enemies, and then both Jews and gentiles try "to molest them and to stone them" (14:1–5). This pattern is repeated in Lystra, where Paul is beaten and stoned—and left for dead—by Jews from Antioch and Iconium (14:19); in Thessalonica, where the Jews attack the house of Jason, who was Paul and Silas' host (17:5–7); in Beroea, where "the Jews of Thessalonica . . . came there too, stirring up and inciting the crowds" (17:13); in Corinth, where the Jews "made a united attack upon Paul and brought him before the tribunal" (18:12); in Ephesus, where the Jews forced Paul to withdraw from the synagogue (19:8–9); and in Greece, where "a plot was made against [Paul] by the Jews as he was about to sail for Syria" (20:3). No wonder that Paul laments in Ephesus that he has served "the Lord with all humility and with tears and with trials that befell me through the plots of the Jews" (20:19). In 2 Corinthians, Paul says, "Five times I have received at the hands of the Jews the forty lashes less one. Three times I have been beaten with rods; once I have been stoned" (11:24–25).[144]

When Paul returns to Jerusalem, after being attacked again and again by the Jews of the Diaspora, he discovers that, even in the Holy City, he cannot escape from their anger and enmity. After agreeing to James' request that he pay for four Christians to undergo a Nazirite ceremony at the Temple, Paul is hunted down by a "crowd" of "Jews from Asia," who call him "the man who is teaching men everywhere against the people and the law," drag him out of the Temple, and try "to kill him" (21:28–31). Oddly enough, although Paul is the victim of violence in this instance, he is treated as a criminal by the Roman tribune who rescues him from the Jews. The tribune asks him if he is the notorious rebel leader called the Egyptian—a man who "recently stirred up a revolt and led four thousand men of the Assassins out into the wilderness" (21:38). Indeed, from this point on, until the end of his life, Paul is a prisoner of the Romans. But his last act documented in Acts of the Apostles is to call together "the local leaders of the Jews" of Rome, to whom he delivers the same message he has been disseminating all over the northern and eastern shores of the Mediterranean Sea for fifteen years. To this, he receives the usual response: "And some were convinced by what he said, while others disbelieved" (28:24). This time, however, there was no violence.

Looking back at the speeches of the four leading speakers in the Gospel of Luke and the Acts of the Apostles, Jack T. Sanders says that all of them say the same thing "over and over in every way possible *ad nauseum*": "[W]ith the unlikely exception of Jesus' statement at the conclusion of the Zacchaeus story, Jesus, Peter, Stephen, and Paul present . . . , *in what they say on the subject*, an entirely, completely, wholly, uniformly consistent attitude towards the Jewish people as a whole. That attitude is that the Jews are and always have been wilfully ignorant of the purposes and plans of God expressed in their familiar scriptures, that they always have rejected and will reject God's offer of salvation, that they executed Jesus and persecute and hinder those who try to advance the gospel, and that they get one chance at salvation, which they will of course reject, bringing God's wrath down upon them, and quite deservedly so." Quoting E. Haenchen, Sanders summarizes the speeches this way: "Luke has written the Jews off." In other words, as Sanders concludes in the final paragraph of his book, "In Luke's opinion, the world will be better off when 'the Jews' get what they deserve and the world is rid of them."[145]

Deicide, Legalism, and Pharisaism

Clearly, if we examine the ideas and actions of the Jews as they are portrayed in the Gospels and the Acts of the Apostles, we can only conclude that these enemies of Christianity were blind, misguided, intolerant, hypocritical, stubborn, disobedient, devious, unjust, self-serving, callous, hard-hearted, hateful, vengeful, punitive, and violent. Both ordinary Jews and their leaders demanded the execution of Jesus, who was not only an innocent man but the Son of God. The chief priests and scribes hunted down disciples of Jesus, like Peter and Silas, and intended to inflict on them a punishment more severe than the beatings they actually received. Unnamed members of the Jewish elite led a systematic persecution against the Christians of Jerusalem, which was apparently based not on their proselytizing in the Temple, but simply on their identification as Christians, and which resulted, in some cases, in their death. Furthermore, according to the leading followers of Jesus—Peter, Stephen, and Paul—the Jews had always been faithless to God, ungrateful for his gifts, disobedient to his laws, and disrespectful to his messengers, the prophets whom they murdered and whose messages they ignored.[146] As C. F. D. Moule puts it: "The agreement or covenant between God and his People, made at Mt. Sinai through Moses, had been broken. God had stood by his People, but they had deserted him."[147]

Quite naturally and logically, before the last half of the twentieth century, the vast majority of Christians writing on the relationship between Jews and Christians in the first century AD relied exclusively on the Gospels and Acts as the basis for their understanding of Judaism and early Christianity. Indeed, these New Testament works have remained the primary sources for many scholars throughout the modern period. Kenneth Scott Latourette, for example, in a book published in 1953, says that Jesus was killed by both Pharisees and Sadducees because of "the offense he had given to their pride." These people, "professedly standing as the guardian of the Jewish heritage [were] both blind to the true content of that heritage and [were] utilizing its championship to obtain for itself pleasure, power, and wealth."[148] "To the informed and unprejudiced observer," Latourette continues, "the charges [against Jesus] were palpably false. They obviously seemed so to Pilate. Yet Pilate yielded to expediency," especially in the face of "a blood-thirsty mob demanding crucifixion."[149]

To be sure, in his condemnation of those responsible for Jesus' death, Latourette includes "the Roman official who ordered it," "the soldiers who carried it out," "the disciples who failed to understand Jesus" and "deserted him," and, indeed, all of humanity: "Since those immediately responsible for the crucifixion were a cross section of mankind, both good and bad, the cross was a condemnation of the entire race, vivid evidence of its stupid perversity and its impotence to save its noblest representative from rejection and humiliating death at the hands of man."[150] However, Latourette particularly singles out "the Jewish leaders who had engineered it"; "the mob who demanded it"; "those Jews such as the one who gave him burial who, lamenting the execution, did nothing to prevent it"; and even "the Jewish religion which, while it had nurtured Jesus, had not prevented its own prostitution by its professed guardians." He adds: "In blindness, selfish fear, and stupid anger they had done to death the rarest spirit ever born of woman, who in his teachings and example had shown the only way by which his own nation could avoid destruction and by which mankind could attain fullness of life."[151]

On the subject of Jesus' death, other scholars have gone so far as to blame the Jews entirely and ignore the Romans altogether. Peter Richardson says, "In agreement with the rest of their Gospels, the writers lay most blame upon the [Jewish] leaders; the 'people' plays a minor part in the drama." Nevertheless, *all* Jews are responsible: "Israel is culpable through the agency of its leaders." Richardson explains that the problem lay in Jewish beliefs and practices: It was "the old ways, old views, [and] old traditions" in which the Jews were "trapped" that "were so largely responsible for the arrest and trial of Jesus."[152] Bammel suggests that "the whole motif of Roman intervention" might be "a literary device" rather than "a tradition based on actual events."[153] Charlotte Klein says that this continued to be a widely held view even in the 1970s: "'The Jews crucified Christ' became a commonplace, despite all attempts—even those of the Second Vatican Council—to introduce less sweeping statements and to explain the circumstances at the time. Despite doubts about the historical accuracy of the trial before the Sanhedrin, most theologians continue to maintain their former view of an irreconcilable hostility between Jesus and the Jews. This hostility is then seen as leading logically to his death."[154]

In making this argument, many scholars deny that Jesus was (or was perceived to be) engaged in actions either threatening or disturbing to the Romans. According to D. R. Catchpole, "[I]t is clearly difficult to believe that Jesus' trial and condemnation" were of concern to the Romans mainly because he "was not involved in indictable political activities . . . The character of Jesus' ministry does, however, provide a coherent and logical prelude for Sanhedrin proceedings." Specifically, Catchpole concludes, "The theological position of Jesus provides a logical and consecutive preparation for a Sanhedrin hearing."[155] Moule explains, "A credible story emerges if only we may assume that the Jewish gravamen"—meaning the significant part of the Jewish complaint—"was 'blasphemy'" and that the Jews persuaded the Romans to execute Jesus for self-serving reasons: "This would be intelligible as a very skilful [sic] attempt on the part of the Jewish leaders to remove a popular but dangerous figure"—that is, to "Pharisaic Judaism," not to the Romans—without incurring unpopularity for themselves."[156]

Joseph Vogt also argues that Jesus was executed by the Jews for religious crimes: "[T]he entry into Jerusalem and the cleansing of the Temple do represent an open attack on the spiritual leaders of the Jewish people. It is the Jewish authorities who are responsible for Jesus' arrest, and their supreme council which interrogates the accused and sentences him to death on the charge of blasphemy. Jesus has to be handed over to the governor for the sentence to be ratified and executed."[157] J. C. O'Neill says, "The charge against Jesus in the Sanhedrin would have been a religious charge," but not based on his attitude toward the Temple, his claim to offer forgiveness, or his rejection of Sabbath restrictions. Rather, O'Neill concludes, "The technical charge upon which Jesus was condemned . . . may well have been that he blasphemed in making himself God."[158] Michael Goulder goes so far as to say that the Jews executed Jesus because he was like Ghandi and Martin Luther King, who "died for their faith": "To love as he loved was bound to evoke the hostility of the authorities . . . To live the life of love, to teach love, and to found the community of love entailed the likelihood of the cross."[159]

Of course, just as the Jews were blamed for Jesus' death, the Romans were held to be entirely innocent of the crime. As Vogt says, Pilate was "undecided," but the Jews "put pressure" on him, and "[h]is hand was forced." And Bo Reicke similarly claims that "Pilate was persuaded to execute Jesus."[160] Indeed, Harold W. Hoehner argues, Pilate sent Jesus to Herod Antipas because he "expected the tetrarch to acquit Jesus." And the fact that Antipas sent Jesus back to Pilate means that he "considered him innocent," supported Pilate's similar judgment, and "absolve[d]" Pilate "from the responsibility of Jesus' death."[161] According to Klein, "Josef Blinzler claims that we should be bound today to come to the same conclusion as the early Christian preachers did about the historical Jewish responsibility." In *The Trial of Jesus* (1959), Blinzler says that the Jews deliberately distorted the charge against Jesus, who was guilty of "calling himself King of the Jews," by emphasizing the "political significance" of his actions; remained throughout their shameful effort dedicated to the "the destruction of Jesus at any price"; and "hinder[ed] Pilate from pronouncing a free and legal judgment by intimidating him with threats and so forcing him to pass sentence of death." The same point, Klein adds later, is made by Heinrich Schlier, in *The Relevance of the New Testament* (1968), and other modern scholars.[162]

In order to blame the Jews for the death of Jesus, it is necessary to exaggerate the power of the Jewish authorities and minimize the power of Pontius Pilate. Reicke's portrait of the Roman prefect suggests that he was merely a minor official who submitted to the priests throughout his years of service, except on a few occasions, when he was compelled to use force to maintain civil order. For example, when Pilate decided to build an aqueduct—a civic project that would obviously benefit the Jewish residents of Jerusalem—he was confronted by angry protesters: "The Jews demonstrated against this too, but Pilate succeeded in getting the work finished with the help of soldiers dressed as civilians." What Reicke fails to mention about what he calls a "creditable" act is that the Jews objected because Pilate funded the project by stealing money from the Temple treasury. Furthermore, Pilate's soldiers dressed up as civilians in order to infiltrate the crowd of Jewish protestors and put down the protest by killing the participants.[163] Other scholars' description of such events illustrates how easy it is to present Pilate positively and the Jews negatively. William K. Klingaman says that Pilate was a "tough-minded veteran military administrator," who was not "squeamish." Indeed, Tiberius appointed him to govern Israel because he had "previously displayed a considerable measure of proven ability and grit." Previous procurators had found the Jews to be "incorrigibly unruly," and they had "failed to grow more mellow" over time. They had "peculiar religious customs," which Pilate's predecessors had respected, but Pilate "was determined to teach [them] to respect" Tiberius. Pilate took money from the Temple treasury to build an aqueduct, but his "expenditures almost certainly fell within the existing limitations on the use" of the money. Nevertheless, he had to endure a protest by "Jewish pilgrims" to Jerusalem who were "most likely fundamentalist troublemakers from the bumptious northern realm of Galilee." Having lost face in his first encounter with these protesting Jews, Pilate later "availed himself of every opportunity to irritate the notoriously thin-skinned residents of Judea."[164]

Traditional scholarly opinion has not only blamed the Jews for the murder of Jesus, however. Until quite recently, students of the Gospels and Acts of the Apostles have also tended to describe the Jews more broadly as the enemies of Christianity in its entirety. Blinzler, for example, says that when Jesus began his mission, one group of Jews, "chiefly the group made up of the religious and political leaders, reacted with skepticism, with unconcealed distrust, then with flat rejection, and finally with deadly hostility."[165] Moule devotes an entire chapter to the ongoing assault on the Christians by Jesus' enemies for many years after the Crucifixion. "Judaism bulks by far the largest among the antagonists of Christianity which have left their stamp on the New

Testament," he says. Jesus' followers "realized that the persecution of a minority by the majority" was characteristic of Judaism throughout its history. It had been the fate "of all the messengers of God before them." Thus, even when the Jews are not directly involved in persecuting Christians, examples of which "are extraordinarily few," they are likely to have promoted it. In Acts, for example. "from start to finish [persecution] is instigated by the Jews." Moule concludes, "So far, then, as our only New Testament narratives go, there is no predisposition to expect other than Jewish origins for persecution."[166]

As I said earlier, no other conclusion is possible for those who accept the New Testament as the word of God and, therefore, as unimpeachable. Based on this assumption, Reginald H. Fuller argues, in a popular work on the Bible addressed to "laymen" rather than scholars, that all of the speeches in the Acts of the Apostles are valid and accurate replications of the words delivered by the followers of Jesus in the first century AD. Fuller grants that "the man in the street" might say that Acts was written at a time "when the original religion of Jesus had turned into a religion about him." However, he contends that this notion has been rejected in modern scholarship. Scholars have shown, he says, that "the speeches in the early parts of Acts . . . are clearly Greek translations of an Aramaic original, that is to say, of the language spoken by the earliest Christians at Jerusalem. Thus they can hardly be dismissed as the free compositions of a later Greek-speaking Christian: the author must have derived them from some primitive source." Fuller makes the same claim about *all* "apostolic preaching," which he calls "a summary remarkably like the early Christian creeds." In other words, the Christianity of the church remained unchanged throughout the early years. Thus, what has sometimes been written off as "accretions and perversions of basic Christianity" is actually authentic.[167]

There were, of course, descriptions of the Jews of first-century Palestine other than those in the New Testament. Besides occasional commentaries on Jews and Judaism written by pagans for the entertainment and edification of non-Jewish readers in the two centuries before and after the time of Jesus, the Jews themselves composed a large number of religious works—now called intertestamental literature—from the second century BC to the first century AD. As time passed, however—particularly as the church gained power and influence in the Roman Empire on its way to gaining complete dominance by the end of the fourth century, the impetus for Christians to consult these historical writings (e.g., by Josephus), philosophical documents (e.g., by Philo), and religious works (e.g., by Ben Sirach) evidently diminished and then disappeared. Or, more accurately, Christians either ignored them or revised them. Thus, largely because there were, *in effect*, no important, relevant, or influential contemporary records of the Jews in the time of Jesus other than the New Testament, ever since the first century AD Christian attitudes toward the Jews have ranged from anger to hatred to unmitigated contempt and rejection. Worse yet, Christians read and heard the New Testament and its account of the Jews and Judaism religiously, in every sense of the word.

The Evolution of Love

Given the growing power of the church, the result was inevitable. As Lieu explains, after the pervasive attacks on Jews in the third century by Christian intellectuals, the treatment of Jews was repeated again and again for the next millennium and a half: "Looking ahead, by the third century we find the systematized collection of arguments and proof texts *Against the Jews*, in Tertullian, Cyprian, Hippolytus and their successors. While it would be wrong to deny any contact between these authors and contemporary Judaism, the arguments they used quickly become standardized and predictable, following well-established themes, and extend from explicit polemic to homiletic, exegetical and liturgical rhetoric."[168] Jon Levenson traces "the intense anti-Semitism evident in many of the classic works in [the] field" of "biblical study" to Christian writings of the first three centuries: "Old Testament theology, in fact, often continues the ancient *adversus Judaeos* [that is, *Against the Jews*] tradition in which the New Testament writers and the church fathers excelled."[169]

When Christianity became the official religion of the Roman Empire in the late fourth century, Jews were henceforth, over a period of decades, deprived not only of some of the privileges they had been granted by Julius Caesar in the first century BC, but also many of the ordinary rights they possessed as residents of the Empire, along with pagans and Christians. In the first two centuries of Christian ascendancy, the Jews were forbidden to marry gentiles, to own land, to purchase gentile slaves, to convert gentiles to Judaism, to practice law, and, as time passed, to in any way participate in the civic life of the communities in which they lived. Church leaders sometimes encouraged Christians to attack Jewish properties, destroy synagogues, burn Torah scrolls, and physically assault the Jews themselves. In the Middle Ages, Jews suffered periodically from expulsions, forced conversions, and massacres. These often brutally punitive actions carried out by Christians in the early years of the church and thereafter were the logical consequences of the unremittingly negative portrait of the Jews and Pharisees in the New Testament.[170]

Given not only the official, but also divinely sanctioned portrait of the Jews in the New Testament and its devastating effect on the political, social, and economic situation of the Jews under Christian domination, it is not surprising that, with few exceptions, up until the last half of the twentieth-century, both the intellectual leaders of the church and members of the scholarly community, who were identical throughout most of the past two thousand years, have similarly treated Judaism as an utterly unworthy and unacceptable faith. Indeed, in John G. Gager's words, "[M]uch of Christian scholarship on ancient Judaism has been shaped by the legacy of early Christian anti-Judaism," which is expressed in the New Testament.[171] As we shall see in chapter 2, this view of the Jewish religion has been supplanted in the last few decades as a result of a reassessment of the Gospels, which has led to the conclusion that these writings, composed, as I said earlier, roughly half a century after Jesus' death—when gentiles in the church began to outnumber Jews, and Christianity and Judaism were slowly separating—were polemical rather than historical. In other words, the picture of the Jews in the New Testament is unreliable at best and reprehensible at worst.

The scholarly accusation that the Judaism of the first century AD was morally bankrupt often focuses on Jewish "legalism," which can be understood in terms of two related doctrines, both of which I will discuss in this and the following sections of this chapter: (1) the belief that obedience to the Law is the ideal expression of religious faith and (2) the belief that salvation can be earned by the performance of legally prescribed actions. On the first point, Gager says that, from the perspective of many scholars, Judaism was "dessicated, legalistic, altogether without appeal to outsiders."[172] This is because legalism ignores *the spirit of the law*, especially insofar as it represents God's intention. Thus, Paul Johnson accuses both the Sadducees and the Pharisees of "legalism, *adherence to the letter of the law.*"[173] One obvious problem with this attitude is that the worshiper need not understand either the meaning or the purpose of the law. He or she simply follows the rules. Another problem is that merely *doing things* is relatively easy. That is, actions can be performed mechanically and insincerely. Indeed, rules can be followed merely for appearance' sake. St. Paul thus rejected legalism, as has the church, but (at least according to traditional scholarship) not the Synagogue, because laws, like rules, can be followed without comprehension and without conviction.

In the view of many scholars, Judaism regarded God as a tyrant who required unquestioning loyalty. And that loyalty could be demonstrated primarily through obedience to God's laws. Johnson makes the point that, by the first century AD, Yahweh had become a terrifying god, whose worship had degenerated into appeasement. The Jews, Johnson says, were "a primitive desert people," whose religion was characterized by "doctrinal certainties and detailed moral teaching," and whose law "had never been fundamentally reformed." It "was administered and enforced by priests and scribes who constituted closed elites" and who "resisted change with fanaticism." So backward were the Jews that their law was "meaningless to a sophisticated, increasingly urban, and commercial community in the first century AD." Indeed, Johnson adds, "God had become a very distant and frightening figure, but the law was an ever-present and weighty reality." It was "a huge and daily burden."[174] In the words of Martin Dibelius, "The Lord of all peoples had become the party leader of the legalists, obedience to the ruler of history had become a finespun technique of piety."[175]

The Jewish law had become onerous not only because obedience to it was required by an all-powerful deity, but also because there were too many laws—to begin with, the 613 rules and regulations recorded in the Jewish Bible. Thus, even if the laws could be followed sincerely, they could hardly be comprehended and appreciated. To Rudolf Bultmann, this is what made the Jewish law impossible to fulfill: "To take [the laws] seriously meant making life an intolerable burden. It was almost impossible to *know* the rules, let alone put them into practice." Many of the ancient moral laws remained in effect, but "Jewish morality became over-scrupulous and pettifogging."[176]

Furthermore, even if these laws could be both understood and followed, the Pharisees, who evidently exercised total control over the Jews of Palestine, had added many additional laws. Johnson says, "Judaism has endless observances, each nested in a cocoon of commentaries."[177] Writing in 1900 and to a large extent representing the dominant view of Judaism before the 1960s and 1970s, Adolf Harnack says: "They thought of God as of a despot guarding the ceremonial observances in His household . . . They saw Him only in His law, which they had converted into a labyrinth of dark defiles, blind alleys and secret passages."[178]

Bultmann argues that—thanks largely to the influence of both the scribes and the Pharisees—among the Jews of the first century AD, "the whole of life was dominated by religion," which was embodied in the Law of Moses. The problems that ancient Jews faced in this regard were (1) that, among these inherited laws, were "many precepts which changing circumstances had rendered obsolete and meaningless"; and (2) that new laws were needed in order "to apply the old laws to the new conditions." These problems were compounded by the fact that even the outdated laws "had still to be obeyed unquestioningly." Furthermore, through what came to be known as the Oral Tradition, the Pharisees "extended [the law] to cover the whole of daily life down to the smallest details."[179]

The same point is made by Bornkamm, who says: "The Pharisees . . . aimed at this: the law is not to be left merely in its sacrosanct letter, but is to be interpreted as obligatory for the present day, and to be applied to all problems of private and public life . . . The exposition of the scriptures, developed and practiced in this movement, led to the addition to the authoritative letter of the Torah a no less obligatory exposition, which on occasion indulged in the oddest subtleties of casuistry."[180] Indeed, according to Bultmann, the problem was not just that there were too many laws, but that they "went into detail to the point of absurdity." And, since "many of the precepts were trivial or unintelligible," they required "the kind of obedience" that must be called "formal" rather than heartfelt.[181]

Of course, if the Pharisees had focused only on the *moral* law, they might have escaped the complete repudiation they received from both Jesus and the scholars. The problem they faced, says Bultmann, was that the Jewish law "inculcated not only morality, but ritualism." Furthermore, "no distinction was drawn between the moral and ritual law in respect of their divine authority."[182] John Riches says that the moral law (touching on "mercy, praise, and thanksgiving") derived from "the prophetic tradition," while the ritual law ("concerning the Sabbath, circumcision and purity") derived from "the priestly tradition." "In practice," Riches argues, underscoring Bultmann's point, "these two strands are interwoven both in the biblical tradition and in the various movements of the post-biblical period of Judaism."[183]

Furthermore, Bultmann says, of the 613 laws of the Pentateuch, 365 are negative. That is, "most of the regulations are . . . prohibitive in character," and over all they lack a "unifying principle."[184] Bornkamm notes that this is what distinguishes Jesus' view of the law from that of the Jews: his emphasis on "the first and greatest commandment," which "plays such an important part in his preaching" and allows his followers to understand that some laws are more important than others. Bornkamm says that the Jews had no basis for differentiating any single law from all the others: "Again we have to realize that this is in no way a natural question for a Jew to ask." Indeed, "[t]here is no lack . . . of Jewish utterances forbidding emphatically any such differentiation between things of greater or lesser importance."[185] This tendency among Jews to treat all laws equally was partly a result of the proliferation of laws and partly because of the belief that all of them had come from God. Thus, in Harnack's words, under the influence of the Pharisees, the law was "weighted, darkened, distorted, rendered ineffective and deprived of its force, by a thousand things which they also held to be religious and every whit as important as mercy and judgment. They reduced everything to one dead level, wove everything into one fabric; the good and holy was only one woof in a broad earthly warp."[186]

Worse yet, Bultmann says, as a result of embracing the tradition of the priests, the Pharisees, unlike the prophets, for whom moral laws were more important than ceremonial laws, actually elevated the latter. Thus, the rules concerning food, ritual performance, purity, and Sabbath restrictions "became the more important of the two, with the result that men lost sight of their social and cultural responsibilities." Indeed, "the whole of life was covered by ritual observances."[187] Bornkamm adds: "The entire life of the individual from morning till night was ritualized to the minutest detail, with prayer and cleansing regulations, with rules for eating and for relations with other people. Above all, the observance of the Sabbath rest became an inexhaustible topic, as we know from Jesus' numerous disputes, and also from the literature of the rabbis."[188]

Again, the kinds of laws we are talking about were not laws governing the relations between human beings, which could form the foundation of a pious, just, and orderly society, but laws governing actions whose only purpose was to placate a tribal god who was indifferent to human needs and unchangeable except by appeasement, like many gods in the pre-Christian Near Eastern pantheon. According to Bultmann, "The Pharisees, in their zeal, imposed upon the laity the laws of purity which had originally applied only to the priesthood."[189] As a result, Charles Guignebert says that the French scholar M. J. LaGrange, author of *Le Judaisme avant Jesus-Christ*, in 1931, similarly charged that the moral leaders of the Jews emphasized obedience over morality: "[T]he Rabbis cared little for the cultivation of piety since for them obedience to the Law was all that mattered."[190]

Insofar as these views emphasize the concerns of the Pharisees and Rabbis, they reflect, as Charlotte Klein notes, the modern influence of Julius Wellhausen, who was particularly contemptuous of the legalistic aspects of Judaism. Unlike Paul Johnson, who argued that the religion of the Jews was undermined by legalism throughout its history, Wellhausen, as we have seen, believed that Judaism acquired its preoccupation with ritual in the post-exilic period. By the second century BC, he says, "Jewish piety 'became hardened and rigid'. It attached the greatest importance to 'forms and externals' and made no distinction 'between minor and major matters in the law'. 'The works of morality were largely set aside; the works of sanctification, fasting, prayer, almsgiving preferred. But nothing was of value unless it was firmly regulated; the important thing was formal exactitude.'" Emil Schurer agreed: "There was no 'true piety, only external formalism': prayer too was 'chained within a rigid mechanism' and consequently became an external work . . . The purity laws simply provided an occasion for 'treating the field of sexual life in a manner which closely resembles the slippery casuistry of the Jesuits'. 'It was a terrible burden which a false legalism had loaded onto the shoulders of the people.'"[191]

According to the accounts in the Gospels, as well as their interpretation by New Testament scholars, the behavior of the Jews was as objectionable as their religion. Especially, insofar as Judaism was represented by the practices of the Pharisees, it was a faith based on the assumption that the Jews were God's elect, as a result of which it was unwelcoming to non-Jews and encouraged pride and self-righteousness. Amy-Jill Levine says that this charge was one among many stereotypes of the Jews: "Jews are narrow, clannish, particularistic, and xenophobic."[192] N. T. Wright notes that St. Paul accused the Jews of particularism—the refusal to include non-Jews in the circle of the saved: "In seeking to establish a status of righteousness, of covenant membership, which will be for Jews and Jews only, [Israel] has not submitted to God's righteousness. The covenant always envisaged a worldwide family; Israel, clinging to her own special status of the covenant-bearer, has betrayed the purpose for which that covenant was made."[193]

Grim as these charges are, Sean Freyne has portrayed the Pharisees as worthy of every conceivable disparaging epithet and guilty of every imaginable sin. Taking the Gospel accounts as the gospel truth, Freyne accuses the Pharisees of being, quite unlike Jesus, preoccupied with protecting themselves "from undesirables."[194] Occupying the extreme opposite side of the moral spectrum from the speaker of the Sermon on the Mount, the Pharisees were loveless and "narrow," as well socially exclusive. Being "parsimonious," "lovers of money," and even "rapacious," they developed a "closed religious system" that "creates social elitism based on their refusal to share their goods with the less well off." The Gospel of Luke, in particular, shows that the Pharisees combined "religious separatism with economic power to establish an elitist control which Jesus challenged." After all, the Gospel also shows that "those who controlled the wealth, namely the Pharisees, were interested only in sharing with those from whom they could expect to receive in return."[195]

For many scholars in this tradition, the Pharisees were not only responsible for a greatly expanded legal system, but also powerful enough to enforce it. Indeed, the idea that the Pharisees virtually ruled over the people of Israel has been a commonplace in Bible studies for centuries. Harnack says, for example, "The priests and the Pharisees held the nation in bondage and murdered its soul. For this unconstituted 'authority' Jesus showed a really emancipating and refreshing disrespect." Even worse, although the Pharisees were at least putatively a *religious* group, their main interest seems to have been power and control. Thus, Harnack says that Jesus struggled with their "wolfish nature and hypocrisy."[196] Freyne argues that, according to the Gospel of Luke, Galilean Judaism, "controlled by Pharisaic elitism," was "more concerned with socio-economic factors than with religious issues of a genuine kind."[197] Freyne adds later, "As the narrative progresses [the Pharisees'] suspicious nature will turn to open hostility, and Jerusalem is clearly seen as their centre of operation, from whence they exercise *their religious control.*" Indeed, in the Gospel of John, "the Pharisees . . . are characterized as the official watchdogs of an orthodox Jewish point of view."[198]

According to William R. Herzog II, the Pharisees were the agents of the high priests: "Owing to the cultural distance between the center and the periphery, those at the center of power and prestige had to monitor the periphery for evidence of compliance and signs of unrest. Typically, rulers sent their retainers to fulfill this role," which was "played by the scribal Pharisees in the Gospels." In other words, the Pharisees "probably came from Jerusalem to monitor compliance and control interpretation of the Torah."[199] Herzog thus agrees with N. T. Wright that the Pharisees were "a first-century version of 'thought police'": That is, they saw themselves and therefore conducted themselves as "moral entrepreneurs and rule enforcers."[200]

Bruce Chilton similarly portrays the Pharisees as guardians of public morality who carried their role as monitors of behavior to an unheard-of extreme. They were "royal nuisances": "sticklers for adhering to the letter of the Law," "busybodies" who stuck their noses into everybody's private activities (including sexual conduct), and enforcers of food laws, which they "fine-tuned," as well as Sabbath restrictions. This preoccupation with legalism became an obsession for Pharisees living closer to the Temple, who "were a testy bunch, innately conservative, not just a little paranoid, and unapologetically self-righteous." Although they had no "official control" over the Temple, they exercised "sway over large numbers of people in Jerusalem" because of their persuasive abilities—people whom they convinced that the purity laws were not only desirable but "necessary." And that allowed the Pharisees to incite mobs to violence, especially against violators of "the caste system," such as Jesus, whom they "stalked" and threatened with stoning.[201]

Nor is this all. Albert Nolan claims that not only the Pharisees, but the Jews in general were not only selfish, but also oppressive and exploitative. That is, it was not the Romans or the Jewish elite or the Pharisees alone who were Jesus' enemies, but *all* Jews, who were, evidently, just being Jews. As Nolan puts it, they were suffering from "the root cause of oppression and domination": their own "lack of compassion." Thus, "[i]f the people of Israel were to continue to lack compassion, . . . the overthrowing of the Romans" would hardly "make Israel any more liberated than before." More precisely, "[i]f the Jews continued to live off the worldly values of money, prestige, group solidarity and power," then "the Roman oppression" would merely be "replaced by an equally loveless Jewish oppression." In short, "there was more oppression and economic exploitation from within Judaism than from without." The problem was that "[t]he middle class Jews who were in rebellion against Rome were themselves oppressors of the poor and the uneducated." That is, "[t]he people had to suffer far more on account of the oppression of the scribes, Pharisees, Sadducees and Zealots than on account of the Romans." Indeed, they were not only hypocritical and insincere, but driven by "greed for money."[202]

According to Riches, as I noted earlier, when Jews put together the books of the Pentateuch, the Five Books of Moses—several centuries before the time of Jesus—they replaced the religion of the Jewish prophets with the religion of the Jewish priesthood. With the standard of worship and behavior in the hands of the latter, it is not surprising that the focus of religious concern shifted from morality, which had been emphasized by the prophets, to purity.[203] As Riches makes clear, this reorientation of Judaism was based on God's explanation of why he established his laws in the first place: "And you shall not walk in the customs of the nation which I am casting out before you . . . I have said to you, 'You shall inherit their land, and I will give it to you to possess, a land flowing with milk and honey.' I am the LORD your God, who have separated you from the peoples . . . You shall be holy to me; for I the LORD am holy, and have separated you from the peoples, that you should be mine" (Lev 20:22–26). In other words, the goal of the Priestly tradition, with its emphasis on purity laws and ritual performance, was to maintain the holiness of the people *by keeping them separate—both spiritually and physically—from others.* Riches concludes, "Thus doing the Law is associated here with not doing as the Gentiles do, and the consequences of doing the Law are contrasted with the consequences of doing as the Gentiles do."[204]

Not surprisingly, according to some scholars, the Pharisees carried these separatist tendencies even further. As F. F. Bruce says, "The Pharisaic concern for ceremonial purity involved not only strict separation from Gentiles, who were beyond the pale of the law altogether, and from Samaritans, whose interpretation of the laws of purity differed from that current among the Jews, but even a considerable degree of aloofness from those of their fellow-Jews who were not so particular about the laws of purity and tithing as the Pharisees themselves were." From this point of view, the Pharisees self-righteously saw themselves as ritually pure and others as ritually impure, especially the vast majority of Jews who were too poor, too far-removed from Jerusalem, too irreligious, or just too lazy to obey God's laws—the so-called *am-haaretz*, the people of the land. "Chief among these latter were the ordinary artisans and peasants," Bruce continues, "who could not devote much time to the study and practice of these laws, and perhaps could not bring themselves to be greatly interested in them." Bruce notes that "a group of ruling Pharisees" in the Gospel of John says of these people: "[T]his crowd, who do not know the law, are accursed" (7:49).[205]

In short, the laws promoted by the Pharisees were not formulated because they served the people, but because they supported the caste system dominated by the priestly class. Harnack argues that since "the governing classes . . . had little feeling for the needs of the people," it was easy for the priests and Pharisees to promote "public worship" and "the cult of 'righteousness'" over "mercy and sympathy with the poor."[206] Martin Marty says that the Pharisees were "well thought of, especially by themselves, for their scrupulosity in keeping the law, but ill thought of when they were judgmental. Marty adds that Jesus saw them as "caring less about persons than about principles and policies."[207] According to John L. McKenzie, "The entire thrust of the sayings of Jesus in the Gospels is in opposition to the legal rigorism and the exclusivism which, it is generally agreed, were traits of the Pharisees based on the principles and the doctrines of Pharisaism. The sympathy with the poor and the needy which runs through the words of Jesus in the Gospel embraces those whom the Pharisees rejected as *am-haares*"—that is, the ordinary people, the people of the land.[208]

Judaism and Quid pro Quo

The second aspect of legalism has to do with the opposition between Christianity and Judaism regarding two different means of achieving salvation: that is, the conflict between Grace and Works. David Christie-Murray says, "Wherever a Christian believes that he can earn salvation by church attendance, adherence to a moral code, Sabbath observance, in short, keeping what he thinks is the Christian version of 'the Law,' he is spiritually a Judaizer"—that is, in effect, a Jew rather than a Christian. "Where a religious man follows a code of behavior or gives his allegiance to a creed because it will win him salvation and heaven, or because his failure will be punished in this world or the next with *delirium tremens*, venereal disease or hellfire, or simply for appearance' sake, he is on the road to heresy."[209] According to Riches, to the ancient Jews, "God's justice is associated with his punishment of the wicked and his rewarding of the righteous, and equally wickedness and righteousness are further defined in terms of disobedience and obedience to the Law.[210] God says to the Jews at Sinai, after the exodus from Egypt, "Now therefore if you will obey my voice, and keep my covenant, you will be my own possession among all peoples, . . . and you shall be to me a kingdom of priests and a holy nation" (Exod 20: 5–6).

Judaism has often been charged with this attitude, which has been condemned because it turns the connection between God and humanity into a king-subject relationship—or, worse, a master-servant relationship—based on fear rather than love. On the other hand, Christie-Murray explains, "true religion" occurs "if a man is so in love with God and his neighbour that he joyfully embraces and accepts a discipline and behavior to express his adoration and philanthropy."[211] In this view, the Jewish faith turned into a *pro forma* obedience to law, as we have seen, and Jewish morality turned into a system of *quid pro quo*—an exchange of meritorious acts for tangible rewards—not an expression of love on the part of humanity and grace on the part of God. "The relation to God," Bultmann says, is thus conceived as a legal contract relation." And that relation is a matter of calculation on both sides. Both God and his subjects are compelled to add up good deeds and subtract bad ones. "An index of this conception," Bultmann adds, "is the absurd dispute in which several rabbis engaged: what will become of the men whose good and bad deeds are equal?"[212]

Like Christie-Murray (and other scholars), Bultmann emphasizes the connection between legalism and what we might call contractualism. Judaism, he says, is "a form of piety which regards the will of God as expressed in the written Law and in the Tradition which interprets it, *a piety which endeavors to win God's favor by the toil of minutely fulfilling the Law's stipulation*."[213] Indeed, not only are these two ideas related; one concept leads to the other: "The legalistic conception of obedience *produced* an equally legalistic conception of divine retribution."[214] The idea that God protects and rewards the obedient and destroys and punishes the disobedient, Riches adds, "finds its fullest exposition in the historical books [of the Jewish Bible] which attempt to give an account of Israel's misfortunes and occasional triumphs in terms of the obedience of the kings to God's Law." This shows that God's justice—this *quid pro quo* system—was understood in relation to "the material and political well-being of the people." However, after many centuries of foreign domination and the clear evidence that the wicked sometimes prosper while the righteous do not, many Jews lost faith in the idea that God's rewards and punishments arrived either immediately or in this life. Thus, "the conventional associations of God's righteousness had to be reworked," and, in some minds, its implementation could be expected only in the future, either after the end-time or in heaven: "[T]he apocalyptic writers increasingly looked forward to a future time of reckoning when the present sufferings of the righteous would be vindicated."[215]

Whether the implementation of this system was intended to take place now or later, however, many scholars saw the Jewish interpretation of God's justice as inherently corrupt. Clearly, an action that is performed for the sake of a reward can hardly be considered virtuous. In other words, as Bultmann points out, "motivation to ethical conduct is vitiated." After all, the phrase "good work" (or "good deed") would seem to refer to something that was done out of kindness, generosity, or love. Something done for gain, however, is obviously merely self-serving. Indeed, such deeds can be performed for a variety of selfish reasons, including not only self-satisfaction, but also a desire for recognition (ambition), a need to compensate for past deeds (sense of guilt), or a wish to avoid punishment (fear). Bultmann relates the third and fourth motives to "supererogation": "the notion of 'good works' that go beyond the required fulfillment of the Law (such as almsgiving, various acts of charity, voluntary fasting, and the like), establishing literal merits and hence also capable of atoning for transgressions of the Law."[216]

Joachim Jeremias attributes these ideas to the Pharisees in particular: They "attached greatest importance to works of supererogation and good works; what is more, the accomplishment of works of supererogation was an integral part of the very essence of Pharisaism and its ideal of meritorious behavior."[217] Kenneth Scott Latourette says, "Their error was their belief that they would earn God's favour by their deeds, or, to put it another way, that they could accumulate merit with God by obedience to His law."[218] Georg Fohrer, emphasizing that this attitude can be found as early as the eighth century BC, comments: "Seen from the viewpoint of the prophets' message, fulfillment of the law appeared merely as a further attempt on the part of the devout individual to place Yahweh under obligation through his own actions."[219] In later Judaism, according to Bornkamm, "The conception of reward . . . has become painfully rigid, and had petrified into a doctrine of retribution meant to throw light on the riddle of history and the life of the individual."[220] This is the aspect of Jewish legalism that Harnack evidently had in mind when he lamented that Jews "had made this religion into an earthly trade, and there was nothing more detestable."[221]

An even deeper problem with this moral program is that all of these motivations can have more serious consequences. First, the actual achievement of recognition can lead to the sin of arrogance and overconfidence, resulting from the certainty that one has done more than enough. Regarding the first issue, Bultmann explains: "[B]elief in the *meritoriousness* of conduct according to the Law easily establishes itself in the Judaism of Jesus' time. In fact, the dependence on good works, the pride in good works, evidently played a fatal part in late Judaism. The religious man expects to be able to call God's attention to his merits, he believes that he has a claim on God."[222]

According to Reginald H. Fuller, the Pharisees acknowledged that the two great commandments, love of God and love of humanity were part of Jewish law, but they did not give them the prominence they were to receive in the New Testament. "All this naturally led to a belief in the saving value of good works, and the sense of pride which a doctrine of merit inevitably entailed." Fuller quotes St. Paul, who says of the Pharisees, "'I bear them witness that they have a zeal for God, but it is not enlightened. For, being ignorant of the righteousness that comes from God, and seeking to establish their own, they did not submit to God's righteousness' (Rom. 10:2–3)."[223]

Latourette, similarly referring to the Pharisees, explains: "This attitude, Jesus saw, bred meticulous care to conform to a set of ethical principles and of ritualistic acts, with a satisfaction in having approximated to them which nourished the deadliest of all sins, pride. Also contributing to pride was the satisfaction of recognition from other men with its associated striving for the approval of men and for place and position, a striving which might even lead one to pray, to undertake ascetic practices, and to perform deeds of mercy for the applause of men." Latourette says later that "the radiant life which God desires for men is not to be had through the meticulous observance of the Law, for no one could ever keep the commands which God had given for men's instruction and guidance, or, if they attempted to win God's favour in that fashion, they would either be in despair, or deceive themselves and be proud of having done so, and thus be guilty of the most deadly of all sins."[224]

Second, the attempt to escape punishment, as Latourette suggests, can lead to apprehension, pathological anxiety, or despair, resulting from the fear or belief that one has done less than enough. Bultmann says, "A further consequence of the legalistic conception of obedience was that the prospect of salvation became highly uncertain. Who could be sure he had done enough in this life to be saved? Would his observance of the Law and his good works be sufficient? ... The prospect of meeting God as their judge awakened in the conscientious a scrupulous anxiety and morbid sense of guilt." To avoid this condition, many Jews turned to asking God for forgiveness, which is why "Jewish literature is full of confessions of sin and penitential prayers." Considering these two extreme (but evidently not unusual) responses to the Jewish concept of justice, Bultmann notes the "remarkable fact that side by side with this sense of sin and urge to repentance we find the 'righteous' proud and self-conscious," as we do in the Parable of the Pharisee and the Publican.[225] Herbert Braun makes the same point: "This polarity results in a peculiar uncertainty of attitude: the devout man is cheerfully confident that he can face the judgement with his achievements ... but at the same time he has the gnawing anxiety that these achievements may nevertheless not be adequate."[226]

It is important to understand how pervasive this view of Judaism was many years ago and how persistent it remains, albeit far less extensively than in the past. Although most scholars have avoided the kind of detailed analysis of legalism that we find in writers like Harnack, Bornkamm, and Bultmann, the accusation that Judaism is or was a debased religion was widespread. One of the ways in which scholars substantiated the superiority of Christianity to Judaism was to emphasize Jesus' opposition to the Jewish faith by contrasting their views, point for point. For example, E. P. Sanders says, "Hundreds, possibly thousands of New Testament scholars have charged Jews with being legalistic, and they have attributed to Jesus the desire to overcome the legalism of his native religion." Indeed, many scholars made a "stark contrast between Jesus, who represents everything good, pure and enlightened, and Judaism, which represents everything distorted, hypocritical and misleading."[227] As Sanders explains elsewhere, "A Christianity that is defined by love of neighbor, belief in God's grace, and good works that do not earn merit, but rather flow naturally from a person's basic religious orientation, needs a Jewish opponent, a religion that denies these views." Christians found their enemy in the Pharisees, who "opposed love, mercy, and grace" and were "legalistic."[228] John P. Meier agrees: "[T]he unique goodness of Jesus' gospel of grace had to be highlighted by being set over against the legalistic, 'works-righteousness' of the Pharisees."[229]

In contrast to Harnack's dark view of Judaism, given above, is his view of Jesus, who did not see God as a despot, but actually "breathed in [his] presence"; did not insist on blind obedience to his laws, but "saw and felt Him everywhere"; and did not spin out "a thousand laws," but "had only one."[230] Bornkamm claims that "there developed, on the ground of Pharisaism and the scribal teaching connected with it, that formalistic legalizing of the law, and a corresponding detailed technique of piety, to which Jesus' message of the divine will stands in sharp contrast."[231] Albrecht Dihle

The Traditional View of Judaism

says that "Jesus [took] issue with the Jews' sense of election and replace[d] pious self-concern with unconditional love of one's neighbor." Herbert Braun similarly accuses the Jews, with their "meticulous obedience" to the Law, of wallowing in "self-glory," while Jesus offered "unconditional" love as well as "joyful and free obedience."[232]

C. H. Dodd says that the "Jewish teachers of [Jesus'] time" established "a quantitative conception of morality," according to which, like a student taking an exam, a person "earned a certain number of marks," the total of which "could be put to [his or her] credit." To Dodd, "the obvious danger" in this ethical program was in "giving the outward act an independent value apart from the disposition which makes it a moral act." That is, it was morally shallow. An additional danger lay in the temptation not only to be proud of one's own achievement of virtue but also to disdain others for not living up to the same standard. Jesus objected to the whole array of sins generated by this misunderstanding of the relationship between God and humanity, including "complacency" and "self-righteousness," "harsh judgment" and "censoriousness," and "self-despair." "In the teaching of Jesus," Dodd says, "goodness is not measurable by any yardstick. It is qualitative and not quantitative at all." Judaism, "starting with the best intentions, . . . had come to encourage this folly and evil," and Jesus insisted that it had lost its way.[233]

As recently as 1996, without emphasizing the inferiority of Judaism to Christianity, Rodney Stark attributed the picture of God as a proponent of love instead of fear to Christianity rather than Judaism. On one hand, he calls "the linking of a highly *social* ethical code with religion" a "distinctive" idea that "came into the world with development of Judeo-Christian thought." What distinguished this moral concept "was the notion that more than self-interested exchange relations were possible" between God and humanity. On the other hand, however, Stark refers only to Christianity as the source of "these revolutionary ideas." The belief "that God loves those who love him" is a "Christian teaching." It was "a new morality" when it was articulated in Matthew 25. And it arose as "something entirely new" when "the moral climate" was dominated by pagan ideas that discouraged mercy and pity as motives for moral action.[234]

Similarly, attacking the Jewish concept of justice, Paul Johnson says: "Jesus was a revolutionary who transformed the entire Judaic religious scheme into something different. It ceased to be a penal system of law and punishment . . . and became an affair of the heart and an adventure of the spirit . . . A faithful soul was not one who obeyed the law but one who, by transforming the spirit, 'entered' the Kingdom. God was not a distant, terrifying Yahweh but 'the Father.'"[235] On the same subject, Fuller argues that, despite the similarities between Jesus' ideas and those of his fellow Jews, the "inner content" of Jesus' idea of God was fundamentally different from that of his Jewish contemporaries: "Later Judaism had pushed God further and further from direct contact with man, had made him more and more 'transcendent,'" intervening "in human life" through supernatural beings, like angels. To Jesus, however, God "is near, is present, is acting, in his demand of obedience and in his offer of salvation." To the Jews, in other words, God was an abstraction; but, to Jesus, he was a father. Indeed, "Jesus dared to call him, as no other Jew had ever dared, by the intimate address, Abba."[236]

Many contemporary scholars regard this contrast between Christianity and Judaism to be a consequence of both New Testament views and subsequent church-generated interpretations. "Tragically," says Raymond E. Brown, "as Christianity began to be looked on as another religion over against Judaism, Matt[hew]'s critique [of Judaism] became the vehicle of a claim that Christianity was balanced and honest while Judaism was legalistic and superficial."[237] Freyne explains that, in order to see Jesus as a divine being, he had to be portrayed as entirely different from the mere humans who rejected him: "An apologetic Christology, especially one endowed with liberal values, required a setting for Jesus' life that was the polar opposite of all that Jesus was held to have affirmed, since discontinuity with his environment was seen as a support for his claims to uniqueness. A view of the religion of Second Temple Judaism as debased and sterile was also an essential ingredient of the picture."[238] According to Levine, "Christian ministers and laity alike depict [Jesus'] Jewish background as the epitome of all that is wrong with the world. If Jesus preaches good news to the poor, . . . 'the Jews' must be preaching good news to the rich. If Jesus welcomes sinners, 'the Jews' must have pushed them away."[239]

Referring to both Church Fathers and modern scholars, John Dominic Crossan says that Christians from the first century AD to the present "have both trivialized and brutalized Judaism in descriptions down through the centuries."[240] Specifically, many contemporary scholars criticize the reduction of Judaism to a religion of Works over Grace as a distortion and misrepresentation. Ben Witherington III comments, "The caricature that all early Judaism was grounded in legalism and works righteousness without any emphasis on grace and God's mercy taking precedence in the way God deals with people is simply false."[241] Richard Elliott Friedman accuses Christians of paying attention to the Old Testament Priestly writers who did, in fact, portray God exclusively as a God of Justice, while ignoring the Old Testaments writers who consistently portray God as the God of Mercy.[242] Thus, W. H. Davies asks, "Was their God aloof and their religion dominated by fear and not by love? Many Christian scholars have often in the past urged that this was so." However, Davies argues, "Judaism did know the love of God for his own and emphasized that as much as it did the fear of the Lord."[243]

Rosemary R. Ruether says that this contrast between Judaism and Christianity began early (presumably in the letters of Paul), continued unremittingly (in the so-called *adversos Judaeos* of the early Middle Ages), and expanded unimaginably into every aspect of morality and religion: "It was the left hand of Christology that generated, almost from the beginning and with growing intensity as time went on, the radical distinction between the believing Church and the blind Synagogue, between the Israel of the spirit and the earthly Jerusalem. Eventually all the dichotomies of salvation between spirit and flesh, light and darkness, truth and falsehood, grace and damnation, life and death, trust and self-righteousness, were projected on the opposition between Church and Synagogue until the Jewish people became the embodiment of all that is unredeemed, perverse, stubborn, evil, and demonic in the world." Furthermore, these "basic dualisms" not only "shaped early Christian understanding," but also profoundly influenced both contemporary scholarship and contemporary preaching. They are "so deeply ingrained in Christian language that modern critical theology and liberal sermonizing still remain largely oblivious to their implications. 'Christian' sincerity and authenticity are, as a matter of course, contrasted with so-called 'Pharisaism.' 'Christian' inwardness is explicated over against something called 'Jewish legalism.'"[244]

In other words, says Donald A. Hagner, "Frequently, . . . a mistaken and unfortunate polarity has been imposed on the data by Christian writers, and this polarity results in a caricature of Judaism and an exaggeration of the uniqueness of Christianity."[245] According to Levine, "Judaism becomes in such discourse a negative foil: Whatever Jesus stands for, Judaism isn't; whatever Jesus is against, Judaism epitomizes the category." As Levine later explains, Jesus "has to have something concrete to oppose. The bad 'system' then becomes, in the scholarship and in the pulpit, first-century Judaism."[246] The essential polarity, according to James Carroll—which he calls the "foundational slander against the Jews"—"is that the 'God of the Old Testament' is the heartless God of the Law, of revenge, of punishment, while the 'God of the New Testament' is the God of love, mercy, and forgiveness."[247]

Providing a crystal-clear example of this kind of scholarly sleight-of-hand, Bultmann says that "the all-important difference between" Judaism and Christianity can be seen in their "conception of God": "For Judaism God has become remote. He governs the world by means of angels, while his relations with man are mediated by the book of the Law," which, Bultmann says, separates Jews "from the outside world" by legalism and ritualism. "For Jesus, however, God's distinction from and transcendence over the world means that he is always the God who comes. He meets man not only in the future judgment, but also here and now in daily life."[248] According to Sanders, and as the aforementioned examples make obvious, the goal of differentiating Christianity from Judaism often went too far: "Earlier generations of scholars sometimes made Jesus so unique (and Judaism so inferior) that the reader is now forced to wonder how it could be that Jesus grew up on Jewish soil. Thus [Wilhelm] Bousset, for example, while conceding some formal similarities between Jesus and his contemporaries . . . , denied any similarity at all on essentials. Although many of Bousset's basic views about Judaism are still unhesitatingly repeated by New Testament scholars, the crudity of his description of Judaism has pretty well disappeared."[249] Sanders emphasizes that Bousset's interpretation of Judaism was not unusual: "It was not, in fact, his own, but was largely derivative. The view of Judaism cannot be simply regarded as a period piece and passed over, however, for two reasons: (1) the use of a denigrating view of Judaism to set off Christianity as superior, which is so clear in Bousset, has continued; (2) his depiction of Palestinian Judaism is still cited as authoritative and standard."[250]

To many contemporary scholars, this negative view of the religion of the Jews is simply attributable to either anti-Judaism or anti-Semitism. James D. Tabor says: "One tendency among scholars of the last century, now largely discarded, was the attempt to strip [Jesus] and his message of its Jewish contexts. The idea was that Jesus, though born a Jew, realized the deficiencies of his obsolete ancestral faith . . . Judaism was seen as a fossilized precursor of the final revelation that Jesus brought to the world. We now understand that such views have no historical basis and in fact are subtle manifestations of Christian anti-Semitism."[251] Illustrating what she calls "the long tradition of scholarly anti-Judaism," Fredriksen says that, according to such scholars as Bornkamm, Jews were the exact opposite of Christians: "One group was simply hierarchical, oppressive, patriarchal, exclusionary, and sexist; the other egalitarian, inclusive, and compassionate."[252]

Often, too, this anti-Judaism has been specifically attributed to German scholars associated with Lutheranism.[253] Meier, for example, argues, "It is the tendency of Bornkamm to read German Lutheran polemics about legalism into the situation of Jesus that especially calls for correction."[254] Unfortunately, says Donald H. Akenson, "despite recent lip-service to the concept of Jesus as a Jewish figure, a strong residual bias towards getting Christianity out of its Semitic phase as quickly as possible remains." Akenson traces this misrepresentation of both Jesus and Judaism to the work of theologians and historians in "the largely teutonic enterprise of 'Higher Criticism,'" represented by Martin Dibelius, Rudolf Bultmann, Ernest Kasemann, and Gunther Bornkamm, who powerfully influenced Bible scholarship in the mid-twentieth century.[255] Martin Hengel more precisely blames "latently anti-Jewish modern liberal German Protestantism," sympathy for which "lasted to the middle of the twentieth century." He cites in an endnote E. Hirsch, who referred to Judaism as "false faith and worship"; and E. Haenchen, in whose work Hengel finds "the strange mixture of antisemitism and modern 'progressive' theology."[256] John Howard Yoder also criticizes what he calls a "Protestant, post-Pietist, rationalist" point of view, "which if not intentionally anti-Semitic, was at least sweepingly asemitic, stranger to the Jewish Jesus."[257]

At this point, some readers will not have to be reminded that the unholy trinity of Germany, Lutheranism, and anti-Judaic views was not born anew in the twentieth century but traces its history back to Julius Wellhausen and beyond. According to Blenkinsopp, Wellhausen, the most famous of all proponents of the theory that Judaism had undergone a severe decline by the first century AD, had an "often expressed distaste for Judaism which, though it can hardly be described as antisemitism, fitted only too well the academic *Zeitgeist* at the time [his] book appeared." On this Zeitgeist, however, without calling Wellhausen's attitude toward Judaism "a racial anti-Semitism," Levenson says that Wellhausen simply "participated in the anti-Semitic culture of his time and place and failed to challenge its theological underpinnings."[258] Indeed, Blenkinsopp adds, "It will be obvious by now that by far the greater number of essays in Old Testament theology emanate from German-language Protestantism," and most of them, as Blenkinsopp makes clear, share the view of Judaism that Wellhausen promoted, which means that Wellhausen's work "made its modest contribution to the 'final solution' of the Jewish problem under the Third Reich."[259]

Fredriksen explains the origins of scholarly anti-Semitism by recalling that Protestantism, under the influence of Martin Luther, developed in opposition to the most notorious expression of Catholicism's *quid pro quo* theory of salvation, the sale of indulgences. The biblical basis for the distinction between salvation by Grace and salvation by Works—and thereby between Protestantism and Catholicism—Luther himself found in the letters of Paul, which praise Jesus for the former and condemn the Pharisees for the latter. The result in Protestant biblical scholarship, Fredriksen says, was the "conflation of Catholic/Pharisee." In short, in Protestant theology, the errors of the Catholics—"works righteousness," "dead legalism," "hypocrisy," and "anxiety about merit"—link modern Catholicism to ancient Judaism: "In describing the Gospel's ancient enemy, Luther made clear the identity of its modern counterpart, and so turned ancient polemic to contemporary use."[260] According to Blenkinsopp, Wellhausen said that the transition from Judaism to Christianity was duplicated by the transition from Catholicism to Protestantism. The Catholic Church was not Christ's creation, "but [in Wellhausen's words] an inheritance from Judaism to Christianity."[261]

Gager similarly argues that "Protestant scholarship in particular engaged in a covert polemic against Roman Catholicism by projecting distasteful aspects of Catholic belief and practice onto Judaism and attacking them in that guise. This process seems to be at work in specifically Lutheran scholarship."[262] Thus, R. E. Brown says that the portrayal of Judaism in the time of Jesus as legalistic arose in "the aftermath of the Reformation." That is, the Protestants of the sixteenth and seventeenth centuries argued that, to the Jews of the first century AD, they "were justified"—or saved—"only if they did the deeds mandated in the Mosaic Law." Such, at least, was Paul's view, and his "condemnation of such a Judaism was used [by Protestants] to refute a legalistic Catholicism that maintained that people could be saved by the good works they performed or had performed on their behalf." Catholics responded by claiming that "justification was a free gift of God that could not be earned by good works." As a result, both Protestants and Catholics proclaimed their unity on this subject and henceforth joined together in accusing "the Jews of Paul's time" of believing that "justification could be merited by good works."[263]

As a further consequence of this achievement of theological agreement, the condemnation of Judaism for embracing the doctrine of Works over Grace has not been limited to Protestant circles. Though educated in Catholic schools, Carroll says that his understanding of Judaism was warped by "German Protestant theology and scholarship, still largely uncriticized for its implicit anti-Judaism," which "in the early 1960s" was "more influential in Catholic circles than ever."[264] Levenson explains that although Catholic scholars have risen "to the top ranks of most branches of biblical studies in the last four decades"—freed as they were from restrictions on their academic study of the Bible by the *Divino afflante spiritu* in 1943—they "have not substantially changed the overwhelmingly Protestant complexion of biblical theology."²⁶⁵

Much of this anti-Judaic view of ancient Judaism has also been attributed to Emil Schurer, the most influential historian of Judaism in the nineteenth century. According to Anthony J. Saldarini, "Many Christian scholars and handbooks are still influenced by the biased picture of Judaism developed by Schurer and perpetuated in numerous introductions and summaries."²⁶⁶ James A. Charlesworth says: "Unfortunately, he succumbed to the tendencies of his day, using the apologetics, even polemics, in some New Testament passages to distort his evaluation of early Jewish piety. It is shocking today to read his claim that in Jesus' time Jewish prayer 'was bound in the fetters of a rigid mechanism.'" The two greatest prayers in the Jewish liturgy, he said—the Shema and the Eighteen Benedictions—were "degraded to an external function."²⁶⁷ Calling Schurer "the author who must bear the greatest responsibility for the wrong view of Judaism in recent studies," Klein says that George F. Moore, in the article referred to earlier, "drew attention to the many basic mistakes and errors" in Schurer's work, including blaming the Jews of Jesus' time for embracing "quite fantastic ideas," being dominated by "an intemperate and not truly religious imagination," and suffering from a reactionary attitude guided by "Jewish self-love."²⁶⁸

Two influential German scholars, writing during the thirties and forties, Walter Grundmann and Gerhard Kittel, were in fact Nazis. Freyne reminds his readers that Grundmann, who wrote *Jesus der Galilaer und Judentum*, "argued that as a Galilean, Jesus was not a Jew!"²⁶⁹ Kittel has been identified by James Carroll and Geza Vermes, among others, as a Nazi-inspired theologian,²⁷⁰ and Grundmann headed a Nazi organization whose task was to cleanse German Christianity of all Jewishness: namely, the Institute for the Study and Elimination of Jewish Influence on German Church Life. Klein discusses these Bible scholars, along with Martin Dibelius, back to back, as examples of "theologians at the time of the Hitler regime who were at pains to detach Christianity from its Jewish roots and to disguise it as 'Aryan.'" All three, Klein adds, are among those "who either still stand for what they taught in the thirties or whose books went into new editions in the sixties." In the book cited above, Grundmann "attempts to show," as Freyne argues, "that Jesus, being mentally and psychologically completely un-Jewish, must have been the same biologically and physically." Kittel's *Theological Dictionary of the New Testament*, "an irreplaceable reference book for exegetes and theologians," Klein says, reveals "traces of a biased or at least scarcely sympathetic approach to Judaism."²⁷¹

Lest it be assumed that the Germans were alone in the anti-Semitic portrait of Judaism, it must be acknowledged that the enterprise began not with Kant, Hegel, and Schleiermacher in the late eighteenth century, but with an Englishman of the seventeenth century, John Lightfoot, of Cambridge University. According to Geza Vermes, Lightfoot was one of the first modern scholars to use "post-biblical Judaica" in his studies by explaining passages in the New Testament "with the help of rabbinic quotations." On one hand, says Vermes, Lightfoot helped make the study of the Hebrew language and Hebrew texts like the Talmud respectable. On the other hand, however, Lightfoot displayed the same kind of contempt for Judaism that became pervasive among German scholars when this kind of scholarship "migrated to the continent" in the next century. "Intending readers of these volumes," says Lightfoot in *Horae Hebraicae et Talmudicae,* "may be frightened away by the ill-repute of their authors who are very badly spoken of by all . . . Their Jewish writings stink." In short, Lighfoot wrote off the Talmud as displeasing and tormenting because its topics are characterized by "stupendous futility" and therefore offer "nothing but nonsense, destruction and poison to drink," which, nevertheless, "the Christians with their skill and industry can covert . . . into useful servants of their studies."[272]

Although there can be little doubt that at least some scholars who have portrayed Judaism negatively were motivated by some kind of religious or racial prejudice, it is also possible to find other reasons for this view. First, to anyone who reads the Bible literally—that is, as an infallible record of the distant past—it is extremely difficult to see the Jews and their religion in any other light. In this context, it is not surprising to find that Freyne, for example, claims that the Gospels are true: "The narratives of Jesus the Galilean that have been left to us in the gospel portraits of his career . . . are an eloquent testimony to just how radical and transforming that experience has, after all, to be." In other words, Freyne's portrait of Jews (and Pharisees in particular) is based on what he believes to be historically reliable accounts.[273] Freyne adds, "[T]here are, indeed, interesting correspondences between the contours of the story of Jesus as narrated and what could plausibly be said of his movement's impact in a Galilean setting. Indeed, not only do broad outlines correspond, but at several points significant details stand up to vigorous critical examination in terms of the historical likelihood." In fact, Freyne finds a match not only between history and the Gospels, but also between the Gospels and the *kerygma*—that is, the Jesus of history and the Christ of faith match up surprisingly well. And, most important in this context, I believe, his faith in the authenticity of the text totally frees him from the charge of bias.[274]

Second, as I suggested earlier, some scholars—without having any kind of prejudice or other disqualifying motivation—sincerely believe, despite the contemporary consensus to the contrary, that Jesus rejected Judaism entirely; and, furthermore, that Christianity succeeded because it was superior to Judaism. This is simply to believe that Christianity is the one true faith. It is also useful to keep in mind that many scholars are quite passionate in their belief, especially in the uniqueness of Jesus and the tragedy of his suffering. Latourette, I think, should be understood to fall into both categories. That is, he believes in the literal truth of the New Testament, and he is genuinely angry about the fate of Jesus. On the one hand, he says of his chapter on the foundations of Christianity: "As will be readily seen from even a casual reading, the preceding pages are written from a conservative viewpoint. They have endeavoured to take account of recent as well as older scholarship, but they are frankly based upon an acceptance of the Gospel records as inspired and conveying accurate information."[275] On the other hand, however, it is clear from Latourette's tone in passages in which he refers to the Passion that it is the inspiration of the text, as much as its accuracy, that deeply moves him.

Fortunately, whether driven by anti-Judaism or not, the traditional picture of Judaism has become an increasingly uncommon view, at least among scholars. Says Meier, "The great challenge to a simplistic (and indeed polemical) view of Judaism at the time of Jesus was given from the Christian side by E. P. Sanders" and other modern scholars. "[F]or all their differences, these scholars represent a turning point in research: simplistic generalizations about 'Late Judaism' (a dreadful misnomer!) being a religion of legalism and fear will no longer be taken seriously by most scholars."[276] N. T. Wright argues that W. D. Davies was the revolutionary in this regard: "Davies' work signals a new attitude to Judaism on the part of post-war scholarship. Until then, Judaism had been regarded . . . as the great exemplar of the wrong sort of religion. It represented human self-effort, legalism, prejudice and pride . . . Jewish [ideas] were irrevocably tainted." Wright adds, "[W]ith Davies the whole scene has changed, in line with the work of Karl Barth, . . . and with the post-war reaction against the vile anti-Semitism which caused the Holocaust."[277] Thanks to these corrections, Franz Mussner says, "[D]istortions of Judaism which have led to its demonization and those hostile images which were developed in the time of the primitive church and which are largely retained to this very day will finally be dismantled."[278]

Chapter Two

The Contemporary View of Judaism

As I said earlier, the idea that the stories in the Bible are true beyond all question or doubt was first challenged during the Enlightenment, when many European and some American intellectuals turned away from orthodox religion and, based on epistemological principles introduced in the seventeenth century, adopted an attitude toward the faiths into which they had been born ranging from outright rejection (atheism) to uncertainty (agnosticism) to what might be called radical minimization (Deism). According to James Carleton Paget: "It is probably in the seventeenth and early eighteenth centuries that the seeds of what we might call the modern study of the historical Jesus are to be found. A number of factors account for this. Some have to do with a growing conviction amongst a minority of Christians that the Bible's witness to truth could not be sustained by a simple appeal to the idea of revelation, but rather by an appeal to reason . . . In this worldview, the Bible's claim to be an inspired document that spoke in some privileged way about divine truth was undermined. It became instead a collection of books whose primary meaning should be located in what its author intended."[279]

In short, as James L. Kugel explains: "'Nature's book'—opened by science—was turning out to be more reliable than that other book, the Bible. At the same time, thinkers such as Francis Bacon (1561–1626) and Rene Descartes (1596–1679) were seeking to examine the very processes of human reasoning and, especially in the case of the latter, to proceed from a radical skepticism that took nothing for granted, including, prominently, the teachings of religion."[280] Several decades before Thomas Jefferson rewrote the Gospels by omitting all of their supernatural claims, a German theologian announced the application of similarly rationalistic standards to the field of Bible study in general. According to Joseph Blenkinsopp, "It has become customary to trace the origins of biblical theology as a distinct discipline to the inaugural lecture of Johann Philipp Gabler delivered (in Latin) at the University of Altdorf on March 30, 1787. As a child of his age, Gabler proposed to set up biblical theology independently of church dogmatics on the basis of scientific, which meant in effect historical, principles. Since then no biblical theology worthy of the name has been able to evade the implications of the historical method."[281]

The traditional view of Judaism was first directly challenged by Gabler's contemporary, Hermann Samuel Reimarus, a German theologian, in a book entitled *On the Aim of Jesus and of His Disciples*. The book was so radical that it could be published only after its author's death, in the late eighteenth century. Reimarus's work was revolutionary because he was among the first scholars in history to question the church's longstanding picture of Jesus and Judaism. He raised new questions about the story of Jesus' life in the context of first-century Judaism because, like Gabler, he embraced a radically new concept of knowledge. He was the product of an age that believed in the possibility of understanding all of human experience on the basis of what educated people considered to be scientific principles. That is, as a man of his time—the Age of Reason, represented as well by Voltaire, David Hume, and Benjamin Franklin—Reimarus believed that he possessed the intellectual capacity and had acquired the analytical skills that would enable him to distinguish between historical facts, which can be verified, and theological assertions (especially regarding supernatural events), which cannot stand up to scientific scrutiny.

What ensued in the wake of Reimarus's book was a series of similar challenges to the New Testament view of Jesus and Judaism. These books were written by university professors—some of whom were fired for their views—who, in the words of Mark Allen Powell, "questioned the accuracy of the Gospels at certain points and sought to supplement the stories with what they thought were reasonable conjectures at other points."[282] Since then, as Powell says, interpretation of the New Testament has become a pitched battle between those who accepted the inherited view of Jesus—the Christ of faith—and those who insisted on understanding him from a historical perspective—the Jesus of history.[283] Joseph B. Tyson explains: "A genuinely biographical interest in Jesus is a peculiarly modern one. Prior to the middle of the eighteenth century, the Christian either accepted the four canonical gospels as strictly accurate historical records or else neglected history altogether. In the post-Enlightenment era, the study of history, along with the study of nature, became an absorbing human enterprise. Since then there has been a flood of books on the life of Jesus."[284]

According to John Riches, Reimarus tried to understand Jesus from a first-century Jewish perspective. In doing so, he denied that Jesus "came above all to reveal the mysteries of the incarnation" and doubted "that Jesus came to found a new religion with its own rites and ceremonies." With no interest whatsoever in either baptism or communion, Jesus simply set out "to reform Judaism from within." He was "executed as an insurgent," not for blasphemy, because his "teaching about the Messiah and the Kingdom was related simply to current beliefs in a future political savior who would free the Jews from foreign rule and re-establish the Jewish Kingdom."[285] Ben F. Meyer notes that whatever its faults, Reimarus's book was prescient: "Reimarus anticipated in remarkable fashion views that would become commonplace in nineteenth- and twentieth-century criticism: Jesus stood wholly within Judaism; the apostles were the founders of Christianity; Paul, who called for belief, is set over against Jesus, who called for trust; the Jesus of history substantially differed from the Christ of faith."[286]

Thanks partly to Albert Schweitzer's reiteration of some of Reimarus's ideas in the early twentieth century and partly to the comprehensive examination of Jesus' words and deeds that followed Schweitzer's book over the succeeding one hundred years,[287] it is now generally understood—at least in the scholarly community—that the traditional concept of Judaism is untenable. Specifically, it has been argued by many historians, Bible scholars, and theologians that the New Testament, the principal source of this concept, is (1) not only inaccurate to some degree because the Bible in its entirety is as flawed as any humanly created document must be, but (2) also misleading because the works written by the Gospel writers were composed to inspire and sustain the faith of their Christian readers and not merely to provide them with objectively verifiable information.

In other words, the Gospels are theological and therefore polemical, not historical and therefore objective and accurate. Among other goals, many scholars have argued, the Gospels were written to denigrate Judaism, to portray Christianity as a superior religion, and to justify the ascendancy of the latter over the former. As Thomas Bokenkotter says: "The Gospels were not meant to be a historical or biographical account of Jesus. They were written to convert unbelievers to faith in Jesus as the Messiah of God, risen and living now in his church and coming again to judge all men. The authors did not deliberately invent or falsify facts about Jesus, but they were not primarily concerned with historical accuracy."[288] According to Morton Smith, "the gospels were written, not merely to record events, but to produce and confirm faith in Jesus the Messiah." Furthermore, the same objective affected Bible scholarship too: "Most of the scholars have not been historians, but theologians determined to make the documents justify their own theological position."[289]

The obvious cause of this polemical approach to the narrative books of the New Testament was not merely the desire to portray Jesus in a positive light, but also, as I said earlier, to discredit the religion he is understood to have left behind. Thus, Alan F. Segal says: "To be read effectively, the New Testament should be read with allowance for its anti-Pharisaic and sometimes anti-Jewish tone. Almost every page of the New Testament reveals an intolerance of its Jewish milieu that is borne of an intensely aggravated family conflict."[290] James Carroll, too, warns against "the deeply problematic legacy of Jew-hatred in foundational Christian texts."[291] And Jack T. Sanders argues that Christians who are interested in bridging the gap between themselves and the Jews "cannot ignore the support that parts of the New Testament give to anti-Jewish sentiment among Christians." Indeed, citing John G. Gager's book on Christian anti-Semitism, Sanders says that "it is a mistake to think that early Christian polemic against the Jews is merely against the Jewish religion ... and not against the Jewish people as such."[292]

The same criticism applies to the traditional German Protestant view of Judaism, written in the second half of the nineteenth century and the first half of the twentieth. One of the earliest objections to this scholarly view was a book by R. Travers Herford, *The Pharisees*, first published in 1924. Herford calls the negative portrait of the Pharisees—and, by extension, the Jews in general—"inadequate and superficial." He considers this interpretation of Pharisaism to be wrong primarily because it does not adequately explain the influence and durability of the movement, which, is, after all, the foundation of modern Judaism: It does not "take account of the consideration that if the Pharisees had been in their real nature and characters such as they are usually depicted, and Pharisaism the organized hypocrisy commonly supposed, such existence and unfailing vitality would have been impossible."[293]

Without an understanding of both ancient Judaism in general and Rabbinism in particular, Herford continues, scholars like Schurer, Bousset, and Wellhausen have been unable "to escape the limitation of view" that results from relying on the Gospels as sources of information on ancient Judaism. These writers, Herford says, argued that Judaism was "degraded . . . at the hands of the Pharisees, into a barren formalism, the descent from prophetic freedom to organised hypocrisy. *A greater misreading of history it is scarcely possible to imagine.*" Again, as Herford explains, the error lies in reading the Gospels literally: "[T]o call the New Testament as the chief witness upon the question of who the Pharisees [and, by implication, the ancient Jews] really were, is false in logic and unsound in history."[294] Herford adds later, "The New Testament shows the controversy from one side only, as indeed is but natural; and nothing can be learned from its pages which directly throws fresh light upon the essential meaning of Judaism."[295] According to John P. Meier: "In general, one may observe that most of the Christian presentations of the Pharisees earlier in this century were uncritical in that they took at face value the presentations of the Gospels . . . The result was more often Christian theology than historical description."[296]

Wellhausen and his contemporaries have by now been roundly criticized by many contemporary scholars for their dismissal of Judaism as a legitimate religion in the first century AD.[297] Clemens Thoma, for example, says that the ideas of this school of thought were "conceived at a time when Christian biblical religious scholarship and exegesis were stamped by apologetics, ignorance of and animosity toward Jews." The result was the misguided view that "Judaism since the Babylonian exile [was] declared to be paralyzing, obscure, ritualized, and under alien influence." Under such circumstances, "Jewish religion was said to have decayed more and more." Henceforth, Jewish "obduracy" made it impossible for Jews "to accept Jesus as the true messiah," as a consequence of which they were forever cursed by God.[298] Stefan C. Reif identifies Paul de Lagarde as "[o]ne of the best known anti-Semitic semitists," who thought of the Jews as 'a repulsive burden with no historical use.'"[299]

According to Albert Schweitzer, Wellhausen also denied any connection between Judaism and Christianity: He "gives a picture of Jesus which lifts him out of the

Jewish frame altogether."³⁰⁰ Jon D. Levenson traces the decline in support for Wellhausen's theory to "the decades following the publication of the *Prolegomena* in 1878," when "archeological excavations produced an exponential growth in our knowledge of the biblical world, much of it as lethal to Wellhausen's reconstructed evolution as it is to the traditionalist's cherished belief in the uniqueness of Israel."³⁰¹ Walter Brueggemann comments: "[T]here is still a widespread assumption of the move [in ancient Judaism] from primitive to ethical to legalistic," which is regrettable because the theory "was not an innocent scholarly matter . . . It is evident that the hypothesis has a distinct Christian bias with an inchoate supersessionism implied . . . Thus, taken at its worst, the hypothesis had an anti-Jewish tilt." However, Brueggemann argues that Wellhausen's "theory of the evolutionary development of Israelite religion in a unilinear fashion is now largely rejected." Indeed, "[b]y the 1970s, the consensus hypothesis of Wellhausianism began to collapse; by the turn of the century, the primary attention given to the hypothesis is by precritical scholars who continue to assault the hypothesis even though it now has few advocates."³⁰²

Writing in the 1960s, the Jewish historian Yehezkel Kaufmann argued that Wellhausen and others misrepresented the history of Judaism by claiming that the sections of the Torah written by the so-called Priestly writer, with their emphasis on ritual and purity, were the strongest (and most recent) influence on the Jews of Jesus' time. According to Ernest S. Frerichs, "The least acceptable element in the Wellhausen program for Jewish biblical scholars was the denigration of Jewish history, the elevation of the preexilic period to a prime status and the corresponding reading of the postexilic period as one of darkness and decline."³⁰³ On the contrary, says Kaufmann, the prophetic books, with their emphasis on morality over ceremony, succeeded, rather than preceded, the composition of the Priestly section of the Torah and therefore exerted the primary influence on the Jews of the first century, whose religion was therefore not degraded, but vital and innovative and even admirable.³⁰⁴

Accepting Wellhausen's assumption that the Priestly books followed the prophetic books, Frank McConnell argues that the final phase in the development of ancient Judaism was not the "priestly aristocracy," as Wellhausen claims, but a period of extraordinary creativity and spirituality. That is, after what McConnell calls "a disaster which was actually a kind of blessing," Judaism "transfigured itself into an intellectual tradition which is, simply, the basis of all Western commentary on literature."³⁰⁵ In other words, some scholars argue that Wellhausen's theory is incorrect whether or not the Priestly writings succeeded the prophetic writings simply because the vitality of Jewish intertestamental literature is enough to demonstrate that Wellhausen and his followers were wrong.

The Pharisees Revisited

Thanks to the work of Kaufmann and other scholars, the Jews of the first century AD are now widely understood to have been something other than morally bankrupt, particularly as a product of the so-called Priestly tradition. They are now believed to have been alive and well—spiritually, at least—insofar as they either continued or at least returned to the moral idealism of the Jewish prophets. In the context of this relatively new understanding of ancient Judaism, it is easy to see why many modern scholars have reexamined the religious character of the Pharisees. What they have discovered is that the putative opponents of Jesus, as they are portrayed in the Bible, may well have been, if not his ideological compatriots, then at least something other than his ideological enemies.

On the one hand, as Jacob Neusner says, the older description of the Pharisees is "part of the cultural background of the West, an aspect of the anti-Semitism nurtured by Christian theology" of the kind proffered by scholars like Wellhausen. On the other hand, however, "a contrary polemic was not lacking." Given the "numerous stories and sayings attributed to the Pharisees before 70 C.E.," preserved by the Rabbis after the fall of Jerusalem, "it was easy for Jewish scholarship to demonstrate not only the theological animus, but also the historical incompetence of those Christian scholars of ancient and modern times who ignored important parts of the Pharisaic record."[306] Frederick J. Cwiekowski comments, "Today the historical setting of the gospels makes us recognize the apologetic and even polemic motives in the Gospels; hence our estimate of the Pharisaic movement in first-century Judaism is much more positive."[307]

Perhaps the most obvious point in the contemporary view of the Pharisees is that they were, in the time of Jesus, not in control of anything—that is, they were unable to impose their religious standards on other Jews. Referring to Martin Hengel's claim that the Pharisees were responsible for the death of Stephen in Acts of the Apostle, Craig C. Hill says that this charge "rests upon an older view of the Pharisees that credits them with more authority than they were likely to have had."[308] Morton Smith argues that John's portrait of the Pharisees "does not fit the facts of the situation before 70, as we know them from earlier sources," which indicate that "the Pharisees before 70 were only one party among many and controlled neither the sanhedrin nor the mass of the people, nor the majority of the synagogues . . . But in John they are practically a para-legal government." Thus, Smith concludes, "it would seem that John's picture of the Pharisees reflects the Jamnian Judaism of his own time [that is, the Pharisees of the late first century] and can never be used with confidence as evidence of Jesus' conflict with members of the sect."[309] Anthony J. Saldarini says repeatedly that, although they always sought it, the Pharisees lacked power after the reign of Alexandra in the first-century BC: "The Pharisees and their leaders such as Hillel and Gamaliel were no more in control during the first century [AD] than were the patriarchs and the sages in the second. They were one of a number of groups competing for power and influence and struggling to forge an identity for the people in the face of increasing pressure from Rome and the need to adapt Jewish life to new circumstances."[310]

In this regard, Joachim Jeremias makes two important points about the Pharisees. First, they were not people of wealth and power, but members of what might be called the middle and lower classes. They were "merchants, artisans and peasants": "In short, the Pharisaic communities were mostly composed of petty commoners, men of the people with no scribal education, earnest and self-sacrificing." Second, "the Pharisees' influence on politics and administration of justice in Palestine before AD 66 must not be exaggerated. Their only real importance during this time was in the realm of religion."[311] Thus, in E. P. Sanders's words, although the Pharisees created "traditions"—or supplementary laws—they "made [them] only for themselves and did not try to force them on everybody." They may have wished to do so, but "they had no actual power."[312] Elsewhere, Sanders argues that the Pharisees had no power either under Herod or after his death: Herod "controlled the Pharisees as he controlled everyone else . . . In the post-Herodian period, individual case after individual case shows that the Pharisees did not control anyone."[313] R. David Kaylor says that the Pharisees "tended to 'live and let live' as long as they were free to live faithfully to the Torah as they interpreted it."[314]

In other words, their influence was limited to the power of persuasion rather than the power of actual control. Fredriksen says: "In circa 30 C.E., the Pharisees were one of a number of groups in Palestine, and a small minority at that. They neither represented nor controlled the Judaism of Jesus' day."[315] According to Burton L. Mack, "[F]or an understanding of the charges leveled against the Pharisees in Q"—i.e., a collection of Jesus' sayings—"it is extremely important to know that the Pharisees were not officials in charge of Jewish synagogues. That is the picture Christians have had in mind and there is absolutely no basis for it whatsoever."[316] Meier says that, in the Gospel of John, "the Pharisees are said to have the power to expel fellow Jews from the synagogue if they profess faith in Jesus as the Messiah (9:22) . . . Such a situation is simply inconceivable in the political and religious conditions of Palestinian Judaism around A.D. 28–30."[317] Commenting on the same passage, L. Michael White argues that the Pharisees described therein are "anachronistically portrayed as religious authorities who oversee piety compliance."[318] Other scholars, as we have seen, emphasize the fact that the standards of the Pharisees simply could not be required; they could only be adopted voluntarily.[319]

This is not to say, however, that the Pharisees were not influential. Arguing against the scholars who claim that the Pharisees were a narrow sect "and that they represented no one but themselves," Irving Zeitlin says that "if any Jewish party became *the* popular movement of the masses, it certainly was the Pharisees." In other words, "The Pharisees had the greatest influence on the ordinary people and the 'support of the masses.'"[320] According to Meier, because the Pharisees influenced both "the mass of Jews who belonged to no party" and the "servants of the people in power"—"low-level bureaucrats, functionaries, and educators"—they may at times have been able to persuade or pressure the high priests and the aristocrats to adopt their views and practices."[321] Thus, says Thoma, although the Pharisees had "limited" influence because they were only members of "a minority party," they were "successful and popular with the masses of the Galilean people."[322] As Sanders explains, "if one asks which of the three parties"—Pharisees, Sadducees, or Essenes—"had the most popular support, the answer will be the Pharisees."[323]

Of course, the question must be asked, how did the Pharisees manage to wield power despite their lack of any official position? The most obvious answer is that they were not the kind of people the Gospels say they were. As Carroll says, "While Jesus lived, the Pharisees would have been completely powerless missionaries, teachers, and low-level administrators. It is only with the elimination of the Temple and its priesthood that the Pharisees emerge as rivals—not of Jesus, but of his movement a full generation removed. That is why they are cast as enemies in the Gospels, which is why, in turn, *almost nothing said by Christians about these particular Jews is true*."[324] What is true, according to Haim Cohn, is that the Pharisees "possessed a wide reputation for piety, tolerance, wisdom," *which formed the basis for their influence*: "This reputation clothed the Pharisees with enormous power, used with remarkable self-restraint."[325] Hyam Maccoby says: "It should be noted . . . that modern scholarship has shown that, at this time, the Pharisees were held in high repute throughout the Roman and Parthian empires as a dedicated group who upheld religious ideals in the face of tyranny, supported leniency and mercy in the application of laws, and championed the rights of the poor against the oppression of the rich."[326]

William K. Klingaman says that the influence of the Pharisees was based on their adoption of "a simple, unassuming lifestyle" as well as their willingness to interact "freely with the masses"; their position as "the nation's foremost scriptural authorities"; and their strong belief in "eternal life," which "opened the door of salvation to every righteous Jew regardless of economic and social status."[327] As Sanders argues, the Pharisees were simply "admired and respected" because of their "popular views" as well as their "learning and piety." Furthermore, they "studied and taught, did their jobs, waited for their chances, acted for the most part with prudence, and occasionally went too far. These miscalculations probably made them all the more popular, since they created martyrs." In this respect, although not in others, Sanders is agreeing with Josephus' assessment of the Pharisees, according to whom "many people followed the Pharisees' rules of worship because they admired their high ideals, expressed 'both in their way of living and in their discourse' (Antiq. 18.15)." Furthermore, "Josephus is claiming that the Pharisees were good and kind and that their devotion to God was admired."[328]

Indeed, many scholars reject in its entirety the idea that the Pharisees were hypocritical, legalistic, or contemptuous of Jews who were less observant or less devout. According to Raymond E. Brown, although "[t]he Gospels often portray the Pharisees as hypocrites and heartless legalists," they were neither.[329] Alan F. Segal similarly rejects the claim that the Pharisees "practic[ed] a hypocritical religion, interested only in the forms, not the substance of religion."[330] Stephen M. Wylen says, "The charge that the Pharisees were hypocritical and legalistic has been convincingly disproved by Christian and Jewish scholars"[331] According to Donald Senior, "Pharisaic devotion to the law should not be seen as a blind embrace of legalism. Their extensive system of oral commentary on the law and its detailed prescriptions was an attempt to make the law livable, not impossible."[332] To Charles Guignebert, "The Pharisees are no longer accused of crushing spiritual religion under a load of minute observances, of losing themselves in a waste of puerile and wearisome detail, or of losing the essential spirit of the Law in the attachment to a formal and hypocritical devotion."[333]

Michael Grant argues that the Pharisees "did not, like certain other groups, consider the divine will to be so fully displayed in the Law that it just had to be obeyed quite literally, without the need for any explanations or glosses."[334] They understood that the Jewish law needed to be explained and interpreted. However, they did not thereby make the laws complicated and overwhelming. Speaking of the Pharisees' reputation for "devising new and difficult twists to put in the law," making "fine-spun distinctions," and thereby making "the law burdensome," Morton Scott Enslin states, "All this is simply not historic."[335] To Paul Winter, "Fulfilling the law was never for [the Pharisees] a matter of external observance only." Indeed, "they saw their vocation from God as the complete fulfillment of the law."[336] Rejecting the idea that the Pharisees were pedantic, obstinate, presumptuous, pettifogging, legalistic, and formalistic, Marcello Craveri says that "we could not, objectively, feel justified in declaring that the violent antagonism to the Pharisees that the Gospels ascribe to Jesus was historically justifiable."[337] According to Sanders, "The rabbis, and presumably the Pharisees, were certainly 'casuists' in a general sense: anyone is who tries to apply a law to a new situation." However, "Rabbinic literature"—and the same is true of that of the Pharisees—"is full of humane and generous casuistry."[338] That is, it was intended to help people rather than hurt them.

As for the charge that Pharisees held unobservant Jews in contempt and kept themselves aloof from them, many scholars have argued otherwise. Sanders explains that, before AD 70, the Pharisees were "lay people who maintained themselves in a relatively high state of ritual purity . . . [S]uch groups were small, voluntary associations which accepted special rules for special reasons." They did not think of themselves as the "righteous" and others as the "wicked." The idea that they saw others as "cut off" from God "is totally without foundation." Nor did they "insist that lay people act like priests."[339] Elsewhere, Sanders says: "Christian scholars sometimes say that meant that Jews would not mingle with Gentiles at all. This is not true, as consideration of elementary facts will make clear. Jews travelled, many lived in pagan cities, and many lived in mixed cities even within Palestine; the idea of self-enclosed ghettoes had not yet arisen."[340]

As Gerd Theissen notes, unlike the Essenes, whose dedication to the purity laws led them to live separately from other Jews, "the Pharisees attempted to practice [these laws] in normal everyday life." In fact, Pharisaism "was the only renewal movement within Judaism which was not involved with an eccentric form of living." Their "demand for purity was interpreted in a reasonable way," and Sabbath laws were "given a strict but practicable form." Furthermore, their "attempt to make rules for all areas of everyday life and to legitimate their programme by the Torah deserves respect." They were criticized by members of more "radical movements" for compromises and inconsistencies. However, Theissen argues, "[i]t was easy from the periphery of society to criticize a group which had a serious concern for 'true living' within the context of a given society."[341] According to Saldarini: "The purity rules, which seem so arcane to modern westerners, regularized life and separated that which was normal and life giving from that which was abnormal or ambiguous and so a threat to normal life. Such a set of categories and rules excluded that which is foreign or strange; their usefulness against the attraction and influence of the Romans and Hellenistic culture is obvious."[342]

Unlike the Sadducees," says Meier, the Pharisees wanted *everyone* to follow all of the Jewish laws and traditions that would enable them to live in a genuinely holy manner. Thus, they "were actively engaged in trying to convince ordinary Jews to observe Pharisaic traditions in their daily lives. However, while the Pharisees struggled to have their views accepted by the common people, they did not consider the common people or other Jews heinous sinners or beyond the pale simply for not agreeing to follow Pharisaic practice."[343] In short, according to Steve Moyise, "there is no evidence" that the Pharisees "were hostile to less observant Jews."[344] Zeitlin agrees: "[T]he term 'Pharisee' has nothing to do with separation from the Gentiles; nor from the alleged uncleanness of the mass of the people . . . There is no evidence to support the view that the Pharisees had set themselves apart from the rest of the people, or from the humbler social levels of society."[345] Thus, says Sanders, it is not only untrue that the Pharisees were either "hypocritical" or "legalistic" but also that, in any way whatsoever, "they despised ordinary people."[346] Like Meier, Sanders claims, "I know of no passage in Jewish literature which indicates that any group which can reasonably be connected with the Pharisees considered the common people beyond the pale."[347]

Furthermore, according to many scholars, the Pharisees not only lacked the vices traditionally associated with them, they in fact possessed a number of positive virtues.[348] To George F. Moore, the accusation that "the Pharisees as a whole were conscious and calculating hypocrites whose ostentatious piety was a cloak for deliberate secret villainy is unimaginable in view of the subsequent history of Judaism." Moore adds, "For it was the men of the Pharisean party who tided Judaism over the two great crises of the destruction of Jerusalem and the war under Hadrian." For this reason, Moore continues, "Judaism is the monument of the Pharisees,"[349] a point also made by James Parkes and Donald Senior.[350] According to Pheme Perkins, "The Pharisees were the ones who were able to restructure Judaism after the destruction of the temple and its cult."[351] Franz Mussner says, "In the Gospels the Pharisees, stylized in a hostile image to an extraordinary degree, are burdened with very negative accents. Scholarly research has already revised this hostile image to a large extent in that it has better illumined the history of Pharisaism and allowed the genuine desires of the Pharisees to be more clearly recognized." Thus, Mussner adds, "The Pharisees were, alongside the Essenes, the most devout people in the Judaism of that time."[352]

More specifically, the piety of the Pharisees manifested itself in two important ways. First, they devoted themselves to adapting the Jewish law to particular circumstances and to what was to them the modern world. As Segal says, the Pharisees tried "to make the laws of Scripture more applicable to the society of their own day." This means that "[t]hey tailored a primitive code of the tenth through fifth centuries B.C.E. to the Hellenistic world."[353] M. Grant says that, "while showing keen anxiety to preserve the distinctly religious character of Jewish life, the Pharisees were also eager to adapt their faith to modern needs."[354] According to Donald A. Hagner, "their earnest quest for righteousness . . . led them to the development of the oral law as a kind of 'hedge' about the written law." They also tried "to bring every area of life in subjection to the law."[355] Justo L. Gonzalez comments: "To them, it was important to be faithful to the law, and for that reason they studied and debated how the law was to be applied in every conceivable situation." In other words, "they sought to make the faith of Israel relevant to everyday situations and to new circumstances under Roman rule and Hellenizing threats."[356]

In this context, it is important to note that, according to Klingaman, the Pharisees were more concerned with ethics than with ritual: They "made no secret of their disdain for the Temple priests, alleging that they substituted an arrogant devotion to arid, archaic rituals for proper ethical behavior."[357] In other words, unlike the stereotype perpetrated by Wellhausen and his contemporaries—i.e., that the Pharisees represented the Priestly tradition and focused on ritual and purity laws—they actually returned to the moral concerns of the great Jewish prophets. Rosemary R. Ruether says: "The development of the oral Torah allowed Judaism to emancipate itself from the Aaronite priesthood and its temple cultus. No longer did the individual Jew need a priestly caste or a sacrificial system to intervene for him with God. Long before the temple actually fell, the Pharisees had been enunciating the way of prayer and study, declaring that acts of repentance, thanksgiving, and loving-kindness were equivalent to, perhaps even better than, the temple sacrifices."[358]

As Gonzalez suggests, their commitment to expanding the law enabled the Pharisees not only to protect Judaism from the influence of Hellenization and to adjust to the complexities of modernism, but also to adjust to new and unexpected experiences. According to Guignebert, "The reason for this is that [the religion of the Pharisees] was a living thing, so that they were peculiarly conscious of the need for expanding the old Jahwism [i.e., worship of Yahweh] and incorporating whatever additions the religious needs of their time demanded."[359] Thus, William M. Thompson says: "All seem agreed that the Pharisees represent a novel and somewhat revolutionary movement within Judaism," the heart of which "was their belief in oral torah, a belief which" among other benefits, "enabled them to remain open to their own experiences as a source of revelation."[360] Thompson quotes Ruether, who says in regard to this modification of traditional Judaism that "it allowed the Pharisees to innovate freely, subject only to that authority which was theirs as the rightful successors of a line of oral tradition that runs back through the *Sopherim* and the prophets to Moses through Joshua."[361]

Second, instead of treating the Jewish law routinely or insincerely, the Pharisees appear to have embraced their faith with deep emotion and true commitment. Saldarini reminds us that Josephus views the Pharisees "as a vital social force which has its base in knowledge and observance of the ancestral laws of Judaism."[362] Segal says that, for the Rabbis, "repentance," which is at the heart of the Jewish faith, requires "intention" as well as "motivation to change one's behavior."[363] Guignebert makes a similar point, arguing that the Pharisees focused on another traditional Jewish concept, *teshubah*, or repentance, which is an attempt to gain forgiveness not merely by doing good deeds, but by undergoing a spiritual transformation.[364] Such ideas may be connected to what Thompson calls "[a] growing personalization in the relationship to the Divine": "[T]he divine is accessible, not simply at temple, but in personal acts of mercy, love, prayer, and study."[365] This idea, in turn, is related to two other ideas associated with Jesus himself: "What is often called the 'Golden Rule' (cf. Matt. 7:12; Luke 6:31) may come from Hillel," says L. Michael White, "and 'summing up the whole Torah in two commandments' was a typically Pharisaic way of thinking (cf. Matt. 22:34–40; Mark 12:28–31)."[366]

E. P. Sanders examines this issue in great detail. First, he argues, the charge that the Pharisees were hypocrites who "were seeking only self-glorification" is false. That is, "their scrupulous definition and fulfillment of the laws" was not "merely external activity that masked inner hypocrisy and self-righteousness." Rather, the Pharisees "thought that God had given them his law and bestowed on them his grace, and that it was their obligation within the loving relationship with God to obey the law precisely." Second, as a consequence of this assumption, the Pharisees "regarded love and devotion to God as standing at the center of their attempt to obey the law in every detail"—a point made by Hillel, when he gave this advice to his fellow Pharisees: "Be of the disciples of Aaron, loving peace and pursuing peace, loving mankind and bringing them nigh to the Law" (Avot 1.12)." Sanders says that the evidence of this understanding appears prominently in the literature of the Rabbis (whom Sanders calls "the spiritual heirs of the Pharisees"), which "so emphasizes the importance of right intention and pure motive, of acting in a spirit of love and humility." In this tradition, "[t]he scholar who studies much is not superior to his fellow, the common person, provided that the latter 'directs the heart to Heaven' (Berakhot 17a)."[367]

Perhaps most tellingly, many modern scholars, in opposition to the Wellhausen hypothesis, see the Pharisees as representatives of the Jewish prophets rather than the Priestly tradition. In other words, they returned to the moral idealism of Isaiah, Jeremiah, and Hosea while preserving some of the cultic practices of the priests. The Pharisees also represented the poor rather than the rich. Joachim Jeremias emphasizes the Pharisees' social consciousness, as well as their devotion to Judaism: "[T]hey represented the common people as opposed to the aristocracy on both religious and social matters. Their much-respected piety and their social leanings towards suppressing differences in class, gained them the people's support and assured them, step by step, of the victory" over the Sadducee on religious issues. They were seen "as embodiments of the ideal life."[368] On the subject of the Pharisees' social concerns, Michael Grant says that, "although they mostly belonged to the middle class themselves, [the Pharisees] often championed the cause of ordinary people and the oppressed."[369] According to Saldarini, the Pharisees have thus been misrepresented as a group that "turned inward"—that is, abandoned their commitment to social reform and focused on cultic matters. Instead of losing their "desire for involvement in political society" or their "emphasis on intra community relations," they seem to have "functioned as a social movement organization seeking to change society" and "sought a new, communal commitment to a strict Jewish way of life based on adherence to the covenant."[370]

Indeed, Sanders argues that, like mainstream Jews generally, the Pharisees embraced what he calls covenantal nomism, which means, first, acknowledging God's grace in his election of Israel (the initiation of the Covenant) and, second, obeying his demand for obedience to his laws (the fulfillment of the Covenant). The concept involved believing "that God would preserve his people as a whole and the nation would obey his law," but also that, by the intertestamental period, God's promise to save the Jews would be fulfilled in the afterlife if not in the present. Sanders justifies his claim that the Pharisees accepted this belief by noting that rabbinic expression of it "appears most fully in the non-legal sections of the tannaitic midrashim (commentaries on the Bible that are attributed to first- and second-century Rabbis)." Again, like other Jews of the time, "they believed that the future was in God's hands and that finally all would come out as it should."[371] Why else, one might ask, would the Pharisees insist on unequivocal loyalty to God and genuine commitment to his demands?

Considering all of these positive attributes, many scholars have suggested that, even if Jesus was not actually a member of the Pharisees' community, he unquestionably shared their desire to make Judaism more meaningful and relevant to ordinary people. "The tragedy for Christians" according to Bernard J. Lee, "is that we have steadfastly missed the genetic connection between Jesus and the Pharisees. There is more insight into Jesus in his continuity with them than in his discontinuity."[372] To Guignebert, "the religion of Jesus appears to be consistent with the general lines and even the spirit of Pharisaic religion."[373] Indeed, Gonzalez says, to the extent that there was "friction" between Jesus and the Pharisees, it was "due to the similarity of their views, rather than to their difference."[374] For example, in believing in the resurrection of the dead and emphasizing the love of both God and mankind, says Geza Vermes, "Jesus is represented as sharing the outlook and winning the approval of the Pharisees."[375] Roland H. Bainton argues that, as a teacher, Jesus "sided politically with the Pharisees against fraternization with Rome and against rebellion."[376] According to Guignebert, the Pharisee's idea of redemption, or *teshubah*, "is surely not far removed from the teaching of Jesus."[377]

Given these similarities, says Meier, "It is hardly a wonder . . . that Jesus would have interacted more with them than with any other Jewish movement or party. Both Jesus and the Pharisees shared a consuming desire to bring all Israel, not just an esoteric sect or a privileged elite, to the complete doing of God's will as laid out in the Law and the prophets." In this context, Meier mentions "the need to respond wholeheartedly to the Law's demands in one's everyday life."[378] Thus, "Even a cursory investigation," Craveri says, "is enough to demonstrate the surprising points of contact between the Pharisaic and the Christian religious conceptions. The views of Hillel and other rabbis recur more often than one might think in the preaching of Jesus, and many of the maxims later brought together in the Talmud are found in identical form in the Gospels."[379] For these reasons, Guignebert claims that the Pharisees provided a bridge that led from Judaism to Christianity: "When all is said, early Christianity arose on a foundation not widely different from that of the *Sopherim* [i.e., the Pharisees], and historically speaking the career of Jesus would be practically inconceivable without the preliminary work accomplished by these men."[380]

Retrojection

Aside from the reasons mentioned earlier in this chapter for questioning the historical accuracy of the Bible (and therefore the accuracy of scholarly books based largely or entirely on biblical accounts), the most widespread argument against the veracity of the Gospels is based on the fact that they were written forty or more years after the Crucifixion. As Robert L. Wilken puts it, "Almost everything we know about Jesus comes from the accounts of his life and teachings in the gospels, . . . written by different authors a generation or more after his death. The events they narrate and the parables and sayings they record were drawn from traditions passed on orally in the early Christian communities, adapted to local interests in the process of transmission over the decades, and shaped according to the aims of each author."[381]

However, the main problem with the Gospel reports of the life of Jesus is not that the Gospel writers were misinformed about Jesus' life or that in the years following his death they misremembered his attitude toward Judaism. Many scholars have pointed out that, whatever the relationship between Jesus and the Jews might have been before the Crucifixion, its description in the Gospels is tainted by the relationship between Christians and Jews at the time of the Gospels' composition. It is generally believed that four or more decades after the Crucifixion the enmity between Jews and Christians was particularly high—that is, in the last quarter of the first century, after the Jewish Revolt, which ended in AD 73. As a consequence of this hostility, the Gospels portray Jesus, the early Christians, and the Jews of the first half of first-century Palestine incorrectly and unfairly. Although this statement is likely to sound questionable to anyone who has not studied the New Testament by examining the biblical scholarship of the last half century, it is widely accepted by contemporary scholars.

In fact, the current scholarly portrait of the major players in the Gospels and the Acts of the Apostles—that is, the view supported by the vast majority of experts in the fields of Bible studies, ancient history of the Near East, and Jewish and Christian theology—is based on the assumption that Jesus did not reject Judaism but remained a practicing Jew and continued throughout his life to embrace Jewish laws and traditions; that the followers of Jesus did not begin to turn their backs on Judaism until after the Jewish Revolt—and then only slowly and sporadically; and that Jesus' Jewish contemporaries, including the Pharisees, were indistinguishable from either Christians or pagans in their commitment to their religion and to the moral standards that emanated from the dominant religions of the Roman Empire in the early years of the Current Era.

Daniel Boyarin sums up the scholarly consensus when he says, "By now, almost everyone recognizes that the historical Jesus was a Jew who followed ancient Jewish ways."[382] According to Wilken, "As an observant Jew, Jesus went regularly to the synagogue on the Sabbath, he celebrated the Jewish festivals and kept the food laws, he asked a blessing before breaking bread, he approved of gifts and offerings in the temple, and . . . he even urged obedience to biblical laws of ritual purity." His goal as a missionary was "to rescue the commandments from being a quotidian set of rules by raising up what was central in Jewish teaching, to love and serve God whose goodness is the source of all good." Based on such claims as these, Karen Armstrong not only points to "the essentially Jewish nature of [Jesus'] career," but also suggests that instead of opposing the Pharisees Jesus might well have been one of them: "Certainly [his] teaching was in accord with major tenets of the Pharisees."[383]

Furthermore, Jesus' disciples "were [also] Jews, and they remained faithful to the traditions and customs of their people, observing the Jewish law, which meant circumcising their male children, abstaining from certain foods, and keeping the Sabbath and holy days. They had no thought of breaking with Jewish ways, nor did they have a mandate to invite non-Jews into their community." Thus, "[t]hey did not constitute a new religion but a 'way' among the Jewish people (Acts 24:14)." To be sure, Wilken concludes, after the first two decades the Christian Jews of Jerusalem were "on [their] way to becoming a religion not only for Jews but also for gentiles—a form, as it were, of Judaism for the nations." In the meantime, however, "Christianity was not a revolt against Israel."[384]

Charlotte Klein explains the historical situation this way. First, "the picture of the Pharisees and scribes given in other historical sources does not correspond to that of the Gospels. It is impossible to explain in detail here the reasons for the contrast. We can only point out briefly that Jewry, after the destruction of the temple in A.D. 70, recognized the Pharisees and their rabbis as its natural religious leaders and the organization of the Jewish religion after the disasters of 70 and 135 as their work. The more the early church came up against the opposition of the Jewish communities, the more urgent it became to portray them as the enemies of Jesus himself." Second, the result was that the Gospels' view of the Pharisees was distorted: "The writings of the New Testament emerged at different times, but all of them after the controversy between the early church and Judaism had already become acute. This conflict is reflected in almost all the books of the New Testament."[385]

In other words, according to Donald Senior, "by the time the gospels were written, Pharisees had become a symbol of opposition to Jesus and prime instigators of his death. The change is due in part to the fact that the early Christian church and orthodox Judaism had drifted further and further apart, especially after the crisis of A.D. 70." Senior adds that, "when we assess the gospel portrait of the Pharisees," we should not overlook "[t]he fact that the Jews generally did not accept the gospel and [that] the efforts of some Jews to thwart the Christian mission led to a fratricidal bitterness" between them. "Certainly some of this tension and polemic helped reduce their image in the gospel story to that of mere opponents and persecutors of Jesus."[386] In short, as these scholars suggest, the Pharisees were unfairly discredited in the Gospels, and Jesus' hostility toward them was irresponsibly exaggerated.[387]

In fact, elsewhere in the New Testament—namely, in the Acts of the Apostles—the Jerusalem church maintained close ties to the Judaism in which every member of that church had grown up. Indeed, Acts shows that these Christians were, in many respects, still Jews. Frederick J. Cwiekowski says, "The earliest Christian community saw itself within the confines of Judaism."[388] This is why, as Marcus J. Borg argues, "it is not clear historically when we should begin using the words 'Christian' and 'Christianity,' if we mean by that a religion distinct from Judaism." Like Cwiekowski, Borg says that "Jesus and his early followers were all Jewish and saw themselves as doing something within Judaism, not as founding a religion separate from Judaism." Even Paul "saw himself as a Jew all of his life," and most, if not all, "of the authors of the New Testament were Jewish." Thus, Borg concludes that the New Testament is best understood "when we see it within the world of first-century Judaism, including the way that world was shaped by the Hebrew Bible." In short, "we understand early Christianity best when we see it as a way of being Jewish."[389]

According to Gerd Theissen, "Earliest Christianity began as a renewal movement within Judaism brought into being through Jesus." That is, Jesus' followers "remained wholly within the framework" of their original faith "and had no intention of founding a new 'church.'" Of course, all this changed after Christians moved into the

Hellenized world outside of Jerusalem, at which time their writings were "addressed to a larger public," and Christianity had "become an independent religion." However, while the members of the church remained in Jerusalem, many Christian Jews "wanted to see the law fulfilled down to the smallest detail"; "felt that scribes and Pharisees were legitimate authorities"; and accepted such practices as sacrifice and fasting. "In some respects," Theissen adds, "they deliberately practised outward conformity, while retaining reservations." However, in terms of exclusiveness, the difference between Christians Jews and Essenes "becomes obvious when we see how little the Jesus movement stood out from the rest of Judaism and how little it was separated from it."[390]

Furthermore, says Cwiekowski, even though they held "out-of-the-ordinary beliefs," they were, like other dissident groups "tolerated by official Judaism in the middle of the first century A.D." This was so because "the earliest believers must have been regarded as Jews who lived devout and modest lives," despite their "eccentric" ideas. Seeing themselves this way, they "continued their association with the temple and their practice of Jewish prayer."[391] They prayed in the Temple (2:46; 3:1; 5:12, 21, 42) and praised the same God that other Jews praised. They were respected by Jews who were not connected to the aristocracy—that is, the vast majority. Indeed, they had "favor with the people" (2:47), who "held [them] in high honor" (5:13).

In fact, they were protected by their fellow Jews from persecution at the hands of the Jewish elite. After Peter and John were arrested, the elders were forced to "let them go, finding no way to punish them, *because of the people*" (4:21; my emphasis), who had "praised God" when they witnessed Peter's healing of "a man lame from birth" (3:1–10). Later, the representatives of the High Priest arrested "the apostles" for the third time, but they did so without "violence, for they were *afraid of being stoned by the people*" (5:26; my emphasis). According to Jack T. Sanders, Luke indicates "that the rulers are unable to move against the church because the people are on the church's side"—the "people" being, of course, the Jews.[392]

On the one hand, the Christian Jews were different from all other Jews in some respects. They healed the sick in Jesus' name; Peter publicly and repeatedly accused the Jews of killing Jesus, albeit "in ignorance" (3:17); and the Jewish authorities ("the priests and the captain of the temple and the Sadducees") arrested Peter and others several times. On the other hand, however, many non-Christian Jews "believed" and joined the community of Jesus' followers (2:47, 4:4). Furthermore, Peter and the other Christian Jews constantly quoted the Jewish scriptures, including the prophets Joel, Isaiah, and Jeremiah; many psalms; and all of the Books of Moses, especially Deuteronomy.[393] The disciples received the Holy Spirit—the same spirit that possessed Jephthah, Samson, Gideon, Othniel, Deborah, and Saul—on the day of the Pentecost, one of the three major Jewish festivals, this one celebrating the Jews' reception of God's law. Until many years after the Crucifixion, Peter did not visit the homes of gentiles ("You yourselves know how unlawful it is for a Jew to associate with or to visit any one of another nation" [10:28]) and avoided eating all non-Kosher food ("Lord, I have never eaten anything that is common or unclean" [10:13]).[394]

R. E. Brown says that, besides regularly praying in the Temple, the early Christians also recited Jewish prayers: "Since they did not cease to be Jewish in their worship, they continued to say prayers that they had known previously, and new prayers would have been formulated according to Jewish models." In short, Brown adds, "This implies that the first Jews who believed in Jesus saw no rupture in their ordinary worship pattern." Brown also notes that the earliest Christian canticles "reflect the style of contemporary Jewish hymnology," including the Magnificat, which is "clearly patterned on the hymn of Hannah, the mother of Samuel, in 1 Sam 2:1–10."[395] Cwiekowski comments, "Many of the early Christians observed the law, were attached to the temple, and seemed to have had no concern for Gentiles or, early on, for a mission beyond the bounds of Judaism." They were simply seen as "a splinter group," a Jewish sect and nothing more—"the sect of the Nazarenes." From the perspective of other Jews, the Christians were "another grouping within the complexity of mid-first century Judaism."[396]

In fact, according to James, the brother of Jesus, *all* of the Christians in Jerusalem were obedient to the Jewish law. Referring to the members of the local church, James and the elders say to Paul, in the late fifties, "You see, brother, how many thousands there are among the Jews who have believed; they are *all zealous for the law*" (21:20; my emphasis). Speaking as a Christian Jew who is about to ask Paul to sponsor the participation of four fellow Christian Jews in an elaborate ritual at the Temple, James is obviously referring to the *Jewish* law, about which members of the church were zealous because, again, they were still Jews.[397] Brown says that, like "all Jews," "the first followers of Jesus" considered the Scriptures to be "authoritative": "Thus, early Christian teaching would for the most part have been Jewish teaching." Indeed, the laws mentioned in the Gospels are actually "the tip of the iceberg, the bulk of which is the unmentioned, presupposed teaching of Israel."[398] That is why, on the day of the Pentecost, Peter addresses the Jews of Jerusalem in the same manner that he addresses Jesus' followers: that is, as "brethren" (1:16; see also 2:29; 3:17), as does Stephen (7:2). Similarly, Peter and John refer to King David as "our father" (4:25), and Stephen refers to Abraham in the same way (7:2).

That is also why, despite the attempt on the part of the chief priests to arrest and imprison the leaders of the Jewish cult that had yet to call itself Christian, the Jerusalem church survived and even prospered. Indeed, the church expanded thanks in part not only to the support of the local Jewish community but also to the fact that thousands of these Jews actually joined the church. After Peter's Pentecost speech to the Jews of Jerusalem, "about three thousand" of them "were baptized" (2:41). Soon after this, "many of those who heard the word believed" (that is, the word which up to this point had been preached *only* to Jews); "and the number of the men came to about five thousand" (Acts 4:4). Later, "the word of God increased, and the number of disciples multiplied greatly in Jerusalem, and a great many of the [Jewish] priests were obedient to the faith" (6:7). Still later, Luke says—presumably referring to the first decade or so of the church's development—"So the church throughout all Judea and Galilee and Samaria had peace and was built up; and walking in the fear of the Lord and in the company of the Holy Spirit, it was multiplied" (9:31), including among its members even a "party of the Pharisees" (15:5).

It was only after the Revolt of AD 66—by which time the church had added many gentile members and had moved into the Diaspora—that its ties to Judaism began to weaken. Rudolf Bultmann says that the church changed dramatically "when gentile-Christian congregations arose for which adoption of the Law and especially circumcision no longer held as the condition for admission to the Congregation and for participation in messianic salvation."[399] As Amy-Jill Levine explains, "By the end of the first century and certainly before the New Testament canon was fixed, the church had become predominantly gentile. Paul's law-free gospel had triumphed over Matthew's insistence that 'not one iota, not one stroke of a letter, will pass from the Law' (5:28)." Mark's claim that Jesus rejected the food laws won out over James' requirement that converted gentiles follow some food restrictions. "Such shifts marginalized Jewish members of the church."[400] For these and other reasons, Christians were compelled to reassess their situation. According to James Carroll, Christians had to deal with "the crisis of the Temple's destruction" and "adjust to the fact that the Lord's return was not imminent," as well as respond to "the influx of Gentile converts."[401]

To many scholars, the increase in the number of gentiles in the church inevitably led to its anti-Judaism. Geza Vermes says that "the new church . . . soon lost its awareness of being Jewish; indeed, it became progressively anti-Jewish." Eventually "there was no longer any Jewish voice in Christendom."[402] Levine notes that "the Jewish identity of Jesus' earliest followers" sooner or later became "eccentricities," and their religious views became "heresies." In the fifth century, St. Jerome wrote to St. Augustine that the Christians who still practiced circumcision, honored the Sabbath, and followed Jewish food laws were no longer acceptable to the church: "Desiring to be both Jews and Christians, they are neither the one nor the other."[403] The idea that Jewish Christianity was marginalized can be seen in the fate of Jesus' brother James in the New Testament. Clearly, although James led the church throughout most of its last twenty to thirty years in Jerusalem, neither he nor his brothers are recognized in the Gospels. As Martin Hengel says, "[I]n all four Gospels James and the brothers play either a negative role or no role at all. This is best explained by the fact that the Synoptic Jesus tradition had already left Jewish Palestine behind and become independent before James took over complete control of the Jerusalem community in the forties and fifties."[404]

Increasingly, Christians were engaged in redefining their faith in relation to the religion they were no longer a part of. Specifically, Harold W. Attridge says, after the fall of Jerusalem, "[t]he Christian movement gradually solidified its internal organization and . . . formalized the structure of its beliefs. In the process, it defined itself over against the people of Israel from which it had emerged and in tension with the larger Hellenistic-Roman society of which it became an increasingly important part."[405] Furthermore, early in this development, Christians were placed in the difficult position of explaining why they were no longer Jews. According to John Dominic Crossan, the answer was, before the end of the century, that the Jews were their enemies.[406] According to Paula Fredriksen, Christians "had to explain to themselves, to potential converts, and, should they be so challenged, to skeptical Jews, how it was that the Jewish understanding of Jewish history and religion was false, and why those who had heard this Christian revelation most directly—Jesus' Jewish audience in Palestine—should have so completely failed to receive it."[407]

At the same time, of the four Jewish factions that existed before the Revolt, according to Josephus, the first-century Jewish historian, three lost their influence after AD 70. The Sadducees, as members of the priesthood, lost their power base when the Romans burned the Jerusalem Temple to the ground. The Zealots were simply defeated by the Romans, to some extent because they were divided among themselves. And the Essenes were driven out of Qumran. Only the Pharisees survived, emerging eventually as the religious leaders of the Jews and the founders of rabbinical Judaism.[408] William K. Klingaman says, "By the end of the first century, leadership of the Jewish communities in the Diaspora had already passed to the Pharisees and rabbis who now served the people as the teachers, interpreters, and guardians of the Law."[409] After AD 70, the now-dominant Pharisees were, like the Christians, engaged in redefining *their* faith, especially in relation not only to the other Jewish factions (which, the Pharisees believed, had led the Jews of Palestine to a humiliating defeat), but also to the Christians, who similarly survived the Revolt relatively unscathed and became increasingly more powerful and influential than they had been several decades earlier.[410]

The Pharisees blamed both the initiation and the failure of the rebellion against Rome on folly and factionalism. Therefore, as Ekkehard and Wolfgang Stegemann explain, the Pharisees' main goal was to establish some kind of unity. This required a resolution of all "disagreements about accepted and deviant behavior, about drawing boundaries regarding Jewish identities, and about a corresponding Jewish way of life." Thus, "[t]he previous multiplicity of diverging groups was replaced by a coalition dominated by moderate Pharisaic groups whose convictions became the core of an ongoing process of integration."[411] One consequence of this view was that, to the Pharisees, whatever threatened to undermine the unity of Judaism was unacceptable. John Shelby Spong says they were suddenly faced with insecurity: "Prior to this fateful year 70, Judaism had been able to tolerate varieties of opinions within its household of faith. Pluralism is always a byproduct of security. But when the survival of this faith tradition—their single claim to the future—was at stake, their level of toleration began to dissipate perceptibly."[412] James M. Robinson comments: "Whatever was left of Judaism had to stand together! The Jewish leaders came together and merged all these parties into a unified Judaism, which soon became the rabbinic Judaism out of which modern Judaism emerged."[413]

In this situation, proselytizing Christians, who had been tolerated (albeit often reluctantly) by most Jews during Jesus' lifetime, were increasingly thrown out of synagogues in the years after the Revolt. Thus, say the Stegemanns, "the previous fractionalism of Judaism was overcome, and, on the other hand, new groups that did not go along with the consensus were excluded."[414] According to Klingaman: "[T]he extraordinary crisis created by the demise of the Jewish state, and the accompanying persecutions inflicted by Rome, induced Judaism to close its ranks in order to ensure its survival, to insist upon a central orthodoxy and cast out the fringe groups that had thrived and caused so much dissension in the first half of the century... And one of the first factions to be ousted from the fold was the community of Jewish Christians."[415] W. H. Davies says that "the Christian Church was increasingly estranged from the Synagogue," the Pharisees "became convinced that Christianity was a menace to Judaism," and Jewish leaders decided "to exclude Christians from the Synagogue."[416] William M. Thompson comments, "It seems clear that the Pharisees rejected the Christian wing of Judaism, viewing it as an example of that 'messianic activism' which had brought the wrath of Rome down upon them and destroyed the temple."[417]

Furthermore. after the Revolt and the destruction of the Temple, Jews and Christians competed for converts. John P. Meier argues that, even during Jesus' lifetime, "both Jesus and the Pharisees were competing to influence the main body of Palestinian Jews and win them over to their respective visions of what God was calling Israel to be and do at a critical juncture in its history."[418] Many years after the Crucifixion, says Carroll, "in this post-Temple period, only the synagogue-based movement generally associated with the Pharisees had survived to compete with the Jesus movement for the legacy of Israel." And both were claiming ownership of the Jewish Bible to justify their respective theologies.[419] According to John G. Gager: "[I]n the latter part of the first century... two important developments had taken place. First, the Pharisees and their successors had emerged as the dominant group within Palestinian Judaism, and second, there was 'competition between the Pharisees and the Christian missionaries for the loyalty of the mass of Jews.'"[420]

In addition, it is important to keep in mind that this competition took place throughout the Diaspora. In the synagogues visited by Paul in the forties and fifties, some members of many congregations were proselytes (pagans who had converted to Judaism) and God-fearers (pagans who attended synagogue services and followed some Jewish laws), who were often susceptible to appeals from Christian missionaries. In the years following Paul's mission, Spong reminds us, as a result of the Revolt of AD 66, Jews who were "dispersed across the Mediterranean by both the accidents of war and the search for economic opportunity" were often vulnerable to appeals from proselytizing Christians. Some "had become weary of the burden of Jewish cultic practices that impeded their abilities to live in their gentile world profitably and comfortably.

So the primary effect of the gentile mission of Jews like Paul and others was to syphon off from the synagogues both the pool of potential gentile converts to Judaism and the more liberal elements of their own Jewish community."[421]

Of course, the competition for proselytes between Christians and Jews created a degree of animosity that did not exist before the war. Says Judith Lieu, "The Sadducean or priestly aristocracy who wielded most power in Jesus's own day recede into the background and increasing obscurity, while the Pharisees assume the dominant role as Jesus's protagonists."[422] And the expulsion of Christians from Jewish houses of worship incited a reaction from Christians. According to Morton Smith, "in the 80s the churches of Matthew and Luke were actively interested in and often hostile to the Pharisees."[423] In fact, this hostility apparently arose in other Christian communities. After the death of Jesus, says Bultmann, "his adherents . . . came more and more into conflict with orthodox Judaism, from which they had separated."[424] As Andre LaCocque explains, since "the Pharisees were the great surviving party after the Roman destruction of the temple in 70 CE, they were . . . the Jewish rivals of the early Christians."[425] According to Hans Kung, "They were now the main opponents of the young Christian communities."[426]

The result of this growing separation between Jews and Christians was that the last third of the first century—unlike the period in which Jesus conducted his ministry, in which many groups were free to claim that they were the "true" Israel—was ripe for more than competition. Although most Jews and Christians evidently lived alongside each other in relative peace,[427] in some communities Christians and Jews saw each other as enemies. As Rosemary R. Ruether explains, "the Church was in tension with the rival teachers of the Law, the rabbinic schools, who formed the teaching class of the synagogues, and with the Pharisees, the superobservant rabbinic leaders. These were the authorities against whom the anti-Judaic line of the Church was to harden during the missionary experience of the first century."[428] This is why Franz Mussner says that, in such circumstances—that is, "in the age of the primitive Church"—the mere presence of "the Pharisees and Pharisaism," especially since it was the only Jewish faction . . . which survived relatively well the catastrophe of the year 70," created mutual hostility.[429] In Carroll's words, the "competition" between Jews and Christians was "fierce and unprecedented."[430] In short, the two groups sometimes faced each other with impatience and, on occasion, anger and resentment.

At this moment in history, it so happens, the Gospels were written. And, as a result, both Jesus and his putative enemies, the Pharisees, were portrayed, for the edification of posterity, from a post-war perspective. And that event could not have occurred at a worse time. For many contemporary scholars, the main problem was that both the Revolt itself and the increasing conflict between Jews and Christians cast a dark shadow over the entire New Testament. In fact, as far as many scholars are concerned, the veracity of the work in its entirety was compromised by the circumstances in which it was composed. Specifically, the roles of both Jesus and the Jews, especially insofar as the latter were meant to be represented by the Pharisees, were mischaracterized. As Cwiekowski explains: "In the popular understanding of many Christians, the Pharisees were a very legalistic and rather hypocritical group very much opposed to Jesus and his teaching. Such a reading of the gospel fails to recognize that the picture of the Pharisees . . . is shaped by the struggles between the increasingly Gentile Christian community and the post-A.D. 70 Jewish community."[431] At the same time, Jesus was portrayed not only as the founder of a new religion but as a fierce opponent of the old one—his new faith being, in every respect, a corrective of the faith he left behind.

Not surprisingly, then, one of the most obvious results of the modern scholarly reassessment of the Gospels is a revision of the way the conflict between Jesus and the Pharisees is now understood. In the Gospels, Jesus appears as *the first Christian* engaged in an ongoing battle with the Pharisees, whereas, in fact, he was, during his lifetime, perceived to be a Jew in an ongoing argument with other Jews. The most important contributions of modern scholarship to our understanding of this subject are (1) the claim that first-century Judaism was characterized by the multiplication of sects, all of which thought they were the "true" Israel and often engaged in harsh criticism of each other; and (2) the understanding that, during the life of Jesus and several decades afterward, Jesus' followers continued to think of themselves as Jews.[432] As a result, even if the disagreements between Jesus and the Pharisees (and others) are accurately recorded in the Gospels, they were inter-tribal—that is, expressions of a conflict between representatives of competing Jewish sects.

As Vermes notes, "First-century Pharisees, Sadducees, Essenes, etc., seem to have coexisted in a spirit of tolerant hostility in clear contrast to the progressively standardized 'orthodoxy' of later ages."[433] Thus, Gillian Clark argues, the exchanges between Jesus and the Pharisees "were 'business as usual' for debates within Judaism . . . , and they do not demonstrate a general distinction between Jews . . . and Christians," particularly if the Jews (as Pharisees) are "characterized"—as they are in the New Testament—"as rule-governed, exclusive, and unable to recognize God's gift of the Messiah," and the Christians are "characterized as socially inclusive and active in mission."[434] Speaking of Jesus' extreme condemnation of the Pharisees in the Gospels, Edward Schillebeeckx says, "This criticism of the Pharisees is still a strictly Jewish affair, not a Grecian-Jewish one; and one finds it also among the Essenes (in the Qumran documents)." That is, Jesus assails the Pharisees, "yet the critique is still a Jewish one."[435]

Meier argues that Jesus' conflict with the Pharisees might also be comparable to the Jewish prophets' conflict with their contemporaries. That is, not only were these kinds of arguments characteristic of the Pharisees of the first century, but the vituperative tone and accusatory content were common in the speeches of the Jewish prophets: "Fiery denunciation was a revered rhetorical tradition from the prophets Amos and Hosea onwards, and Jesus the prophet saw himself as standing in their line."[436] Meier adds: "Granted the long tradition of fiery denunciation used by Israelite prophets against their opponents, we need not be surprised if Jesus the prophet spoke in a similar fashion against his opponents, including the Pharisees. Such verbal attacks by the historical Jesus must not be read as an attack on Judaism from without, as they so often have been read in later Christian history."[437] According to Gager, "many of these disputes, or at least the specific identification of these opponents, represent occasions not so much from Jesus' lifetime as from later times, the times of the gospels themselves, which have been read back into Jesus' career."[438]

The truth is, as far as many scholars are concerned, even assuming that Jesus actually argued with some of his contemporaries, it was only in the post-70 period that this conflict could have been interpreted as a Christian-Jewish confrontation. That is, like other Jews, Jesus questioned the bad behavior of some of his fellow Jews, and they, in turn, questioned him. However, says Donald H. Akenson, "[w]hatever arguments he had with them were fought within a shared frame of reference and in modes of discourse that were mutually comprehensible."[439] Jack T. Sanders adds: "Such debate [not on the law itself but on the *interpretation* of the law] is entirely normal within the Palestinian Judaism of Jesus' day and later. During this time the two schools ('houses') of Hillel and Shammai debated with each other."[440] Crossan explains: "In sectarian debates [in the Gospels and elsewhere], Christian Jews attacked Pharisaic Jews." However, although "[t]he polemical crescendo charts the increasing alienation of Christian Jews over against Pharisaic Jews," it tells us "nothing" about "the relative merits" of either Jesus or the Pharisees. "All such name-calling, no matter how bitter, is intra-Jewish strife."[441]

Ironically, as Sanders's reference to the ongoing conflict between the schools of Hillel and Shammai suggests, diversity reigned even within Pharisaism, which is why argumentation flourished among its members. According to Anthony J. Saldarini, "Internally, the Pharisees had their own vision of how society should be but rabbinic literature also indicates that they had many disagreements within their small and diverse movement."[442] Thus, Mussner argues that the Pharisees cannot be portrayed "as a uniform mass."[443] And Irving Zeitlin says, "[P]rior to AD 70 'Pharisaism', so-called, far from being a monolith, was a rather complex and heterogeneous religious movement."[444] According to Bart D. Ehrman, "Pharisees had serious disputes among themselves concerning how to interpret and implement [some] laws."[445] Akenson explains: "Instead of a tightly-disciplined party, with central control and unified admission requirements throughout their domain, the Pharisees should be considered to have been a tendency, a constellation of small groups that had overlapping views." To be sure, they were interested in the interpretation of Jewish laws. "Crucially," however, Akenson adds, "one should not see this legal interest as indicating a rigidity in religious outlook or practice." The Pharisees were remarkably flexible, because they were beginning to operate according to a body of laws that was later called the 'Oral Torah.'"[446]

Indeed, Meier argues, unlike the Essenes—many of whom lived separately from other Jews and maintained extremely strict laws of purity—the Pharisees "shared in what we might call 'mainstream' or 'common' Judaism . . . [They] might develop and mold these basic elements of the Law to fit their own views, but the basic elements were something they held in common with all Jews."[447] David Flusser agrees: "Fundamentally, the Pharisaic philosophy of life was in line with non-sectarian universal Judaism, while the Sadducees turned into a counter-revolutionary group that denied the validity of the oral tradition and saw belief in a future life as an old wives' tale."[448] It seems fair to say, therefore, that, despite the claim to the contrary among traditional scholars, debates between Jews and Christians, like other debates between (and within) other Jewish groups, did not signify either irremediable enmity or irreparable separation between the participants. Thus, Meier warns against taking this portrayal of Jesus' confrontation with Pharisees too seriously: "[E]specially in view of the tragic history of later Christian polemic, it must be stressed that the biting rhetoric used by Jews, including Jesus, in religious debates with their coreligionists should not be translated into a rejection of Judaism in general or of the Jewishness of one's adversaries in particular."[449]

Considering the short- and long-term consequences of this kind of misrepresentation, Clemens Thoma suggests that it was the starting point for Christian anti-Judaism: "It is one of the historical tragedies of theology, of the Gospel proclamation, and of humanity in general that the polemics of Jesus against the Pharisees were misinterpreted by absolutizing them and giving them the wrong emphasis. In the second century CE, Gentile Christians no longer understood the genre of Jewish 'polemics,' and Christian anti-Pharisaism became one with anti-Judaism."[450] In this context, it is clear that the Gospel writers' negative view of the Pharisees enabled them to portray the conflict between Jesus and his fellow Jews as something other than an intra-Jewish argument. Indeed, as the Gospels portray these disputes, it looks as though the Jews and Christians disagreed on *everything*. That is, there was no common ground between them. In this respect, the arguments are presented as irreconcilable conflicts *between the first Christian, Jesus, and his Jewish enemies, the Pharisees*. As Gager explains, "[I]nternal disputes between different Jewish groups" turned into "a situation in which the Jews, as a people, stand *against the Christians*."[451]

It is important to recognize, however, that, according to many scholars, the Gospels' misrepresentation of the relations between Jesus and the Pharisees went much further than this. They argue that the conflict between Christians and Jews after AD 70 was superimposed *more or less comprehensively* on the encounter between Jesus and the Pharisees in AD 30. On this view, the Gospel writers not only mischaracterized the nature of the relationship between Jesus and his fellow Jews, but also misrepresented the content of their arguments, the extent to which they actually disagreed, and the degree of mutual hostility these disagreements engendered. Indeed, the same circumstances that turned the intra-Jewish debate between Jesus and the Pharisees as well as other Jews into a Jewish-Christian debate also transformed Jesus into a defenseless victim of both verbal attacks and, ultimately, murder and transformed the Jews—especially the Pharisees—into the worst imaginable perpetrators of this villainy. According to Charles Guignebert, "It was in reality the Christians who . . . conceived the idea of setting up the 'hypocritical' Pharisees in such strong contrast to Jesus, and their attitude is explained by the resistance which they had encountered from Pharisaic orthodoxy in their own efforts to win the support of the Jews"[452]—that is, a generation or two after the Crucifixion.

Some scholars are inclined to accept the Gospel portrait of the Pharisees but allow for some degree of distortion.[453] Lawrence H. Schiffman, for example, agrees that the conflict was exaggerated but states this idea tentatively: "The New Testament accounts" of these disagreements "presage the later Jewish-Christian schism and *may even be* a reflection of it."[454] According to J. T. Sanders, "the conflict belongs to the early days of the Jewish Christianity *as well as to the life of Jesus*."[455] Michael Grant contends that "the violence of the conflict between the Pharisees and scribes on the one hand, and Jesus on the other, *may have been . . . to some extent* exaggerated by the Gospels." That is, "the Gospels *somewhat* exaggerate [Jesus'] hostility."[456] Referring to Jesus' criticism of the Pharisees in Matthew 23, James Parkes says that, when we understand the conflict between Jews and Christians "at the time when the gospels were being written down, . . . it ceases to be surprising that there is this *additional vehemence* in the denunciations put into the mouth of Jesus."[457] Meier says, "Gospel stories that narrate a pronouncement of Jesus about the Law *might be* basically historical while the presence of the Pharisees as the debating partners in the stories *might be* a later Christian creation."[458]

Lieu, however, argues that the Gospel writers "tell the story of Jesus in the light of their own experience, and that on their pages Jesus' encounters with *his* contemporaries *reflect more than a little* about the early Christians' own encounter with theirs."[459] Saldarini similarly makes the point that because the Gospels were written in "the last third of the first century" they fail to provide "first hand witness to what happened in the life of Jesus." What they offer instead is both a retrojection and a misrepresentation: "They often project onto the life of Jesus later controversies between the Christian and Jewish communities and may simply reflect a later author's misunderstanding of traditions at his disposal and of Palestinian society." Furthermore, their goal is polemical rather than historical: "In all cases the gospel writers have woven Jesus' opponents into a dramatic narrative which is controlled by their purposes in writing the narrative rather than by a desire to faithfully reproduce the events of Jesus' life. Thus the Pharisees, scribes and Sadducees undergo mutation for dramatic and theological purposes." It is not that the arguments between Jesus and others never occurred, but that "the disputes have been refined and reworked to fit the later needs of the Christian community and that Pharisees are often added to the narrative in Matthew, Luke and John, and perhaps to the Markan narrative as well."[460]

After his general characterization of the Gospel depictions of Jesus and the Pharisees, Saldarini argues that Mark "is reflecting something of the mid-first century situation"—that is, "if not the experience of Jesus," then "the experience of the early Christian community." Furthermore, since "[i]n the background of Matthew's polemic against the scribes and Pharisees are the Christian and Jewish communities of Matthew's day," his list of Pharisaic attributes in chapter 23 "is so polemical . . . that little reliable historical information can be gleaned from it." In Luke, the Pharisees, who "function as a stereotyped opposition to Jesus," are mischaracterized as "rich and powerful patrons of the peasants" and "powerful community leaders in Galilee." Despite the fact that John's treatment of the Pharisees "differs greatly from that in the synoptic gospels," it is similarly part of "a simplified and unhistorical view of Jewish leadership" before the Revolt of 66 AD. Specifically, "the Pharisees were only one among many political and religious forces" at the time. Thus, "John's view of the Pharisees probably fits his community's experience of Judaism and the Pharisees in the mid-first century."[461]

Despite his acknowledgement that some of the most important aspects of the relationship between Jesus and the Pharisees as reported in the Gospels are nonhistorical, Saldarini nevertheless insists repeatedly that the Pharisees, as "opponents of Jesus," did in fact compete with him for influence on and control over the Jews of Palestine. First, they disagreed: "The Pharisees' beliefs and behavior as Jews were different enough from those of Jesus and the early Christians, as well as other Jewish groups, to provoke disputes and factional competition and conflict." Second, Jesus and the Pharisees were not only "minor social forces" with "similar interests," they also "sought to influence the people in similar ways." In other words, the Pharisees "perceived Jesus as a threat to their power," and their "opposition . . . is reasonable and expected." Thus, the idea that Matthew (and presumably the other Gospel writers) is *totally* "projecting the post-Jamnia situation of Judaism and Christianity back on the life of Jesus . . . is most probably overstated," which means that he is not "reading the late first century situation back into the life of Jesus on a grand scale." Furthermore, "the contention that the early church put the Pharisees in all the Galilean disputes . . . lacks cogency."[462]

Yet again, it is important to note that many scholars have gone one step further by suggesting that the portrayal of the Pharisees in the Gospels was not merely exaggerated, but, if not invented whole-cloth, then at least *largely* created to serve the church's special needs in the late first century. Carroll says, "This conflict found its way into the second, third, fourth iterations of the story Christians were telling each other and newcomers"—by which he presumably means the last three Gospels—"which is how the Pharisees came to be pressed into service as the main antagonists of Jesus, even though *they had been no such thing*." In other words, as I noted earlier, Carroll argues that "*almost nothing said by Christians about these particular Jews [i.e., the Pharisees] is true.*"[463] According to Marcello Craveri, "In truth, the hatred toward the Pharisees that emerges from the Gospels is imputable not to Jesus but to the first Christians."[464] Ruether contends that "[t]here was probably no such 'meeting' between Jesus and the

Pharisees in a manner that one can say literally that the Pharisees, as a school, evaluated and rejected Jesus' teaching in his own lifetime. The importation of the Pharisees into the controversy stories . . . was primarily a creation of the Church out of its later conflict" with the Pharisees' "teaching tradition."[465]

Several scholars have described this view as widely shared, if not universal. According to Bernard Lee, "It is generally acknowledged today that much of the polemic between Jesus and the Pharisees is the argument of the early church read back into Jesus' life."[466] Lieu contends that it is "widely assumed in New Testament scholarship that the early church's continuing and allegedly increasingly tense relations with the Jews of their own age further shaped the way those traditions were preserved, interpreted and retold."[467] "In fact," Guignebert argues, "it is increasingly clear that the long-established habit of looking upon the religion of Jesus as a reaction against Pharisaism is erroneous."[468] E. P. Sanders says, "It is noteworthy that several recent works have sharply diminished or even eliminated the role of the Pharisees as substantial opponents of Jesus."[469] To Brown, this view is commonplace: "Few doubt that this picture [of Pharisees as hypocrites and legalists] is hostilely exaggerated, reflecting later polemics between Christians and Jews."[470]

The extent to which the Gospel writers are charged with exaggeration or fabrication depends largely on which Gospel or Gospels scholars are referring to. It is generally understood that Mark and Luke are less critical of the Pharisees than Matthew and John. This suggests that the picture of the Pharisees darkened as time passed and that, while Mark is relatively mild in his anti-Pharisaism, John is unequivocally harsh. "As we trace the history of the New Testament traditions," says Schiffman, "they move from disputes with Pharisees, scribes, and chief priests to polemics against the Jews and Judaism, from the notion of some Jews as enemies of Jesus to the demonization of the Jewish people as a whole."[471] According to Meier, "The polemic already heard in Mark becomes increasingly vitriolic in the later Gospels of Matthew and John." That is, "both . . . evince the tendency to make the Pharisees *the* enemy of Jesus during the public ministry. They thus reflect the struggle of the early church with the embryonic rabbinic movement of the post-70 period, anachronistically identified with the Pharisees of Jesus' day."[472]

The Stegemanns also insist that the treatment of the Pharisees in Matthew and John "must be understood" in the context of the relationship between Jesus and Judaism "in the period after 70 C.E." That is, "[t]he exaggerated and polemically distorted portrait of the Pharisees and scribes (especially in the Gospel of Matthew) can be interpreted against this background." The fact that the Pharisees and scribes are connected and that both appear as the leaders of Judaism is "understandable only in the situation after 70."[473] Thus, Thompson says, "Scholars are increasingly agreed that Matthew's and John's Gospels need to be understood against the background of post-70 Judaism."[474] After a long discussion of the subject, Meier similarly concludes: "The Pharisees of Matthew and John are largely the post-70 Pharisees and their allies who are swiftly on their way to becoming the early rabbis of tannaitic Judaism. Hence one must take great care in using either Matthew's or John's Pharisees to reconstruct the historical Pharisees who interacted with Jesus ca. A.D. 28–30."[475]

Among the synoptic Gospels, scholars pay special attention to Matthew's chapter 23. Parkes says, "There is an unmistakable increase in hostility in the tone of the three synoptists if they are read in the historical order of their appearance." He adds, "Nothing in Mark or Luke "corresponds to the violence, bitterness and thoroughness of the famous denunciations of chapter twenty-three" of Matthew.[476] Norman Perrin and Dennis C. Duling argue that "the diatribe against 'the scribes and Pharisees' in Matthew 23 does not reflect a conflict between Jesus and the scribes and Pharisees of his day, but one fifty years later between Matthew and their descendants spreading their influence from Jamnia."[477] James D. Tabor refers to Matthew's Pharisees as "shadowy figures": "Again and again throughout the Gospel of Matthew, the 'scribes and Pharisees' of Jesus' time appear as villains, pictured in garb and demeanor more appropriate to that of the rabbis and sages of early Rabbinic Judaism than that of the scribes and retainers of Herodian Galilee."[478]

Vermes says that the debates between Jesus and the Pharisees in the Gospel of Matthew reflect later conflicts outside of Palestine: They "mirror the controversies with Pharisees in which Jewish Christians and Pauline Christians in the diaspora were engaged in the second half of the first century A.D. They are anachronistically backdated by Matthew to the life of Jesus and have substantially contributed to the blackening of the name of the Pharisees." Vermes particularly disputes the authenticity of Matthew 23: "[I]t is very likely that the anti-Pharisee diatribes put into the mouth of Jesus in chapter 23 of Matthew did not originate with him."[479] Thus, speaking generally of the treatment of the Pharisees in the Gospel of Matthew, J. T. Sanders claims that "there is a broad consensus today that Matthew in its present form stems from a Christian community that is most in conflict with Pharisaism—that is, with emerging rabbinic Judaism after the destruction of Jerusalem."[480]

In discussions of the Gospel of John, scholars emphasize the Christian-Jewish rather than the Christian-Pharisee conflict, noting that in *this* Gospel John expresses a rejection of *all* Jews, not just their leaders. J. T. Sanders argues that, "[a]s the Jesus tradition develops"—that is, from Mark to John—"there is a tendency for this conflict to be merged into a general Christian-Jewish conflict."[481] Brown says that John uses the term "the Jews" in a "hostile" manner "for those of Jewish birth who distrust or reject Jesus and/or his followers." To the extent that the term refers to ordinary Jews as well as members of the Jewish elite, its use "may be an attempt to portray the Jewish opponents in the synagogues of John's time—opponents who are persecuting John's community (16:2) even as Jewish opponents in Jesus' time were remembered as persecuting him."[482] "Like Matthew and Luke," according to Howard Clark Kee and his co-writers, "John may also be dealing with the problem of the relation of Christianity to Judaism ... [B]ut he goes much further in stressing the intensity of the Jewish rejection, and the contrast between the old and the new."[483]

Many scholars, like Brown and Kee, attribute John's picture of the Jews to retrojection. That is, like the conflict between Jesus and the Pharisees in the synoptic Gospels, the conflict between Jesus and the Jews in general in the Gospel of John was shaped by the conflict in the post-70 period. According to L. Michael White, the "denunciations" of the Jews in the Gospel of John are indicative of the later Jewish-Christian conflict. They "are symbolically very powerful, because they are paired with liturgical and confessional elements and thus make John's polemic some of the most inflammatory anti-Jewish rhetoric in the early Christian tradition. The Gospel of John thus represents a social situation in which there is much greater separation between the Christian community and its Jewish neighbors."[484] Citing a number of "anachronistic passages in John," M. Smith says that "John's picture of the Pharisees reflects almost entirely the Jamnian Judaism of his own time and can never be used with confidence of Jesus' conflicts with members of the sect."[485]

Referring to the vicious exchange between Jesus and the Jews in chapter 8 of this Gospel, Hengel argues: "This heightened controversy with a caricature of Jesus among opponents explains the intensification of the polemic againstthe Jews in the two late Gospels which today is rightly complained about: this is typical of the tribulations of the church on the threshold of the second century."[486] Elaine Pagels makes the same point regarding Jesus' caricature of the Jews: "Most scholars agree that Jesus probably did not make these accusations, but that such strong words reflected bitter conflict between a group of Jesus' followers to which John belonged (c. 90–100 C.E.) and the Jewish majority of their city, especially the synagogue leaders."[487] Meier adds, "Clearly, to take every Gospel story involving the Pharisees as a video-taped replay of the historical events from ca. A.D. 30 or to ignore the massive expansion of the Pharisee's role in the Gospels of Matthew and John as part of their polemical agendas is to abandon the quest for the historical Jesus in favor of Christian theology."[488]

Who Killed Jesus?

This picture of the break between Judaism and Christianity, which increased substantially after the Revolt of AD 66, and its adverse effect on the portrayal of the Jews and Judaism in the Gospels has become the standard interpretation over the past fifty years.[489] It is important to say, however, that the separation between these two religions did not occur quite so abruptly and completely everywhere in the Roman Empire. In many communities, as I said earlier, Christians and Jews lived together peacefully and amicably. Geza Vermes says that "the split reflected in John between Judaism and Christianity, with followers of Jesus being expelled from the synagogue, is hardly conceivable before the turn of the first century A.D."[490] James D. Tabor reminds us that, after all, Luke "seems proud to report that the Jerusalem Church was attractive to Pharisees and Jewish priests, and that the apostles were held in high regard by their fellow Jews."[491] Furthermore, the Christian mission to the Jews, first led by Peter, clearly continued for long after the first century. Partly for this reason, Jewish Christians still outnumbered gentile Christians in some areas. Rodney Stark says that "Jews were the largest sources of [Christian] converts until well into the second century."[492] Thus, Ekkehard and Wolfgang Stegemann have concluded that "everyday relations between confessors of Christ and Jews were relatively harmonious." The Stegemanns add later that social conflicts are rarely reported in the New Testament and that "negative encounters between Christ-confessing groups and Diaspora synagogues took place at most sporadically."[493]

Furthermore, some Christians continued to be influenced by Jewish ideas and practices at least until the fourth or fifth century.[494] In the second century, church leaders refused to accept a version of the New Testament, composed by a Christian named Marcion, that was limited to Paul's letters and Luke's Gospel stripped of all Jewish influences and references. Stark comments, "To me, the Marcion affair suggests that the mission to the Jews remained a very high priority far later than has been recognized."[495] In the fourth century, says Robert L. Wilken, "particularly in greater Syria, some Christians attended the synagogue on festival days and were attracted to Jewish rites," especially "in those communities where Jews had become Christians and also where Christians lived alongside Jews—which was the case in many cities."[496] Christians in Antioch were still attending synagogue services and celebrating Jewish holidays, much to the chagrin of the Bishop of Antioch, St. John Chrysostom, who delivered eight virulently anti-Semitic sermons in an effort to dissuade Christians from engaging in Jewish activities.[497] Similarly, as I noted earlier, St. Jerome complained sometime around AD 400 that a group of Jewish Christians, called Nazarenes, still "practice[d] circumcision, celebrate[d] the Sabbath, and follow[ed] Jewish dietary regulations."[498] In fact, considering the persistence of Jews and Judaism in the world of Christians and Christianity, it might seem surprising that the earliest surviving Christian texts, besides Paul's letters, strongly suggest that the divide between Judaism and Christianity began immediately and increased both precipitously and comprehensively after the Jewish war of AD 66.

The fact is, however, that Christian hostility toward Jews, which is so amply illustrated in the Gospels and Acts of the Apostles, was made permanent by its inclusion in these works. Although they were not originally assumed to be sacred texts or even expressions of the official views of the church,[499] their importance grew as time passed, particularly their influence on interactions between Christians and Jews. Before, during, and after their composition, a series of events occurred that eventually resulted in the transformation of these documents into a validation of the church's growing criticism of, hatred for, hostility toward, and violence against the Jews: (1) the Crucifixion of Jesus, (2) Paul's rejection of law-obedience as a means of salvation for Christians, (3) the noncontingent admission of gentiles into the church, (4) the

Roman defeat of the Jews in the Revolt of AD 66, (5) the destruction of the Temple, (6) the movement of the church into the Diaspora, (7) the delay of the Parousia, (8) the assumption of church leadership in the second and third centuries by Greek-educated pagans, (9) the spectacular growth of the church from a few thousand in the first century to more than thirty million by the middle of the fourth century, and (10) the establishment of Christianity as the official religion of the Roman Empire.

In this context, it is important to revisit the passage from James Carroll that I quoted at the beginning of chapter 1: "It is at this point"—by which Carroll means "the Roman War, the loss of the Temple, the dispersal from Jerusalem, the readiness of the Gentiles to be recruited"—"that something unprecedented and truly dangerous began to happen. 'Jews' became the embodiment of the other. Because the conflict was cast as one between good and evil, . . . 'the Jews' now became identified in the minds of Christians with the devil. An ethos of fulfillment became an ethos of demonization." In other words, at some point in the midst of what Carroll calls a series of "accidents of history," two thousand years of Christian anti-Semitism began: "Once Christian became 'Christian,' once the embattled Jewish sect became the mostly Gentile 'Church,' the structure of the foundational story was set, the ground of Christian memory, the longest lie. The Jews would be the archenemy of Jesus, and of his people, from then on."[500]

Specifically, this enmity was rooted in the consequences of these historical accidents. The Jews were blamed for the Crucifixion. Paul's non-Jewish theology alienated prospective Jewish converts. The increase in the number of gentiles in the church diminished the importance of Jewish beliefs and practices. The Jews became intolerant of dissent after losing the war against the Romans. According to John Shelby Spong, the loss of the Temple eliminated the meeting place and common ground of Judaism and Jewish Christianity.[501] The church's move to the Diaspora increased the marginalization of Jewish Christianity. The delay of the arrival of the Kingdom of God, says Wayne A. Meeks, reduced the appeal of Christianity to Jews. The dominance of Greek-educated Christians contributed to the Hellenization and de-Judaization of the Christian faith.[502] The growth of the church threatened the existence of Judaism. And the triumph of Christianity allowed the church to punish the Jews for their sins against Christianity.

Clearly, some of the events mentioned by Carroll influenced the way Jews were portrayed in the Gospels. Indeed, as we have seen, the biblical Christian denigration of Jews is a consequence of Jewish-Christian conflicts that occurred long after the death of Jesus. For many contemporary scholars, these events helped to enhance, enshrine, and immortalize the anti-Judaism that these scholars find in the New Testament. Spong says: "It is because of the forces of history that Jewish books that we call Gospels written in a Jewish style came to be read exclusively by gentile people who knew not the ways of the Jews . . . It was, furthermore, on the basis of these gentile interpretations that the creeds, theological systems, and ecclesiastical superstructures of the Church were erected."[503]

Furthermore, many scholars argue that what Carroll and others call the "demonization" of the Jews, which was itself a product of anti-Judaism, led directly to the ongoing anti-Semitism of Europe and even the Nazi Holocaust. As Frederick J. Cwiekowski explains: "Relations between Judaism and the first three generations of Christians were at times stormy. Reflections of the sometimes bitter tensions between the two groups are a permanent record in several of the New Testament writings. The polemics in some of these texts had a role in encouraging in later centuries a reprehensible anti-Semitism that at times seriously compromised the Christian element of the history between the two groups."[504]

Referring to "the increasing alienation of Christian Jews over against Pharisaic Jews," which was misrepresented in the Gospels as something other than an "intra-Jewish" battle, John Dominic Crossan says, "It is absolutely important after two thousand years of Christian anti-Judaism and the final obscenity of European anti-Semitism, to emphasize that point as strongly as possible."[505] Speaking of the treatment of Jews in the Gospel of John, Meeks argues that "this way of talking," that is, the Christians' "way of stigmatizing their enemies"—the Jews—"would bear the bitter fruit of Christian anti-Semitism."[506] Making the same point, Rosemary Ruether says that "it is easy to see how [the] Christian myth" of Jews as "carnal Israel" and Christians as spiritual Israel "could be translated into anti-Semitic racism."[507] Elaine Pagels claims that, although "Jesus' followers did not invent the practice of demonizing enemies within their own group," they "carried this practice further than their Jewish predecessors had taken it, and with enormous consequences."[508] Edward Schillebeeckx takes this charge one step further: "Christians share the blame for a Western anti-Semitism that made possible the Nazi *Endlosung*."[509]

As these comments suggest, the persistent and profoundly negative portrait of the Jews in the New Testament resulted in a similarly enduring and deeply negative attitude toward the Jews in the real world.[510] However, most scholars argue that it was less this picture of a righteous Jesus battling unrighteous Jews that led to this attitude than the loud and clear claim that the Jews—*all of them, everywhere and forever*—were responsible for the death of Jesus. It is evident in both the public speeches of proselytizing Christians, such as those reported in Acts of the Apostles and in the Passion narratives of the Gospels, that the evangelists laid the blame for Jesus' Crucifixion on the Jews rather than the Romans. Indeed, the transformation in which Jesus' Jewish opponents turned into sons of the devil is the same transformation in which Jesus' Jewish opponents became his murderers. Diarmaid MacCulloch sums up this point of view: "It is painful but necessary to remind Christians of the centuries-old heritage of anti-Semitism festering in the memories of countless ordinary twentieth-century Christians on the eve of the Nazi takeover ... Without the long Christian centuries of characterizing the Jews as Christ-killers, the Nazis would not have been so easily able to manipulate otherwise decent ordinary folk."[511]

Speaking of the Passion narrative, in which the Crucifixion is the culminating event, Marcus Borg and John Dominic Crossan argue that "two thousand years of theological anti-Judaism and even racial anti-Semitism derived from this story."[512] Martin Marty calls the Gospel accusation that the Jews killed Jesus "one of the roots of Christian anti-Judaism, the biggest blot on" the story of Christianity.[513] Donald Senior agrees: "One of the most tragic and shameful blots on Christian history has been the use of the passion story as an excuse for anti-Semitism."[514] Sean Freyne says that "the generalizing tendencies with regard to the Jewish involvement [in the death of Jesus], especially in the First and Fourth Gospels, has promoted the charge of deicide being levelled at the whole Jewish people in later anti-Jewish, Christian polemic."[515] Noting that the evangelists make the encounter between Jesus and the Jews a manifestation of a "cosmic war" between good and evil, Pagels says that the "violence epitomized in the execution of Jesus . . . has vindicated Jesus' followers and demonized their enemies." That is, "[h]aving cast the Jews" as the "symbol of all evil," the Gospel of John, in particular, "can arouse and legitimate hostility toward Judaism," which, in the words of Reginald Fuller, "has been abundantly and tragically actualized in the course of Christian history."[516]

Of course, if the Jews had actually been the prime movers behind the execution of Jesus, as the Gospels contend, it would be hard to accuse the evangelists not only of fomenting anti-Judaism, but also of being motivated by it. However, from the point of view of many scholars, the Gospel accounts of Jesus' Passion are simply fictitious. H. Conzelmann and A. Lindemann contend that these stories are statements of faith rather than historical claims: "[O]ne would misunderstand the passion narrative(s) if they were regarded to be an attempt to reconstruct the course of events with historical accuracy. Just as in the earlier part of the Gospels, the Christological interest predominates here as well. The passion story interprets the Christian confession and has been shaped exclusively with this interest in mind."[517] More directly, Crossan says that the Passion is "magnificent theological fiction, to be sure, but entailing a dreadful price for Judaism."[518] James Charlesworth claims that one of the purposes of his book "is to disclose that this account does not derive from ancient history; it is medieval—even modern—fiction."[519] According to Morton Smith, "the stories are fictitious; their true function seems polemic—to make Jesus' death result from the Jewish authorities' rejection, as blasphemous, of the formal statement of his true nature and rank."[520]

At the center of this widespread distrust among scholars of the historical accuracy of the Passion is a similarly widespread questioning of Jesus' trials.[521] John McKenzie says, "These narratives are loaded with uncertainties and ambiguities."[522] Smith argues, "The accounts of interrogations and trials . . . are unscrupulous dramatizations of uncertain events."[523] Gunther Bornkamm contends that "Jesus' trial before the Jewish High Court" is based on theology rather than history: It "has been elaborated by the Gospels in the spirit of faith in Christ . . . Looked at from the historical point of view, the story arouses critical doubts."[524] John P. Meier notes that Friday, the day of the trials, is so overloaded with events as to be unbelievable.[525] To Joseph Tyson, the evangelists' "picture of a Jewish trial that issued in a Roman execution over the protests of the chief Roman authority" is "incomprehensible" largely because "the earliest tradition pointed to Rome as the party responsible for the death of Jesus."[526] William M. Thompson says that the accounts "of the various trials are contradictory (and there were apparently no Christian witnesses) . . . Scholars even debate whether the council could have lawfully met."[527] McKenzie agrees: "Commentators have often noticed that the Talmud prohibited nocturnal sessions. I am more impressed with the practical difficulties of holding a meeting of seventy people at night in the illumination available in Roman times."[528] Bruce Chilton believes that Pilate "did not interrogate Jesus . . . and could not have done so directly for the simple reason he did not speak Aramaic, any more than most Romans of his class, but only Greek and Latin."[529]

Bart D. Ehrman doubts that Jesus could have been accused of blasphemy, as he is in Mark, since it is questionable whether he even committed that crime. "It seems unlikely, then," he concludes, "that the trial proceeded in the way it's described in Mark, our earliest source."[530] Bornkamm says that "there is not one single instance of a person's ever being accused of blasphemy and sentenced to death by the Jewish authorities because he claimed to be the Messiah. There is no mention of an abuse of the name of God."[531] Crossan questions whether the Romans would have bothered with anything as formal as an official trial for such an insignificant criminal: "I am very unsure what level of Roman bureaucratic authority was empowered to eradicate a peasant nuisance like Jesus . . . It's difficult for the Christian imagination, then or now, to accept the brutal informality with which Jesus was probably condemned and crucified."[532] William R. Herzog II goes so far as to say that there were no trials: "Jesus was never tried to determine his innocence or guilt. There never was a 'trial of Jesus.' To speak of a trial is an anachronism" that overlooks the typical practices of the Romans in the first century.[533] E. P. Sanders argues that since there were no followers of Jesus in attendance at the trial, virtually nothing can be known about it: "*That anyone, even someone close to the scene, knew precisely who did what is unlikely*. That the *internal motives* of the actors were known by those on whom the evangelists drew seems impossible."[534]

All of this might strike the non-scholarly reader as preposterous. However, over the past half-century, historians and students of the Bible have been exploring the day-to-day realities of life in the Roman Empire during the first century AD. One of the most interesting facts that scholars have uncovered is the way the Roman government dealt with threats to its hegemony in provincial territories.[535] Typically, the Romans established in each province a connection with the indigenous aristocracy, whose responsibility was to collect taxes and maintain order. As N. T. Wright explains, "The Romans liked to run their huge empire through local power brokers on whom they could rely to collect the taxes and keep the population under control." Their job was "particularly to suppress unrest."[536] In Palestine, under the governance of the procurator

The Evolution of Love

or prefect, the Jewish elite were the constituted power, whose leader, the high priest, could be both appointed and deposed by his Roman superior. Serving at the will of the Roman governor, the high priest was expected to keep the peace and faced dismissal if he failed to do so. During the period between AD 6 and the Jewish Revolt in AD 66, eighteen high priests were hired,[537] all of them presumably retained or dismissed on the basis of their success in suppressing political dissent. The elite had to walk a fine line by satisfying the Roman overlords without offending the Jewish populace.[538]

E. P. Sanders says, "The impression is overwhelming that the chief priests took the lead in mediating between the Romans and the populace: they were held responsible by the Romans"[539] Thus, after his year (or more) of healing and preaching, his royal entry into Jerusalem, and his attack on the Temple, Jesus was arrested by the Temple police. In Ehrman's words, "[I]t makes sense that a local offender would first be brought before the local authorities. In the case of Jesus, it was the high priest Caiaphas and his ruling 'council,' called the Sanhedrin."[540] In this context, the Sanhedrin would be likely to arrest anyone who threatened the social order, not because he challenged the authority of the Jewish aristocracy, whose ongoing status and power were underwritten by the Roman prefect, but who might be perceived by the prefect to be potentially dangerous. Thus, says Sanders, "if the Jerusalem leaders thought that Jesus would attract the hostile attention of Rome, they would have been quick to single him out as an undesirable troublemaker."[541] Which, of course, they did.

As Paula Fredriksen explains, it was not that the Jews were offended by Jesus' claim to be the Son of God, jealous of his success in converting many Jews to a new religion called Christianity, or worried about his threat to the laws pertaining to the Sabbath, purity, food, and ritual. Rather, "since the priests were the middlemen between the populace and the Roman occupation government," their fear that Jesus "might inspire popular agitation, and so provoke Roman hostility," compelled them "to forestall disaster by handing him over to Pilate," thereby fulfilling their political responsibility.[542] That is, it was not sensitivity, jealousy, or religiosity that motivated the Sanhedrin, but survival.[543] In this respect, the words of "the chief priests and the Pharisees" in the Gospel of John reveal the real motives of these Jewish leaders: "If we let him go on like this, the Romans will come and destroy our holy place and our nation" (11:47–48), to which Caiaphas, the high priest, famously responds: "[I]t is expedient for you that one man should die for the people, and that the whole nation should not perish (11:47–50)."[544]

Both Caiaphas and the others agree on the problem. And despite Caiaphas' apparent criticism of them—"you do not understand"—both agree on the solution. They realize that they cannot "let him"—that is, Jesus—"go on." Pagels comments: "John shows the council members concerned about the disturbances Jesus arouses among the people, a plausible motive for their judgment, for they want to protect their own constituency from the risk of Roman reprisals, even at the risk of wrongful execution."[545] Herschel Shanks and Ben Witherington III say that the Jewish priests in Jerusalem always responded to "messianic figures or Jewish revolutionaries" in the same way because, if the troublemaker "aroused the suspicions of Rome," it "might lead to their loss of political power."[546] Thus, Chilton asks, "How could Herod Antipas and the Romans respond other than violently to the news that a disciple of John the Baptist was using messianic terms to refer to himself?"[547] And Smith argues: "Between the certainty of Jesus' power and the certainty of Roman power the high priests hardly hesitated long. We have seen that the fear of a messianic uprising and consequent Roman intervention, which Jn. 11.48 puts in their mouth, is completely credible."[548]

Two additional facts are important. First, although Pontius Pilate is portrayed as an innocent bystander in the Gospels, he was well known as a brutal ruler who was not easily intimidated by his subjects and who displayed little concern for their religious interests.[549] Helmut Koester says that Pilate offended the Jews on several occasions and, although he backed down the first time he encountered Jewish resistance, he otherwise reacted swiftly and violently: "He did not hesitate to order on-the-spot executions by his soldiers." In short, he seems to have learned what he had to do in order to maintain control over the rebellious Jews. Indeed, he was removed from office for acting "recklessly and brutally" a few years after the Crucifixion.[550] Thus, Michael Grant comments, although in the Gospels Pilate "shows an undignified feebleness and vacillation," he was in fact "a man who had already held down one of the worst trouble spots in the empire for a number of years."[551] According to Joseph B. Tyson, "He is presented at one and the same time as convinced of Jesus' innocence and anxious for his release, as holding the power of life and death in his hands, and as succumbing to the insistence of the people he governed, even though they offered no evidence for their charges."[552] Pagels says, "Other first-century writers, Jewish and Roman, describe a very different man. Besides Josephus, Pagels adds that Philo, "a respected and influential member of the Alexandrian Jewish community, describes Pilate as a man of 'ruthless, stubborn and cruel disposition,' famous for, among other things, ordering 'frequent executions without trial.'"[553]

Second, Roman prefects like Pilate were notorious for executing rebels (including those only *perceived* to be rebels) without any concern for due process. Vermes says that "self-proclaimed Jewish redeemer figures," of which the Jewish historian Josephus names many and among whom Jesus is the most famous, incurred a great risk "in the powder keg of Palestine in the first century A.D."[554] What Vermes means is that, when Pilate was faced with rebelliousness, especially from a Galilean with a "messianic reputation," he reacted in the same way that Romans did everywhere in the Empire when they faced opposition. As Ehrman explains, "The central government in Rome was not overly concerned about how the governors achieved" their objectives. They "were given virtually free reign to do whatever was necessary to rule." For example, if a riot broke out or if a self-proclaimed messianic leader arose, as they sometimes did in the half century or more before the Jewish Revolt, governors "could send out the troops." Then, even "if several thousand people were killed in the process, well, maybe next time the masses wouldn't be so quick to be a troublemaker."[555] In addition, "[i]f someone was perceived to be a troublemaker there was no need to follow anything that would strike us as due process, at least for non-Roman citizens in the provinces—no requirement of a trial by jury, for example, or for a careful cross-examination of all witnesses."[556]

Considering that, according to contemporary accounts, Pontius Pilate was not a reluctant executioner who was fair-minded and temperate and that Roman governors in the provinces were unrestrained by procedural rules in their responses to civil unrest, it is difficult to accept the Gospel versions of the circumstances that led to Jesus' death. Thus, while scholars "differ over who was actually responsible," says White, "[a]lmost all would agree that it was ultimately Pilate; that the main reason was political (rather than 'blasphemy' or heresy); and that the Jewish population had nothing to do with it or say about it."[557] Donald Senior claims, simply, "Jesus was executed by the Romans. About that there is no doubt." Furthermore, "the charge against [him] was not religious but political." He was "executed as a political insurgent."[558] After spending a chapter exploring the subject, E. P. Sanders similarly concludes that "Jesus was executed by the Romans" and that "he was [highly probably] executed for sedition or treason, as would-be king."[559] According to Chilton, the claim that the Jews were responsible for Jesus' death "is historically inaccurate . . . Nothing could be further from the truth." Later, Chilton says that "the realities of power in Rome and Jerusalem, as well as Pilate's own temperament, make the theory of general Jewish guilt for the death of Jesus completely implausible in historical terms."[560]

Borg and Crossan note, after all, that crucifixion was "a very definite type of capital punishment for those such as runaway slaves or rebel insurgents who subverted Roman law and order." Intended to be "a calculated social deterrent," it was not used to punish "[o]rdinary criminals," but genuine threats to the status quo, such as Jesus as well as the "two other rebels against Rome" who were executed with him.[561] Similarly, Jürgen Moltmann says, "Crucifixion was a punishment for crimes against the state." It was "a political punishment for rebellion against the social and political order of the *Imperium Roman*." Therefore, "Jesus was condemned by Pilate as a political rebel."[562] According to Koester, "in the case of Jesus, Pilate was quick in sentencing a potential agitator."[563] So, "in the end," says Tabor, "the Romans crucified Jesus for sedition—his claim to be the rightful King of the Jews."[564]

Of course, it goes without saying that Jesus was *not* a revolutionary; however, as Stephen M. Wylen argues, in the eyes of the Romans (and therefore in the eyes of the Jewish officials), "[a]ll leaders who attracted a following were potential revolutionaries."[565] Thus, the fear may have been misplaced, but it was nevertheless real. Noting that Jesus was a "political suspect," Conzelmann and Lindemann conclude that "Jesus was not only executed in keeping with Roman instruction, but he was also sentenced by the Romans."[566] Clyde L. Manschreck says that Jesus' "tie" to the Zealots, through Simon Zelotes, "and the crowds that Jesus attracted apparently caused Rome to think that [he] might be the center of an incipient revolt, a factor which contributed to his crucifixion."[567]

N. T. Wright provides a comprehensive overview of this subject. First, Jesus' words and actions appeared to be threatening: "Talking about someone new being in charge was dangerous in Jesus' day . . . Someone behaving as if they possess some kind of authority is an obvious threat to established rulers and other power brokers." That is, "If either Herod or the high priest heard that someone was going around announcing that God was becoming king, they would smell trouble at once." Second, Jesus was perceived to be a threat because his "actions and sayings were ramming home the point, dangerous though it was, that the present rulers were being called to account and were indeed being replaced." He seemed to be "a rebel leader . . . setting up an alternative government, establishing his rule, making things happen in a new way." Third, everyone understood–or at least *thought* they understood—Jesus' purpose. Especially in choosing twelve disciples, he was "reconstituting God's people, Israel, around himself." People interpreted Jesus' movement in relation to the predictions of the prophets, who "had spoken of the day when all the tribes would be united again." Fourth, those who could not accept the replacement of the old regime with a new one had no alternative except to eliminate the perpetrator. Thus, Jesus was "executed on the charge of being a would-be rebel leader, a 'king of the Jews.'" And, "[l]ike many thousands of young Jews, he died by crucifixion." This side of Jesus' arrest and execution has been ignored, Wright adds, because "[o]ur culture has become used to thinking of Jesus as a 'religious' figure rather than a 'political' one. We have seen those two categories as watertight compartments, to be kept strictly separate. But it wasn't like that for Jesus and others of his time."[568]

The Gospel writers tell a different story for two reasons. First, as we have seen, relations between Jesus' followers and the Jews slowly deteriorated after the Crucifixion. Judith Lieu says: "It is . . . widely assumed in New Testament scholarship that the early church's continuing and allegedly increasingly tense relations with the Jews of their own age further shaped the way those traditions were preserved, interpreted, and retold. Thus, already in the New Testament Gospels Jewish responsibility for the death of Jesus is heightened and Roman responsibility correspondingly downplayed."[569] Stanley Cook makes a similar point: "Anti-Jewish feeling cannot be ignored, least of all in Matt., xxvii, 24 f., which whitewashes the Roman Procurator Pilate and harshly intensifies the guilt of the Jews."[570] To Senior, "Christian concentration on Jewish involvement in the death of Jesus stemmed, in part, from the hurt and perplexity caused by the fact that by and large the Jewish people had not accepted the gospel message."[571] Carroll says: "So as Christians felt themselves and their movement to be mortally challenged by the refusal of their fellow Jews to affirm their messianic understanding of Jesus, it was a small step to lay the actual death of Jesus at the feet not so much of Rome as of these rejecting Jews."[572] Thus, as Wylen explains: "In the decades after the crucifixion, as the young Christian church shifted its missionary activities from the

Jews to the Roman Gentiles, the church shifted blame away from potential Christians, the Romans, and toward the Jews who had rejected Christianity."[573]

Wylen says this shift reflected yet another retrojection: "In shifting blame, the gospels represent this missionary concern of their own period rather than the historical realities of Jesus' time."[574] Smith agrees: The charges "by the high priest and sanhedrin"—making "Jesus' death result from the Jewish authorities' rejection"—"are the retrojected reactions of the Jews opposing the church in which this tradition was formed." More precisely, Smith argues that "the passages shifting the blame for Jesus' conviction from the high priests, by degrees, to 'the Jews' are polemic misrepresentations; they are matched by many apologetic elements representing Pilate as convinced of Jesus' innocence, anxious to release him, and yielding only reluctantly to the high priests' . . . demand for his execution—all these are incredible inventions to show that Christianity and its founder were really innocent in the eyes of the Roman judge: Jesus was not a deservedly condemned criminal, but the victim of a political deal. When such propaganda, and the novelistic elements . . . are set aside, little reliable information remains."[575] Ruether says that the goal of the evangelists was not only to "shift the blame" from Jews to Romans, but also change the charge against Jesus from a political crime to a religious one: "This suggests that the purpose of this shift was not merely one of apologetics toward the Gentiles, but one, first of all, of polemic toward the Jewish religious tradition."[576]

Referring to the claim that Jewish crowds called for Jesus' death and willingly took the blame for his execution, Thomas Sheehan argues that such charges, "which were later written into the accounts of Jesus' passion, are the products of a bitter polemic between early Christianity and Judaism and have helped cause the horrors of two millennia of anti-Semitism."[577] Arguing that "the account of Jesus' passion was eventually 'heard' in an antiJewish way," Brown agrees with Sheehan: "Sometimes the early Christian communities encountered the hostility of local synagogue leaders, and they saw a parallel between this hostility and the treatment of Jesus by the authorities of his time. Now, however, the issue was no longer on an intraJewish level: That other group, the Jews, were doing things to us Gentile Christians and were responsible for the death of Jesus."[578]

Second, the increasingly gentile church preferred to avoid offending the Romans. M. Grant says that "the evangelists, in their desire after the Jewish Revolt to incriminate the Jews and deny any serious dispute between the Christians and Romans, made Pilate so indecisive because they wanted to show that they had not been *really hostile* to Jesus, and had even attempted, unsuccessfully, to save him."[579] Chilton argues that the reason for this attitude was practical: "The desire to remove blame from the Romans for the crucifixion that only they could have been responsible for is understandable. After all, the earliest Christians had to live under the hegemony of officials like Pilate." Therefore, "[t]hey wanted to ingratiate themselves with their Roman rulers, and to charge antagonistic synagogue leaders with instigating every conceivable form of violence against them"[580] According to Perrin and Duling, Christians understood that, given the delay in the Parousia, they might have "to live in the Empire for a considerable period of time." To help his readers "come to terms" with this reality, "the author of Luke-Acts [presumably, like the other Gospel writers] consistently presents Roman authorities as sympathetic to the Christian movement."[581] Thus, say the Stegemanns, the suggestion that "both the Jewish and Roman authorities were aware of Jesus' innocence . . . is without doubt a tendentious presentation, which cannot simply be explained on the basis of later experiences; it reveals, rather, an apologetical interest in warding off the criminalization of Christians in the Roman empire."[582]

Chapter Three

The Pentateuch

ONE OF THE OBSTACLES to an appreciation of Judaism is its early adoption and subsequent retention of various rituals (including circumcision and Temple sacrifice) and food and purity laws. On the one hand, many of these practices were in force elsewhere in the Near East. Most ancient societies offered sacrifices to their gods and established a system of taboos, often pertaining to food and everyday human activities. E. P. Sanders points out that "religion *was* sacrifice"—for example, "in Rome, Greece, Egypt, and Mesopotamia" as well as "most other parts of the ancient world."[583] "Circumcision," says George Foot Moore, was "customary among peoples of unrelated races in widely remote quarters of the globe . . . According to Herodotus (ii, 104), it was practised by the Egyptians, the Ethiopians (Nubians), the Phoenicians, the 'Syrians of Palestine,' and further by certain tribes in Asia Minor, and by Colchians . . . , all of whom he believes to have got the custom from Egypt."[584] According to Alan F. Segal, "The concept [of purity laws] is widespread in ancient and modern cultures." Indeed, many "ritual actions are typical of much of the world's religious practice."[585]

On the other hand, however, the particular laws promulgated by the Jews were originally intended to enable them to maintain their ethnic and national identity. Robert Wright explains: "One bias [of ancient societies] is called ethnic marking," which occurs when "an ethnic group works to preserve, or initially construct, a cohesive identity" by "highlight[ing] differences between itself and nearby peoples."[586] The Jews distinguished themselves from all other cultures by calling themselves "the chosen people." To be sure, many tribal societies saw themselves as superior to other tribal societies, sometimes calling themselves "human" and referring to others as "non-human." The new, second-millennium migrants to the Indus Valley, for example, called themselves Aryans, meaning "noble" or "honorable." All other tribes or groups were obviously not so special.[587] According to John A. Wilson, the ancient Egyptians "made a distinction between 'men', on the one hand, and Lybians or Asiatics or Africans, on the other . . . In other words, the Egyptians were 'people'; foreigners were not."[588]

However, the Jews, being a very small minority in an especially volatile region of the Near East (and living between the powerful Egyptians to the south and the equally powerful Assyrians, as well as other Mesopotamian nations, to the east), may also have been influenced by feelings of vulnerability and weakness, rather than national pride. Bernhard W. Anderson says of Israel's difficult position in the Middle East: "From earliest times the Fertile Crescent was the scene of a fierce struggle for land. As we have seen, this coveted area periodically was invaded by peoples from Arabia, Asia Minor, the Caucasian highlands, or Egypt . . . Palestine was, by virtue of its geographical location, inevitably drawn into the incessant conflict. This little country was the place where small nations rudely and brutally fought for Lebensraum, or 'living space,' and where big nations fought their wars of empire."[589] According to Walter Brueggemann, "The land of Israel that primarily concerns the Old Testament is endlessly an arena of contestation between Egyptian power in the south and the sporadic imperial ambitions of the powers in the north."[590]

Thus, from this perspective, Jewish "exclusivism" was a matter of survival rather than superciliousness. Moore argues that it was motivated by "self-preservation, and nothing more"—especially under foreign domination. Many food and purity laws "had the effect of putting hindrances in the way of intercourse with the heathen," but they were not invented for that purpose. "They were ancient customs, the origin and reason of which had long since been forgotten. Some of them are found among other Semites, or more widely."[591] G. Ernest Wright attributes Israel's claim to have been chosen by God to the belief that in liberating them from Egypt God had treated the Israelites with special favor. That is, "she was merely giving the one plausible explanation of the historical fact that . . . she was freed by the wonderful work of this one true God."[592] Karen Armstrong says: "Israel was a newcomer in the family of nations, born of trauma and upheaval, and constantly threatened with marginality. The Israelites developed a counteridentity and a counternarrative: they were different from the other nations in the region, because they enjoyed a unique relationship with their God, Yahweh."[593]

No doubt, the prophets moved Judaism closer to universalism—the idea that, in Moore's words, "God would one day be acknowledged and served by all mankind."[594] In the language of contemporary theology, however, the ancient Jews were, at least in their early years, particularists rather than universalists. They sometimes forbade intermarriage, they established special holy days commemorating important events in their own history, and they revered their own national heroes.[595] Again, these were not unusual religious practices in the late second and early first millennia BC. However, they unquestionably put Judaism in a unique category in the so-called Axial Age of the mid-first millennium. Despite the fact that the new religions of Buddhism, Zoroastrianism, Platonism, and Taoism, were founded in India, Persia, Greece, and China, respectively, they were not limited in their appeal to particular ethnic groups or particular nations. All of these new religions turned their backs on the older religions they threatened to replace—not only the polytheism, but also the focus on ritual, taboos, and other more-or-less tribal practices.

Judaism changed, but, like the "new" Hinduism of the Baghavad Gita and the Upanishads, it did not repudiate its past.[596] And the result was that, although the writings of the prophets not only focus on morality rather than ritual, but also reach toward universalism, Judaism never lost its identity as a *Jewish* religion, meant, at least initially, *only* for Jews.[597] Not that the Jews did not proselytize and not that their attempt to attract converts was unsuccessful. But surely the inclusion of their own national history and the celebration of their own ancestors as an indispensable part of their faith must logically have made Judaism less appealing to non-Jews than Buddhism or Platonism, for example. Anderson says, "Judaism is the religion of a people who have a unique memory that reaches back through the centuries to the stirring events of their Bible, events that formed them as a people with a sense of identity and vocation"[598]

The second obstacle to an appreciation of Judaism is, as I said in the introduction, despite the fact that in many respects this religion moved away from its tribal roots and the particularist tendencies that characterized its earliest phase, it is not always easy to distinguish the new from the old. On the one hand, there can be little doubt that, by the time Deuteronomy was written and the prophets announced their revolutionary doctrines, Judaism had departed from its earlier Pentateuchal concern with ritual and purity laws. John J. Collins says that, after Deuteronomy, "cultic rituals would henceforth play a much smaller role in the lives of most of the people" of Israel. For example, "Purity concerns are not prominent in Deuteronomy."[599] Israel Finkelstein and Neil Asher Silberman argue that Deuteronomy signals a new emphasis on social justice: "[I]t is important to note that the book of Deuteronomy contains ethical laws and provisions for social welfare that have no parallel anywhere else in the Bible. Deuteronomy calls for the defense of what we would call today human rights and human dignity. Its laws offer an unprecedented concern for the weak and helpless in Judahite society."[600]

On the other hand, however, it is sometimes hard to say exactly what Judaism was (and still is) to the extent that it was (and still is) connected to the older practices. Indeed, the problem is complicated by the fact that Deuteronomy retains some old-fashioned elements, such as the claim that Moses wrote it as well as the insistence that Jewish armies were required by God to destroy entire populations (including children and animals). Similarly, the prophets, whose works can be roughly dated, are not in total agreement on the relationship between morality and ritualism;[601] and both Psalms and Proverbs were written over many centuries and therefore cannot always be identified with a particular historical period or with a singular moral vision.

In fact, part of the problem is that nobody knows for sure exactly when any of the books of the Pentateuch were composed (as opposed to written), and the same may be said of Joshua, Judges, 1 and 2 Samuel, and 1 and 2 Kings. Finally, as Julius Wellhausen claimed in the nineteenth century, the Pentateuch is a composite work made

The Pentateuch

up of intermingled passages written by four (or more) different writers. Exodus, for example, as Collins notes, consequently offers two versions of many stories, including the creation, the flood, Abraham's visits to foreign kings with Sarah, God's covenant with Abraham, and Sarah's repudiation of Hagar.[602]

Third, although it is generally understood among Jews, with the special exception of the Orthodox and Ultra-Orthodox, that large portions of the Jewish Bible are legendary or mythological, it is often impossible to determine where myth ends and history begins. According to William A. Irwin, "[w]e wrong this whole body of literature when we appraise it primarily as history, for it was composed for a variety of purposes, most of them quite apart from systematic record of the past."[603] Thus, as Jack Miles has said, "Myth, legend, and history mix endlessly in the Bible, and Bible historians are endlessly sorting them out."[604] It has long been taken for granted, given the scientific evidence, that everything up to the story of Abraham was fictional: namely, the stories of the Creation, Adam and Eve, the Tower of Babel, and Noah. According to Kaufmann, Genesis contains the "most ancient" material in the Bible, particularly chapters 1–11, which "have long been recognized as drawing upon ancient Near Eastern materials. It may be further observed that these early legends are characterized by an almost unique folkloristic naivete."[605] Anderson says that both "the sovereignty of the God of the Exodus" and "the unity of *Israel* as God's people" were "pushed back" to the age of the patriarchs. "Strictly speaking, this results in an oversimplified picture."[606]

In fact, more recently, archeologists have raised a number of questions about the historical validity of the patriarchal stories, especially the interconnected genealogy of the patriarchs themselves. Armstrong argues, for example: "Even the biblical account suggests that Israel was not descended from a single ancestor, but consisted of a number of different ethnicities—Gibeonites, Jerahmeelites, Kenites, and Canaanites from the cities of Hepher and Tirzah—who all became part of 'Israel.' These groups and clans seem to have bound themselves together by a covenant agreement."[607] According to Anderson, "By the time of the Yahwist, these miscellaneous traditions [i.e., stories of the patriarchs] had already been fairly well adapted into the story of a single family bound together by the relation of father to son: Abraham, Isaac, Jacob, Joseph. The Yahwist, however, was primarily responsible for giving to the patriarchal period a unity that did not actually exist until the time of the Tribal Confederacy or the United Monarchy."[608]

Questions have also been raised about the stories of Joseph and his brothers, and even the escape from Egypt, including the journey through the desert and the meeting between Moses and God on Mt. Sinai.[609] Brueggemann says: "The critical conclusion that the ancestral narratives in Genesis are not historical has been followed by a widely shared critical judgment that the events of the thirteenth–eleventh centuries (Moses, Joshua, Samuel) are not historical, and the existence of David and Solomon is now widely contested. More radical critics, drawn to more negative critical judgments, raise issues about the historicity of Hezekiah and Josiah, so that clear historical ground for what the Bible asserts is at the earliest, for the most radical judgments, in the sixth or even fifth centuries."[610] Gerhard von Rad comments: "As far as I can see, Israel finally went over to the prosaic and scientific presentation of her history with the Deuteronomistic history. Thus, right down to the sixth century, she was unable to dispense with poetry in drafting history, for the Succession Document or the history of Jehu's revolution are poetic presentations, and are indeed the acme of poetic perfection."[611]

Finkelstein and Silberman argue that "recent discoveries of archeology . . . have revolutionized the study of early Israel and have cast serious doubt on the historical basis of such famous biblical stories as the wanderings of the patriarchs, the Exodus from Egypt and conquest of Canaan, and the glorious empire of David and Solomon."[612] Other scholars, as well, contend that there is little historical evidence that the Jews were ever in Egypt and little physical evidence that 600,000 men and their families spent forty years in the Sinai.[613] There have also been questions raised as to whether the Jews fought many (or even some) battles in Canaan before the establishment of the monarchy.[614] The history of the monarchy itself raises uncertainties because there are two somewhat dissimilar accounts of the leaders of Israel in Kings and Chronicles. Miracle stories, such as those associated with Elijah and Elisha, have been challenged, and, in the post-exilic period, many biblical works are widely understood to be intentionally fictional, such as the books of Job, Esther, and Daniel.

Brueggemann says that, "over time, the community that produced the Old Testament appropriated much of [the]common material' that was available in the Near East, including Canaan, "and made use of it in its liturgic practice and in its theological self-understanding." The question is not whether this kind of borrowing occurred, but "the extent to which Israel *appropriated* such material, the extent to which it radically *transformed* the material, and the extent to which it *rejected* the material that it found inimical to its own theological commitments."[615] At the furthest extreme, according to Martin Goodman, "it has been suggested that the whole history of the Jews before the third century BCE was invented at that time by the compilers of the Bible."[616] Acknowledging that "[s]ome scholars believe that the entire history of Israel was created out of whole cloth" sometime between the sixth and second centuries BC, Robert N. Bellah nevertheless rejects "the so-called minimalist theory" because he finds no reason for post-exilic Jews to have made up the entire story: "I see no reason why the inhabitants of a small province under Persian or Greek rule would have any need to create the history of the unified, then divided, then obliterated monarchy, or the Moses/Exodus epic either."[617]

Particularly keeping in mind the kinds of changes in theology and religious practices that occurred in the Axial Age religions, what we can say for sure is that in ancient Israel the concept of God and the rules of morality underwent significant changes from the pre- to post-exilic periods. Indeed, if we examine the first four books of the Pentateuch, we can see a fairly confusing idea of God, who is not always omniscient, not always rational, and not always moral. Richard Elliott Friedman reminds us that in early Judaism God is characterized by "blatant anthropomorphisms": God not only walks in the Garden and calls out to Adam and Eve, but "personally makes [their] clothes, personally closes Noah's ark, smells Noah's sacrifice, wrestles with Jacob, and speaks to Moses out of the burning bush." Later, "God personally speaks the Ten Commandments out loud from the heavens over Sinai."[618]

One problem is that the Jewish God, throughout the Pentateuch, is not only called by various names (Elohim, Yahweh, El Elyon, and El Shaddai, among others), but also characterized by various attributes, such as strength, jealousy, wisdom, vengefulness, disappointment, anger, righteousness, and love. According to Brueggemann, "Over time functions that had been assigned in religious interpretation to a variety of gods accrued to the person of YHWH who was then understood as a complex character with a rich internal life."[619] Jack Miles says, "The God whom ancient Israel worshiped arose as the fusion of a number of other gods whom a nomadic nation had met in its wanderings." Specifically, Miles explains, one can see in the Jewish God a number of "clearly distinguishable tints": "Here the sky blue of El, there the earth tones of 'the god of your father,' over the blood red of Baal or Tiamat or the evergreen memory of Asherah." These are the sources of or influences on the early Jewish conception of deity: El, who was the sky god of the Semitic peoples; "the god of your father," who was the Jewish version of the Mesopotamian personal god; Baal, who was the Canaanite war, storm, and fertility god; and so on.[620]

In the Beginning

There can be little doubt that, as Robert Wright argues, the God of the Pentateuch is omnipotent, but he is sometimes neither omniscient nor omnipresent.[621] That is, he does not know everything since he often either visits particular locales or sends representatives in order to find out the facts on the ground. After Adam and Eve eat the forbidden fruit, God arrives in the Garden of Eden to chastise them, but does not know exactly where they are: "And they heard the sound of the Lord God walking in the garden in the cool of the day, and the man and the woman hid themselves . . . But the Lord God called to the man, and said to him, 'Where are you?'" (3:8–9). God then asks Adam, "Have you eaten of the tree of which I commanded you not to eat? (3:11). And He asks Eve, "What is this that you have done?" (3:13). In the story of Adam and Eve, God is consistently portrayed as if he has physical attributes and lacks the kind of knowledge that one expects in an all-knowing deity.

Similarly, when Cain reacts negatively to God's rejection of his offering, "[t]he Lord said to Cain, 'Why are you angry, and why has your countenance fallen?'" (4:6). After Cain murders his brother, God asks, "Where is Abel your brother? . . . What have you done?" (4:9–10). Later, when God appears to Abraham in the guise of "three men," he asks, "Where is Sarah your wife?" (18:9). After God tells Abraham that Sarah will have a son in her old age and she laughs in response, God asks Abraham, "Why did

The Evolution of Love

Sarah laugh?" (18:13). And when God says to Abraham that he has heard an "outcry against Sodom and Gomorrah," he explains that he must visit those cities in order to verify this claim: "I will go down to see whether they have done altogether according to the outcry which has come to me; and if not, I will know" (18:20–21).

In all of these cases, one would expect an omniscient God to possess the answers to his questions without asking anyone for help. Surely, by the time he visited Eden, God knew where Adam and Eve were and what they had done. Similarly, he must have known why Cain was disappointed and what crime he had committed as a result of his anger. And God certainly knew that Sarah was in her tent, why she laughed, and whether or not Sodom and Gomorrah were in fact as bad as he heard they were. On the other hand, it could be argued that sometimes God was testing his auditors—that is, he was trying to determine whether they would willingly accept responsibility for their sins. In this light, part of the story of Adam and Eve is that they not only refused to admit their guilt, but tried to hide from God, which is merely dramatized by his question "Where are you?" Adam says, "The woman whom thou gavest to be with me, she gave me the fruit of the tree, and I ate." And Eve says, "The serpent beguiled me, and I ate" (3:12–13).

Indeed, God may have asked Cain why he was angry in order to point out that he should simply try harder: "If you do well, will you not be accepted?" God also warns Cain to "master" sin, which is "couching [sic] at the door" and ready to capture him (4:6-7). Furthermore, God knows exactly what Cain has done since he curses him without waiting for him to confess. Cain compounds his crime by answering God's question with the evasive and irresponsible answer, "[A]m I my brother's keeper?" (4:9-11). Finally, God's question about Sarah's laugh may actually be a criticism of her inadequate understanding of God's power. "Is anything too hard for the Lord?" he asks. Also, she tells God that she did not laugh, but he knows better. "No, but you did laugh," he says, without any recrimination (18:13–15).

Nevertheless, it remains true that "two angels," representing God, actually go to Sodom, stay at Lot's house, and find clear evidence that the "outcry" God heard about the sinfulness of Sodom and Gomorrah is true (19:1-9). Yet again, it may be that the angels have come to Sodom only to rescue Lot and his family since they immediately warn Lot of the imminence of God's destruction and literally seize Lot and his family and drag them out of Sodom when they linger, except for Lot's "sons-in-law," who believe that the angels are "jesting." After all, Lot is saved because "the Lord [is] merciful to him," and the angels tell him not that they have only now become convinced that Sodom is worthy of destruction, but that they "are about to destroy this place, because the outcry against its people has become great before the Lord, and *the Lord has sent [them] to destroy it*" (19:12–16; my emphasis).

On the other hand, "the Lord" himself stays behind to discuss the fate of Sodom with Abraham. Instead of saying that the city will definitely be destroyed, God finally agrees with Abraham that he will spare Sodom if he can find ten "righteous" persons (gender unspecified) dwelling there (18:23–32). Assuming that God is being sincere in his promise, the decision has yet to be made, and it is presumably not made until "the men of Sodom, both young and old, all the people to the last man" arrive at Lot's front door and ask to have Lot's visitors turned over to them for sexual purposes (19:4–9). Furthermore, if God were in fact all-knowing he would know that there are not ten good people in the cities he is about to destroy.

Whatever one might say about God's omniscience, it is certainly true that, as these stories make clear, the people whom God created were, in the majority of cases, unworthy of his support, let alone sympathy. In other words, except for Noah, Isaac, and Joseph, the major characters in Genesis commit all kinds of sins. They tell lie after lie, deny their responsibility for their actions, violate their agreements, encourage deception, compete deviously for affection, and deceive even their closest relatives. As we have seen, Adam and Eve not only disobey God's prohibition, but also refuse to acknowledge their guilt. Cain, the first murderer, denies that he has done anything wrong. The father of Noah and a descendant of Cain, Lamech kills a man who has wounded him and refers to himself as "avenged . . . seventy-sevenfold" (3: 23–24).

Such incidents demonstrate that even if God knows everything that *has already happened*, he remains unaware of future events. He is not only surprised but disappointed with the behavior of Adam and Eve, Cain, all of Noah's contemporaries, the builders of the Tower of Babel, the residents of Sodom, Lot's wife, Jacob's sons and grandsons, and Shechem. Before the Flood, the narrator of Genesis says: "The Lord saw that the wickedness of man was great in the earth, and that every imagination of the thoughts of his heart was only evil continually. And the Lord was sorry that he had made man on the earth, and it grieved him to his heart" (6:5–6). There is little reason to doubt that God experienced the same grief in response to the other acts of "wickedness" that occur again and again in the book of Genesis. In short, he expected more.[622]

After the Flood and up to the time of Jacob, there are any number of acts committed by major figures in the Bible that, although they are unpunished by God, are likely to strike the modern reader as either self-serving or mean-spirited, or both. Twice Abraham lies to foreign kings about his relationship to Sarah, calling her his sister in order to save himself from harm: "Say you are my sister, that it may go well with me . . . and that my life may be spared on your account." In Egypt, after Sarah is introduced as Abraham's sister, she is taken into the Pharaoh's house, and Abraham is given servants and animals in return. However, the Pharaoh, "afflicted . . . with great plagues" by God, gives Sarah back to Abraham and angrily dismisses both of them (12:10–20).

The editors of *The Oxford Annotated Bible*, Herbert G. May and Bruce M. Metzger, comment on this incident: "The narrative does not moralize about the white lie but rather portrays the Lord's rescue of Sarah from the jeopardy into which Abraham's self-interest had placed her" (15).[623] Notably, as Abraham says, Sarah is "a woman beautiful to behold," and she is "taken into Pharaoh's house" because Pharaoh's princes tell him that she is "very beautiful." Since Abraham receives "sheep, oxen, he-asses, menservants, maidservants, she-asses and camels" from the Pharaoh, who, we are told, "dealt well" with him, it almost looks as if Abraham simply sold Sarah to the Pharaoh.[624]

The same thing happens when Abraham and Sarah sojourn to Gerar after the destruction of Sodom and Gomorrah (20:1–18). Abimelech, King of the Philistines, takes Sarah from Abraham, but God intervenes. In a dream he says to Abimelech, "Behold, you are a dead man, because of the woman you have taken; for she is a man's wife." Abimelech responds: "Lord, wilt thou slay an innocent people? . . . In the integrity of my heart and the innocence of my hands I have done this." Since God threatens to destroy not only the king but "all that are" his—that is, his "people"—Abimelech returns Sarah to Abraham with this complaint: "You have done to me things that ought not to be done." After Abraham explains his actions to the king, he is given not only "sheep and oxen, and male and female slaves," but also, as the king explains to Sarah, "a thousand pieces of silver," which he describes as her "vindication in the eyes of all who are with [her]; and before everyone [she is] righted." God had, in fact, rendered the king's wife and female slaves infertile, a malady healed only after Abraham asks God to forgive Abimelech.

In both instances, Abraham puts the kings in extreme jeopardy—God punishes them with plagues or barrenness—although he fails to hold Abraham accountable. At any rate, Abraham himself does not object to either king's apprehension of Sarah. Only God demurs and threatens the duped kings with severe penalties, despite their innocence. Indeed, Abimelech is so impressed by the power of Abraham's God that he also offers Abraham the right to live in his territory: "Behold, my land is before you; dwell where it pleases you." Shortly after this, the king says to Abraham: "God is with you in all that you do; now therefore swear to me here by God that you will not deal falsely with me or with my offspring or my posterity." Abraham swears, and the two men later make a covenant (21:22–32).

Similarly, Sarah twice treats her Egyptian handmaid, Hagar, unjustly—or, at least cruelly. As Susan Niditch says, the story "prods the modern reader (as well as the classical rabbis) to worry about God's fairness and about Abraham's excessive passivity."[625] First, Sarah offers Hagar to Abraham as a wife in order to provide him with an heir. Then, offended by Hagar's "contempt" for her, Sarah "dealt harshly with" her, as a result of which Hagar runs off to the wilderness. Abraham had said to Sarah, "Behold, your maid is in your power, do to her as you please." Encouraged to return to Sarah and "submit" to her by "an angel of the Lord" (16:1–9), Hagar is once again sent away, this time by Abraham, because Sarah saw their two sons playing together and objected to "the son of this slave woman" being Abraham's "heir with [her] son Isaac" (21:8–14). This time, we are told that Abraham finds the situation "very displeasing," but whether he is upset with Sarah or Hagar is not immediately clear. The latter seems to be the case since God says to Abraham, "Be not displeased because of the lad and because of your slave woman; whatever Sarah says to you, do as she tells you, for through Isaac shall your descendants be named." Although God does not condemn Sarah for her jealousy and inhumanity, he saves Hagar twice in the wilderness and promises to make her son, Ishmael, "the ancestor of the Bedouin tribes of the southern wilderness."[626]

The command "Do to her as you please" occurs again when Lot, Abraham's nephew, is confronted by the entire male population of Sodom. They demand that he turn over the two men whom he has welcomed into his home as sojourners (and who are actually two angels). Lot offers the Sodomites an alternative that allows him to honor the rules of hospitality: "Behold, I have two daughters who have not known man; let me bring them out to you, and *do to them as you please*; only do nothing to these men, for they have come under the shelter of my roof" (19:8; my emphasis). No comment is necessary.

Jacob's career begins when he refuses to share his pottage with his twin brother, Esau, who has come "in from the field, and he was famished." Jacob agrees to feed Esau if his brother is willing to give him his birthright as the first-born son of Isaac. Esau agrees because, as he says, "I am about to die; of what use is a birthright to me" (25:29–34). Jacob appears again when Isaac, who is near death, sends Esau out to bring him a "savory" dish before he gives his older son his blessing. Having overheard this conversation, Rebekah commands Jacob, whom she prefers to Esau, to help her prepare food for Isaac, to put on Esau's clothes, and to put kidskin on his hands and neck—all of this to deceive Isaac into thinking that Jacob is Esau and thereby to allow Jacob to receive Isaac's blessing. Jacob proceeds to lie to his father when he claims to be Esau and says that he prepared the food quickly because "God granted [him] success."[627]

After Isaac blesses Jacob, Esau shows up, hears that his father has already blessed Jacob, and "crie[s] out with an exceedingly great and bitter cry." To both Esau and Isaac, Jacob is clearly a thief, who, according to Esau, has lived up to his name, which means either "heel" or "supplanter." Isaac says, "Your brother came with guile, and he has taken away your blessing." Esau replies, "Is he not rightly named Jacob? For he has supplanted me these two times. He took away my birthright; and behold, now he has taken away my blessing." John L. McKenzie comments: "There is no hint in the story itself that the blessing and the promises are taken from an undeserving heir and given to a more worthy bearer. Jacob does not appear as a more worthy bearer." Indeed, McKenzie says later, "There is no doubt that Jacob, in contrast with Abraham and Isaac, is not a moral hero."[628] When Rebekah overhears Esau's promise to kill Jacob, she sends her favorite son away, again with Isaac's blessing, to marry one of her brother Laban's daughters and thereby escape his brother's wrath (27:1—28:5).

We next meet Jacob on his way to Laban's house, when he sees God in a dream that begins with "angels of God . . . ascending and descending" on a ladder that "reache[s] to heaven." It is important to recall that, when he was blessed by Isaac, Jacob told his father that "the Lord *your* God granted me success" (27:20; my emphasis), indicating that he had yet to accept Isaac's God as his own. Yet when he awakens from his dream, Jacob is convinced that he has actually seen God: "Surely the Lord is in this place ... This is none other than the house of God, and this is the gate of heaven." Yet again, grand though his vision is, Jacob remains an unbeliever. In fact, he says that he will accept God as *his* God only under certain conditions: "Then Jacob made a vow, saying, 'If God will be with me in this way that I go, and will give me bread to eat and clothing to wear, so that I come again to my father's house in peace, *then the Lord shall be my God*'" (28:10–21; my emphasis).[629]

At least partly based on Jacob's pledge, there can be little doubt that God is on Jacob's side from this point on. However, when Jacob finally reaches Laban's house, falls in love with Rachel, and begins to serve Laban for seven years for the right to marry her, it becomes equally clear that God cannot protect Jacob from the deceptions practiced by Laban. Jacob's uncle tricks him into marrying Rachel's older sister, Leah, and then forces Jacob into working seven more years in order to marry Rachel. After Laban promises to pay Jacob for his many years of labor, he hides the animals that he agreed to give him. When Jacob, who feels cheated by Laban, secretly leaves for home and takes his wives and goods with him, at God's urging, Laban accuses Jacob of cheating him. In addition to the fact that both daughters resent each other in their competition for Jacob's love, Rachel not only steals Laban's idols, but tells her father, who is desperately searching for his precious goods, that she is menstruating and therefore has to remain seated on a camel's saddle in which the idols are hidden (29:4—31:35).

Jacob's next exploit has to do with his fear of his brother, Esau, whom he cheated twice, twenty years earlier. Jacob prays to God to save him from the wrath of Esau, who, Jacob believes, could "come and slay us all" (32:11). To appease his brother, Jacob offers Esau nearly six hundred goats, sheep, rams, camels, cows, and asses. He sends out servants, each with a different group of animals and each group spaced behind the other so that Esau will be overwhelmed when he finds out from every servant that these animals are gifts to him from his brother. As Jacob explains, "I may appease him with the present that goes before me, and afterwards I shall see his face; perhaps he will accept me" (32:13–20). That night, "until the breaking of the day," Jacob wrestles with "a man" who is actually God or an angel of God. His opponent seems to be a divine figure because he stops the fight merely by touching Jacob's thigh, blesses Jacob and renames him Israel (which God does again in 35:9–10), and elicits from Jacob the sense that he has "seen God face to face" (32:24–30).

That morning, when Jacob sees Esau approaching him with four hundred men, he goes out to meet him, "bowing himself to the ground seven times." However, it turns out that Esau is no longer angry and vengeful, but happy to see his brother; at least initially unwilling to accept his gifts because, as he says, "I have enough"; and even eager to have some of his men accompany Jacob home. Jacob says after Esau's warm greeting, "[T]ruly to see your face is like seeing the face of God, with such favor have you received me." At this point, evidently relieved beyond words, he "urge[s]"

Esau so strongly to accept his gift—because, like Esau, he has "enough"—that Esau appears to have little choice but to accept it (33:1–11, 15).

Our final example of Jacob's persistently questionable behavior has to do with his daughter Dinah's rape by a man named Shechem, the son of a prince, who evidently falls in love with Dinah after he sexually assaults her: "[H]e loved the maid and spoke tenderly to her" after "he seized her and lay with her and humbled her" (34:1–3). When Shechem and his father, Hamor, come to Jacob and his sons to ask them to give Dinah to Shechem "in marriage" and promise to give them "as marriage present and gift" anything they ask for, including intermarriage with Hamor's daughters as well as land in Hamor's territory, Jacob's sons (and, presumably, Jacob himself) "answered Shechem and his father Hamor deceitfully" (34:8–13).

On the one hand, "the men were indignant and very angry, because [Shechem] had wrought folly in Israel by lying with Jacob's daughter, for such a thing ought not to be done" (34:7). On the other hand, however, Jacob and his sons concoct a horribly vengeful plan that punishes *all* of Hamor's people. Jacob's sons tell Hamor that they will give Dinah to Shechem only on the condition that "every male of you be circumcised," after which the intermarriage that Hamor offered would take place. Hamor announces this to "the men of his city," orders "every male [to be] circumcised," and adds, "These men are friendly with us; let them dwell in the land and trade in it" (34:14–24). What was the patriarchal response? "On the third day, when [the men in Hamor's city] were sore," two of Dinah's brothers "took their swords and came upon the city unawares, and killed all the males," including the prince and his son. "And the sons of Jacob came upon the slain, and plundered the city, because their sister had been defiled; they took their flocks and their herds." Furthermore, "all their wealth, all their little ones and their wives, all that was in the houses, they captured and made their prey" (34:25–29).

The denouement of Genesis, the story of Joseph, focuses on Joseph's career in Egypt, which underscores the fulfillment of God's promises to Abraham and his heirs by demonstrating that Joseph, like his forebears, lived a long life, produced many offspring, survived adversity, and achieved prosperity.[630] As for adversity, partly because Joseph is his father's favorite (37:3), his brothers plan first to kill him and then, under Reuben and Judah's influence, decide to put him into a pit, with the intention of selling him to passing traders (37:18–27). Stolen from the pit by Midianites or Ishmaelites, Joseph is sold as a slave and eventually becomes the right-hand man of Potiphar, the captain of the Egyptian guard (37:28, 39:1–6). In the meantime, Joseph's brothers kill a goat, dip Joseph's robe in blood, and bring the robe to Jacob, who had given it to Joseph as a special gift. Jacob says, "It is my son's robe; a wild beast has devoured him; Joseph is without doubt torn to pieces." After this, "Jacob rent his garments, and put sackcloth upon his loins, and mourned for his son many days" (37:29–36). Betrayed by Potiphar's wife and sent to prison,[631] Joseph is freed after two years by the pharaoh himself because he successfully interprets the king's dreams (39:7—41:38).

The Evolution of Love

As for prosperity, Joseph eventually becomes the second-in-command of all Egypt (41:39–57). In fact, the narrator of Joseph's saga says repeatedly that Joseph succeeded because God was with him (39:2–3, 41:38–39, 45:3–8). Furthermore, in the end, having saved Egypt from the ravages of the famine that he predicted, Joseph is reconciled with his brothers; reunited with his father and his only "full" brother, Benjamin; and able to witness his father's blessing of Jacob's sons, Manasseh and Ephraim. The theological pinnacle of Genesis occurs when Joseph's brothers repent for their sins (42:21–22, 50:15–17) and Joseph implicitly forgives them (45:5). He interprets their unequivocally evil act as, unbeknownst to them (or anyone else), an expression of God's will, his plan to allow them all to survive by bringing Joseph to Egypt and providing him with salvific powers: "[D]o not be distressed, or angry with yourselves, because you sold me here; for God sent me before you to preserve life." God intended "to preserve for you a remnant on earth, and to keep alive for you many survivors. So it was not you who sent me here, but God" (45:5–8).

In fact, God was evidently not only saving Joseph's family, but the Egyptians as well: He made it happen "so that many people should be kept alive" (50:20). On this point, Anderson says, "Joseph, elevated to the position of prime minister of Egypt, saved the land from famine and brought security and prosperity to Egypt."[632] Instead of either punishing or forgiving his brothers, Joseph says, "Fear not, for am I in the place of God? As for you, you meant evil against me; but God meant it for good, to bring it about that many people should be kept alive, as they are today" (50:19–20). Only God can help us or harm us, Joseph says. And, in so saying, he presages a later and wiser age, in which these sentiments are dominant—not, as they appear to be in Genesis, an afterthought.

Despite the fact that the stories in Genesis are not historically reliable, they are worth retelling in some detail for several reasons. First, as I suggested earlier, they reveal how at least some ancient Jewish writers viewed human nature. Specifically, these stories illustrate the depravity of nearly everyone in the book of Genesis, all of whom God created, including the patriarchs and matriarchs, who are otherwise vaunted and revered as the founders of Judaism. As Gerhard von Rad observes, the patriarchs are hardly model citizens: "As is well known, a great deal of mischief has been caused by the widespread idea that the patriarchs were patterns of pious behavior before God. The question whether and where the story-tellers want to provoke 'imitation' is not so very easy to answer."[633] To be sure, Abraham and Lot obey the laws of hospitality, Isaac blesses Jacob wholeheartedly despite his younger son's theft of Esau's birthright, and both Esau and Joseph famously forgive their brothers.[634] But Genesis is otherwise so filled with immoral acts that one wonders where God is hiding after destroying the entire population of the world except for Noah and the entire population of Sodom and Gomorrah except for Lot and his daughters.

According to G. Ernest Wright, despite God's "loving and merciful acts" (e.g., his saving of innocent people like Noah and Lot, his ongoing support of all the patriarchs, his provision of children to Sarah, Rebekah, and Rachel), "a deep, basic, and fundamental infection exists in the heart of man, with the result that wherever he moves he finds himself doing that which *he knows to be wrong.*" Furthermore, the failure of the author of this material to "preach at us" is part of his effort to allow the stories to speak for themselves. As "a man of great faith," he also possesses "great understanding of the nature of man." And his stories are illustrations of the pervasiveness and persistence of human evil. That is, to Wright, Genesis is, more than anything else, a testament to human depravity: "Together [the stories therein] form a powerful and profound portrayal of the problem of universal man. That problem is *sinful rebellion against the Creator and against man's created nature.*"[635] As von Rad says, Genesis traces in great detail "the growth of sin," which God "punishe[s] . . . with increasingly severe judgments."[636]

In fact, framed as it is by Cain's murder of Abel and Joseph's brothers' attempt to get rid of him, the book of Genesis is a long and painful meditation on the dominance in human life of both sex and violence. Furthermore, although many of the accounts under both headings are indispensable to our understanding of the narrative as a whole, some of them are either inexplicable or gratuitous, such as the song of Lamech, in which, as I noted earlier, he boasts of murdering someone who injured him (4:23–24);[637] the marriage of an unidentifiable group of men called "the sons of God" and "the daughters of men" (6:2–4); Noah's curse on his grandson Canaan because Canaan's father, Ham, "saw the nakedness" of Noah (9:22–27);[638] the destruction of the Tower of Babel and the scattering of people all over the earth;[639] Lot's offer of his virgin daughters to the Sodomites, who are trying to gain sexual access to Lot's angelic guests (19:6–8);[640] Rachel's agreement with Leah to allow her sister to have sex with their husband, Jacob, in exchange for some mandrakes, which were, at the time, "thought to have aphrodisiac properties which stimulated conception."[641]

The same kinds of events occur in the story of Joseph and his brothers, including Reuben's sexual encounter with Bilhah, Jacob's concubine (35:22), followed later by his father's deathbed condemnation of this act (49:4); God's murder of Er, Judah's oldest son, for some unspecified "wicked" act (38:7); Judah's sexual encounter with his daughter-in-law Tamar, who has become a "harlot" because Judah failed to have his son Shelah marry her after the death of her husband;[642] and Judah's initial condemnation of Tamar to death by burning for becoming pregnant out of wedlock, although he later realizes that the child is his (38:15–30).[643] Some stories, morally objectionable though they may be to a modern reader, at least underscore the need, under God's direction, for Abraham's heirs to propagate. One such story tells of Lot's daughters' seduction of their father after their prospective husbands are killed in the destruction of Sodom and Gomorrah (19:31–38). Another is God's murder of Onan for "spill[ing] his semen on the ground" rather than consummate a levirate marriage with Tamar, his brother Er's widow (38:8–10).[644]

What is just as striking in Genesis as the presence of evil actions on the part of God's favorites, as well as many secondary characters, is the almost complete absence of good actions on their part. That is, except for Joseph, none of the patriarchs or matriarchs stand out for being generous, kind, merciful, or forgiving.[645] The examples of human decency usually crop up in odd places, such as, for example, in the stories of King Abimelech, who is ready to do almost anything to accommodate Abraham; Esau, who is quite willing to forget Jacob's hostile acts of the past and reestablish their brotherly relationship; Prince Hamor, who, like Abimelech, wants to compensate for an immoral act by offering Jacob's sons anything they want; Ephron the Hittite, who offers Abraham a free burial space for Sarah; and the pharaoh of Joseph's time, who seems to understand Joseph's passionate attachment to his family and wants to help Jacob and his sons in any way possible. One might assume that all of the leading figures in Genesis are in fact righteous in some sense of the word, but one could hardly conclude that, without definitions or illustrations, their stories could be construed as in any way instructional and the characters themselves exemplary.

Furthermore, God's rewards and punishments fail to illustrate any standard of right and wrong. God punishes the residents of the land of Shinar for building the Tower of Babel and wanting to "make a name" for themselves. He inflicts plagues on a pharaoh even though he has done nothing wrong except believe Abraham's lie. And he threatens Abimelech with death for the same reason. Worse yet, God allows Jacob's sons to murder the entire population of Hamor's city for the sin of Shechem. At the same time, despite their sins—both small, as in the case of Abraham and Sarah, and large, as in the case of Rebekah and Jacob—the patriarchs and matriarchs survive unscathed. Indeed, they are never punished or even chastised for their sins. Abraham and Sarah lie; Sarah, with Abraham's approval, sends Hagar and Ishmael away because she is resentful of her handmaid's presence; Rebekah urges Jacob to deceive his father; Jacob himself is consistently manipulative, deceptive, ingratiating, and vengeful; Rachel and Leah compete, resentfully, for Jacob's affection; and Joseph's brothers plot to either kill him or sell him into slavery.[646] Yet again, no one is punished. As John J. Collins says of God's response to Jacob's deception of his father, "[N]o moral judgments are made."[647]

The second reason for looking closely at the stories in the book of Genesis is what they tell us about the earliest Jewish conception of God's covenant. What is surprising about it is that God's requirements for all of the patriarchs are rather limited. As G. E. Wright explains, "[T]he central theme is that of the promise of God."[648] As I said earlier, God promises Abraham, Isaac, and Jacob land, progeny, fame, and blessings (regarding, e.g., protection and prosperity): "Go from your country," he says to Abraham, "and your kindred and your father's house to the land that I will show you. And I will make of you a great nation, and I will bless you, and make your name great. I will bless those who bless you, and him who curses you I will curse; and by you all the families of the earth shall bless themselves" (12:1–3, 7). The covenant is reaffirmed by God when he calls himself Abraham's "shield," promises him a "reward" as well as a son, and conducts a covenantal ritual (15:1–11).

God not only repeats this promise to Abraham in 13:14–16; 15:1, 5, 13–15, 18–21; 17:1–16; and 22:16–18; he also predicts that Sarah will give birth to a son and cures the barrenness of Rebekah and Rachel. God promises Abraham that he will make a covenant with Isaac (17:19, 21). Furthermore, God says that he will establish his covenant with all of Abraham's descendants "throughout their generations for an everlasting covenant." God tells Isaac not to go to Egypt, promises to "fulfil the oath which [he] swore with Abraham" (26:2–3), and tells Isaac to "fear not" because God is with him (26:24). God makes the same pledge to Jacob (28:13–15) and later tells him, when conflicts with Laban come to a head, "Return to the land of your fathers and kindred, and I will be with you" (31:3). Jacob is blessed again in 35:9–12.

Indeed, the covenant could be regarded as "everlasting," as God says to Abraham in 17:7, 8 (where God promises Abraham "everlasting possession" of Canaan), 13, and 19, only if it is unconditional—that is, only if it requires *nothing at all from anyone*. After all, that is also the case with God's covenant with Noah, which God calls "everlasting" (9:16) and of which God says, "I establish my covenant with you, that never again shall all flesh be cut off by the waters of a flood" (9:11). Before this statement, God makes it absolutely clear that his promise is not contingent on anything that human beings do or fail to do since he knows that human evil is not only inborn but ineradicable: "I will never again curse the ground because of man, for the imagination of man's heart is evil from his youth, neither will I ever again destroy every living creature as I have done" (8:21).

Jack Miles says, "As God makes his various appearances to the three patriarchs and repeats his promises of land and progeny, he does not even once make his promise conditional on observance of any existing, much less new, laws"—with the exception, of course, of circumcision, which is a ritual and not a moral requirement.[649] Wright similarly comments: "In God's covenant with Abraham, . . . the emphasis is almost solely on God's part of the agreement . . . Nothing is said there about Israel's part of the agreement, except that the people must perform the rite of circumcision as the sign and seal of the covenant." Wright adds later: "[T]he whole emphasis is upon God's promise to the patriarch. here God commits himself, and Abraham is the one who receives the promises and acts upon them in faith."[650] And well he should since, as Marcus J. Borg reminds us, "[i]n the stories of the ancestors, God saves Israel from the abyss of nothingness again and again."[651]

Of course, it is not that God requires nothing. It is that he promises people *everything* and asks for very little from them in return. He tells Noah to build an ark, to bring animals on board, and to "[b]e fruitful and multiply" (6:14, 19–20, 8:17). The rules Noah must live by are remarkably simple. He is to refrain from eating meat that has not been drained of blood. He is also not to shed "the blood of man" (9:4–6). o the patriarchs, God's message is even simpler. Initially, the covenant is, at God's direction, confirmed by a ritual that requires Abraham to bring to God a heifer, a she-goat, and a ram, each three years old, as well as a turtledove and a pigeon. Abraham then cuts the animals, but not the birds, in two, and finally lays "each half over against the other. Later, after Abraham has fallen asleep and has heard a more detailed summary of God's promise, "a smoking fire pot and a flaming torch passed between these pieces" (15:9–10, 17). The editors of *The Oxford Annotated Bible* explain: "The covenant ceremony described in vv. 7–12 and 17–18 rests on an early tradition, as evidenced by the ancient ritual of making a covenant by cutting animals in two (Jer. 34:17–19) and passing between the parts... The presence of God is symbolized by fire (see Exod 3.2 n.) passing between the pieces" (17–18).[652]

Still later, God establishes two more requirements. First, Abraham must "walk before [God], and be blameless" (17:1). Second, Abraham must circumcise himself and all of his family as well as his servants: "Every male among you shall be circumcised. You shall be circumcised in the flesh of your foreskin, and it shall be a sign of the covenant between me and you. He that is eight days old among you shall be circumcised; every male throughout your generations, whether born in your house, or bought with your money from any foreigner who is not of your offspring... So shall my covenant be in your flesh an everlasting covenant. Any uncircumcised male who is not circumcised in the flesh of his foreskin shall be cut off from his people; he has broken my covenant" (17: 9–14).

Besides being "blameless" and circumcising every male, the only religious act God seems to require of his followers is to build an altar and either offer a sacrifice or perform some other kind of ritual at the places where he has spoken to them. God asks Jacob to "go up to Bethel, and dwell there; and make there an altar to the God who appeared to you" (35:1). Both before and after this scene, in 28:18 and 35:14, Jacob "poured oil on the top" of the pillar.[653] Before this, without God's direct request, "Noah built an altar to the Lord... and offered burnt offerings on the altar" (8:20). At Shechem (and perhaps shortly afterward near Bethel), Abraham "built there an altar to the Lord, who had appeared to him" (12:7–8). At Beersheba, Isaac "built an altar" after "the Lord appeared to him" (26:24–25). More memorably, of course, Abraham offers up a ram "as a burnt offering instead of his son" after an angel of the Lord speaks to him (22:13).

The significance of these ritual acts is that they constitute the only means of worship by the Israelites before the introduction of liturgical practices after the appearance of God on Mt. Sinai. This feature of these actions is suggested in Genesis 35 when, after hearing God's demand that he go to Bethel and build an altar, "Jacob said to his household and to all who were with him, 'Put away the foreign gods that are among you, and purify yourselves, and change your garments... So they gave to Jacob all the foreign gods they had, and the rings that were in their ears,'" which Jacob hid under a tree near Shechem (vv. 2–4).[654] On the one hand, Collins comments: "There is a striking discrepancy between the manner of worship practiced by the patriarchs and what is commanded later in the Bible."[655] On the other hand, however, the incident might well have marked a moment in their history when the Israelites took a step closer to the monotheism that began to emerge at Sinai and was established during the period of the great prophets.

What should be obvious in God's covenantal requirements in Genesis is their emphasis on ritual rather than moral probity, which leads us to the third reason for reexamining the first book of the Pentateuch. It is important to understand that, in explaining what he wants the patriarchs to do in exchange for his remarkable largesse, God is very specific about the ritual requirements, but quite vague about his moral demands. The problem is that, in the absence of any definitions anywhere in Genesis, "walking with or before God" and being "blameless" are almost meaningless. And the same judgment applies to the word "righteousness," which is used to describe Abraham in 15:6 and 18:19.[656] In the latter instance, on the way to Sodom, God says to his accompanying angels that he has asked Abraham to "charge his household after him to keep the way of the Lord by doing righteousness and justice" (18:19). Noah is also called "righteous" and "blameless," and he is said to have "walked with God" (6:9, 7:1).

However, in Genesis, these terms have no moral content. The editors of *The Oxford Annotated Bible* say that "righteousness" means standing "in right relationship to God" (8). G. E. Wright comments: "Righteousness is maintaining the covenant, which means fulfillment of our vows to obey God. Sin is the violation of covenant and rebellion against God's personal lordship."[657] Yet again, it seems fair to say that all of these terms mean nothing more than "obedience." And, at most (at least in Genesis), obedience means obeying ritual requirements—cutting up animals, performing circumcisions, and setting up pillars—that is, nothing grand enough to be called walking with God, maintaining the covenant, fulfilling vows, or acting righteously and blamelessly.

To be sure, Abraham displays a sense of justice or fairness when he generously gives Lot the opportunity to choose the land he will occupy (13:12) and when he asks God to save Sodom and Gomorrah if he finds as few as ten righteous residents there (18:23–32). And whatever else is signified by Abraham's willingness to sacrifice his son Isaac at God's behest, it is, to God, a sign of Abraham's loyalty: "[N]ow I know that you fear God" (22:12). But what exactly these terms required, beyond obedience to specific commands and kindness in general, remains elusive. God tells Isaac that Abraham "kept my charge, my commandments, my statutes, and my laws" (26:5). However, except for God's rather vague "charge" to Abraham to be righteous and just, such things as moral or religious "statutes" and "laws" did not exist in Abraham's day. God made requests (or, perhaps, delivered something that could be called commandments), but these could not have been understood to be either "laws" or "statutes," since the terms conventionally apply to rules for communities, not individuals.

Furthermore, God seems to have defined righteousness as nothing more than faith, rather than any kind of moral action. And what is faith? Wright says: "Faith is simply believing what God has said, what God has promised; it is the knowledge that what he has said he will do. Faith is not a series of propositions which are either believed or not believed. It is instead that trust in God that leads one to follow him in whatever situation one may find oneself, a trust which waits on the Lord even in times when one is fearful for his life."[658] Armstrong makes the same point but emphasizes that God's requirement of faith distinguishes him from other gods in the ancient world: "[E]ven though these early tales show the patriarchs encountering their god in much the same way as their pagan contemporaries, they do introduce a new category of religious experience"—faith. "Today we tend to define faith as an intellectual assent to a creed, but . . . the biblical writers did not view faith in God as an abstract or metaphysical belief . . . In the Bible, Abraham is a man of faith because he trusts that God would make good on his promises, even though they seem absurd."[659]

We get a clearer idea of the human relationship to God in Genesis when we consider not only other means of worship, such as the performance of moral acts, but also other motivations for worship, such as love or fear. According to Wright, the motive for worship in Genesis is hope, and sin is a consequence of uncertainty: "[S]in is born of doubt and nourished by anxiety. It is a failure to believe God's promises. This led Abraham and his wife to assert their own wills and to plunge themselves deeper into trouble."[660] Later in the Bible, God will add fear to his various methods for promoting human cooperation by including threats of punishment along with promises of reward. Ultimately, the picture will include heaven and hell, in addition to poverty and wealth. And, at some point in the future, the covenant will be described as an act of love on the part of God, intended to elicit a corresponding act of love on the part of humanity. Before this, God reminds his people of his gifts, especially his liberation of the Israelites from slavery in Egypt and suggests that one good turn deserves another. God has been good to the Jews, so the Jews should be good to God and to each other.

But these concepts do not appear until God has learned by experience that, as far as mere human beings are concerned, fear is a stronger motive than hope, and that love is a more enduring and more creditable motive than either. Yehezkel Kaufmann says: "The faith of the Torah has a naïve, popular character, quite different from that of prophecy"—that is, the writings of Isaiah, Amos, Micah, and Hosea. "Its image of deity is highly anthropomorphic; its conception of apostasy is primarily as disbelief in God's ability to conquer the obstacles of the desert and the Canaanites. Contrast the prophetic idea of apostasy as the forgetting of God's past kindnesses, straying after the lusts of the heart, and lack of faith in his prophets."[661]

In this respect, the book of Genesis could be said to reveal to the reader exactly how God was viewed in the earliest days of Judaism. Specifically, although God himself considered Noah, Abraham, Isaac, Jacob, and Joseph to be worthy of his special concern, the writer's purpose throughout the period covered by the first book of the Pentateuch was to demonstrate God's undying commitment to Abraham and his progeny, with a particular fondness for second-born sons—*but not to establish moral standards*. That is, if such positive attributes as righteousness, blamelessness, and faithfulness are seldom mentioned and nowhere defined or explained in Genesis, the reason, obviously, is that, like other gods of the second millennium, the Jewish God was not originally understood to be, *first and foremost*, a moral being.

To be sure, the God of Genesis punishes evil. However, it is equally clear that his human creations were never called upon to follow a particular moral code. They were required only to believe God's promises, and the only law they were expected to follow without objection or complaint was God's demand for circumcision (17:10–14). As Kaufmann explains, to the Israelites of this time, "moral sin is not a historic, national sin that taints all Israel and is to be reckoned as a cause of its downfall." Thus, when Genesis "speaks of the causes of national punishment and exile," it does not mention "social-moral injunctions." Rather, the Torah, up to that point, focuses on apostasy as the great national sin, especially in the form of idolatry."[662]

Considering that, in all of Genesis, God neither establishes anything that could be called moral laws nor even bothers to define any moral terms, some scholars have suggested that the God who appears in this book was, like many gods in the ancient world, a tribal deity. Brueggemann says, "The usual critical account . . . is that YHWH was a tribal god who, through a series of contested interpretations, came to be dominant for Israel among the gods and eventually—as late as the sixth century—gained hegemony until Israel in doxology could attest YHWH as the only God."[663] Before his ultimate transformation, this God requires loyalty, which is demonstrated merely by the performance of symbolic acts. But he is indifferent to morality, except of course for his prohibition against murder and his objection to certain kinds of sexual activity. Miles comments: "God's prohibition of bloodshed after Cain's murder of Abel is a genuine ethical demand, and after the flood he repeats and slightly expands this prohibition. But generally speaking, through the book of Genesis, God is concerned with reproduction, not with morality."[664]

Indeed, Miles says that "God shows little sustained interest in ethics" until after he delivers the Ten Commandments in the book of Exodus. "The point is not that there are no laws or customs," many of which existed in all of the tribal societies of the ancient world, "but that observing them is not material to the patriarchs' relationship with God."[665] Wright comments: "Not until the later covenant at Sinai (Exodus 19–24) would the nation's responsibilities be made clear." The point is that religious knowledge "comes in and through a community of life." That is, "The knowledge of God is not formed in us in our solitariness . . . Knowledge is not conveyed or communicated apart from a social form or structure of thought and experience. In the Bible, that structure is the covenant society."[666] Kaufmann says: "Later legend seized upon Abraham and made him the father of Israelite religion. But the absence of the essential motifs of Israelite religion in patriarchal times indicates that it was not then that the monotheistic idea came into being."[667]

The final reason for paying attention to the stories in Genesis, despite the fact that they might not tell us anything about the actual history of the Israelites, is that they also reveal how the ancient Jews defined their God not only as a partner in a covenantal relationship but as one kind of deity among many that were worshiped in the Near East in the second millennium BC. Specifically, the Jewish God of the patriarchs is a friend, a companion, who offers assurance, promises protection, and asks for nothing in return but faith, which is nothing more than confidence that this supernatural being can live up to his promises. According to Anderson, this god is El (or Elohim), who was worshiped in the religion that "the Hebrews . . . brought with them" from Mesopotamia and that "in many respects was like the nature religion of the Fertile Crescent."[668]

Armstrong says: Unlike Yahweh, "Abraham's god El is a very mild deity. He appears to Abraham as a friend and sometimes even assumes human form. This type of divine apparition, known as an epiphany, was quite common in the pagan world of antiquity."[669] The ancient world would have recognized that this god—who shows up in ordinary, earthly situations, delivers personal messages to individuals, and guarantees success as well as survival—is not the celestial storm god (e.g., Yahweh) who wins wars and conquers enemies. Rather, he is similar to the so-called *personal god* of the pagans, the household deity who is more a good friend than a storm or sky god. This god comes and goes without fanfare; indeed, no one other than the recipient of his message knows that he has arrived. He is focused on the patriarchs almost exclusively; he provides counsel to them alone; and, while he might punish others, including even the innocent, he never hurts or harms in any way his favorites, his blessed ones. Thus, Anderson says, the Israelites "lived by a venture of faith, trusting that the future was in the hand of their personal God."[670]

Often, of course, the personal god shows up in the form of an angel, who is a mediator or messenger and not God himself. Anderson says of the personal god in association with the patriarchs: "In each case, the family God manifested himself personally to the patriarch and gave demands and promises. Therefore, the deity was known by the name of the patriarch who received the revelation: the God of Abraham, the God of Isaac, and the God of Jacob."[671] According to Thorkild Jacobsen, "The personal god can help a man in his undertakings, can give him standing and respect in his community." Thus, in Genesis, Jacob the patriarch promises, "[I]f the god will only comply with his wishes, then he will be there right away and adore him." That is, "the way of obedience, of service and worship, is the way to achieve protection; and it is also the way to earthly success, to the highest values in Mesopotamian life: health and long life, honoured standing in the community, many sons, wealth."[672]

Two additional issues are raised in Genesis, neither of which is completely resolved in the remainder of the Jewish Bible and both of which are intimately related: first, the extent to which God controls the events in the universe, and second, the extent to which human beings are responsible for their actions. As we have seen, Joseph explains to his guilt-ridden brothers that he does not hold them accountable for harming him. That is, although they quite correctly recall that they conspired against him, Joseph explains that their hostility was part of God's plan to get him to Egypt in order to be able to provide for his family during the famine. As Anderson argues, "The story affirms that affairs were not governed by the evil designs of men, or by the economic stresses that led to Jacob's migration to Egypt, but by the overruling providence of God, who makes all things serve his purpose." Thus, "despite the vicissitudes in their encounters with God, the patriarchs retain "the unshakable confidence, which dominates the Yahwist's epic like a symphonic theme, that Yahweh's promise does not fail. He is lord of history. Events are linked together in his purpose: history presses forward toward the goal he has in view."[673]

The issue here is not merely that God is shown to be responsible for the success of Abraham in his war against the four kings (14:20), for the pregnancies of the matriarchs, and for the prosperity of their husbands. All of these positive results are consequences of God's commitments to his people and their loyalty to him. The question in regard to Joseph's brothers is whether God has so much control over human actions that, at least on occasion, he can either force people to commit sins or use their (presumably) freely chosen bad actions to bring about results that he desires. One such action occurs when God makes the pharaoh reject Moses' request to free the Israelites enslaved in Egypt, which will allow God to show the Egyptians that he is God (Exod 7:1–5). Another such action occurs in the case of Joseph's brothers.[674] Cook says that besides "let[ting] men sin and suffer"—that is, act as independent agents—God also "tempts (tests) them, lays stumbling-blocks before them, hardens their hearts, causes them to be deceived, and gives them laws which are subsequently denounced."[675]

The second issue arises because, as I said earlier, in the book of Genesis God never bothers to state with any depth or breadth exactly how he wants people to act. Indeed, according to James L. Kugel, "for a long time, keeping divinely established laws was a notion hardly mentioned," including the moral laws that would later be announced in Exodus.[676] We have already seen that this compels us to regard God as amoral—that is, as the kind of god who is more interested in obedience, especially regarding ritual laws, than in morality. The other consequence is that, despite God's power, his followers simply have no idea how to behave. As Collins says, "One problem was, how did the people who lived before Moses, such as the patriarchs know what to do?"[677] And, in that case, it can be argued, *they had no responsibility for their actions*. Did Cain know that murder was forbidden? Did Noah's contemporaries understand why they were being destroyed? Did the residents of Sodom and Gomorrah realize they were being punished for sodomy? And did either of Judah's two sons know that they had sinned?

The point is that one can hardly attribute the misery that many humans in Genesis suffer to their own moral failure. Logically, there can be no moral violation in the absence of a moral code, which Israelites did not receive from God in that book of the Bible. As G. E. Wright acknowledges, not only does God fail to define "faith" in his earliest covenants, he also fails to explain what he means by the claim that man is made in the image of God (1:26): "The Church accepts it as a noble, an exalted, view of man, but when we come to ask what it means, we are perplexed. The statement is hard to define because no one in the Bible ever attempts to clarify it for us."[678] Elsewhere, although Wright emphasizes the simultaneously "dependent and responsible relationship existing between man and God," which, Wright says, is "made perfectly clear in Gen. 2–3," he nevertheless asks, "Why is this noble creature of God confronted with so much misery, trouble, and sorrow?"[679]

The Exodus

Although neither question was ever satisfactorily answered, the second of the two was far less pressing after God gave the Israelites the Ten Commandments, as well as hundreds of ancillary laws. Indeed, after that event, the "knowledge of God' came to mean not merely an awareness of God's reliability, but an understanding of God's will as it is expressed in his legislative decrees. According to Jeremiah, as God himself explains: "Did not your father . . . do justice and righteousness? He judged the cause of the poor and needy: then it was well. *Is not this to know me?*" (22:15–16; my emphasis). In other words, as Walter Brueggemann says, quoting Isaiah 11:9, "knowledge of God" came to mean more than faith. It "concerns covenantal fidelity, adherence to YHWH's sovereignty, and *obedience to YHWH's commands.*" In other words, "walking in God's ways" became more than an empty phrase. To know is to learn, and to learn is to be taught by God. As Isaiah says, "Come ye and let us go up to the mountain of the Lord . . . and He will teach us of His ways and we will walk in His paths" (2:3). G. E. Wright explains that this concept "involves both an inner and outer obedience in which man's total being finds its true unity, happiness, and fulfillment," apart from which "there is no communion; and apart from communion there is only disintegration, misery, and death."[680]

Isaiah also shows that, although one may hear God say, "[D]o what is right" (56:1), unless that command is spelled out in detail, it is unlikely to be followed, as the events in Genesis demonstrate. As Brueggemann explains, the command at the beginning of Isaiah 56 "is not given any particular substance. In the poetry that follows, however, the substance of the summons becomes clear," as it does in Exodus and in all of the works of the prophets. In the next few verses of chapter 56, Isaiah says that "obedience consists in a welcome inclusiveness," as well as "justice for the oppressed and sustenance for the poor and the homeless . . . In sum, this poetry anticipates a community acutely committed to the enactment of Torah justice."[681] According to James Muilenburg, "Yahweh reveals what Israel needs above all things else to know."[682]

Thus, in the later books of the Pentateuch, God assumes the role of Teacher as well as Judge, who first passes this responsibility on to Moses, through Jethro, when Jethro says, "[Y]ou shall teach them the statutes and the decisions, and *make them know the way they must walk and what they must do*" (Exod 18:20; my emphasis). As God explains to Moses, "I will give you the tables of stone, with the law and the commandment, which I have written for their instruction" (Exod 24:12; see also Deut 4:1–14). Eventually, God is no longer limited to the black-or-white option of either ignoring his people's sins or destroying them for their misdeeds. Rather, using the instrument of chastisement, he is committed to teaching his people not only by instructing them, but also by punishing them more mildly with the intention of changing their behavior without ending their lives. Honoring the Davidic covenant and speaking of King David, God says, "If his children forsake my law . . . then I will punish their transgression with the rod and their iniquity with scourges; but I will not remove from him my steadfast love" (Ps 89:30–33; see also 2 Sam 7:14–16).

In this way—and perhaps *only* in this way—the Covenant is everlasting. That is, its violations result in the kind of correction administered by a father to a child, not by a sovereign to a subject or a master to a slave. And, thus, the God of Wrath merges with the God of Mercy and adds forgiveness to his repertoire of reactions to sin: "As a father has compassion for his children, so the Lord has compassion for those who fear him. For he knows how we were made; he remembers that we are dust" (Ps 103:13–14; see also Deut 8:5). Brueggemann comments, "The operational words concerning Yahweh's propensity are *steadfast love, mercy,* and *compassion.* The statement concludes with an allusion to Genesis 2:7 and the affirmation that human persons are made from dust (clay), and do not have great staying power. In their fragility and weakness, human persons violate YHWH; and YHWH knows this and is therefore ready to act in generosity."[683] Clearly, God does not act on this assumption in the book of Genesis.

As I said earlier, God's explicit and extensive presentation of his rules and regulations in Exodus enables his people to gain a clear understanding of his moral as well as his cultic expectations. This is why Moses can say to God, even after the Ten Commandments have been given, because he wants more clarity (that is, more *knowledge of God*), "Now therefore, I pray thee, if I have found favor in thy sight, *show me now thy ways, that I may know thee* and find favor in thy sight" (Exod 33:13). In this way, the religion of the Israelites took a large step toward a definition of God as more than the two-dimensional figure that he appears to be throughout the book of Genesis. In Exodus, furthermore, God calls himself the father *of Israel*, whom he refers to as his "first-born son" (4:22–23). And, at least once, he claims for himself many of the attributes he displays more often in the works of the prophets: "The Lord, the Lord, [is] a God merciful and gracious, slow to anger, and abounding in steadfast love and faithfulness, . . . forgiving iniquity and transgression and sin" (34:6).[684]

Also, like God in Genesis, who speaks to the patriarchs in a friendly and respectful way, God in Exodus is said to have spoken "to Moses face to face, as a man speaks to his friend" (33:11). Nevertheless, the latter God is distinguished by the fact that he speaks exclusively to Moses, who is always recognized as God's special emissary, while God in Genesis is quite willing to talk to anyone, including not only the patriarchs and the other important personages in these early stories like Adam, Eve, Cain, Noah, and the matriarchs, but also such decidedly minor characters as Hagar, Lot, Abimelech,

The Evolution of Love

the pharaoh, Laban, and the serpent. In Exodus, evidently, God is more exalted, less accessible, and more intimidating. At the same time, however, he is both more complicated and more clearly defined. His moral program is elaborate, and his expectations are imposing, but he is, as well as a terrifying presence, a father and a teacher.

In fact, for most scholars, God, or Yahweh, in Exodus is, among other kinds of deity, a warrior god, who either defeats or helps defeat the enemies of his people. Celebrating the liberation of the Israelites from Egypt, Moses and his fellow Israelites call Yahweh "a man of war," who is worthy of worship because of his power and majesty and glory (Exod 15:3, 6, 11). Jack Miles says of Yahweh in the book of Exodus: "[T]his is a deity who has not previously shown himself to be a warrior. Now, suddenly, unexpectedly, he has shown himself an invincible warrior, defeating the mightiest military power the Israelites knew."[685] As Stanley Cook explains, "Yahweh is a God of War; he is the Lord of Hosts, the armies whose captain ["the commander of the Lord's army" (Josh 5:15)] confronted Joshua before his attack upon Jericho." This God "can intervene as a veritable storm-god, like the earlier gods of storm and war in Palestine and neighboring lands . . . He will call for the sword against the nations," as he does in Jeremiah 25:29, "and devote men to destruction," as he does in Deuteronomy 7:1–2.[686]

Sharing some attributes with "Shamash, the Sun-god, Hadad (also called Baal), the Storm and War-god," and various goddesses, Yahweh was worshiped in similar ways. "[I]ndeed," says Cook, "among the Psalms are passages which could well have been used in the worship of Palestinian deities other than Israel's Yahweh." In Psalm 58, "[H]e will bathe his feet in the blood of the wicked" (v. 10); in Psalm 69, he is asked to blot the wicked "out of the book of the living" (v. 28).[687] Karen Armstrong says that "Yahweh's cult was very similar to Baal's, and some of Baal's hymns were even adapted for use in Yahweh's temple in Jerusalem."[688] Although most scholars thus agree that Yahweh is not very different from other warrior gods of the Near East, Armstrong says that "his provenance" is hard to determine. "In pagan antiquity," she explains, "gods were often merged and amalgamated, or the gods of one locality accepted as identical with the god of another people."[689]

To be sure, the warrior god does not make his first biblical appearance in Exodus. As the destroyer of all of humanity except for Noah and his family, this god appears briefly at the beginning of Genesis. From the destruction of Sodom and Gomorrah to the end of the first book of the Pentateuch, however, the Jewish God is no longer the god of wrath and vengeance and destruction. That is, the warrior god is later no longer front and center. In fact, starting after "the Lord rained on Sodom and Gomorrah brimstone and fire" and ending in the early chapters of the book of Exodus, when God inflicts on the Egyptians a series of plagues, including the death of the Egyptian firstborn, this period witnesses only two deaths at the hand of God: Judah's two rebellious sons, Er and Onan.

However, it is not as if God is transformed in chapter 12 of Genesis, when he speaks to Abraham for the first time. In fact, both the God who befriends the

The Pentateuch

patriarchs and the God who kills masses of people appear intermittently throughout the Torah.[690] According to Brueggemann, "YHWH's sovereign power and YHWH's compassionate engagement are not in tension, but are taken together in Israel's life and praise and prayer."[691] The friend of the patriarchs is replaced at times by the God of wrath, who not only destroys whole cities, but also kills off everyone on earth except a single family. Indeed, he has to be persuaded by Abraham to be reasonable, at least from Abraham's point of view, and not kill the innocent along with the guilty. In defense of Abimelech, Abraham prays to God to refrain from punishing the king, even though God knows that he is innocent, since he earlier said to Abimelech, "Yes, I know that you have done this in the integrity of your heart" (21:6, 17). In defense of the residents of Sodom and Gomorrah, Abraham says to God, "Shall not the Judge of all the earth do right?" (18:25).

In short, as many scholars have argued, the God of Israel who appears throughout the Jewish Bible is not two or more different gods but one—that is, a combination of many gods, including Elohim, Yahweh, El Shaddai, and El Elyon, the last of whom Melchizedek praises for helping Abraham win his battle against the king of Elam, among others, who had captured Lot and his family (14:19–20). That is, the God who is heard walking through the Garden of Eden and who speaks in a stern but measured voice to Adam and Eve, Cain, and Noah is the same God who speaks more gently and supportively to the patriarchs, more fiercely to Moses on Mt. Sinai, and far more angrily and threateningly to the traveling Israelites in the book of Numbers. Anderson says: "Careful reading of the narrative in Exodus 3 discloses that two terms for deity are used alternately. At times, the general term translated 'God' (Hebrew: 'Elohim) is used (3:1, 4, 11, 12, 13); sometimes the special Hebrew word Yahweh is found (3:2, 4, 7, 15). This is one of the evidences that have led many scholars to conclude that the narrative represents a blending of sources J and E, so closely that they can hardly be separated."[692]

Nevertheless, it is notable that God almost always appears to his beneficiaries in Genesis as if he is a friend who has stopped by for a casual conversation, instead of the mighty God who appears to Moses in the book of Exodus and calls to him out of a burning bush. The scene in Exodus has a number of special features, including proximity to a holy site (Horeb, "the mountain of God"), a miracle (the bush is not consumed by the fire), an experience quite special to the participant ("I will turn aside and see this great sight"), an exclamatory greeting ("Moses, Moses!"), a warning that this holy ground requires unusual behavior ("Do not come near; put off the shoes from your feet"), the participant's extreme fear ("And Moses hid his face, for he was afraid to look at God"), an announcement, not of personal aid, but of liberation for an entire people ("Come, I will send you to Pharaoh, that you may bring forth my people, the sons of Israel, out of Egypt"), and two additional miracles (a rod turns into a snake, and Moses' hand becomes leprous for a moment) (Exod 3:1—4:5).

There is only one parallel in Genesis—when God appears to Jacob in a dream—because in that book God typically presents himself as a family mentor: "I am the Lord," he says to Jacob, "the God of Abraham your father and the God of Isaac" (28:13). And, again, this is because he sometimes takes on the role of the personal god of Mesopotamia. As Miles says, as God becomes "the God of Abraham," he "seem[s], often enough, more like a friend of the family than like the Judge of all the earth." However, Miles says elsewhere, "as monotheism emerges in Israel, Israel's God combines features otherwise best described as those of Canaanite El and the Mesopotamian personal God." "The Lord God," Miles continues, is both "the creator" and "the destroyer": "The fate of nations, witness Sodom, is in his hands, but he can also stoop to direct involvement in the private life of an individual man."[693] Yahweh explains to Moses that he failed to introduce himself to Abraham under his present name: "I am the Lord [that is, Yahweh]. I appeared to Abraham, Isaac, and Jacob, as God Almighty [that is, as El Shaddai], but by my name the Lord I did not make myself known to them" (6:2–3).[694]

Thus, God, speaking rather frighteningly out of the burning bush, tells Moses to say "to the people of Israel, 'The Lord, the God of your fathers, the God of Abraham, the God of Isaac, and the God of Jacob, has sent me to you'" (Exod 3:15). God's message, however, reveals that he is not merely the familial and familiar god of the patriarchs, but the avenger, Yahweh, the God of War. Like the God who wipes out the entire population of two cities in Genesis, the God of Exodus tells Moses that he intends to punish Egypt for "what it has done to" his people. True, they have been enduring "the affliction of Egypt" for four centuries, but things have evidently become intolerable.[695] Hearing their "cry," Yahweh tells Moses that he will compel the pharaoh to release the Israelites. Yet, instead of simply demonstrating his power to the pharaoh and showing that he is capable of destroying Egypt, Yahweh drags out the punishment by imposing ten more or less increasingly ruinous plagues on Egypt.[696] Most importantly, the first nine punishments are ineffective not because they are innocuous, but because, as Yahweh explains to Moses, he "will harden [the pharaoh's] heart" and thereby make him unwilling to liberate his Jewish slaves. Indeed, Yahweh will not merely frighten the pharaoh into cooperating, but actually "smite Egypt" and also allow his people to "despoil" their enemies by taking their "jewelry of silver and of gold" (3:20–22; 7:3; 14:4).[697]

In the tenth plague, Yahweh "smote all the first-born in the land of Egypt, from the first-born of Pharaoh who sat on his throne to the first-born of the captive who was in the dungeon, and all the first-born of the cattle" (12:29). As a result of this mass execution, the pharaoh virtually expels the Israelites. He says to Moses and Aaron, "Rise up, go forth from among my people, both you and the people of Israel; and go, serve the Lord, as you have said" (12:31). But the plagues represent only the first of Yahweh's violent acts in Exodus. The next mass murder occurs when "Moses stretched forth his hand over the sea," and the Egyptian army—"the chariots and the horsemen and all the host of Pharaoh"—drowned in the sea, which the Israelites had crossed

The Pentateuch

after Moses "divided" the waters (14:21–28). After this, Yahweh promises to send an angel before his people in order to guide them to the land now occupied by Amorites, Hittites, and Canaanites, among others, whom Yahweh will "blot" out: "I will send my terror before you, and will throw into confusion all the people against whom you shall come, and I will make your enemies turn their backs to you" (23:23–27).

Still later, after the Israelites worship the Golden Calf, Yahweh says, "I have seen this people, and behold, it is a stiff-necked people; now therefore let me alone, that my wrath may burn hot against them and I may consume them" (32:9–10). Shortly after this, he says to Moses, "Whoever has sinned against me, him will I blot out of my book . . . I will visit their sin upon them." Then, giving full vent to his anger, "the Lord sent a plague upon the people, because they made the calf which Aaron made" (32:33–35). Finally, Yahweh reiterates his hostility to the current residents of the Promised Land: "I will drive out before you the Amorites, the Canaanites, the Hittites," and others. And the Israelites are required to "tear down their altars, and break their pillars," as well as other religious symbols (34:11, 13).[698]

Just as Yahweh's first appearance to Moses is, befitting a god of violence, a pyrotechnical display, so his entry into public speaking, on Mt. Sinai—which, he tells Moses, is planned so that "the people may hear when I speak to you" (19:9)[699]—is accompanied by extraordinary accoutrements. On the one hand, Yahweh "goes before" the Israelites continuously in a pillar of cloud during the day and in a pillar of fire at night (13:21–22). On the other hand, however, his descent onto the mountain in order to deliver his laws to Moses is preceded by a mass consecration of all of the Israelites who will attend the event (including garment washing, boundary marking, and sexual abstinence) and enhanced by a massive thunderstorm: "[T]here were thunders and lightnings, and a thick cloud upon the mountain, and a very loud trumpet blast, so that all the people who were in the camp trembled." Yahweh descends in fire, the mountain quakes, and the Lord speaks thunderously (19:10–19).[700]

The purpose of this spectacular self-presentation, as Moses explains, is to impress the audience with Yahweh's power and thereby to encourage them to obey his commandments: "And Moses said to the people, 'Do not fear; for God has come to prove you, and that the fear of him may be before your eyes, that you may not sin'" (20:20). Clearly, the God of Genesis did not need to instill fear into the patriarchs since he did not demand very much from them. But the God of Exodus introduced a new concept of the human-divine relationship, based on high moral standards covering a wide range of activities, requiring strict observance, and involving serious consequences for disobedience.[701] A similar point may be made about the ten plagues, all of which Yahweh evidently planned to deliver from the very beginning. After all, he told Moses to tell the pharaoh that he would "slay [his] first-born sons" if he failed to comply (4:23).

However, it is not that Yahweh is trying to punish the Egyptians as much as possible by hardening the pharaoh's heart and thereby compelling him to refuse to let the Israelites go into the wilderness in order to pray to their god, although, as James

The Evolution of Love

L. Kugel reminds us, God did promise to punish the Israelites' future slave masters in Genesis 15:13–14: "I will bring judgment on the nation which they serve."[702] Rather, as Yahweh says repeatedly, his intention is to impress on the pharaoh and his people that he is not only the God of Israel, but also the Lord of Creation and the King of the Universe. When Moses and Aaron first visit the pharaoh, they pass on his message: "Thus says the Lord, the God of Israel, 'Let my people go, that they may hold a feast to me in the wilderness.'" Of course, the pharaoh is unimpressed by this command because he has never heard of this deity: "Who is the Lord, that I should heed his voice and let Israel go? I do not know the Lord, and moreover I will not let Israel go" (5:1–2). As May and Metzger explain, "The contemptuous Pharaoh, whose absolute power was enforced by his deification in Egyptian religion, knew many gods; but this 'god,' the Lord, was unheard of and a request made in his name carried no authority."[703]

Thus, before their next visit, Yahweh says to Moses and Aaron that he will ultimately "lay [his] hand upon Egypt" and free his people. Then his purpose will be fulfilled: "And the Egyptians shall know that I am the Lord" (7:4–5). Accordingly, Moses repeats this message to the pharaoh (7:17) again and again (8:10, 9:29, 11:9, 14:4). Before the seventh plague, however, Yahweh explains his intention more fully: "[T]his time I will send all my plagues upon your heart . . . that you may know that there is none like me in all the earth. For by now I could have put forth my hand and struck you and your people with pestilence, and you would have been cut off from the earth; but for this purpose have I let you live, *to show you my power, so that my name may be declared throughout all the earth*" (9:14–16; my emphasis). However, Yahweh is not interested in impressing only the Egyptians, as he explains to Moses: "I have hardened his heart . . . that you may tell in the hearing of your son and your son's son how I have made sport of the Egyptians, and what signs I have done among them; that you may know that I am the Lord" (10:1–2).[704]

Besides being morally demanding, as well as prepared to demonstrate both his ability and willingness to punish wrongdoing, Yahweh also differs from his earlier incarnation in Genesis in that he elevates his interlocutor, Moses, to a position far above that of the patriarchs. One reason for this difference is that Yahweh has a massive following and is faced with a communication dilemma: Either he addresses all Israelites at the same time or he speaks to a special intermediary whose function is to pass his messages on to his people. Yahweh also gives Moses powers that none of the patriarchs had—not only the ability to perform what would have been regarded at the time as magical acts and which Yahweh calls "miracles" (4:2–9, 21), but, far more significantly, the destructive acts that Moses (and sometimes Aaron) initiates by raising the rod that Yahweh gives him (4:17), including all of the plagues, except the killing of the Egyptian first-born.

Using "the rod of God," Aaron "lifted [it] up . . . and struck the water that was the Nile," turning the water into blood (7:20). To bring on the plague of frogs, "Aaron stretched out his hand over the waters of Egypt" (8:6); and to bring on the plague of gnats, he struck "the dust of the earth" (8:17). Moses threw ashes "toward heaven" to make boils (9:10); he "stretched forth his rod toward heaven" to bring hail (9:23); he "stretched his rod over the land of Egypt" and brought locusts (10:13); and he "stretched out his hand toward heaven," bringing the plague of darkness (10:22). Finally, pursued by the Egyptian army, Moses twice "stretched out his hand over the sea": first, to divide the waters so that the Israelites could cross on dry land; and, second, to allow the water to "come back upon the Egyptians" and thereby destroy "the host of Pharaoh that had followed them into the sea" (14:21–28).

In fact, Yahweh gives Moses so much power that he seems to be able to solve every problem that arises. He satisfies the Israelites' hunger by reporting their "murmurings" to Yahweh, who provides them with quail in the evening and manna in the morning (16:12–15). Moses satisfies the Israelites' thirst by purifying the "the water of Marah" and by getting water from a rock. First, he throws a tree into the water and, later, strikes a rock with his magical rod, both under God's direction (15:25; 17:6–7). And Moses protects the Israelites from attack by the Amalekites by appointing Joshua to organize an army while Moses holds "the rod of God in [his] hand." "Whenever Moses held up his hand, Israel prevailed." So, with the help of Aaron and Hur, Moses brings victory to the Israelites (17:8–13).

Finally, in an act that is conspicuously not directed or guided by Yahweh, Moses, his "anger burn[ing] hot," not only breaks the tablets given to him by Yahweh, but burns the Golden Calf made by the Israelites, mixes it with water, and makes the people drink it (32:19). What has Moses done? According to the editors of *The Oxford Annotated Bible*: "Moses subjected the people to a trial by ordeal . . . Those who suffered ill effects from drinking the water and pulverized metal were regarded as guilty and fell in a plague" (110).[705] Furthermore, Moses tells the sons of Levi, who pledge themselves "to be on the Lord's side" in this matter, "Put every man his sword on his side . . . and slay every man his brother, and every man his companion, and every man his neighbor," which, according to the narrator, results in the death of "three thousand men" (32:25–28).

Moses is also able to carry on an extended dialogue with Yahweh in which he sometimes raises objections to Yahweh's decisions, the earliest of which relate to Moses' initial unwillingness to assume the role he is asked to play.[706] Moses suggests to Yahweh that he is too ordinary to do what Yahweh asks him to do, and Yahweh says, "I will be with you" (3:11–12). Moses asks Yahweh for his name, and Yahweh simply tells him (3:13–14). And Moses says that no one will believe that he is representing God himself, so Yahweh enables him to perform three miracles (4:1–9). After Moses tells Yahweh that he is "not eloquent" enough to communicate his message, Yahweh says: "Who has made man's mouth? Who makes him dumb, or deaf, or seeing, or blind? Is it not I, the Lord? Now therefore go, and I will be with your mouth and teach you what you shall speak" (4:10–12).

The Evolution of Love

After Moses continues to demur, God angrily suggests that Aaron can do the job of communicating to the people. Indeed, Yahweh goes so far as to say that Moses "shall be to [Aaron] as God" (4:16). That is, Aaron "shall be [his] prophet" (7:1). After the pharaoh responds punitively to Moses' request to free the Israelites, Moses complains twice more to Yahweh. To the first complaint ("Why didst thou ever send me?"), Yahweh reassures Moses that he will honor his covenant with the patriarchs by both liberating the Israelites from Egypt and bringing them to the Promised Land (5:22—6:8). To the second complaint ("Behold, the people of Israel have not listened to me"), Yahweh spells out his plan in more detail, making Moses "as God to Pharaoh" (7:2), deliberately hardening the pharaoh's heart, and not only freeing his people but also destroying the Egyptians (6:12; 7:2–9). Listing Moses' special features in Exodus, Kugel asks, "Did not all this . . . suggest that [Moses] was, or became, superhuman, halfway between God and humanity?"[707]

Subsequently, Moses plays the role of God's anger-management counselor. After the Israelites have worshiped the Golden Calf, Yahweh says to Moses, as I noted earlier, "I have seen this people, and behold, it is a stiff-necked people; now therefore let me alone, that my wrath may burn hot against them and I may consume them." Moses successfully dissuades Yahweh from carrying out his threat by telling him that the Egyptians will use this mass murder to discredit him and that his rejection of the Israelites would constitute a violation of his covenant with the patriarchs. Quite surprisingly, rising from the position of God's instrument, Moses becomes God's moral guide. He says to Yahweh, "Turn from thy fierce wrath, and repent of this evil against thy people (32:9-13). And equally surprisingly, Yahweh repents (32:14). Indeed, as Brueggemann says, more often than not "YHWH seeks to meet Moses' resistances and objections," presumably because, ultimately, he "is a God who answers hurt, who is attentive to the voiced pain of Israel."[708]

Moses' next encounter with Yahweh is even more shocking. After the Levites' execution of three thousand men—at Moses' behest and as punishment for worshiping the Golden Calf—Moses tells the Israelites that he will try to "make atonement for [their] sin" by revisiting Yahweh and putting the case before him. After Moses acknowledges to Yahweh that "this people have sinned a great sin," he actually tries to force Yahweh's hand by offering up his own life if Yahweh refuses to forgive the Israelites: If you will not "forgive their sin, . . . blot me, I pray thee, out of thy book which thou hast written" (32:30–33). Since Yahweh has already said that even if he killed all of the other Israelites, he would spare Moses' life (32:10) and since Yahweh has already promised not to wipe out the entire nation (32:14), it seems logical to conclude that Moses is making a Christlike atonement not only to save lives, many of which he himself has already taken, but to induce Yahweh to fulfill the promise that Moses reminded him of earlier (32:13): "to lead the people to the place of which I have spoken to you" (32:34).

It seems, then, that Yahweh agrees to a compromise. First, he will punish those who are guilty—specifically, by "send[ing] a plague upon the people" (32:35), which will either confirm the punishment that Moses has already imposed or add an additional punishment. That is, as he says, "Whoever has sinned against me, him will I blot out of my book" (32:33). Second, however, Yahweh will also live up to his promise to take the Israelites to the Promised Land—not by leading them personally, as he has done up to this point, but by sending his angel to "go before" them (32:33). To make his position clear, Yahweh repeats this message in the next passage, in greater detail. To Moses he says: "Depart, you and the people . . . to the land of which I swore to Abraham, Isaac, and Jacob, saying, 'To your descendants I will give it'" (33:1)—which rather precisely corresponds to Moses' request in 32:13. Yet, again, Yahweh will not accompany the Israelites because he remains too angry to be near them: "I will not go up among you, lest I consume you in the way, for you are a stiff-necked people" (33:3). Rather, Yahweh will "send an angel," "drive out the Canaanites" and others, and lead his people "to a land flowing with milk and honey" (33:2–3).[709]

Having solicited and received from Yahweh a promise not to punish the Israelites by killing all of them and a reaffirmation of his promise to bring them to the Promised Land, Moses then attempts to change Yahweh's mind about not personally leading his people out of the wilderness. By this time, Moses has established the practice of consulting Yahweh regularly at the so-called tent of meeting, which is pitched outside the Israelite camp.[710] The narrator reports, "Thus the Lord used to speak to Moses face to face, as a man speaks to his friend" (33:11). In one of his final confrontations of this kind with Yahweh, at least as attested in Exodus, Moses says, "See, thou sayest to me, 'Bring up this people'; but thou hast not let me know whom thou wilt send with me. Yet thou hast said, 'I know you by name, and you have also found favor in my sight.'" To this apparent request for a personal favor, Yahweh responds, "My presence will go with you, and I will give you rest."

Presumably to clarify the meaning of Yahweh's promise, Moses says that if this is not the case, then Yahweh should not "carry us up from here." The reason is that, without Yahweh's presence, two consequences will arise. First, Moses says, "How shall it be known that I have favor in thy sight, I and thy people?" Second, he adds, "Is it not in thy going with us, so that we are distinct, I and thy people, from all other people that are upon the face of the earth?" To this, Yahweh says, "This very thing that you have spoken I will do; for you have found favor in my sight, and I know you by name" (33:12–17). Finally, between Yahweh's presentation of the new tablets to Moses on Mt. Sinai and his reiteration of the Covenant, Moses says again—as if Yahweh needed to be reminded or Moses needed to be reassured—"If now I have found favor in thy sight, O Lord, let the Lord, I pray thee, go in the midst of us, although it is a stiff-necked people; and pardon our iniquity and our sin, and take us for thy inheritance" (34:9).

Perhaps Moses' most outrageous request is to ask Yahweh to show him his "glory" (33:18). The passage is problematic because God's glory appears to the Israelites

The Evolution of Love

before Yahweh gives them quail meat and manna: "[A]nd behold, the glory of God appeared in the cloud" (16:10). Later, the same vision appears when Moses "went up on the mountain" for the first time: "The glory of the Lord settled on Mt. Sinai" in the form of a cloud. "Now the glory of the Lord was like a devouring fire on the top of the mountain in the sight of the people of Israel" (24:15–17). In the final few verses of Exodus, God's glory is described as a permanent presence in the Israelite camp: "Then the cloud covered the tent of meeting, and the glory of the Lord filled the tabernacle." Indeed, "throughout all their journeys the cloud of the Lord was upon the tabernacle by day, and fire was in it by night, in the sight of all the house of Israel" (40:34, 38).

Nevertheless, in response to Moses' request in chapter 33, Yahweh works out an elaborate scheme in which his intermediary will be able to see his glory as no one else has ever seen it (33:19–23). Perhaps, however, the "glory" that Yahweh intends to show to Moses is not so much his visible, but his spiritual self—that is, his true identity as a moral being—which he displays immediately afterward in the next chapter: "And the Lord descended in a cloud and stood with him there, and proclaimed the name of the Lord. The Lord passed before him, and proclaimed, 'The Lord, the Lord, a God merciful and gracious, slow to anger, and abounding in steadfast love and faithfulness, keeping steadfast love for thousands, forgiving iniquity and transgression and sin, but who will by no means clear the guilty'" (34:6–7).

In response to this extraordinary and unprecedented display of covenantal values, as Kugel describes it, "Moses made haste to bow his head toward the earth, and worshiped" (34:8). Kugel says of Yahweh's self-description: "[N]owhere else had God's traits of character, as it were, been set forth as such. It was as if, in response to an earlier request of Moses—'I pray You, show me Your glory' (Exod. 33:18)—God now revealed to his prophet something of His very nature."[711] Noting the repetition of this passage in six psalms, three prophets, Nehemiah, 2 Chronicles, and several non-canonical works, Kugel concludes that "from a very early period, the qualities of divine mercy and compassion mentioned in this verse, along with God's assertion of his faithfulness to Israel and willingness to forgive sins, became central items in the Israelites' thinking about God."[712] Indeed, shortly after Moses' request and God's compliance, God says to Moses, "Behold, I make a covenant. Before all your people I will do marvels, such as have not been wrought in all the earth or in any nation" (34:10).

As time passes and as these events illustrate, Moses' stature grows and grows. Even before the tenth plague and as a result of his confrontations with the pharaoh and his performance of several miracles, Moses achieves great fame in Egypt, both among his own people and among the Egyptians: "[T]he man Moses was very great in the land of Egypt, in the sight of Pharaoh's servants and in the sight of the people" (11:3). Furthermore, even before Yahweh gives the Ten Commandments to the Israelites, Moses, like Joshua and Gideon, becomes the official judge of the tribes, whose special function both before and after Jethro's reform is to adjudicate special cases that require Moses "to inquire of God," a function that only he is able to perform (18:15).[713]

The Pentateuch

Thus, given a similar role in Deuteronomy, Marcus J. Borg contends, Moses clearly emerges as "the greatest of all prophets." Indeed, "[o]ther than God"—since "he towers over the Pentateuch"—"he is the central figure is Israel's primal narrative."[714]

Finally, on the occasion of Moses' return to Mt. Sinai to receive the new tablets of the law from Yahweh, he says to Moses, "Moses alone shall come near to the Lord" (24:2). At the critical moment "on the mountain," Moses enters the cloud in which God is hidden, where he remains, again, for "forty days and forty nights" (24:18). Earlier Yahweh had said to Moses, "Lo, I am coming to you in a thick cloud, that the people may hear when I speak with you, and may also believe you for ever" (19:9). Descending from Mt. Sinai a second time, carrying the new tablets on which God has written the Ten Commandments, Moses undergoes a transfiguration: "Moses did not know that the skin of his face shone because he had been talking with God. And when Aaron and all the people saw Moses, behold, the skin of his face shone, and they were afraid to come near him" (34:29–30).

Recall that Moses begins his public career and his unique relationship to God not just modestly, but reluctantly and self-effacingly. Chapter by chapter, he acquires more confidence, more power, and more faith until he could be said to assume a semi-divine status: He alone has direct access to God, and God wants him to be believed "forever." Gerhard von Rad notes that, according to the writer who calls God Yahweh, God says that he himself "will bring Israel out" of Egypt (3:16). However, according to the writer who calls God Elohim, God tells Moses, "*You* are to bring Israel out" (3:10; my emphasis). Furthermore, this writer "pushe[s] Moses much more into the foreground as the instrument of God in effecting the deliverance." Indeed, "Moses is now the miracle-worker, in fact almost to the point of being a magician: it is through his intervention with Pharaoh and at the Red Sea and elsewhere that the history receives its momentum."[715]

Alan F. Segal reminds his readers that in the first century AD Philo said "that Moses was virtually divine."[716] It is worth remembering also, as I noted earlier, that Yahweh tells Moses twice that he is God—at least to both Aaron and the pharaoh. Given Yahweh's unwillingness to address his people directly, he has no choice but to depend entirely on his human agent. The problem is that, if Moses is not believed, neither is Yahweh (4:8). Thus, Moses is not transfigured only once, but every time he speaks with God, after which he must veil his face—aglow with "the radiant glory of the Lord," according to the editors of *The Oxford Annotated Bible* (114)—in order to reduce or eliminate the fear of the Israelites. This is the glow that St. Paul many centuries later interpreted to be a consequence of "beholding the glory of the Lord" and thereby "being *changed into his likeness*" (2 Cor 3:18; my emphasis).

This brings us to a consideration of the prospective believers, the Israelites, who leave Egypt at Moses' behest, solve problems with Moses' help, and understand Yahweh's messages—including his disappointments, his interventions, and his laws—only through Moses' communications. Yahweh's view of the Israelites (supposedly descendants of the patriarch Jacob, or Israel) is consistently negative, filled as it is with expressions of anger and name-calling (especially in chapter 32). And, although he is apparently more sympathetic, Moses is similarly frustrated by their infidelity as well as their tendency to blame him, instead of Yahweh, for their difficulties (e.g., 14:10–11; 16:8). However, it must be said in defense of these people that they are constantly beset by problems ranging from abuse and oppression in Egypt to fear and confusion in the wilderness.

The first obstacle to an understanding of the Israelites is the paucity of information we have about them, especially regarding their four centuries in Egypt. When did their enslavement begin? Did their situation change abruptly or worsen gradually? Did they see themselves as an independent group? Were they organized into tribes? To what extent were they connected to their religious heritage? Did they continue to circumcise their sons and build altars to God? Were they aware of their common history and the events that originally brought them to Egypt? How much had their religious views and practices been influenced by the Egyptians? Were they in any sense monotheists or henotheists? Knowing the answers to such questions would help us to assess the Israelites' equivocations and uncertainties. But we have almost no information. As Brueggemann says, "We do not know, in this case, if the slaves knew anything of YHWH or of the Genesis promises. If they do, they do not here make an appeal to YHWH or to YHWH's promises." That is, although Yahweh responds to their expression of utter despair, their cry is not specifically addressed to him.[717]

In fact, we have no assurance in the text that the Israelites were actually descendants of Jacob. At one extreme, John McKenzie claims, "[S]cholars are reasonably assured thatthe body which Moses led was not the twelve tribes of Israel, as they are identified."[718] Brueggemann says: "The ones who cry [in 2:23] are defined in the text as 'the Israelites,' but in truth it is likely that the cry was [from] a ragtag band of needy, powerless slaves who are preoccupied with their own suffering. If this band of slaves constituted Israel, then in this instant Israel is a sociological entity of those who suffer the abuse of being cheap, exploited labor in the Egyptian Empire." Brueggemann allows for the possibility that they are the "children of Abraham" rather than just suffering workers, but, again, he emphasizes the fact that their cry was "addressed to no one in particular" even though it was heard by Yahweh.[719]

Based partly on Joshua's command to his followers that they "put away the gods that [their] ancestors served beyond the river and in Egypt" (Josh 24:14), Tullock says that the people who left Egypt included both Semites and non-Semites—that is, both Israelites and a "mixed crowd" (12:28) "who presumably were non-Israelite."[720] Anderson argues that they were not Israelites at all, but "a motley group; not only the family of Joseph but a 'mixed multitude' (12:38) representing Habiru [i.e., Semites, who are assumed to have been Hebrews by some scholars] of other origins. Indeed, it is historically inaccurate to speak of these people as 'Israelites' at this stage, although the narrative does so repeatedly. Only later, as they shared the experiences of the desert and remembered a common history, were they forged into a community, the people Israel."[721]

A second theory posits that most Jews were originally Canaanites and that only a relatively small number of Jews came from Egypt. According to Richard Elliott Friedman, "Some investigators . . . have concluded that, historically, only a small portion of the ancient Israelites were actually slaves in Egypt." Moses and a few others have Egyptian names, some of whom might have been Levites, who are distinguished by the fact that they owned no land in what became Israel, perhaps because they arrived later than the others. The writer called E was a Levite, who may have brought with him not only the story of El's announcement of his name, Yahweh, but also the entire story of Moses and liberation.[722]

Although he agrees that there were "Semitic slaves in Egypt in the late second millennium," that "[o]ne papyrus records the passage into Egypt of an entire tribe during a drought," that another papyrus "reports the pursuit of runaway slaves who had escaped to the desert," and that a plague-like "epidemic" of some kind occurred in the fourteenth century, John J. Collins says that such incidents "fall far short of establishing the historicity of the exodus." Indeed, Collins believes archeologists' claims "that the material culture of early Israel, in the central highlands of Palestine, was essentially Canaanite," not Egyptian. "If there was an exodus from Egypt, then, it must have been on a small scale." Furthermore, "the genre of the stories in Exodus is legendary and folkloristic," which means that the claim that six hundred thousand Jewish men and their families left Egypt at the same time, as well as all of the "miraculous incidents"—presumably including Moses' birth and rescue, the story of the burning bush, the defeat of the Egyptians, and the appearance of God on Mt. Sinai—are simply fictional.[723] As James Muilenburg explains: "On such important questions as the time and circumstances of the entrance into Egypt, the number and identity of the tribes, the length of the Egyptian sojourn, the date of the Exodus, and the location of Sinai, we are not in a position to give any decisive answer."[724]

T. J. Meek agrees with Friedman. On the one hand, he says, "It is difficult to understand how Moses could have induced his people to leave Egypt under the guidance of a god of whom they knew absolutely nothing and of whom they had no previous experience." Thus, he concludes, "there is good ground for the belief that [in Egypt] Yahweh was early known to the Hebrews, at least in some circles close to Moses."[725] On the other hand, however, again like Friedman, Meek says that "only a part of the Hebrews went to Egypt," "that the number in Egypt was comparatively small and hence not the whole nation," and "that there were Hebrews in Palestine . . . all the time that there were Hebrews in Egypt and that only a comparatively small group ever went to Egypt."[726] At the other extreme, Jon D. Levenson rejects both theories: "To put it mildly, the evidence that those who escaped in the exodus were a racially and religiously heterogeneous underclass is slim. The basis for the currently popular idea that Israel originated as a group of disenfranchised Canaanite peasants is only slightly more substantial."[727]

Nevertheless, all of these arguments are worthy of notice because they have a strong bearing on our understanding of the attitude of the "Israelites" after their escape from Egypt. That is, if they had not been a unified community, they would have been less able to give each other the kind of moral support that comes from group unity. And if they had had no collective attachment to the traditions of the patriarchs, then they might have had a difficult time believing in the strange God who made grandiose promises and subjected his followers to an unexpectedly long and arduous journey. However, on this issue, we are certain of nothing. Werner H. Schmidt, in fact, attributes the entire story of slavery in Egypt to "conditions connected with Solomon's building activity," which involved the kind of "forced labor" that the writer of Exodus wrote into the pre-monarchial history of the Israelites. Schmidt says that it might have been nothing more than an etiological answer to "the sapiential question What is humanity?"—or, more narrowly, Where did we come from?[728]

Moses first addresses the Israelites, represented by their elders, in 4:29–30, by telling them what Yahweh told him: that God is aware of "their sufferings" and that he intends "to deliver them out of the land of the Egyptians, and to bring them to . . . a land flowing with milk and honey" (3:7–8). Although "the people believed" and "bowed their heads and worshiped" (4:31), they spend the rest of the book of Exodus vacillating between faith and infidelity—trust and doubt. William M. Ramsay says: "[I]f we look in the chapters that follow [the Israelites' escape from Egypt] for a repeated phrase or idea, one immediately strikes us: 'And the people complained' (15:24; cf. 16:2, 12; 17:3; and recall 2:14). Realistically and factually, these Israelite historians make no effort to idealize their ancestors."[729]

This theme underscores the single most important difference between Genesis and Exodus. In the former, God's help is constant and effective, and at least some of his promises are fulfilled rather quickly. As von Rad says, "[T]he promise of a land was certainly originally made with reference to an imminent realisation."[730] Furthermore, the initially barren matriarchs become pregnant, as promised, and the patriarchs prosper. The Israelites in Egypt continue to multiply and grow strong (Exod 1:7), as they did in Genesis. However, their size and influence reaches a point at which they are perceived to be a threat that requires the Egyptians "to afflict them with heavy burdens" (1:11). In addition, the patriarchs not only hear from God directly, but also have the opportunity to respond to him when necessary. In Exodus, the people can neither understand God's words (though they can hear his voice) nor see God's face (though they can see his "glory").[731] Indeed, they cannot even approach him closely without risking death. As Muilenburg explains: "There is something fearful, terrifying, even demonic in him. The whole mountain quakes at his descent, and the people tremble before the awfulness of the theophany."[732]

Although they are liberated from their oppressive lives in Egypt, the Israelites face numerous problems. Living in the wilderness (or desert), they have difficulty with survival issues (hunger and thirst, as well as military attack [17:8–16]), and periodic displays of anger and violence by both Yahweh and Moses. Since their only food, besides quail meat, is manna—which is supplied to them by God but with which they are completely unfamiliar (16:15) and are forced to consume it daily "for forty years" (16:35)—they may also have suffered from boredom. In the book of Numbers, they clearly complain, through tears, that they are tired of manna and would much prefer meat, perhaps because the manna is neither tasty nor nourishing: "O that we had meat to eat! . . . [B]ut now our strength is dried up, and there is nothing but this manna to look at" (Num 11:4–9). Living in tents, the Israelites—in addition to gathering manna, measuring it, grinding it in mills or beating it in mortars, boiling it in pots, and making cakes out of it (Num 11:7–8)—cared for their animals but constructed no buildings and planted no fields in the desert. They appear to trudge from place to place, following the cloud in which Yahweh dwells, until they arrive at Kadesh, an oasis south of Canaan, where the Israelites "spent most of the forty-year sojourn in the wilderness."[733]

Whether moving or stopping, however, they appear to have little clarity regarding their destiny, certainly wondering where they are going and when they will get there. And while they wait impatiently for directives they receive not from God himself, but from Moses, Moses leaves them for forty days without telling them how long he will be away. Thus, when "Moses delayed to come down from the mountain," the people say to Aaron, "Up, make us gods, who shall go before us; as for *this Moses, the man who brought us up out of the land of Egypt*, we do not know what has become of him" (32:1; my emphasis). Besides showing that they are plunged into deeper uncertainty by Moses' unexplained absence, this demand suggests that the Israelites have a very tentative connection to Yahweh, whom they are quite prepared to replace with other gods. And despite his alleged fame in Egypt, they appear to have surprisingly little familiarity with Moses, referring to him as "this Moses." Nor does it help that Aaron, quite possibly equally uninformed about Moses' (or God's) plans, responds to the people's request to make an idol without any hesitation whatsoever.

Worst of all, the Israelites seem to be punished in this case (and again and again) for overreacting to their dilemma, although it is difficult for a modern reader to interpret their responses to their rather extraordinary situation as either excessive or unreasonable. John H. Tullock reminds us that "Egypt, even with its slavery, did provide at least a minimum of food and plenty of water to drink. In contrast, the Sinai made Egypt look like the Garden of Eden."[734] Levenson says that in Egypt the Israelites were not in fact slaves attached to individual families, but slaves of the pharaoh. Thus, their bondage was "state slavery," a kind of "forced labor."[735] But whether this was more or less onerous than domestic slavery is not at all clear. Indeed, McKenzie argues that "[t]he 'slavery' from which [Moses] liberates his countrymen was the ordinary life of the Egyptian peasant, who seems to have been more contented with his lot than most peasants."[736] Thus, as Bernhard Anderson says: "Freedom in the desert was, to many of the pilgrims, a poor substitute for slavery in Egypt. Water was scarce, there was no food; existence was precarious." The situation was so bad that "the people cried out: 'Is Yahweh among us or not?'" (17:7).[737]

In the Wilderness

As a story of the exodus, the book of Numbers (or, in Hebrew, In the Wilderness) begins where the book of Exodus ends, immediately after Moses' second descent from Mt. Sinai. The narrative traces the journey of the Israelites from Sinai to the Promised Land and basically continues the story of the three-way relationship between Yahweh, Moses, and the people of Israel. According to May and Metzger, the editors of *The Oxford Annotated Bible*: "Many of the traditions [in this book] portray Israel's murmuring, occasioned by the people's precarious existence in the wilderness. The people are pictured as faithless, rebellious, and blind to God's signs" (160). Indeed, in Numbers, the "murmuring" of the Israelites, the anger and vengefulness of Yahweh, and the frustration and sense of helplessness of Moses are far more extreme than they are in Exodus.[738]

The Israelites complain or rebel seven times about (1) "their misfortunes" generally (11:1), (2) having no "meat to eat" (11:4), (3) the formidable enemy in Canaan (14:1–4), (4) the leadership of Moses and Aaron (as well as the superior position of the priests over the Levites; 16:3, 13), (5) Yahweh's murder of the rebelling Levites (16:41), (6) the lack of "water for the congregation" (20:2), and (7) the "worthless food" (21:5). Several of these complaints, especially concerning food and water, echo passages in Exodus (14:11–12, 15:22–24; 16:2–3, 14; 17:1–3). However, the murmurings of the Israelites are not only more frequent in Numbers, but also more likely to elicit extreme reactions by both Moses and Yahweh. In this respect, the appropriateness of Moses' and Yahweh's response to the people's laments and protests is even more questionable in Numbers than it is in Exodus.

In Exodus, Yahweh hears the same kinds of complaints and responds by simply solving the problems raised by the Israelites. When they are frightened by the approach of the Egyptian army, Yahweh tells Moses to divide the sea so that the people will be able to escape. When they are hungry or thirsty, he provides them with food and water. The only time Yahweh is angry with his people in Exodus is when they worship the Golden Calf, at which moment he calls them "stiff-necked," expresses his "wrath," and threatens to "consume them" completely (Exod 32:9–10). In Numbers, Yahweh almost invariably reacts to his people's complaints with "anger," "fierce anger," or "wrath." Indeed, his contempt and its destructive expression at Sinai become the model for his reaction to many of the complaints in Numbers: His anger turns into

The Pentateuch

fire, and the fire consumes some portion of the people (11:1; 16:47)—sometimes, however, only the guilty parties (11:33–34; 14:36–37; 16:31–32; 21:6–9).

In Exodus, as we have seen, Yahweh threatens to "consume" all of the worshipers of the Golden Calf and "make a great nation of Moses." However, because of Moses' mention to Yahweh of his concern for his reputation among the Egyptians and Moses' reminder of his promise to the patriarchs, Yahweh sends a plague only to some of the Israelites (32:11–14, 35). In Numbers, in his reaction to the Israelites' fear of fighting a strong enemy in Canaan (14:1–4), Yahweh threatens to "strike [the complainers] with pestilence and disinherit them" and make of Moses "a nation greater and mightier than they." Again, however, Moses talks him out of it by mentioning Yahweh's concern for his reputation among the Egyptians *and* "the nations who have heard [his] fame" and by reminding him not of his promise to the patriarchs, in Genesis, but of his "promise" in Exodus (34:5–8): that he is "slow to anger, and abounding in steadfast love, forgiving iniquity and transgression" (Num 14:13–19).

In the Numbers version of his reactions to disobedience and dissatisfaction, Yahweh is always persuaded by Moses to modify his punishment—to reduce it from total to partial destruction. Even then, however, Yahweh has a difficult time cooling off. In the last-mentioned instance, he not only destroys "the men whom Moses sent to spy out the land" and who afterward gave "an evil report" (14:37), he also denies all of the Israelite men over twenty years old the privilege of reaching Canaan: "[N]one of the men who have seen my glory and my signs which I wrought in Egypt, and yet have put me to the proof these ten times and have not hearkened to my voice, shall see the land which I swore to give to their fathers; and none of those who despised me shall see it" (14:22–23).

Furthermore, Yahweh tells Moses to say to these men that their "dead bodies shall fall in this wilderness" and that, although their "little ones"—males under age twenty—"shall know the land which [the older males] have despised," they too will be punished. They "shall be shepherds in the wilderness forty years and will suffer for [their fathers'] faithlessness, until the last of [their fathers'] dead bodies lies in the wilderness" (14:22–23, 31–33; see also 26:64–65 and 32:10–11). Then, when the repentant men, having been denied the very thing they left Egypt for, try to atone for their sin by fighting the Amalekites and Canaanites, Yahweh no longer supports them, as Moses warns them, and they are defeated by the armies of the people who inhabit Canaan (14:39–45).[739]

Yahweh's response to the Israelites' request for meat in both Exodus and Numbers clearly illustrates the difference between the books. In Exodus, when the Israelites ask for meat, Yahweh simply sends them quail, which will be his people's evening meal to supplement their morning meal of manna. Yahweh responds without any anger or recrimination. In Numbers, however, his gift of quail is accompanied by an angry tirade, which he delivers to Moses: "You shall not eat one day, or two days, or five days, or ten days, or twenty days, but a whole month, until it comes out at your nostrils and becomes loathsome to you, because you have rejected the Lord who is among you" (11:19–20). In addition, in order to punish the Israelites even more severely for their complaint, Yahweh kills "the rabble" who asked for meat in the first place: "While the meat was yet between their teeth, before it was consumed, the Lord was kindled against the people, and the Lord smote the people with a very great plague" (11:33).

The excessiveness of Yahweh's vengefulness in Numbers is illustrated by his treatment of Miriam. When she and her brother Aaron question their secondary position to Moses, particularly considering his marriage to Zipporah, a Midianite, Yahweh not only simply asserts his preference for Moses, but also gives Miriam (but not Aaron) a seven-day case of leprosy, which results in her expulsion from the Israelite camp for one week. When both Aaron and Moses "beseech" Yahweh, quite passionately, to heal her, he responds, "If her father had but spit in her face, should she not be shamed seven days?" (12:1–15). As the editors of *The Oxford Annotated Bible* explain, "The punishment cannot be less than the defilement of being spat upon by her father, the sign of a curse" (179), which tells us that Yahweh, in the role of a father, figuratively spat in his daughter's face as a punishment for her misbehavior.

More generally, the difference between the two books is shown in two ways. First, in Numbers, Yahweh regards all of the Israelites' complaints as personal attacks on him—both his power, insofar as it is represented by his "signs," and his commitment, which is demonstrated by his ongoing support. The people have "rejected the Lord" (11:20), "despised" and disbelieved him (14:11, 23), "despised" the land that he has promised them (14:31), and "despised [his] word" (15:31)—attitudes that they reveal by speaking frankly and desperately to Moses. To stop this unceasing reaction, Yahweh asks Moses: "How long shall this wicked generation murmur against me?" (14:27, 35). Thus, after performing a miracle with Aaron's rod, Yahweh tells Moses to keep the rod "as a sign for the rebels, that you may make an end of their murmurings against me, *lest they die*" (17:10; my emphasis).

So deeply is Yahweh offended by this behavior that he often threatens to kill everyone, until Moses talks him out of it (14:12, 16:20, 16:45). Eventually, of course, Yahweh kills tens of thousands of Israelites. And, even before they get to Canaan, under Yahweh's direction, the Israelites wipe out the entire population of small kingdoms whose kings refuse to allow them safe passage though their lands. In Heshbon, for example, they "slew" not only the king and his sons, but "all his people, until there was not one survivor left" (21:25). On the verge of their invasion of Canaan, Yahweh orders the Israelites to "drive out all the inhabitants of the land before you" and all of their idols, which means, as Yahweh explains in Deuteronomy, his people "must utterly destroy" their enemies "and show no mercy to them" (7:2).

This point is shown most clearly when some of the Israelites "play the harlot with the daughters of Moab," which results from their worship of Baal. The "daughters of Moab" are ritual prostitutes in Midian who celebrate fertility by engaging in sexual acts with worshipers of Baal. In this instance, Yahweh does exactly what he has done before: He orders the execution of the Israelite chiefs and the slaying of all Israelite men who worshiped this foreign god (25:4–5). Only the action of Pinehas, Aaron's son, who kills both an Israelite and his Moabite paramour, prevents Yahweh from "consum[ing] the people of Israel in [his] wrath," although 24,000 are destroyed in Yahweh's plague before Yahweh stops it (25:6–11). So far, his response to the outright infidelity of the Israelites is like his response to their disloyalty when they worshiped the Golden Calf in Exodus. In Numbers, however, Yahweh goes one step further. For one thing, he orders Moses to "[h]arass the Midianites, and smite them" (25:16). "Avenge the people of Israel on the Midianites" (31:1).

The reason for this is not entirely clear, since nothing in the narrative suggests that anyone but Yahweh's own people are responsible for their involvement with the Midianite women. That is, not only are the Midianite men completely free of guilt, but also (as far as we know) the women do nothing unusual to attract the Israelite men. The Israelites were evidently drawn to the Midianite women who were acting as ritual prostitutes in what Jack Miles calls "the orgiastic worship of Baal of Peor."[740] This is the sense in which they "invited the people to the sacrifices of their gods" (25:2–3). Nevertheless, Yahweh visits a plague on these people by commanding the Israelites "to execute the Lord's vengeance on Midian" (31:3).

Nor is this all. After Yahweh's army kills "every male" as well as the "the kings of Midian"; takes "captive the women of Midian and their little ones," as well as "their goods" and domestic animals; and burns "their encampments"; Moses accuses "the officers of the army" of failing to kill enough Midianites. Thus, he orders them "to kill every male among the little ones, and kill every woman who has known man by lying with him" (31:17). The Israelites are also ordered to keep the Midianite virgins for themselves. What is even more shocking in this passage is that the Israelites are punishing the residents of Shittim, on the east side of the Jordan, where the people of Israel are not going to settle (although they later change their minds about this).

The point is that the Israelites are directed to wipe out the residents of Canaan, where they intend to live permanently, in order to remain uninfluenced by the local religion. As Bernhard Anderson says, Yahweh is, in such passages, a shockingly brutal deity, who is quite willing to kill people whose only sin is that they are not Israelites: "Considering the terrible suffering involved in the conquest of Canaan, especially for the defeated people, it is difficult for most of us to understand the Israelite conviction that God was actually taking part in the struggle. Yahweh is seemingly portrayed as a God of holy war who ruthlessly demands the *herem*—the wholesale destruction of Israel's enemies as a sacrifice to him."[741]

As the editors of *The Oxford Annotated Bible* explain, "This holy war is based on the fear of the corrupting influence of Canaanite culture" (210; see also 113), especially Canaanite religion. As Yahweh commands: "[I]f you do not drive out the inhabitants of the land before you, then those of them whom you let remain shall be as pricks in your eyes and thorns in your sides, and they shall trouble you in the land

The Evolution of Love

where you dwell. And I will do to you as I thought to do to them" (33:55–56). This is why Yahweh's orders always include destroying not only the idols of his enemies, but also their holy places (e.g., Exod 23:24; 34:11–16). Thus, as far as Moses (and perhaps Yahweh as well) knows at this point,[742] the Midianites do not represent a long-term threat to the Israelites' exclusive devotion to him. In short, the complete destruction of Shittim is not a protective measure, but an expression, as I noted above, of "the Lord's vengeance" (31:3).

The charge that the Israelites are, in fact, simply rejecting Yahweh for no good reason is not supported by the text. Rather, Yahweh's interpretation of his people's motive for complaining about their situation appears to be a reflection of his self-regard and hypersensitivity. On the one hand, in Exodus, the Israelites seem to have suffered from the deliberate oppression of the Egyptians. In Deuteronomy, Egypt is referred to twice as a "house of bondage" (6:12; 8:14) and once as "the iron furnace" (4:20). In Exodus, the Israelites not only seem to have been enslaved for hundreds of years, but also, for an undetermined period of time, subjected to a deliberate attempt to oppress them because they had become "too many and too mighty." The new king said that, in order to prevent them from supporting an enemy invasion and escaping from Egypt, they should be monitored by "taskmasters" whose job was "to afflict them with heavy burdens." The Egyptians' "dread of the people of Israel . . . made the people of Israel serve with rigor, and made their lives bitter with hard service" (1:8–14). Furthermore, the king ordered "the Hebrew midwives" to kill all of the first-born sons of the Israelites. This plan failed, but the king later told *all* Egyptians to kill the first-born sons of these people (1:15–22).

Thus, as Walter Brueggemann says, "The regime of Pharaoh is remembered as stifling and exploitative in every regard, whereby the underlings in their pain and resentment are completely silent." However, when this king dies, "Israel, the slave community, enters history when it finds its voice. Its initial utterance, after a long, unbearable silence, is the raw, unrestrained, undifferentiated shriek of pain."[743] In this context, it could reasonably be said that—with Yahweh's liberation, his ongoing support on the journey through the wilderness,[744] and his gift of "a land of milk and honey"—any complaints reflect, if not contempt for the Liberator, the Redeemer, at the very least, ingratitude on the part of the formerly enslaved Israelites.

On the other hand, however, as I suggested earlier, regardless of the conditions in Egypt, as far as the Israelites are concerned, their choice, at times, appears to be between life in Egypt and death in exile. Pursued by the pharaoh and his army after their escape, the Israelites remind Moses that they initially rejected his offer to free them: "Is not this what we said to you in Egypt, 'Let us alone and let us serve the Egyptians?' For it would have been better for us to serve the Egyptians than to die in the wilderness" (Exod 14:12; 17:3). "Why does the Lord bring us into this land, to die by the sword? Our wives and our little ones will become a prey; would it not be better for us to go back to Egypt?" (Num 14:3). Indeed, according to Brueggemann, it "is found to be a place without a viable life-support system. That deficiency evokes in Israel a wish to return to its slavery."[745] To Jeremiah, the wilderness is "a land of deserts and pits," "a land of drought and deep darkness," and "a land that none passes through, where no man dwells" (2:6). The Deuteronomist calls it "great and terrible" because of "its fiery serpents and scorpions, and thirsty ground where there was no water" (8:15).

Otherwise, the choice is between plenty of food in Egypt and hunger in the desert: "Would that we had died by the hand of the Lord in the land of Egypt, when we sat by the fleshpots and ate bread to the full; for you have brought us out into this wilderness to kill this whole assembly with hunger" (Exod 17:3). "We remember the fish we ate in Egypt for nothing, the cucumbers, the melons, the leeks, the onions, and the garlic" (Num 11:4–5; 21:5). "And why have you made us come up out of Egypt, to bring us to this evil place? It is no place for grain, or figs, or vines, or pomegranates; and there is no water to drink" (Num 20:5). For all of these reasons, Miles says, "[h]istorically, it is quite possible that, though the Israelites were enslaved in Egypt, they were not, in fact, being worked to death, much less threatened by the (surely mythical) slaughter of their infant males . . . It is also possible . . . that after long residence in Egypt the Israelites had largely forgotten the God of their fathers in whose name Moses ordered their emigration. Given this set of circumstances, they could easily have regretted their decision to follow Moses into the lethal harshness of the Sinai desert."[746]

As for Yahweh's saving acts in the wilderness, some scholars have suggested that many of them could have been interpreted as natural events. John H. Tullock, for example, explains all of the plagues as "natural phenomena." That is, the Nile turns red when "red soil washe[s] down from the Ethiopian highlands." "Frogs . . . were common when the Nile flooded." And gnats (or mosquitoes) "bred in the stagnant pools of water."[747] Water could be found at oases, and quail sometimes fell from the sky because their flight from oasis to oasis was tiring. Manna simply grew in the desert. Even the waters of a small or shallow lake could be separated by a change in the weather. As G. Ernest Wright says, "As a result of the wind, the waters, presumably rather shallow, were driven back; but when the Egyptians tried to follow, their chariot wheels floundered in the mud (Ex. 14:25), and they were trapped when the water returned."[748] Anderson argues, furthermore, that Yahweh's so-called miracles were not really intended to prove his power: "These signs were not proofs given to convince men once and for all that God is sovereign, however. The narratives of the Exodus show that their meaning was not self-evident to those who witnessed them."[749]

The most obvious example of the unconvinced is the pharaoh, who, even after Yahweh's murder of the Egyptian first-born and the successful departure of the Israelites, was still not converted to Yahwism, even though Yahweh's purpose was to demonstrate his supernatural status to the Egyptians and the rest of the world. As I noted earlier in this chapter, Yahweh commands Moses, before the plague of hail, to tell the pharaoh: "I will send all my plagues upon your heart, and upon your servants and your people, that you may know that there is none like me in all the earth . . . [F] or this purpose have I let you live, to show you my power, so that my name may be declared throughout the earth" (Exod 9:14–16).[750] Obviously, that did not happen. "Furthermore," says Anderson, "the Israelites, though they had witnessed the signs performed by Moses, did not believe him ... Even after their successful escape across the Red Sea they murmured in disbelief and longed for the fleshpots of Egypt."[751]

While the people complain more in Numbers than they did in Exodus and while God complains more about the people, Moses' stature in the later book is raised even higher than it was in Exodus. First, he is referred to by the narrator as meeker "than all men that were on the face of the earth" (Num 12:3), which perhaps explains why he appears to be so reluctant in Exodus to take on the job of God's mediator (Exod 3–4). Furthermore, in defense of his elevation of Moses above Aaron and Miriam, Yahweh explains that he is more than a prophet. That is, his position is unparalleled in the world: "If there is a prophet among you, I the Lord make myself known to him in a vision, I speak with him in a dream. Not so with my servant Moses; he is entrusted with all my house. With him I speak mouth to mouth, clearly and not in dark speech; and he beholds the form of the Lord" (Num 12:6–8). Furthermore, Moses continues in his role as the chief judge of the people because he is the only judge who is able to seek God's counsel (9:8; 15:34–35; 27:5). And he remains not only the people's representative to Yahweh, but also Yahweh's moral guide as well as his representative to the Israelites.

Again and again, Moses appeals to Yahweh's reasonableness, whether it is his sense of justice, his concern for his reputation, his willingness to keep his promises, or his willingness to forgive. For example, when Yahweh threatens to kill all of the Israelites after Korah objects to Moses' leadership, Moses and Aaron fall on their faces, which they often do in their responses to opposition, and say to Yahweh, "O God, the God of the spirits of all flesh, shall one man sin, and wilt thou be angry with all the congregation?" (16:22). In every instance, Yahweh modifies his initial judgment, as I said earlier, and either stops spreading the plague by which he destroys the Israelites *en masse* or limits his punishment to the sinners rather than killing the entire congregation.[752]

What distinguishes Moses in Numbers from Moses in Exodus is (1) the expansion of his ongoing role as Yahweh's conscience;[753] (2) his utter frustration with the unbearable responsibility of serving both the rebellious Israelites and their vengeful deity; and (3) what can only be regarded as his victimization at the mercy of an ungrateful master. At the very beginning of Numbers, when the Israelites complain about eating manna day after day, "Moses [is] displeased." It might seem that he is upset with the people, but they are actually "weeping"—"every man at the door of his tent," as well as his family. In fact, Moses is expressing a concern that, in Exodus, elicits Yahweh's prompt response, without recrimination. There, Yahweh is immediately and uncritically compliant: "At twilight you shall eat flesh, and in the morning you shall be filled with bread; then you shall know that I am the Lord your God" (Exod 16:12).

In Numbers, however, Moses' displeasure is actually with Yahweh, to whom he says, "Why hast thou dealt ill with thy servant? And why have I not found favor in thy sight, that thou dost lay the burden of all this people upon me? Did I bring them forth, that thou shouldst say to me, 'Carry them in your bosom, as the nurse carries the suckling child, to the land which thou didst swear to give their fathers?'" (11:10–12). Yahweh reacts to Moses' complaint by appointing seventy men to share the responsibility of governance: "[T]hey shall bear the burden of the people with you, that you may not bear it yourself alone" (11:17). And, once more, Moses' stature is pushed to the limit, according to von Rad: "His *charisma* was so tremendous that a mere portion of it, even when it was distributed over seventy elders, threw the recipients out of their normal psychic state and stimulated them to ecstasy": "Then the Lord . . . took some of the spirit that was upon [Moses] and put it upon the seventy elders; and when the spirit rested upon them; they prophesied" (Num 11:25).[754]

Yahweh takes extreme measures in this instance—perhaps the only time in Numbers that he responds unstintingly to Moses' concerns—because Moses' frustration is absolute. Moses says to Yahweh (again) that he would rather die than go on in the same way: "If thou wilt deal thus with me"—that is, if this situation remains unchanged—"kill me at once, if I find favor in thy sight, that I may not see my wretchedness" (11:15).[755] What follows, besides the easing of Moses' burden by Yahweh's extension of the Holy Spirit to seventy elders among the Israelites, is clearly a perpetuation of Moses' need to accommodate both Yahweh and the Israelites and a deepening of his apparently unresolvable dilemma. That is, the Israelites continue to complain, and Yahweh continues to treat their concerns not as genuine expressions of disappointment, fear, and deprivation, but as personal insults, representing disobedience, rebellion, and infidelity. That is, Moses' problem persists.

Thus, it comes as something of a shock that Yahweh not only forbids the adult males among the Israelites to reach Canaan and forces them and their families to remain in the desert for as long as it takes for the last man over twenty years old to die, but also forbids Moses to reach the Promised Land. The precipitating event for this reaction is easy to miss in the narration. Thus, the question is not only how Yahweh could punish his esteemed "servant" so severely, but also what Moses could possibly have done to merit this curse. Particularly compared to the patriarchs in Genesis and to everyone else in Exodus and Numbers, Moses is called upon to sacrifice far more in terms of burdens borne and disappointments endured. Furthermore, he is the most lauded of God's followers—indeed, by Yahweh himself—and the least interested in rewards and recognition. Finally, he is willing to die for his people, which, ironically, he does.

Yahweh's condemnation of Moses occurs after the penultimate complaint of the Israelites, who find themselves once more without water for themselves and their cattle. When Moses and Aaron, soliciting Yahweh's help, fall on their faces in front of the tent of meeting, Yahweh orders Moses to "tell the rock" in front of them "to yield its water." Gathering the thirsty Israelites together, Moses says to them, "Hear now, you rebels; shall we bring forth water for you out of this rock?" After Moses hits the rock twice with the rod given to him by Yahweh, the "water came forth abundantly." However, not having expressed any anger about the latest request from his people, Yahweh now says to both Moses and Aaron—though, given the weight of his statement, with surprisingly little emotion—"Because you did not believe in me, to sanctify me in the eyes of the people of Israel, therefore you shall not bring this assembly into the land which I have given them" (20:2–12). Since Moses appears to accept this judgment without protest, we are forced to assume that he understood his sin. Yahweh explains his reason to Moses later in Numbers: "[Y]ou rebelled against my word in the wilderness of Zin . . . to sanctify me at the waters before their eyes" (27:14). In Deuteronomy, he says: "[Y]ou broke faith with me in the midst of the people of Israel . . . [Y]ou did not revere me as holy in the midst of the people of Israel" (32:51).

However, this too is somewhat non-explanatory. That is, although it is clear that Moses and Aaron are being accused of failing to "sanctify" Yahweh or "revere him as holy," we are not told exactly what they failed to do. Thus, Richard Elliott Friedman comments: "Theological interpreters have pondered this passage for centuries, trying to understand just what the nature of Moses' offense was."[756] The options are, first, that Moses "struck the rock instead of talking to it"—that is, he simply disobeyed God.[757] Second, "he called the people 'rebels'"—that is, he insulted God's people. Third, he attributed the act to himself and Aaron instead of Yahweh: "Shall *we*" perform the miracle, or "Shall *God*?"[758] Comparing the Numbers version of this story with the Exodus version, where Yahweh has no negative reaction, however, Friedman notes that there was no offense "in the earlier version." Thus, Friedman says that the author of the story, the Priestly (or P) writer, "has gone out of his way to introduce it into the story."[759]

It is also problematic that Moses three times reports in Deuteronomy that, when Yahweh forbade all the adult males among his people from entering the Promised Land, he also forbade Moses: "Not one of these men of this evil generation shall see the good land which I swore to give to your fathers . . . You also shall not go in there" (1:35, 37). Moses twice says to his people that "the Lord was angry with me *on your account*, and he swore that I should not cross the Jordan . . . For I must die in this land" (4:21–22; 3:26; my emphasis). Thus, the editors of *The Oxford Annotated Bible* comment, "Here Moses is not punished for his own sin, but vicariously bears the divine wrath on Israel's account" (215–16).

To be sure, whatever Yahweh's reason may be for denying Moses the right to enter the Promised Land, his charge against Moses does not diminish Moses' reputation. Indeed, particularly because God's justification for his extreme reaction remains obscure, it simply adds to the impression that Yahweh is both hypersensitive and unjust. This view is underscored by the fact that, throughout the final book of the Pentateuch, Deuteronomy, Moses is presented as the last prophet, the most important mediator of Yahweh, and the communicator of Yahweh's final message. In the last lines of Deuteronomy, the narrator says, "And there has not arisen a prophet since in Israel like Moses, whom the Lord knew face to face, none like him for all the signs and the wonders which the Lord sent him to do in the land of Egypt, ... and for all the mighty power and all the great and terrible deeds which Moses wrought in the sight of all Israel" (34:10–12).

Of course, what this mixed picture of Moses illustrates is, if not Yahweh's inconsistencies or other shortcomings, at least the different treatments of both God and Moses from book to book in the Pentateuch. If we look back at three of the first four books of this surprisingly diverse collection—Genesis, Exodus, and Numbers—we see three quite different views of God. Indeed, if we add Leviticus to the list, given its almost total concentration on cultic issues (priestly responsibilities, purity laws, and guidelines for rituals, including sacrifices), we can identify four versions of the Jewish deity. It should be unsurprising, therefore, to find in the book of Deuteronomy yet another portrayal of the Supreme Being.

What is interesting about these different portraits is the fact that they are not entirely independent of each other. In fact, each successive description retains, to some degree, aspects of its predecessor(s). Thus, the personal adviser of Genesis survives in the God of Exodus, who advises Moses—indeed, not occasionally, which is the case in Genesis, but frequently and even, one might say, continually. Both the mild-mannered guide of Genesis and the cosmic lawgiver of Exodus—now, however, focused on ceremonial matters—reappear in Leviticus. And these two figures, as well as the priestly mentor of Leviticus, are active in Numbers.

In Deuteronomy, as we have learned to expect, all of these deities return: Moses, instead of the patriarchs, passes on the message of Yahweh; the message is a body of laws, as it is in Exodus; the laws pertain to both moral and cultic concerns, as they do in Leviticus; and Moses both reminds the Israelites of their failure to follow God's rule and prepares them for war, as he does in Numbers. However, as we have also learned to expect, yet another feature is added to the Pentateuchal picture of God in Deuteronomy: the loving God, who not only asks for love in return, but also revives the covenantal promises of the preceding books of the Jewish Bible. According to the editors of *The Oxford Annotated Bible*, "Here the legal tradition of the book of Exodus (for example, the Decalogue or the Covenant Code) is not just repeated; it is reinterpreted in contemporary terms, so that the promises and demands of the covenant were brought near to every worshiping Israelite" (214).[760]

The Covenant arises as a major subject in Deuteronomy when Moses equates it with the Ten Commandments: "The Lord spoke to you out of the midst of the fire ... And he declared to you his covenant, which he commanded you to perform, that is, the ten commandments" (4:12–13). Moses reminds the Israelites that although these commandments were given to them long ago, they are still in effect today: "Not with our fathers did the Lord make this covenant, but with us, who are all of us alive this day" (5:2–3). Indeed, the reason for Yahweh's (and Moses') renewed emphasis on the

The Evolution of Love

Covenant is that the Israelites are on the verge of entering Canaan and establishing a settled community. That is, now, for the first time, knowledge of these laws is imperative: "And the Lord commanded me to teach you statutes and ordinances, that you might do them in the land which you are going over to possess" (4:14).

As the editors of *The Oxford Annotated Bible* comment, "Loyalty to the covenant"—which is to say, obedience to the Decalogue—"is the condition for life in Canaan" (229). And this is why, as many scholars have noted, the Covenant Code, throughout the Pentateuch, is meant not for the semi-nomadic Israelites in the wilderness and certainly not for the Hebrew slaves that they were in Egypt—although many of the Covenant laws were influenced by the organizational and operational features of pre-agricultural tribal life—but for the lives they are soon to live in the Promised Land. John J. Collins says, "These laws were formulated in a settled agrarian community; they are not the laws of nomads wandering in the wilderness."[761]

What is new in this book is a message that was almost completely absent from Genesis and not as clearly stated in either Exodus or Numbers: the idea that the Israelites are not merely required to obey Yahweh by refraining from expressing their dissatisfaction and avoiding idolatry—the two main sources of anger and frustration for Yahweh in Exodus and Numbers. Rather, they must obey *a large portion of the body of laws* that appear in all of the first four books of the Pentateuch. Thus, in Deuteronomy, Moses repeatedly and emphatically makes the Covenant contingent on *obedience to laws*, which may well be considered the central theme of Deuteronomy, not on obedience only to the direct orders and unannounced expectations of Yahweh: "And now, O Israel, give heed to the statutes and the ordinances which I teach you, and do them, that you may live, and go in and take possession of the land which the Lord, the God of your fathers, gives you" (4:1). Moses repeats this command in 4:9–20, 6:1–9, 10:12–22, and more briefly in chapters 11 and 26. Twelve individual laws are restated in 27:15–26; Moses orders the Levites to read the laws aloud every seven years (31:9–13); God orders Moses to compose a song of warning against disobedience (vv. 19–22); and Moses orders the Levites to place a copy of the laws next to the ark of the covenant—"that it may be there for a witness against you" (vv. 24–26).

Moses recites the Ten Commandments again (5:6–21), underscores the importance of obedience (chs. 8–10), and spells out the consequences of following or not following these laws in 4:21–28; 6:12–15; 7:10–14; and 8:19–20. "Behold," Moses says later, "I set before you this day a blessing and a curse: the blessing, if you obey the commandments of the Lord your God, which I command you this day, and the curse, if you do not obey the commandments of the Lord your God, but turn aside from the way which I command you this day" (11:26–28). In chapter 28, Moses specifies precisely the rewards and punishments—the blessings and curses—that God will impose on the Israelites in response to their obedience (vv. 1–14) or disobedience (vv. 15–68). In chapter 29, he warns against the danger to the entire community by even a single disobedient "man or woman or family or tribe, whose heart turns away this day from the Lord our God and to go and serve the gods of those nations; lest there be among you a root bearing poisonous and bitter fruit" (v. 18). Finally, in chapter 32, Moses quotes God as saying that infidelity will result in massive and brutal punishment: "And I will heap evils upon them; I will spend my arrows upon them; and they shall be wasted with hunger, and devoured with burning heat and poisonous pestilence; and I will send the teeth of beasts against them, with venom of crawling things of the dust" (vv. 23–24).

In light of these dire prospects, Moses warns the Israelites not only to take the laws of God seriously, but to make sure that their children take them seriously as well: "[Y]ou shall teach them diligently to your children, and shall talk of them when you sit in your house, and when you walk by the way, and when you lie down, and when you rise. And you shall bind them as a sign upon your hand, and they shall be as frontlets between your eyes [i.e., as *tefillin,* or phylacteries]. And you shall write them on the doorposts of your house and on your gates [i.e., as *mezuzot*]" (6:7–9). Based on these passages and others (11:18; 17:18; 27:3; 31:10), Yehezkel Kaufmann says that "Deuteronomy is the first to conceive of a Torah book, the possession of the people, to be studied" not only by parents and children, but also by kings and priests. "The very style of Deuteronomy," Kaufmann continues, "repetitive and hortatory, is inspired by this purpose."[762]

What is also new in Deuteronomy, as I said earlier, is the picture of Yahweh as the God of Love. This is so despite Miles's claim that Deuteronomy means "second law," which suggests that "virtually everything in this last book of the Pentateuch has already been recounted or enjoined in the first four books."[763] According to the editors of *The Oxford Annotated Bible*, "A new element is added to the theological tradition: the Lord's election of Israel was based upon his love. Israel's obedience, therefore, should be motivated by a responding love" (223). William M. Ramsay says, "No other book of the Old Testament so emphasizes the command to love God."[764] And Werner H. Schmidt makes exactly the same point, adding, furthermore, that "the book acquired immense importance, took deep hold on the life of the people," and "exercised" a "far-reaching indirect influence" on ancient Judaism.[765] "Indeed," says James L. Kugel, "from an early period ... Lev. 19:18 seems to have been exalted as a central principle and the epitome of all the Torah's laws concerning relations between human beings."[766]

It is important, of course, to recognize that the word *love* derives, to some extent, from political treaties of the Near East in which mutual love is better interpreted to mean mutual respect than mutual affection. As Miles explains, "That [God] does not require love as we might ordinarily understand the word is clear from" the fact that God uses the words *love* and *fear* interchangeably. Thus, Miles asks: "What does the Lord require, then, love or fear? An easy answer is that he requires both, but in fact the two are alternative words for essentially the same attitude. Historical critical scholarship has made the point by stressing that the love in question is not a spontaneous, interpersonal emotion but covenant love."[767]

However, in this covenant document, Moses explains Yahweh's harsh treatment of the Israelites, especially in Numbers, as both an unprecedented gift and an act of kindness. That is, his persistent threat not only to end his commitment to the Covenant but to completely destroy his followers was not really a manifestation of his anger and contempt, but part of a conscious program that was a manifestation of his graciousness and mercy. As Collins puts it, "Deuteronomy puts the emphasis on compassion." In fact, Collins adds, "The recollection of the experience of slavery as a reason to be compassionate is typical of the rhetoric of Deuteronomy." Collins next goes through a list of laws in the Covenant Code of this book, illustrating its emphasis on social justice: "Some of these concerns are already found in the Book of the Covenant in Exodus, but they are more developed in Deuteronomy." Thus, the book is characterized by its "generally humane attitudes."[768]

Indeed, Moses insists, on a practical level, that Yahweh's angry responses to his people's disobedience were not merely expressions of his anger and hostility. They were, in fact, educational rather than punitive. As Moses suggests in 8:5, they were a series of chastisements, done for the purpose of helping the Israelites understand their relationship to God: "Out of heaven he let you hear his voice, that he might discipline you." The reason is that "he loved your fathers and chose their descendants after them." Therefore, he "brought you out of Egypt with his own presence, by his great power, driving out before you nations greater and mightier than yourselves, to bring you in, to give you their land for an inheritance, as at this day" (4:36–38). Moses says later, "And consider this day . . . the discipline of the Lord your God, his greatness, *his mighty hand and his outstretched arm*, his signs and his deeds which he did in Egypt and to all his land" (11:2–3; my emphasis).

More specifically, indicating that the entire purpose of the exodus was educational for the Israelites and investigative for Yahweh, Moses says: "And you shall remember all the way which the Lord your God has led you these forty years in the wilderness, that he might humble you, testing you to know what was in your heart, whether you would keep his commandments, or not. And he humbled you and let you hunger and fed you with manna, which you did not know, nor did your fathers know; that he might make you know that man does not live by bread alone, but that man lives by everything that proceeds out of the mouth of the Lord" (8:2–3). Anderson says that "through these trials Yahweh was uniting and disciplining his people for the historical task that lay ahead of them."[769]

In this respect, Yahweh's relationship with the Israelites was part of a unique and spectacular blessing, which echoes 11:2–3 (cited above): "For ask now . . . whether such a great thing as this has ever happened or was ever heard of . . . [H]as any god ever attempted to go and take a nation for himself from the midst of another nation, by trials, by signs, by wonders, and by war, by *a mighty hand and an outstretched arm* . . . ?" (32:34). In fact, that "mighty hand" held the people "he loved": "[A]ll those consecrated to him were in his hand" (33:3). Again: "The eternal God is your dwelling place, and underneath are the everlasting arms" (33:27). The editors of *The Oxford Annotated Bible* comment, "God is a place of refuge and, like a parent, his *everlasting arms* support his children" (261).

This image of Yahweh reaching out with his mighty arm and holding the Israelites in his hand is reflected in the occasional reference to Yahweh in Deuteronomy as his people's father. Early in the book, Moses says, "The Lord your God who goes before you will himself fight for you, just as he did for you in Egypt before your eyes, and in the wilderness, where you have seen how the Lord bore you, *as a man bears his son*, in all the way that you went until you came to this place" (1:30–31; my emphasis). "Know then in your heart that, as a man disciplines his son," Moses continues, "the Lord your God disciplines you" (8:5). "You are the sons of the Lord your God" (14:1). In his song, Moses asks the Israelites: "Is not he your father, who created you, who made you and established you?" (32:6).

So strong is the emphasis in Deuteronomy on love as the principal driving force in the human-divine relationship that Moses urges the Israelites not to assume that God chose them because of their merit—that is, because they earned it. Moses says to them, "Know therefore, that the Lord your God is not giving you this good land to possess because of your righteousness" (9:4–6). Anderson comments: "In his marvelous grace he selected this people . . . solely because he spontaneously set his love upon a small, insignificant band of slaves in Egypt . . . Election is an act of divine grace that should evoke consecrated service rather than the proud feeling of being God's favorite (7:6–11)."[770] In other words, God is fulfilling his promise to his people as an act of love—one might say, as a father provides for his children. As Moses claims to have said twice to Yahweh at Kadesh, they are "thy people and *thy heritage*," saved, again, by God's "mighty hand" and "outstretched arm" (9:26, 29; my emphasis). James Muilenburg comments: "Yahweh's choice of Israel is not explained by Israel's genius for religion, by her native endowment, by the purity of her ethical life, or by any merit by Israel at all, but rather by the divine mercy. Above all, in the covenant relationship Yahweh manifested his love and mercy to Israel."[771]

To be sure, the first four chapters of Deuteronomy serve as an introduction to the book *as a covenant*, or treaty, and therefore lay out exactly what the Lord, the suzerain, has done for the Israelites, his vassals, which is exactly what such treaties began with in the ancient Near East.[772] What follows in Deuteronomy (chs. 5–28) is what ordinarily comes next in such agreements: a very detailed explanation of the mutual obligations of the two parties, beginning with the Ten Commandments and a revision of the old Covenant Codes from preceding books of the Bible. The Covenant concludes (chs. 29–30), as Near Eastern treaties commonly did, with a list of consequences that will follow any and all failures to comply with the terms of the treaty.

Nevertheless, this formal document is so laden with expressions of affection, especially the words *love* and *heart*, that it is difficult to see Deuteronomy as nothing more than a conventional ancient document. Thus, Collins warns, "Deuteronomic theology should not be construed too narrowly as a legalistic religion." This is because "[i]ts core teachings were love of God and of one's neighbor."⁷⁷³ Indeed, what follows Moses' recitation of the commandments is the famous Hebrew prayer, the Shema, which calls upon the Israelites to love Yahweh as much as he loves them: "Hear, O Israel: The Lord our God is one Lord; and you shall love the Lord your God with all your heart, and with all your soul, and with all your might" (6:4; 10:12–13; 11:13, 18; 30:6). The editors of *The Oxford Annotated Bible* explain that the words *heart*, *mind*, and *soul* "express the idea of loving God"—not passively, formally, or routinely—but "with the full measure of one's devotion" (223). Kugel says, "So it was that Deut. 6:4–5 (and soon enough, the whole paragraph of Deut. 6:4–9) came to occupy a special place in Judaism."⁷⁷⁴

Anderson comments on such passages: "This does not mean that one should love God in different ways, for these terms [i.e., *heart*, *mind*, and *soul*] overlap in meaning. Israel is to love God in one way: with the unswerving, complete, steadfast loyalty that is the very foundation of the covenant community."⁷⁷⁵ After all, Moses says later, "the Lord, out of all the peoples on the face of the earth . . . [has] set his love upon you and chose you . . . because the Lord loves you, and is keeping the oath which he swore to your fathers" (7:6–8). "Know therefore that . . . (God) keeps covenant and steadfast love with those who love him and keep his commandments" (7:9; 11:1; 30:16, 20). If you do so, Moses continues, "God will keep with you the covenant and the steadfast love which he swore to your fathers to keep; he will love you, bless you, and multiply you" (7:12–13; 5:33; 6:3). Thus, even Miles concludes, "Something more than loyalty underlies the relationship" between God and humanity. "For covenant love has been preceded by the more mysterious, gratuitous love that established the covenant in the first place."⁷⁷⁶

In this context, the Covenant Code in Deuteronomy should be understood as something more than the codes that appear in earlier books of the Pentateuch. On the one hand, the codes in Exodus and Leviticus should be seen in the light of traditional tribal values that led to the formulation of social rules and regulations whose purpose was to maintain ancient societies that were united by kinship ties and therefore dedicated to preventing political marginalization, social isolation, and economic neglect or exploitation. In other words, communities were organized for the purpose of self-preservation and social harmony. As A. T. van Leeuwen argues, "the tribal organization . . . remained important as a basic principle and as an ideal" through the time of the prophets. That is, "the Torah perpetuated a fairly primitive nomadic structure of human relationships," and it "remained firmly rooted in the Mosaic Covenant."⁷⁷⁷ As Franz Mussner adds, the Ten Commandments "form the core of the Torah of Israel, its 'covenantal fundamental charter.'" And they are "statements of the 'natural moral law,'" not "statements of revelation."⁷⁷⁸

On the other hand, however, in Deuteronomy, the Covenant Code is not merely a practical matter. G. E. Wright says that in this book "legal requirement is not the center of the relationship between God and his people. Rather, the relationship is one of love and grace; as God has loved us, so we should love him."[779] "Thus," in Anderson's words, "the basis for ethical responsibility is not dutiful obedience to a law code, but an inward, personal response to Yahweh's sovereign deeds of kindness and benevolence."[780] Quoting another writer, Mussner says that, in Deuteronomy, the love of God is best expressed by the love of humanity, which is "not the simple expression of the morality of kinship[;] . . . rather it is theologically motivated by the love of YHWH for the people and for the stranger and rests, as the other commandments of YHWH, on the covenant relationship."[781]

That is, the Covenant Code is not a set of rules justified by the goal of survival, but a set of moral standards both driven by love and authorized by God. The Israelites are commanded to protect the poor and the exploited not because these people are literally their brothers and sisters, but because God is, as Karen Armstrong says, "on the side of the impotent and the oppressed." The point is that, although the idea needs no clarification or explanation in kinship groups, it does in more complex societies. In such situations, as Jesus later noted, people need to be reminded of their brotherhood and sisterhood—their *spiritual* kinship. Armstrong continues: In this sense, the God of Deuteronomy "is a God of revolution," who "has inspired an ideal of social justice."[782] As Marcus J. Borg explains, "social justice" in this context demands that "the social system as a whole" establish justice comprehensively, effectively, and systemically: "Do [the structures of society] produce a large impoverished class or result in a more favorable distribution of resources? Do they benefit some at the expense of many or serve all equally?"[783]

This is why, for many scholars, the Covenant Code in Deuteronomy is widely understood to be neither an add-on nor a supplement, but the very core of the book and the very heart of the Jewish religion. On the one hand, Ramsay argues, "We see the concept of covenant repeated over and over in the Bible until it is clear that it is the heart of the biblical faith."[784] On the other hand, however, it is clearly *in Deuteronomy* (as well as in the work of the prophets) that the importance of the Covenant is raised to this level. As Armstrong says, "In his last sermon, Moses is made to give a new centrality to the covenant and the idea of the special election of Israel."[785] That is, according to Anderson, "Deuteronomy, influenced in part by Hosea's message, returns to and deepens the meaning of the original Mosaic covenant. Yahweh's gracious and undeserved love, manifested in his deeds of benevolence on behalf of Israel (6:20–23), should awaken Israel's response: love of God and, as a corollary, love of fellow-men."[786]

T. G. Soares sees this view of God as the product of the ethical development of the Jews: "The advancing humaneness of the people under the influence of their religious leaders resulted"—especially in Deuteronomy—"in modifications of the harsher customs of the earlier days." Furthermore, "[t]he sense of kindness" led to an even stronger tendency to support the disenfranchised.[787] Roland de Vaux comments: "This code seems designed to replace the old code by taking account of a whole social and religious revolution; it also reveals a change in spirit by its appeals to the heart and by the tone of exhortation in which its prescriptions are often couched."[788] Ramsay says: "Deuteronomy echoes the cry of the prophets such as Micah 6:8. To love the Lord is to mirror the love of God. God had liberated them. Now Israel is to liberate the oppressed." In this regard, Ramsay adds, Deuteronomy looks like the founding document for "a constitutional monarchy," except for the important fact that it repeatedly calls for "that social justice which prophets such as Amos and Micah had proclaimed as the essence of the will of God."[789]

To Kaufmann, it was not the content of the Covenant Code that distinguished it from other ancient bodies of law. Rather, it was, as early as the events in Exodus, "a prophetic revelation, an expression of the supreme moral will of God." Furthermore, "God revealed himself not to a visionary, a priest, or a sage, but to a whole people."[790] Yet again, in the book of Exodus, in some sense the revelation comes and goes. The people go back to obeying two laws: one, from Genesis, trust in God; and one from Exodus, the first commandment, believe only and exclusively in Yahweh. On the brink of entering a world in which a community would be established, civic responsibilities expanded, and therefore *all* laws enforced, the Deuteronomist, like the prophets, "speak[s] impassionedly of guilt and the consequences of wrongdoing." Kaufmann goes on to say that this condemnation of sin "is not primitive, but rather the highest stage of morality, transcending the individual. Indeed, "[s]ociety has a duty to educate each member and look after his deeds . . . because society as a whole is under a covenant obligation to eradicate evil from its midst and cause justice to prevail."[791]

The Israelites could understand that necessity only because they had completed their journey through the wilderness. According to G. E. Wright, they began to see that "in the wilderness their forefathers became a people."[792] As Anderson says, they came to this realization, at least to some degree, even as early as their stay in Sinai: "Despite enemy attack, lack of food and water, and the murmurings of the people, the indomitable Moses led the pilgrims on until at last they staggered into the oasis of Sinai. Here they had an opportunity to reflect upon the experiences that had brought them together. Here they came to understand in a deeper way the nature of the community into which they had been called. The particular nature of this community is expressed in the covenant relationship between Yahweh and his people." Anderson adds later, "It is apparent, then, that 'the rabble' (Num. 11:4) under Moses' leadership did not become a stable, unified community overnight. A powerful, centripetal force, the redemptive action of Yahweh, had pulled them toward the center of a common covenant allegiance."[793]

Chapter Four

The Covenant

As I said in the introduction, Judaism is difficult to define. First, there is not now and never has been an officially approved doctrine of Judaism. Karen Armstrong says that, to the Pharisees, as to the Rabbis, "there was no single authoritative reading of scripture."[794] Catholics are Catholics insofar as they accept the Nicene Creed, and many Protestants identify themselves through the Westminster Confession, but Jews have no collectively and universally affirmed summary of their faith.[795] This is largely because there is not now and never has been an officially approved authority that could formulate such a doctrine. Presumably, all of the Jewish congregations in the world could get together and approve a creed or confession, but that has never occurred and probably never will. And, even if it happened, no one would have to pay any attention to it.

Josephus identified four different Jewish sects in Palestine in the time of Jesus (exclusive of the Samaritans, who self-identified as Jews), and even today there are not only Reform, Conservative, and Orthodox Jews, but also Hassids, Reconstructionists, Lubavitchers, and others. Thus, when Baruch Spinoza, the famous seventeenth-century philosopher, was excommunicated, he was merely excluded by his synagogue in Amsterdam and shunned by many of its members. He remained a Jew, however, simply because no established body of Jewish leaders had the power to deprive Spinoza of his Jewish identity. The question of who is a Jew is also complicated by the fact that the term has both a religious and an ethnic meaning. It can be said that Jews are Jews by birth, regardless of their devotion to one doctrine or another.

Second, as I also said in the introduction, since Judaism has been in existence for more than three thousand years, it has undergone numerous changes. Starting as members of a tribal religion, Jews worshiped many gods. During the monarchy, Mark S. Smith argues, they not only prayed to Yahweh, Baal, and Astarte, but also regarded the sun, moon, and stars as deities. Even when these many gods were conflated into one, called Yahweh, he was, for some time, considered to be one God among many. He was distinguished from other gods merely by the fact that he belonged to Israel alone.[796] The Jews saw him as other ancient people saw their tribal gods: as possessing human traits and features (anger and jealousy as well as body parts),[797] as properly worshiped by appeasement (ritual and sacrifice, including at first human sacrifice), and as indispensable for satisfying the needs of his followers (e.g., for winning wars and attaining prosperity). In short, the religion of the Jews was similar to what it was for other ancient people.[798] Somehow, instead of this more or less generic faith, Jews eventually came to see their God as moral and universal, developed an ethical code as a means of worship, and embraced the idea that God was a father who merited their love instead of a king who demanded their obedience. Even in this extraordinary transformation, Judaism underwent a change similar to that experienced by other first millennium BC religions, including those of China, India, Persia, and Greece.

Although Judaism strongly resembled other ancient religions at its birth and for several centuries afterward, it is unique because it developed a legal system that, at least as an ideal, has endured for centuries. The rules established by the Jews of the late second and early first millennia BC, known as the Covenant Code, were created to help this pre-urban agricultural society—which specialized in raising sheep, goats, and cattle and growing grapes, figs, and olives—to maintain its way of life by guaranteeing that people treated each other as brothers and sisters. As Roland de Vaux explains, this simply means that the Code was intended to preserve tribalism: "The clan had common interests and duties, and its members were conscious of the blood-bond which united them: they called each other 'brothers.'"[799]

Although the form of the Covenant was based on legal contracts and international treaties, it was, in fact, a spiritual agreement. As G. E. Wright says, "The major point to be noted is that God is known in his covenant as the great suzerain whose prior acts of love and mercy call forth a response of love and service from his people." In other words, the Covenant between God and his people was not a *quid pro quo* agreement in which both parties promise to exchange favors—*this* for *that*—but a statement of understanding that one party, the beneficiary of previous favors, will respond in kind out of gratitude. As Wright later explains, "the relationship is one of love and grace: as God has loved us, so we should love him with all our heart and soul and strength, for obedience must be rooted in love."[800]

This meant specifically that the Jews, who had benefitted from God's love, especially by being freed from slavery in Egypt, were forbidden to exploit each other. After all, they had been assured that, despite their poverty, they would not perish or even suffer irremediably. And, in recompense, they were required to do everything they could to maintain the integrity of their society. The rules themselves were not unique. In fact, they were indistinguishable from the rules of all cultures that were socially tribal, economically agricultural, and politically egalitarian—that is, ruled by elders in ordinary circumstances and, temporarily, by military leaders (called judges) when necessary. In this respect, John J. Collins says of the laws of Exodus, "they stand in the legal tradition of the ancient Near East" and represent, at best, "a modest advance over the Near Eastern precedent."[801]

Such laws would not have been accepted in the second millennium by Egypt, Babylonia, and Persia because these states were no longer tribal, no longer rural, and no longer led by elders. They were urban agricultural societies, characterized by class differentiations and dominated by kings who were protected by priests and warriors.[802] These laws were attractive in Israel and other pre-urban nations because, as Robert N. Bellah says, the consequences of "economic growth" that characterized societies transitioning from rural to urban were "destabilizing." Small farmers, who typically fell into debt and sometimes became dependent on money lenders, were ultimately "sold into slavery" or were bought out by large landowners. "All of this greatly undermined the effectiveness of the extended kinship system."[803] Again, the rules were unique because they were endowed with a longevity that enabled the prophets in the monarchial period as well as the followers of Jesus to appeal to a standard of ethics that actually existed in the distant past and could be revived to create a society or community similarly characterized by justice and mercy.[804]

To be sure, although the Covenant Code in Deuteronomy was purportedly written, as the code in Exodus was, for a society undergoing a transformation from rural to urban, the fifth book of the Pentateuch was actually "discovered" in the seventh century BC (2 Kgs, chs. 22–23), long after the urbanization of Samaria and Jerusalem and long after the glory days of the monarchy under David and Solomon. According to Benjamin Uffenheimer, the Code, which was amended "during the period of the First Commonwealth," was "meant to meet the conditions created by the process of urbanization, which reached its pinnacle during the reign of King Solomon and later on during the reign of the Omri dynasty in northern Israel." The "central provision" of the amendments—"the return of all lands to their original owners" (Lev 25)—was "designed to restore the original parceling of the country between the tribes according to their size at the time of the Israelite conquest." And "the ancient laws of inheritance (Num. 27:9–11; 36:1–9)" were intended to preserve "the ancestral plot" for individual landowners. Uffenheimer says that the laws pertaining to the "three concentric life cycles"—the Sabbath, the Sabbatical year, and the Jubilee—mandated recurrent social and economic attempts to re-establish the egalitarianism of tribal life and recall "the principle of freedom based upon the utopian social concept of divine kingship."[805]

By this time in Jewish history, Israel had fallen into the same state of corruption and exploitation that characterized other urban agricultural societies, many of which had suffered from the apparently inevitable problems of urbanization for more than a millennium. As Theodore H. Robinson explains, in the later ninth century BC, "there grew up a class of wealthy subjects who used their traditional liberty to amass fortunes for themselves." As a result, "a complete change had come over the social and economic structure of Israelite society. The old peasant of the Naboth type had almost completely disappeared, and the land was now parceled out into large estates, worked by tenant farmers or serf labor... There was a great gulf between [the absentee owner] and the actual workers, whose abject misery excited the pity of men like Amos and Isaiah, and called for their strong denunciations."[806]

A mere glance at the writings of the prophets not only underscores the prominence of these issues when Deuteronomy was presumably written, but also the negative influence on the fate of Israel fomented by both the political turmoil of the Middle East at the time and the failure of the Jewish monarchy to maintain the integrity of the Jewish faith and protect the Jewish state from foreign invasion and conquest, first by Assyria in the eighth century and by Babylonia in the sixth, the latter of which resulted in the destruction of the Jerusalem Temple and the city of Jerusalem itself. It should be understood that Deuteronomy was thus composed in a situation of extreme suffering and conflict and uncertainty. And the resurrection and revision of its central focus, the Covenant Code, must be understood to be an urgent "response to the momentous events" of the time, in James Muilenburg's words, which threatened to destroy the Jewish people, as well as their land and their religion. "The great events of the seventh and sixth centuries," says Muilenburg, "left their literary precipitate in the form of such works as" many psalms and prophecies, as well as "the Deuteronomic Code." "No period of comparable extent is so rich in biblical writings of the first importance."[807]

In this context, it is easy to understand why Deuteronomy may well be the most unusual book in the Jewish Bible. As von Rad explains, the Jews of the exilic and postexilic periods had a clear sense of their estrangement from God and an equally clear sense of its cause: "Our fathers sinned, and are no more; and we bear their iniquity," says the author of Lamentations (5:7), a sentiment echoed by many of the prophets. Israel engaged in this pervasive self-admonition, von Rad says, because the entire nation "looked on its relationship with God as threatened" and tried desperately to reverse the situation. Thus, like Isaiah and Jeremiah, the author of Deuteronomy pulls out all the stops and offers a plea for repentance that embodies in every aspect the sense of urgency that he clearly felt. Thus, the "Deuteronomic style, which is characterized by a ceaseless repetition of set phrases, is out and out paranetic, a wooing and imploring form of address." It is first of all an obviously "intensive preaching activity" that is a desperate "summons to obedience." Fulfilling this goal "in an extremely militant fashion," it is "pervaded by the feeling of a great anxiety lest Israel might possibly" ignore God's last offer of salvation.[808]

The clearest sign of the Deuteronomist's desperation is the extent and variety of Moses' inducements: first, the unity, comprehensiveness, and clarity of his message, which provides its audience with an unprecedented opportunity to understand God's demands fully and definitively; second, the most extravagant collection of promises and threats in the entire Bible, which appeals to the people's hopes and fears; third, the most heartfelt effort to remind them of God's steadfast love, which appeals to their sense of gratitude to God and their responsibilities to each other; fourth, strong assurances that their obligations in both categories are really quite easy to satisfy and should not be understood to be onerous; and, finally, a sympathetic picture of Moses, who, in his "farewell sermon" to Israel, is portrayed as neither a God-inspired miracle worker nor a heroic ("Promethean") defender of the people but as an obedient servant of Yahweh, and who endures without resistance the most extreme disappointment of all: God's refusal to allow him to enter the Promised Land. In short, Moses is presented as a model of what he is encouraging every Israelite to be—the faithful follower of God's will who earnestly and passionately urges his fellow Jews to adopt the love and devotion that he so persistently displays.

To the first point, von Rad says, "[N]ever again did [Israel] express herself so comprehensively and in such detail as to the meaning of the commandments and the unique situation into which Jahweh's revelation of his will put her." The Deuteronomist returns to the scene of God's most extraordinary saving act, his gift of the commandments at Mt. Sinai, which is intended to remind his readers that they are once again "between election and fulfilment." That is, "Israel is in very great danger of missing Jahweh's call to her." And what the author offers—"for once"—is "a work that has unity of thought, internal balance, and finish," an achievement that raises the question "when and where was Israel ever again able to clothe a great literary work in so completely uniform a style and diction?" It not only "bears one theological stamp throughout," it is "*the* revelation of Jahweh" because it is "an artistic mosaic" in which "is gathered the total expression of" Israel's past. Its unity is remarkable because it embraces "many originally independent traditions," which, "far from compromising the whole wealth of traditions," now characterizes a work that can legitimately be called "Torah" because it represents "something like a totality of teaching," a summary of *everything* the ancient Jews needed to know.

In what von Rad calls "lavish terms," Deuteronomy offers Israel a means of restoring its relationship to Yahweh and thereby earning a reward of unprecedented magnitude as well as avoiding a punishment equally unmatched elsewhere in the Bible. The reward is nothing less than "a paradise upon earth" since "it is in every respect the all-sufficient prerequisite of the perfect bliss of the people of God." Noting that "the saving blessings held out to the people are for the most part material—fertility in man and beast, peace from enemies, political greatness"—the Deuteronomist nevertheless makes every effort to underscore the idea (1) that the principal motivation for faith should not be hope and fear, but love, and (2) that the gifts God promises are a continuation of his past blessings, which should induce gratitude rather than expectation. As von Rad explains: "It would, however, be a mistake to take the land as the real subject of the Deuteronomic preaching. The constant logic of all these addresses is rather this: since Jahweh has shown you such faithfulness in all these matters, and will continue to do so, it is your duty to love him in return, and to keep his 'statutes and judgments.'"

That is, despite the Deuteronomist's blunt (and, indeed, over-the-top) appeal to motives lying somewhere between need and greed, he is—in agreement with scholars like G. E. Wright—opposed to the idea that the legalistic concept of *quid pro quo* is the moral foundation of the relationship between God and Israel. Thus, as von Rad points out, the legalism in Deuteronomy is itself at least one of the reasons that "the Deuteronomic preacher has so frequently to combat the idea of self-glorification," which would, of course, be the result of promoting the belief that salvation is a reward for obedience: "Israel is not to ascribe to her own prowess what she owes solely to the guidance of Jahweh" (8:17, 9:4-6). Indeed, "[t]his summons to gratitude lets us see the strength of the preacher's appeal to the inner disposition, in fact to the heart." Faced with "signs of a perilous weakening in the tradition of faith"—the loss of "an immediate relationship to the commandments and cultic regulations of Jahweh"—the Deuteronomist is compelled to "appeal all the more emphatically for the inward acceptance of the commandments." As the Shema makes clear (6:4), the writer of this book wanted to give its message "an inward reference," which he achieves by "laying it on heart and conscience." And his "unremitting call to 'remember' Jahweh, his commandments, his acts, etc., . . . corresponds to the urge for subjective actualisation."

According to von Rad, the principal means by which the importance of legalism is undermined (or at least diminished) in Deuteronomy, as Wright similarly argues, is the claim that God selected the Israelites *before* he imposed his requirements on them. That is, "the obedience which Deuteronomy demands is in no sense the prerequisite of election. The order is rather the reverse." God says to his people in chapter 27, "[T]his day you have become the people of the Lord your God. You shall therefore obey the voice of the Lord your God, keeping his commandments" (vv. 9-10). This obedience is thus not required in exchange for God's favor—his election of Israel as well as his liberation of them from slavery—but simply "Israel's return of the divine love bestowed upon her." In this sense, "[t]he many imperatives in Deuteronomy are therefore appeals . . . for gratitude to be shown in action." And the action is often *in*action since so many of God's commands require nothing more than the kind of restraint that societies typically demand of their members—against lust, greed, and selfishness—and which Deuteronomy considers "easy to fulfil." Thus, despite the fact that "there are a certain number of cases where the reception of the blessings of salvation is in actual fact conditional," they too "are prefaced by a declaration of Jahweh's election and his love."[809]

The Pentateuch Revisited

The Jewish Covenant, which is generally considered to be the main subject of Deuteronomy, was at first an agreement between God and Abraham. It was a contractual relationship in which each party promised to do something for the other. What we now call the Covenant Code, which spells out the rules of the Covenant, can be found in Exodus 21-23, Leviticus 17-26, and Deuteronomy 12-26. There is some evidence that some of these rules, like much of the rest of the Torah, were in force as early as 1200 BC, after the exodus and before the establishment of the Jewish monarchy. In fact,

Yehezkel Kaufmann says: "The whole political background of the Torah's narratives, laws, and songs points to the pre-conquest period. There is a promise of kingship, and a few allusions to events of the first days of the monarchy. But this is the limit of the Torah's historical horizon." Thus, except for I Samuel 10, "the Torah legislation reflects . . . the early 'kingdom of God,' based on the primitive democracy that existed in pre-monarchic Israel. The tribes are headed by chiefs; the people by a prophet-judge."[810] At this time, the Jews not only lived without a king, they also worked as independent farmers and dwelt in small villages. We know from the books of Joshua, Judges, and 1 Kings that such political and economic conditions prevailed before Saul, David, and Solomon became kings in the tenth and ninth centuries.[811]

We know from archeologists that the Israelites lived in villages in the hill country west of the Jordan, in which houses were similar in size; there was no class system; there were no palaces or temples or luxury goods; and the farmers were self-sufficient. According to Israel Finkelstein and Neil Asher Silberman, "The discovery of the remains of a dense network of highland villages–all apparently established within the span of a few generations—indicated that a dramatic social transformation had taken place in the central hill country of Canaan around 1200 BCE. There was no sign of violent invasion or even infiltration of a clearly defined ethnic group. Instead, it seemed to be a revolution in lifestyle. In the formerly sparsely populated highlands from the Judean hills in the south to the hills of Samaria to the north, far from the Canaanite cities that were in the process of collapse and disintegration, about two-hundred fifty hilltop communities suddenly sprang up. Here were the first Israelites." Furthermore, say the authors, "there is no evidence of social stratification in these villages, no sign of administrative buildings for officials, large residences of dignitaries, or the specialized products of highly skilled artisans."[812]

The Covenant Code consists of lists of commandments, which, as I said, had the general goal of preserving the communities of small farmers, helping them retain their land, and protecting them from exploitation or oppression by both residents (those who aspired to power and wealth) and outsiders (those who aspired to conquest and domination). According to Richard A. Horsley and Neil Asher Silberman, these laws "enabled the people of Israel to maintain a stable system of social relations, economic welfare, and local autonomy." Furthermore, these writers add: "These laws"—which also governed "property rights, personal morality, festivals, Sabbaths, and Sabbatical years"—were "not abstract religious dogma or standards of individual ethics." Rather, they provided the ancient Jews with "a down-to-earth constitution, a code of conduct and handbook of instructions by which they could survive on the land in their families and villages and perhaps even prosper in a challenging—if not overly productive—physical environment."[813]

Some of the laws had no doubt been in effect during the nomadic period, from the Exodus to the settlement of Canaan, but these mainly pertained to social relations and political concerns rather than economic issues, which increased significantly when the Jews became small farmers. All of the laws of the Covenant were based on two assumptions: (1) that obedience is an act of piety because God wants his children to obey him and (2) that compliance is a practical necessity insofar as the rules guarantee security and survival even without God's support. As God is quoted as saying in Deuteronomy, "There will . . . be no one in need among you, because the Lord is sure to bless you in the land that the Lord your God is giving you as a possession to occupy, if only you will obey the Lord your God by diligently observing this entire commandment that I command you this day" (15:4–5). Or, more simply, "You shall observe my statutes and faithfully keep my ordinances, so that you may live on the land securely" (Lev 25:18).

G. E. Wright says that the intention of the Holiness Code in Leviticus (17–26) is expressed in the words "Thou shalt love thy neighbor as thyself" (19:18). "This is the summary of the whole economic life of the people. The whole purpose of their economic and social life is that they shall love their neighbor, particularly the poor and unfortunate, by assisting them according to need."[814] Thus, people were encouraged to take care of widows, orphans, and strangers—that is, those who were likely to be indigent. At harvest time, for example, farmers were required to leave grain at the edges of their fields, as well as grapes on their vines for the poor: "When you reap the harvest of your land, you shall not reap your field to its very border, neither shall you gather the gleanings after your harvest. And you shall not strip your vineyard bare, neither shall you gather the fallen grapes; you shall leave them for the poor and for the sojourner: I am the Lord your God" (Lev 19:9–10). In Deuteronomy, these leavings are for "the sojourner, the fatherless, and the widow." And, for those who comply with this demand, "God [will] bless [them]in all the work of [their] hands." The act is not done to merit a reward, however; rather, it is an act of gratitude for what God has done for his people: "You shall remember that you were a slave in the land of Egypt; therefore I command you to do this" (24:19–22).

There were two additional methods by which the indigent were taken care of by members of the tribe. First, every seventh year—that is, every Sabbatical year—farmers were required to leave their land uncultivated, and the poor were welcome to reap the harvest. Although the fields might not yield much grain, at least the fruit trees would bear an abundant crop of grapes, olives, and figs. God says, "For six years you shall sow your land and gather in its yield; but the seventh year you shall let it rest and lie fallow, that the poor of your people may eat . . . You shall do likewise with your vineyard, and with your olive orchard" (Exod 23:10–11).[815]

Second, in an attempt to help the indigent more often, every third year, instead of every seventh year, farmers had to pay a tithe to support the Levites as well as the poor. God says through Moses in Deuteronomy, "[Y]ou shall take some of the first of all the fruit of the ground which you harvest from your land that God gives you, and you shall put it in a basket, and you shall go to the place which the Lord will choose, to make his name to dwell there." The gift is given to "the Levite, the sojourner, the

The Covenant

fatherless, and the widow" (26:2, 12). The poor "shall come and eat and be filled; that the Lord your God may bless you in all the work of your hands that you do" (15:29).

Not only were these groups to be taken care of in terms of their needs; in fact, people were forbidden to abuse them in any way whatsoever. God says, "You shall not wrong a stranger or oppress him, for you were strangers in the land of Egypt. You shall not afflict any widow or orphan. If you do afflict them, and they cry out to me, I shall surely hear their cry." The punishment for this sin is neither a warning nor a mere chastisement, but death: "[A]nd my wrath will burn, and I will kill you with the sword, and your wives shall become widows and your children fatherless" (Exod 22:21–24). The need to protect strangers is reiterated in Exodus 23:9; in Leviticus, God says that "the stranger who sojourns with you shall be to you as the native among you, and you shall love him as yourself" (19:34). In Amos, God says he will punish Israel for these transgressions: "[T]hey sell the righteous for silver, and the needy for a pair of shoes—they that trample the head of the poor into the dust of the earth, and turn aside the way of the afflicted" (2:6–7). In addition, God will punish the Samarians "who oppress the poor, who crush the needy." They will be picked up with fishhooks and "cast forth into Harmon" (4:1–3). Concerning those who are disabled or old, God says in Leviticus, "You shall not curse the deaf or put a stumbling block before the blind" (19:14), and you shall respect the aged: "You shall rise up before the hoary head, and honor the face of an old man" (19:32).

It was also mandatory for people to care for clan members who were indigent, for whatever reason. As Roland de Vaux explains, "The members of the family in this wider sense had an obligation to help and protect one another. There was in Israel an institution which defined the occasions when this obligation called for action; it is the institution of the *go-el*," which basically means "to protect."[816] Thus, God says in Leviticus, "If your brother [i.e., your kinsman] becomes poor, and sells part of his property, then his next of kin [presumably, the *go-el*] shall come and redeem what his brother has sold." However, the obligations did not end with that act of largesse. "If your brother becomes poor, and cannot maintain himself with you, you shall maintain him; as a stranger and sojourner, he shall live with you." If he "sells himself" to his brother, his brother cannot "make him serve as a slave." He shall become "a hired servant" and then be freed after a number of years. At that time, he will leave with his children "and go back to his family, and return to the possession of his fathers." The idea is that kinsmen cannot rule over kinsmen "with harshness," but, clearly, must treat them only with kindness and generosity. Finally, if your kinsman "becomes poor and sells himself" to pay off his debts, "then after he is sold he may be redeemed; one of his brothers may redeem him, or his uncle, or his cousin may redeem him, or a near kinsman belonging to his family may redeem him; or if he grows rich he may redeem himself" (Lev 25: 25, 35–41, 47–49).

The special attention paid to relatives in these passages reminds us that the entire Covenant Code, especially the care and concern shown for the helpless, is a characteristic feature of the rules governing tribal societies at all times and in all places. It is important to remember that nomadic tribes, whose members are almost always related to each other by blood, treat each other on the basis of kinship. This means that, without class differences, participating in similar tasks, and interacting on the principle of reciprocity, tribal members are inclined to take responsibility for each other, especially close family members. "The primitive pastoral life," says T. G. Soares, ". . . was simple in its social structure. The wealth of the clan was practically held in common, although the head would determine the proportions in which it should be enjoyed by the various members . . . There was no beggar or pauper; all shared the fortunes of all."[817] de Vaux adds: "The bond of blood, real or supposed, creates a certain solidarity among the members of a tribe . . . This solidarity is seen above all in the group's duty to protect its weak and oppressed members."[818]

The same rules remained in place even when the Jews settled among the Canaanites and adopted an agricultural lifestyle. Since they found fertile fields that enabled them to raise grain, fruit, and beans as well as continue to feed their cows, goats, and sheep, they were able to transform their economic system. Nevertheless, although in the long run this change brought about many difficulties that arose inevitably out of agriculturalism, many aspects of their culture stayed the same. The blood bond, says de Vaux, "is a very strong feeling, and persists long after the settlement in Canaan."[819] Susan Niditch notes that "village life in the agricultural and pastoral modes continued to flourish throughout Israel's history." Even during the monarchy "the vast majority of people continued to live in villages," which means that "kinship ties based in village life and the bonds of kinship groups to ancestral lands must have remained important in the sociology of ancient Israel."[820]

Over time, however, family ties slowly weakened; orphans and widows depended more and more on the solidarity of the clan or tribe, rather than the family; and variations in personal skill, work habits, and luck resulted in widening gaps between rich and poor. Ironically, under these circumstances, the Covenant rules, emphasizing collective responsibility for the less fortunate, became even more important than they had been during the nomadic period. As de Vaux says, "The social ideal was that every man should live 'under his vine and under his fig tree'" (Mic 4:4, Zech 3:10).[821]

However, it was not only widows and orphans who became indigent, in which cases they had lost a husband or a father. It was also entire families who, because of the economic uncertainties inherent in agricultural ventures, lost their family farms and therefore lost their livelihood. Niditch says: "Life on the frontier would have been difficult, plagued by drought, mudslides on the terraces, competition from other settlers, and roving bandits. This form of subsistence agriculture does tend to make for a high level of interaction and cooperation between the genders." To be sure, these conditions changed when, "[b]y the mid-tenth century B.C.E., Israelites had made the transition from a society of kinship-based groups . . . to a young state."[822] de Vaux explains: "Alienation of family property and the development of lending at interest led to the growth of pauperism and enslavement of defaulting debtors or their dependents. This destroyed that social equality which had existed at the time of the tribal federation and which still remained as an ideal."[823]

Even before these changes occurred, the Covenant Code had addressed the causes directly. In these documents, people were encouraged to lend needy persons money (or its equivalent in goods) when they faced adverse circumstances, natural (as in drought) or human (as in a creditor demanding a loan payment). God says in Deuteronomy that lending is to be done in a generous and inoffensive manner: "If there is among you a poor man, . . . open your hand to him, and lend him sufficient for his need, whatever it may be. Take heed lest there be a base thought in your heart . . . You shall give to him freely, and your heart shall not be grudging, when you give to him" (15:7–10).

Three other laws represented an attempt to prevent the negative effects of exploitative lending. First, in all of the codes, lending with interest is recognized as a serious social problem and is therefore strictly forbidden. God says in Exodus, "If you lend money to any of my people with you who is poor, you shall not be to him as a creditor, and you shall not exact interest from him" (22:25). God tells Moses in Leviticus that a poor man cannot be charged interest on loans or provided with food "for profit" (25:36). And in Deuteronomy, the prohibition applies not just to the poor, but to everyone: "You shall not lend upon interest to your brother, interest on money, interest on victuals, interest on anything that is lent for interest" (25:19).

To the prophet Ezekiel, righteousness includes, among many other virtues, "not lend[ing] at interest." (18:8). Indeed, this sin is the equivalent of shedding blood or committing extortion (22:12). de Vaux says, "When an Israelite fell on hard times and was reduced to borrowing, he should have found help among his clan or tribe. Lending to the poor is a good deed," as the psalmist makes clear: "[T]he righteous is generous and gives . . . He is ever giving liberally and lending" (37:21, 26; see also Ps 112:5). And he does not charge interest on his loans: "All this concerns loans without interest," says de Vaux, "the only kind of loan allowed by the Code of the Covenant" and in Psalm 15, wherein the righteous man is, among other things, one "who does not put out his money at interest" (v. 5).[824]

Second, items used as collateral for loans were sometimes not returned to the borrower although they were often meant to be merely symbolic pledges.[825] Ezekiel says that a righteous man "restores to the debtor his pledge" (18:7). In the Covenant Code, indispensable goods, such as cloaks and mill-wheels, were either forbidden for this use or required to be returned by nightfall: "If ever you take your neighbor's garment in pledge, you shall restore it to him before the sun goes down; for that is his only covering, it is his mantle for his body; in what else shall he sleep? And if he cries to me, I will hear, for I am compassionate" (Exod 22:26–27; Deut 24:12–13).[826] "No man shall take a mill or an upper millstone in pledge; for he would be taking a life [i.e., a livelihood] in pledge" (Deut 24:10). To be sure, there were more extreme cases.

Job complains that the wicked "take the widow's ox for a pledge" and even "take in pledge the infant of the poor" (24: 3, 9). Third, lenders, who were evidently inclined to be rude and imposing, were required to act in a generous and inoffensive manner. For example, they could not burst into someone's house and demand collateral but had to wait politely outdoors: "When you make your neighbor a loan of any sort, you shall not go into his house to fetch his pledge. You shall stand outside, and the man to whom you made the loan shall bring the pledge out to you" (Deut 24:10–11).

Although many of these laws may have been written before the monarchy, they remained relevant because Israel often dealt with economic adversity, especially in the post-exilic period. In the fifth century BC, for example, the Jews—led by the governor, Nehemiah, in the midst of building a wall around Jerusalem—suffered not only from the distraction of that project and defending themselves against their enemies, but also from famine. Their concerns were typical of the kinds of issues faced by residents of monarchial societies, particularly, as in this case, under the rule of foreign kings. The people complained: "We have borrowed money for the king's tax upon our fields and our vineyards . . . [W]e are forcing our sons and daughters to be slaves, and some of our sons and some of our daughters have already been enslaved; but it is not in our power to help it, for other men have our fields and our vineyards." Nehemiah says that he called together "the nobles and the officials" and accused them of charging interest and appropriating land. "I and my brethren and my servants are lending [the people] money and grain. Let us leave off this interest. Return to them this very day their fields, their vineyards, their olive orchards, and their houses," as well as the taxes the people had already paid (Neh 5:1–12). In this instance, Nehemiah's nobles and officials agreed to comply.

In the days of the prophets, if not earlier, the Covenant Code touched on two other concerns that affected the day-to-day lives of ordinary people. First, people were required to treat employees and servants fairly and humanely. Foreign slaves had the benefit of living with the family who owned them and had at least a chance to develop personal relationships with their masters. Although servants and slaves existed in Israel in the nomadic period, hired workers were a rare phenomenon, even when Jews first established an agrarian society in Canaan. As villages turned into cities and as small-landowners lost their farms because of debt or disaster, the number of laborers increased. Soares says: "The lot of the hireling was a hard one. He was practically at the mercy of his employer, for he had little opportunity to appeal to the courts of justice."

Thus, Soares continues, "[i]n both the Deuteronomic and Levitical Codes it was found necessary to require that the laborer should receive his wages at the end of the day": "You shall not oppress a hired servant who is poor and needy; whether he is one of your brethren or one of the sojourners who are in your land within your towns; you shall give him his hire on the day he earns it, before the sun goes down (for he is poor, and sets his heart upon it); lest he cry against you to the Lord, and it be sin in you" (Deut 24:15; see also Lev 19:13).[827] A glance at the writings of the prophets reveals that workers suffered because they were sometimes abused and either paid late or not at all. Jeremiah says, "Woe to him who builds his house by unrighteousness and his upper rooms by injustice; who makes his neighbor serve him for nothing, and does not give him his wages." This kind of person is guilty of "dishonest gain," "shedding innocent blood," and "practicing oppression and violence" (22:13, 17). Job's lament for the circumstances in which laborers worked indicates that they were sometimes denied the leavings in fields and orchards, possessed neither clothing nor shelter, and went hungry and thirsty despite working as food gatherers and processors (24:6–12).

Unlike slaves in the most economically advanced and highly urbanized societies in the Middle East—Egypt, Persia, and Mesopotamia—slaves in ancient Israel (at least before the monarchy) were not, except under the rule of foreign powers, employed by the state to construct public buildings, in which cases, they were treated, almost inevitably, impersonally and insensitively. According to Soares, "The more common slavery [in Israel] was agricultural and domestic, where the servants as members of the patriarchal household carried on the duties of the house and farm, and were comfortably cared for and generally kindly treated." This was more likely to be the case, however, for Hebrew slaves rather than foreign ones. The former, who became slaves (or, more accurately, indentured servants) because they lost their patrimony, were "the subjects of increasing consideration in the various codes of law."[828] "Hebrew slaves," according to Exodus, "shall serve six years, and in the seventh shall go out free, for nothing" (21:2). In Leviticus, the release comes not in the Sabbatical year, but at the Jubilee, the fiftieth year, at which time many other reversals are to occur (25:40–41). In Deuteronomy, the freed slave (or indentured servant) not only goes free, but he is generously provided for by his master at the end of six years: "[Y]ou shall furnish him liberally out of your flock, out of your threshing floor, and out of your wine press" (15:12–14).

Foreign or alien slaves were less highly regarded, although they were not unprotected by the law. On the one hand, "[t]hese captives male and female became perpetual bond servants and their children after them." That is, they were slaves for life. God says to Moses: "As for your male and female slaves whom you may have: you may buy male and female slaves from among the nations that are around about you. You may also buy from among the strangers who sojourn with you and their families that are with you, who have been born in your land; and they may be your property." These slaves and their children can be passed on to the slave owner's children (25:44–45).

On the other hand, however, foreign slaves gained certain rights because they were required to be circumcised (Gen 17:12–13), in which case they could participate in the Sabbath (Exod 20:10), the Passover seder (Exod 12:44), and, Soares says, "all the [other] festivals which were joyously celebrated by the Hebrew family (Deut 12. 12, 18; 16. 11–14)." The rule that limits the punishment that may be imposed on owners who beat their slaves to death seems harsh because by modern standards it is: "When a man strikes his slave, male or female, with a rod and the slave dies under his hand, he shall be punished," unless the slave survives a day or two, in which case the owner escapes any punishment (Exod 21:20–21). However, it should be remembered, since slaves were universally considered to be their owners' private property, even this small attempt to hold owners responsible for their lethal actions was exceptional.[829]

The other area in which the Covenant Code benefitted people in ancient Israel is related to the justice system, which underwent a significant change when the Jews settled in Canaan. The system that had been in place was typical of nomadic societies. Judicial issues were decided more or less informally by tribal chiefs or elders. There was little concern about the adequacy of these judges because there were no great differences in the ability of tribal members to influence the administration of justice. A problem arose, however, when the ancient Jews became farmers and were sooner or later faced with disparities in wealth and power. Soares comments: "As soon as some members of the group become stronger than others they have the ability to exercise oppression. There must be some umpire to whom to appeal."[830]

The first solution to this problem was to establish a court system: "You shall appoint judges and officers in all your towns which the Lord your God gives you, according to your tribes; and they shall judge the people with righteous judgment" (Deut 16:18).[831] The second solution was to establish guidelines to prevent the perversion of justice, particularly by protecting the poor. According to George Foot Moore, the effort was successful: "Nowhere is the endeavor to develop the highest possible principles of the Law in ordinances and regulations more conspicuous than in the sphere of judicial procedure."[832]

In these circumstances, according to de Vaux, the intention was less to punish wrong-doers than to protect the innocent, especially the weak and helpless: "The role of the judge . . . was not so much to impose a sentence as to settle a dispute while respecting justice. He was more a defender of right than a punisher of crime."[833] Thus, many of the laws of the Covenant Code remind everyone of their responsibilities to those who are vulnerable to oppression and exploitation. God says in Exodus, "You shall not pervert the justice due to your poor in his suit. Keep far from a false charge, and do not slay the innocent and righteous, for I will not acquit the wicked" (23:6–7). In Deuteronomy, God says through Moses that everyone who is vulnerable to abuse should be protected: "You shall not pervert the justice due to the sojourner or to the fatherless" (25:17). Isaiah addresses the problem this way: "Woe to those who decree iniquitous decrees, and the writers who keep writing oppression, to turn aside the needy from justice and to rob the poor of my people of their right, that widows may be their spoil, and that they may make the fatherless their prey!" (10:1–2).

Of course, it was not enough to create a judicial system and identify the principles by which it should operate. It was also necessary to make sure that people who actually participated in the system acted fairly.[834] In the circumstances described by Isaiah, judges were under pressure to favor the rich over the poor and the powerful over the powerless. Indeed, Soares says, it was "probably" this problem that inspired the creation of the Book of the Covenant in the first place: "The official judges were peculiarly liable to venality. The development of the landed nobility, the sharpening of the contrast between the rich and the poor, the entrance into the social stage of commercialism—all these things gave opportunities to the judge to render valuable services to litigants who were in a position to give him a bribe."[835]

Thus, the Covenant laws urge judges to maintain their impartiality and both plaintiffs and defendants to refrain from exercising undue influence. God says to judges in Leviticus, "You shall do no injustice in judgment; you shall not be partial to the poor or defer to the great, but in righteousness shall you judge your neighbor" (19:15). In Exodus, God charges judges not to take bribes, "for a bribe blinds the officials, and subverts the cause of those who are in the right" (23:8). In Deuteronomy, judges are once again asked not only to avoid taking bribes, but also to maintain impartiality: "Justice, and only justice, you shall follow, that you may live and inherit the land which the Lord your God gives you" (16:19–20).

The other participants in any trial were the witnesses, who were also susceptible to outside influence and in danger of violating a general prohibition against slander: "You shall not go up and down as a slanderer among the people, and you shall not stand forth against the life of your neighbor" (Lev 19:16).[836] This was evidently a major problem since God addresses it in the ninth commandment: "You shall not bear false witness against your neighbor" (Exod 20:16). God says later in Exodus, suggesting that a witness could be swayed by either an interested party or public opinion : "You shall not utter a false report. You shall not join hands with a wicked man, to be a malicious witness. You shall not follow a multitude, to do evil; nor shall you bear witness in a suit, turning aside after a multitude, so as to pervert justice" (23:1–2).

In Deuteronomy, the violation of this law is addressed in more detail, and the violator is threatened with severe punishment: "If a malicious witness rises against any man to accuse him of wrongdoing, then both parties to the dispute shall appear before the Lord, before the priests and the judges who are in office in those days;[837] the judges shall inquire diligently, and if the witness is a false witness and has accused his brother falsely, then you shall do to him as he had meant to do to his brother; so you shall purge the evil from the midst of you." In other words, the false witness is to receive the punishment that would have been given to the victim of the falsehood. And the punishment is severe because the goal is to prevent this crime (and sin) from being repeated by others: "And the rest shall hear, and fear, and shall never again commit any such evil among you." The operative principle here, of course, is the *lex talionis*: "Your eye shall not pity; it shall be life for life, eye for eye, tooth for tooth, hand for hand, foot for foot" (19:15–21).[838]

There were, of course, some aspects of the Covenant Code that were not duplicated elsewhere in the Middle East at the end of the second millennium BC and the beginning of the first. Kaufmann says that, "[d]espite the existence of class divisions among the people, particularly in late monarchic times, Israelite law—as distinct from other ancient Near Eastern law—recognizes no class privileges. Slaves apart, the law makes no distinction between patrician and plebeian, rich and poor, propertied and proletariat."[839] G. E. Wright comments: "[T]he covenant theology meant that the Near Eastern common law in Israel had to be revised in such a way as to provide for the equality of all citizens before the court of law . . . In Israel, . . . all classes of society, no matter what their social status may have been, were included" in the application of the *lex talionis*.[840]

Furthermore, punishments for violations of Covenant laws were generally less harsh than violations of such laws elsewhere in the region. de Vaux says that the Covenant "is distinguished from other Eastern codes . . . by the humaneness of its sentences. Bodily mutilation is exacted only in one very special case (Dt 25: 11–12) . . . Flogging is limited to forty strokes, 'lest the bruises be dangerous and your brother be degraded' (Dt 25:3)." Furthermore, Werner H. Schmidt adds: "Contrary to widespread false impression, OT criminal law is by no means based universally on the principle of talion, that is, "the principle of requital for an injury by an exactly similar injury done to the offender . . . Requital of like with like—a life for a life, an eye for an eye, a tooth for a tooth—comes into play only in connection with particular crimes among particular persons (Exod 21:22f.; Lev 24:17ff.; cf. Deut 19:15ff.)."[841]

The *lex talionis*, de Vaux explains, universal in the region, "seems to have lost its force" in Israel because it was usually replaced by "the principle of proportionate compensation," which applied, for example, to "a wound inflicted in a fight." The penalty was "payment of compensation and medical expenses (Ex 21:18–19)." In fact, "[o]nly in one case is strict retaliation exacted: the guilty murderer must die and cannot buy his freedom" (Num 35: 31–32; Deut 19:11–12).[842] God also spends a good deal of time carefully distinguishing between what modern criminologists might call first- and second-degree murder, the first of which is punishable by death while the other requires exile to a city of refuge (Num 35:9–34).

The Covenant Code was also distinguishable from other contemporary legal codes because, although other societies' laws were believed to have come from a divine source (e.g., Shamash, god of justice in Babylonia, gave the law to King Hammurabi), only Israel claimed that God was not just the source of Jewish laws, but also the *partner* in the Covenant with his people. As de Vaux explains: "[S]ince these pacts governed Israel's dependence on Yahweh, not on a human suzerain, the Israelite law, for all its resemblances in form and content, differs radically from the clauses of the Oriental 'treaties' and the articles of their 'codes'. It is a religious law. It establishes the principles of the Covenant with Yahweh: its aim was to ensure that this covenant remained in force . . . God was not merely a guarantor of the Covenant"—as he was in Hittite, Assyrian, and Babylonian codes—"he was a party to it, and no Oriental code can be compared with the Israelite law, which is ascribed in its entirety to God as its author."[843]

Furthermore, G. E. Wright argues, the law "was not God's special gift to [the king] alone. He was as subject to it as was the nation as a whole." For this reason,

The Covenant

"[t]otalitarianism was lifted from the earthly to the heavenly sphere. The law thus envisaged a security and a freedom for the individual, who was not to be unrighteously oppressed by human power."⁸⁴⁴ According to de Vaux, this is also why, "[u]nlike all other Eastern laws, its prescriptions are often supported by a justifying motive," which could be practical, moral, or historical. The last of the three is most commonly a reference to the fact that God liberated the Jews from slavery in Egypt. That is the principal rationale for kindness to both slaves and sojourners: The Israelites were slaves before and sojourners after that event.⁸⁴⁵

Another difference between the Jewish code of laws and all others derives from the fact that the leader of Israel had no legislative power. Before the establishment of the monarchy at the end of the eleventh century, Israel was ruled, in the loosest possible sense, by figures whose primary roles were judge and warrior. And after Israel acquired a monarch, he was not endowed with the power to make laws. Thus, while in other Middle Eastern countries the laws were attributed to and enforced by an earthly king, in pre-monarchial Israel the laws were attributed *only* to God. de Vaux says: "In Israel, . . . the historical books never allude to any legislative power of the king." That is, "the king could add nothing to the authority of a law to which he himself was subject."⁸⁴⁶ "The tribes do not go the way of their neighbors and establish a monarchy," Kaufmann says, "because they believe simply and strongly that YHWH rules them through his messengers." On the one hand, a group of leaders "arose out of the ancient tribal council of elders" and ruled in "normal times." On the other hand, "in time of trouble the people looked for the appearance of an apostle-savior," who, starting with Moses and ending with Samuel, "represent the kingdom of God."⁸⁴⁷

In these circumstances, it is not surprising that, when the monarchy was established in Israel, it was limited as no other monarchy in the Near East was. Again, Wright says that God gave the law not to the king, but to the people. Thus, he "could never have the absolute power over the people which other kings of the day had." This meant, specifically, that the king could neither appropriate land nor suppress dissent. As Wright explains: "Law could not be set aside in Israel by the king as it could be set aside in the totalitarian Canaanite regime . . . Ancestral law was hallowed and private right was respected in Israel."⁸⁴⁸ Furthermore, as Moshe Weinfeld explains, the Assyrians assumed that "the emperor's actions always reflect[ed] the will of his god, while Isaiah makes a clear distinction between the divine mission and the human fulfillment of it."⁸⁴⁹ As the writer of 2 Kings says repeatedly of the kings who governed the Jews after David: They "did what was evil in the sight of the LORD."

King Ahab, for example, was unable to either purchase or seize Naboth's vineyard (I Kgs 21). And the prophet Nathan could publicly (and with impunity) accuse King David of murder and adultery (2 Sam 12:9). As everyone knew, de Vaux says, "[t]he monarchical institutions produced . . . a class of officials who drew a profit from their posts and the favours granted them by the king." Thus, everyone knew what to expect when kingship was instituted in Israel. And the prophets inveighed against them when they arrived on the scene: "The rich were found mostly among the influential people, and many passages in the Prophets condemn the two together."[850] Speaking of the author of I and II Kings, Wright says, "[O]ur historian proceeds to describe the procession of Israel's kings"—that is, after David. "His purpose is to interpret Israel's life under the monarchy, and his judgment is that the institution was a virtual failure."[851] Second, the ancient Jews maintained the belief that, no matter what political system they established, they would remain under the kingship of God. Evidently, the compromise they worked out was to accept, in the face of external threats, the need for a permanent leader and the need as well, given their loyalty to the *real* King, to impose serious limits on his authority.

Three passages in the Jewish Bible stand out as indications that the ancient Jews only slowly and reluctantly accepted monarchy, perhaps for two reasons. First, in the pre-monarchial period, they could easily see in the surrounding societies that kings were, all too often, a threat to the kind of personal freedom they had enjoyed under the rule of elders and judges. Furthermore, in the post-monarchial period, the Jews could easily look back at their own history and conclude that the Jewish experience with kingship was an almost complete disaster. As Gerhard von Rad explains, "The king actually did conscript the young men of the country population in order to put them on his garrisons as regular soldiers. He laid hands on landed property to set up estates of his own throughout the country; and from the country population, too, he drew the labour forces for these estates. Other landed property he confiscated as rewards for his henchmen (I Sam. xxii. 7). He taxed the whole population to defray the expenses of his court (I Kings iv. 7, xx. 15): indeed, even womenfolk were not safe from his requisition for he needed them as perfumers, cooks, and bakers."[852]

In the book of Judges, Gideon is visited by an angel of God and commanded to drive the Midianites out of northern Palestine. Several points in the narrative are worth noting insofar as they illustrate the dominance of God and the subordination of his earthly representatives. First, Gideon is not a self-appointed ruler who was driven by a quest for power. Rather, he is chosen by God, whose angel says to him, "The Lord is with you, you mighty man of valor." Second, unimpressed by the angel's praise, Gideon says to the angel: "Pray, sir, if the Lord is with us, why then has all this befallen us?" Third, Gideon asks why he has been chosen since he is hardly a man of "might." His clan is "the weakest in Manasseh," and he is "the least in [his] family." Furthermore, he has been interrupted in the rather humble act of "beating out wheat in the wine press, to hide it from the Midianites."

Fourth, Gideon demands that the angel prove his divine identity by undergoing no fewer than three tests: "[S]how me a sign that it is thou who speakest with me." Fifth, although Gideon accepts God's command that he destroy the altar of Baal and construct an altar to God, he performs these acts at night "because he was too afraid of his family and the men of the town to do it by day." Sixth, Gideon accepts God's command that he cut his army in half so that everyone will recognize his victory as entirely

The Covenant

the work of God. Seventh, Gideon is empowered *solely* by the Holy Spirit: "{T}he spirit of the Lord took possession of" him. And eighth, Gideon turns down the request "from the men of Israel" that he assume the kingship of Israel. He says, conspicuously as a representative of the Kingdom of God, "I will not rule over you, and my son will not rule over you; *the Lord will rule over you*" (6:7—8:23; my emphasis). Indeed, every detail of the story is obviously intended to demonstrate that Gideon is not a hero in the traditional sense, but entirely an instrument of God. In fact, God chooses a man who, though sometimes skeptical and even defiant, is essentially weak, humble, timid, and equivocal. Clearly, the kingdom is *God's, not Gideon's.*

In Deuteronomy, before he describes the kind of kingship he will allow, God establishes a court of appeals, the pinnacle of his judicial system. It will be centrally located, run by Levitical priests, and empowered to make final and unchallengeable decisions. In other words, this is a religiously grounded court that preserves the traditional Israelite theocracy against the secular power of the king.[853] This idea is stated unequivocally since, after saying four times that the judgments of this court are absolute, God warns: "The man"—presumably including the king—"who acts presumptuously, by not obeying *the priest who stands to minister there before the Lord your God, or the judge*, that man shall die; so you shall purge the evil from Israel. And all the people shall hear, and fear, and not act presumptuously" (17:8–13; my emphasis). Then (and only then), God says to Moses that, if the people decide to have a king, he must be someone whom "the Lord your God will choose."

Furthermore, God insists that the king may not have too many horses, too many wives, or too much silver and gold. In order to make sure that the king does not depart from these restrictions, God says that "he shall write for himself in a book a copy of this law." And the king is not to read it only once, but "all the days of his life." The purpose of this demand is to make sure that the king remains conscious of his subservience to God and continues to obey God's rules—that is, "that he may learn to fear the Lord his God, by keeping all the words of this law and these statutes, and doing them." Indeed, the king must remain aware that he is really no better than *anyone* else—"that his heart may not be lifted up above his brethren, and that he may not turn aside from the commandment" (17:14–20). The point is that, whereas the decision of the judicial priest is totally binding, the decision-making power of the king is circumscribed. *He can neither make the law nor change it.*

In I Samuel, God goes into even greater detail regarding the restrictions he imposes on the future King of Israel.[854] The story begins with "the elders of Israel," who, noting that Samuel is old and that his sons "do not walk in [his] ways," implore him to "appoint for [them] a king to govern [them] like all the nations." As a traditionalist, abiding by the practices in place in pre-monarchial times, the "displeased" Samuel prays for guidance from God, who tells him to obey the elders' wishes and not to feel hurt, "for they have not rejected you, but they have rejected me from being their king over them." Though granting the elders' request, God nevertheless requires Samuel to "solemnly warn them, and show them the ways of the king who shall reign over them."

According to God himself, the prospective king is not merely, like the prospective king in Deuteronomy, subject to extraordinary temptations—i.e., to accumulate horses, wives, and precious metals. He will be, according to Samuel's warning to the elders, which is stated in "all the words of the Lord," not just tempted, but ineluctably and insatiably gluttonous and acquisitive and possessive. The king will take their sons and use them as horsemen, commanders, farmers, and weapons-makers; he will take their daughters and use them in a variety of tasks; he will take their fields, vineyards, and orchards; and he will take their servants and animals. Finally, Samuel says to the elders, "[A]nd you shall be his slaves."[855] They will cry out, "but the Lord will not answer [them] in that day." The story ends with the elders' refusal to drop their demand and God's acquiescence: "Hearken to their voice and make them a king" (8:1–21).[856]

The Prophets

Although hostility to the idea of monarchy is not frequently expressed in the Jewish Bible, its importance is nevertheless underscored by the persistent judgment against the kings of Israel from the reign of Solomon to the reign of Josiah. Bernhard W. Anderson comments: "Not one king of Israel escapes the historian's blacklist, and his judgment falls pretty severely on the kings of Judah too. Only two southern kings (Hezekiah and Josiah) come off with a clean record; six receive a grade of only 'passing,' . . . and ten 'flunk.'"[857] G. Ernest Wright says, "With king after king the historian [in II Kings] affirms," as I said earlier, "that he 'did evil in the sight of the Lord' and led the people to do evil" (e.g., 15:18, 24; 16:2; 17:2; 21:2, 20), Later, Wright adds, "God's controversy with the kings of his people had come to an end with the destruction of the monarchy, temple, and state. The history of Israel within her land had begun with hope and triumph and promise and conquest. It ends in sadness, bloodshed, and destruction."[858]

In this context, it is important to note, as Roland de Vaux reminds us, "that apart from [Deuteronomy 17:14–20] the king is nowhere mentioned in the Deuteronomic Code."[859] Speaking of the warning against kingship in I Samuel, anomalous as that passage may be in this and subsequent books of the Bible, the editors of *The Oxford Annotated Bible* comment: "The evils described here and in the Deuteronomy passage seem to be mainly those of the reign of Solomon, and it is probable that the resentment against the monarchy arose at this time and never ceased, becoming a part of the thought of many of the prophets and of the Deuteronomic writers." Later, referring to I Kings 11:1–43, which describes "the dark side of Solomon's reign,"—and in which God's dissatisfaction with Solomon is clearly stated (11:9)—the same editors say that "the writers knew the tragedies that followed . . . and sought to probe their causes. In this connection, Deut. 17:14–20, from the same school of writers, should be carefully considered" (340, 432).

Indeed, according to Daniel C. Maguire, this resentment initiated a revolution—or at least a return to the revolution that had been interrupted by the monarchy: "For two hundred remarkable years, this revolution worked until Israel succumbed to temptations of royalty. Then the prophets rose to protest the decadence and recall the original vision."[860] That is, as Werner Schmidt says, "The prophets became corrective critics of the kings."[861] Gaalyah Cornfeld comments: "There was a fundamental conflict between prophets and kings, which grew more intense toward the end of the Kingdom of Judah. Although the relationship went back to the beginnings of the monarchy in Israel (e.g., Samuel and Saul and David), there were basic tensions and difficulties as royal policies and practices diverged more and more from prophetic standards of divine righteousness."[862] Von Rad explains: "If we bear in mind that the great period of the prophetic movement, which runs from the ninth to the seventh century B.C., can be described as an era of internal disintegration, in which political and economic life had long ago asserted their independence and autonomy, and in which Jahwism was already precariously thrown back on the defensive and now found its representative only in the countryside—in these circumstances this phenomenon has for the historian contemplating it the appearance of the eruption of a long-dormant volcano."[863]

To be sure, the prophets of ancient Israel were not necessarily opposed to monarchy on principle or inclined to blame the kings of Israel exclusively for the sins of the Jews.[864] Rather, they spread the blame to everyone who was in a position to exert some influence over the people: their religious leaders (priests and official prophets) and the rich and powerful (merchants and traders), as well as the secular authorities (kings and princes), for the evils they believed their fellow Jews indulged in. In the words of James Muilenburg, quoted by Abraham J. Heschel, among the most "striking" and "pervasive" aspects of the prophetic writings is "the denunciation and distrust of power in all its forms and guises." Heschel comments: "The prophets repudiated the work as well as the power of man as an object of supreme adoration." They rejected arrogance, angry kings, "the oppressors," and others who relied on power to force their will on the weak and vulnerable.[865] Thus, William M. Ramsay says, "We shall see that many of the prophets whose words formed books of the Bible denounced the injustice and the faithlessness to the Lord of the rulers of their day."[866]

In this opposition, the prophets shared with other Axial Age revolutionaries an attitude that appears to have arisen at a moment in history when nation states had, in becoming urban agricultural societies, abandoned the values that characterized the tribal societies from which they had developed.[867] No longer united to others by kinship ties, divided from the wealthy by class differences, and subjected to exploitation and taxation, the peasants and workers of Israel faced the same problems that motivated religious rebels in China and India. According to Karen Armstrong, "[W]ealth was confined to the upper classes, and the gulf between rich and poor became distressingly obvious." Thus, "it was not surprising that prophets rose up in the name of Yahweh to attack the government."[868] Von Rad says: "These were the men who proceeded to stronger and stronger attacks on existing institutions, and altogether denied their legitimacy in the eyes of Jahweh. Polemic against internal conditions became the almost exclusive form in which their *charisma* found expression . . . In actual fact it was against the holders of the high offices, kings, priests, and prophets, that these prophets turned, and reproached them with their failure to comply with the will of Jahweh."[869]

As Yehezkel Kaufmann comments: "In the twilight of the northern kingdom, the social cleavage and the evils that it entailed grew more acute. Masses of people became impoverished, and the rift between ideal and reality became more critical. Out of this rift, classical prophecy was born." Thus, "[t]he distinctive feature of classical prophecy is its vehement denunciation of social corruption."[870] Besides the rise of syncretism, the assumption of statehood, and the threat of foreign imperialism, von Rad similarly attributes the disintegration of ancient Israel to economic changes: "Because of the burden of taxation, the peasant, economically weak, became less and less able to remain a free man on his own land—his old influential and honourable status as a free man liable for military service dwindled away, and ownership of land came more and more into the hands of capitalist-town-dwellers. The country people became increasingly proletarianised (Is. V. 8; Mic. II. 1f.)."[871]

In the middle of the eighth century BC, Amos, the earliest of the Hebrew prophets, "denounced Israel, as well as her neighbors, for reliance upon military might, and for grave injustice in social dealings, abhorrent immorality, and shallow, meaningless piety."[872] The injustice that Amos objected to, especially in the Northern Kingdom and its capital, Samaria, arose because, as James D. Newsome Jr. explains, the wealth that was accumulated in the reign of Jeroboam II "was not . . . equally shared among all classes in society. Amos' words portray an economic polarization which produced a very wealthy class of merchants and rulers," who were complacent, self-indulgent, and oppressive. Thus, the situation was ripe, as it was for all of the Hebrew prophets, for social criticism based on the Covenant Code.[873] James Muilenburg says that, to Amos, "[e]very social wrong—profiteering at the expense of the poor, commercial dishonesty, intemperance, bribery, social callousness, distortion of justice, luxury, and extravagance—is an offence to Yahweh."[874]

In this regard, says John J. Collins, Amos and the other prophets "were traditionalists, calling Israel back to the observance of its original norms." Nevertheless, Collins adds, Amos and the others "were highly original figures who changed the nature of Israelite religion" by insisting on the concept of "moral obligation."[875] Ramsay says: "Two things especially make this 'minor' prophet a book of major importance: (1) no other Old Testament prophet more resoundingly voiced God's demand for justice for the oppressed; and (2) oracles attributed to Amos were the first words of a prophet to make up a written book of the Bible. Amos was by no means the first of Israel's prophets; Nathan, Elijah, Elisha, and many others had preceded him. But something new happened with regard to Amos's prophecies: somebody wrote them down. Indeed, they are among the first written words of all our scripture. The recording of Amos's stormy warnings against injustice was a first step in the birth of the Bible we study today."[876] Muilenburg notes that Amos is also "the first to set the religious faith of Israel completely free of nationalism, and his message rises to a height not before attained." Thus, in this prophet's words, "we have a great advance in the history of religion, for this is the first appeal to an international morality."[877]

As Newsome acknowledges, the Covenant Code is not directly referred to by Amos, although "the idea of the covenant is implicit in Amos' thought." Like the other prophets, Amos shows "an awareness that without the grace of God Israel would have long ago been destroyed by its enemies."[878] This is why Amos—again, like most of the other prophets—refers to God's liberation of the Jews from Egypt as a reminder of his willingness to keep his side of the covenantal agreement (2:10, 3:1, 9:7). According to Heschel, God's justice was thus not "mechanical": "Israel proved faithless, but again and again God had overlooked and forgiven, hoping that Israel might see the error of her way and repent." Speaking of Amos' song of lament (4:6–13), Heschel says that God's repetition of the refrain "yet you did not return to me" emphasizes God's mercy rather than his justice.[879]

Making a general charge against the rich, mostly for explicit violations of the Covenant Code, Amos quotes God as saying that "they sell the righteous for silver, and the needy for a pair of shoes—they that trample the head of the poor into the dust of the earth, and turn aside the way of the afflicted; a man and his father go in to the same maiden, so that my holy name is profaned; they lay themselves down beside every altar upon garments taken in pledge" (2:6–8; see also 8:6). "Woe to those," the perpetrators of these crimes, God says, "who are at ease in Zion, and to those who feel secure on the mountain of Samaria . . . Woe to those who lie upon beds of ivory, and stretch themselves upon their couches," who wine and dine and sing and revel, while others suffer and starve (6:1, 4–7).[880]

The wealthy women of Samaria "oppress the poor" and "crush the needy" (4:1).[881] The dwellers in "the house of Israel . . . trample upon the poor and take from him exactions of wheat," "afflict the righteous," "take a bribe, and turn aside the needy" (5:11–12). They "have turned justice into poison and the fruit of righteousness into wormwood" (6:12). The merchants are also guilty of wanting the Sabbath to pass so they can "make the ephah [i.e., a measuring unit, less than a bushel] small and the shekel great, and deal deceitfully with false balances" (8:4–5). T. G. Soares summarizes these charges and puts them into historical perspective: "Amos appears in Israel as the first challenger of the fundamental policies and practices of the nation. Prophets before him had often challenged the particular acts of kings. He went deeper and brought a message to the people that concerned itself with the fundamental basis of their life."[882] Thus began the prophetic project.

Slightly later in the eighth century, according to the editors of *The Oxford Annotated Bible* (1088), "Hosea spoke as a native to his own people [in the Northern

Kingdom], who were suffering from war with Assyria and in virtual anarchy," which, of course, he attributed to their sins against God. As Newsome explains, "Hosea possessed an unusually profound appreciation for the historical tradition of Israel and he did not hesitate to cite these in his effort to remind his people of their spiritual responsibilities." Thus, he accuses the "people of Israel" with serious crimes and even with violating the Covenant (6:7, 8:1).[883] As Collins notes, however, Hosea regarded the Covenant as a marriage agreement rather than a political treaty, for which reason the people's worship of Baal was an act of marital infidelity rather than a breach of contract.[884] Thus, the sins of Israel were extreme and ran across the entire spectrum of the laws of the Decalogue: "There is no faithfulness or kindness, and no knowledge of God in the land; there is swearing, lying, killing, stealing, and committing adultery; they break all bounds and murder follows murder" (4:1–2).[885]

The only problem is that, except for the metaphorical "harlotry" of the Jews, representing their idolatry, which Hosea emphasizes quite strongly in his first three chapters, these crimes remain somewhat unspecified as to perpetrators and victims. Amos tells us who does what to whom, but Hosea is more circumspect. Nevertheless, it is evident that priests and prophets are at least partly responsible because they have not taught the people well: "My people are destroyed for lack of knowledge, because you have rejected knowledge" (4:4–9). The result is sin and greed (4:7–9) as well as robbery and murder (6:8–9). According to John H. Tullock, "More priests and prophets meant more leaders to lead them astray, since the people followed their leaders. The Lord's priests had led the people to the worship of Baal," and in this way "had brought them to destruction and punishment."[886] Unfortunately, the merchants were not much better. God says, "A trader, in whose hands are false balances, he loves to oppress. Ephraim has said, 'Ah, but I am rich, I have gained wealth for myself'; but all his riches can never offset the guilt he has incurred" (12:7–9).

Although Hosea does not accuse the leaders of Israel of the crimes that Amos mentions, his attitude toward the monarchy is negative throughout.[887] God says at the beginning of the prophecy that he "will punish the house of Jehu for the blood of Jezreel, and [he] will put an end to the kingdom of the house of Israel" (1:4). According to Newsome, God is angry at Jehu because he "wiped out the preceding dynasty of Omri," an event "for which Israel will suffer."[888] Later, God shows his contempt for Gilgal, where Saul was celebrated as Israel's first king and where God "began to hate" Saul's supporters: "Because of the wickedness of their deeds I will drive them out of my house. I will love them no more; all their princes are rebels," perhaps a reference to the series of self-appointed and regicidal kings who ruled Israel after the assassination of Jeroboam II's son, Zechariah. As Heschel notes, "Within ten years following Jeroboam's death [Israel] had five kings, three of whom seized the throne by violence."[889]

Thus, God says, "[T]hey devour their rulers. All their kings have fallen; and none of them calls on me" (7:7). "They made kings, but not through me.[890] They set up princes, but without my knowledge" (8:4). Finally, God taunts the Israelites for choosing a king in the first place, since neither that king nor his successors will be able to protect them from God's vengeance: "Where now is your king, to save you; where are all your princes, to defend you—those of whom you said, 'Give me a king and princes.' I have given you kings in my anger, and I have taken them away in my wrath" (13:10–11). In this context, it is easy to understand why Hosea suggests that the people's corruption, wickedness, false dealing, and evil appear to please the political leaders: "By their wickedness they make the king glad, and the princes by their treachery" (7:1–3). After all, the kings themselves had "plowed iniquity" and "reaped injustice" because of their criminal acts, as well as their reliance on military might (chariots, warriors, and war; 10:13–14).

Isaiah addressed the people of Judah, the Southern Kingdom, in the late eighth and early seventh centuries, "that critical period in which the Northern Kingdom was annexed to the Assyrian empire." In this judgment, "Isaiah attacks social injustice as that which is most indicative of Judah's tenuous relationship with God" (*The Oxford Annotated Bible*, 822). Isaiah begins vaguely, accusing Israel (in God's words), of being a "sinful nation, a people laden with iniquity, offspring of evildoers, sons who deal corruptly" (1:4). "Wash yourselves; make yourselves clean," God says; "remove the evil of your doings from before my eyes" (1:16).[891] However, Isaiah quickly gets to a clear assignment of guilt, which lies with the rich and powerful: "[S]eek justice, correct oppression; defend the fatherless, plead for the widow" (1:17). As Newsome says, the problems that inspired Amos also inspired Isaiah, since "much of the same economic polarization which characterized the Northern Kingdom of Jeroboam II must have been true of Uzziah's Judah." Thus, Newsome adds, "The tone of Isaiah's oracles during this period is very similar to [that] of his great predecessors Amos and Hosea in that he indicts the nation for its arrogance and greed."[892]

Like the capital of the North, Samaria, the city of Jerusalem had become unjust, unrighteous, and murderous because its "princes are rebels and companions of thieves. Every one loves a bribe and runs after gifts. They do not defend the fatherless, and the widow's cause does not come to them" (1:21–23). More specifically, "The Lord enters into judgment with the elders and princes of his people: 'It is you who have devoured the vineyard, the spoil of the poor is in your houses. What do you mean by crushing my people, by grinding the face of the poor?'" (3:14–15). Soares says, "The evil, to Isaiah's mind, was that the strong and privileged, not satisfied with the advantages they enjoyed by reason of their very condition as such, not only did not realize the fraternal responsibility of generosity to the weak, but actually took every opportunity of exploiting them."[893]

To be sure, Isaiah also condemns divination and idolatry (2:6–8); wanton women (3:16); and moral confusion, self-inflation, drunkenness, and bribery (5:20–23). Like the other classical prophets, he delivers "oracles" against Judah's enemies, including Assyria and Egypt (chs. 30–31). But his focus is clearly on the crimes of the rich against the poor: the elder and the prophet, head and tail, "who lead this people and lead them astray," as well as the godless and wicked who insatiably devour their "neighbor's flesh" (9: 15–20); the landowners "who join house to house, who add field to field, until there is no room, and you are made to dwell alone in the midst of the land" (5:8);[894] the judges "who decree iniquitous decrees, and the writers who keep writing oppression, to turn aside the needy from justice and to rob the poor of my people of their right," including widows and orphans (10:1–2); and "the priest and prophet [who] reel with strong drink" (28:7).[895]

Finally, Isaiah condemns the leaders of Judah: the "scoffers, who rule this people in Jerusalem! Because you have said, 'We have made a covenant with death, and with Sheol we have an agreement'" (28:14–15).[896] In these criticisms, he is expressing his contempt not only for the sins that the other prophets typically rail against, but also for Judah's faith in wars and treaties: "Isaiah's utter distrust of worldly power, . . . for the scepter and the pomp of the wicked rulers (14:5, 11), for their arrogance, pride, and insolence made it impossible for him to approve of any military alliance" and any dependency on military might, both of which, to Isaiah, reflected a rejection of God's power to make all things right.[897] Heschel reminds us that Isaiah "acted out the shame of a prisoner of war by going about naked and barefoot for a period of three years, a dramatic way of saying that this would be the fate of the people if they, instead of relying on the grace and power of God to deliver them, relied on the weapons and instruments of war."[898]

Micah, "a younger contemporary of Isaiah," prophesied at a time when the circumstances in Judah were similar to what they were "in the ministries of Hosea and Isaiah" (*The Oxford Annotated Bible* 1123). Like Isaiah, in particular, Micah is concerned about the sins of the powerful. Newsome says that, to Micah, "a love of power and money has caused the leaders of the nation to cheat and oppress common men and women."[899] They are "those who devise wickedness and work evil upon the beds!" When they wake up the next day, "they perform it, *because it is in the power of their hand.* They covet fields, and seize them; and houses, and take them away; they oppress a man and his house, a man and his inheritance" (2:1–2; my emphasis).[900] Micah asks the ruling powers, "Hear, you heads of Jacob and rulers of the house of Israel! Is it not for you to know justice?" The answer is resoundingly no, of course, but in the most horrific language in all of the writings of the prophets. These rulers not only "hate the good and love the evil." Like cannibals, they "tear the skin from off my people and their flesh from off their bones; who eat the flesh of my people, and flay their skin from off them, and break their bones in pieces, and chop them up like meat in a kettle, like flesh in a caldron" (3:1–3).[901]

As Newsome notes, Micah's delivery was different from that of earlier prophets: "In contrast to the preaching of Amos and Hosea which employed certain oratorical and/or literary devices to achieve maximum effectiveness, that of Micah appears to be relatively blunt and straightforward. In fact, the very crudeness of his metaphors may have caused them to fall with greater impact upon the ears of his hearers."[902] According

The Covenant

to Muilenburg,: "A peasant farmer from the Sephelah, [Micah] knows the harsh and grudging life of the poor. He speaks out in bitter outrage at the injustices done to those who have neither power nor capacity to resist, but with deep compassion for those who suffer from the devices and machinations of shrewd and prosperous men."[903] Micah says once more to the leaders of the two kingdoms that they "abhor justice and pervert all equity"; they "build Zion with blood and Jerusalem with wrong." These leaders "give judgment for a bribe," and the religious leaders, too, are guilty: Jerusalem's "priests teach for hire, [and] its prophets divine for money" (3:9–11), just as religion in Samaria is corrupted by images and idols.

Thus, even half way through his relatively brief assault on the values of his contemporaries, only seven chapters long, Micah has challenged what the editors of *The Oxford Annotated Bible* call "all classes of Israelites," but especially those who were in control: "Not only the prince and the judge, but the best and most upright of Jerusalem's inhabitants were corrupt" (1129).[904] Micah continues, with a long peroration "in the voice of the Lord": "Can I forget the treasures of wickedness in the house of the wicked, and the scant measure that is accursed? Shall I acquit the man with scales and with a bag of deceitful weights? Your rich men are full of violence; your inhabitants speak lies, and their tongue is deceitful in their mouth . . . The godly man has perished from the earth, and there is none upright among men; they all lie in wait for blood, and each hunts his brother with a net. Their hands are upon what is evil, to do it diligently; the prince and the judge ask for a bribe, and the great man utters the evil desire of his soul; thus they weave it [i.e., the net] together, the best of them is like a brier, the most upright of them a thorn hedge . . . Put no trust in a neighbor, have no confidence in a friend, guard the doors of your mouth from her who lies in your bosom." Sons and daughters rebel against parents, and "a man's enemies are the men of his own house" (6:9—7:6). As the editors note, "[T]he godly man's enemies" were those who were closest to him. The leaders had poisoned everyone, and "[t]here was no basis for mutual confidence" anywhere (1129).[905]

Jeremiah, also a Judean, prophesied at the end of the seventh and the beginning of the sixth centuries BC. According to this prophet, God's initial complaint is that his people have forsaken him by turning to idols: "[T]hey have burned incense to other gods, and worshiped the works of their own hands" (1:16). In his longest sustained complaint about his people's idolatry, God warns Jeremiah that "the kings of Judah, its princes, its priests, and the people of the land"—that is, the rich and powerful—"will fight against" him (1:18–19), for "the rulers," as well as the priests and prophets (2:8), have "defiled" the land by turning their backs on God (2:4—3:10).[906] Indeed, Jeremiah comes back again and again to the evils committed by priests and prophets, including idolatry (2:26–27), false prophecies (5:31; 6:13), ungodliness, and wickedness (23:11). The prophets, particularly, have led people astray, committing adultery, lying, and supporting "evildoers" (23:13–14).[907]

185

Thus, "the Lord of Hosts" concludes: "Do not listen to the words of the prophets who prophesy to you, filling you with vain hopes: they speak visions of their own minds, not from the mouth of the Lord. They say continually to those who despise the word of the Lord, 'It shall be well with you'; and to every one who stubbornly follows his own heart, they say, 'No evil shall come upon you'" (23:16–17). Later, God accuses men, women, and children of making "cakes for the queen of heaven," or Ishtar (7:18), and he inveighs against them again, at greater length, in 44:15–28. The editors of *The Oxford Annotated Bible* explain: The Jewish refugees in Egypt "return to the worship of the queen of heaven (7:16–20), which was the Babylonian-Assyrian goddess Ishtar, goddess of the star Venus . . . First introduced, presumably, by Manasseh (2 Kg.21.1–18), suppressed by Josiah (2 Kg.23.4–14), and restored by Jehoiakim (2 Kg.23.36–24.7), the cult was especially popular among women, who had an inferior role in the cult of the Lord" (972). Jeremiah also charges "the sons of Judah" with sacrificing their children, presumably to pagan gods (7:30–31).

It does not take long, however, for Jeremiah to get around to his other main topic—wickedness, which is manifested in both greed and injustice.[908] The prophet says that there is in Jerusalem no "one who does justice and seeks truth," either among "the poor, [who] have no sense," or "the great, [who] know the way of the Lord" but reject it (5:1, 4–5). Then God lists the sins of the Israelites, especially the wealthy, who "set a trap" and "catch men" and thereby "have become great and rich," as well as "fat and sleek." Their "wickedness" is boundless, for "they judge not with justice the cause of the fatherless, to make it prosper, and they do not defend the rights of the needy" (5:26–29). In short, "there is nothing but oppression" in Jerusalem (6: 7; see also 6:28–29).

However, Jeremiah does not limit his criticism only to the very rich and the very poor. God later says that the people of Israel—meaning *everyone*—will be forgiven "if [they] truly execute justice one with another, if [they] do not oppress the alien, the fatherless, or the widow, or shed innocent blood in this place, and if [they] do not go after other gods" (7:5–7).[909] Yet, he adds, "They hold fast to deceit, they refuse to return . . . [N]o man repents of his wickedness," and each one "turns to his own course, like a horse plunging headlong into battle" (8:5–6). Furthermore, "from the least to the greatest every one is greedy for unjust gain" (8:10). And everybody Is guilty of adultery, treachery, dishonesty, untrustworthiness, deception, unrepentance, and oppression (9:2–8). God thus commands Jeremiah to "go to the house of the king of Judah" and tell him: "Do justice and righteousness, and deliver from the hand of the oppressor him who has been robbed. And do no wrong or violence to the alien, the fatherless, and the widow, nor shed innocent blood in this place" (22:1–3).[910]

Throughout his prophecy, Jeremiah indicts the leaders of Judah and Israel, including the wise, the mighty, and the rich, who fail to "practice steadfast love, justice, and righteousness" (9:23–24), which means they fail to obey the demands of the Covenant, to which Jeremiah, like all of the prophets, is deeply devoted (11:3–11). With

The Covenant

the specific prohibitions of the Covenant Code in mind, God curses "him who builds his house by unrighteousness, and his upper rooms by injustice; who makes his neighbor serve him for nothing, and does not give him his wages." He continues: "Did not your father eat and drink and do justice and righteousness? Then it was well with him. He judged the cause of the poor and needy: then it was well ... But you have eyes and heart only for your dishonest gain, for shedding innocent blood, and for practicing oppression and violence" (22:13–17).[911]

The deeper problem for this prophet, however—and an idea that is anomalous among the Hebrew prophets, at least in its explicitness—is that the cause of human evil is not willful disobedience, but innate human depravity. Schmidt notes that, to Jeremiah, "Evil has become as it were humanity's 'second nature' ..., of which people are neither able (13:23; cf. 4:22, etc.) nor willing (6:16; 8:5) to divest themselves." God implies this when he says, "Though you wash yourself with lye and use much soap, the stain of your guilt is still before me" (2:22).[912] But he is quite explicit in what may be the most well-known verse in in the book of Jeremiah: "The heart is deceitful above all things, and desperately corrupt; who can understand it?"[913]

For this reason, God warns, "Cursed is the man who trusts in man," but "[b]lessed is the man who trusts in the Lord." The first is "a shrub in the desert"; the other is "a tree planted by water" (17:5–9). It is unclear how knowing this is supposed to affect human behavior, except to make people mistrustful of their fellow human beings. Furthermore, regardless of the implication that human beings are not responsible for their actions, God says clearly that he rewards the good and punishes the bad: "I the Lord search the mind and try the heart, to give every man according to his ways, according to the fruit of his doings" (17:10).[914]

Ezekiel preached in the first half of the sixth century BC, before and after the destruction of Jerusalem in 587, mostly in Babylon, but also in the Holy City. In Ezekiel's prophecy, God announces that he has been betrayed by the residents of Jerusalem: "[S]he has wickedly rebelled against my ordinances more than the nations, and against my statutes more than the countries around her ..."[T]herefore ... I will execute judgments in the midst of you in the sight of the nations" (5:6–8). Accusing Israel several times of committing "abominations," God says, "Your doom has come, injustice has blossomed, pride has budded. Violence has grown up into a rod of wickedness" (7:10–11). These charges remain vague until God identifies "the stumbling block of [Israel's] iniquity," a religious crime rather than a moral one, involving worshipping idols made of silver and gold: "Their beautiful ornament they used for vainglory, and they made their abominable images and their detestable things of it" (7:19–20).[915]

After accusing Israel of several more abominations, God repeats his general charges: "The guilt of the house of Israel and Judah is exceedingly great; the land is full of blood, and the city full of injustice" (9:9). And again, God settles on another religious crime, this time involving the prophets, or, more properly, diviners, "who prophesy out of their own minds," who are "like foxes among ruins" and who "have spoken falsehood and divined a lie" (13:1–6). When God summarizes the sins of the Israelites after their departure from Egypt, he includes idolatry and Sabbath violations, but little else. That is, "they rebelled against me," says God, but their sins were religious, not moral (20:5–39).

At this point, it becomes quite clear that, because Ezekiel was a priest, his concerns differed at least somewhat from those of most of the other prophets. Nevertheless, he could hardly avoid some consideration of the moral laws in the Covenant Code.[916] Thus, on the one hand, consistent with his interest in his own religious laws, God says: "If a man is righteous and does what is lawful and right—if he does not eat upon the mountains or lift up his eyes to the idols of the house of Israel, does not defile his neighbor's wife or approach a woman in her time of impurity, . . . he is righteous" (18:5–6, 9). Newsome says: "When Ezekiel describes sin, it is most often in cultic terms, a view which harmonizes well with Ezekiel's vocation as a priest . . . This is not to say that Ezekiel was unconcerned with personal immorality, but his emphasis in describing sin is upon the legal and cultic aspects of righteousness before God."[917]

On the other hand, however, consistent with God's moral laws, if a man "does not oppress any one, commits no robbery, gives his bread to the hungry and covers the naked with a garment, does not lend at interest or take any increase, withholds his hand from iniquity, executes true justice between man and man, walks in my statutes, and is careful to observe my ordinances," he is also righteous (18:7–9). Furthermore, God says, "Behold, the princes of Israel in you, every one according to his power, have been bent on shedding blood. Father and mother are treated with contempt in you; the sojourner suffers extortion in your midst; the fatherless and the widow are wronged in you" (22:6–7).[918] In short, as the editors of *The Oxford Annotated Bible* say, "This writ of indictment contains a catalogue of sins . . . reminiscent of the regulations in the Holiness Code," which, though they represent a priestly emphasis, nevertheless reflect the concerns of the Covenant Code in general (1026). Yet, the final chapters of Ezekiel's prophecy are devoted to a description of the restored Temple, a focus that underscores Ezekiel's special commitment to the priestly orientation.

Second, or Deutero, Isaiah, chapters 40–55 of the book of Isaiah, is believed to represent the ideas of an unknown prophet who preached around the time of the Persian conquest of Babylonia, in the sixth century. In this prophecy, God refers several times to his Covenant with Israel, which he describes as his special gift to the Jews and which he regards as a source of enlightenment, a foundation of righteousness, a means of liberation, and a guide to survival (42:6–7, 49:8–10). Thus, as we have learned to expect, God is also concerned about his people's violation of the Covenant Code, including idolatry (42:17, 45:20), which he satirizes at length in 44:9–20. This is consistent with God's ongoing portrayal of himself as the creator of the universe, the source of all knowledge, and the incomparable ruler of the world (40:10–28, 45:1–26), "who brings princes to nought," "makes the rulers of the earth as nothing" (v. 23), "tramples kings under foot," and "makes them like dust with his sword" (41:2). "The

The Covenant

Lord goes forth like a mighty man, like a man of war he stirs up his fury; he cries out, he shouts aloud, he shows himself mighty against his foe" (42:13).[919]

In this role, God laments the suffering of Israel: "[T]his is a people robbed and plundered, they are all of them trapped in holes and hidden in prisons; they have become a prey with none to rescue" (42:22). In response to this suffering, God offers support: "He gives power to the faint, and to him who has no might he increases strength" (40:31). He does this, out of his omnipotence, by destroying their enemies: "Even the captives of the mighty shall be taken, and the prey of the tyrant be rescued, for I will contend with those who contend with you, and I will save your children" (49:25). Thus, he says: "[F]ear not, for I am with you . . . I will strengthen you, I will help you" (41:10, 13).

It is important to note, however, that Second Isaiah's portrait of God as cosmic warrior is accompanied by his portrait of God as a loving father, who is as tender and affectionate as the warrior-God is fierce and punitive. That is, the Covenant is also an expression of compassion and everlasting love (54:7–10; 55:3). God starts by advising his prophet to "[s]peak tenderly to Jerusalem" (40:1). After all, God says, the people of Israel are those "in whom [his] soul delights" (42:1) and to whom he says, "I love you" and "I am with you" (43:4–5). This is because they are his "servant," whom he has "chosen," as well his sheep, whom he "will feed," "gather the lambs in his arms, and gently lead those that are with young" (40:11). As God says repeatedly, he "formed" the people of Israel (43:1); he "made" them and "formed [them] from the womb" (44:2; 46:3; 49:5).[920]

Thus, God is not only the father of Israel, but also the mother: "Can a woman forget her sucking child, that she should have no compassion on the son of her womb? (49:15). Finally, he is the "husband" of Israel, who "has called [her] like a wife forsaken and grieved in spirit" (54:5–6). And, instead of threatening his people's enemies with his great power, he offers the kind of help that the Covenant Code promises: "When the poor and needy seek water, and there is none, and their tongue is parched with thirst, I the Lord will answer them, the God of Israel will not forsake them" (41:17). He will release the prisoner, feed the hungry, and "will have compassion on his afflicted" (49:9–10, 13). "I am he that comforts you," says the Lord (51:12).

What is missing in Second Isaiah, however, is made clear by examining what is included in Third, or Trito, Isaiah, chapters 56–66 of the book of Isaiah. Specifically, this is the set of moral demands—for love, justice, and righteousness—that appears so frequently and prominently in the work of most of the other Jewish prophets. To be sure, God says to his people in Second Isaiah, "O that you had hearkened to my commandments" (48:18), but he indicates what he means only later and somewhat vaguely: "Seek the Lord while he may be found, call upon him while he is near; let the wicked forsake his way, and the unrighteous man his thoughts; let him return to the Lord, that he may have mercy on him" (55:6–7).

On the contrary, Third Isaiah begins with the familiar command: "Keep justice, and do righteousness . . . Blessed is the man who does this, and the son of man who holds it fast, who keeps the sabbath, not profaning it, and keeps his hand from doing any evil" (56:1–2). In the following chapter, Third Isaiah offers what Newsome calls "one of the finest statements in the Old Testament concerning the nature of true worship, a favorite theme of the Third Isaiah: "For thus says the high and lofty One who inhabits eternity, whose name is Holy: 'I dwell in a high and holy place, and also with him who is of a contrite and humble spirit, to revive the spirit of the humble, and to revive the heart of the contrite' (57:15.)"[921] Again, in the language of the Covenant Code, God says, "[I]f you pour yourself out for the hungry and satisfy the desire of the afflicted, then shall your light rise in the darkness" (58:10).

Indeed, chapter 59, which reads like a confession by the prophet himself, provides an overall summary of the Covenant violations of which the people of Israel and the rest of the world are guilty: "For your hands are defiled with blood and your fingers with iniquity; your lips have spoken lies, your tongue mutters wickedness. No one enters suit justly, no one goes to law honestly; they rely on empty pleas, they speak lies, they conceive mischief and bring forth iniquity . . . The way of peace they know not, and there is no justice in their paths; and they have made their roads crooked, no one who goes in them knows peace . . . Justice is turned back, and righteousness stands afar off; and truth has fallen in the public squares, and uprightness cannot enter" (vv. 3–4, 8, 14).

These passages connect Third Isaiah to Amos, Hosea, Micah, and Isaiah. Newsome says, "[T]he mention of *mishpat* and *tsedhaqah* [justice and righteousness] together (v. 9)—"Therefore justice is far from us, and righteousness does not overtake us"—"recalls the tradition of the prophets of old."[922] And Third Isaiah's announcement that "[t]he Spirit of the Lord God is upon [him] because the Lord has anointed [him] to bring good tidings to the afflicted" connects the Covenant Code to the mission of Jesus, who says in Luke 4:18–19, "[H]e has sent me to bind up the brokenhearted, to proclaim liberty to the captives, and the opening of the prison to those who are bound; to proclaim the year of the Lord's favor." With these covenantal words, Jesus introduced himself to the members of a synagogue in Nazareth more than half a millennium after they were uttered by Third Isaiah.

Even among some of the lesser known prophets, the focus is on morality. Zechariah, for example, calls for "true judgment" as well as "kindness and mercy" and rejects not only the oppression of the helpless, but also *any* "evil against your brother in your heart" (7:9–10; see also 8:16–17)—all related, specifically, to the Ten Commandments, all based on the "covenant" between God and his people (9:11), and all driven by God's "compassion" (1:16; 10:6; 12:10). Habakkuk, too, says Schmidt, "complains about injustice and violence," first regarding "legal and economic oppression within Israel itself": "Behold, he whose soul is not upright in him shall fail, but the righteous shall live by his faith" (2:4).[923] After this verse, the prophet delivers his "woes"—"a common feature of the prophetic oracles"[924]—against the leaders of Babylonia, who engage in acts of injustice and violence: "Woe to him who heaps up what is not his own . . . and loads himself with pledges"; "to him who gets evil gain for his house, to set his nest on high, to be safe from the reach of harm"; "to him who builds a town with blood, and founds a city on iniquity"; and "to him who makes his neighbors drink of the cup of his wrath, and makes them drunk, to gaze on their shame" (2:9–15).

It is clear that, with their emphasis on morality, the prophets transformed Judaism from a cultic religion to the kind of ethics-centered faith that flowered midway through the first millennium in the words and works of Lao-Tse, Buddha, and Plato. "[I]n the subversive literature of the Israelite prophets," Andre LaCocque says, "moral imperatives take precedence over the offering of sacrifices."[925] They did this in two ways: first, as I have argued, by reviving the moral core of the Covenant Code. According to G. E. Wright, "The prophetic protest against social iniquity was based squarely on the covenant law in the attempt to see that this law was unconditionally enforced."[926] As Kaufmann says: "Classical prophecy shares with the popular religion the belief that Israel is subject to the moral and religious obligations of a covenant made with YHWH in ancient times." More specifically, he adds: "The prophetic demands for social justice echo, for the most part, the ancient covenant laws. But they go beyond the early religion in raising these matters to the level of factors decisive for the national destiny."[927]

Second, the prophets elevated morality by quite deliberately and emphatically stating that cultic religion without it is not religion at all. Heschel says: "Amos and the prophets who followed him not only stressed the primacy of morality over sacrifice, but even proclaimed that the worth of worship, far from being absolute, is contingent upon moral living, and that when immorality prevails, worship is detestable."[928] After laying out his Covenant principles and accusing his people of violating them (2:6–8), God, in the prophecy of Amos, charges the Israelites with performing rituals merely for show [929]: "Come to Bethel, and transgress; to Gilgal and multiply transgression; bring your sacrifices every morning, your tithes every three days; offer a sacrifice of thanksgiving of that which is leavened, and proclaim freewill offerings, publish them; *for so you love to do, O people of Israel!*" (4:4–5; my emphasis).

Later, after another statement of his Covenant ideals (5:10–15), God famously and unequivocally repudiates festival celebrations, worship services, sacrifices, and hymn-singing when these religious acts are unaccompanied by morality: "I hate, I despise your feasts, and I take no delight in your solemn assemblies." As for sacrifices, God "will not accept them" or even "look upon them." And as for "the noise of songs" or "the melody of [their] harps," he "will not listen."[930] God wants *mishpat* and *tsedakkah*, without which religion is meaningless: "But let justice roll like waters, and righteousness like an ever-flowing stream" (5:21–24).[931] Collins goes so far as to suggest that "[i]n the case of Amos, the rejection [of the cult] is unequivocal." This is because, for Amos, "to serve God is to practice justice." Thus, "sacrifices, even if offered at great expense, were not only irrelevant to the service of God, but actually an impediment to it."[932]

In the prophecy of Hosea, after indicating precisely the extent to which he insists that his people abide by Covenant values,[933] God says, "I desire steadfast love and not sacrifice, the knowledge of God, rather than burnt offerings" (6:6). Later, God accuses the Israelites again: "They love sacrifice; they sacrifice flesh and eat it; but the Lord has no delight in them. Now he will remember their iniquity, and punish their sins; they shall return to Egypt"—that is, to slavery. "For Israel has forgotten his Maker, and built palaces; and Judah has multiplied fortified cities, but I will send a fire upon his cities, and devour his strongholds" (8:13–14). Finally, God says, "They shall not pour libations of wine to the Lord: and they shall not please him with their sacrifices" (9:4).

Addressing the residents of the Southern Kingdom, in the prophecy of Isaiah, God asks, "What to me is the multitude of your sacrifices?" He continues: "I have had enough of burnt offerings of rams and the fat of fed beasts; I do not delight in the blood of bulls, or of lambs, or of he-goats." Then, as he did in the book of Amos, God rejects every kind of cultic practice: not only sacrifices, but also celebrations of the new moon and the Sabbath, solemn assemblies, "appointed feasts," and prayers. All these, he "cannot endure" and his "soul hates" for "they have become a burden" rather than a blessing.[934] What God wants is for his people to wash the blood from their hands; "cease to do evil, learn to do good; seek justice, correct oppression; defend the fatherless, plead for the widow" (1:10–17), just as he had demanded in Amos' prophecy: "Seek good, and not evil . . . Hate evil and love good, and establish justice" (5:14–15).

The pattern in these alternating condemnations of ritual and commendations of morality is repeated in both Micah and Jeremiah. In the work of the former, God rejects both sacrifices and libations and then asks, "[W]hat does the Lord require of you but to do justice, and to love kindness, and to walk humbly with your God?" (Mic 6:6–8).[935] In Jeremiah, God first complains that "this people . . . have not given heed to [his] words; and as for [his] law, they have rejected it." Of course, God is not talking about the cultic law, which "this people" have followed, one might say religiously but not effectively: "To what purpose does frankincense come to me from Sheba, or sweet cane from a distant land? Your burnt offerings are not acceptable, nor your sacrifices pleasing to me" (6:20). Then he explains why these acts are meaningless by accusing Judeans of failing to "amend [their] ways," which they can do only by executing justice, refraining from oppressing aliens, and forswearing idolatry (7:5–6). God returns to his assault on ritual by reminding his people that "in the day that I brought you out of the land of Egypt, I did not speak to your fathers or command them concerning burnt offerings and sacrifices" (7:22), a point also made in Amos 5:25. Jeremiah later reports that God told him: "Do not pray for the welfare of this people. Though they fast, I will not hear their cry, and though they offer burnt offering and cereal offering,

The Covenant

I will not accept them; but I will consume by the sword, by famine, and by pestilence" (14:11–12).

Finally, Third Isaiah offers a slightly different treatment of the subject of the role of ritual in the practice of Judaism. Having urged his people to embrace contrition and humility, God shows that he is as little interested in fasting as he is in sacrifice, libation, and other kinds of worship. His people request "righteous judgments" from God, which they believe they have earned by fasting and humbling themselves before God. However, God finds their religion shallow and their humility false because their other activities—particularly their interactions with other people—reveal their lack of integrity. Thus, when they ask, "Why have we fasted, and thou seest it not?" the Lord answers: "Behold, in the day of your fast you seek your own pleasure, and oppress all your workers. Behold, you fast only to quarrel and to fight and to hit with wicked fist" (58:2–4).

This kind of religious practice will not reach God's ear, nor will this kind of submissiveness make God responsive. The fast that God chooses for his people is for them "to loose the bonds of wickedness, to undo the thongs of the yoke, to let the oppressed go free, and to break every yoke" (58:6). It is also "to share [their]bread with the hungry, and bring the homeless poor into [their] house; when [they] see the naked to cover him, and not to hide [themselves] from [their] own flesh" (58: 7). In short, only *their* "righteousness" is able to evoke *his* righteousness: "Then you call, and the Lord will answer." Lift the yoke, God continues, "pour yourself out for the hungry and satisfy the desire of the afflicted" (58:8–10), and honor the Sabbath without "going your own ways, or seeking your own pleasure, or talking idly" (58:13).

Obviously, the prophets' insistence that following moral laws is more important than following cultic laws was not simply a preference for one kind of obedience over another. According to many scholars, the prophets' primary focus on person-to-person relationships (involving moral actions) and only secondary focus on the human-divine relationship (involving cultic actions) reflects what we might call their ethical maturation. "The sea-change in the history of ancient Israel," says Ben F. Meyer, "was, in fact, from ethnic to religious community," which involved "the rise of prophets who would effect a change in the nation's self-understanding."[936] As Kaufmann explains, "There is thus a recognizable development between the viewpoint of the Torah and that of later Judaism. In between have come the prophets, with their insistence on the conditional value of the cult. Post-prophetic Judaism continued to support this view, while avoiding "the more extreme formulations of this position." Specifically, they "stress[ed] the idea that the moral goodness is the chief part of piety."[937]

Summing up this revolutionary idea, Wright says: "What God wants is not simply pious acts in church; he wants a righteous national life from his people. And anyone who thinks that worship can be used as a substitute or as a cover for social responsibility . . . must understand that God hates this kind of worship and will have nothing to do with it."[938] Thus, as John Dominic Crossan explains, noting this development (and despite some similarities between the ancient Jews and their Near Eastern neighbors), nothing "diminishes in any way the far, far more serious way in which righteousness and justice, especially as protective of the widows and the orphans, the poor and the wretched, were taken in the Bible. There it was the righteousness of God that was at stake."939

Discussing this difference, Samuel Umen says, "It is very difficult for us to realize what a tremendous advance in religious thought was marked by this view of the prophets as to what constitutes true worship." Everywhere in the world, Umen says, "religion was identified with ritual and sacrifices, and . . . in these the whole religious life centered." The limitation of this religious practice was that it was self-interested and materialistic. "The primitive conceptions at the root of the sacrificial cult are most apparent in in the twofold purpose which it was thought to serve. Sacrifices were regarded, on the one hand, as the medium by which man might enter into or renew communion with the deity." By this means, "the offerer expected from the deity, not spiritual gifts, but purely material blessings, such as a plentiful harvest, numerous flocks, long life, or, for the nation at large prosperity, conquest, and so on." The prophets found this idea of religion "grossly materialistic" and therefore argued that God's people should pray "not for their temporal welfare, not for the gratification of their material wants, but to satisfy the needs of their soul" as well as the demand of God for what Uman earlier calls "righteous conduct."940

As this passage suggests, the guiding idea of the prophets—that humanity's righteousness is an expression of God's righteousness—is based on God's message to Moses: "[T]herefore be holy, for I am holy" (Lev 44, 45). Crossan comments, "It is almost a cliché that the biblical Jewish prophets demanded social justice as [their] covenantal responsibility . . . *Social justice was for them the human face of divine justice.*"941 Indeed, in the course of their moral development, the ancient Jews seem to have adopted the idea that love of God is best represented by love of humanity. According to Soares, Amos, emphasizing justice, "reaches out to the great truth that *Jehovah is only to be served through the social relationships of men.*" And Hosea, emphasizing love, makes the same point: "It is . . . *love of man to man which he sees as the only bond of the social organism.*"

Both of these prophets, Soares adds, rejected the idea "that Jehovah was like a jealous monarch asking for praise and tribute and offering, when all his wish was to see [his people] living together in mutual justice and love, *acknowledging him with the love that was the answer to his own.*"942 In short, he was the best of kings. Thus, although I said earlier that the prophets were not opposed to monarchy on principle, this statement must be modified. Given the prophetic view of God as guide and father and partner, as well as *benevolent* king, Robert N. Bellah contends that there was no need, after Moses, for a mediator between God and his people. "It is this understanding," says Bellah, "that the prophets challenge: for them God related directly to the people . . . What the prophets insisted on was that the king had no monopoly in relation to Yahweh." Indeed, Hosea "rejected kingship altogether": "Where now is your king to save you?" asks God. "It is I who answer and *look after you*." (13:10, 14:8; my emphasis).[943]

Two characteristics of the prophets' writing made their work particularly effective among their contemporaries as well as among their successors. First, referring to all of the prophets, Crossan says, "The consistent tradition . . . repeats the same themes over and over again. It is not the eccentric vision of an individual here or there but the constant vision of a tradition involving this God, this people, this land, this justice." Crossan adds: "The tradition extends from Hosea, Isaiah, and Micah in the second half of the eighth century, through Jeremiah at the end of the seventh century, into Ezekiel and Zechariah at the start and end of the sixth century."[944] Second, the prophets not only shared a revolutionary vision but also presented it with unusual clarity and eloquence. As William A. Irwin argues, in their works "Israel's literature reached its maturity." Indeed, they "brought Hebrew writing to such excellence that the period of approximately two hundred years . . . is well considered Israel's classic age."[945]

Repentance

In chapter 1, we saw that Judaism has often been characterized as a religion of Works rather than Grace. That is, especially according to scholars before the last half of the twentieth century, salvation and survival in Judaism were assumed to be based on doing good works and gaining divine rewards as well as avoiding sins and thereby evading divine punishments This was, after all, the assumption held by all ancient peoples, who believed that the gods had to be placated or appeased by sacrifices or compelled by magic to behave in ways that benefitted their worshipers. However, it is clear that by the eighth century BC, if not earlier, the ancient Jews began to develop a very different understanding of the requirements for gaining blessings and escaping curses. Instead of believing God to be a stern judge who administers rewards and punishments impersonally and automatically, the prophets understood God to be a loving Father who responds to his children's behavior fairly but mercifully. This was based on the assumption that God is not only the majestic and transcendent Lord of the universe, and certainly not one of the many gods of nature, but also a deeply feeling and accessible parent.[946]

Not merely either satisfied or dissatisfied with human actions, God could be joyful, hurt, disappointed, pleased, impatient, remorseful, or wrathful. He could experience this wide range of emotions because he was a partner in a loving relationship. And, therefore, he could no more impose the ultimate punishment, death to all of his sons and daughters, than he could stop loving them. This is why the post-Torah books of the Jewish Bible are strewn with expressions of yearning, waiting, hoping, pleading, and questioning. God feels betrayed when his people turn to idols or otherwise fail

The Evolution of Love

to abide by his laws, and his people feel abandoned when God withdraws his support from them.[947]

This is also why the issue of repentance arises again and again in the works of the prophets, who collectively formulated this new concept of God. After all, the prophets emerged in the midst of disappointment on both sides of the human-divine relationship. And, although they made some attempt to define that relationship insofar as it governs the day-to-day life of God's people, in both good times and bad, the prophets found themselves in the worst of times. For this reason, they focused less on sustaining the status quo (alienation from God) than on trying to recover the status quo ante (reconciliation with God).[948] They understood God to be the creator of the universe, the source of their laws, the teacher of their ethics, and the guide to their salvation. In their present situation, however, God was the unhappy Father, from whom the prophets heard the terms of forgiveness for sins and thereby conveyed to their fellow Jews what God expected them to do. Thus, as Robert Bellah says, they "were angry men speaking for an angry God, yet, critically, a loving God, willing to forgive the truly repentant."[949] In short, according to Robert R. Wilson, the prophets suggest that "Israel's future is the result of its present activities and that future disaster can be avoided if people will change their present behavior."[950]

Of course, if forgiveness were merely contingent on good works, the solution would have been simple. Both God and the prophets, however, the latter because they had access to God's expectations, understood that actions are meaningful only when they are sincere.[951] And, assuming that God's people sinned because of who they were, they could stop sinning only if they changed. That is, their sins were not merely a matter of accident or error, mistake or misjudgment, but an expression of their moral inadequacy. And their turn away from sin was possible only if they became morally competent. That was the only way God could be brought to believe that his children were not just going through the motions. Good works matter only if they are not merely acts of obedience, but expressions of love.

The prophets recognized the fact that the failure to follow God's moral laws could be neither expiated nor atoned for, especially by merely ceremonial acts. God's forgiveness could not be gained by an act of self-denial either by punishing oneself or by repaying God. Even the Priestly tradition supported this idea. According to Anderson, "[L]est sacrifice should become just an end in itself, leading a person to suppose that he could have the benefits of divine grace and still continue in his stubborn, rebellious, and self-centered way, the priestly law affirmed categorically that sacrifice is not effective in the case of deliberate sin—sin 'with a high hand' (Num 15:30)." Anderson continues: "Sacrifice, said the priests, is effective only in the case of 'hidden sins'—the sins that come to light when one's life is exposed to the light of God's revelation. And even then it must be accompanied by confession and repentance."[952]

To the prophets, in particular, forgiveness could be achieved only if the sinner acquired a new understanding, became a different person, and thereby established a new relationship to both God and humanity. This concept represented a shift from expecting justice to praying for mercy, from paying a price to practicing virtue, from earning forgiveness to asking for grace.[953] Moore explains that "in no ancient religion is normal piety so pervaded by the consciousness of sin, the need of repentance, and the conviction that man's sole hope is the forgiving grace of God." The prophets of the eighth century and their successors, he continues, "combated the prevalent notion that God can be propitiated by gifts and offerings and that sin can be expiated by multitudinous and costly sacrifices." On the contrary, "the only way to avert [God's] wrath is sincere and thorough-going amendment."[954] As Yehezkel Kaufmann says: "[R]epentance [is] conceived of as an act of will, a change of heart in man which is answered by a change of the will-to-punish on the part of God. Mercy and compassion overbalance justice."[955]

Kaufmann argues that this concept "receives its full expression in the book of Jonah," which demonstrates the limitations of its main character's implicit belief that morality can be sustained only on the basis of God's offer of rewards and punishments, particularly the "ancient idea that sin must be punished." According to Kaufmann, Jonah's "view is here challenged." The narrative demonstrates that "a change of heart and action is itself capable of atoning for sin." In the words of the Bible, threatened by God with being "overthrown," the king of Nineveh "made proclamation" that his people should refrain from eating and drinking, cover themselves with sackcloth, "cry mightily to God," and "every one turn from his evil way and from the violence which is in his hands." At this point, God forgave their sins. When he observed their repentant acts—"how they turned from their evil way"—he refrained from further punishment (3:4–10).[956]

Of course, most of the other prophets would see the expiatory acts of self-denial and wearing sackcloth as inconsequential, sincerely undertaken though they evidently were, and, not incidentally, required by God. Concerned principally with moral change, the prophets would regard the cry to God and the turn away from evil and violence as the important acts of repentance, especially assuming that Nineveh is adequately described in the prophecy of Nahum as bloody, dishonest, and acquisitive (3:1) as well as a betrayer of nations (3:4)—that is, guilty of immoral acts. As Moore explains, "the transparent primary sense of repentance in Judaism is always a change in man's attitude toward God and in the conduct of life, a religious and moral reformation of the people or the individual." Moore adds later, "Repentance, as a turning from sin unto God, involves not only desisting from the sinful act, but the resolve not to commit it again, the abandonment of an evil way of life with the stedfast [sic] purpose no longer to walk in it."[957]

To the other prophets as well, God is not an accountant, preparing a balance sheet of debits (or sins) and credits (or expiations), but a Father waiting for his prodigal son or daughter to return, hoping that his wayward child will change, undergo a transformation, and acquire the capacity to act justly and righteously.[958] The old way is simply represented by a God who distributes rewards and punishments based on good and bad actions that earn one response or the other. The new way is represented by a God who both educates and chastises. As God explains in the prophecy of Jeremiah, "Your wickedness will chasten you, and your apostasy will reprove you" (2:19). Later, God says in the same work, "I will chasten you in just measure, and I will by no means leave you unpunished" (30:11). Still later, God says that he heard his people appealing to him: "Thou hast chastened me, and I was chastened, like an untrained calf; bring me back that I may be restored, for thou art the Lord my God. For after I had turned away I repented; and after I was instructed, I smote upon my thigh; I was ashamed, and I was confounded, because I bore the disgrace of my youth" (31:18-19).

In other words, God provides the means for acquiring knowledge of his ethical standards and punishes violations of those standards in order to correct misbehavior and encourage remorse (manifested by shame), understanding (acquired through instruction), and reformation (coming after repentance). In Isaiah, God describes his punishment of his people as a kind of purification or refinement: He "will smelt away [their] dross as with lye and remove all their alloy" (1:25).[959] Then he will forgive them, but this cannot occur, says Moore, without repentance—"that is, contrition, confession, reparation of injuries to others, and a reformation of conduct undertaken and persisted in with sincere purpose and out of religious motives."[960]

Of course, the old way still survives in the writings of the prophets, especially the idea that God offers rewards and punishments. Thus, in Amos, God says, by way of moral correction, "Seek good, and not evil, that you may live . . . so God will be with you" (5:14-15). In Isaiah, God tells his people, "If you are willing and obedient, you shall eat the good of the land; But if you refuse and rebel, you shall be devoured by the sword" (1:1:19-20. In Obadiah, God uses the *lex talionis* to indicate how he will deal with sin: "As you have done, it shall be done to you" (v. 15). Third Isaiah says of God, "[A]ccording to their deeds, so will he repay" (59:18). God says, "For I the Lord love justice, I hate robbery and wrong; I will faithfully give them their recompense" (61:8). In Zechariah, he says more positively, "If you walk in my ways and keep my charge, then you shall rule my house and have charge of my courts, and I will give the right of access among those who are standing here" (3:7).

God says in Second Isaiah, "Keep justice, and do righteousness, for soon my salvation will come, and my deliverance be revealed. Blessed is the man who does this, and the son of man who holds it fast, who keeps the sabbath, not profaning it, and keeps his hand from doing evil" (56:1-2; see also 58:9-14). After all, this formula goes back to the Covenant announced in the book of Exodus by Moses: "Behold I set before you this day a blessing and a curse; the blessing, if you obey the commandments of the Lord your God, which I command you this day, and the curse, if you do not obey the commandments of the Lord your God, but turn aside from the way which I command you this day, to go after other gods which you have not known" (12:26-28; see also 30:15-20).

The Covenant

Elsewhere, however, God clearly states that his forgiveness for Israel's sins is not a *quid* for his people's *quo*. In Ezekiel, God says to the "house of Israel," "And you shall know that I am the Lord, when I deal with you for my name's sake, not according to your evil ways, nor according to your corrupt doings" (20:44). Consequently, Daniel prays for grace and mercy rather than justice and recompense: "Now therefore, O ourGod, hearken to the prayer of thy servant and to his supplications, and *for thy own sake*, O Lord, cause thy face to shine on thy sanctuary . . . O Lord, hear; O Lord forgive; O Lord, give heed and act; delay not, *for thy own sake*, O my God, because thy city and thy people are called by thy name" (9:17–19; my emphasis). God says in Second Isaiah, "I, I am he who blots out your transgressions for my own sake, and I will not remember your sins" (43:25). Perhaps this is why God adds, "For as the heavens are higher than the earth, so are my ways higher than your ways and my thought than your thoughts" (55:9). That is, unlike humanity, he does not operate on the principle of *quid pro quo*.[961]

Nor is salvation gained by Israel's accumulation of good deeds, God says to Ezekiel, just as damnation is not inevitable for the wicked: "The righteousness of the righteous shall not deliver him when he transgresses; and as for the wickedness of the wicked, he shall not fall by it when he turns from his wickedness." That is, if the righteous one "trusts in his righteousness and commits iniquity, none of his righteous deeds shall be remembered." And, if the wicked one "turns from his sin and does what is lawful and right, . . . [n]one of the sins that he has committed shall be remembered against him" (Ezek 33:12–16). Referring to Ezekiel's definition of repentance, Kaufmann says: "No decree of God concerning man is final; man need not pine away in sin . . . The task of the prophet is to warn men away from sin, and this warning has meaning, for if men repent they will not be held accountable for the sins of the past—not even of their own past."[962] In short, one's latest act erases all previous acts. There is no balance sheet.

The situation of the Israelites and Judeans is the same in all of the writings of the prophets. The ancient Jews, in ignorance, have turned their backs on God. This betrayal is manifested in two principal ways: first, in the sin of idolatry and, second, in the crime of injustice. In every case, God offers forgiveness, but he requires something in exchange. In almost every instance, what he demands is not a gift for himself, but a change in the supplicant that results in a change in his or her relationship to God. In Jeremiah, God invites his people to restore their faith in him by asking not for a penitential act or a sacrifice of some kind, but for a "return," by which he means a reunion with him in the deepest sense. The point is, as I said earlier, Israel did not merely disobey its king and is therefore only able to recover its former position through self-effacement or submission. Rather, Israel betrayed a loving relationship, the suspension of which resulted in pain and disappointment on the part of a loving God.

To be sure, as a powerful king, God is often wildly angry with and vengeful against his faithless people, but, as a partner in a relationship based on the Covenant, he is also sometimes simply hurt and saddened about their unwillingness to return: "[I]f you will not listen, my soul will weep in secret for your pride; my eyes will weep bitterly and run down with tears, because the Lord's flock has been taken captive" (Jer 13:17). God weeps because he "yearns for" his lost people (31:20).[963] Jack Miles says that in Isaiah God "goes most deeply into himself, providing the most searching inventory of his own responses to the agony occasioned in his own life by the agony he has inflicted on his chosen people."[964] As Bernhard Anderson says, "God's purpose is not to destroy, but to heal." His anger is intended to create "crises that shake the very foundations of human self-sufficiency." And the result, in Hosea's prophecy, for example, is that after a period "of cleansing and purgation, there would be a new beginning."[965]

The people of God will therefore not be judged as if they were slaves or subjects, but treated mercifully, as if they were God's children or even his wife. "Return, faithless Israel," says God in Jeremiah, "I will no longer look on you in anger, for I am merciful . . . Only acknowledge your guilt, that you rebelled against the Lord your God and scattered your favors among strangers" (3:12–13)—that is, established relationships with other gods. "I thought you would call me, My Father, and would not turn from following me. Surely, as a faithless wife leaves her husband, so have you been faithless to me, O house of Israel" (3:19–20). In Hosea, God says of the people to whom he expects to be reconciled: "And in that day . . . you will call me, 'My husband,' and no longer will you call me, 'My Ba'al' . . . And I will betroth you to me for ever" (2:16, 19). In Third Isaiah, God says to his people: "[Y]our Maker is your husband, the Lord of hosts is his name . . . For the Lord has called you like a wife forsaken and grieved in spirit, like a wife of youth when she is cast off" (54:5–6).

In this context, the Covenant is less like a business agreement than a marriage contract. Abtaham Heschel says: "In contrast to our civilization, the Hebrews lived in a world of the covenant rather than a world of contracts . . . [God's] relationship to His partner is one of benevolence and affection . . . [W]hat obtains between God and Israel must be understood, not as legal, but as a personal relationship, as participation, involvement, tension."[966] It is not a deal-making arrangement, but a pledge of eternal love. As God goes on in Third Isaiah: "For a brief moment I forsook you, but with great compassion I will gather you, with everlasting love I will have compassion on you . . . For the mountains may depart and the hills be removed, but my steadfast love shall not depart from you, and my covenant of peace shall not be removed, says the Lord, who has compassion on you" (54:7–10).

Indeed, the theme of *chesed*, "steadfast" or "everlasting love," is repeated again and again, not only throughout the works of the prophets, but also throughout the psalms. And the point is therefore made emphatically that God will never sever the tie or abandon his promise to his people. "Return to the Lord, your God, for he is gracious and merciful, slow to anger, and abounding in steadfast love, and repents of evil" (Joel 2:13; my emphasis). As Micah explains: "Who is a God like thee, pardoning iniquity and passing over transgression for the remnant of his inheritance? He does not retain his anger for ever because he delights in steadfast love. He will again have compassion upon us, he will tread our iniquities under foot. Thou wilt cast all our sins into the depths of the sea. And thou wilt show faithfulness to Jacob and steadfast love to Abraham, as thou hast sworn to our fathers from the days of old" (7:18–20). In Jeremiah, God has "compassion" on his people; that is, he loves them "with an everlasting love" (30:18, 31:3).[967] And God says in Third Isaiah, "Seek the Lord while he may be found, call upon him while he is near; let the wicked forsake his way; and the unrighteous man his thoughts; let him return to the Lord, that he may have mercy on him, and to our God, for he will abundantly pardon" (55:6–7).

Tied to God by *chesed*, a truly penitent person will have to "swear, 'As the Lord lives,' in truth, in justice, and in uprightness" (Jer 4:2), but the words alone will not be sufficient.[968] To fix a broken relationship, God demands not merely words or even oaths, but actions. Perhaps not surprisingly, the change that God requires is not only abandoning idolatry, but also embracing the moral law, which his people have heard but often failed to obey. Thus, according to Jeremiah, God says to them, "Amend your ways and your doings," by which he means not just their religious activities, but also their ethical behavior: "For if you amend your ways and your doings,"—that is, "if you truly execute justice one with another, if you do not oppress the alien, the fatherless or the widow, or shed innocent blood in this place"—"then I will let you dwell in this place, in the land that I gave of old to your fathers for ever" (7:5–7). These crimes are, of course, the abrogations of the moral imperatives that we have seen over and over in both the Covenant Code and its recapitulation in the writings of the prophets. In Isaiah, God says, "When you come to appear before me, . . . cease to do evil, learn to do good; seek justice, correct oppression; defend the fatherless, plead for the widow" (Isa 1:16–17).

Indeed, the transformation that God calls for ideally results in either the recovery or the acquisition of *tsedakkah*, or righteousness. As God explains in Isaiah, "Zion shall be redeemed by justice, and those in her *who repent by righteousness*. But rebels and sinners shall be destroyed together, and those who forsake the Lord shall be consumed" (1:27–28; my emphasis). In Zephaniah, God warns: "Seek the Lord, all you humble of the land, who do his commands; *seek righteousness*, seek humility; perhaps you may be hidden on the day of the wrath of the Lord" (2:3; my emphasis). In short, as God says in Hosea, "Sow for yourselves righteousness, reap the fruit of steadfast love" (10:12). Again: "So you, by the help of your Lord *return*,"—that is, "hold fast to love and justice, and wait continually for your God" (12:6; my emphasis). Heschel comments: "Questioning man's right to worship through offerings and songs, [the prophets] maintain that the primary way of serving God is through love, justice, and righteousness."[969]

In Ezekiel, God says: "If a man is righteous and does what is lawful and right . . . he shall surely live." And what Ezekiel means by "righteous" includes not only not eating "sacred meals in pagan high places,"[970] not practicing idolatry, and not "defil[ing] his neighbor's wife" (18:5–6). The word also refers to someone who (in a passage I quoted earlier) "does not oppress any one, but restores to the debtor his pledge, commits no robbery, gives his bread to the hungry and covers the naked with a garment, does not lend at interest or take any increase, withholds his hand from iniquity, [and] executes true justice between man and man" (18:7–8). T. G. Soares says, "As one reads the prophesies of Ezekiel it seems as if the greatest emphasis is upon the sin of idolatry and of the worship of other gods." However, as I noted earlier, Soares emphasizes Ezekiel's objection to these activities as moral as well as cultic. Furthermore, "[t]he social quality of Ezekiel's preaching is clear enough."[971]

All of this is explained by God when he says in Hosea, "I desire steadfast love and not sacrifice," because he is not simply rewarding good behavior and punishing bad but establishing a relationship with a morally conscious human being. Thus, as I noted earlier, he desires "the knowledge of God, rather than burnt offerings" (6:6). In Isaiah, too, God complains that "Israel does not know, my people does not understand" (1:3). To solve this problem, God presents himself as a teacher, a common idea in the works of the prophets as it is in Deuteronomy. In Jeremiah, God says to his people: "Return, O faithless children . . . And I will give you shepherds after my own heart, who will feed you with knowledge and understanding" (3:14–15). Generally speaking, the kind of knowledge God provides is the most useful kind. According to the prophets, he is "wonderful in counsel, and excellent in wisdom" (Isa 28:29). He "will be the stability of your times, abundance of salvation, wisdom, and knowledge" (33:6). At the end-time, God says in Jeremiah, when he will make a new covenant with his people, "they shall all know me" (31:34.). As Hosea says, "I will betroth you to me in faithfulness; and you shall know the Lord" (2:20). Until then, however, the people will suffer in ignorance.

As in the Pentateuch, however, this knowledge is not merely the awareness of God's existence or even the awareness of his name. Rather what is required is the knowledge of God's laws, the understanding of the means by which wisdom leads to salvation. The problem, God explains in Ezekiel, is that his "people know not the ordinance of the Lord" (8:7). Thus, God says in Jeremiah, "For my people are foolish, they know me not; they are stupid children, they have no understanding. They are skilled in doing evil, but how to do good they know not" (4:22). This, and this alone, according to God in Hosea, explains "the controversy" which he has "with the inhabitants of the land": "There is no faithfulness" to God and no "kindness" to others because there is "no knowledge of God" (4:1). In Jeremiah, God says that his people "proceed from evil to evil, and they do not know me" (9:3). God asks them to be conscious of the path to redemption by remembering the path to sin: "Set up waymarks for yourself, make yourself guideposts; consider well the highway, the road by which you went." And then, "Return, O virgin Israel" (31:21).

The wisdom that God teaches leads to salvation because it explains the standards that God has established for human behavior, directed both to himself and to the rest of humanity. Isaiah says that, at the end-time, "all the nations shall . . . go up to the mountain of the Lord and that he may teach us his ways and that we may walk in his paths" (2:2–3; Mic 4:2). In Second Isaiah, God says, "I am the Lord your God, who teaches you to profit, who leads you in the way you should go" (48:17). Thus, he is worth knowing because no one knows more than he does: "Who has directed the Spirit of the Lord, or as his counselor has instructed him? Whom did he consult for his enlightenment, and who taught him the path of justice, and showed him the way of understanding?" (40:13–14). God says in Jeremiah, the only truly wise person is the one who "understands and knows [God], that [he] is the Lord who practices steadfast love, justice, and righteousness" (9:24). And, of course, he is the Lord who demands these standards among his people.[972]

It is important to understand that "knowledge of God" in the works of the prophets and elsewhere in the Jewish Bible is not merely an intellectual matter. On the subject of *daath elohim*, knowledge of God, Heschel argues that "knowing" in Hosea's prophecy involves more than dispassionate understanding. In fact, "Hosea seems to have seized upon the idea of sympathy as an essential religious requirement. The words *daath elohim* mean *sympathy for God*, attachment of the whole person, his love as well as his knowledge." Furthermore, the feeling is mutual. Love—or *chesed*—goes both ways.[973] Indeed, God sometimes urges his people to comprehend his message not with their minds, but with their hearts. In Isaiah, God suggests that they will be able to "turn and be healed" only if they "understand with their hearts" (6:10). God says to Ezekiel, "Son of man, all my words that I shall speak to you, receive in your heart" (3:10). In Third Isaiah, he says that those "who know righteousness" are "the people in whose heart" his law is written (51:7), which is presumably why, in Jeremiah, he promises to "write [the law] upon their hearts" when he makes a new Covenant with Israel and Judah in the future. Then, and presumably *only* then, "they shall all know me" (31:31–34).

For most scholars, knowing with the heart is not merely an emotional experience, but a deeper and more comprehensive kind of knowing. Franz Mussner argues that the prophets and other biblical writers use the word *heart* in the way that modern writers use the word *conscience*: "The organ in the human being which hears the instruction of God is called in the Old Testament not 'conscience,' but 'heart.'" Elsewhere, Mussner explains: "As *vox theologica*, 'to know' in the Old Testament does not mean the rational, speculatively won insight of reason." It is "rather a holistic personal act in the sense of acknowledgement, trust, entrusting, giving oneself over, believing. 'To know' describes the correct attitude toward God which is born out of the center of existence."[974] Thus, Bernhard Anderson says: "[T]his is a knowledge which includes the *will* as well as the mind. Hosea was talking about the language of the heart—that is, the response of the whole person to God's love. To know Yahweh means to respond to the claim he makes upon one's devotion, to obey his will in society where the poor and needy cry for help."[975]

The Evolution of Love

In this context, it is not surprising that the prophets often describe repentance as a change of heart rather than mind. Sometimes, God says that the human heart requires a complete cleansing. For example, he says in the prophecy of Jeremiah, "O Jerusalem, wash your heart from wickedness, that you may be saved" (Jer 4:14). Similarly, he says in Isaiah: "Wash yourselves; make yourselves clean; remove the evil of your doings from before my eyes." Sometimes, God insists that repentance requires "whole-heartedness" because anything less is a "pretense" (Jer 3:9). Indeed, the same criticism applies to those who "draw near [God] with their mouth and honor [him] with their lips, while their hearts are far from [him]." Their fear of God is nothing more "than a commandment of men learned by rote" (Isa 21:13). In this respect, an uninformed heart, an evil heart, and a divided heart are different ways of describing the same spiritual shortcoming. God says in the prophecy of Joel, "Yet even now . . . return to me *with all your heart*"—that is, completely. In Deuteronomy, Moses commands Israel "to fear the Lord your God, to walk in all his ways, to serve the Lord your God *with all your heart and with all your soul*" (10:12; my emphasis). And God says in Jeremiah that he will hear his penitents and they will find him only when thy seek him "with all [their] heart" (29:12-13).

All this suggests that God does not merely require good deeds, such as acts of mercy and justice; rather, he asks for the kind of internal change that enables the performance of good deeds. As Newsome explains, "It is not only a commitment to the keeping of the law . . . but also one which involves a reorientation of the heart."[976] "Circumcise yourselves to the Lord," Jeremiah says, "remove the foreskin of your hearts"—in other words, *change profoundly* (4:4; see also Deut 10:16; 30:6). In fact, in Ezekiel, God seems to give a new definition of exactly what he means by repentance. He says, "Repent and turn from all your transgressions, lest iniquity be your ruin. Cast away from you all the transgressions which you have committed against me, and *get yourselves a new heart and a new spirit!*" (18:30-31; my emphasis). God's point in this demand—the idea that the old heart and old spirit will not work—suggests that real devotion involves even more than a pledge or an affirmation. Indeed, God's people can mend their broken relationship with him only by undergoing a moral transformation.[977]

The prophets also make it clear that knowledge of self is as important as knowledge of God. And this means, first and at the very least, awareness of one's guilt, one's responsibility for sin. In Jeremiah, God says, "Return, faithless Israel, . . . I will not look on you in anger, for I am merciful . . . Only acknowledge your guilt, that you rebelled against the Lord your God" (3:12-13). God later laments, the people "hold fast to deceit, they refuse to return. I have given heed and listened, but they have not spoken aright: no man repents of his wickedness, saying, 'What have I done?'" (Jer 8:5-6). In Third Isaiah, God says in a passage I quoted earlier, emphasizing the role of contrition in the process of repentance: "I dwell in the high and holy place, and also with him who is of a contrite and humble spirit, to revive the spirit of the humble, and to revive the heart of the contrite" (57:15; see also 66:2). In the prophecy of Ezekiel,

The Covenant

God says that the people of Israel must first "remember [their] evil ways, and [their] deeds that were not good." (Ezek 36:31).

Second, they must "loathe" themselves for their sins in order to be forgiven (36:31). In Hosea, God says to his people that he will have nothing to do with them "until they acknowledge their guilt and seek [his] face, and in their distress they seek [him] . . . After two days he will revive us; on the third day he will raise us up, that we may live before him. Let us know, let us press on to know the Lord'" (5:15; 6:2–3). This passage, brief though it is, covers virtually every aspect of the process of repentance. The first step, remorse, requires the acknowledgement of sin, the confession of "guilt." The second step, understanding, requires a "return" to God and an acceptance of his ways. And the final step is a profound change in the penitent, who henceforth willingly "press[es] on to know the Lord." This is what the prophets meant, says Moore, by "a transformation *not only of conduct but of character*," which is the indispensable "moral aspect of repentance."[978]

Finally, sometimes repentance even requires suffering. God says in the prophecy of Joel, do it "with fasting, with weeping, and with mourning"—that is, with abnegation, with sorrow, and with a sense of loss. "And rend your hearts and not your garments" (2:12–13)—that is, have a *real* experience rather than a symbolic one—indeed, one that is painful as well as sad. In Hosea, God says, "Come let us return to the Lord; for he has torn, that he may heal us; he has stricken, and he will bind us up." (6:1–2). How could anything less than a heart-rending and life-changing experience elicit from God the grace, mercy, and love that he often promises? Thus, God laments in Hosea, "They do not cry to me from the heart" (7:14). When they do, he says, "I will heal their faithlessness; I will love them freely" (14:4).

While repentance arises first and most emphatically in the works of the prophets, it is also important in the book of Psalms, a subject we will examine in the next chapter. For now, it is important to remember that the concept also appears in Deuteronomy, although it is hardly as important there as it is in either of the other two collections. It is useful to keep in mind that the Covenant in Deuteronomy, though based on the mutual love between God and his people, is nevertheless presented throughout this book as a classic or textbook example of a *quid pro quo* agreement. It is based on the idea that the Israelites were being offered the possession of the Promised Land in exchange for their obedience to a modified version of the laws presented in the book of Exodus. It is necessary to remember, however, that the Israelites are offered a reward despite their past record of disobedience and infidelity. Furthermore—and this is where repentance enters the story—they will remain God's people because, even if they sin in the future, they will be able to ask for forgiveness and then be forgiven![979]

We noted in the preceding chapter that Moses, in Deuteronomy, repeatedly demands strict obedience from the Israelites. It is important to note, as well, considering his offer of many rewards for obedience as well as many punishments for disobedience, that he may be uncertain that God's people have either the willingness or the capacity to comply. This also might be why Moses' description of the act of acquiescence makes it sound surprisingly easy. Moses quotes God as saying again and again, "[G]o in and take possession of the land" that is "before you" and "which the Lord swore to your fathers" (1:8, 21; 4:1; 6:18; 8:1). And Moses himself says to the Israelites: God's commandment "is not too hard for you, neither is it far off. It is not in heaven, that you should say, 'Who will go up for us to heaven . . . ? But the word is very near you, it is in your mouth and in your heart, so that you can do it" (30:11–14).

Indeed, God assures the Israelites that he will make the enemies of the Israelites—in this case, the present occupants of the Holy Land—afraid of them, as he did in the past: "This day I will begin to put the dread and fear of you upon the peoples that are under the whole heaven, who shall hear the report of you and shall tremble and be in anguish because of you" (2:25). Thus, says Moses, the Israelites have nothing to fear on their part, especially since God himself will help them: "You shall not fear them; for it is the Lord your God who fights for you" (3:22; 7:17–24; 9:1–3; 20:1–4). In fact, Moses says: "The Lord your God himself will go over before you; he will destroy these nations before you, so that you shall dispossess them . . . Be strong and of good courage, do not fear or be in dread of them: for it is the Lord your God who goes with you; he will not fail you or forsake you (31:3, 6; see also 11:23–25).

Moses also reminds the Israelites that they can rely on God's help now because he helped them in the past, particularly by choosing them out of all the nations of the world, liberating them from Egypt, leading them across the desert, and taking them to the Promised Land: "[H]as any god ever attempted to go and take a nation for himself from the midst of another nation . . . ?" (4:34). "We were Pharaoh's slaves in Egypt; and the Lord brought us out of Egypt with a mighty hand" (6:21). "[T]he Lord your God has chosen you to be a people for his own possession, out of all the peoples that are on the face of the earth" (7:6). "And you shall remember all the way which the Lord your God has led you these forty years in the wilderness" (8:2). "[Y]ou shall rejoice in all the good which the Lord your God has given to you and your house" (26:11). "You have seen all that the Lord did before your eyes in the land of Egypt" (29:2).

Furthermore, God destroyed the enemies of the Israelites in the course of their journey, as Moses explains in great detail in 2:24—3:21. In brief, "[T]he Lord our God *gave all into our hands*" (2:36; my emphasis), including Sihon the king of Heshbon and Og the king of Bashan. "And because he loved your fathers and chose their descendants after them, and brought you out of Egypt with his own presence, by his great power, driving out before you nations greater and mightier than yourselves, to bring you in, to give you their land for an inheritance, as at this day; know therefore this day, and lay it to your heart, that the Lord is God in heaven above and on the earth beneath; there is no other" (4:37–39).

As if all this might not be enough to persuade the Israelites, Moses also offers several rewards to the Israelites for obeying God's laws and complying with his orders to invade Canaan. On the one hand, in his most formulaic description of God's positive

The Covenant

reinforcement program, Moses modestly tells the Israelites: "Therefore you shall keep his statutes and commandments . . . *that it may go well with you*, and with your children after you, and that *you may prolong your days in the land* which the Lord your God gives you for ever" (4:40; see also 5:16, 29, 33; 6:2–3, 18; 12: 25, 28; 22:7; 30:16; my emphasis). The major features of this offer—well-being and long life, as well as land—should remind us of the promises God made to the patriarchs in the book of Genesis. After all, Moses is careful to remind the Israelites that God has already fulfilled his prediction (in Genesis 22:17; 26:4; and Exodus 32:13) that Joseph's family of seventy members would expand miraculously in the future: "[T]he Lord your God has multiplied you, and behold, you are this day as the stars of heaven for the multitude" (Deut 1:10; 10:22; 28:62)—that is, "as he swore to your fathers," word for word (13:17).

On the other hand, however, God also offers the Israelites an incredible laundry list of gifts that far exceed in value and extent the substantial but in no sense spectacular gifts God promised the patriarchs. First, when they take over Canaan, they will inherit not just land, but an already developed civilization, featuring "great and goodly cities, which you did not build, and houses full of all good things, which you did not fill," as well as already hewn cisterns and already planted "vineyards and olive trees" (6:10–11). Second, the land itself will, with God's blessing, yield grain, wine, and oil; their herds and flocks will flourish (7:13). "For the Lord your God is bringing you into a good land, a land of brooks of water, of fountains and springs, flowing forth in valleys and hills, a land of wheat and barley, of vines and fig trees and pomegranates, a land of olive trees and honey, a land in which you will eat bread without scarcity, in which you will lack nothing, a land whose stones are iron, and out of whose hills you can dig copper. And you shall eat and be full" (8:7–10; see also 11:8–15).

Third, aside from the infrastructure of Eden, the Israelites will be granted perfect health: "You shall be blessed above all peoples; there shall not be male or female barren among you, or among your cattle." Furthermore, "the Lord will take away from you all sickness; and none of the evil diseases of Egypt, which you knew, will he inflict upon you but he will lay them upon all who hate you" (7:14–15). And, fourth, God will give the Israelites wealth, fame, and power: "The Lord your God will make you abundantly prosperous in all the work of your hand" (30:9). Moses thus warns the Israelites not to forget God "when you have eaten and are full, and have built goodly houses and live in them, and when your herds and flocks multiply, and your silver and gold is multiplied." After all, "the Lord your God is he who gives you power to get wealth" (8:12–13, 18). And, more than that, "he will set you high above all nations that he has made, in praise and in fame and in honor" (26:19). "And all the peoples of the earth shall see that you are called by the name of the Lord; and they shall be afraid of you. And the Lord will make you abound in prosperity . . ."[A]nd you shall lend to many nations, but you shall not borrow. And the Lord will make you the head, and not the tail; and you shall tend upward only, and not downward" (28:11–13).

The Evolution of Love

The common ground between Deuteronomy and the prophets is, first, the recent, if not the present, sinfulness of the Israelites, who are now reminded by Moses of their failure to trust God, which is the basis for the danger they have continually put themselves in. In 1:19–46, Moses retells the story of their reluctance to invade Canaan because of the negative report of the spies, God's rejection of almost all of the adult males who refused to fight, and their subsequent change of mind, which contradicted God's orders. In 9:7–21, Moses recounts their rebellion at Mt. Sinai, their worship of the Golden Calf. And in 23:15–18, Moses provides an overview of their rebelliousness: "[Y]ou waxed fat, you grew thick, you became sleek . . . You were unmindful of the Rock that begot you, and you forgot God who gave you birth." Interwoven throughout Deuteronomy is the threat that God will destroy the Israelites if they fail to obey the commandments at the present time: "I call heaven and earth to witness against you this day, that you will soon utterly perish from the land," which "will be utterly destroyed. And the Lord will scatter you among the peoples, and you will be left few in number among the nations where the Lord will drive you" (4:26–27; see also 6:14–15; 9:19–20; 11:16–17).

Mass destruction sounds bad enough, but just as the rewards for obedience are grandiose, so are the punishments for disobedience. The extraordinary and unprecedented suffering that sinful Israelites will be forced to endure is documented at great length and in great detail in chapter 28. Moses says: "The Lord will send upon you curses, confusion, and frustration, in all that you undertake to do, until you are destroyed and perish quickly, on account of the evil of your doings, because you have forsaken me." Your land will be cursed with pestilence, heat, drought, and mildew; rain will come down as dust. Locusts will eat your grain, and worms will consume your grapes. Your body will be cursed with consumption, fever, inflammation, boils, ulcers, and scurvy; your mind with suffer from madness and confusion. Your enemies will triumph: "and you shall be only oppressed and robbed continually." You will marry an unfaithful woman, and you will build a house and not be able to live in it. All of your animals will die; and your children will be taken away. "All these curses shall come upon you and pursue you till you are destroyed." "And your dead body shall be food for all birds of the air, and for beasts of the earth" (28: 15–46). There are twenty more verses dedicated to this subject, which include a woman who eats her just-born children (28:56–57) and a forced return of the Israelites to Egypt: "And the Lord will bring you back in ships to Egypt and there you shall offer yourselves for sale to your enemies as male and female slaves, *but no man will buy you*" (v. 68; my emphasis; see also 30:17–18).

Needless to say, this is a series of warnings that could hardly be either exceeded in horror or more likely to discourage Moses' audience from rejecting what Moses calls the way of life and embracing what he calls the way of death (30:15, 19). Along with the magnificent rewards that God has promised the Israelites for their obedience, these extremely dire punishments for their disobedience reflect what must be understood to be an overwhelmingly appealing and appalling expression of Moses' sense of danger, reflecting his fear that the Israelites will not comply—a last, desperate attempt to make them understand the consequences of their decision to disobey. Indeed, at the end of this tirade, Moses offers the Israelites a final opportunity: the certainty that, despite their past and even their present sinfulness, they can be saved. And this is where the idea of repentance enters the story.

Moses explains that any punishment by God, including even the devastation wrought by a single reprobate—an individual, a family, or a tribe—that leaves "the whole land brimstone and salt, and a burnt-out waste, unsown and growing nothing" (29:18, 23) could still be reversed and repaired by a "return to the Lord your God." That is, Moses says to his fellow Israelites, renewed obedience—repentance—"with all your heart and with all your soul" would allow God to "restore your fortunes, and have compassion upon you," resulting in your possession of the land and the fulfillment of God's promise to "make you more prosperous and numerous than your fathers" (30:2, 5). Thus, whether they remain in their present fallen state or fall into sin again, the Israelites will be afforded another chance to "again obey the voice of the Lord, and keep all his commandments." This reversal is possible "if you turn to the Lord your God with all your heart and all your soul." And, as a consequence, "God will make you abundantly prosperous in all the work of your hand" (30:8–10).

It is not as if this option arises only at the end of Deuteronomy. Early in this book, Moses says to the Israelites: Even if "you forget the covenant of the Lord your God," and you are scattered "among the peoples" as a result (4:23, 27), it will still be possible for you to "seek the Lord your God." If you do, "you will find him, if you search after him with all your heart and with all your soul." This will happen if "you return to the Lord your God and obey his voice, for the Lord your God is a merciful God; he will not fail you or destroy you or forget the covenant with your fathers which he swore to them" (4:29–30). Under these circumstances, "the Lord may turn from the fierceness of his anger, and show you mercy, and have compassion on you" (13:17). The key to forgiveness, Moses says twice in chapter 30, is "loving the Lord your God" (vv. 16, 20). And, in his song, written at the behest of God to give one last warning to the Israelites, Moses says that "the Lord will vindicate his people and have compassion on his servants, when he sees that their power is gone, and there is none remaining, bond or free" (32:36). Thus, in the end, God "makes expiation for the land of his people" (32:43). That is, according to the editors of *The Oxford Annotated Bible*, God "cleanses or purges the land and its people of guilt" (p. 259). Blessing "the children of Israel before his death," Moses says of God, "Yea, he loved his people" (33:2).

Chapter Five

A Crisis of Faith

Yahweh, the God of Judaism, differs from many of the gods of other ancient civilizations for several reasons. First, of course, he is the *only* God, a concept that developed as early as the eighth century BC, at which time other countries in the Middle East remained polytheistic.[980] Second, he is a moral God, who can be counted on to act on the principles of justice and mercy, which distinguishes him from many ancient gods who at least sometimes acted self-indulgently and amorally.[981] Third, he is a God who established moral standards for his worshipers, requiring righteousness rather than obedience to rules.[982] Fourth, he is a God who treats all of his followers equally, instead of favoring the royal family and members of the aristocracy.[983]

It must be emphasized, however, that God does not always appear in this guise in the earliest phase of Judaism, which is recorded in the first four books of the Torah. He is described in the aforementioned terms, as I suggested in chapter 4, in the first millennium BC, when religions in several of the urbanized societies of the world underwent a similar change, not only in their vision of God, but also in their modes of worship and in their definitions of morality. As we have seen, the prophets of Israel thoroughly revised Judaism in all these respects. And the transformation of the Jewish faith is also discernible in the Psalms, the Proverbs, and other writings that were composed in the exilic and post-exilic periods. "In this trying period," says Samuel Umen, "the Jews were called upon to rethink and re-evaluate their God concept, their mode of worship, their whole approach to their God, their religion, and their life." Specifically, Umen explains: "From the idea of a National God, they advanced to the idea of a Universal God. Their God who heretofore could be reached by their intermediaries the priests now became their personal God to whom they could open their hearts. As a substitute for the sacrifices offered in their behalf by the priests in the holy Temple, they introduced—prayer."[984]

Scholars often refer to the major Jewish writings of the mid-first millennium BC, the body of work that was the product of this process of change and maturation, as a consistent and unified expression of what might be called the essence of Judaism.

A Crisis of Faith

This is a valid judgment insofar as the prophets, the Deuteronomist, and the psalmists focus on the Covenant Code and its portrayal of the ideal relationship between human beings as based on compassion and guided by the principles of justice and mercy. Indeed, the covenant idea, as I have emphasized—derived from the Decalogue and accompanying laws in Exodus and Leviticus, especially the twofold commandment in Leviticus to love not only God, but both neighbor and stranger—runs from those origins forward to the prophets and Deuteronomy and onward to the Pharisees and the Rabbis, without much deviation.

It must be said, however, that these works are not entirely in agreement on the subject of God's distribution of rewards and punishments. The point is that the idea of God as a promoter and protector of *a particular kind of moral order* changed over time and was particularly challenged in the post-exilic period. In short, the concept of God and his relationship with humanity underwent serious transformations—not insofar as God was understood to be the creator and administrator of the universe, but only insofar as he was understood to be both the creator and the enforcer of a system of moral guidance based strictly on the principle of justice: that is, the idea that, in response to people's moral actions, God gives everyone what he or she deserves, precisely determined by his or her adherence to or departure from the laws identified and explained in the Pentateuch.

On the one hand, the basis for morality and God's enforcement of it in the book of Psalms shifts back and forth between a strict application of the concept of *quid pro quo* and the assumption that God's rewards and punishments are not automatic but influenced by his mercy as well as his justice. On the other hand, the prophets are in agreement in their view that, although the Jews of the first millennium BC were justly punished by God for their infidelity—that is, their suffering was the consequence of their sin—God, in his mercy, offered them the possibility of forgiveness to the extent that they were willing to repent (see, e.g., Jer chs. 3–4).

Although Deuteronomy retains the concept of morality that appears in the works of the prophets, it does not focus on repentance for past sins as a means of gaining forgiveness. Rather, it emphasizes obedience as a means of attaining salvation in the future. In addition, the prophets, unlike either the psalmists or even the Deuteronomist, promise not only well-being, security, and longevity—that is, the kinds of rewards that might accrue to people who have created a fair and just society—but a veritable transformation of the human condition: an end to any and all natural disasters, disease, and war, as well as all social and psychological maladies, including political domination, economic exploitation, interpersonal conflict, and individual suffering of any kind and for whatever reason.

The Evolution of Love

The Old View in the Psalms and Proverbs

Many of the psalms reflect the religious ideas of early Judaism, which are, in many respects, indistinguishable from the religious concepts of other ancient people. El (or Yahweh) was assumed to be one of many gods, a defender of the tribe of Israelites, and a warrior capable of protecting his subjects against both human adversaries and natural disasters. In exchange for providing help in all kinds of enterprises, especially war, he expected to be honored by sacrifices, flattered by obedience, and praised by all of his beneficiaries in song and ceremony. His rewards for these acts of subservience were security, prosperity, and power; and his punishments were not only the absence of those more or less material gains but also suffering, exile, and death. He was, in short, the God of the Pentateuch, though without the more positive attributes, such as love and forgiveness, which God possesses in Deuteronomy.

Polytheism is evident in a number of psalms, especially those that deal with a "council of gods" or a "divine council," starting with Psalm 82: "God has taken his place in the divine council; in the midst of the gods he holds judgment" (v. 1). Patrick D. Miller comments: "Yahweh was envisioned seated on a throne in his temple or palace surrounded by a nameless host of divine beings who rendered service to the enthroned deity (1 Kings 22:19; Isa. 6:1–4). Yahweh took counsel with them and commissioned them with tasks."[985] The editors of *The Oxford Annotated Bible* explain that the psalmist is using "a conception, common to the ancient Near East, that the world is ruled by a council of gods." The God of the Jews says to the other gods that, "[b]ecause they govern the earth unjustly, they shall all perish like mere human beings" (720): "You are gods," he says, "sons of the Most High, all of you; nevertheless, you shall die like men, and fall like any prince" (vv. 3–7). In Psalm 58, the psalmist asks, "Do you indeed decree what is right, you gods? Do you judge the sons of men uprightly? Nay, in your hearts you devise wrongs; your hands deal out violence on earth" (vv. 1–2).[986]

The same idea occurs in several other psalms. In Psalm 89, the writer asks: "For who in the skies can be compared to the Lord? Who among the heavenly beings is like the Lord, a God feared in the council of the holy ones, great and terrible above all that are around him" (vv. 6–7). In Psalm 95, the psalmist says that "the Lord is a great God, and a great king above all gods" (v. 3). And the writer of Psalm 77 asks, "What god is great like our God?" (v. 14). Clearly, in these psalms, using phrases like "heavenly beings," "holy ones," and "all gods," the psalmists are referring not to angels, but to the array of gods worshiped everywhere in the ancient world, compared to whom Yahweh is always distinguished by his power, justice, mercy, and compassion. The other gods "have neither knowledge nor understanding, and they walk about in darkness" (82:5). According to Karen Armstrong, "As archeologists have discovered, most of the population worshiped other local gods besides Yahweh, and Baal worship flourished in Israel until the sixth century. But by the ninth century, some Israelites were beginning to cut down on the number of gods they worshiped . . . A small group of prophets . . .

A Crisis of Faith

wanted to worship Yahweh alone, and were convinced that he could provide for all the wants of his people." Elijah—whose name means 'Yahweh is my God!'—"is the first prophet on record to insist on the exclusive worship of Yahweh."[987]

Technically, of course, the Jewish faith expressed in these psalms is not polytheism, but henotheism, the worship of one god, with the understanding that other gods exist. As Franz Mussner puts it, "[P]olytheism was denied and only a single God was honored . . . without questioning the existence of other national deities."[988] Elsewhere in the psalms, although God is not identified as the leader of the Divine Council, he is called "the God of gods" (84:7), one among many, albeit superior to the others, a description that occurs again in Psalm 136: "O give thanks to the God of gods" (v. 2). The psalmist says in Psalm 86, "[T]hou alone art God" (v. 10), which sounds monotheistic, but earlier in the same psalm he says not only, "Thou art *my* God" (v. 2; my emphasis), as if he were distinguishing his god from all the others, but also "There is none like thee among the gods, O Lord" (v. 8). In Psalm 138, the writer says, "I give thee thanks, O Lord, with my whole heart; before the gods I sing thy praise" (v. 1). After all, asks the writer of Psalm 113, "Who is like the Lord our God? (v. 5), partly because as the writer of Psalm 147 says, "He has not dealt thus with any other nation; they do not know his ordinances" (v. 20). Therefore, "[b]lessed is the nation whose God is the Lord" (33:14). In other words, there are nations who have other gods, but all the worse for them: "Those who choose another god"—besides 'the Lord,' or Yahweh—"multiply their sorrows" (16:4).

In some psalms, "other gods" are treated ambivalently. On the one hand, they are portrayed as nothing more than statues. On the other hand, however, they are referred to as actual gods who are, though inferior to Yahweh, nevertheless real. In Psalm 96, the psalmist says that "all the gods of the peoples are idols." Yet, Yahweh "is to be feared above all gods" (vv. 4-6). The writer of Psalm 97 makes the same point: "All worshipers of images are put to shame, who make their boast in worthless idols." However, this psalmist also returns immediately to the idea that other gods are not *merely* idols, but also the actual gods of other nations. And these gods, ironically, worship Yahweh: "[A]ll gods bow down before him" (v. 7). The same double message appears in Psalm 135, where the writer mocks the idolatry of other faiths: "The idols of the nations are silver and gold, the work of men's hands. They have mouths, but they speak not, they have eyes, but they see not, they have ears but they hear not, not is there any breath in their mouths. Like them be those who make them!—yea, every one who trusts in them! (vv. 15-18). Earlier, however, the psalmist says, "For I know that the Lord is great, and that our Lord is above all gods" (v. 5; see also Ps 115).

Of course, God is described in the psalms as dwelling on "high" (138:6)—in fact, "high above all nations" as well as "above the heavens," which enables him to "look far down upon the heavens and the earth" (113:4-6). In Isaiah, God being "the high and lofty One who inhabits eternity," he says, "I dwell in the high and holy place" (57:15). However, since the gods of ancient religions are often said to live in heaven or above

213

it, it is significant that the God of the psalms as well as the book of Daniel is frequently referred to (more than a dozen times in both books) as the "most high" God. He is defined in Psalm 97 as not only highest "over all the earth," but also "exalted far above all gods" (v. 9). That is, the superlative "most high" suggests throughout these works that Yahweh is the highest *among other high gods*. In Psalm 83, for example, the writer says, "Let them know that thou alone, whose name is the Lord, art the Most High over all the earth" (v. 18).

In many psalms, Yahweh is also portrayed as a tribal god rather than a god who represents all of humanity. That is, although he is acknowledged as the creator of the universe, he belongs to the tribe, to the Jewish nation. I do not mean to suggest that the Jewish God never achieved universality. There can be little doubt that in both Deuteronomy and the works of the prophets he is often portrayed as a god who is quite different from the typical pre-Axial Age deity who welcomes solicitation and adulation, offers his worshippers support and protection, and is therefore understood to be responsive to human needs not out of love, but because of either obligation or manipulation. In the psalms, however, God sometimes matches the kind of God who not only had these characteristics, but also was identified as the God who belonged to the ancient Jews and to no one else.

In Psalm 33, as we have seen, the psalmist says, "Blessed is the nation whose God is the Lord" (v. 12). It must be remembered that in making this claim, the psalmist does not mean that his nation's god is God. It means that his nation's god is *Yahweh* (or, in most of the psalms from 42 to 83, *Elohim*). And the same point applies to statements in which God is referred to as "ours": "[T]his is . . . our God for ever and ever" (48:14) or "[H]e is our God" (97:7). These claims do not refer to a generic, universal god, but to a specific god, the God of the Covenant, and no other. In Psalm 148, the writer claims that God "has not dealt thus with any other nation; they do not know his ordinances. Praise the Lord!" (v. 20).

Certainly, as I said earlier, like many gods of the ancient world, Yahweh was originally understood to be a warrior god. As Armstrong notes, during David's reign in Judah, the king was seen as "the earthly counterpart of the divine warrior."[989] In Exodus, Moses says, "The Lord is a man of war," "glorious in power," who "shatters the enemy." He continues: "Who is like thee, O Lord, among the gods? Who is like thee, majestic in holiness, terrible in glorious deeds, doing wonders?" (15:3, 6, 11). In many psalms, God is described in exactly the same terms. In Psalm 2, the psalmist warns earthly kings (presumably besides King David) to be fearful of God's wrath and power: "Now, therefore, O kings, be wise; be warned, O rulers of the earth. Serve the Lord with fear, with trembling kiss his feet, lest he be angry, and you perish in the way; for his wrath is quickly kindled" (vv. 10–11). In Psalm 9, we are told that God "rebuke[s] the nations," "destroy[s] the wicked," and "blot[s] out their name" (v. 5). Indeed, God "rain[s] fire and brimstone" on them (11:6). In Psalm 24, Yahweh is referred to as "strong and mighty, . . . mighty in battle!" (v. 8). Therefore, King David

A Crisis of Faith

(and his successors) can always be confident of victory: "Now I know that the Lord will help his anointed; he will answer him from his holy heaven with mighty victories by his right hand" (20:6).

In exchange for their loyalty, God was expected to protect his worshipers from their enemies by defending them, fighting for them, or helping them fight for themselves. In the first instance, God simply protects his people's security and well-being. Thus, says the psalmist, "All my enemies shall be ashamed and sorely troubled; they shall turn back, and be put to shame in a moment" (6:10; see also Pss 35:4, 26; 40:14). "When evildoers assail me, uttering slanders against me, my adversaries and foes, they shall stumble and fall" (27:2). With this assurance in mind, the psalmist in Psalm 3:1–3 asks God to serve as his "shield": "O Lord, how many are my foes! Many are rising against me; many are saying of me, there is no help for him in God." In Psalm 144, King David says, "Rescue me from the cruel sword, and deliver me from the hands of aliens, whose mouths speak lies, and whose right hand is a right hand of falsehood" (v. 11).

Less aggressively, God provides his people with a "a hiding place" in which he "preserve[s]" them "from trouble" and "encompass[es]" them "with deliverance" (32:7). The petitioner in Psalm 17 says to God, "Keep me as the apple of the eye; hide me in the shadow of thy wings, from the wicked who despoil me, my deadly enemies who surround me" (v. 8–9). This is why the psalmists say again and again that "all who take refuge" in God are "[b]lessed" (2:11; 37:39–40; 46:1; 59:16; 91:9), including the king: "The Lord is ... the saving refuge of his anointed" (28:8). Indeed, "none of those who take refuge in him will be condemned" (34:22). "The children of men take refuge in the shadow of [God's] wing" (36:7). And the psalmists say repeatedly, "O Lord my God, in thee do I take refuge" (7:1; 16:1; 11:1; 18:2; 25:20; 31:4; 43:2; 46:7; 62:7; 64:10; 71:1, 3; 73:28; 94:22; 118:7). The writer of Psalm 143 asks for the same protection: "Deliver me, O Lord, from my enemies! I have fled to thee for refuge!" (v. 9; see also 17:7; 69:18).

Alternatively, though less often, the petitioner asks for (and expects) God's direct intervention: "Arise, O Lord! Deliver me, O my God! For thou dost smite all my enemies on the cheek, thou dost break the teeth of the wicked" (3:7). "Arise, O Lord, confront them, overthrow them! Deliver my life from the wicked by the sword" (17:13). In Psalm 18, the writer describes God's actions in his defense as spectacular. The psalmist was "encompassed," "assailed," and "entangled" by the "cords" and "snares" of death, all inflicted on him by his enemies. In response, God caused the earth to reel and the mountains to tremble. Smoke, fire, hailstones, lightning, and hot coals came out of him. Darkness covered the earth, and God scattered and routed the enemy. Finally, God exposed "the channels of the sea" and "the foundations of the world" (vv. 7–15).

With this kind of protection, it is logical for the petitioner to say: "Contend, O Lord, with those who contend with me; fight against those who fight against me! Take

The Evolution of Love

hold of shield and buckler, and rise for my help! Draw the spear and javelin against my pursuers! Say to my soul, 'I am your deliverance!'" (35:1–3). In Psalm 60, the psalmist says confidently, "With God we shall do valiantly; it is he who will tread down our foes" (v. 12; see also 108:13). After all, God himself says of King David that he "will crush his foes before him and strike down those who hate him" (89:23).[990] The king thus appeals to God in Psalm 59: "Rouse thyself, come to my help, and see! Thou, Lord God of hosts, art God of Israel. Awake to punish all the nations; spare none of those who treacherously plot evil" (vv. 4–5). "O my strength, I will sing praises to thee" (v. 9).

The expectation that God will help on these occasions is based on his covenantal vows and his history of saving the Jews from their enemies, from the exodus onward, a subject summarized in great detail in Psalms 78 and 106. Sometimes, victory for the psalmist in such circumstances is possible only because God guides and strengthens and even arms those who obey him: "Blessed be the Lord, my rock, who trains my hands for war, and my fingers for battle" (144:1). In Psalm 18, the writer claims to have defeated his enemies on his own: "I pursued my enemies and overtook them; and did not turn back till they were consumed" (v. 38). However, he expresses his gratitude to God and acknowledges that he did not accomplish this task alone: "Yea, by thee I can crush a troop, and by my God I can leap over a wall . . . Thou hast given me the shield of thy salvation, and thy right hand supported me, and thy help made me great" (vv. 29, 35). In Psalm 44, the writer says to God, "Through thee we push down our foes; through thy name we tread down our assailant" (v. 5). In Psalm 21, the psalmist says to the king, "If [your enemies] plan evil against you . . . they will not succeed. For you will put them to flight" (vv. 21:11–12). The reason is not that the king is powerful, but that God supports him. The psalmist tells God that the king's "glory is great through [his] help; splendor and majesty [he] dost bestow upon him" (v. 5).

It is consistent with these activities of God to demand from his worshippers not only gratitude, but gifts, in the form of sacrifices. Simply put, the writer in Psalm 4 tells his fellow worshippers to "offer right sacrifices, and put [their] trust in the Lord" (v. 3; see also 76:11–12; 96:8; 107:21–22). In Psalm 5, the psalmist clearly understands that Yahweh is not about to grant his request without some kind of compensation. Thus, first he makes his plea: "Give ear to my words, O Lord, give heed to my groaning. Hearken to the sound of my cry, my King and my God, for to thee do I pray." Then he promises God a reward: "I prepare a sacrifice for thee, and watch" (vv. 1–2). The same pattern recurs in Psalm 27. The writer praises God for providing him with a "stronghold," fending off his enemies, and otherwise protecting him, in response to which he "will offer in his tent sacrifices with shouts of joy" (vv. 1–6). In Psalm 54, the writer asks for protection from "insolent" and "ruthless" men; expresses confidence that God will help him; and concludes by promising God, "With a freewill offering I will sacrifice to thee . . . [f]or thou hast delivered me from every trouble" (vv. 6–7).

In Psalm 56, the psalmist announces that he is invulnerable, but entirely owing to God's help: "What can man do to me?" To this, he responds, "My vows to thee I must perform, O God; I will render thank offerings to thee. For thou hast delivered my soul from death" (vv. 11–13). In Psalm 66, the psalmist is grateful for "what [God] has done for" him, in response to which he promises God: "I will come into thy house with burnt offerings; I will pay thee my vows, that which my lips uttered and my mouth promised when I was in trouble. I will offer to thee burnt offerings of fatlings, with the smoke of the sacrifice of rams; I will make an offering of bulls and goats" (vv. 13–16). The psalmist in Psalm 116 says exactly the same thing. He asks, "What shall I render to the Lord for all his bounty to me?" He answers: "I will pay my vows to the Lord . . . I will offer to thee the sacrifice of thanksgiving" (vv. 14, 17).

The recipients of God's favors repay him not only by offering sacrifices, but also by literally singing his praises. The latter actions have a twofold purpose. First, they express the people's gratitude for God's willingness to satisfy their needs. Second, the songs of praise spread the news of God's extraordinary deeds throughout the world. Praise in these two senses is what God explicitly requests when he says that he is responding positively to his people "for His name's sake." That is, God helps them partly because they glorify his *name*—his *reputation* as a righteous and responsive deity. The oldest use of this phrase appears in Psalm 106, where it refers to Exodus 32:11–14, which describes Moses' appeal to God to spare the Israelites after he threatens to destroy them for their disobedience. The psalmist says, "Yet [God] saved them for his name's sake, *that he might make known his mighty power*" (v. 8; my emphasis).

Surprisingly, this concept also appears occasionally in the works of the prophets. In Isaiah, God says, "For my name's sake I defer my anger, *for the sake of my praise* I restrain it for you, that I may not cut you off" (48:9; my emphasis). In Jeremiah, the people say to God, "Do not spurn us for thy name's sake; *do not dishonor thy glorious throne*" (14:21). In every instance, as the italicized passages indicate, God appears to be concerned about his reputation for being powerful, his capacity to elicit praise, and his reputation for honor. This passage in Ezekiel, in which God speaks to the Israelites, makes the point clear: "It is not for your sake, O house of Israel, that I am about to act, but for the sake of my holy name, which you have profaned among the nations to which you came . . . I will vindicate the holiness of my great name, which . . . you have profaned" (36:22–23).

In many psalms a number of these and other concepts are tied together to form a constellation of related terms that, collectively, portray the relationship between God and his people in what appears to be pre-exilic terms: (1) "praise" of God as an expression of people's thankfulness for his protection, (2) "sacrifice" as another symbol of gratitude, (3) "glorification" of his works as a method of Jewish proselytization, (4) "God's name" as the object of glorification, (5) "steadfast love" as another motive for God's ongoing support, (6) "righteousness" as God's most important feature, (7) "trust" as an expression of people's confidence in God's covenantal promises, and (8) "fear" as an aspect of people's uncertainty in the face of God's extraordinary power.

The Evolution of Love

In Psalm 7, for example, the psalmist says, "I will give to the Lord *thanks* due to his *righteousness*, and I will sing *praise* to the *name* of the Lord, the Most High" (v. 17). In Psalm 22, the writer says to God, "I will tell of thy *name* to my brethren; in the midst of the congregation I will *praise* thee: You who *fear* the Lord, praise him! All you sons of Jacob, *glorify* him, and stand in awe of him, all you sons of Israel!" (vv. 22–23). In Psalm 86, the psalmist *thanks* God and promises to *glorify* his *name*, desires to *fear* him, and acknowledges his *steadfast love* (vv. 11–13). In Psalm 131, the psalmist both praises and thanks the Lord, lauds his "wonderful works" as well as his righteousness, and says he will "provide for those who fear him" (vv. 1–3, 5). All of these passages, which can be duplicated in more than one-third of the psalms, depict God as a king who needs to be appeased by sacrifices, honored by adulation, and feared rather than loved—that is, a God who was worshiped in the pre-prophetic period, but who was later understood very differently as a result of the writings of Amos, Hosea, and Isaiah, as well as the Deuteronomist.

In the history of religion, this kind of god was also expected to offer rewards for "good" behavior. However, in the book of Psalms the passages in which this behavior is referred to are often unexpectedly general. In the very first psalm, the writer says, "Blessed is the man who walks not in the counsel of the wicked, nor stands in the way of sinners, nor sits in the seat of scoffers; but his delight is in the law of the Lord" (vv. 1–3). In Psalm 18, the psalmist explains that God "recompensed" and "rewarded [him] according to [his] righteousness; according to the cleanness of [his] hands," by which he means that he "kept the ways of the Lord"—obeying his "ordinances" and "statutes" (vv. 20–24). Similarly, the writer in Psalm 19 says that God gives "great reward" for "keeping" his "law," "testimony," "precepts," and "commandment" (vv. 7–11), although none of these psalmists specifies which or what kind of law or commandment God has in mind. "Surely, there is a reward for the righteous," says the writer of Psalm 58, but he too fails to say just what "righteous" means (v. 11).

On the one hand, in these psalms, God demands not merely obedience but obedience to *moral laws*. Furthermore, in the tradition of the prophets and the Deuteronomist, he is inclined to demand respectful imitation rather than blind subservience. As the psalmist in Psalm 5 says to God, "Thou dost bless the righteous" (v. 12). God does so, according to the traditional explanation in the Pentateuch, because he insists that his people obey him by embracing his moral standards and imitating his actions: "You shall be holy; for I the Lord your God am holy" (Lev 19:2). As George Foot Moore explains, this verse can be understood to mean "If ye make yourselves holy, I impute it to you as though ye hallowed me." In other words, God is worshiped ("hallowed") when his people follow his laws, especially his *moral* laws, a point stressed by Jesus, when he says to his disciples, "Truly, I say to you, as you did it to one of the least of these my brethren, you did it to me" (Matt 25:40).[991]

In Psalm 11, the psalmist says that "the Lord is righteous, he loves righteous deeds" (v. 7). In Psalm 94, the psalmist says that "the Lord will not forsake his people

". . . for justice will return to the righteous, and all the upright in heart will follow it" (vv. 14–15; see also 18:20–24). In Psalm 37, the "righteous" man is counseled to "do good" because the Lord "uphold[s]" him (vv. 3, 17). Thus, in Psalm 7, the penitent asks for God's help because he has lived righteously: "[J]udge me, O Lord, according to my righteousness and according to the integrity that is in me" (v. 8). After all, God tests "the minds and hearts" of everyone, and, because he is both a "righteous God" and "a righteous judge," he "saves the upright in heart" (vv. 8–11). In Psalm 34, the writer says, "The eyes of the Lord are toward the righteous, and his ears toward their cry . . . When the righteous cry for help, the Lord hears, and delivers them out of all their troubles" (vv. 15, 17).

On the other hand, however, "righteousness" remains undefined. Thus, in Psalm 24, we are told that God blesses those who have "clean hands and a pure heart" (vv. 4–5; see also 73:1), but the only specific misbehavior this psalmist condemns is lying.[992] In Psalm 81, the writer says that God would feed with "the finest" wheat and honey anyone who listened to him, refused to worship other gods, and "walk[ed] in [his] ways" (vv. 13–16; see also Ps 128:1). In Psalm 84, the message is equally vague: "No good thing does the Lord withhold from those who walk uprightly" (v. 11). In Psalm 97, we are told that God "loves those who hate evil; he preserves the lives of the saints; he delivers them from the hand of the wicked," and he also rewards "the upright in heart' (vv. 10–11). In Psalm 125, the psalmist asks God to "do good . . . to those who are good, and to those who are upright in their hearts!" (v. 4). But we never really discover what it means to walk uprightly or to walk in God's ways, except that these phrases obviously indicate that God's worshipers are supposed to be obedient in some sense of the word.

Indeed, the same point applies to the rewards themselves. Besides military protection, they are as nonspecifically defined as are the good deeds that evoke them. Some rewards are material. Thus, in Psalm 1, the psalmist says of the follower of God's law, "In all that he does, he prospers." (v. 3). Similarly, in Psalm 128, God promises to those who fear him "a share in the prosperity of Jerusalem." To those who "follow his ways," God says, "You shall eat the fruit of the labor of your hands; you shall be happy and it shall be well with you" (v. 1–2, 4). In Psalm 34, we are told that "those who seek the Lord lack no good thing" (v. 10). In Psalm 37, the writer says: "[T]rust in the Lord and do good; so you will dwell in the land, and enjoy security. Take delight in the Lord, and he will give you the desires of your heart." Furthermore, "the meek shall possess the land, and delight themselves in abundant prosperity" (v. 11). And "there is posterity for the man of peace" (v. 37). In Psalm 75, the psalmist says that "the horns of the righteous shall be exalted" (v. 10).[993] In Psalm 81, God will feed those who listen to him "the finest of the wheat" and "satisfy" them with "honey from the rock" (v. 16). In Psalm 84, God "bestows favor and honor" and other blessings "to the man who trusts in [him]" (v. 11–12). Sometimes, but far less often, the rewards are spiritual. In Psalm 11, the writer says that "the upright shall behold [God's] face" (v. 7).

Otherwise, as we saw above—in his role as rock, fortress, salvation, deliverer, stronghold, shield, and refuge (18:1)—that is, as the warrior god—God provides his people with security as well as prosperity by protecting them from those who threaten them, whether they happen to be invading armies or personal enemies. In Psalm 5, those who are good will be defended from those who are evil (v. 11). In Psalm 34, the Lord "delivers [the righteous] out of all their troubles . . . and saves the crushed in spirit" (vv. 17–18). It might be claimed that anyone who read or heard about these vaguely defined rewards and responsibilities would be likely to know what they mean. However, unless the psalmists distinguished between moral and cultic obligations, for example, a clarification that the prophets seldom failed to make, their readers or listeners might not have known exactly what to do or what to expect.

After all, the psalms were written as individual works, which means that ambiguities or uncertainties in one psalm cannot be said to be corrected or clarified by looking at other psalms. As Jack Miles notes, the psalms are so diverse "in content and occasion" that it is "difficult to specify what [they] collectively say about God." All are "spoken in the present tense," although the circumstances that occasioned them are more often than not lost in the quite distant past. "The second mitigating factor for a synthetic reading of the Psalms," Miles continues, "is the fact that a great many of them are altogether without specification as to time and place."[994]

The book of Proverbs, which offers some of the same ideas as the earlier psalms, is a product of religious teachers whose goal was to educate Jewish youth and to provide adults as well with moral instruction. Although this work was compiled as late as the early third century, it may well cover a period of time similar to that of the psalms and therefore similarly express some of the concepts of God, worship, and morality that prevailed before the age of the prophets.[995] According to the editors of *The Oxford Annotated Bible*, this collection of sayings "includes much older material from the long tradition" of moral teaching "in the wisdom deemed necessary for the good life." Indeed, the proverbs in the Jewish Bible not only go back to the early years of the Jewish faith, they also reflect a long Middle or Near Eastern tradition that reaches back even further into that region's history.[996]

On the one hand, T. G. Soares says that some of the later proverbs appear to have come out of the time of "contact between east and west [that] came about in the Greek period," meaning, one assumes, some time after the conquest of the Middle East by Alexander the Great. Soares notes that "the later books of wisdom"—certainly Job and Ecclesiastes, if not Proverbs itself—"emanated for the most part from Alexandria," where "the process of fusion between Hebrew and Greek thought went forward rapidly."[997] On the other hand, however, what is referred to as "wisdom" literature, of which Proverbs is a part, initially came out of the Fertile Crescent, particularly Egypt and Babylonia, as early as the middle of the third millennium BC.

To be sure, Israel was not exposed to this material until the establishment of the monarchy, particularly the reign of Solomon. Anderson says that "there is good

A Crisis of Faith

reason to believe that [Israel's] wisdom tradition received its greatest impetus during Solomon's reign" and that, in fact, some proverbs written between 1000 BC and 600 BC were directly influenced by a well-known Egyptian collection of proverbs.[998] Yehezkel Kaufmann goes so far as to say that Jewish proverbs are thoroughly derived from regional sources: "The abundant material of cognate cultures at our disposal today shows beyond question that Israelite wisdom belongs to the common sapiential legacy of the ancient Near East. Hardly anything in biblical wisdom (apart from its monotheistic viewpoint) cannot be paralleled in the literatures of Egypt and Mesopotamia." Thus, Kaufmann adds, the book of Proverbs lacks "a distinctively Israelite element"—such as any references to the Covenant, cultic practices, or historical events or personages.[999] Anderson notes that this literature "seems to stand apart from the rest of the [biblical] books . . . The prophetic themes that dominate the Pentateuch and the prophetic writings—Israel's election, the Day of Yahweh, the covenant and the Law, the priesthood and the Temple, prophecy and the messianic hope—are dealt with hardly at all."[1000]

For most scholars, Proverbs is a body of teachings that is secular in two ways. First, its instruction is derived not from God's communication to humanity through intermediaries like Moses, Elijah, and Isaiah, but from everyday experience.[1001] According to Kaufmann, "Like its non-Israelite counterparts, biblical wisdom is not a prophetic revelation, but the teaching of reason." Based on "understanding and discernment," Kaufmann says, '[i]t conceives of morality rather as a kind of natural law that God implanted in the hearts of men.'"[1002] As Anderson explains, throughout the Near East, where this tradition flourished, the man of wisdom "gave counsel with the insight derived from his keen observation of life, from years of experience, and from wide acquaintance with the fund of ancient wisdom."[1003] Furthermore, says Anderson, instead of deriving lessons from the history of Israel alone—the focus of biblical writers almost everywhere else in the Jewish Bible—the writers of the wisdom literature, especially the book of Proverbs, based their understanding of the human situation on "the wide expanse of human experience."[1004]

Second, the book of Proverbs is secular because it concentrates less on the responsibility of the individual to the community, which is the focus of the Covenant Code and the prophets, than on the means by which the individual can achieve what we might call the good life.[1005] Robert Alter says, "The usual scriptural focus on the distinctiveness of Israel and its covenantal relationship with God is entirely absent; revelation and, arguably, theological perspectives are not much in evidence."[1006] The fourth or third century BC compiler of these sayings was strongly influenced by the (then) popular concept that Wisdom is a prophetess who offers her followers "knowledge" that comes from God. This knowledge will enable them to survive and succeed: "So you will walk in the way of good men and keep to the paths of the righteous. For the upright will inhabit the land, and men of integrity will remain in it; but the wicked will be cut off from the land, and the treacherous will be rooted out of it" (2:20–22).

However, the question answered by this collection of sayings was not so much "What does God want us to do?" Rather, it was "What does life itself teach us?" John McKenzie reminds us that "Egyptian and Mesopotamian wisdom were quite secular" insofar as they ignored "religion as a factor in the skills of living." This is because "the basic wisdom was how to live successfully in the human community. This is the wisdom which the young man in Proverbs is urged to learn from his parents"—that is, not from priests or prophets and not from the Bible, but from the tradition established by sages or sophists, which is called "folk wisdom"—in their "attempt to build character" rather than save souls. "The wise man would do no wrong, McKenzie adds, not because it is morally wrong but because it is foolish." That is, actions are unacceptable not because they are immoral, but because they are impractical. And the moral agent is concerned not about sin, but about folly.[1007]

As Anderson explains: "Many of the proverbs give the impression of being rather 'secular,' although this term may be too modern to do full justice to the ancient appeal to common sense. It is true that the oldest proverbs show a positive, healthy view toward worldly affairs. Reflecting on various courses of human conduct, the sage suggests that the good life can be won through diligence, sobriety, and prudence, and that the marks of the good life are success, well-being, and a long and fruitful life."[1008] Indeed, much of the advice is purely practical since certain activities generate their own positive or negative results, regardless of their moral desirability. "Here," says Miles, "the only punishment is self-inflicted; it is simply the predictable, built-in consequence of foolish behavior."[1009] Gerhard von Rad explains: "[F]or the men of the ancient world, . . . man was the prisoner of his own actions in a very radical sense. With every good and evil deed he enters upon a nexus of fate. Good and evil alike have to fulfil themselves upon their agent, for the act is in no sense ended with the deed itself."[1010] According to Werner Schmidt, "The writers [in this tradition] like to formulate act-consequence connections, which show that a person's destiny follows from his or her own behavior": Laziness leads to poverty. Self-indulgence makes success difficult. Failing to discipline children encourages them to be irresponsible.[1011]

"In this respect," Anderson says, "the proverbs are quite similar to the prudential advice given by sages in Babylonia, Egypt, and elsewhere. Many of the biblical proverbs deal with ordinary problems that hinder a man from attaining fullness of life: laziness (6:6–11; 24:30–34), drunkenness (23:20–21, 29–35), relations with harlots (5:9–10), unwise business dealings (6:1–5), and so on." Anderson adds, "Judged by the frequency of the nagging-wife theme, the sage seems to have been greatly troubled by this problem." (He cites Proverbs 27:15–16; 17:1; 19:13; 21:9, 19; 25:24.)[1012] It is confirmative of Anderson's view that the final twenty-plus verses of the book of Proverbs constitute what the editors of *The Oxford Annotated Bible* call "an acrostic on the ideal housewife" (803). And, in the penultimate chapter, the writer refers to ants, badgers, locusts, and lizards as "exceedingly wise" (30: 24–28). In this context, it is not surprising to encounter Herodotus' characterization of the Egyptians as "slavishly devoted to ritual, most scrupulous about ceremonial cleanliness and prescribed forms, but without the slightest indication of spirituality or of a working ethics."[1013]

Indeed, although many members of ancient Near Eastern cultures believed that their death would be followed by a divine judgment that would determine their future state of being, morality was either an irrelevancy or at best a minor consideration. Gordon Childe says that in gaining "a favourable verdict the appropriate spells and ritual purity were supposedly the essential factors." Since "moral virtues" were at least "helpful," people insisted on their relative innocence. However, "the attainment of immortality was not presented as a motive for moral virtue. Still less did an Egyptian or Sumerian pray to his god . . . to help him to be honest, just, or charitable."[1014] As J. E. Manchip White describes "The Judgment of the Dead" in Egypt, the dead man's heart was weighed on a pair of scales against "the feather of Maat," while the dead man "adjured [his heart] not to inform against him" by revealing not violations of "religious morality," but "almost entirely offences against the law, primarily the law of property."[1015] According to Henri Frankfort, the principal method by which the Egyptian judges were persuaded to grant immortality was magic. To be sure, the dying preferred to be buried with a copy of their Declaration of Innocence, but the method by which they prevented their heart from revealing their secret sins was including in their coffins a spell written on a scarab.[1016]

Although the Wisdom literature tends to leave God out of the picture, he was universally seen as the architect of the system. Thus, on the one hand, von Rad says: "It cannot be said, of course, that Israel derived the knowledge of these connexions especially from Jahweh—they were much too obvious for that. They were in fact a basic element in the general understanding of life, and, as such, more a part of that ancient oriental philosophy of life in which Israel also participated." In this regard, von Rad continues—that is, "in view of the existential connexion between act and consequence"—"it is out of place to speak of a 'doctrine of retribution,' for the idea of retribution, in that it understands 'punishment' as an additional forensic act, implies a legal way of thinking which is wholly foreign to this whole range of ideas." The ancient Jews saw the act-consequence connection as a truth "confirmed in daily experience" and therefore "anything but a theological theory." In fact, "the frequent assertion of the nexus between sin and calamity, in themselves still stand outside of theology" and must be understood in an entirely secular manner.[1017]

On the other hand, however, for Israel, with its "belief in Jahweh as the universal cause, it was impossible to understand such an elemental process except in relation to his power." Thus, "these beneficial or baneful results of an act were referred back to Jahweh himself with the utmost immediacy." As the creator of all things, God had to have been the creator of the moral design of the universe, an idea that is absent in the earlier Proverbs, but increasingly present as time passed—that is, "in the later reflexions of the Wisdom literature." Thus, von Rad says, in a number of proverbs, God is portrayed "as the one who weighs and tests the hearts of men" (Prov 16:2; 17:3; 21:2). He does so because he is concerned about morality: "The eyes of the Lord are in every place, keeping watch on the evil and the good" (15:3). He hates "the wicked," for whom "[t]here is severe discipline," and "loves him who pursues righteousness" (vv. 9–10). "A further step in this direction," von Rad adds, is taken by another group of maxims which speak very directly of the displeasure (or pleasure) which God has in certain practices or ways of human behavior,"[1018] particularly violations of the Covenant Code.

Thus, some scholars disagree with Kaufmann that the writers of proverbs are generally indifferent to the kinds of religious values and moral issues that affect the entire community, especially the indigent and vulnerable. Walter Brueggemann acknowledges that "the way in which a covenantal ethic relates to such a sapiential inventory" is not entirely obvious. However, he says that "even Israel's wisdom materials are shot through with covenantal awareness; it is clear all through the wisdom teaching that members of society are all deeply responsible with and for one another and that the cohesion of the community is derived from the rule of the creator-redeemer God." Brueggemann adds that, in this respect, the wisdom traditions in the Old Testament and the Near East developed separately.[1019] As Soares argues, "[T]he most serious economic evil remained still, as in the prophetic times, that the rich and powerful took advantage of their opportunity to oppress the poor and weak. They '*devour the poor from off the earth*' (30:14), as Micah had already said."[1020] Thus, the book of Proverbs virtually begins with a reference to the importance of "righteousness, justice, and equity" (1:3). Indeed, God himself teaches these principles, provides "wisdom for the upright," and protects "those who walk in integrity," guard "the paths of justice," and "preserve the way of his saints" (2:6–9).[1021]

Furthermore, these ideals, which are stated again and again, are not merely to be understood as doctrine, but, as Wisdom says, deeply felt and welcomed "into your heart" (2:10; see also 2:2; 3:1). God advises, "Let your heart hold fast my words; keep my commandments, and live" (4:4, 21; 6:21; 23:26). Thus, readers are urged to be righteous (11:18)—specifically, to have pity on the poor (19:17; 21:13; 28:8). In Proverb 31, an unknown king, called Lemuel, advises other kings: "Open your mouth for the dumb, for the rights of all who are left desolate. Open your mouth, judge righteously, maintain the rights of the poor and needy" (vv. 8–9). In fact, echoing the sentiments of some of the prophets, the writer of Proverb 21 says, "To do righteousness and justice is more acceptable to the Lord than sacrifice" (v. 3). Although the Egyptians also paid extensive attention to some purely secular (and even trivial) issues, says Frankfort, they too "were firmly convinced that one should live according to common human decency."[1022]

In several proverbs, the writers claim that wealth itself is worthless: "He who trusts his riches will wither" (11:28); "Riches do not last for ever" (27:24); "Do not toil to acquire wealth" (23:4–5; see also 28:22). However, some writers state that wealth is inferior to poverty only if it is unaccompanied by faith and virtue: "Better is a little with the fear of the Lord than great treasure and trouble with it" (15:16; see also 16:8); "It is better to be a lowly spirit with the poor than to divide the spoil with the proud"

(16:19; see also 19:1); "Better is a poor man who walks in his integrity than a rich man who is perverse in his ways" (28:6; see also 28:11). Furthermore, some things are better than wealth: "A good name is to be chosen rather than great riches" (22:1); and "wisdom is better than jewels" (8:11; see also 16:16). Of course, "sinners" are to be avoided, especially when they promise "all precious goods" to "fill [their] houses with spoil" by "ambush[ing] the innocent" and thereby "get[ting] gain by violence" (1:11–19). However, it is often not greed alone that is the problem, but, as in this case, only "greed for unjust gain" (15:27). "Wealth hastily gotten [or "gotten by vanity" (KJV)] will dwindle, but he who gathers little by little will increase it" (13:11).

Of course, when we examine the book of Proverbs in its entirety, it is clear that the pursuit of wealth is a legitimate, even honorable enterprise. That is, wealth acquired through legal means is simply the just compensation for hard work: "A slack hand causes poverty, but the hand of the diligent makes rich" (10:4). "A rich man's wealth is his strong city; the poverty of the poor is their ruin" (10:15). Indeed, "the blessing of the Lord makes rich" (10: 22). "The ransom of a man's life is his wealth" (13:8). And Wisdom says, "Riches and honor are with me, enduring wealth and prosperity" (8:18; see also 3:16). At the same time, poverty is greatly to be avoided. It is the punishment for loving pleasure (22:17), avoiding obvious responsibilities (24:30–34), and indulging in sleep (20:13). Along with "disgrace," it will "come to him who ignores instruction"—that is, whoever ignores the counsel proffered throughout the book of Proverbs (13:18). In short, as Soares says, "[W]ealth in general is regarded in the Proverbs as a reward for piety and uprightness, . . . while poverty is the result of folly."[1023]

Furthermore, even the most noble sentiments in the Proverbs, which remind us of the high ethical standards of the prophets, are tainted or even undermined by their goals or motives. For example, readers of Proverbs are urged not to "rejoice" when their enemy falls and not to "pay the man back for what he has done" (24:17, 29). In Proverb 25, the writer carries these admonitions one step further: "If your enemy is hungry, give him bread to eat; and if he is thirsty, give him water to drink" (v. 21). However, the goal of this act of kindness, stated in verse 22—"you will heap coals of fire on his head"—is not very noble, as the editors of *The Oxford Annotated Bible* note: "[T]he best way to take vengeance on one's enemy is to be merciful to him" (797). Notably, St. Paul quotes this passage in Romans 12:20, which the editors of *The Oxford Annotated Bible* interpret this way: "To heap burning coals . . . is to make the enemy feel ashamed by meeting his *evil* with *good*" (1373). That is, what at first looks like one of the most generous admonitions of both the Old and New Testaments—"Love your enemies"—turns out to be an act of hostility. In addition, this act of pseudo-kindness will elicit God's gratitude, at least in the Jewish Bible: "[T]he Lord will reward you" (25:22).

Indeed, what consistently diminishes the call for righteousness throughout this work is the idea that it should not be pursued for the reasons the prophets suggest: that is, as an expression of compassion for humanity or even loyalty to Yahweh. Rather, as William M. Ramsay says, "Proverbs does not usually urge the reader to be generous

The Evolution of Love

because of divine commands, but because one can see that it pays."[1024] Chief among the most prominent concepts in Proverbs, according to the editors of *The Oxford Annotated Bible*, is the belief "that reward and punishment follow in this life" (769).[1025] That is, the reason for being righteous is simply that it is rewarded. And, of course, this view of the relationship between God and humanity is perfectly consistent with everything else we know about early Judaism, as well as every other religion in the ancient world until the middle of the first millennium.

God announces this moral principle clearly in Proverb 24: "I will render to the man according to his work" (v. 29). That is, everyone gets what he or she deserves. In Book II of Proverbs, the section running from 10:1 to 22:16, the writers restate this formula, again, in the simplest possible terms: "[O]ne who sows righteousness gets a sure reward" (11:18). Indeed, throughout this proverb, righteousness "delivers" its possessor from all kinds of adversity, including "death" and "trouble" (vv. 4, 8) while providing all kinds of benefits, including "honor" and "favor" (vv. 16, 27). At the same time, "[t]he wicked shall not be unpunished" (11:21; 24:20). "He who despises the word brings destruction on himself, but he who respects the commandment will be rewarded" (13:13).

Not surprisingly, the rewards and punishments for good and bad actions are often described as wealth and poverty, respectively: "In the house of the righteous is much treasure, but trouble befalls the income of the wicked" (15:6). "Honor the Lord with your substance and with the first fruits of all your produce; then your barns will be filled with plenty, and your vats will be bursting with wine" (3:9–10; see also 10:4, 22; 13:18; 14:24; 21:17). Lady Wisdom herself says that she "endow[s] with wealth those who love [her], and fill[s] their treasuries" (8:20–21). God says in Proverb 1, "[H]e who listens to me will dwell secure and will be at ease, without dread of evil" (v. 33). "[T]he upright man will inherit the land, men of integrity will remain in it" (2:21). A father advises his son to acquire wisdom, prize her, and love her; in response, he says, "[S]he will keep you," "guard you," "exalt you," "honor you," and "embrace you." At last, "[s]he will place on your head a fair garland; she will bestow on you a beautiful crown" (4:6–9). As a recipient of these rewards, the writer of Proverb 8 says, "Riches and honor are with me, enduring wealth and prosperity" (v. 18). Considering the consequences of bad behavior—vulnerability, poverty, insecurity, and dishonor—it is logical for the book to begin with the statement "The fear of the Lord is the beginning of knowledge" (1:7; see also 9:10). Indeed, fear itself, in the sense that it counsels obedience to God's will, thereby leads to good health (3:8), long life (10:27), confidence (14:26), protection from harm (19:23), hope (23:17–18), and praise (31:30).

In this context, although the rules of conduct in the book of Proverbs are said to have come from God, as the passages above suggest, they are not necessarily godly. What distinguishes the moral code promoted by Wisdom from other ethical concepts in ancient Israel is that it was based *exclusively* on the *fear* of God, which, in turn, was based on the expectation of rewards and punishments, or *quid pro quo*. As we have seen, the prophets believed that moral conduct should be based on the Covenant and its establishment of mutual love as the basis for all interactions between God and humanity. That is, to the prophets, ethical decisions should be motivated by love rather than fear, altruism rather than egoism, and compassion for others rather than desire for wealth.[1026] The follower of wisdom is guided by caution and moderation rather than holiness. As McKenzie says, "Here the utilitarian character appears without ambiguity," since the "wise man," who is also "the virtuous man," acts "for reasons of prudence" and not for reasons of compassion, gratitude, or even social responsibility.[1027]

After all, if the consequences of behavior are invariably matched to either rewards or punishments, it is wise—but not necessarily good or even moral—to act in order to be rewarded, unless trained animals, subjected to a regimen of behavior modification, can be said to be moral. In fact, according to Miles, God is rendered almost irrelevant to the process, except for the fact that he established it: "God continues to be honored as the creator, through Wisdom, of a world which enjoys in general an immanent moral order—a world, in other words, in which reward for the good and punishment for the wicked is on the whole a natural and therefore automatic outcome."[1028]

The New View

The psalms are a particularly interesting subject of study because they span such a long period of Jewish history, from at least the early years of the monarchy in the tenth century to the time of Ezra and Nehemiah. According to Bernhard W. Anderson, "the Psalter is a condensed account of the whole of Israel's history with God from the time of David down to the late period of the Old Testament."[1029] Although the psalms might have been collected in their present form as late as the first century AD, many of them date from pre-exilic times.[1030] At the beginning of this period, the Jewish nation was independent, experimenting with monarchy for the first time, and moving away from the village life that characterized the pre-monarchial phase of Jewish history. At the end of this period, the nation was totally dependent on Rome, the last of several conquering nations which had dominated the people of Israel for several centuries.

The Jews had come to the end of almost half a millennium of monarchy, under which they had experienced expansion and contraction, glory and shame, and benevolence and cruelty. Furthermore, they had watched their nation embrace urbanization, commercialization, and internationalization. Cities like Samaria, in Israel, the Northern Kingdom, and Jerusalem, in Judea, the Southern Kingdom, had grown into cosmopolitan urban centers. Owing to increased job specialization and concentration of wealth, the people were divided into sometimes embattled social classes. And they watched their nation engage in both risky and costly interactions with powerful nations—Babylonia, Assyria, and Egypt—that were interested in conquest and domination and not at all in the well-being of their weak and vulnerable "enemies."

At the same time, Judaism itself had undergone even more radical changes, especially from polytheism to monotheism; from tribalism to universalism; and, regarding the relationship between God and humanity, from king and subject (or patron and client) to parent and child. Although it is difficult to trace these changes in the psalms, it is possible to see in many of them expressions of ideas different from those that we have just examined. Thus, although many psalms and the vast majority of proverbs can be seen as giving voice to a form of Judaism that was in many ways supplanted by the nobler and more inspiring message of the prophets, a substantial number of psalms deserve to be treated with the same level of respect that both Jews and Christians have shown to the words of Hosea, Jeremiah, and Isaiah. Indeed, both Jews and Christians have turned to these psalms in precisely the same way they have turned to the prophets by including them in their liturgies and, no doubt, reading them in moments of private prayer for the purpose of meditation or consolation.[1031]

Part of the reason for this attention is a result of historical events in the life of ancient Israel that challenged many people's faith in the moral system articulated in Deuteronomy. Indeed, we know that political and social upheavals in many of the urban agricultural societies of the same period culminated in a similar challenge across the globe. After all, the rise of radically new religions in the Axial Age of the mid-first millennium is often attributed to concerns about and objections to living conditions in the societies in which these religions arose. According to Karen Armstrong: "The sages of the Axial Age did not create their compassionate ethic in idyllic circumstances. Each tradition developed in societies . . . that were torn apart by violence and warfare as never before." To be sure, from what we know of ancient Israel at the time, change of this kind appears to have been inevitable. As Armstrong says, "During the sixth century, Israel embarked fully upon its Axial Age,"—at which time, "the catalyst of change was the experience of unbridled, shocking violence."[1032] It was one thing to have lived through the failed monarchies of four centuries. It was quite another, however, to have to endure the conquest and domination of both the Northern and Southern kingdoms by Assyria and Babylonia, respectively, which succeeded that failure.

Scholars particularly point to the year 586 BC, when Judea was invaded by Babylonia, the Jews of the Southern Kingdom were conquered, and the Temple was destroyed. James Muilenburg says: At this moment, "a new period was inaugurated in the history of biblical religion. The traditional faith had then to be read in the light of an event, catastrophic for Israel's political life and consequently supremely fateful for the quality of faith enshrined in the sacred history. Faith in a historical revelation was seriously threatened, and not a few came to conclusions of hopelessness that the facts of history seemed only too eloquently to warrant. The literature following 586 B.C. bears witness to the character of the transformation that took place."[1033] And Muilenburg is referring not only to the book of Job and Lamentations but also to the many psalms that appear to have been composed in the dark shadow of that grim historical situation.

A Crisis of Faith

This is why Jack Miles describes turning from the psalms to the proverbs as moving from one world to another: "Reading Proverbs after reading Psalms is rather like leaving the steamy murmur of a crowded church where hidden agonies and immoderate hopes have all been on sometimes painful display and stepping into the busy briskness of the marketplace outside the church door—close enough to be sure, but still outside. The stakes out here in the daylight may be much lower, the only eloquence a rough-and-ready tartness of repartee, yet there is something bracing about the change. Everyone still believes in God, indeed casually refers to him in every other sentence, but everyone also seems to have other business than his in hand and to be relying on mother wit, as we might well put it, rather than on father or grandfather God, for the Lord God is indeed beginning to seem an elderly relative still nominally the head of the house but no longer very active as the manager."[1034] Robert Alter similarly characterizes the move from Psalms to Proverbs as a sea change because their purposes were different, the Psalms being "expressive" while the Proverbs are "didactic" and "hortatory."[1035]

Perhaps the most noticeable difference between one Judaism and the other is, as Miles suggests, the disparity between the two in levels of confidence, optimism, and certainty regarding God's responsiveness to human needs. Unlike the writers we have already considered, the other (presumably later) psalmists did not always see God as an object of fear and hope, based on his threat to punish bad actions and reward good ones. Against the tone of cheerful expectation, which we see in many proverbs and which accompanies God's assurances that virtue will gain favor as certainly as wickedness will not, is the cry of despair that we encounter in psalm after psalm, emanating from the fact that the lockstep requital described in many psalms and almost all the proverbs is not quite so certain. As Walter Brueggemann explains, these psalms "affirm" two of God's characteristics. First, he is "compassionate" and eager to answer everyone's plea for help. Second, however, he "is not an automaton who automatically answers," which means that "cries addressed to YHWH sometimes go unheeded."[1036]

Thus, as many psalms demonstrate, Judaism rests on the assumption that God acts out of love, not obligation, and that his followers hope for his help, but do not expect it as something they necessarily deserve. As Amy-Jill Levine explains, the traditional view that "Jews follow Torah in order to earn God's love or a place in heaven" is a "misconception." Thus, it is not true that Judaism is "a religion of 'works righteousness' rather than of grace." Rather, she continues: "This view fails to observe that the election of Israel is based on grace, not merit or works."[1037] In short, the righteous do not follow rules merely out of fear and hope, but as a consequence of genuinely loving both God and humanity and acting accordingly. Being righteous and upright is, therefore, less a reward-seeking attitude rooted in obedience than a natural expression of being in a special relationship with God and his people. According to H. Conzelmann and A. Lindemann, "In Judaism commandment and obedience are not primarily formal entities . . . [R]ather, they are related to one's total relationship with

God. Obedience to God's commandment is not an external, obligatory exercise for the Jew, but is by all means related to all of his thoughts and desires."[1038]

Indeed, in many psalms, the writer reveals that God's system of rewards and punishments is simply not working. That is, relying on God's readiness to recompense good and evil has been disappointing and even disillusioning. Thus, in these psalms, as Miles says, the "hidden agonies" of the petitioners are on "painful display" because God is sometimes slow to respond to his believers' requests for help. As Anderson explains: "The remembrance of Yahweh's deeds"—a common theme throughout the psalms—"can also have the effect of plunging an individual or the whole Israelite community into bewilderment about the present situation of suffering and distress," whether this was a personal matter or one of the many crises that the Jewish people endured in the exilic and post-exilic periods. Anderson continues: "Although 'theoretical atheism' was unknown in the Old Testament period, Israel was affected from time to time with the feeling that Yahweh had abandoned his people. When one considers that Israel, situated in a storm-center of world politics, so often suffered deeply, it is not surprising that fully one third of the Psalter consists of laments in which a suppliant cries to God 'out of the depths' (Ps. 130:1)."[1039]

Unlike the earlier psalms, according to Anderson, these so-called laments "reflect a growing concern about theodicy, or the justice of God's administration of earthly affairs, which came to be a burning issue in Judaism."[1040] It is not, however, that in the psalms Jews revised their collective view of God's response to human behavior. Rather, they raised a serious question that was raised more directly in the story of Job and more definitively in the long lament of Koheleth. Muilenburg explains: "That God punished sin and rewarded righteousness was the foundation of Israel's religious ethic. So when affliction and sorrow and pain came, when the unjust persecutor got the better of his victim, when the dark spells of uncanny forces laid the sufferer low on his deathbed, the mind endured tortures deeper than any physical pain. Many a cry breaks forth out of the night of despair."[1041] In Psalm 6, the petitioner says, "O Lord, rebuke me not in thy anger, nor chasten me in thy wrath. Be gracious to me, O Lord, for I am languishing; O Lord, heal me, for my bones are troubled. But thou, O Lord—how long?" (vv. 1–3). This woeful cry arises again and again in the psalms, revealing what must be recognized as an expression of doubt about the traditional Jewish concept of the divine-human relationship: i.e., that God *owes* the petitioner some kind of compensation for loyalty, good works, or obedience.[1042]

Another reason for the uncertainty of his people is that God not only *gives* his laws but must also *teach* them. Thus, as William M. Ramsay says, although most psalms were written "for worship," "some psalms were written to instruct the hearer, to teach the reader how to live."[1043] The idea is that, for a variety of reasons, people are dependent on God's help to follow his commandments. Psalm 119 is a running commentary on this concept, which is based on the assumption that neither God's demand for obedience nor people's desire to obey him is sufficient to prevent ordinary

A Crisis of Faith

human beings from sinning. Clearly, the petitioner understands his situation in this regard. He knows that the blameless are blessed, but also that he can achieve blamelessness only if he "knows" the Law in the deepest sense. Thus, he says to God, "I will praise thee with an upright heart, when I learn thy righteous ordinances" (v. 7). This learning, however, is not easy: "How can a young man keep his way pure?" (v. 9). "My soul cleaves to the dust" (v. 23). "[T]he godless have subverted me with guile" (v. 78). "I have gone astray like a lost sheep" (v. 176).

Therefore, the petitioner requests, "[T]each me thy statutes! Make me understand the way of thy precepts . . . [S]trengthen me according to thy word! Put false ways far from me; and graciously teach me thy law! . . . I will run in the way of thy commandments when thou enlargest my understanding!" (vv. 26–28). "Teach me good judgment and knowledge . . . [T]each me thy statutes" (vv. 66, 68). "[G]ive me understanding that I may learn thy commandments" (v. 73). "[T]each me thy ordinances" (v. 108). "[G]ive me understanding, that I may know thy testimonies!" (v. 125; see also 144, 169). Now, evidently owing to God's help, the petitioner is able to say, "I have more understanding than all my teachers . . . I understand more than the aged . . . Through thy precepts I get understanding" (vv. 99–104). Nevertheless, he continues in verse after verse to implore God not only for protection against his enemies, but also for the ability to sustain his adherence to God's laws.

Similarly, in other psalms, the writers argue that either because worshipers lack the will or commitment or because God's laws are not entirely clear or understandable, they require his help either to interpret the laws or to carry them out. In Psalm 25, the psalmist says, "Good and upright is the Lord; therefore he instructs sinners in the way. He leads the humble in what is right, and teaches the humble his way" (vv. 8–9). Thus, "Who is the man that fears the Lord? Him will he instruct in the way that he should choose" (v. 12). In most instances in which the concept of God-as-teacher arises, the psalmist is a supplicant who has sinned and therefore requests both forgiveness and instruction. In Psalm 94, the writer says that God both "chastens" and "teaches."[1044] And "[b]lessed is the man whom thou dost chasten, O Lord, and whom thou dost teach out of thy law" (v. 12).

In Psalm 25, the psalmist, obviously eager to gain his mercy and comprehend his commandments, asks God, "Make me to know thy ways, O Lord, teach me thy paths. Lead me in thy truth, and teach me . . . (vv. 4–5). In Psalm 73, the supplicant says that he was "stupid and ignorant" and therefore acted "like a beast" toward God. Thus, he appeals to him, "Thou dost guide me with thy counsel" (vv. 22–24). In Psalm 27, the psalmist says, "Teach me thy way, O Lord; and lead me on a level path because of my enemies" (v. 11). In Psalm 139, the writer says, "Search me, O God, and know my heart! Try me and know my thoughts! And see if there be any wicked way in me, and lead me in the way everlasting!" (vv. 23–24). In Psalm 51, in which the petitioner asks God to "create in [him] a clean heart" (v. 10), he also says to God, "Behold, thou desirest truth in the inward being; therefore teach me wisdom in my secret heart" (v.

6).[1045] The psalmist in Psalm 90 asks God to "teach us to number our days that we may get a heart of wisdom" (v. 12; see also 139:23).

To be sure, no petitioner directly expresses the idea that the Deuteronomic theodicy is inoperative. Many of the psalms, however, no longer appeal to God's willingness to reward and punish. Rather, as I said earlier, God is assumed to be moved not by his sense of obligation, but only by his mercy, his undying compassion. Thus, the psalmist in Psalm 6 adds, "Turn, O Lord, save my life: deliver me *for the sake of thy steadfast love*" (v. 4; my emphasis). Similarly, in Psalm 5, the petitioner asks God to hear his cry for help, but he does not rest his case on the sacrifice he has just offered or on anything else he has done to earn God's favor. On the one hand, he speaks to God as a defender of high moral standards, to whom the behavior of his enemies should be abhorrent: "For thou art not a God who delights in wickedness; evil may not sojourn with thee. The boastful may not stand before thy eyes; thou hatest all evildoers" (vv. 4–5). On the other hand, however, the psalmist appeals to God's "steadfast love" (v. 7).[1046]

This appeal to God's *graciousness* and *mercy* is a strong indication that God's response to petitioners is spontaneous, not automatic, and unpredictable, not inevitable. Indeed, the words *graciousness* and *mercy* often appear together (and are, to a large extent, synonymous) with *compassion*, *steadfast love*, and *faithfulness*. This idea is introduced in Exodus 34: "The Lord passed before [Moses}, and proclaimed, 'The Lord, the Lord, a God merciful and gracious, slow to anger, and abounding in steadfast love and faithfulness, keeping steadfast love for thousands, forgiving iniquity and transgression and sin, but who will by no means clear the guilty.'" (vv. 6–7). In Psalm 145, God is first described as great, glorious, mighty, majestic, and wondrous (vv. 3–6). But he is also said to be abundantly good, righteous, gracious, merciful, slow to anger, steadfastly loving, compassionate and "good to all" (vv. 7–9). Later, God is more specifically described as "faithful in all his words," "gracious in all his deeds," "uphold[ing] all who are falling," "rais[ing] up all who are bowed down," "just in all his ways," "kind in all his doings," and "near to all who call upon him." Furthermore, God satisfies "the desire of every living thing" and "preserves all who love him." (vv. 8, 13–18).

In Psalm 86, the writer calls God "good and forgiving, . . . merciful and gracious, slow to anger, and abounding in steadfast love and faithfulness." Then he pleads, "Turn to me and take pity on me" (vv. 5, 15). In Psalm 103, the psalmist says that God "satisfies you with steadfast love and mercy" (v. 4). He refers to God as "merciful and gracious, slow to anger, and abounding in steadfast love." God, he continues, "will not always chide, nor will he keep his anger for ever" (vv. 89). "Gracious is the Lord, and righteous; our Lord is merciful," says the writer of Psalm 116:5. Thus, in psalm after psalm, the supplicant says to God, "Be gracious" (4:1; 6:2; 9:13; 26:11; 27:7; 30:10; 31:9; 41:4, 10; 56:1; 119:58). He is asking God to be more than fair, more than law-enforcing, and more than judgmental: "Be mindful of thy mercy, O Lord, and of thy steadfast love, for they have been from of old" (25:6). In Psalm 77, the writer asks,

"Will the Lord spurn me for ever, and never again be favorable? Has his steadfast love for ever ceased? . . . Has God forgotten to be gracious? (vv. 7-9).

One manifestation of God's graciousness is his willingness to consider his side of the Covenant with his people—his contractual obligation to help them—as inviolable. That is, no matter what the Jews do in terms of their obligations to God, including rejecting him completely, as he often accuses them of doing, God promises that he will stand by his commitment to support and sustain them. In Psalm 111, God is said to be "gracious and merciful" as well as "ever mindful of his covenant" (vv. 4-5). "He sent redemption to his people; he has commanded his covenant for ever" (v. 9). In Psalm 74, the writer asks God not to "forget the life of [his] poor for ever." Then he reminds God of his obligations that he himself articulated in his agreement with the Jews: "Have regard for thy covenant; for the dark places of the land are full of the habitations of violence. Let not the downtrodden be put to shame; let the poor and needy praise thy name" (vv. 19-21).

The psalmist begins Psalm 89 by saying he will sing of God's "steadfast love . . . for ever . . ." For God's "steadfast love was established for ever" (v. 1-2). Then he repeats the terms of God's eternal covenant with David (vv. 3-4, 19f.), including his pledge that his "hand shall ever abide with him" (v. 21) and his promise never to withdraw his "steadfast love" or to suspend the covenant (v. 28). Finally, before the psalmist asks God why he appears to have abandoned these obligations, God says of David: "If his children forsake my law and do not walk according to my ordinances, . . . I will punish their transgression with the rod and their iniquity with scourges; but I will not remove from him my *steadfast love*, or be false to my faithfulness. *I will not violate my covenant, or alter the word that went forth from my lips*" (vv. 30-34; my emphasis).

In Psalm 106, after summarizing the history of Israel's "iniquity"—her disobedience to God—at length (vv. 6-42), the psalmist comments: "Many times he delivered them, but they were rebellious in their purposes, and were brought low through their iniquity. Nevertheless he regarded their distress, when he heard their cry. *He remembered for their sake his covenant, and relented according to the abundance of his steadfast love.* He caused them to be pitied by those who held them captive" (vv. 43-46; my emphasis). From the perspective suggested by these three passages, God reacts to Israel's persistent—and apparently unrelenting—violation of their contractual relationship to him by equally persistently forgiving them.

One reason for this pattern of forgiveness is that human beings are, by their own admission, unable to live up to God's expectations. That is, given the limitations inherent in humanity, people have no chance, without God's help, of following his will. The psalmist in Psalm 39 suggests that human life is too brief and insignificant even to be worthy of God's notice: "Lord, . . . my lifetime is as nothing in thy sight. Surely every man stands as a mere breath! Surely man goes about as a shadow!" Furthermore, the entire purpose of existence is uncertain: "Surely for nought are they in turmoil; man heaps up, and knows not who will gather" (vv. 4-6).[1047]

In Psalm 19, the psalmist praises God for his law, which "reviv[es] the soul," "mak[es] wise the simple," and "rejoic[es] the heart." He also appreciates the fact that "there is great reward" for obeying these precepts and commandments. However, this achievement is insufficient because of his and others' inability to know when they have committed a violation: "But who can discern his errors?" the psalmist inquires. Thus, he asks God to help him to refrain from sinning: "Clear thou me from hidden faults. Keep back thy servant also from presumptuous sins; let them not have dominion over me! Then"—and presumably *only* then—"I shall be blameless, and innocent of great transgression." Finally, the supplicant concludes with a prayer for assistance as well as forgiveness: "Let the words of my mouth and the meditation of my heart be acceptable in thy sight, O Lord, my rock and my redeemer" (vv. 7–14).

In the most famous lament on this subject of human inadequacy, the writer of Psalm 8 asks God, "[W]hat is man that thou art mindful of him, and *the son of man that thou dost care for him*?" (v. 4; my emphasis). So sinful are we, indeed, that we are undeserving of God's help: "*If thou, O Lord, shouldst mark iniquities, Lord, who would stand? But there is forgiveness with thee, that thou mayest be feared*" (130:3–4; my emphasis). In Psalm 78, the writer says that God, speaking of ordinary mortals, "remembered that they were but flesh" (v. 39), so "he, being compassionate, forgave their iniquity, and did not destroy them" (v. 38). In Psalm 103, the psalmist says that since God "knows our frame" and "remembers that we are dust," "[h]e *does not deal with us according to our sins, nor requite us according to our iniquities*" (vv. 14, 10; my emphasis).

In Psalm 143, the petitioner acknowledges that he is completely unable to live up to God's standards: "Hear my prayer, O Lord; give ear to my supplications! In thy faithfulness answer me, in thy righteousness! Enter not into judgment with thy servant; for *no man living is righteous before thee*" (vv. 1–2; my emphasis). In other words, as the writer of Psalm 49 says, "Truly no man can ransom himself, or give to God the price of his life, for the ransom of his life is costly, and can never suffice" (vv. 7–8). However, this writer adds, "God will ransom my soul from the power of Sheol"—the place of the dead (v. 15). The importance of these passages is that they explain why human beings cannot expect to *earn* either forgiveness or salvation. They are simply too weak to make any claims on God, who is, perforce, forgiving. Notably, this is also the explanation of grace that St. Paul provides.

Not surprisingly, many supplicants in the psalms not only admit their helplessness nut also confess their guilt—their unworthiness. Indeed, it is clear that forgiveness cannot occur without confession and repentance. "In the period with which we are concerned," says George Foot Moore, as I noted in chapter 4, "in spite of all the calamities of the age, religion was more healthy-minded; nevertheless, in no ancient religion is normal piety so pervaded by the consciousness of sin, the need of repentance, and the conviction that man's sole hope is the forgiving grace of God." Moore says elsewhere, "In the case of man as well as God the condition of forgiveness is repentance and confession." Furthermore, in the case of human beings, reparation is also required:

"We shall see," Moore adds, "that in the case of a wrong done to a fellow man by deed or by word, in his person, property, or honor, reparation is the indispensable condition of divine forgiveness; and that for offenses against God, good works, especially charity . . . , is one of the things that cause the revocation of divine decree."[1048]

In Psalm 32, the writer explains the importance of confession in what amounts to a series of steps, from sin to forgiveness: "Blessed is he whose transgression is forgiven, whose sin is covered. Blessed is the man to whom the Lord imputes no iniquity, and in whose spirit there is no deceit. When I declared not my sin, my body wasted away through my groaning all day long . . . I acknowledged my sin to thee, and I did not hide my iniquity; I said, 'I will confess my transgressions to the Lord'; then thou didst forgive the guilt of my sin" (vv. 1–5). The supplicant in Psalm 66 says, "If I had cherished iniquity in my heart, the Lord would not have listened" (v. 18).

However, it is necessary to add, once again, that nothing is guaranteed; no response from God is certain. This is evidently why in many appeals the petitioners feel they are compelled to throw themselves totally on God's mercy. In Psalm 51, the psalmist says, "Have mercy on me, O God, according to thy steadfast love; according to thy abundant mercy blot out my transgressions" (v. 1). In fact, this sinner not only acknowledges his sins, he also says to God, "[T]hou art justified in thy sentence and blameless in thy judgment" (v. 4). Furthermore, he asks God to "create in [him] a new heart," as if to suggest that he is incapable of acting righteously on his own (v. 10).[1049]

In Psalm 25, the writer says, "Remember not the sins of my youth, or my transgressions . . . For thy name's sake, O Lord, pardon my guilt, for it is great" (vv. 7, 11). Here the writer does not expect a reward for his confession. Rather, he appeals on two other grounds: first, he reminds God of his concern for his "name"—his reputation for forgiveness, an appeal also made in Psalm 79 ("Help us . . . for the glory of thy name . . . for thy name's sake" [v. 9]). Second, he merely asks for relief from his suffering: "Turn thou to me, and be gracious to me; for I am lonely and afflicted. Relieve the troubles of my heart, and bring me out of my distresses. Consider my affliction and my trouble, and forgive all my sins" (25:16–18). Similarly, in Psalm 38, the penitent asks God for forgiveness because, as a result of his sin and God's rebuke, his health is poor, his wounds grow foul, his loins are burning, his heart is in tumult, he is alienated from friends and kinsmen, and his senses are not working (vv. 1–14). "I confess my iniquity, I am sorry for my sin," he says. But all he can do is "wait" for God's grace: "Do not forsake me, O Lord! . . . Make haste to help me, O Lord, my salvation" (vv. 18–22).

Although many of these psalms reveal serious concerns about God's willingness or readiness to implement his *quid pro quo* system, they do not reveal any doubts about the moral foundation of that system. That is, although these psalms express a widespread uncertainty and anxiety about God's *application* of his ethical principles, they do not express any concern about the ongoing *validity and importance* of those principles. Indeed, the psalms in question not only continue to see God as he is portrayed in the works of the prophets and the Deuteronomist—i.e., that he is just and righteous, as well as merciful and compassionate—but also, unlike the older psalms, spell out exactly what it means to be worthy of love and worship.

Indeed, as Muilenburg notes, although they clearly and unambiguously express both pain and anguish, some psalmists also restate their faith in the traditional Jewish theodicy. Thus, on the one hand, "[t]he large number of such psalms illustrates how real this problem was . . . In Ps. 73, the greatest of all the psalms on this subject, a lonely man reveals the depth and stress of the problem which tortures him." On the other hand, however, this man, like other psalmists, "finally comes to think and live by his faith and his awareness of the presence and fellowship of God: 'Though my flesh and my heart waste away, God is the rock of my heart and my portion forever' (73:25–26)."[1050] This is why Collins says that "the psalms as a whole are animated by trust rather than fear": "Even though I walk through the darkest valley, I fear no evil; for you are with me" (23:4).[1051] The "darkness" in the psalms is often real and tangible, but it never entirely destroys the psalmists' hope. Remarkably, the supplicants keep on seeking and pleading for help, evidently because they trust that sooner or later God will respond. Brueggemann comments: "It is remarkable that in Israel's practice of faith, that in the face of cries unanswered, Israel continues to address YHWH in urgency. That is, lack of divine response does not cause a cessation in the cry."[1052]

Psalm 22 illustrates this point by starting with the most extreme statement of hopelessness in the entire book of Psalms: "My God, my God, why hast thou forsaken me? Why art thou so far from helping me, from the words of my groaning? O my God, I cry by day, but thou dost not answer; and by night, but find no rest" (vv. 1–2. From this expression of almost complete despair, however, the petitioner moves on (1) to remind God that he saved the psalmist's "fathers" and served as his God from birth (vv. 3–11); (2) to reveal to God the extent of his suffering (mocked by others, physically wasted, and tormented by "evildoers"; vv. 12–18); (3) to promise God that he will praise him in the Temple (vv. 22–26); and (4) to assure God that everyone on earth ("the families of the nations") will "praise the Lord," "worship before him," and "tell of the Lord to the coming generation" (vv. 27–31). In other words, the psalmist is certain, despite his initial fears, that God will "hasten to [his] aid," "deliver [his] soul," and "[s]ave [him] from the mouth of the lion" (vv. 19–21).

Gerhard von Rad offers two additional explanations for this reversal from pessimism to optimism in the psalms, including, first, "the consolation which was given to the men praying, after they had recited their prayer of lament," and, second, the attainment "of a deeper and more personal relationship to God." That is, the mere articulation of their suffering led some people to experience a "change of mood" that "derived from the comfort which the suppliant received" either from others who heard him or from the sheer relief of acknowledging his or her suffering. The other consolation was based on the idea that prayer, involving both humble petition and sincere confession, might lead to "a retreat into the realm of the most sublime communion with God."[1053]

A Crisis of Faith

It must be emphasized, of course, that the appeal to God for mercy rests on the assumption that he is concerned about the plight of both those who have brought their misfortune on themselves—that is, the sinners who have repented—and those who are either victims of circumstances (drought, famine, political change, or economic dislocation) or, as Psalm 22 reveals, victims of outright oppression and exploitation. In other words, in some psalms God is shown to be not only responsive to the lost sheep who have acknowledged their sin and asked for forgiveness, but also responsive to people who are not victims of their own misdeeds but victims of other people's acts of neglect, abuse, or tyranny. That is, the God of these psalms is not merely a tribal God, ready to do favors for his people, or the God of *quid pro quo*, automatically distributing rewards and punishments. Rather, he is a universal God, who is ready to show compassion for all victims of either misfortune or injustice.

God's compassion for the poor and marginalized is evident, for example in Psalm 147, in which God is praised for his graciousness because he "gathers the outcasts of Israel. He heals the brokenhearted and binds up their wounds . . . and lifts up the downtrodden" (vv. 1–3, 6). "For though the Lord is high," says the psalmist in Psalm 138, "he regards the lowly" (v. 6). In Psalm 41, God is blessed because he "considers the poor! The Lord delivers him in the day of trouble; the Lord protects him and keeps him alive; he is called blessed in the land . . . The Lord sustains him on his sickbed; in his illness thou healest all his infirmities" (vv. 1–3). In Psalm 68, God is praised by "the righteous" for his "goodness" (vv. 3,10): "Father of the fatherless and protector of widows is God in his holy habitation. God gives the desolate a home to dwell in; he leads out the prisoners to prosperity" (vv. 5–6).

Given God's disposition to help those who are suffering for reasons other than their own sins, the psalmist in Psalm 69 asks for God's help: "Let the oppressed see it and be glad . . . For the Lord hears the needy and does not despise his own that are in bonds" (vv. 29–33). In Psalm 70, the psalmist says, "I am poor and needy; hasten to me, O God! Thou art my help and my deliverer" (v. 5). In Psalm 44, the petitioner says, "Rise up, come to our help! Deliver us for the sake of thy steadfast love!" (v. 26). In Psalm 72, the psalmist says, "May [the king] defend the cause of the poor of the people, give deliverance to the needy, and crush the oppressor" (vv. 1–4). After praying that this righteous king defeat all other kings, the writer concludes: "For he delivers the needy when he calls, the poor and him who has no helper. He has pity on the weak and the needy, and saves the lives of the needy. From oppression and violence he redeems their life; and precious is their blood in his sight" (vv. 12–14).

All of these descriptions indicate that God is not only merciful but righteous. In other words, all of the forgoing petitions derive from the belief that God not only forgives repentant sinners and responds compassionately to victims of injustice but also embraces a code of right and wrong, which he spells out explicitly and repeatedly in many of the psalms. That is, unlike many of the psalms we studied in the first section of this chapter, many of the psalms we are examining in this section provide a clear and comprehensive definition of what righteousness and wickedness are. Simply put, righteousness means the same things to the psalmists as it does to the prophets: supporting the poor and the needy, feeding the hungry, releasing the prisoners, and protecting the oppressed—as well as forgiving the repentant. As these passages suggest, to both prophets and psalmists—that is, to both groups of interpreters of Judaism—God is principally venerated because he stands for social justice. And wickedness is any violation of social justice.

Thus, like most of the prophets and unlike the psalmists we discussed earlier in this chapter, some psalmists understand that what God wants is not gifts of sacrifice in exchange for material rewards but acts of righteousness performed for their own sake—or, better, for the sake of humanity. Their main focus is on the relationship between the individual and other human beings, which is, as we have seen, the concern of the Covenant Code and its reiterations in writings outside the Pentateuch. As A. T. van Leeuwen explains: "The duty to protect widows, the orphaned and the poor was a generally accepted ideal in the East. With Israel the ideal became a central, unconditional and paramount command, firmly grounded in that *sedhaqah* [meaning righteousness] which God had shown in his election of Israel. Israel saw herself, in relation to the Lord, as being in the position of the neighbor, with all that that implies of solidarity and support."[1054]

Who is the righteous person? In Psalm 106, the psalmist says, "Blessed are they who observe justice, who do righteousness at all times!" (v. 3). That is, the righteous are the people who avoid the sins of the wicked, including, in Psalm 10, pursuing and seizing the poor, crushing the hapless, ambushing and murdering the innocent, greedily seeking gain, renouncing God, cursing, and practicing deceit, oppression, mischief, and iniquity (see also 62:10; 73:1–12; 94:3–7; 109:16–17). The *tzaddik*, or righteous one, however, is not only just, but also kind, generous, merciful, and forgiving. Psalm 112 is almost entirely devoted to a description of this person, "who fears the Lord" and "greatly delights in his commandments." He or she "deals generously and lends," as well as "conducts his affairs with justice . . . He is not afraid of evil tidings; his heart is firm, trusting in the Lord . . . He has distributed freely, he has given to the poor; his righteousness endures for ever" (vv. 1, 5–9).[1055]

In Psalm 15, according to the editors of *The Oxford Annotated Bible*, the psalmist asks, "Who shall be admitted to the worshiping congregation?" The answer is "Only those who have the requisite moral qualities" (664)—that is, those "who walk blamelessly, do "what is right," and speak the truth. More specifically, this means someone who refrains from slandering and reproaching others, despises bad people and honors good, and avoids both lending at interest and taking bribes (vv. 1–5). In Psalm 37, the psalmist praises those who "do good" (vv. 3, 27)—not only by trusting God and "wait[ing] patiently for him," but also by avoiding anger and arrogance, generously giving to the poor, and lending "liberally" (vv. 5, 7, 8, 11, 21, 26). In Psalm 7, the writer says, "O Lord, . . . if there is wrong on my hands, if I have requited my friend with evil or plundered my enemy without cause, let the enemy pursue me and overtake me" (vv. 3–5).

However, as we noted earlier, God also expresses his morality by pledging assistance to those who have not necessarily acted righteously: that is, generously, fairly, or responsibly. As we have seen, besides the righteous, who in some sense have *earned* God's appreciation—that is, they have done what God asked them to do—God also saves the suffering, who are hungry or needy or despondent not because of their sins, but because of their misfortune. As von Rad explains: "The conviction that those whose legal standing was weak and who were less privileged in the struggle of life were the objects of Jahweh's particular interest reaches far back into the history of the people of Jahweh ... In fact, a great number of references understand these poor quite frankly and directly as those who can justifiably expect the divine protection. This state of being poor also includes a defencelessness and helplessness, as a result of which these men who pray designate themselves as cast upon Jahweh alone."[1056]

What is striking about God's embrace of these people is that his concern for them is not merely an expression of his pity or mercy.[1057] Rather, as I suggested earlier, God saves the indigent, helpless, and oppressed for the same reasons that he saves the righteous: *both* justice and mercy. Being downtrodden, they are either victims of those who have violated the standards of righteousness or they are potential victims of such people. Clearly, God is merciful toward them—that is, he "pities" them—but he also supports them out of a sense of fairness: "I know that the Lord maintains the cause of the afflicted, and *executes justice for the needy*" (140:12). Von Rad comments: "This conception of the poor practically contains a legal claim upon Jahweh; and it was precisely this which later made it a self-designation of the pious upon Jahweh"—i.e., in the self-descriptions of the Essenes at Qumran and the Christians in Jerusalem as "the poor." "Thus as self-designations the pious and the wretched became in the end of great importance for interpreting and filling out the concept of the 'righteous.'"[1058]

In this regard, those who suffer are indistinguishable from God's other favorites. On the one hand, "Surely the righteous shall give thanks to thy name; the upright shall dwell in thy presence" (140:12–13). On the other hand, however, so will the sufferers. The reason is that the psalmists—in this respect, very much like the prophets—regarded all suffering of the helpless (whether present or prospective) not as a consequence of their own misbehavior—laziness, immorality, or self-indulgence—but as a result of a political and economic system that permits oppression, exploitation, and social indifference. Thus, Daniel C. Maguire argues: "The distinctive feature of Jewish justice is the *stress on redistributive sharing and remedial systemic changes that favor the poor*. Its distinguishing accent is on what we call today social and distributive justice, not on individual (or commutative) justice."[1059]

This is, after all, the main theme of God's message to the Divine Council in Psalm 82: "*Give justice* to the weak and the fatherless"—meaning either that it is simply unjust that they are weak or fatherless or that their weakness and fatherlessness make them vulnerable to injustice. God continues, "[M]aintain the right of the afflicted and the destitute"—meaning either that the afflicted or destitute have the *right* to be relieved of their affliction or destitution or that they have a *right* to be protected from potential oppression or exploitation. And God concludes, "Rescue the weak and needy; deliver them from the hand of the wicked"—meaning either that the weak or needy are such because of the predations of "the wicked" or that they should be saved from the abuse to which their condition makes them susceptible (vv. 3–4; my emphasis).

Speaking generally of the ideas and practices of Judaism, John Dominic Crossan says (in a passage I cited earlier): "None of those Mesopotamian, Ugaritic, or Egyptian parallels diminishes in any way the far, far more serious way in which righteousness and justice, especially as protective of the widows and the orphans, the poor and the wretched were taken in the [Jewish] Bible." Crossan cites, among other passages in the Bible, the address to God in Psalm 99: "[L]over of justice, thou hast established equity; thou hast executed justice and righteousness" (v. 4).[1060] Indeed, Moore says, Judaism considers it a "duty" of the righteous to protect and redeem the suffering and a "right" of the suffering to be redeemed: "Attention may . . . be called to the fact that the ordinary, and one may say technical, name for almsgiving in Judaism is *sedakah*, a right, or just, act, and that it is taught not only that it is the duty of those who have means thus to relieve the need of others, but that the poor have a right to such relief—a right of which God declares himself the vindicator" in Deuteronomy 15:9.[1061]

Thus, although we hear in Psalm 7 that a "righteous God" is one who "saves the upright in heart" (vv. 9–10)—that is, the morally deserving, who have what Moore calls "rectitude" or "integrity"—we discover elsewhere that he also saves either the victims of injustice or those who are in danger of being treated unjustly. In Psalm 34, the psalmist says that "[w]hen the righteous cry for help, the Lord hears," but he is also "near to the brokenhearted and saves the crushed in spirit" (vv. 17–18). In Psalm 146, God "*executes justice for the oppressed*" and "gives food to the hungry." He "sets the prisoners free," "opens the eyes of the blind," "lifts up those who are bowed down," "loves the righteous," "watches over the sojourners," and "upholds the widow and the fatherless" (vv. 6, 8–9; my emphasis)—again, not out of mercy, but out of a sense of justice. In Psalm 10, God is asked to "hear the desire of the meek" and to "*do justice to the fatherless and the oppressed*" (vv. 17–18; my emphasis; see also 35:10).

In Psalm 10, the psalmist condemns a long series of crimes by the wicked against the disenfranchised, after which he concludes, "O Lord, thou wilt hear the desires of the meek; thou wilt strengthen their heart, thou wilt incline thy ear to *do justice to the fatherless and the oppressed*, so that the man who is of the earth may strike terror no more" (vv. 2–3, 7–10, 17–18; my emphasis). The psalmist in Psalm 72 begins to define righteousness by linking it with justice, as many psalmists do: "Give the king thy justice, O God, and thy righteousness to the royal son! May he judge thy people with righteousness, and *thy poor with justice!*" (vv. 1–2). As the editors of *The Oxford Annotated Bible* say, "The king is to be the guarantor of justice for the helpless" (709–10).

A Crisis of Faith

Just as the psalmists in these poems clearly condemn the suffering of the poor, they praise the punishment of the wicked. On the one hand, in some psalms the "enemy" is nothing more than the antagonist of the king or of some other official. In such cases, "the wicked" are not wicked objectively, but only because they are offensive to the psalmist. Thus, In Psalm 68, the writer says that "God will shatter the heads of his enemies, the hairy crown of him who walks in his guilty ways." God will, in fact, allow his people to avenge themselves on their opponents: "I will bring them back from the depths of the sea, that you may bathe your feet in blood, that the tongues of your dogs may have their portion from the foe" (vv. 21–23).

On the other hand, however, some psalmists identify "the wicked" as those who exploit or oppress the indigent and the vulnerable.[1062] In Psalm 109, the supplicant asks God to punish someone who "did not remember to show kindness, but pursued the poor and needy and the brokenhearted to their death" (v. 10). In Psalm 5, the psalmist says to God, "Make them bear their guilt, O God, let them fall by their own counsels; because of their many transgressions cast them out, for they have rebelled against thee" (v. 10). In Psalm 9, the writer praises God for exercising "righteous judgment" by punishing those who have inflicted suffering on the weak and helpless: "Thou hast rebuked the nations, thou hast destroyed the wicked; thou hast blotted out their name for ever and ever . . . The Lord is a stronghold for the oppressed . . . For the needy shall not always be forgotten, and the hope of the poor shall not perish for ever" (vv. 4–5, 9, 18). In Psalm 107 (called "A group thanksgiving for pilgrims" by the editors of *The Oxford Annotated Bible*, 790]), the writer says that the politically powerful eventually pay for their crimes against the poor: "When [the hungry] are diminished and brought low through oppression, trouble, and sorrow, [God] pours contempt upon princes and makes them wander in trackless wastes, but he raises up the needy out of affliction, and makes their families like flocks. The upright see it and are glad" (vv. 39–42).

I have concluded my discussion of the psalms with what some readers might consider to be the dark side of this collection of poems—that is, those in which God seems to countenance and even encourage vengeance and violence. Of course, it must be acknowledged that these psalms are not exceptional. As we have seen, many psalms are addressed to a warrior God, who is called upon to destroy the psalmists' enemies, sometimes in a cruel and bloodthirsty way, as in Psalm 137, which starts out so tenderly, with a reference to the plight of the Jews in captivity in Babylonia, and ends with this threat in recompense for the destruction of the Temple in Jerusalem: "Happy shall he be who requites you with what you have done to us! Happy shall he be who takes your little ones and dashes them against the rock!" (vv. 8–9). Furthermore, we find in I Samuel the story of King Saul's destruction of both male and female Amalekites, as well as children and infants, all done at God's behest. And we also read of God's disappointment that Saul, his newly anointed representative on earth, failed to destroy not only the king of the Amalekites, but also the country's domestic animals (vv. 5, 9).

The Evolution of Love

In short, there can be little doubt that the picture of Yahweh as Lord of hosts and merciless avenger actually existed. However, as I said at the beginning of this chapter, this picture changed over the centuries. And, although we cannot be certain that the idea of revenge, supported by a deity whose main virtue was his power and might, simply faded out entirely, there is substantial textual evidence that a significant modification occurred. As Charles Guignebert puts it, "[A] new and very different impulse . . . was manifested in the psalms," which "are imbued with a spirit of warm and spontaneous personal piety, that seems like a direct heritage from the religion of the prophets."[1063]

The differences between the older and newer views of God and his relationship to his people are evident when we compare what we can fairly certainly identify as representative examples of pre- and post-exilic Judaism. In what is considered to be one of the two or three oldest psalms, the 29th,[1064] the focus is on God's grandiosity: "Ascribe to the Lord . . . glory and strength," as well as a thunderous, powerful, and majestic voice, which breaks the cedars of Lebanon, shakes the wilderness of Kadesh, strips the forests bare, and breathes fire. If we compare this psalm to the 23rd, it is easy to see that the war-mongering king has become a soul-restoring shepherd, who satisfies wants and encourages righteousness. In Psalm 23, the psalmist does not laud God's power to destroy his or his people's enemies. Rather, he emphasizes God's trustworthiness, which is manifested in his protectiveness, his provision of food and "comfort," and his promise of "goodness and mercy."[1065]

As Miles says, the psalms move toward "*sedeq* and *hesed*"—God's righteousness and love—"rather than to his prowess in battle or his bounty."[1066] On the one hand, Miles notes that "steadfast love" (*hesed* or *chesed*), as well as "kindness and faithfulness," are connected with the Covenant and represent "the loyalty that binds liege and vassal rather than any more tender or personal feeling." On the other hand, however, he adds that the understanding of God was slowly changing in the first half of the first millennium BC and that such uses of the word *chesed* in the psalms and prophets at the very least meant "loving pity." Later, Miles says that in every mention of "steadfast love" as well as "righteousness" the psalmist "is reclaiming the covenant and extolling the law."[1067]

Thus, the consensus of contemporary scholars is that the psalms, especially those that reflect the ideals expressed in the works of the prophets, represent Judaism at its best, particularly in terms of their eloquence and their overall moral vision. G. Ernest Wright says, "While the individual psalms differ greatly in their quality of utterance, even those unlearned in biblical lore cannot fail to be impressed and inspired by the depth of feeling and sheer lyric beauty of many of the psalms, a depth and beauty that appear even in translation." Indeed, he continues, "[A]ll of the psalms . . . speak to the whole being of man with a power possessed equally by no other devotional literature in the Bible."[1068]

As Muilenburg reminds us, the uncertainty expressed by the supplicants in these psalms rests on the assumption that God is neither an abstract principle nor a purely transcendent entity, but "an intense reality," whose "anthropomorphic and anthropopathic" portrayal is revelatory of both his accessibility and unpredictability: "For Yahweh was personal. He entered into relationship with those who called upon him."[1069] In this respect, many of the psalms are not doctrinal and instructional statements, but prayers. And although many of them served liturgical purposes, they nevertheless express personal feelings and therefore indicate a connection to God that is not formal, priest-mediated, and collective but spontaneous, inward, and individual. As John J. Collins argues, "There can be little doubt that most of the psalms originated as emotive expressions." Thus, Collins concludes: "The book of Psalms is not a book of moral instruction. It is primarily a record of ancient Israel and Judah at prayer."[1070] And, in the psalms, the supplicants pray without ceasing.

Regarding the psalms in general, Miles notes, the focus on the individual led to "the universal assumption that God is a friend intimately acquainted with the supplicant," that this "personal relationship with God" led to "the new centrality of the law as meditation and delight," and that the change from "aggressive public and political themes to the quiet study of the law" was accompanied by "the shift from national to personal and family welfare."[1071] According to R. Travers Herford, "The book of Psalms stands alone, not only in the Old Testament, but in the literature of the world . . . [They] were hymns of religion, felt to be fresh and living, and for that reason, and no other, the men who made the Synagogue and gave to its worship the means of utterance, turned to the Psalms to supply their need."[1072]

For such reasons, based on the major Jewish texts, including the book of Psalms, as well as everything else we know about ancient Judaism, most contemporary scholars regard it as a religion based on a just and merciful moral code and a strong emphasis on inward devotion rather than ritual and sacrifice. According to Brevard S. Childs, "God's redemptive purpose in the world was seen only in the tangible shape of the Israel who did justice, loved kindness, and walked humbly with her God."[1073] Regarding God's justice, Herford explains, Judaism can be summed up in three principles: "first, that God is just; second, that there is an intrinsic difference between doing right and doing wrong; third, that the whole duty of man is to do the will of God."[1074] Regarding God's mercy, Guignebert says, the heart of the ordinary Jew "was filled with unbounded gratitude to Jahweh, who had proved himself not merely a just God, but a God of pity and love, the true Father of his people." The idea of the fatherhood of God "had a place both in the Scriptures and in the Schools, and was a source of religious poetry, as the Psalms of David and the Psalms of Solomon testify."[1075]

The Evolution of Love

Disillusionment

One could argue that the differences between the two views of God are attributable to the passage of time—particularly in response to changing circumstances. That is, it is logical to conclude that, over time, predictions and prophecies that were not eventually fulfilled had to be either redefined or abandoned. Such, for example, is the idea of the future Kingdom of God in Christianity, which either has been reinterpreted by scholars, theologians, and the church itself as a kingdom that arrived with the first coming of Jesus or has been simply ignored or dismissed, as Albert Schweitzer argues in *The Quest of the Historical Jesus* and Martin Werner explains at great length in *The Formation of Christian Dogma*. To appreciate some of the fundamental differences among the aforementioned Jewish writings, it is important to understand that two kinds of speculations about the future became similarly problematic in ancient Israel.

The first is the one we touched on above: the idea that God or the gods reward and punish virtue and vice in a strictly lockstep manner—that is, not only automatically but rather quickly—as many ancient peoples believed and as the earliest psalms as well as the Deuteronomist repeat again and again. Surely, it is the case that, as the Jews continued to be not only dominated, but also often oppressed and exploited by other nations, from the Assyrian invasion to the Roman occupation, at least some Jews began to lose faith in God's responsiveness to the pleas of supplicants, whether they were innocent or guilty and despite their willingness to repent in the latter case. Therepeated cry "How long?" in the psalms and even occasionally in the prophets (Isa 6:11; Hab 1:2; Zech 1:12) is an indication that the wait for God's merciful intervention often took far longer than expected and that the *quid pro quo* theory appeared to some people to be flawed, if not entirely wrongheaded. No doubt, this disappointment was exacerbated by the fact that the nations perceived by the Jews to be evil went unpunished, despite their cruelty and injustice (e.g., Jer 12:1).

The second example of unfulfilled expectations is the predictions of the prophets, many of which were restated by a group of writers, from Daniel onward, who wrote apocalypses, all of which also made promises that were never fulfilled. What is most important about these prophecies is that they all assumed that the current (and to some degree increasingly) painful and disappointing situation of the Jews would come to an end because God would intervene, as he did in Egypt in the second millennium BC. Isaiah and the other prophets held out the prospect that the *Yom Yahweh*, the Day of the Lord, was coming: "Wail, for the Day of the Lord is near; as destruction from the Almighty it will come!" (Isa 13:6; Jer 46:10; Zeph 1:7; Zech 14:1).[1076] However, the promise that God would "punish the world for its evil" (Isa 13:11; see also chs. 24–26; Jer 46:10; Ezek 30:2–3) as well as reward some small segment of the world for its virtues—both the result of God's miraculous intervention and his creation of utterly new conditions for human existence—was never carried out. The Deuteronomist's expectation that Israel would turn into a glorious Eden was not fulfilled.

A Crisis of Faith

Besides the persistent cry of impatience and frustration in many psalms and often in the prophets, three post-exilic works, in particular, illustrate what might be considered to be a small but eloquent expression of disillusionment with some of the major aspects of ancient Judaism: two canonical works, the book of Job and Ecclesiastes, and one apocryphal work, 2 Esdras. It is clear that, as time passed in the post-exilic period, some (if not many) Jews became more and more frustrated by the absence of any significant change in their political, social, and economic situation under the domination of one foreign ruler after another. And to the extent that this situation continued to be both tragic and intolerable, they began to lose faith that God would ever reward their piety or relieve their suffering, let alone fulfill the promises he made in both Deuteronomy and the works of the prophets. According to W. O. E. Oesterley and Theodore H. Robinson, the subject of the book of Job "is one which might have exercised the mind of any thoughtful Israelite after the exile," especially considering that this work was written, by most accounts, in the fifth or fourth century BC.[1077] This is because, as Dan Cohn-Sherbok says, it "was written at a later stage in biblical history as Jews became increasingly perplexed by God's justice."[1078]

There are many reasons to be impressed by the book of Job, including its literary qualities, the seriousness and relevance of its subject, and the tendency among scholars to see it—for both of these reasons—as a major world classic. Robert Alter, noting "the greatness of the Hebrew poetry of Job," says that the story is told in a style "that is often distinct both lexically and imagistically from its biblical counterparts" and thus "displays a virtuosity that transcends all other biblical poetry."[1079] According to Oesterley and Robinson, this work is the "highest point reached by the practical ethics of the Old Testament."[1080] Beyond this achievement, Gaalyah Cornfeld says, the book of Job is "one of the indisputably great classics of world literature."[1081] To G. Ernest Wright, it is "one of the great classics of all literature," particularly because of its "elevated style" and "sophisticated language."[1082] And Georg Fohrer comments, it is "a poetic work of the highest order," partly because it "shows its author to be an almost unequaled master of baroque imagination and great learning."[1083] The immediate relevance of the book of Job to the lives of fifth- or fourth-century Jews is suggested by Karen Armstrong: "For the first time in Jewish religious history, the religious imagination had turned to speculation of a more abstract nature. The prophets had claimed that God had allowed Israel to suffer because of its sins; the author of Job shows that some Israelites were no longer satisfied by the traditional answer."[1084]

Despite its reputation as a literary masterpiece, however, the book of Job is almost universally regarded as difficult to interpret, if not entirely incomprehensible. Mayer Gruber, for example, cites "its elaborate arguments"; "its highly poetic language, which is particularly ambiguous"; and a variety of "structural issues."[1085] The problematic structural problems include (1) the relationship between the prose framework, which is drawn from an old folk tale and confirms traditional moral and theological ideas, and the poetic core, which is contentious and heterodox;[1086] (2) later additions, such as chapter 28, which praises the wisdom tradition, although the rest of the book seems to challenge it, and the speeches of Elihu, which, like some verses in Ecclesiastes, were added to "normalize" the work, thereby making it acceptable to orthodox readers;[1087] and (3) passages that have been attributed to the wrong speaker, especially in chapters 25–27. For such reasons, William M. Ramsay calls this work "very puzzling."[1088] G. Ernest Wright considers it to be "the most difficult book in the Old Testament to translate."[1089] Oesterley and Robinson argue that "there are passages which defy translation as they stand."[1090] And Gerhard von Rad says that understanding the middle section of the book "is made extremely difficult by the lack of a clear progression of thought and a clearly fixed subject of conversation."[1091]

No doubt partly because of some of these issues, the story itself is burdened with contradictions and ambiguities. It is unclear, for example, whether the author intended to debunk, criticize, or support the idea that God rewards virtue and punishes vice. In this respect, the book of Job may be said to raise more questions than it answers. On one hand, the author seems to question the idea that all suffering comes from sin, as Job's friends contend. This issue is important because the causal connection between humanity's disobedience and God's punishment is an essential feature of the Judaism of Deuteronomy, the Prophets, the Proverbs, and many of the psalms. Job seems to question this theory by arguing that, despite his loss of health, children, and animals, he is innocent of doing anything that would merit not just this extreme punishment, but virtually any punishment at all. And God seems to settle the question by angrily announcing to Job's friend Eliphaz at the end of the narrative that he and his associates have been unjust to Job: "My wrath is kindled against you and against your two friends; for you have not spoken of me what is right, as my servant Job has." Job's friends are told to make a ritual sacrifice on Job's behalf, thus apologizing to Job for their error, and he is free to either accept or reject their symbolic show of remorse. If he prays for their forgiveness, God will not "deal with [them] according to [their] folly" (42:7–8). Furthermore, just as Job's friends are at least verbally punished, Job is rewarded for speaking correctly of God—indeed, he is given "twice as much as he had before" (42:10).

Thus, Alter, for example, argues that the book of Job presents a "challenge to the biblical consensus view of reward and punishment."[1092] Ramsay says that the book "is clearly an attack on that theology." Indeed, Ramsay adds, "The traditional view, still maintained by most commentators, is that . . . God's ways are a mystery beyond a mortal's understanding, and that no human has a right to make demands on the Almighty."[1093] G. E. Wright contends that "Job was written to explode the common notion of the wise men . . . that deity rules the world in a moralistic way, so that one can assess his goodness in the sight of God on the basis of his prosperity." Wright adds, "The reason is that there is a mystery in God's dealing with man, and in the last analysis no human formula is capable of resolving that mystery completely."[1094]

Gruber claims that the three main themes of the book of Job are (1) that human suffering is undeserved; (2) that those who argue otherwise inevitably mischaracterize both the sufferer and God; and (3) that, "in the Lord's argument, the reasons for suffering—if there are any—are simply beyond human comprehension."[1095] Walter Brueggemann says that God's "self-announcement"—his long response to Job at the end of the story—"is an invitation for the reader of the book to think and live outside any reductionist wisdom and, by inference, outside any reductionist Torah requirements."[1096] In short, as Derek Kidner notes, whereas in the book of Proverbs the note of uncertainty is brief and anomalous—"How then can man understand his way?" (20:24), one writer asks—"in Job, what was no more than a passing cloud in Proverbs now blots out the very sky."[1097]

On the other hand, however, this conclusion is problematic because no one in the story, including not only Job's friends, but both Job and God himself, actually repudiates the traditional biblical concept of rewards and punishments. That God supports the program is demonstrated by his treatment of Job and his friends at the end of the story. To put it simply, they are, respectively, rewarded and punished—or, at least in the case of Job's friends, threatened with punishment. And, more important, Job is outraged not because he objects to the concept, but because he believes that—not only in his case, as far as he can tell, but, more demonstrably, for all of humanity—it has not been fairly applied. Thus, he demands a trial (over and over) in order to determine whether he is mistaken about his own behavior or God has mistakenly charged him with wickedness.

In fact, Job is willing to accept God's punishment if only God will explain why he deserves it. After all, God twice praises Job at the beginning of the story: He "fears God and turns away from evil" (1:8, 2:3), a statement that seems to imply that there is a causal relationship between Job's fear of God and his willingness to obey him. Thus, while it may not be the case that Job has been virtuous because he hopes to gain earthly rewards, it is clear that he has avoided wickedness because he wishes to evade earthly punishment. Furthermore, Job never questions God's control over everything in the universe: "In his hand is the life of every living thing and the breath of all mankind" (12:10).

Thus, other scholars have suggested that it is not the *quid pro quo* theory that the author of Job attacks, but its rigid application and its arrogant defense, both of which are represented by Job's friends. Kidner argues that, while "one may easily conclude that the book of Job is designed as an attack on the older wisdom school," this conclusion "is too sweeping." Rather, the object of the author's scorn is not the theory defended by Job's friends, but their manner of expressing it: "the arrogance of pontificating about the application of these truths, and of thereby misrepresenting God and misjudging one's fellow men."[1098] Oesterley and Robinson acknowledge that "[o]ur first perusal of the book may have left us with the feeling that the essential theme is handled in a confusing and uncertain fashion." However, they offer three interpretational options, one of which is to apply the charge of arrogance not only to Job's friends, but also to Job himself: "Here we have the position of a reader of the popular story and of the poem, who felt that there was one serious fault in Job's character which needed correction. Throughout the debate he has insisted on his substantial righteousness," but Job's utter self-abasement at the end demonstrates that he understands his sin, implicitly accepts his punishment, and thereby withdraws his objection to God's moral program.[1099] Indeed, "the most common interpretation," according to Jack Miles, is that although Job "insist[s] on his own righteousness" and "demand[s] that God explain why his servant must suffer," he also believes that God will eventually exonerate him, for which reason (presumably) he finally *"repent[s] of what he said."*[1100]

Another issue that obfuscates the meaning of the story is that God's view of Job appears to be contradictory. The most obvious proof of this is the fact that God initially praises Job to Satan; later criticizes him directly for being misguided, faultfinding, and contentious; and finally rewards him—and not his friends—for being "right" in what he has "spoken" of God! At first, God calls Job not only "blameless and upright," but also superior to everyone else "on the earth" (1:8, 2:3). After nearly thirty chapters of Job's argument with his friends, however, God denounces him for his ignorance: "Who is this that darkens counsel by words without knowledge?" (38:2). Two chapters later, God also accuses Job of arrogance: "Will you put me in the wrong? Will you condemn me that you may be justified?" (40:8).[1101] And, finally, God indicates that, while he disapproves of Job's friends, he approves of Job, so much so that, as I said earlier, he restores to his "servant" "twice as much as he had before" (42:10). The question that remains unanswered, of course, is not whether Job was right, in some sense, and his friends were wrong, but what they were right and wrong about.

It should not be forgotten, in this context, that God's attitude toward Job in chapters 38–41 of the book of Job is unreservedly hostile. And this hostility is manifested not only in God's serious charges against him, but also in his absolute unwillingness to answer Job's fundamental questions: Is he innocent or guilty? If innocent, why is he being punished? And, if guilty, what exactly is his crime? Gruber says that "the speeches of the Lord raise the argument to a new level entirely, and then close off all further conversation without ever answering any of the deep and painful questions that have been raised along the way."[1102] Instead of responding to Job's desperate and urgent appeal for some kind of explanation (6:8–13; 7:11–21; 9:2–20, 25–35; ch. 10; 13:17—14:22), God offers Job nothing more than a series of rhetorical questions the purpose of which is to point out that Job was neither a witness to nor capable of imitating God's wondrous creation of every aspect of the cosmos, including the earth and the sea, morning and night, life and death, the weather, the stars, the animals, the birds, and two monsters, the Behemoth and Leviathan (38:4—39:30, 40:15—41:34). As Miles says, "in his furious speech to Job, the Lord never directly claims to be just, only to be almighty."[1103]

A Crisis of Faith

Job responds to God in chapter 40 with striking humility and reticence, as if to acknowledge not only God's stature, but also the unanswerability of his questions: "Behold I am of small account; what shall I answer thee? I lay my hand on my mouth" (40:3). Then God repeats the patronizing and problematic command to Job that he delivered when he first appeared to him "out of the whirlwind" (in 38:3): "Gird up your loins like a man"—as if Job were behaving immaturely or irresponsibly]; "I will question you, and you shall declare to me" (40:7). God tells Job that he has accused God of wrongdoing and condemned God merely to justify himself. Notably, despite his later praise of Job and reward for speaking correctly of God, God does not acknowledge at this juncture that Job is right about anything.

However, God's main point seems to be not that Job has incorrect opinions, but that he is being audacious. Thus, in effect, he says to Job, When you can do what I can do, I will take you seriously. Specifically, and perhaps with a jab at Job for asking questions at all, God mentions that he alone is able to abase the proud and "bring him low," as well as "tread down the wicked." If you can do that, God concludes, "[t]hen will I acknowledge to you, that your right hand can give you victory" (40:10–12, 14). The implication, of course, is that only God can provide victory: "Have you an arm like God, and can you thunder with a voice like his?" (40:9). Otherwise, be quiet!

In fact, God seems to imply that Job's inability to accept his mysterious ways is nothing more than a consequence of Job's own limitations. Robert Wright argues that, although "Job was allowed to interrogate God himself about the seeming injustice of it all," he was eventually "forced to settle for this answer: you wouldn't understand."[1104] According to Alter, some readers "have complained that [God's response] amounts to a kind of cosmic bullying of puny man by an overpowering deity." Instead, however, "it rousingly introduces a comprehensive overview of the nature of reality that exposes the limits of Job's human perspective, anchored as it is in the restricted compass of human knowledge and the inevitable egoism of suffering."[1105]

When "Yahweh answers Job out of the whirlwind," says Bernhard Anderson, his speech "is not so much an answer as a series of ironical questions that make Job's questions irrelevant. The effect of the questions is to remind Job that he is a creature whose finite standards are ineffective for judging the Creator." Indeed, so evasive is God at the very moment when both Job and the reader expect him to provide them with a precise and nuanced clarification of Job's strengths and weaknesses that one may wonder what the book of Job is all about. As Anderson explains, its subject is neither "the problem of suffering" nor "the question of divine justice." Thus, "the reader who approaches the book expecting to find an answer to these questions will be disappointed. Indeed, it is doubtful whether the author had any intention of trying to answer them."[1106]

It must be noted, of course, that if God's purpose in chapters 38–41 is to cow Job into submission—to elicit from him not only the self-abasement that Job expresses in chapter 40 ("I am of small account") and chapter 42 ("I despise myself")—the effort is hardly worth it. Job clearly knows that God is a superior being who is in no way either disposed or obliged to respond to an ordinary human being. Thus, Alter says that although "Job's final recantation begins by a recognition of God's omnipotence, . . . he had conceded this attribute all along in his complaint against God, raising doubts not about divine power but about divine justice."[1107] Job acknowledges God's terrifying power as well as his extraordinary achievements when he says: "[H]ow can a man be just before God? If one wished to contend with him, one could not answer him once in a thousand times. He is wise in heart, and mighty in strength—who has hardened himself against him, and succeeded?" After all, Job continues, God "removes mountains, "overturns them," "shakes the earth," and "commands the sun." He "alone stretched out the heavens, and trampled the waves of the sea." In addition to making the constellations, he "does great things *beyond understanding*, and marvelous things without number" (vv. 4–10; my emphasis). Here, as Gruber says, "Job anticipates what he will be told by the Lord in 38–41. Humankind is too insignificant to understand an explanation of how God rules the cosmos even if such an explanation were to be forthcoming."[1108]

Job returns to the subject of God's power when he acknowledges that in God's "hand is the life of every living thing and the breath of all mankind." Furthermore, God possesses wisdom, might, counsel, and understanding. He "overthrows the mighty," "makes nations great," and generally controls the actions of the powerful, including counselors, priests, and "the chiefs of the people of the earth" (12:10–24).[1109] Job is, therefore, "terrified at his presence," "in dread of him," and faint-hearted (23:15–16). In this context—that is, given Job's unmitigated fear that God will comply with his unquenchable desire to stand before him—it is not surprising that Job "repents . . . in dust and ashes," the authenticity of which is suggested by the fact that the phrase was uttered by Abraham when he similarly questioned God: "Behold, I have taken upon myself to speak to the Lord, I who am but dust and ashes" (Gen 18:27).[1110]

However, although God accuses Job of ignorance and arrogance—charges, incidentally, that are not accompanied by physical punishment, but, soon after, by physical rehabilitation—God does not charge him with past sins, thereby acknowledging his innocence, which is also confirmed by God's restoration of substantially more than Job's status quo ante.[1111] Furthermore, Job's prediction comes true: "I know that my Redeemer lives, and at last he will stand upon the earth; . . . then from my flesh I shall see God, whom I shall see on my side" (19:25–27). Even if Job is talking about the appearance of a "Vindicator" other than God, as the editors of *The Oxford Annotated Bible* argue, he nevertheless retains his belief that God will respond to him: "In his utmost destitution, rejected by friends, deprived of heirs, attacked by God, uncertain of future fame, Job's faith leaps for a moment to the certainty that after death his most cherished wish will be fulfilled" and that 'he will see God'" (631). Indeed, his wish is fulfilled *before* his death. As Job had also predicted, "when [God] has tried me, I shall come forth as gold" (23:10).

It is important to note that God confirms Job's virtue not only by doubling his wealth and restoring his children to him, but also by appearing to him in person, which evokes from Job his famous response: "I had heard of thee by the hearing of the ear, But now my eye sees thee" (42:5–6). According to the editors of *The Oxford Annotated Bible*, "God has not justified Job, but he has come to him personally; the upholder of the universe cares for a lonely man so deeply that he offers him the fulness of his communion. Job is not vindicated but he has obtained far more than a recognition of his innocence: he has been accepted by the ever-present master-worker, and intimacy with the Creator makes vindication superfluous. The philosophical problem is not solved, but is transfigured by the theological reality of the divine-human rapport" (655).

The reader might not entirely agree with the editors' last point, but certainly Job is rewarded by God both materially and spiritually. In this respect, it is clear that he has not been brow-beaten into submission, since God's response to him is not only not the assault that he anticipated, but, in fact, restorative rather than punitive. Indeed, Job humbly repents not because he is intimidated by God's power,[1112] but because he is redeemed by God's presence. As Yehezkel Kaufmann says, "In the theophany and the discourse with man, God's ultimate grace shines forth, the grace of revelation. This is the supreme favor. Not what he said, but his very manifestations the last, decisive argument."[1113]

According to von Rad, however, even the *content* of God's response to Job is at least an indirect answer to his basic question. That is, although most readers regard God's reply as off the mark, it nevertheless asserts the reality of God's justice, at least in the sense and to the degree that the entire universe is not only orderly because God created and measured it—land and sea, light and darkness, birth and death, and all earthly creatures and heavenly constellations. It is also a place in which "the sons of God shouted for joy," the wicked "of the earth . . . are shaken out of it," and even the raven is provided its prey "when the young ones cry to God, and wander about for lack of food" (38:7, 13, 41). Thus, despite the fact that "God's answer deals with something completely different from what Job asked about," it "insists upon the absolute marvellousness of his management of the world." In short, "If Job's holding fast to his righteousness was a question put to God, God gives the answer by pointing to the glory of his providence that sustains all his creation."[1114]

It is also important to understand that this theophany is not merely a reward for Job's undying faith, which pleases God and elicits from him an act of grace. Some scholars have noted that the story of Job is much more than merely a thirty-chapters-long, more or less randomly arranged series of complaints culminating in a demonstration of God's mercy. Rather, the narrative carefully traces Job's *development*—mentally, emotionally, and spiritually—and presents the appearance of God as a culmination of Job's evolution from one level of consciousness to another—from darkness to light, from merely human knowledge to divine wisdom. In this view, God appears to Job at the end of his *via negativa*, his journey into the depths of despair, the spiritual voyage into darkness that traditionally culminates in revelation. Indeed, his suffering is so extreme and his despair so deep, even from the beginning, that he curses his own birth (3:1–2; 10:18) and complains that his losses are too much to bear, which is why his "words have been rash" (6:3). He says to God, "I will give free utterance to my complaint" (10:1).

As time passes, Job is not only abandoned by both respectable colleagues and needy beneficiaries, but also severely criticized by his so-called friends, whose response to him is not a random attack but a carefully orchestrated provocation delivered by three quite different individuals,[1115] with different styles and temperaments,[1116] whose growing chorus of accusations are increasingly hostile and mean-spirited: Job's well-meaning comforters" move "ever further from reality" as "they pass from gentle probings for some hidden sin, to stern rebukes for [Job's] intemperate language (e.g., ch. 15), and finally to inventing a fictitious catalogue of crimes for him (22:5ff.)."[1117] In fact, these charges provoke Job to understand his situation in broader and broader terms so that his expanding awareness corresponds to his increasing despondency and carries him upward spiritually as well as downward emotionally.

As von Rad says, Job changes from "the man wholly sheltered in his faith and his commitment to God" to "one sinking into all the depths of abandonment by God, and accusing him"—"blasphemous and scorning"—only to arrive thereafter at "quite a different spiritual and religious" place.[1118] And as he "moves forward," according to Oesterley and Robinson, "each step he takes is made possible by something that the friends say." Thus, starting with "simply a cry of pain," Job learns from Eliphaz, who tells him to "repent and submit to God," that "it is God who is responsible." From Bildad's claim that "God is 'righteous'" and Zophar's suggestion that Job "can never reach God," Job thinks of proving his righteousness before God in a court of law. The scholars conclude: "Our first perusal of the book may have left us with the feeling that the essential theme is handled in a confusing and uncertain fashion. It is only when we recognize the fact that Job is the result of a growth in which three main stages can be distinguished," all of them identified with the three cycles in each of which Job serially encounters each of his three friends.[1119]

Ironically, of course, as Job evolves into an independent thinker, relying solely on his own experience, and unable to refrain from expressing his defiance and despair, his friends become not only increasingly insulting and accusatory, but also "more and more traditional . . . until it would appear that they have to nothing more to say."[1120] In contrast to Job, Anderson says, "The three friends were too smug in their orthodoxy, too sure of the answers to life's enigmas, too confident that God was bound by their logic." Furthermore, while Job grew in sympathy, "their rigidity prevented them from having any real sympathy for Job."[1121] Thus, as his friends turn into objects of God's unmitigated scorn, Job moves toward reconciliation. As a sign of his moral growth, just as he eventually reverses some of his worst accusations against God,[1122] Job also reverses his wish that "those who opposed him"—his friends—"would get

A Crisis of Faith

the punishment they deserved."[1123] This reversal occurs when Job asks God "not to deal with [them] according to [their] folly," but to forgive them in exchange for their request to him to be absolved (42:8).

"Step by step," says Kaufmann, Job "passes from his own case to generalized observations."[1124] According to Ramsay, citing the views of Gustavo Gutierrez, "one can see in Job's speeches a gradual turning away from himself." Increasingly, "he identifies with all of suffering humanity." And this transformation prepares Job "for his encounter with God."[1125] To be sure, Job starts with a long lament for his own suffering, which expresses itself as a death wish (3:1–26). After his first encounter with Eliphaz, however, he asks a question about humanity: "Has not man a hard service upon earth, and are not his days like the days of a hireling?" (7:1–2). Later, Job accuses God of "destroy[ing] both the blameless and the wicked"; "mock[ing] at the calamity of the innocent"; and giving "the earth . . . into the hand of the wicked" (9:22–24). However, in the first twenty chapters of the story, these brief excursions into the world of empathy turn into a more extensive discussion by Job of the plight of "man" only in chapter 14, which begins, "Man that is born of woman is of few days, and full of trouble. He comes forth like a flower, and withers" (vv. 1–22).

To be sure, Job focuses on his own problems in 10:1–22, 16:1–22, and 19:1–29. But he returns to the broader problems that beset all of humanity soon enough: "Why do the wicked live, reach old age, and grow mighty in power?" "How often is it that the lamp of the wicked is put out? That their calamity comes upon them? That God distributes pains in his anger?" (21:7–17). The wicked are not punished for oppressing the poor, the fatherless, and the widow, while these victims must forage in the fields, the wilderness, and the desert. "From out of the city the dying groan, and the soul of the wounded cries for help; yet God pays no attention to their prayer." Murderers and adulterers go free (24: 5–17).

Job not only expands his awareness of suffering by seeing his own problems in relation to those of humanity at large; he also turns away from his "friends," who continually disappoint him, and turns *to God*. In chapter 7, he says, "Therefore I will not restrain my mouth; I will speak in the anguish of my spirit; I will complain in the bitterness of my soul" (v. 11). In the same chapter, says G. E. Wright, "his misery so overcomes him that he begins to address God directly."[1126] Since the question that increasingly preoccupies him is whether or not God is just, Job eventually decides to go to the source. "What is man," he asks God, "that thou dost make so much of him, and that thou dost set thy mind upon him, dost visit him every morning, and test him every moment?" (vv. 17–18). His strongest complaint to God is, of course, that he is innocent. And his second strongest complaint is that God has abandoned him. According to Anderson, "Throughout his spiritual struggle, Job is tortured by the remoteness and hiddenness of God . . . With increasing clearness he sees that a great gulf is fixed between the Creator and the creature, between the righteousness of God and the righteousness of man . . . He knows that God is 'God and not man'—the

Wholly Other, the Transcendent One."[1127] Just as he understands that his friends are completely worthless as guides to solace as well as salvation, he also realizes that God is equally remote but remains his only hope for redemption.

Job combines these two complaints into one when he asks God to provide him with an opportunity to present his case to him, face to face: "Why dost thou not pardon my transgression and take away my iniquity?" (7:21). "Why dost thou hide thy face, and count me as thy enemy?" (13:24). "O that I knew where I might find him, that I might come even to his seat! I would lay my case before him and fill my mouth with arguments" (23:3–4). At first, in chapters 9 and 10, responding to Bildad's suggestion that he appeal to God, Job expresses the deepest doubt that God will acknowledge his innocence. At the end of his speech, he says to God, "Let me alone that I may find a little comfort before I go whence I shall not return"—that is, Sheol, the land of darkness, gloom, and chaos (10:20–22). However, Job never abandons his hope for salvation, since even in Sheol, God might "remember" him: "Thou wouldst call, and I would answer thee" (14:15).

In fact, in chapter 19, having reached what Anderson calls "the very limits of thought, where momentarily his vision is enlarged,"[1128] Job says, "I know that my Redeemer lives, and at last he will stand upon the earth; . . . then from my flesh I shall see God, whom I shall see on my side, and my eyes shall behold, and not another" (vv. 25–27).[1129] On Job's certainty of redemption, Kidner comments, "For all its ebbing and flowing, that conviction inches its way forward, to reach a point"—or, more accurately, higher and higher points—in 14:13–15, 16:19–21, 17:3, and 19:25–27—the last of which Kidner calls "the greatest saying of all."[1130] And, in the words of Oesterley and Robinson, it is underscored at the end of Job's final "appeal to Yahweh to appear and pronounce on the case": "Oh, that I had one to hear me! (Here is my signature! Let the Almighty answer me!") (31:35).[1131]

Significantly, God satisfies Job's passionate wish in this passage by appearing to him immediately after he expresses it, at the end of his elaborate declaration of his innocence in chapters 29–31. That is, Job's last appeal is nothing less than a courtroom presentation of what the editors of *The Oxford Annotated Bible* call his "final defense" or "final plea" (640) and what G. E. Wright calls "the final summary of his case."[1132] Alter notes that in 19:25–27 Job's claim *I know my Redeemer liveth* "in fact continues the imagery of a legal trial to which Job reverts so often."[1133] Therein, Job argues in great detail that he has always followed the Covenant to the letter, helping the poor, the fatherless, and the widowed. He was righteous and just. He took it upon himself to investigate "the cause of him [he] did not know." He defeated the unrighteous and the predatory. He gave counsel that was never contradicted. He supported the fearful and comforted mourners (29:12–25).

According to the editors of *The Oxford Annotated Bible*, Job reiterates his innocence by listing in chapter 31 all of the sins he has *not* committed: "To convince God and men of his innocence, Job reviews his past behavior in the form of sixteen oaths, covering varying aspects of religious and moral misdeeds. The poet offers by implication the evidence of a refined ethical consciousness" (642). Again, the presentation elicits exactly what Job hopes for, the appearance of God—"now my eye sees thee"—which, though hardly an explanation of human suffering, is explicitly an act of reconciliation and, at least implicitly, an acknowledgement of Job's innocence. Even if the latter is not earned by Job's final plea, it is certainly provided in response to his final repentance. In this respect, Job has, indeed, "come forth as gold" (23:10), for, having passed through his dark night of the soul, he has been transformed by his experience: "Surely there is a mine for silver, and a place for gold which they refine . . . Men put an end to darkness, and search out to the farthest bound the ore in gloom and deep darkness" (28:1, 3). It is important to understand, as Marcus Borg reminds us, that *"[s]eeing* God is classical language for a mystical experience: an intense, immediate experience of the sacred." As such, regardless of the content of his response, God's appearance alone should be seen as an affirmation of Job's virtue, particularly his personal integrity.[1134]

To be sure, the book of Job marks yet another development in the history of ancient Judaism. After all, it is the first major work in this tradition to offer, at the very most, ambiguous support for one of the major themes of the works that precede it: the idea that God rewards virtue and punishes vice. Of course, this ambiguity is not entirely new, since it arises in the book of Psalms whenever the psalmists, like Job, ask God for some kind of response to their cry for help, forgiveness, or consolation. Indeed, since Job expresses the same kind of desperation and despair that appears quite often in the psalms, the middle chapters of Job's story (excluding the interruptions of Job's friends) could be considered a long psalm-like lament. Fohrer says, "In Job's dispute with God, Job's challenges are chiefly modeled after the psalms of lament (a 'narrative account' of distress and protestation of innocence)."[1135]

This is especially the case when Job cries, "How long wilt thou not look away from me," and when he asks, "Why dost thou not pardon my transgression and take away my iniquity?" (7:19, 21)—echoing Psalm 13: "How long, O Lord? Wilt thou forget me for ever? How long wilt thou hide thy face from me?" (v. 1; see also Pss 22:1–2, 55:1–2, 69:1–3). Indeed, there are quite specific echoes in Job of the sentiments expressed in Psalms 77 (1–10) and 88 (1–18). Furthermore, Job repeats the essential question of Psalm 8: "What is man that thou dost make so much of him, and that thou hast set thy mind upon him, dost visit him every morning, and test him every moment?" (7:17–18; cf. Ps 8:4). And later he laments, "Man that is born of a woman is of few days, and full of trouble. He comes forth like a flower, and withers; he flees like a shadow, and continues not" (14:1–2). "Surely," says the psalmist, "man goes about as a shadow!" (39:6). "Man is like a breath, his days are like a passing shadow" (144:4).

At the same time, also like many of the psalmists, Job maintains his innocence and asks God for a chance to defend himself against God's charges. The supplicant in Psalm 7 says, "[J]udge me, O Lord, according to my righteousness, and according to the integrity that is in me" (v. 8).[1136] "Hear a just cause, O Lord" pleads the writer of Psalm 17; "attend to my cry! Give ear to my prayer from lips free of deceit! From thee let my vindication come" (vv. 1–2). And the penitent in Psalm 26 directly asks for a courtroom hearing of some kind: "Vindicate me, O Lord, for I have walked in my integrity, and I have trusted in the Lord without wavering. Prove me, O Lord, and try me; test my heart and my mind" (vv. 1–2; see also Ps 54:1–2). Job similarly wants God to explain why he is suffering: "Do not condemn me; let me know why thou dost contend against me" (10:2). I would lay my case before him and fill my mouth with arguments. I would learn what he would answer me . . . There an upright man could reason with him, and I should be acquitted for ever by my judge" (23:3–7). Thus, Job asks God to suspend his punishment and allow him to defend himself: "Then call, and I will answer; or let me speak, and do thou reply to me. How many are my iniquities and my sins? Make me know my transgression and my sin" (13:20–23).[1137]

The point is that, in the fifth or fourth century BC, when the book of Job was written, some indeterminate number of Jews had reached a point at which serious questions about God's moral governance of the universe were not only unavoidable, but unanswerable. "In the entire book [of Job]," says Fohrer, "there are only a few verses that do not contain echoes of and similarities to other books of the OT . . . It remains true, however, that the poet is living through a crisis of the theological wisdom system"—indeed, "the crisis convulsing the traditional faith of his time." Thus, although he was "Immersed in the material and motifs of the OT," he "had to find his own path to secure foundations."[1138] That the author of Job actually found that path is not entirely clear. And, if two other Jewish works of a later time—Ecclesiastes and 2 Esdras—are any indication, some Jewish writers and thinkers continued to have a difficult time discovering their own "secure foundations." "This skepticism," says Kidner, Old Testament scholar G. von Rad "saw as the end of a road on which, in his opinion, Israel had already set foot in losing faith in God's action in history."[1139]

Like the book of Job, Ecclesiastes, written in the third century BC, is a wisdom book. It repeats the statement from Proverbs that our survival, if not our salvation, depends on the "fear [of] God" (8:14); praises wisdom as superior to strength and weapons of war (9:16, 18); and, as we shall see, focuses on socially, rather than morally, useful advice. This work, however, goes one step beyond the book of Job: it clearly and unequivocally rejects the belief that God rewards good behavior and punishes bad.[1140] As the editors of *The Oxford Annotated Bible* comment: "Ecclesiastes contains the reflections of a philosopher rather than a testimony of belief. The author seeks to understand by the use of reason the meaning of human existence and the good which man can find in life" (805). However, according to Anderson, the result is a "bold challenge to orthodox Judaism" which "was regarded as dangerously close to heresy." Indeed, this challenge was so strong that "the book was touched up here and there to make it more palatable to orthodox taste." A conclusion was added in 12:12–14 that warns the reader not to take the ideas in the book too seriously—"much study is a weariness of the flesh"—and more than half a dozen passages were added to mitigate the charge of heresy.[1141]

According to some scholars, partly because of these interpolations, as well as the loose structure of the book—which is typical of wisdom literature generally—Ecclesiastes nevertheless presents the reader with some interpretational problems. Says R. Gordis, "There is scarcely one aspect of the book, whether of date, authorship or interpretation, that has not been the subject of wide difference of opinion."[1142] Alter argues: "The movement of Qohelet's thought is freewheeling and associative. It includes segments of maxims and perceptions that clearly belong together thematically... Beyond that, it is hard to find architectonic design in the book."[1143]

Although Ecclesiastes is regarded as a more or less random collection of proverbial comments, it is actually better appreciated if it is treated as an experience-based confession that moves from despair in the face of God's apparent moral indifference to extremely guarded optimism based on the prospect of the quite limited opportunities for either satisfaction or happiness. The early chapters of the book concentrate on the "vanity" of every conceivable activity and the futility of the search for meaning. Koheleth, the putative author (whose name simply means that, as a teacher or preacher, he is addressing an *ecclesia*, or assembly), says, "All is vanity" (1:1) and goes on to include in his list of futile efforts and achievements "toil" (1:3; 2:21–22; 3:9; 4:8), "pleasure" (2:1), "great works" (2:4), "wisdom" (2:15), fame (4:13–16) and "wealth" (5:10, 13–14).

These chapters are notable for the repetition of three phrases. First, the author has examined everything "under the sun." Second, in response to every potential source of meaningfulness, he says that "this also is vanity." And, third, for that reason, every conceivable human activity is "a striving after wind." As Alter explains, the Hebrew word *hevel* can mean not only *vanity*, but *futility, absurdity, insubstantiality, ephemerality,* and *elusiveness*.[1144] According to Koheleth, the conclusion of his quest for meaning drove him into a state of despair. "I hated life," he says, "because what is done under the sun was grievous to me; for all is vanity and a striving after wind" (2:17). "I turned about and gave my heart up to despair over all the toil of my labors under the sun" (2:20). "And I thought the dead ... more fortunate than the living" (4:2).

Several aspects of human nature and the human condition caused this transformation. First, Koheleth says, nothing ever changes. That is, "[T]here is nothing new under the sun" (1:9). This is so because God made the world in such a way as to render ineffectual and therefore useless all human efforts to change anything for the better: "What is crooked cannot be made straight" 1:15; 7:13). Nature operates in an unending cyclical manner: "The sun arises and the sun goes down" (1:5). It is perhaps good news that "[f]or everything there is a season," but Koheleth concludes his list of seasonally appropriate activities with the grim question "What gain has the worker from his toil?" (3:1–9). his question compels us to challenge the popular interpretation of the passage: i.e., that human activities will succeed if they are performed at the right time or, as Anderson explains the passage, "Each time is an opportunity sent from God."[1145] At the very least, it suggests (1) that there is a fixed balance between positive and negative experiences (and also that killing, breaking down, mourning, separating, losing, rending, hating, and fighting wars are inevitable), and (2) that some events—such as birth and death—are completely outside of human control.[1146]

Indeed, the editors of *The Oxford Annotated Bible* interpret 3:1–15 to mean that *everything* falls into this category: "*Everything happens at the time fixed for it*" (807; my emphasis). As Koheleth comments: "I know that whatever God does endures for ever; nothing can be added to it, nor anything taken from it; God has made it so, in order that men should fear before him" (3:14). Thus, it is not merely that nothing changes, but also that God is in total control of everything that happens: "God . . . has appointed a time for every matter, and for every work" (3:17). "For every matter has its time and way, although man's trouble lies heavy upon him" (8:7). Koheleth makes it very clear that both pleasure and pain come from God. All enjoyment "is from the hand of God" (2:24). It is "God's gift to man" (3:13; see also 5:18–19; 8:15; 9:7). At the same time, all frustration and disappointment also come from God, including the inevitably futile search for wisdom (1:13; see also 3:10; 8:17).[1147] "As you do not know how the spirit comes to the bones in the womb of a woman with child, so you do not know the work of God who makes everything" (11:5).[1148]

Second, Koheleth claims that the moral system that is questioned in the book of Job is simply nonexistent. As Ramsay says, Ecclesiastes "over and over affirms that there simply is no pattern of reward and punishment or any other discernible order in life as its author has seen it."[1149] "In my vain life," Koheleth says, "I have seen everything; there is a righteous man who perishes in his righteousness, and there is a wicked man who prolongs his life in his evil doing." The lesson, therefore, is to avoid excess either way. That is, avoid being "righteous overmuch" and "[b]e not wicked overmuch" (7:16–17). Koheleth at first believed that wisdom was better than folly because "the wise man" can see while "the fool walks in darkness." However, he soon "perceived that one fate comes to all of them. Then he said to himself, "What befalls the fool will befall me also; why then have I been so very wise . . . For of the wise man as of the fool there is no enduring remembrance, seeing that in the days to come all will have been long forgotten. How the wise man dies just like the fool!" (2:13–16).

In fact, death is the single most important event that renders the *quid pro quo* system invalid. Both men and beasts have the same fate: "All go to one place; all are from the dust, and all turn to dust" (3:18–20; see also 6:6). And death awaits all human beings regardless of their virtues or vices: "[O]ne fate comes to all, to the righteous and the wicked, to the good and the evil, to the clean and the unclean, to him who sacrifices and him who does not sacrifice. As is the good man, so is the sinner; and he who swears is as he who shuns an oath. This is an evil in all that is done under the sun, that one fate comes to all" (9:2–3). The result is, as Koheleth says in his most famous comment on the subject: "[T]he race is not to the swift, nor the battle to the strong, nor bread to the wise, nor riches to the intelligent, nor favor to the men of skill; but time and chance happen to them all" (9:11).

Third, human beings are incapable of understanding why things are the way they are. One problem is that they are unable to recall past events: "There is no remembrance of former things, nor will there be any remembrance of later things yet to happen among those who come after" (1:11). nother problem is that the future is equally inaccessible to them: "[M]an may not find out anything that will be after him" (7:14). Thus, "who knows what is good for man while he lives the few days of his vain life, which he passes like a shadow? For who can tell man what will be after him under the sun?" (6:11; see also 8:6; 10:14). "In the morning sow your seed, and at evening withhold not your hand; for you do not know which will prosper, this or that, or whether both alike will be good" (11:6).

Denied knowledge of the past as well as knowledge of the future, human beings are also unable to understand the present. Koheleth says that when he tried "to search out by wisdom all that is done under heaven," he discovered that "it is an unhappy business that God has given to the sons of men to be busy with." Having "seen everything," he concluded that it was "a vanity and a striving after the wind." Furthermore, he realized that the more you know, the sadder you are—that "in much wisdom is much vexation" and that "he who increases knowledge increases sorrow (1:13–18; see also 3:10–11; 7:23–25; 11:5). This is why, as Koheleth later explains, he lost sleep and gained nothing except the realization that the understanding he searched for could not be found: "However much man may toil in seeking, he will not find it out; even though a wise man claims to know, he cannot find it out" (8:16–17).

Fourth, Koheleth's experience leads him to believe that human nature is unalterably and universally evil, the result of which is that, even if God maintained a program of moral reward and punishment, no one could escape the latter. The main problem is that everyone is motivated by competitiveness and insatiability: "Then I saw that all toil and all skill in work come from a man's envy of his neighbor" (4:4). "[T]he eye is not satisfied with seeing, nor the ear filled with hearing" (1:8). "He who loves money will not be satisfied with money; nor he who loves wealth with gain" (5:10; see also 4:8). "All the toil of a man is for his mouth, yet his appetite is not satisfied" (6:7). This is because, in so many words, he cannot have his cake and eat it: "When goods increase, they increase who eat them; and what gain has their owner but to see them with his eyes?" (5:11). The result of these maladies is that no one is perfect: "Surely there is not a righteous man on earth who does good and never sins" (7:20; see also 7:29). Thus, although "God will judge the righteous and wicked," he will be unable to make any distinctions because "in the place of justice, even there was wickedness, and in the place of righteousness, even there was wickedness" (3:16–17).

Koheleth also sees manifestations of human evil simply because some people have power over others: "I saw all the oppressions that are practiced under the sun. And behold, the tears of the oppressed, and they had no one to comfort them!" This problem is pervasive and unchangeable because "[o]n the side of their oppressors there was power, and there was no one to comfort them" (4:1). The "high official"—who oppresses the poor and violently takes away "justice and right"—"is watched by a higher, and there are yet higher ones over them." The bureaucracy of power is immovable, and besides, "a king is an advantage to a land with cultivated fields" (5:8–9). Koheleth also advises his readers to "[K]eep the king's command" because "he does whatever he pleases." No one can question him because his word is "supreme." That is, "[h]e who obeys a command will meet no harm" (8:2–5). Thus, "man lords it over man to his hurt," and no one can (or should) do anything to prevent it (8:9).

Although both Job and Koheleth fall into a state of deep despair, it is important to distinguish between the personal, emotional, and physical aspects of Job's suffering and the more or less intellectual or philosophical aspect of Koheleth's.[1150] Indeed, Job's physical pain, social isolation, and actual loss of all of his children, all of his possessions, and all of his relationships with friends, family, and God make his situation not only utterly intolerable, but also salvageable only by God himself. Koheleth is not in physical pain, he has not been abandoned by friends and family, and he has no reason to believe that God is either capable of or interested in saving him by changing the circumstances of his life. To Koheleth, God is unquestionably in control of the universe. However, he is not perceived to be prepared to interfere with Koheleth's situation. In fact, God's last word in the Jewish Bible is expressed in the book of Job. And his last intervention in the affairs of his people occurs in the same biblical text. Thus, although Koheleth is not suffering in the way that Job is, he is left to his own devices, quite ready to make whatever adjustment is necessary, and ready to examine his situation as a means of achieving his survival, if not his salvation.

In his attempt to deal with his revolutionary realization of his precarious position in the universe, Koheleth first acknowledges that he can achieve some satisfaction by pursuing modest goals and experiencing small, though transient, pleasures.[1151] Work itself can provide some kind of "enjoyment" (2:24). That is, one "can take pleasure in all his toil" (3:13). Indeed, "there is nothing better than that man should enjoy his work" (3:22). It is, after all, "the gift of God" (5:19; see also 8:15). Koheleth does not explain how or why work, or toil, which achieves nothing permanent and apparently nothing worthwhile, can provide satisfaction, let alone pleasure or enjoyment. Nevertheless, he concludes, do it because "it is your portion in life": "Whatever your hand finds to do, do it with your might; for there is no work or thought or knowledge or wisdom in Sheol, to which you are going" (9:10).

Along with work, Koheleth claims, eating and drinking (2:24) are the only human activities that are worthy of pursuit: "I know that there is nothing better for [people] than to be happy and enjoy themselves as long as they live; also that it is God's gift to man that every one should eat and drink" (3:12–13; see also 5:18). "I commend enjoyment, for man has no good thing under the sun but to eat and drink, and enjoy himself" (8:15). "Go, eat your bread with enjoyment, and drink your wine with a merry heart; for God has already approved what you do" (9:7). These appear to be not only modest, but trivial and inconsequential satisfactions, which can be justified only because, in Koheleth's view, they are all we have: "Bread is made for laughter, and wine gladdens life, and *money answers everything*" (10:19; my emphasis). "In the day of prosperity be joyful, and in the day of adversity consider; God has made the one as well as the other" (7:14).

In other words, what makes these activities worthy of pursuit is simply that, as Koheleth argues from chapter 4 through chapter 9, *something is better than nothing*. Although he says early on that the unborn—"he who has not yet been" (4:3)—is better off than either the living or the dead (4:3) and later claims that sorrow is better than laughter (7:3) and that "the end of a thing" is better than "its beginning," (7:8), he also says that "a living dog" is better than "a dead lion" (9:4). The formula—*x* is better than *y*—which Koheleth returns to repeatedly in the central chapters of Ecclesiastes, represents the author's connection to the wisdom tradition, this formula being an important motif in Proverbs. It also represents his evidently desperate decision to accept the depressing facts of life—the futility of human effort, cosmic meaninglessness, the pervasiveness of evil, and the inevitability of death—rather than yield to the utter hopelessness expressed by Job's wife: "Curse God, and die" (2:9).

In fact, Koheleth demonstrates his unwillingness to give up on the wisdom tradition entirely when he offers his readers the same standard of behavior that appears in Proverbs, which is based on the importance of succeeding in the world, as opposed to following God's covenant demands as they are expressed in the Prophets, Psalms, and Deuteronomy. As Werner Schmidt says, "In style and intellectual stance Qoheleth's associations are with proverbial wisdom; he even takes over its language and insights."[1152] Readers are advised to control their passions: "Better is the sight of the eyes than the wandering of desire" (6:9). And they are told to protect their reputation: "A good name is better than precious ointment" (7:1). Koheleth also recommends patience over pride (4:13), "the rebuke of the wise" over "the song of fools" (7:5), poverty and wisdom over wealth and folly (7:8), personal grooming over carelessness (9:8), deference to rulers over protest (10:4, 20), and hard work over "sloth" and "indolence" (10:18)—all of which are similarly recommended in one form or another in Proverbs.[1153]

Emphasizing worldly success, the author of Ecclesiastes shows that he is still connected with at least one biblical tradition. At the same time, however, he also reveals how far he has moved from the principles of the Covenant, particularly the concern for the suffering of ordinary people, especially the disenfranchised, such as fatherless children, husbandless wives, and country-less visitors. "For all his questionings," says Kidner, Koheleth "has no quarrel with conservative wisdom, as long as it is not the means of either hiding the darker facts of life which it is his mission to expose,"[1154] or honoring the covenant responsibilities that Job takes very seriously. We have already noted that Koheleth believes that a wise person ignores the injustices perpetrated by kings and their bureaucratic subordinates, nor does he give "the slightest indication," says Alter, "as in Psalms or elsewhere, that God will rescue them from their suffering, and without any exhortation, as in the Prophets, that we must act to rescue them." Indeed, Alter says later, referring to 10:6, Koheleth "accepts established hierarchies and thinks something is out of joint if the foolish (or the lowly) are on top and the wise (or the rich) on the bottom. A similar sentiment is expressed in the next verse [v. 7] in his dismay over slaves mounted on horseback."[1155]

All of this may or may not represent the thinking of a large number of Jews. What is apparent, however, is that a new portrait of God seems to have emerged in both Job and Ecclesiastes. He is portrayed as increasingly disengaged, increasingly unwilling or unable to intervene in the affairs of humanity, and increasingly indifferent to the moral standards of the Covenant. Alter says, speaking of God in Ecclesiastes, he "is clearly not the same deity as the one imagined in the dominant currents of biblical theology." Unlike the God of earlier biblical texts, this one does not assume either that "humanity [is] expected] to fulfill a grand destiny" or that "dereliction" from this achievement "triggers His wrath and brings down His punishment." Indeed, Koheleth's God "seems to be a stand-in for the cosmic powers-that-be, for *fate or the overarching dynamic of reality that is beyond human control.*" Indeed, "his sense of life is often readily translatable into post-theistic terms: the world is a theater of continuing frustration and illusion; that is the way that *God/fate/the intrinsic constitution of reality* has determined that it should be."[1156]

Later, commenting on Proverb 3:15, Alter refers to God's will as "a matter of *luck*," which is yet another way of describing not so much what Alter calls God's "absolute determination of events, beyond all human control" but the *absence* of his determination, since, whatever its source, the ultimate cause of or influence on everything beyond human effort appears to be random, unpredictable, and unfathomable—that is, expressive of no discernible moral intention.[1157] G. E. Wright comments: "The author of Ecclesiastes is not a disbeliever in God"—a statement Wright evidently makes in the face of at least some evidence to the contrary. "He believes," Wright continues, "but he does not have much use for theology, certainly not for the type which the leaders of the wisdom movement espoused. It is useless to try to talk about God's moral government of the world, or to penetrate into the secrets of life in relation to God."[1158] Thus, just as many scholars' argue that Koheleth's God is sovereign—i.e., totally engaged in human life and totally in control of everything that happens—some scholars regard Koheleth as a Deist, suggesting that God is disengaged from the world and that circularity and unpredictability are simply built into the cosmos, which he created but no longer manages or controls.[1159]

Von Rad does not regard Koheleth as either "a nihilistic agnostic" or a "cynical hedonis[t]." The author of Ecclesiastes believes that life is "completely encompassed by God" and therefore has no doubt "about Jahweh's existence and power." Indeed, he clearly expresses his intention to "please" God by attaining "prosperity" (7:14) and by engaging in the few activities that can yield at least a small amount of pleasure or satisfaction: eating and drinking, toil (2: 25, 3:13), and marriage (9:9). Nevertheless, Von Rad considers Ecclesiastes to be a tragedy because it expresses "the despair of a wise man" for whom life has "lost all meaning" and to whom any sign of God's moral involvement in human life—"his readiness to interfere drastically in history or in the life of the individual"—has disappeared. Specifically, "Ecclesiastes no longer sees a fate-bringing connection between act and consequence in any shape or form. The idea of the fate-bringing sphere, which in earliest Israel was built into the foundations of the understanding of life, can in Ecclesiastes hardly now be discerned even in outline. He had long ago lost the belief that events in the external world correspond to human behaviour, and are turned towards man in benefit or in punishment."[1160]

Chapter Six

Apocalypse

THE SKEPTICISM REPRESENTED BY the books of Job and Ecclesiastes did not end with the latter work, in the third century BC. This fact is demonstrated by the appearance at the end of the first century AD of a work we shall examine more closely later in this chapter, 2 Esdras. To be sure, one could hardly argue that these three writings together represent a major shift in the theology and morality of ancient Judaism. However, their very existence and the persistence over more than half a millennium of their revolutionary view of God's administration of justice suggests that to some degree, at some level, and in one way or another the Jews of the post-exilic period were not unanimous in their faith in the moral program defined in the major works of the Jewish Bible.

Indeed, as von Rad reminds us and as we have seen in earlier chapters, the skepticism that is expressed in the book of Job and Ecclesiastes—at least in the form of doubt and uncertainty about God's moral management of the universe—appeared much earlier, not only in many of the psalms but also among the older prophets: "This skepticism is not so very late; even the pre-exilic prophets encountered an astonishingly detached attitude on their contemporaries' part."[1161] Isaiah, for example, feels compelled to say to the evil-doers who mockingly invite God to demonstrate his righteousness, which has evidently not been manifest: "Let him make haste, let him speed his work that we may see it; let the purpose of the Holy One of Israel draw near, and let it come, that we may know it" (5:19). The question "How long?" appears in a dozen psalms and in the prophecies of Isaiah, Jeremiah, Habakkuk, and Zechariah. To be sure, in these works God always answers the question "Wilt thou keep silent?" (Isa 64:12) positively. However, the mere fact that the query was raised so frequently shows that doubts arose surprisingly early and persisted for centuries.

Like Job and Koheleth, Ezra, the main character in 2 Esdras, is "troubled" and "agitated" by what he perceives to be the unreasonableness of God's system of rewards and punishments (3:1-3). As Robert H. Pfeiffer notes, this "gloomy" work "reflects the tragic aftermath of the destruction of Jerusalem in A.D. 70 and was written about twenty years later."[1162] Also, like Job and Koheleth, Ezra not only experiences an emotional shock initiated by what he believes to be the irrationality of God's actions and inactions, he never receives an adequate answer to his questions. What he is given by his spiritual advisor, the angel Uriel, is the claim that mere human beings are unable to understand God's ways and that everything will be made clear sometime in the future.

This late first-century work—which has been described as "the most widely circulated Jewish apocalypse in antiquity and continuing into the Middle Ages"[1163]—represents two trends in ancient Judaism that evidently continued into what we now call the Common Era. First, 2 Esdras deals with what Pfeiffer calls the "problem of theodicy." Second, it offers a solution to that problem, insofar as it describes a future world in which God's rule is clearly operative. The work examines whether it is possible "to prove the justice and love of God in a world where there seems to be no relationship between man's behavior and man's lot." That is, it attempts to answer the question "Does God no longer care for his beloved chosen people"? Pfeiffer says: "The first part is an impassioned discussion of the problem of God's love and justice in this world filled with sin and woe; the second is a solution of the problem, on the basis of faith and hope, in the world to come. But the solution fails to satisfy the disheartened and pessimistic author."[1164]

According to the editors of *The New Annotated Oxford Bible*, 2 Esdras does, in fact, reflect a contemporary religious dilemma: "Chapters 3–10 contain the author's wrestling with some of the central questions confronting the Jewish people in the first century A.D. These include in particular the question of how to affirm God's justice, wisdom, power, and goodness, given the many evils and trials that beset the human community" (300 AP). Ezra underscores the weight of these "evils and trials" when, after hearing a series of unsatisfying responses to his concerns, he gives a long list of "the sorrows of Jerusalem," including the destruction of the Temple, the abuse of children, the murder of priests, the defilement of wives and virgins, and the enslavement of men (10:21–23). Ezra receives a series of visions, none of which are either self-explanatory or consoling, even after their interpretation by Uriel. Uriel promises, as he has all along, to "light in [Ezra's] heart the lamp of understanding" (14:25), but the Job-like Ezra continues to believe that "the world lies in darkness, and its inhabitants are without light" (14:20).

Besides being an expression of disillusionment, in the tradition of the prophets and many psalms, as well as the book of Job and Ecclesiastes, 2 Esdras is a kind of writing technically known as apocalyptic, which, as a literary genre, is almost always intended to be uplifting and sustaining. As Bernhard W. Anderson explains, *apocalypse* derives from the Greek word *apokalyptein*, meaning "to uncover, reveal." And the way apocalyptic literature achieves its positive goal, Anderson continues, is by presenting "God's revelation concerning the end-time, the coming of the Kingdom of God."[1165] Quoting Adela Yarbro Collins, Raymond E. Brown says, "Apocalypses are 'intended to interpret present, earthly circumstances in light of the supernatural world and of the future, and to influence both the understanding and behavior of the audience by means of divine authority.'"[1166]

According to Lester L. Grabbe, "The whole phenomenon of apocalypticism takes up not only personal survival and judgement of the individual but the end of the world, cosmic cataclysm, final judgement of all living, new heavens and a new earth." Typically, Jewish apocalyptic works thus focus on *eschatology*, which "refers to the concept of 'last things': the end of life, the end of the world, final judgement, life after death."[1167] The end-time is not to be feared, however, nor is the final judgment to be averted. The theory is that the present situation—politically, economically, and socially—is so unbearable that its termination is not only desirable but necessary. Thus, Anderson says, such works are often "written in times of persecution."[1168] According to Brown, "[W]hen the circumstances are desperate because of captivity or oppression, the prophet may offer hope in terms of return to the homeland or the destruction of the oppressor and a restoration of the monarchy." Indeed, Brown continues, "although apocalypses may be written "[w]hen the circumstances . . . are prosperous and comfortable," they are most often addressed to those living in times of suffering and persecution—so desperate that they are seen as the embodiment of supreme evil."[1169]

Although different groups of Jews saw the end-time (the *eschaton*) in different ways, the expectations of many Jews were influenced by the prophetic idea of *Yom Yahweh*, the Day of the Lord, at which time all men and women would be judged by God and rewarded or punished appropriately.[1170] Anderson explains: "Israel understood that her life was involved in a great drama which, under the direction of God, was moving toward final consummation. In the pre-exilic period, this hope found expression in the popular doctrine about the coming 'Day of Yahweh'—the day when Yahweh would vindicate Israel by humbling her foes and raising her to a position of prestige and blessing in the world."[1171]

The idea remained popular, as is evidenced by its adoption by many apocalyptic writers, particularly in the intertestamental period and modeled on the apocalyptic vision of Daniel. In such writings, D. S. Russell says, "the writer depicts the overthrow of the wicked and the triumph of the righteous, either in this world or in the world to come, in an earthly kingdom or in a heavenly, in their physical bodies or in renewed 'spiritual' bodies; the Messianic Kingdom, temporal or eternal, is ushered in and heralds or inaugurates the Age to Come when God's purposes will triumph and he will live with his people for evermore."[1172] As N. T. Wright comments, "There was no shortage of people in the first century claiming prophetic inspiration, speaking urgent words from YHWH to his suffering and anxious people, sometimes promising them immediate and spectacular supernatural deliverance."[1173] Indeed, as James Parkes says, a "flood of Messiahs . . . sprang up in the first half of the first century A.D."[1174] And Louis H. Feldman reminds us that several of the most important leaders of the Revolt of AD 66 were self-described messiahs, among whom "Josephus mentions at least ten . . . who probably were regarded as messiahs by their adherents."[1175]

Apocalypse

According to Russell, the "purpose" of this kind of belief "was a very practical one, to inspire the nation with a new courage and with fresh hope in the ultimate victory of good over evil."[1176] Indeed, Anderson calls apocalyptic literature, which was based on this vision of the future, "the most popular" kind of writing in the intertestamental period because "[i]n troubled times, when faith was put to the severest tests, men hoped for the coming kingdom."[1177] In this context, it is useful to remember that most of the works of the prophets, one of the major influences on apocalyptic literature, as Ben Witherington III notes, were also "written during very dark days of Israel." He explains that "from the exilic period on, an increasing stress was placed on eschatological and apocalyptic elements in prophecy, not surprisingly as it appeared less and less likely that the Davidic earthly 'good old days' would ever return prior to the Day of Yahweh."[1178]

Quoting A. Y. Collins, John Dominic Crossan identifies the specific problems that typically generate such grandiose visions: "[A]pocalyptic faith often correlates with marginality, cognitive dissonance, and relative deprivation." "Marginality" refers to a group or individual who is "anomalous, peripheral, or alien." "Cognitive dissonance" occurs when there is a "disparity between expectations and reality." And "deprivation" refers to the plight of the victims of "catastrophes and disasters." However, as the history of the exilic and post-exilic period demonstrates, the Jews found themselves in this position almost continuously. Thus, Crossan sees the apocalyptic movement in ancient Israel as a response to the culmination of these problems and a last-ditch effort to maintain a shred of hope in the face of utter hopelessness: "Apocalypticism is the counterattack of those who perceive themselves to be marginalized," disappointed, and oppressed "at a level too profound for any less radical solution." The problem is, Crossan continues, that "[t]he disease is fatal; only transcendental intervention can effect a cure."[1179]

Before the arrival of what some of the apocalyptists call the Day of the Lord—that is, the Day of Judgment, which will precede the final glorious transformation—Grabbe adds, God presents a series of terrifying signs, which include "the reversal of normality: the world is turned upside down; the expected order of society has become its opposite; nothing is the way it should be. Chaos has re-entered the cosmos." This turmoil ends, however, "because God will soon intervene to bring an end to all human suffering."[1180] All Jews (or all of humanity) will be judged by God: The good, who are presently suffering, will be rewarded; and the evil, who are presently thriving, will be punished. That is, the Kingdom of God will not only bring present conditions to an end but also create a new cosmos in which pain, exploitation, oppression, and sin will be eliminated. E. P. Sanders comments: "The hope for restoration presupposes God's loyalty to the covenant with Israel and, in most of the expressions of it which are still available, the expectation that Israel would show its loyalty to God by obeying his law," all of which results in "restoration."[1181]

The earliest apocalypses were composed by the great Jewish prophets for a variety of reasons, all of which underscore what Russell calls the "deep ethical concern" of all the apocalyptists, early and late.[1182] First, Isaiah and others felt the need to explain that the Jews were suffering because of their own sinfulness: "[T]hey have transgressed the laws, violated the statutes, broken the everlasting covenant. Therefore a curse devours the earth, and its inhabitants suffer for their guilt" (Isa 24:5–6). Second, the prophets wanted to reassure their people that God's moral code remained intact and that the desolation on earth would end when God gave both Jews and their enemies exactly what they deserved. Isaiah says, "[T]he Lord will punish the host of heaven ... and the kings of the earth" (24:21). Ezekiel warns that God will destroy the entire "people of Israel," whom he refers to as "a nation of rebels" (2:3). Jeremiah says that God will punish Egyptians, Philistines, Moabites, and many other foreign nations (46–51). According to Zephaniah, he will kill all of "the wicked," which means "all the inhabitants of the earth" (1:3, 18).

Third, however, the prophets, as well as the apocalyptists after them, also intended to use both the present suffering of their people and the future destruction of some or all of humanity as admonitions and not irreversible punishments. Thus, they promised that, if the residents of "the house of Israel" repented, God would return them to their homeland and provide them with the prosperity and happiness that their righteousness deserved. Zechariah says, "For there shall be a sowing of peace; the vine shall yield its fruit, and the ground shall give its increase, and the heavens shall give their dew; and I will give the remnant of this people to possess all these things" (8:12). In other words, after he acts justly by punishing evil people, God will act mercifully by rewarding good people—according to some prophets, far beyond their just deserts. As Isaiah claims: "He will swallow up death forever, and the Lord will wipe away tears from all faces ... It will be said on that day, ... let us be glad and rejoice in his salvation" (25:9).[1183]

In the intertestamental period, Anderson says, apocalyptic works, all strongly influenced by the prophets,[1184] described the final judgment in "extravagant language" and also redefined the last "struggle" as an event of "superhistorical or cosmic proportions."[1185] Russell says that "the emphasis" in later apocalyptic works "came increasingly to be laid not so much on God's judgment within time and on the plane of history, as on his judgment in a setting beyond time and above history; the idea of judgment was no longer confined to the living but was extended to include the dead"; and "the Final Judgment" was applied individually rather than collectively.[1186] Shaye Cohen says that some of the later apocalyptists introduced the idea that the present suffering of the Jews was not a result of their sins but part of a grand scheme in which a profound change in the lives of the Jews would occur because God planned it that way, not because of their repentance.[1187]

Apocalypse

Intertestamental

Like these Jewish apocalyptic writings, many of the other Jewish works of the intertestamental period, from 200 BC to AD 100, demonstrate that the moral ideas of the Covenant Code, which had been restated by the prophets and the psalmists, continued to be expressed despite the continued domination of Palestine by foreign powers (Ptolemies, Seleucids, and Romans) and the ever-increasing influence of Hellenization on the countries of the Near East as well as the entire Mediterranean basin. Indeed, one might say that the same balance of continuity and diversity that characterizes many of the post-prophetic writings—such as many of the psalms, the book of Job, Ecclesiastes, and the book of Daniel—is maintained in such works as *The Wisdom of Solomon*, the stories of the Maccabees, Tobit, *Ben Sirach*, and 2 Esdras. Furthermore, like the stories of Daniel and Esther, canonized tales of Jewish life in the Diaspora and under the rule of foreign kings, the writings of the intertestamental period often deal not only with Jews living outside of Palestine (e.g., in Alexandria, Nineveh, and Babylonia), but also with the struggle on the part of these Jews to preserve their religious heritage in the face of extreme opposition.

In fact, it could be argued that the book of Daniel, written in the 160s BC, provided a template for Judith, Tobit, and 4 Maccabees, especially in relation to the stories of Daniel and his friends, which, according to the editors of *The Oxford Annotated Bible*, "illustrate how faithful Jews, loyally practicing their religion, were enabled by divine aid to triumph over their enemies" (1067). In several of the stories, Daniel, who is the recipient of God's "favor and compassion" (1:9), is able to interpret two of King Nebuchadnezzar's dreams, translates a prophetic written message for King Belshazzar, and shares three visions of the future with Belshazzar and two other kings. In addition, Daniel survives unharmed a close encounter with hungry lions, and his three friends (Shadrach, Meshach, and Abednego) survive a fire that kills everyone else exposed to it. In almost every instance, the kings who witness these examples of prophecy and immunity to death honor the Jews who perform these miracles and respect the Jewish God who made them possible (3:29; 4:37; 5:29; 6:25–27).

After Daniel's first dream analysis, Nebuchadnezzar "fell upon his face, and did homage to Daniel, and commanded that an offering and incense be offered up" to the Jewish deity, whom the king calls the "God of gods" and the "Lord of kings" (2:46–47). The kings pass decrees that permit the Jews living in their kingdoms to worship freely, and Daniel is promoted to higher and higher positions in the Babylonian, Median, and Persian governments that he is said to have served. Thus, says William M. Ramsay, "when freed of fanciful misrepresentations, Daniel has brought a message of steadfastness and hope to millions who pray, 'Thy kingdom come'; for this is a book about the kingdom of God."[1188] Moshe Weinfeld comments: "The concept which dominates later eschatology about a new ideal kingdom built on the ruins of a former ruthless empire was actually conceived for the first time"—that is, by Isaiah—"in the eighth century B.C. It was motivated by feelings of suppression and subjugation to the Assyrian empire. Similar eschatological hopes"—such as those expressed in the book of Daniel—"were given expression whenever a new empire rose and oppressed nations. The Israelite prophets who acted at the rise of the world's first empire"—from Isaiah onward—"were thus the first in world history to raise their voice against imperial tyranny and to depict instead a glorious picture of mankind living in harmony under divine guidance."[1189]

The author's optimism about the prospects for the acceptance of Judaism in the gentile world may have been prompted by the success of the Maccabean revolt against Antiochus Epiphanes, during whose brutal reign the author wrote his account of Daniel's rising influence in kingdoms run by Israel's conquerors. It might also have been the author's own visions, which are quite possibly the basis for Daniel's visions, that inspired his expectation of a bright future for the Jews: "And the kingdom and the dominion and the greatness of the kingdoms under the whole heaven shall be given to the people of the saints of the Most High; their kingdom shall be an everlasting kingdom, and all dominions shall serve and obey them" (7:27). Clemens Thoma says that the author of Daniel is simply announcing that he and other Jews "unswervingly keep to the covenantal obligations toward the God of Israel"; they remain "prepared to risk [their] lives"; and they consider themselves to be "radically responsible for the people of God."[1190]

In this and other ways, the book of Daniel bears a strong resemblance to the visions of the other prophets of ancient Israel, among whose works this book is included. Daniel tells Nebuchadnezzar that he must "break off [his] sins by practicing righteousness, and [his] iniquities by showing mercy to the oppressed" or face God's severe punishment (3:24–27). Like Shadrach and his two friends, he refuses to worship the gods of the pagans, despite the threat of death (3:18, 6:10). And, in a long prayer to God, Daniel acknowledges that God keeps his Covenant and offers "steadfast love" to those who "keep his commandments"; admits that he and his fellow Jews "have sinned and done wrong and acted wickedly and rebelled, turning aside from [God's] commandments"; and implores God to show "mercy" and offer "forgiveness" (9:3–10). Notably, like some of the psalmists, Daniel says that he is not asking God to reward him for good works (9:18).

Like Daniel, Tobit, the main character in an apocryphal work that was written between the two testaments, lives in exile. Having been taken into captivity by the forces of King Shalmaneser, Tobit resides in Nineveh, Assyria. He is a pious Jew, who proudly describes himself as "walk[ing] in the ways of truth and righteousness" and "performing acts of charity" (1:3).[1191] Unlike all of his relatives, who "sacrificed to the calf that King Jeroboam had erected," Tobit "alone went often to Jerusalem for the festivals," giving sheep and cattle to the priests, grain and fruits to the Levites, and money to the widows and orphans (1:5–8). He refuses to eat "the food of the Gentiles" (1:18), feeds and clothes the needy, and buries dead Jews, many of whom have been killed by the new king, Sennacherib (1:17–19). At one point, he is reported on for secretly removing the dead bodies, sought for punishment by the king, and forced to flee Nineveh, as a result of which he loses his property and hides until the king is assassinated (1:19–21).

After Tobit returns to Nineveh, he buries yet another murdered Jew, an act which elicits contempt from his neighbors: "He has already been hunted down to be put to death for doing this, and he ran away," they say; "yet here he is again burying the dead" (2:8). Tobit's kinsman, Raguel, tells Tobias, Tobit's son, that Tobit is "a good and noble father" and "an upright and beneficent man" (7:7), as does Tobit's friend Gabael (9:6). In his prayer, offered to God after he goes blind and feels "much grief and anguish of heart" because he is unable to support his family, Tobit calls God righteous, just, merciful, and truthful. Like Daniel, he apologizes for his sins and those of his ancestors (3:2–3). He concludes with a wish to die: "[R]elease me to go to the eternal home, and do not, Lord, turn your face away from me" (3:6).

Some of Tobit's advice to his son, Tobias, is drawn from the Wisdom tradition. For example, Tobit tells Tobias to avoid pride, idleness, drunkenness, and fornication; to get good counsel; and to marry within his tribe. The reward, of course, is prosperity: "You have great wealth if you fear God and flee from every sin and do what is good in the sight of the Lord your God" (4:21; see also 4:5–6). However, despite the influence of "certain Gentile writings," says D. S. Russell, the story's "entire moral and spiritual outlook is shaped by the Old Testament Scriptures."[1192] That is, Tobit's main focus is clearly on the values of the prophets and the psalmists. He tells Tobias to pay workers their wages in a timely manner and to follow the Golden Rule; (4:12–18). Indeed, his main religious activity, besides burying the dead, is almsgiving, which he recommends to his son: "[G]ive alms from your possessions, and do not let your eye begrudge the gift when you make it." Give much or little, Tobit adds, depending on your wealth (4:7–8; see also 4:16). As the editors of The *New Oxford Annotated Bible* comment, "Deuteronomy's doctrine of retribution (i.e., the idea that, ultimately, the righteous are rewarded and the wicked punished) provides the basic theology for Tobit" (1 AP). Tobit tells his son, "Do not turn your face from anyone who is poor, and the face of God will not be turned away from you" (4:7).

The middle chapters of the story deal with Tobias' visit to Tobit's kinsman, Raguel, in Media (Persia). Tobias is guided by the angel Raphael, disguised as Azariah, a relative of Tobit's, who arrives in response to Tobit's heartfelt prayer and is sent by God to both test and help Tobit and Tobias (12:14). Raphael tells Tobias to extract the gall, heart, and liver of a fish, which he later uses to cure Tobit's blindness and to drive away a demon who has cursed Raguel's daughter, Sarah. Raphael suggests that the two travelers stop at the home of Raguel, where Tobias meets Sarah and marries her. The final chapters of the story return to its central ethical message. Raphael repeats Tobit's moral sentiments: "Do good[,] and evil will not overtake you." Furthermore, righteousness is better than wealth because "almsgiving saves from death and purges away every sin. Those who give alms will enjoy a full life, but those commit sin and do wrong are their own worst enemies" (12:7, 9–10). Finally, Raphael adds, echoing the prophets, "Prayer with fasting is good, but better than both is almsgiving with righteousness" 12:8).

In both a long prayer to God and a deathbed speech to Tobias and his seven sons, Tobit prophesies that Israel's suffering will end, and the nation will be visited by all of the world's people, bearing gifts (13:11–17). The Jewish exiles will return to Israel and rebuild Jerusalem, and the nations of the world will worship Yahweh (14:5–6). Particularly citing the prophet Nahum's grim prediction about the destruction of Assyria, Tobit says, "For I know and believe that what God has said will be fulfilled and will come true; *not a single word of the prophecies will fail*" (14:4; my emphasis). Ramsay comments: "Tobit's real point is the example of strict Jewish piety in a Gentile culture. Tobit observes the ceremonial law, he gives generously to the poor, and he prays devoutly."[1193]

Like Job, Ezra, the main character in 2 Esdras, complains about the suffering of others as well as his own. Ezra's concern in the early pages of this work is God's willingness to punish the Jews, who are supposedly God's own people, and his apparent unwillingness to punish the enemies of the Jews. Indeed, most of this story consists of a dialogue between Ezra and God's representative, the angel Uriel, whom Ezra asks for an explanation of God's ways and remains to the very end unsatisfied with Uriel's responses to his questions and accusations. Ezra begins: "I was troubled as I lay on my bed, and my thoughts welled up in my heart, because I saw the desolation of Zion and the wealth of those who lived in Babylon. My spirit was greatly agitated, and I began to speak anxious words to the Most High" (3:1–3). Clearly, as R. Travers Herford says of 2 Esdras, "[t]o read that book is to understand the close connection between Apocalyptic and despair. It is indeed a mournful book, and the writer plainly indicates his perplexity that devotion to Torah should have ended in such colossal disaster."[1194]

Ezra is particularly struck by the fact that Israel has been destroyed, and Babylon is flourishing. He says to God, "You handed over your city to your enemies" (3:27). He then asks why Babylonia is ruling over Israel since the Babylonians are no better than the Jews. When he visited Babylonia, Ezra says, he "saw ungodly deeds without number," a fact that deeply affected him: "My heart failed me, because I have seen how you endure those who sin, and have spared those who act wickedly, and have destroyed your people, and protected your enemies, and have not shown anyone how your way may be comprehended" (3:28–31). Here it is the apparent contradiction that disturbs Ezra. Why are some sinners punished and others not merely forgiven, but rewarded? Ezra also believes that God's treatment of the Jews is a betrayal of his promises. God chose Abraham for himself, made "an everlasting covenant with him," and "promised him that [he] would never forsake his descendants" (3:13–15). Thus, Ezra asks God "why Israel has been given over to the Gentiles in disgrace; why the people whom you loved has been given over to godless tribes." This is particularly galling to him because the old agreements and understandings of the past seem to have died away: "[T]he law of our ancestors has been brought to destruction and the written covenants no longer exist" (4:23).[1195]

Ezra's most important concern, however, is not that God has been unjust to the Jews by favoring their enemies or by breaking his promises to them. Rather, Ezra believes that God's entire reward and punishment system is inherently unworkable. This is because, morally speaking—as far as Ezra can determine—no one can be distinguished from anyone else. And this is because everyone is a sinner. Ezra introduces this argument by providing a brief overview of moral history from Adam onward. Adam's descendants, like the father of all humanity, "transgressed" by doing "ungodly things." And the descendants of Noah were "more ungodly than their ancestors" (3:9-13). God chose David—"[Y]ou raised up for yourself a servant"—"but the inhabitants of the city [that David built] transgressed, in everything doing just as Adam and all his descendants had done" (3: 25-26). Ezra speculates that the delay in the Judgment Day may be a result of the pervasiveness of evil: "O sovereign Lord, all of us also are full of ungodliness" (4:38-39). Later, Ezra says simply, "[W]ho among the living is there that has not sinned, or who is there among mortals that has not transgressed your covenant" (7:47). "For all who have been born are entangled in iniquities, and are full of sins and burdened with transgressions" (7:68).[1196]

Ezra's charge that all human beings are ungodly is based on the assumption that the heart itself is evil. That is, humanity is biologically sinful. Ezra says that "the first Adam, *burdened with an evil heart*, transgressed and was overcome, as were also all who descended from him. Thus the disease became permanent; *the law was in the hearts of the people along with the evil root*; but what was good [that is, the law] departed, and the evil [that is, the root] remained" (3:21-22; my emphasis). The descendants of David followed the descendants of Adam because "they also had the evil heart" (2:26). Thus, we are evil because "an evil heart has grown up in us, which has alienated us from God, and has brought us into corruption and the ways of death, and has shown us the paths of perdition and removed us far from life—and that not merely for a few but for almost all who have been created" (7:48).

Uriel had earlier promised to explain the role of the evil heart: "I will you show you the way you desire to see, and will teach you why the heart is evil" (4:4). But what he actually says to Ezra is that a mere human being cannot "comprehend the way of the Most High."[1197] In response to this evasion, Ezra falls on his face and says to Uriel, "It would have been better for us not to be here than to come here and live in ungodliness, and to suffer and not understand why" (4:11-12). Later, Uriel says, simply, that the end cannot come until the evil have been punished. On the one hand, "the age is hurrying swiftly to its end." On the other hand, however, "It will not be able to bring the things that have been promised to the righteous in their appointed times, because this age is full of sadness and infirmities" (4:26-27). What is important to notice in 7:48 is Ezra's inclusion of himself as a sinner along with everyone else: He too has had an evil grow up in him; he too has been alienated from God; and he too has been far removed from life. And this is what underscores his lament: He is as guilty as all the others: "But now the mind has grown with us, and therefore we are tormented, because we perish and we know it... What does it profit us that we shall be preserved alive but cruelly tormented" (7:64, 67; see also 7:75).

The high point of his grief comes later in chapter 7, when Ezra offers a long and painful complaint, aimed at everyone, including himself, that although much has been offered, nothing will be gained: "O Adam, what have you done? For though it was you who sinned, the fall was not yours alone, but ours also who are your descendants. For what good is it to us, if an immortal time has been promised us, but we have done deeds that bring death? And what good is it that an everlasting hope has been promised to us, but we have miserably failed. Or that safe and healthful habitations have been reserved for us, but we have lived wickedly? (7:118–20; see also 121–26). Ezra ends his eloquent dirge in chapter 7 with what appears to be not only an admission of sinfulness, for himself as well as all of humanity, but also a clear confession of human responsibility: "What good is it... that the faces of those who practiced self-control shall shine more than the stars. For while we lived and committed iniquity we did not consider what we should suffer after death" (7:126).

Elsewhere, however, although he never states it directly, Ezra strongly implies that God himself is responsible for the miserable fate of mankind. Indeed, the real drama in 2 Esdras lies in Ezra's hesitant but growing willingness to broach this subject. After all, this is really the most striking injustice of all because it cannot, under any circumstances, be explained or understood. A *quid pro quo* system in which the good are blessed and the evil are cursed may be too demanding (so that only a few can achieve godliness) or administered unfairly (so that the undeserving go unpunished for their sins), but Ezra seems to suggest that the system is illogically and unexplainably rigged because *God himself is in control of everything*. And, therefore, he is as much the creator of the "evil heart"—the human proclivity to sin—as he is the creator of humanity.

Ezra begins his discussion of this problem in his initial summary of God's treatment of the patriarchs and their descendants. On the one hand, he says to God, after the Jews were liberated from the Egyptians: "You bent down the heavens and shook the earth, and moved the world, and caused the depths to tremble, and troubled the times. Your glory passed through the four gates of fire and earthquake and wind and ice, to give the law to the descendants of Jacob, and your commandment to the posterity of Israel" (3:18–19). In short, God made a grand, earth-shattering effort to provide his people with a clarification of his expectations of them. Ezra's objection is that God did nothing to enable them to follow his rules.

In Ezra's words, "Yet you did not take away their evil heart from them, so that your law might produce fruit in them" (3:20). Despite his enormous and unquestionable power, Ezra says to God, "every nation walked after its own will; they did ungodly things in your sight and rejected your commands, *and you did not hinder them*" (3:8;

my emphasis). Indeed, God "appointed death" for Adam and "brought the flood upon the inhabitants of the world" (3:7,9). But the fault was neither Adam's nor humanity's: "For the first Adam, *burdened with an evil heart, transgressed and was overcome*, as were also all those who were descended from him" (3:21; my emphasis). "This is my first and last comment," Ezra says later: "it would have been better if the earth had not produced Adam, or else, when it had produced him, had restrained him from sinning" (7:116).

It is not hard to see that Ezra is treading lightly on this subject, reluctant as anyone would be to blame God directly for the sins of mankind.[1198] For, as both Ezra and God certainly knew, it was not "the earth" as an independent and supernatural force that created Adam. Here "earth" (in 7:116) is a euphemism for God, introduced earlier in the chapter: "O earth," Ezra says—when he might otherwise have said, "O God"—"what have you brought forth, if the mind is made out of the dust like the other created things? For it would have been better if the dust itself had not been born, so that the mind might not have been made from it. But now the mind grows with us, and therefore we are tormented, because we perish and we know it" (7:62–64). Thus, in response to Uriel's explanation that "the earth . . . provides a large amount of clay from which earthenware is made, but only a little dust from which gold comes," Ezra says, woefully: "Then drink your fill of understanding, O my soul, and drink wisdom, O my heart. *For not of your own will did you come into the world, and against your will you depart, for you have been given only a short time to live*" (8:2, 4–5; my emphasis).

Finally, Ezra drops the pretense that human beings are made by the "earth." That is, Uriel's persistent unwillingness to deal directly with Ezra's questions, says Pfeiffer, "raises the problem of theodicy . . . to a tragic pitch."[1199] That is, Ezra argues, echoing Isaiah, that God is entirely in charge. In Isaiah's words, God says, "I made the earth, and created humankind upon it; it was my hands that stretched out the heavens, and I commanded all their host" (45:12).[1200] As Ezra puts it: "O Lord above us, . . . you alone exist, and *we are the work of your hands*, as you have declared. And because *you gave life to the body* that is now fashioned in the womb, and furnish it with members, what you have created is preserved amid fire and water, and for nine months the womb endures your creature that has been created in it. But that which keeps and that which is kept *shall both be kept by your keeping . . . [A]nd afterward you will still guide it in your mercy*. You have nurtured it in your righteousness, and instructed it in your law, and reproved it in your wisdom" (8:6–12). In short, with God in total control of his creation—from conception to adulthood, as virtual father, mother, and teacher—he alone is responsible for the results. However, if God fails in his task, what then? Thus, Ezra asks, "If then you will suddenly and quickly destroy what with so great labor was fashioned by your command, to what purpose was it made?" (8:14).

Ezra makes the same point when he compares the relation between God and his creation to the relation between a farmer and his crop. Ezra says that God's law did not "produce fruit" in his people because "the law was in the hearts of the people

The Evolution of Love

along with the evil root" (3:20, 22). Ironically, however, Uriel is the first to extend the metaphor completely. "[T]he evil about which you ask me has been sown," he says—meaning the godless acts of humanity—"but the harvest of it has not yet come," meaning that punishment has not yet been given. "If therefore that which has been sown is not reaped," he continues, "and if the place where the evil has been sown does not pass away, the field where the good has been sown will not come," meaning that this world must pass away before the new world arrives (4:28-29). Then Uriel says that the seed planted by the farmer is analogous to the evil that God implanted in humankind: "For a gram of evil seed was sown in Adam's heart from the beginning, and how much ungodliness it has produced until now—and will produce until the time of threshing comes! Consider now for yourself how much fruit of ungodliness a grain of evil seed has produced. When the heads of grain without number are sown, how great a threshing floor they will fill!" (4:30–432).

It is not clear that Uriel understands that the parallel between God and farmer underscores Ezra's argument: That is, if the crop fails, one cannot blame the crop. Perhaps this is why Ezra returns to the metaphor when he makes a clear statement about God's responsibility for the actions of humanity: "O Lord above us, grant to your servant that we may pray before you, and give us a seed for our heart and cultivation of our understanding so that fruit may be produced, by which every mortal who bears the likeness of a human being may be able to live" (8:6). Later, Uriel reintroduces the metaphor by saying that, although "the farmer sows many seeds in the ground," only some will survive. "[S]o also those who have been sown in the world will not be saved" (8:41). Ezra responds: "If the farmer's seed does not come up" because it has received either too little or too much rain, "it perishes."

Then Ezra broaches what he evidently considers to be the real implications of the analogy. He says to God, "But people, who have been formed by your hands and are called your own image because they are made like you, and for whose sake you have formed all things—have you also made them like the farmer's seed?" Ezra backs away from this charge—"Surely not, O Lord"—perhaps because he wants to avoid offending God, but he returns to it later in 9:31–37. In this passage, according to the editors of the *The New Oxford Annotated Bible*: "The seer draws the contrast between the vessel that contains a precious object [i.e., the land or the human heart] and the object it contains [i.e., a seed or God's law]. The latter may be used up or destroyed, but normally the former survives. [That is, the crop dies, but the land endures.] With us it is just the opposite; God keeps alive the divine law, but Israel, its receptacle, is destroyed" (325 AP). Ezra's point is that this makes no sense.

The conflict between Ezra and God remains unresolved at the end although Ezra has been granted seven revelations. The book is, after all, technically at least, an apocalypse, which describes the end-time and thereafter. The problem is that these visions fail to answer most of Ezra's questions, which leaves him frustrated by the fact that Uriel has been either unable or unwilling to satisfy Ezra's desperate desire to understand the human condition. Indeed, one of the surprising characteristics of the exchange between the two main personages in the story is what it reveals about both of them. On the one hand, it is hard not to admire Ezra because of his humility, his compassion, his courage, and his intelligence. On the other hand, it is difficult to take Uriel seriously.

Time after time, Uriel either gives Ezra a conventional answer or avoids Ezra's question altogether. Indeed, Uriel's theology appears to be based solely on a kind of cold-hearted justice rather than warm-hearted mercy. To be sure, Uriel generously and repeatedly assures Ezra that God recognizes his virtues (6:32; 8:47–50; 10:57; 13:53–55) and will not include him among the condemned because he has "a treasure of works stored up with the Most High" (7:77; 8:51–54; 10:50; 13:56). Indeed, the rewards for righteousness are boundless because the life to come will be a paradise in which "plenty is provided, a city is built, rest is appointed, goodness is established, wisdom perfected," and evil and illness and death are "banished" (8:52–53).

At the same time, however, the sinners will not only be excluded from paradise, but punished in a hell of "thirst and torment" (8:59). Indeed, "such spirits shall not enter into habitations, but shall immediately wander about in torments, always grieving and sad, in seven ways." In the last of the seven ways, "they shall utterly waste away in confusion and be consumed with shame, and shall wither with fear at seeing the glory of the Most High in whose presence they sinned while they were alive, and in whose presence they are to be judged in the last times" (7:80, 87). Uriel's justification for this severe retribution is that the ungodly are not merely ignorant or neglectful of (or even indifferent to) God's law, but *willfully hostile to God himself*: "Therefore do not ask any more questions about the great number of those who perish. For when they had opportunity to choose, they despised the Most High and were contemptuous of his law, and abandoned his ways. Moreover, they have even trampled on his righteous ones, and said in their hearts there is no God." In short, they have "defiled God's name . . . and have been ungrateful to him" (8:55–60; see also 7:19–24).

Thus, in the closing pages of 2 Esdras, Ezra is left with three unanswered questions: (1) Why are so few of God's people going to be saved? (2) Why, if God made them and shaped them, are so many going to be punished? And (3) why is God unwilling to show them any mercy? Ezra simply cannot get past the idea that God is "now called" merciful to the unborn, gracious to the repentant, patient to unredeemed sinners, and both bountiful and compassionate to all (7:132–37). urthermore, God "is called the giver, because if he did not give out of his goodness so that those who have committed iniquities might be relieved of them, not one ten-thousandth of humankind could have life, and [called] the judge, because if he did not pardon those who were created by his word and blot out the multitude of their sins, there would probably be left only very few of the innumerable multitude" (7:138–40).

Uriel's view is quite different. On Judgment Day, he says: "The Most High shall be revealed on the seat of judgment, and *compassion shall pass away, and patience shall be withdrawn. Only judgment shall remain*, truth shall stand, and faithfulness shall grow strong. Recompense shall follow, and the reward shall be manifested; righteous deeds shall awake, and unrighteous shall not sleep. The pit of torment shall appear, and opposite it shall be the place of rest; and the furnace of hell shall be disclosed, and opposite it the paradise of delight" (7:33–36; my emphasis).

Of course, because Ezra and Uriel never reach agreement on these issues, the reader is hard-pressed to decide what the author of 2 Esdras wants his audience to believe. On the one hand, God asks Ezra to spend his next forty days writing seventy books, based on God's inspiration, which Ezra says had a powerful effect on his assigned task: "[M]y heart poured forth understanding, and wisdom increased in my breast" (14:40). On the other hand, if 2 Esdras, the book, is the product of that inspiration, it seems evident that it had little effect on Ezra's theological position. Perhaps the book was written to dramatize what we referred to earlier in this chapter as the older view of God versus the newer, a contrast that is exhibited in the book of Psalms, wherein the contradictions that plague Ezra also remain unresolved.

That is, Uriel's God is, as we have seen, not only fierce, unforgiving, and punitive, but also unmotivated to explain his system of retribution; whereas Ezra's God is (again) patient, loving, and merciful. Uriel's God is, as he often says, beyond human comprehension, whereas Ezra's God (or at least his *ideal* God) is logically and rationally understandable, even by mere human beings. In fact, the two opposing concepts of God seem to reflect the opposing personalities of the two main characters, which I referred to earlier. Uriel is emotionally disengaged and therefore uninterested in Ezra's questions. Ezra is compassionate and eager to learn as much as he can about God and his intentions. As the editors of *The New Oxford Annotated Bible* explain: "The fact that the angel cannot seem even to understand Ezra's concern is not for himself but for the myriads of sinners doomed to perish is a good indication that the author of 2 Esd 3–10 thinks as Ezra does" (322–23 AP).[1201]

Sirach (or *Ben-Sira*), named for the author, otherwise known as Ecclesiasticus, written in the first century BC, draws from the ideals of the major Jewish texts of the mid-first millennium. As Pfeiffer explains: "Sirach's ideas on personal piety are inspired by the Prophets and by the Psalms (stressing morals and prayer), but also by the Pentateuch (stressing righteousness, or obedience to God's law). He was convinced that God rewarded piety on this earth (for he still believed that at death men's ghosts gathered at Sheol: 14:16; 17:27–28; 41:4); but in view of the misery of many pious people he concluded that the highest rewards were of the spirit, such as communion with God (2:7–11; 34:13–17), and, after death, continued remembrance (44:8; 13:15)."[1202]

However, as Pfeiffer notes, "[t]he most original and interesting parts of *Ecclesiasticus* deal with practical matters: observations on human life and counsels for attaining happiness and success."[1203] That is, this work also derives from the Wisdom tradition. As we saw in the book of Proverbs, works in this tradition focus on a kind of middle-class moral code in which the goal is social and economic success, and sin is any act that threatens to interfere with the attainment of that goal. The standard is not right and wrong as they are related to the sacred and the profane, but as they are related to prudence and recklessness. Patience is an important virtue (Sir 1:23, 2:4), friendship is a useful acquisition (6:5–17, 22:19–26), wicked women are to be avoided (25:13—26:27), and pride is a terrible vice (10:9; 23:4; 32:12).

What is particularly interesting about these moral values is that they are nowhere authorized by God; rather, they are justified by experience: "An educated person knows many things, and one with much experience knows what he is talking about" (34:9). And violations of these rules are not punished by God but penalized by public condemnation, as in the case of loudness or any violation of conventional social rules. In some instances, the violation is simply self-destructive, as in the case of drunkenness or any form of over-indulgence. To be a sinner in the conventional biblical sense is to offend God. To be a sinner in the Wisdom tradition is to offend parents, employers, and generally people of power and influence.

Sirach begins with the idea that the female figure of Wisdom was, as Proverbs claims, created by God before anything else (1:4). God gives wisdom to those who either love him (1:10) or fear him (1:12). Indeed, to fear God is both the "beginning" and the fulfillment of wisdom (1:14, 16). Wisdom "came forth from the mouth of the Most High" (24:3), was told to "take her dwelling" among the Jews (24:8), and offers her fruit to all who hunger and thirst for knowledge (24:19–23). Wisdom is powerful enough to uplift the lowly (11:1). However, in its fullest sense, wisdom is intended only for those who have "the opportunity of leisure"—that is, "little business" (38:24). Farmers, artisans, smiths, and potters are indispensable for the survival of the city—"they maintain the fabric of the world" (38:34)—but they are not sought out for their wisdom, "nor do they attain eminence" or serve as judges or participate in governance (38:24–33).

Unlike those who "rely on their hands" (38:31), the "scribe" is the esteemed seeker of wisdom, past and present, who preserves, interprets, and explains texts for everyone, including rulers. He prays to God, who fills him "with the spirit of understanding," and he is ultimately honored and remembered (39:1–15). Less grandiose, but useful and helpful, are the rewards of Wisdom for her other followers (4:1–19; 6:18–37). Indeed, "she fills their whole house with desirable goods, and their warehouses with her produce." Furthermore, she makes "peace and perfect health to flourish" (1:17–18; see also 4:12–15; 15:1–6)

Many of the sins identified in *Sirach* are, as I said, the kinds of actions forbidden in the book of Proverbs, but in few other Jewish texts. Besides fearing God and obeying him wholeheartedly, the author of this work also advises against "hypocrisy" and self-exaltation (1:28–30), laziness and foolishness (22:1–18), and excessive drinking (31:25–30). In chapter 4, the author is particularly concerned about more or less trivial social issues: "Watch for the opportune time . . . [and] do not be ashamed to be yourself . . . Do not show partiality . . . or deference . . . Do not refrain from speaking at the proper moment" (vv. 20–23). The author adds in chapter 5: "Stand firm for what you know, and let your speech be consistent. Be quick to hear, but deliberate in answering. If you know what to say, answer your neighbor; but if not, put your hand over your mouth" (vv. 10–12). And he adds in chapter 11: "Do not praise individuals for their good looks, or loathe anyone because of appearance alone . . . Do not boast about wearing fine clothes, and do not exalt yourself when you are honored . . . Do not answer before you listen, and do not interrupt when another is speaking" (vv. 2, 4, 8; see also 32:1–12).

The editors of *The New Oxford Annotated Bible* note that the author stresses the need for moderation and self-control (6:2–4; 18:30—19:4; 22:27—23:27) in every aspect of life: behavior with women (9:1–9), the use of wealth (14:3–19; 31:1–11), raising children (30:1–13; 42:9–14), and dining with important people (31:12–24). Since many of these actions are neither encouraged nor forbidden by God, he is not involved in their punishment. Indeed, as I noted earlier, many of these actions bring about their own negative results: "Honor and dishonor come from speaking . . . Shame comes to the thief . . . And do not become an enemy instead of a friend; for a bad tongue incurs shame and reproach . . Evil passion destroys those who have it, and makes them a laughingstock of their enemies" (5:13–14; 6:1,4).

Although the author encourages his readers not to act solely for the purpose of earning God's approval (11:23), he also recognizes that God plays a role in the distribution of rewards and punishments. Thus, on the one hand, he says, "Do not offer [God] a bribe, for he will not accept it" (35:14). Authenticity is distinguished from its opposite as *intention* is distinguished from rote obedience. On the other hand, however, "it is easy for the Lord on the day of death to reward individuals according to their conduct" (11:26). In this way, "everyone receives in accordance with one's deeds" (16:14). God rewards the obedient individual by making him "like a son of the Most High" (4:10). Furthermore, good deeds can be accumulated and used to compensate for bad deeds: "Lay up your treasure according to the commandments of the Most High, and it will profit you more than gold. Store up almsgiving in your treasury, and it will rescue you from every disaster" (29:11–12). Equally, the disobedient person is condemned to suffering: "To all creatures, human and animal, but to sinners seven times more, come death and bloodshed and strife and sword, calamities and famine and ruin and plague. All these were created for the wicked" (40:8).

Although this advice seems to be based on a rather strict application of the *quid pro quo* principle, God's enforcement of this moral system is not absolute because God is "compassionate and merciful," especially insofar as "he forgives sin and saves in time of distress" (2:11). Thus, God "makes room for every act of mercy" (16:14), and anyone who fears him can "wait for his mercy" (2:7). Specifically, "to those who repent he grants a return" (17:24; 29). God's mercy is particularly revealed in his ongoing effort to chastise his people in order to guide them to wisdom and righteousness: "Great as his mercy, so also is his chastisement" (16:12). This is because he has "compassion . . . for every living thing" and therefore wants all of his people to succeed. Thus, "He rebukes and trains and teaches them, and turns them back, as a shepherd his flock. He has compassion on those who accept his discipline and who are eager for his precepts" (18:13–14; see also 2:2–5). Indeed, Wisdom herself is his intermediary in this regard: "[A]t first she will walk with them on tortuous paths"; "she will bring fear and dread upon them, and will torment them by her discipline"; and "she will test them with her ordinances" (4:17).[1204]

Furthermore, despite the obviously very strong influence of the Wisdom tradition on this work, the author of *Sirach* remains committed to the values expressed in the Covenant Code (18:11–13, 20–21; 21:1, 5). For these reasons, God is worthy of both trust and fear (2:1–18). As I said, however, God does not reward actions that are self-rewarding or punish actions that are self-punishing. He approves of moderation in all things, but he is also concerned about acts of justice and mercy, the performance of which is truly worthy of reinforcement and, ultimately, salvation. He is equally concerned about the failure to perform such acts, which is worthy of discouragement and, ultimately, damnation. Under the first headings fall acts of kindheartedness, which are represented by these commands in chapter 4: "My child, do not cheat the poor of their living, and do not keep needy eyes waiting. Do not grieve the hungry, or anger one in need. Do not add to the troubles of the desperate, or delay giving to the needy. Do not reject a suppliant in distress, or turn your face away from the poor. Do not avert your eye from the needy, and give no one reason to curse you . . . Give a hearing to the poor, and return their greeting politely. Rescue the oppressed from the oppressor . . . Be a father to orphans, and be like a husband to their mother" (vv. 1–10).

These statutes are, as we know from the prophets and the psalms, especially important because they require God's people to imitate him, as the author of *Sirach* shows in chapter 35, wherein God appears as the ideal dispenser of justice and mercy: God "will not show partiality to the poor; but he will listen to the prayer of one who is wronged. He will not ignore the supplication of the orphan, or the widow when she pours out her complaint . . . Indeed, the Lord will not delay, and like a warrior will not be patient until he crushes the loins of the unmerciful and repays vengeance on the nations; and he destroys the multitude of insolent, and breaks the scepters of the unrighteous; until he repays mortals according to their deeds; and the works of all according to their thoughts" (vv. 16–17, 22–24). Like some of the prophets, the author of *Sirach* says that sacrifices offered by bad people are unacceptable to God (34:18–19). Furthermore, moral acts—performed, for example, by "one who heeds the commandments," by "one who returns a kindness," or by "one who gives alms"—can substitute for ritual acts, and implicitly have the same, if not more, spiritual efficacy (35:1–9).

The intertestamental works we have so far examined appear to be quite consistent with the mainstream Judaism of the Jewish Bible. In particular, they retain the two principles of Jewish theology and religious practice that dominate the writings of the prophets and the psalms. First, they portray God as the dispenser of justice and mercy. Second, they emphasize the primary importance of these values in human relationships. On the one hand, ancient Jewish writings never abandoned these ideals. On the other hand, however, two historical events exposed worldwide Jewry to Greek culture, which clearly influenced Jewish thinking during the intertestamental period. First, Hellenization was imposed on the entire Near East after the Alexandrian conquest in the fourth century. Second, Jews came into more direct contact with Hellenism when they moved out of Palestine, both voluntarily and involuntarily, into lands, both east and west of their homeland, that were firmly embedded in Greek religion, philosophy, and social life. Indeed, this influence is clear in at least one canonical work, Ecclesiastes, which seems to have been deeply affected by Greek ideas.

Another example is a non-canonical work, *The Wisdom of Solomon*, which, according to the editors of *The New Oxford Annotated Bible*, "was composed in Greek, by an unknown Hellenistic Jew, probably in Alexandria" (57 AP). Since the book was written in the city that also produced Philo, the great Jewish philosopher of the first century AD, it should come as no surprise to anyone that *The Wisdom of Solomon* "is clearly a product of Hellenistic culture."[1205] As Ramsay says, being "addressed to scoffers," the book deals with a problem that was more likely to arise in a Hellenized community. And the solution was more likely to be found there, the promise of "a future life": "But the souls of the righteous are in the hands of God, and no torment will ever touch them" (3:1). Thus, Ramsay concludes, "The Wisdom of Solomon seems here to reflect the Greek concept of the immortal soul."[1206]

However, the editors of *The New Oxford Annotated Bible* also claim that *The Wisdom of Solomon* "is intensely Jewish" (57 AP). As in *Sirach*, for example, God is characterized as just: "[H]e will put on righteousness as a breastplate and wear impartial justice as a helmet" (5:18). And he is merciful: "[T]he faithful will abide with him in love, because grace and mercy are upon his holy ones" (3:9). God "pronounce[s] judgment in uprightness of soul" (9:3), and "severe judgment falls on those in high places" (6:5). As for "those who utter unrighteous things, . . . justice, when it punishes will not pass them by" (1:8). At the same time, God is the "Lord of Mercy" (9:1), and he has "not neglected to help [his people] at all times and in all places" (19:22). In its combination of Jewish religion and Greek philosophy, Russell says that *The Wisdom of Solomon* has "two objectives—first to win back apostate Jews and to establish pious Jews in their faith, and secondly to demonstrate to the heathen in a language and thought they could understand the truth of Judaism and the folly of paganism."[1207]

Otherwise, *The Wisdom of Solomon* is, as its title suggests, a work in the Wisdom tradition, with Wisdom portrayed as a celestial female figure, as she is in both *Sirach* and Proverb 8, who is nevertheless available to sincere admirers and pursuers of her gifts: "Wisdom is radiant and unfading, and she is easily discerned by those who love her, and is found by those who seek her" (6:12). In chapters 7 and 8, Solomon himself is quoted on the value of wisdom, based on passages from 2 Kings (3:6–9) and 2 Chronicles (1:8–10).

Apocalypse

In this work, God's justice, as we might expect, is exercised on the basis of his distribution of rewards and punishments. On one hand, "the souls of the righteous are in the hand of God, and no torment will ever touch them" (3:1). Indeed, they will attain immortality as well as God's eternal protection: "[T]he righteous live forever, and their reward is with the Lord; the Most High takes care of them. Therefore they will receive a glorious crown and a beautiful diadem from the hand of the Lord, because with his right hand he will cover them" (5:15–16). On the other hand, the unrighteous will suffer because they have not "discerned the prize for blameless souls" (2:22). Therefore, "the ungodly will be punished as their reasoning deserves, those who disregarded the righteous and rebelled against the Lord; for those who despise wisdom and instruction are miserable. Their hope is vain, their labors are unprofitable; and their works are useless. Their wives are foolish, and their children evil; their offspring are accursed" (3:10–13).

This condemnation seems to emanate from God's uncompromising wrath, but it is tempered, as it is in *Sirach*, by God's fairness and mercy. The author of *The Wisdom of Solomon* says to God, "You are righteous and you rule things righteously, deeming it alien to your power to condemn anyone who does not deserve to be punished" (12:15). He continues: "Although you are sovereign in strength, you judge with mildness, and with great forbearance you govern us" (12:18). Furthermore, God's people are reminded, God has treated Israel's enemies much more harshly than he has treated the Jews. That is, "while chastening us you scourge our enemies ten thousand times more" (12:22).[1208]

Two points alluded to in the preceding two paragraphs help to explain God's mercy in *The Wisdom of Solomon*. First, partly owing to its Greek influence, this work emphasizes more strongly than either the book of Proverbs or *Sirach* the role of reason in moral decision-making. The author explains that the "ungodly" made a "covenant" with death because "they reasoned unsoundly, saying to themselves, 'Short and sorrowful is our life, and there is no remedy when a life comes to an end, . . . and we were born by mere chance'" (1:16; 2:1–2). As the author continues, it becomes clear that, as he understands it, evil is not merely a consequence of selfishness, greed, anger, lust, or impulsiveness. Rather it is the result of a conscious choice that derives from a theory about the human condition: Death is inevitable, life is meaningless, and therefore morality has no foundation.

In short, people do bad things because they have lost faith in the moral order of the universe, and they have discovered no justification for moral behavior. They say: "Come, therefore, let us enjoy the good things that exist, and make use of the creation to the full as in youth . . . Let none of us fail to share in our revelry; everywhere let us leave signs of enjoyment, because this is our portion, and this is our lot" (2:6, 9). However, they not only feel inclined to pursue pleasure; they also feel entitled to oppress the poor, the widow, the old, and the weak: "But let our might be our law of right" (2:10–11). They are even moved to "lie in wait for the righteous man" because he "opposes [their] actions" and "reproaches [them] for sins" (2:12–13). In this effort, they are cynically testing God, "mak[ing] a trial of his forbearance," by condemning the righteous "to a shameful death" (2:17–20). "Thus they reasoned," the author concludes, "but they were led astray" (2:21).

Second, the author of *The Wisdom of Solomon* offers a cure for this problem by stating, again more emphatically than either the book of Proverbs or *Sirach*, that God tries to influence our understanding of the human condition by teaching us, especially through chastisement. Since "perverse thoughts separate people from God" (1:3), it takes "a holy and disciplined spirit," offered by Wisdom, to reunite people and God (1:5). As for "the righteous" who have died, they were "disciplined a little," and "they are at peace ... because God tested them and found them worthy of himself; like gold in the furnace he tried them" (5:3–6). The author says to God, "[W]hen they were tried, though they were being disciplined in mercy, they learned how the ungodly were tormented when judged in wrath." They were "tested ... as a parent does in warning," and, therefore, "through their own punishments the righteous had received benefit" (11:9–10, 13).

In other Wisdom works, chastisement sometimes appears to be a kind of negative reinforcement, in its worst form nothing more than an attempt to associate sin with pain. In this work, however, the discipline imposed by God appears to be educational. The author says to God, "For your immortal spirit is in all things," as followers of Plato believed. "Therefore you correct little by little those who trespass, and you remind them and warn them of the things through which they sin, so that they may be freed from wickedness and put their trust in you, O Lord" (12:1–2). At the end of the process, God does not expect salivation, but repentance: "But judging them little by little you gave them an opportunity to repent" (12:10). "But you are merciful to all," the author says, "and you overlook people's sins, so that they can repent" (11:23). Thus, God is a teacher, as well as a trainer: "Through such works you have taught your people that the righteous must be kind, and you have filled your children with good hope, because you give repentance for sins" (12:19). The result, ideally of course, is a community characterized by "a holy and *disciplined* spirit" (1:5; my emphasis).

Clearly, on the one hand, this work criticizes some of the kinds of sins that are more likely to be criticized in the proverbs than in the psalms. In the first chapter, the author condemns "blasphemers": God "knows what is said, therefore those who utter unrighteous things will not escape notice." Then, the author condemns all kinds of verbal sins: "Beware then of useless grumbling, and keep your tongue from slander; because no secret word is without result, and a lying mouth destroys the soul" (vv. 7–11). He also condemns sexual misbehavior: "defiling of souls, sexual perversion, disorder in marriages, adultery, and debauchery" (14:26). Furthermore, the saving virtues are not only justice and mercy, but those typical concerns of Wisdom literature, "self-control and prudence," which are not just morally desirable but "profitable" (8:7).

On the other hand, however, the author emphasizes the idea that God's motivation is love: "But you, our God, are kind and true, patient, and ruling all things in mercy. For even if we sin we are yours, knowing your power; but we will not sin, because we know that you acknowledge us as yours" (15:1–2). In fact, in *The Wisdom of Solomon*, God loves not just *his* people, but "all people" (12:13; my emphasis) and even "all things that exist" (11:24). Out of love, God also condemns the violations of covenant law: oppressing the poor, the widows, and the old (2:10), as well as murder, theft, deceit, and corruption (14:25); holds kings to a higher standard of righteousness (6:1–9); and reminds his people, as many of the prophets and psalmists do, of the saga of the early Israelites, who during the exodus, "were being disciplined in mercy" (10:15—11:20).

Written in the first century AD, 4 Maccabees is awash in Greek ideas and thereby represents, except for the small body of Jewish-Gnostic works, the furthest reach into Hellenism that ancient Israel attempted. The work is based on two stories that first appeared back-to-back (in written form) in 2 Maccabees: the tale of Eleazar and the tale of the seven brothers, which are here conflated. Fourth Maccabees tells the story of Eleazar, a Greek-educated Jew, and the rest of his family, including his wife and their seven sons, who are threatened with torture and execution. Even in the more-or-less oral/folk sources of the narrative, the characters stand up against King Antiochus Epiphanes, who historically tried to wipe out Judaism by forbidding circumcision, Torah-reading, food restrictions, and ritual practices.

All of the Jews in the story unflinchingly reject the king's request that they eat non-kosher food, and they accept their fate without any hesitation, reluctance, or attempt to negotiate. They are offered the opportunity to pretend to eat the forbidden food, but all of them refuse. As a result, they die horrible deaths, as evidently many Jews did at the time, with the collective understanding and justification that they are setting an example for other Jews. The Greek features of the story are the ideas (1) that the reward of virtue is immortality, (2) that reason is the best defense against sin, and (3) that the death of one person can expiate for the sinfulness of others (although, of course, this idea appears in Deuteronomy as well).

What is impressive in 4 Maccabees is its complex study of both reason and emotion, which occupies the first half the work. We are told at the beginning that reason ("rational judgment") is the highest virtue—"because it is the guide of the virtues" (1:30)—and that its primary function is to control emotions, "not for the purpose of destroying them, but so that one may not give way to them" (1:1–2, 6). It is as if the emotions are garden plants (they are "planted" in human beings [2:21]), and reason is the gardener, who "weeds and prunes and ties up and waters and thoroughly irrigates, and so tames the jungle of habits and emotion" (1:29). Thus far, the ideas are entirely Greek.

The connection to traditional Judaism is the insistence throughout that the highest philosophy teaches religious truths. The "master cultivator" is both obedient and rational, both righteous and virtuous: "Now reason is the mind that with sound logic prefers the life of wisdom," which is "the knowledge of divine and human matters and the causes of these," which, in turn, is "education in the law, by which we learn divine matters reverently and human affairs to our advantage" (1:15–17).[1209] For Eleazar, the author's most pious of Jews and most exemplary of rationalists, "piety" *is* "devout reason," and true philosophy is wholehearted religious fervor: "What person who lives as a philosopher by the whole rule of philosophy, and trusts in God, and knows that it is blessed to endure any suffering for the sake of virtue, would not be able to overcome the emotions through godliness?" (7:16, 18, 21).

The author's analysis of emotion is based generally on Stoic philosophy. The editors of The *New Oxford Annotated Bible* state that the author's definition of wisdom—"rational judgment, justice, courage, and self-control" (1:6, 18; 2:23)—are "the four cardinal virtues of the Platonic and Stoic traditions" (342 AP).[1210] The same may be said of his discussion of emotions, which are grouped according to the particular virtue each emotion threatens or inhibits. In short, the function of reason is to dominate the psychological forces that threaten to evade or overwhelm reason. Thus, gluttony and lust "hinder self-control" (1:3). And self-control dominates "the desires," "appetites," and "impulses" (1:31, 35). Malice "hinder[s] one from justice" (1:4). And justice inhibits "lust for power, vainglory, boasting, arrogance, and malice" (2:15). Anger, fear, and pain "stand in the way of courage" (1:4). And, logically (although the author does not say it), courage can triumph over these emotions, which is, of course, the subject of the story of Eleazar and his family (see, especially 6:10–11, 15:23–30). Emotions can also be divided into two categories: pleasure and pain. Still other emotions, desire and delight, precede and follow pleasure, respectively; and fear and sorrow precede and follow pain. Both pleasure and pain have "malevolent" tendencies—or "manifestations"—that are connected with either the soul ("boastfulness, covetousness, thirst for honor, rivalry, and malice") or the body ("indiscriminate eating, gluttony, and solitary gourmandizing") (1:20–27).

Two ideas distinguish 4 Maccabees from the vast majority of Jewish works of the intertestamental period: the immortality of the soul and expiation. As Willis Barnstone explains: "The reward for [Eleazar and his family's] resolve is the immortality of the soul in Heaven. Unlike 2 Maccabees, from which the story of the martyrs is taken, the souls, rather than the body, are saved after bodily death. In fact, even the souls of the wicked persist—in eternal fire and torment, however, rather than in the eternal happiness promised for the virtuous."[1211] The author says that, like the patriarchs, "as many as attend to religion with a whole heart . . . do not die to God, but live to God," a point he later repeats when he says that Eleazar's wife encouraged her sons "to die for the sake of God" and thereby to "live to God" (16:24–25). More precisely, the author says that Eleazar and his family "were deemed worthy to share in a divine inheritance," by which he means that they "have received pure and immortal souls from God," while Antiochus "is being chastised after his death" (18:3, 23, 5).

Apocalypse

The expiation that occurs in 4 Maccabees is a result of Eleazar and his family's martyrdom, which, from the point of view of the author, aided Eleazar's fellow Jews by removing Antiochus Epiphanes from the domination of Israel. We are told in the first chapter that because of the family suicide, "they conquered the tyrant, and thus their native land was purified through them" (1:11). Indeed, Eleazar himself says before his death: "You know, O God, that though I might have saved myself, I am dying in burning torments for the sake of the law. Make my blood their purification, and take my life in exchange for theirs" (6:27). The author concludes, since "the tyrant was punished, and the homeland purified," the martyrs became "a ransom for the sin of our nation." Furthermore, "through the blood of those devout ones and their death as an atoning sacrifice, divine Providence preserved Israel" (17:21–22).

The story consists of several speeches by members of Eleazar's family addressed either to each other or to the king. One after another, Eleazar, his wife, and his seven sons, having been arrested for conspicuously flouting the new laws, explain why they refuse to submit to the king's demands, even in the face of death. Eleazar says that he is moved by piety—that is, his "reverence" for both "the only living God" and the law established by him. He adds, "[N]or will I transgress the sacred oaths of my ancestors concerning the keeping of the law, not even if you gouge out my eyes and burn my entrails" (5:24–25, 29). He further explains that he is also motivated by the desire to avoid setting a bad example by engaging in an act of "impiety" (6:18–19). The narrator observes that "as many as attend to religion with a whole heart, these alone are able to control the passions of the flesh, since they believe that they, like our patriarchs Abraham, Isaac and Jacob, do not die to God, but live to God" (7:18–19).

The wife of Eleazar and the mother of the boys has the last word. Speaking of her husband to her sons, she says: "While he was still with you, he taught you the law and the prophets." He read to them about all of the martyrs—the Jews who, in most instances, died for their faith. "He reminded you of the scripture of Isaiah, which says, 'Even though you go through the fire, the flame shall not consume you.' He sang to you songs of the psalmist David, who said, 'Many are the afflictions of the righteous.' He recounted to you Solomon's proverb: 'There is a tree of life for those who do his will.' He confirmed the query of Ezekiel, 'Shall these dry bones live?' For he did not forget to teach you the song that Moses taught, which says [in God's words], "I kill and I make alive: this is your life and the length of your days" (18:10–19).

The Essenes at Qumran

If we step back from these particular works and ask where Judaism stood in the first century AD, especially on the subjects of theology and morality, we find ourselves, as I suggested in chapter 2, in the midst of an incredibly diverse collection of interpretations, which were the inevitable consequence of external influences and the ongoing assessment of inherited beliefs in relation to historical events. Out of the Wisdom tradition from Mesopotamia and Egypt, the Zoroastrianism of Persia, and the various isms that came from the cultural traditions of Greece and Rome, Judaism emerged as a variety of sects—including not only the Pharisees, the Sadducees, and the Jewish Christians, but also the Zealots, the Essenes, and the Samaritans, all of whom reacted in different ways to (1) the Judaism of the first millennium BC; (2) the religious ideas and practices from other countries that Jews encountered through the centuries, especially in the current intertestamental period; and (3) the political and cultural domination of the Romans that would endure for many more centuries. According to Louis H. Feldman, citing the Jerusalem Talmud, "there were 24 sects of heretics at the time of the destruction of the Temple,"[1212] all of them self-identifying as Jewish and many calling themselves the only "true" representatives of Judaism.

These sects were also affected by the fact that, with the exception of less than a century of self-rule under the Hasmonians, the Jews of ancient Israel had been dominated by foreign powers since at least the sixth century BC. Lester L. Grabbe says, "[F]or centuries after the conquest of Jerusalem by Nebuchadnezzar's army in 587/586 BCE, the Jewish nation seems to have submitted to foreign domination . . . In reality Judah had been under Assyrian rule for much of the last century even of the monarchy."[1213] The question was, according to James L. Kugel, where was God? "If God had long ago determined Israel to be His own people, how could anyone account for the fact that this people was now being kicked around by the imperial army of a foreign power, indeed, by a nation that worshiped false gods, while our God stood on the sidelines?"[1214] As time passed, it is clear that discontent increased, while Jewish nationalism remained strong. As Lee I. E. Levine says, "For 300 years, since the successful Maccabean revolt in the second century B.C.E., nationalist aspirations had been a significant factor in Jewish history, often finding expression in revolts or attacks on Jewish neighbors."[1215]

The problem was that, except for the success of the Maccabees, all of these efforts failed. For many Jews, therefore, frustration turned into despair, desperation fomented irrationality, and what the Christian historian Eusebius refers to as "madness" prompted not only more rebellion (*Ecclesiastical History*, Bk. 4, Ch. 6), but also messianism (the hope that God would send a leader capable of defeating the enemies of the Jews) and apocalypticism (the hope that God would also establish peace and prosperity as permanent features of a transformed world). Commenting on the last revolt (in AD 132), Levine says that it may have been initiated not because of any particular event but because its leaders were "so intoxicated by religious dreams of national restoration that any kind of rational reading of the international political and military map was beyond [their] capacity."[1216] Of course, the same point may be made about all the other failed revolts after the Maccabean rebellion. Nahum N. Glatzer argues that "the apocalyptic visions" that proliferated in the intertestamental period "were composed against the background of national calamity and disappointment at the failure of Messianic hopes to materialize."[1217]

Apocalypse

These sects arose partly because of this widespread frustration and partly because, with the passing of Herod and his unrelenting suppression of dissent, the government of Palestine lost some of its ability to maintain control over its subjects. Except for Caiaphas and two others, the high priests who headed the Judean government on behalf of the Romans ruled for an average of less than three years during the sixty-year period before the Revolt of AD 66. And the Jewish citizens of Palestine deeply resented the priestly establishment and the Roman government as much as they had resented Herod. According to Anthony J. Saldarini, "The emergence of a diversity of groups in Jewish society fits the pattern of agrarian empires when they become large and complex." Furthermore, such sects "thrive when society's central authority is weak, disorganized or unaccepted by much of the population, exactly the sociological conditions pertaining in first century Palestine."[1218]

Thus, there were "many organizations of zealous Jews which provided a program for defending and reforming Judaism in the face of Roman and Hellenistic pressure," including not only the Pharisees and the Sadducees, but also rebel leaders like Judas, who founded the Zealots; Jesus, the leader of the Nazarenes; and Simon bar Giora, who also led a messianic movement—all of whom "easily gathered modest groups of enthusiastic followers who strove to convince other Jews to join them in seeking influence and power over social policy." Saldarini emphasizes that these attempts were characterized by "polemics and invective which bear witness to the social, political and religious strife among Jewish groups" and "testify" to the conflict and competition that reached their peak in the first century AD.[1219]

Two prominent Jewish sects of the first century AD reveal how strongly messianism and apocalypticism influenced the thinking of the Jews of that time: the Essenes in the desert at Qumran and the Christians in Jerusalem.[1220] According to most scholars, Qumran was settled by Essenes as early as the second century BC in protest against the ruling Hasmoneans, who not only took the priesthood away from the heirs of Aaron, but also remained open to the Hellenizing influences that the Maccabees had fought against in opposition to the Seleucid King Antiochus IV. Geza Vermes describes the Essenes—who regarded all other Jews as "wicked and corrupt"—as a separatist religious group whose "communities were distributed throughout the towns and villages of the land as well as . . . Qumran." They saw themselves as "the one true Israel, the Church of God's elect." As both apocalyptists and messianists, the Essenes "believed that they would, during their lifetime, participate in the great battles of Light against Darkness, and that they would see and share with the triumphant Messiah the fruits of his victory."[1221] Vermes adds that the Dead Sea Scrolls, which have enabled scholars to thoroughly examine the ideas and practices of the ancient Essenes, "reveal one facet of the spiritual ferment"—nurtured, we might add, by the desperation and frustration we referred to earlier—"which culminated in a thorough examination and reinterpretation of the fundamentals of the Jewish faith."[1222]

The Essenes saw themselves as "the remnant which held fast to the commandments of God" (*The Damascus Rule* [DR] III; see also Hymn 10) and therefore established strict rules governing membership (who could be admitted), initiation (how new members were to be instructed), and behavior (what they could and could not do). Vermes explains the rigid hierarchy at Qumran, which was justified by the fact that different members had passed through different stages of spiritual purification and moral education: "It would appear that status within the Community was invested with particular importance. We meet constantly in the Scrolls the phrase, 'each man according to his rank' as well as the injunction that every member of lesser rank should show deference and obedience towards his senior."[1223]

According to Theodor H. Gaster, the Essenes' view of themselves as the holy remnant was based on the belief that they were "specially 'enlightened,'"[1224] thanks partly to the divine knowledge acquired by their deceased leader, the Teacher of Righteousness,[1225] and partly to their rigorous entrance requirements (including annual exams during the initiate's first two years), vigilant observation and frequent correction of members (based on strict rules whose violations could result in either suspension or expulsion and whose obedience could lead to advancement in the community hierarchy), and constant study of the Jewish law (which was thought to be conducted in the company of angels, required the presence of a priest, and was directed by the Guardian of the community).

The process of initiation and training was demanding because initiates were assumed to have come from the profane world of false values and sinful behavior, which required that they undergo conversion from sinfulness to sinlessness—that is, abandon "the dominion of Satan" and "no longer follow a sinful heart" (*The Community Rule* [CR] I). The need for rigorous training was particularly strong because the Essenes had what Vermes calls a "profound awareness of human frailty, unworthiness, and nothingness."[1226] In recognition of humanity's innate evil, *The Community Rule* states that "through the spirit of true counsel concerning the ways of man . . . all his sins shall be expiated that he may contemplate the light of life. He shall be cleansed from all his sins by the spirit of holiness uniting him to His truth, and his iniquity shall be expiated by the spirit of uprightness and humility" (III). Thus, upon "entering the Covenant," all members of the holy community heard the Levites "recite the iniquities of the children of Israel, all their guilty rebellions and sins during the dominion of Satan." Afterward, everyone confessed his past sins and shouted, "We have strayed!" (CR I).

This thoroughgoing expiation was, unsurprisingly, accompanied not only by an initiatory bath but by regular ritual baths thereafter: "And when his flesh is sprinkled with purifying water and sanctified by cleansing water, it shall be made clean by the humble submission of his soul to all the precepts of God" (CR III). Furthermore, according to *The War Rule* (WR), "No man entering the house of worship shall come unclean and in need of washing" (XI). Hannah K. Harrington says that members of the community had to bathe before every meal because they were expected to follow the Old Testament's requirements for priests: "Apparently, the sect has combined the priestly purification instructions with the command to all Israel to wash after contact with impurity," which was nearly everywhere.[1227]

Although this emphasis on purity, hierarchy, and ritual suggests that the Essenes were mere legalists, content to display their piety by obeying what most people consider to be minor laws and performing expiatory rather than genuinely moral actions, they were also committed to the spirit of the laws, particularly the moral requirements of the Covenant. Millar Burrows says: "The covenanters were not wholly preoccupied with matters of ritual purity and the observance of sacred times. Their devotion to the law included moral and social righteousness as well."[1228] The goal of the community was to instill in every member's heart the "fear of the laws of God," which included "a spirit of humility, patience, abundant charity, unending goodness, understanding, and intelligence," as well as trust in God's deeds and lovingkindness, zeal for justice, "steadfastness of heart," and understanding.

At the same time, members were taught to avoid greed, unrighteousness, haughtiness, deceit, cruelty, folly, insolence, lewdness, and blasphemy (CR IV; see also VIII). As Gaster argues, their intention was not to impress God or the other members of the sect or outsiders, but to "see the *simplice lume* of Dante, the 'infused brightness' of Saint Theresa"—in short, to "achieve an intimacy, a communion with the eternal, unchanging things."[1229] Robert A. Kugler says, "The community that resided [at Qumran] revered the sacrificial cult and priests as the means for establishing communion with God."[1230]

Concluding his essay on this subject, James C. VanderKam says: "There can no longer be any question about the importance of the law of Moses and elaborations of it in the [Dead Sea] scrolls."[1231] *The Damascus Rule*, for example, warns against exploiting the poor, widows, and the fatherless (VI). As Vermes explains, "The obligations imposed by the [Essenes'] New Covenant were materially the same as those implicit in the Old; namely, perfect obedience to the teachings of Moses and the Prophets." Indeed, Vermes argues: "As far as the Law itself was concerned, the revelations granted to these sons of Zadok, the sect's priestly hierarchy, added fresh severity and rigour to a legal code already strict in itself... In addition to its increased severity, the Community's interpretation of the Law was distinguished by its claim to infallibility,"[1232] which encouraged the Essenes to aggressively "rebuke" violations within the community and impose severe punishments for them (CR V-VI, VIII-IX). As Harrington explains: "For Qumran, human holiness does not come simply by obedience to the law. That is a given, but holiness must increase by emulating God to the best of one's ability. Greater holiness is achieved by discovering and fulfilling God's perfect will."[1233]

Seeing themselves as members of the army of the sons of Light against the army of the sons of Darkness—that is, pitted in a fight to the death against their profoundly and irremediably evil enemies—the Essenes at Qumran went so far as to separate themselves entirely from the rest of the Jews in ancient Israel and, like the Christians, created a sharing community in which all property was held in common. Although residents of areas outside of Qumran "were still not subject to the rule of common ownership of property," they were forbidden to "receive anything from the sons of the Pit"—the sinful world of non-Essenes—"except for payment" (DR XII). Still, "[t]hey had to hand over to the Guardians and the Judges the revenue of two days out of every month, and from this fund aid was given to the widows and orphans, the sick and aged, etc., in their midst." Full-fledged members of the community, however, put their property and income "in the hands of the Bursar," whose duty was "to administer this common property for the benefit of his companions."[1234]

It should be noted, however, that the residents of Qumran were united not only by the sharing of material goods, but also by the command to love one another: "For according to the holy design, they shall all of them be in a Community of truth and virtuous humility, of lovingkindness and good intent one towards the other and (they shall all of them be) sons of the everlasting Company" (CR II). Furthermore, according to *The Damascus Rule*, "A man shall seek his brother's well-being and shall not sin against his near kin" (VI-VII). Indeed, as Hans G. Kippenberg explains, the Qumranites carried the principle of social justice further than the Covenant Code required: "Here the obligations toward the needy, widows, and orphans already postulated in the Old Testament, are even increased. The community of Qumran protects also the unmarried women who did not have any free male relatives (go'el); it takes care of the redemption of its fellows who fell into slavery abroad; it offers the traveling Essenes protection and shelter; it assists the dying; it helps the indigent who live by manual work; and it protects the fatherless." In short, "there should be nobody in [the supervisor's] community who is persecuted and oppressed."[1235]

Similarly, In *The Community Rule*, not only are compassion and sympathy required for dealing with the disenfranchised, but restraint, humility, and absolute respect are required for dealing with other members of the community. Specifically, there was to be no deceit, obstinacy, impatience, insult, indifference, malice, revenge, foolish speech, interruption, slander, or any kind of negative reaction to a member of the community (VII), all of which violations of the principle of brotherhood required various forms of penance, including, as I said earlier, temporary exclusion and complete expulsion. According to "the Rule for the Guardian of the Camp," the leader at Qumran was expected to "love" the members "as a father loves his children, and shall carry them in all their distress like a shepherd his sheep. He shall loosen all the fetters which bind them that in his Congregation there may be none that are oppressed or broken" (DR XIII).

Clearly, the idea of sharing was motivated by several goals. It was, first, a means of establishing the principle of equality throughout the community. That is, at least in terms of material possessions, everyone was on the same level. As Burrows notes, "Josephus mentions the great attachment of the Essenes to one another, and Philo speaks of the extraordinary spirit of equality and fellowship . . . The ideal of equality [also] found expression among the Essenes in the repudiation of slavery."[1236] In this respect, the Dead Sea sectaries restored the spirit of tribal society by embracing egalitarianism, as well as kinship through brotherhood. Second, it was a means of providing the members of the sect with ample time to perform their duties, particularly the time-consuming tasks of independent study and group discussion of the laws. Third, contributions to the common fund at Qumran provided the group with the financial wherewithal to "give to the fatherless," as well as "succour the needy, the aged sick and the homeless, the captive taken by a foreign people, the virgin with no near kin, and the ma[id] for whom no man cares" (DR XIV).

Fourth, giving up their possessions enabled the members of the Qumran community to minimize the main threats to their spirituality: greed, materialism, and ambition. The writer of Hymn 16 thanks God for allowing him (as well as all those who recited these words) to avoid the temptations faced by non-members of the sect: "Thou hast not placed my support in gain, [nor does] my [heart delight in riches]; thou hast given me no fleshly refuge." While others may "pride themselves in possessions and wealth, . . ."[the soul] of Thy servant has loathed [riches] and gain, and he has not [desired] exquisite delights." According to *The Community Rule*, among the precepts that had to be followed by the Master of the community was the command to leave to "the men of perdition"—all the outsiders who clung to ordinary values and would therefore meet with an ordinary fate—"wealth and earnings like a slave to his lord and like a poor man to his master" (IX).

Speaking of the "princes of Judah"—that is, the Jewish ruling class—*The Damascus Rule* says that they "have wallowed in the ways of whoredom and wicked wealth," specifically by, among other things, "hav[ing] acted arrogantly for the sake of riches and gain" (VIII). Elsewhere in the Damascus Rule, "riches" are identified as one of "the three nets of Satan" (IV). Thus, the Essenes at Qumran were advised to avoid "the sons of the Pit" and to "keep away from the unclean riches of wickedness acquired by vow or anathema or from the Temple treasure; they shall not rob the poor of His people, to make of widows their prey and of the fatherless their victim . . . They shall love each man his brother as himself; they shall succor the poor, the needy, and the stranger" (VI).

Finally, the adoption of poverty as a way of life was also a means of purification—that is, an indispensable part of living what Vermes refers to as "a holy life": "For them, 'perfection of the way' was the true remedy against the disease of sin and guilt, and mortification (poverty, purity, and self-abnegation) the vehicle of healing and life."[1237] Thus, like the early Christians of Jerusalem, the Essenes at Qumran described themselves as "the poor" (*The War Rule* XI, XIII), both of which usages, Gaster says, "bore the specific sense of 'ascetic.'"[1238]

In at least a few hymns, the writer (possibly the Teacher of Righteousness) refers to himself as "the poor one" (Hymns 3, 5, and 8) and, in two of these works, refers to the traditional covenantal view that God saves "the poor" along with other suffering and oppressed people, among whom the writer includes himself: "But Thou, O my God, hast succoured the soul of the poor and the needy against one stronger than he; thou hast redeemed my soul from the hand of the mighty" (Hymn 3). "Thou hast preserved the soul of the poor one in the den of lions . . . Thou hast closed up their teeth, O God, lest they rend the soul of the poor and needy" (Hymn 8). In Hymn 9, the writer says, "I thank thee, O Lord, for thou hast not abandoned the fatherless or despised the poor." He then thanks God for helping "the humble" and "causing all the well-loved poor to rise up together from the trampling."

The role of God in the Dead Sea Scrolls is similar to the role described by other religious writers and thinkers for whom human beings are innately unworthy of salvation: St. Paul, St. Augustine, and John Calvin. That is, God at Qumran was, as I said earlier, believed to be responsible for everything, especially for both offering salvation and providing the means for attaining it. Since, as sinners, human beings were assumed to be unworthy of God's offer of eternal life, they were wholly dependent on his forgiveness to receive anything at the end-time besides eternal punishment. As Vermes says, "the sectary" in the Scrolls "is amazed by the blessings showered on him and expresses himself in the Hymns in tones of self-abasement . . . With all this awareness of blessing and salvation, and balancing any tendency toward arrogance, comes the constant reminder that all goodness and truth proceed from God and that no act of virtue can be accomplished without His help."[1239]

Thus, the writer of Hymn 11 says to God: "I have not relied [upon the works of my hands], to raise up [my heart], nor have I sought refuge in my own strength. I have no fleshly refuge, [and Thy servant has] no righteous deeds to deliver him from the [Pit of no] forgiveness. But I lean on the [abundance of Thy mercies] and hope for [the greatness] of Thy grace." The author of *The War Rule* makes the same point: "Many times hast Thou also delivered us by the hand of our kings through Thy lovingkindness, and not in accordance with our works by which we have done evil, nor according to our rebellious deeds" (XI).

On the one hand, although the Essenes of Qumran believed there was no way to *earn* salvation, they seem to have believed that salvation could in fact be achieved by membership in the sect, which, in turn, they maintained by all the traditional ways of demonstrating their total commitment to God, including belief in his promise of salvation, knowledge of his laws, and performance of his commands. In this respect, the religious program at Qumran remained a *quid pro quo* system. It was rooted in all of the promises stated in the Torah and other books of the Jewish Bible—the recurrent idea that God will provide long life and prosperity in exchange for trust, understanding, and obedience. After all, the two ways offered to humanity in the Dead Sea Scrolls—the way of Light and the way of Darkness—are reflections of the choices offered in Psalm 1: "Blessed is the man who walks not in the counsel of the wicked, . . . but his delight is in the law of the Lord, and on this law he meditates day and night" (vv. 1–2).

Apocalypse

At Qumran, the blessing was not merely God's reward of long life and prosperity, but permission to participate in the great war between the forces of good and evil and to enjoy the extraordinary results of victory—eternal life and eternal happiness: "The war of the heavenly warriors shall scourge the earth; and it shall not end before the appointed destruction which shall be forever and without compare" (Hymn 5). In the aftermath of war, the soldier of God was expected to "walk before [him] in the land [of the living], into paths of glory and [infinite] peace which shall [never] end" (Hymn 11).[1240]

What followed from this view was the belief that the Guardian (or Master) at Qumran needed to screen, examine, teach, encourage, monitor, correct, and sometimes penalize the members of the brotherhood in order to help them stand by their oath, profit from his guidance, and *choose* to follow the rules that would allow them to retain their membership in the sect. Thus the urgency of the Master's cry in Hymn 1: "O just men, put away iniquity! Hold fast [to the Covenant], O all you perfect of way; [O all you afflicted with] misery, be patient and despise no righteous judgement!" Indeed, in the same Hymn, the Master says that he has offered "healing to those . . . who repent, prudence to the simple, and steadfastness to the fearful of heart, . . . [and] a counsel of truth and understanding to the upright of way." After all, "a merciful God" who "pardon[s] those who repent of their sin" and, at the same time, "visit[s] the iniquity of the wicked" is a God who can be loved "freely"—that is, *by choice*, as an act of individual volition and expressive of a capacity for self-determination (Hymn 22). Only the truly free agent can repent, confess to having "a perverse spirit" or "a perverse heart" and thereby be forgiven, pardoned, strengthened, purified, and cleansed by "a merciful and compassionate" God (Hymns 1, 5, 10, 12, 22, 23).

On the other hand, however, the community at Qumran claimed that human beings are *utterly* unable to earn salvation, period. As Burrows says: "They believed that all things were ordained by God. Even the existence of evil and the struggles between good and evil in human society and in the individual soul were part and parcel of the divine plan."[1241] In *The Community Rule* Hymn, the writer says, "For mankind has no way, and man is unable to establish his steps since justification is with God and perfection of the way is out of His hand. All things come to pass by His knowledge; He establishes all things by His design and without Him nothing is done" (XI). Righteousness, I know," says the writer of Hymn 7 to God, "is not of man, nor is perfection of way of the son of man: to the Most High God belong all righteous deeds." The writer of Hymn 22 addresses God with the same message: "I know . . . that righteousness is not in a hand of flesh, [that] man [is not master of] his way and that it is not in mortals to direct their step. I know that the inclination of every spirit [is in thy hand]." And the writer of Hymn 20 says, "By Thy goodness alone is man righteous."

The writer of Hymn 12 asks, therefore, whether anyone can claim to deserve God's reward: "Who, when he is judged, shall be righteous before thee? For no spirit can reply to Thy rebuke nor can any withstand Thy wrath." "For thine, O God of knowledge, are all righteous deeds and the counsel of truth; but to the souls of men is the work of iniquity and deeds of deceit." In fact, the overriding message of the Hymns is simply that God alone is responsible for everything and that human beings can achieve nothing: "Clay and dust that I am," says the writer of Hymn 15, "what can I devise unless Thou wish it, and what contrive unless Thou desire it?" In Hymn 19, the writer asks: "And how shall I speak unless Thou open my mouth; how understand unless Thou teach me? How shall I seek thee unless Thou uncover my heart, and how follow the way that is straight unless [Thou guide me?]."

The question arises, of course, if all righteousness comes from God, how can one person be saved while another is damned? Furthermore, why should anyone be saved if everyone is evil? And why should anyone be punished if everyone is made evil by the Creator? The first and third questions, raised by Ezra in 2 Esdras, remain unanswered in that work and generally unaddressed in religious writings of all kinds. Among the few serious attempts to deal with these issues, the one offered implicitly by St. Paul and explicitly by St. Augustine and John Calvin is called predestination. And this is the explanation we find in the Dead Sea Scrolls.

The writer of Hymn 21 says that God "[divided men] into good and evil in accordance with the spirits of their lot"—a phrase that means "the spirits that they were allotted by God." "They believed strongly," says Burrows, "in the doctrine of divine election—so strongly, indeed, that their belief has even been called fatalistic. A favorite word of the Manual of Discipline [*The Community Rule*] is the one used in the Old Testament for the lot that was cast to determine matters of dispute or doubt." In the Qumran document, Burrows continues, the word "is used for the destiny allotted by God to each man, somewhat as we commonly speak of a man's lot in life." Quoting Josephus, Burrows concludes that "the Essenes believed everything that happened to be determined by destiny," which has been called by one scholar "a deterministic theology."[1242]

Commenting on the cosmic conflict between the spirits of Light and Darkness, G. Ernest Wright says that, to the Essenes, all men are born into one or the other: "All men are predestined as it were, to live under one of these two spirits; hence all men can be divided into two groups, the children of light and the children of darkness."[1243] According to *The Community Rule*: "From the God of Knowledge comes all that is and shall be. Before ever they existed He established their whole design, and *when, as ordained for them, they come into being, it is in accord with His glorious design that they accomplish their task without change . . . Those born of truth spring from the fountain of light, but those born of falsehood spring from a source of darkness.* All the children of righteousness are ruled by the Prince of Light and walk in the ways of light, but all the children of falsehood are ruled by the Angel of Darkness and walk in the ways of darkness" (CR III; my emphasis).

Similarly, the writer of the first Hymn says that God did not make *everyone* evil but designed the distribution of good and evil before he created mankind: "Thou didst establish their destiny before ever they were." As the writer of Hymn 22 explains: "I know that the inclination of every spirit [is in Thy hand]; *Thou didst establish [all] its [ways] before ever creating it,* and how can any man change Thy words?" Then he explains that God made some people "just" and some people "wicked": "*Thou alone didst [create] the just and establish him from the womb* for the time of goodwill, that he might hearken to Thy Covenant and walk in all [Thy ways] . . . But *the wicked Thou didst create for [the time] of Thy [wrath], Thou didst vow them from the womb* to the Day of Massacre, for they walk in the way which is not good" (my emphasis). Burrows says: "Paul too emphasizes divine election and foreordination as the ground of man's salvation. The problem of reconciling this doctrine with commands and exhortations implying freedom of choice is left unresolved in the Dead Sea Scrolls, as it is in Paul's epistles."[1244]

The Christian Jews

The Christian Jews of the first century differed from the Essenes in a number of ways.[1245] After emerging from the small towns of Galilee, they settled in Jerusalem and more or less—at least for a generation—remained indistinguishable from their non-Christian neighbors. Unlike the Qumran sectaries, who lived in the desert, rejected the Temple and its priesthood, and embraced an ascetic lifestyle, the Christian Jews turned away from John the Baptist—"clothed with camel's hair," with "a leather girdle around his waist," and eating "locusts and wild honey" (Mark 1:6)—who may actually have been a product of the Qumran community, as G. E. Wright suggests.[1246] Furthermore, unlike the Essenes, the Christian Jews believed that their leader was not only divine, but in fact the Son of God; a miracle worker with supernatural powers and a healer, whose spiritual endowment enabled him to bring the dead back to life; and a redeemer of mankind, whose death would atone for the sins of humanity. In addition, as John P. Meier emphasizes, the Christian Jews continued to worship at the Temple.[1247] They also proselytized militantly but did so outside of Israel and among gentiles as well as Jews. Finally, the Christian Jews gradually broke away from their Jewish origins and eventually established a new religion.

Nevertheless, both Essenes and Christians were products of the messianic movement that emerged in the intertestamental period. As James L. Kugel explains, "During the last century BCE, expectations of the coming of such a future king had reached a fever pitch, at least in some segments of Jewish society. Among these expectants were the followers of Jesus of Nazareth."[1248] For this and other reasons, the similarities between the two Jewish groups are strong enough to suggest that the various Jewish sects of the first century, though embracing a wide range of ideas and practices, remained connected by a number of core beliefs that distinguished them from many other contemporary religions.

Both Essenes and Christian Jews called themselves the "true" Israel, "the elect," "the poor," and "the Sons of Light."[1249] They also believed that they had been provided with "a New Covenant" by their martyred leader and founder.[1250] "On *sexual* matters," Meier says, "Jesus and the Essenes tend in the same direction: stringent standards and prohibitions." As "extreme conservatives" on this subject, Meier adds, "[b]oth Jesus and the Essenes demand strict restraints on thoughts and actions that could lead to improper sexual activity . . . Jesus and at least some Essenes practiced celibacy, while affirming monogamous marriage for most people."[1251] Both groups practiced baptism, had meals in common, and, unlike the other Jewish sects, committed their beliefs to writing in the hope that their members would better understand in what ways and to what degree their respective faiths differed from those of others.

Theodor Gaster briefly discusses the "many parallels which these texts afford" in the organization of the Essenes at Qumran and that "of the primitive Christian Church."[1252] For example, both Essenes and Christians established a hierarchical organization led by bishops and guided by twelve leaders representing the twelve tribes of Israel.[1253] Wright says, "The Qumran community organized its common life along lines which suggest certain features of the later Christian organization. The Damascus Document speaks of officials known as 'visitors' or 'assessors,' the exact verbal equivalent of the New Testament *episcopoi* or 'bishops' (A.V.)." Furthermore, both "followed the way (cf. Acts 9:2) under the authority of twelve laymen."[1254] Noting the common acknowledgment of twelve leaders, Millar Burrows also mentions the similarity between the position of Peter in the Jerusalem church and that of the Qumran superintendent described in the scrolls.[1255] Craig A. Evans says that the Essenes intended to commemorate the twelve tribes by inscribing their names on the shield of their leader, thus signifying, as in Mark 3:14 and Matthew 19:28, that all the tribes of Israel would be restored.[1256]

Regarding the life and ideals of the Qumran sect and those of the early church of Jerusalem, Burrows says, "A spirit of love and unity was cultivated in both."[1257] Jesus' Sermon on the Mount quite clearly demonstrates that he made the same demands on his followers that the Teacher of Righteousness made on the Essenes at Qumran, especially in his insistence that his disciples honor "the law and the prophets" (a phrase that Bernhard W. Anderson says "was a standing expression for Jewish scripture" [1258]): "For truly, I say to you, till heaven and earth pass away, not an iota, not a dot, will pass from the law until all is accomplished. Whoever then relaxes one of the least of these commandments and teaches men so, shall be called least in the kingdom of heaven; but *he who does them and teaches them shall be called great in the kingdom of heaven. For I tell you, unless your righteousness exceeds that of the scribes and Pharisees, you will never enter the kingdom of heaven*" (Matt 5:17–20; Luke 16:17; my emphasis). Later in the Gospel of Matthew, when a young man asks Jesus how he can attain "eternal life," Jesus replies, "If you would enter life, keep the commandments" (Matt 19:16–17; Mark 17:19; Luke 19:18–20). The editors of *The Oxford Annotated Bible* comment, "The question concerns the way of life which Jesus will guarantee as satisfying God" (1196).

Apocalypse

It should be remembered that, despite his reputation among scholars of the past for repudiating the Jewish law, more recent scholars have insisted that Jesus honored the Ten Commandments as well as the ancillary laws of the Torah. Undoubtedly, he disagreed with the Pharisees' adoption and defense of a large body of oral laws, which he referred to as their "tradition." But the textual evidence, especially in the synoptic Gospels, demonstrates that while he *interpreted* the sacred laws of the Torah—as did the Pharisees and the Essenes, as well as the Sadducees and the Samaritans—Jesus was hardly as extreme as some other Jews. E. P. Sanders says: "Several stories in the Gospels concern Jesus' relationship to the Jewish law. These passages create the impression that Jesus was lax about observance of the Law, but on closer examination we shall see that there are no clear instances of actual transgression."[1259]

For example, Jesus criticizes the scribes and Pharisees for engaging in trivial religious acts, such as "tith[ing] mint and dill and cumin," while "neglect[ing] the weightier matters of the law, justice and mercy and faith." However, it is easy to forget or ignore Jesus' unwillingness to dismiss the legitimacy of tithing: "[T]hese"—i.e., matters of justice, etc.—"you ought to have done," he adds, but "*without neglecting the others*" (Matt 23:23; Luke 11:42; my emphasis).[1260] The first part of this passage has frequently been cited by scholars because of the strong assumption in the scholarly community that, even if Jesus found the moral laws of Judaism to be acceptable, he certainly rejected the laws associated with the Priestly tradition, including rules governing purity, the Sabbath, and sacrifice. Sanders says, however, representing, again, the views of many contemporary scholars, "It is most unlikely that Jesus attacked sacrificial practice or purity distinctions, and very improbable that he sought Gentile equality in the Temple."[1261]

In an earlier passage in the Gospel of Matthew, Jesus again emphasizes the priority of morality (maintaining cordial relations with others) over ritual (making a sacrifice at the Temple). However, like the prophets, who made the same distinction, he does not deny the importance of ceremony in the practice of Judaism: "So if you are offering your gift at the altar, and there remember that your brother has something against you, leave your gift there before the altar and go; first be reconciled to your brother, and then come and offer your gift" (5:23–24). Jesus uses the example to illustrate the need (in the preceding verse) to refrain from anger: "I say to you that every one who is angry with his brother shall be liable to judgment" (5:22). However, this does not mean that the peacemaker should not return to the Temple and complete the ritual that he or she temporarily interrupted in order to fulfill a more important and therefore more pressing obligation.

When we compare Jesus' reinterpretations of Jewish laws on divorce, oath-taking, and Sabbath observance to the Essenes' complete repudiation of the Temple and the priesthood, to the Sadducees' rejection of everything except the Pentateuch as holy scripture, or to the arguments between the two leading Pharisees, Hillel and Shammai, we realize that Jesus' innovations were typical of the kinds of disagreements that Jews had with other Jews. In light of this fact, many contemporary scholars have argued that Jesus not only embraced Judaism as much as any of his fellow Jews did but also had no intention of creating a new religion.[1262] Many scholars have noted that most, if not all of Jesus's moral pronouncements were Jewish in origin, including, for example, the Golden Rule (which Jesus himself calls "the law and the prophets" [Matt 7:12]) and the Lord's prayer (which, according to many scholars, is based on the Kaddish, a traditional Jewish prayer).

Jesus clearly agreed with his fellow Jews that the essence of Judaism was the doctrine of love, particularly as it is expressed in what many Jews called the Two Commandments, one referring to the first five of the Ten Commandments and the second referring to the last five. The first and overriding commandment was based on the Shema, from Deuteronomy 6:5–6: "[Y]ou shall love the Lord your God with all your heart, and with all your soul, and with all your might. And these words which I command you this day shall be upon your heart." The second commandment, from Leviticus 19:17–18, was generally understood to be a way of fulfilling the first (and, incidentally, provides the basis for the passage I cited above, from Matt 5:22–24): "You shall not hate your brother in your heart, but you shall reason with your neighbor, lest you bear sin because of him. You shall not take vengeance or bear any grudge against the sons of your own people, but you shall love your neighbor as yourself." John J. Collins says that these were the "core teachings" of the Jewish Bible: "The saying attributed to Jesus in the Gospels (Matt 22:34–40; Mark 12:28–31; Luke 10:25–28) on the twofold greatest commandment sum up at least one strand of Deuteronomic theology."[1263]

In two of the three synoptic Gospels, Jesus shared with a Jewish interlocutor an equal and mutual appreciation for the importance of this formulation. In the Gospel of Matthew, when he was asked, "Which is the great commandment?" he simply identified "these two commandments" as the foundation of "all the law and the prophets" (22:40). In the Gospel of Mark, however, when Jesus gave a similar answer to that question, he was praised by the scribe who asked it and who added—quoting 1 Samuel, Hosea, and Micah—that loving God and humanity "is much more than all whole burnt offerings and sacrifices." In response to this, Jesus said to him, "You are not far from the kingdom of God" (12:28–34). Similarly, in the Gospel of Luke, when Jesus was asked by a lawyer, "Teacher, what shall I do to inherit eternal life?" Jesus replied by asking his interlocutor, "What is written in the law?" Here it was the lawyer who quoted these passages from the Pentateuch, in response to which Jesus said, "You have answered right; do this, and you will live" (10:25–28)—that is, eternally.

Jesus taught that, in addition to following the commandments, his disciples actually had to go beyond them. That is, in order to exceed the "righteousness . . . of the scribes and Pharisees," he urged them in the Antitheses (Matt 5:21–48) not only to obey God's laws, but to avoid even the emotions that drive people to break them, especially within the brother- and sisterhood of his disciples. Like violations of the rules at Qumran, violations within the Christian community were evidently reportable to

Apocalypse

something that Jesus calls "the council," and "whoever says, 'You fool!' shall be liable to the hell of fire" (5:22). Indeed, "if any one strikes you on the right cheek, turn to him the other also" (5:39). Two principles are at work here: (1) "Love your enemies and pray for those who persecute you, so that you may be sons of your Father who is in heaven" (5:44); and (2) Vengeance belongs to God and not to men. Thus, "if you forgive men their trespasses, your heavenly Father also will forgive you; but if you do not forgive men their trespasses, neither will your Father forgive your trespasses" (6:14–15). That is, "Judge not that you be not judged. For with the judgment you pronounce you will be judged, and the measure you give will be the measure you get: (7:1–2). That is, *quid pro quo*.

Although the Essenes at Qumran displayed a strong dislike for everyone outside the cult, they insisted, as we have seen, on a similarly high standard of affection and loyalty within the brotherhood, based on the fundamental idea "that they [must] love all the sons of light" and be "of good intent one towards the other" (CR I, II). They were encouraged to criticize each other "in truth, humility, and charity," but they were told not to hate any of the brothers for any reason (CR III-IV).[1264] No one was to respond to "his companion" either obstinately or impatiently (CR VI). Anger, malice, and revenge were also forbidden (CR VII; see also DR IX), along with ill-temper, obduracy, and envy (CR V). Indeed, in *The Community Rule* Hymn, the members promise: "I will pay to no man the reward of evil; I will pursue him with goodness." Finally, as if they had read the Sermon on the Mount, the Qumran brothers say, "For *judgement of all the living is with God* and it is He who will render to man his reward" (my emphasis).

This level of compassion and generosity was imperative for both the Essenes and the Christian Jews because both groups believed that their single most important obligation was to imitate God—specifically, by replicating his acts of mercy, of which they felt themselves to be the beneficiaries. As Jesus says to his disciples, "You received without pay, give without pay" (10:8). Given their vision of themselves as undeserving and irredeemable sinners, the Qumran sectaries were particularly impressed by God's infinite capacity for mercy and his willingness to forgive even the worst of evildoers. Throughout the Hymns, the Qumran Master thanks God for forgiving sins (12, 17, 23; see also DR IV), rewarding obedience (7) and repentance (1), and offering mercy and grace (15, 16, 22; see also CR Hymn). In Hymn 18, he says, "Blessed art Thou, O God of mercy and compassion . . . Rejoice the soul of Thy servant with Thy truth and cleanse me by Thy righteousness. Even as I have hoped in Thy goodness, and waited for Thy grace, so hast Thou freed me from my calamities in accordance with Thy forgiveness; and in my distress Thou hast comforted me for I have leaned on Thy mercy."

Less convinced of the absolute depravity of mankind and, indeed, focused on "the lost sheep of the house of Israel"—evidently, the sick and the sinful (Matt 10:5–8; 15:24; 18:12–14)—Jesus was committed to healing the suffering. However, as many of the psalms suggest, some of the suffering were victims who simply needed help, the disenfranchised to whom he promised early entry into the Kingdom of God; and some of them were sinners who needed to undergo a spiritual change in order to be accepted into the kingdom. Throughout the synoptic Gospels, Jesus asks members of the latter group—the lost sheep—to repent. In the Gospel of Matthew, his preaching, after the arrest of John the Baptist, is expressed in the commandment, "Repent, for the kingdom of heaven is at hand" (4:17; Mark 1:15). In the Gospel of Luke, he says, "I have not come to call the righteous, but sinners to repentance" (5:32). "I tell you, there will be more joy in heaven over one sinner who repents than over ninety-nine righteous persons who need no repentance" (Luke 15:7). The prodigal son repents and confesses his sin, and his father, out of "compassion," welcomes him home (Luke 15:21–24). The tax collector confesses his guilt and asks for mercy, which God grants him because "he humbles himself" and is thereby "exalted" (18:13–14).

Elsewhere, Jesus berates a variety of people for failing to repent and thereby rendering themselves unable to enter the kingdom of God. In the Gospel of Matthew, he "began to upbraid the cities where most of his mighty works had been done, because they did not repent" (Matt 11:20). Later, he criticizes the chief priests and elders for ignoring the message of John the Baptist. Because they "did not afterward repent, and believe him," they will enter "the kingdom of God" after the repentant tax collectors and harlots (21:32). In the Gospel of Luke, after he hears of Pilate's murder of Galileans, Jesus tells "the multitudes": "[U]nless you repent you will all likewise perish" (13:3, 5). So important is the connection between repentance, forgiveness, and entrance into the kingdom of God, that Jesus tells his disciples: "Take heed to yourselves; if your brother sins, rebuke him, and if he repents, forgive him." Indeed, Jesus continues, whether "your brother" continues to sin, he must be forgiven as long as he repents: "[A]nd if he sins against you seven times in the day, and turns to you seven times, and says 'I repent,' you must forgive him" (17:3–4; Mark 6:12). After his resurrection, Jesus tells his disciples to carry this message all over the world: "[R]epentance and forgiveness of sins should be preached in his name to all nations" (24:47).

Looking over such passages as these, Norman Perrin concludes: "If one asks the natural question: In what way is the kingly activity of God primarily known? then the answer of the teaching of Jesus is abundantly clear: In the forgiveness of sins. According to the gospel tradition, this is the central specific aspect of Jesus' proclamation of the Kingdom."[1265] Furthermore, according to Acts of the Apostles, this is the message that Jesus' disciples got as well. After the Crucifixion, in his first speech to his fellow Jews in Jerusalem, Peter says, "Repent, and be baptized every one of you in the name of Jesus Christ for the forgiveness of your sins" (2:38). In his second speech, he says, "Repent therefore, and turn again, that your sins may be blotted out" (3:19). And in a brief speech to the Sanhedrin, Peter says of Jesus: "God exalted him at his right hand as Leader and Savior, to give repentance to Israel and forgiveness of sins" (5:31). Peter later tells Simon, the Samaritan magician, to repent and thereby earn God's forgiveness: "Repent therefore of this wickedness of yours, and pray to the Lord that, if possible, the intent of your heart may be forgiven you. For I see that you are in the gall of bitterness and the bond of iniquity" (8:22).

When they extend their mission to the gentiles after Peter's revelation in Joppa, the Christian Jews of Jerusalem remain committed to repentance as the centerpiece of their message. In response to Peter's description of his conversion of Cornelius in Caesarea, Jesus' followers in Jerusalem say, "Then to the Gentiles also God has granted repentance unto life" (11:18). As the leader of the gentile mission and, like other Christians, one of "God's offspring," Paul later explains to the Athenians that they must repent because everyone will be judged by the resurrected Messiah on *Yom Yahweh*: "[N]ow [God] commands all men everywhere to repent, because he has fixed a day on which he will judge the world in righteousness by a man whom he has appointed, and of this he has given assurance to all men by raising him from the dead" (17:29–31). In Miletus, Paul reminds "the elders of the [Ephesus] church" that he has been "preaching the kingdom" (20:25), by which he means "testifying both to Jews and to Greeks of repentance to God and of faith in our Lord Jesus Christ" (20:21). In self-defense, after his arrest by the Romans, Paul says to King Agrippa that he has done nothing more threatening than preaching to everyone "that they should repent and turn to God and perform deeds worthy of their repentance" (26:20).

The Christian Jews who established a religious community, perhaps in Syria,[1266] and wrote what Bart D. Ehrman calls "the first 'church manual' to have survived from early Christianity" similarly established rigorous standards for entrance into the community and for retaining membership in it. In their brief instructional text for initiating gentiles into the sect, called *The Didache* (or *Teaching*) *of the Twelve Apostles*, these Christian Jews begin with the so-called Two Ways (1:1–2), "the way of the righteous" and "the way of the wicked," derived from the first psalm (1:2) and reiterated by Jeremiah (21:8).[1267] The "way of life" includes strict obedience to the covenant laws of Leviticus, love of God and love of humanity, as well as the Golden Rule and a number of other commands similar to those in the Sermon of the Mount.[1268] Although the manual is "moderate" on food laws and baptismal requirements, according to Joseph B. Tyson, the emphasis on the Two Ways is "a perfectionist ideal."[1269] Furthermore, Aaron Milavec emphasizes the carefully organized steps required of every initiate, from "preparing the candidate for abusive treatment at home" to bringing him or her from "humble beginnings" to "an exalted end."[1270] John Dominic Crossan says that the sect is "always tolerant except where intolerance is absolutely demanded and articulated."[1271]

Indeed, *The Didache* concludes with the admonition that initiates must aim for nothing less than moral excellence, not only by "seeking the things pertaining to [their] souls," but also by understanding that "the whole time of [their] faith will not be of use to [them] if in the end time [they] should not have been perfected" (16:2). This goal is underscored, according to Milavec, by the fact that the title of the text should be translated *training* rather than *teaching* because it "was normally used to refer to a prolonged apprenticeship under a master" and is defined in the *Theological Dictionary of the New Testament* as "a continued activity with a view to a gradual, systematic, and therefore all the more fundamental assimilation."[1272] Crossan explains: "The *Didache* is willing to be gentle and delicate in demanding full perfection of everyone . . . But it is not willing to create two classes of Christians . . . All alike are called to perfection and should get as close to it as possible." Speaking of the *Didache*'s final plea for total obedience, Crossan says, "One must take very seriously . . . this final warning in the apocalyptic section that concludes the *Didache*."[1273]

Of course, both the Essenes and the Christian Jews (whether in Jerusalem or elsewhere) could embrace such unusually high standards of behavior at least partly because they believed that God rewarded men and women for living up to these ideals and punished them for failing to do so. In Hymn 3, the Essene writer says that his enemies, "the conceivers of Vanity, shall be prey to terrible anguish . . . and the gates [of Hell] shall open . . . and the everlasting bars shall be bolted on all the spirits of Naught." In Hymn 7, the writer says to God that "those who please Thee shall stand before Thee forever; those who walk in the way of Thy heart shall be established for evermore." The writer of *The Community Rule* explains that "the children of men" walk in both the way of truth and the way of falsehood: "And the whole reward for their deeds shall be, for everlasting ages, according to whether each man's portion in their two divisions is great or small" (IV).

In the Gospel of Matthew, Jesus promises his followers that, although there are no rewards for loving those who love them (5:46) or for making a public display of their piety (6:1–7), their "reward" for suffering as followers of Jesus "is great in heaven" (5:12; Luke 6:23). Indeed, if they love their enemies, give alms "in secret," pray and fast in private, and refrain from "heap[ing] up empty phrases" in their appeals to God, he will "reward" them (6:4, 6:18; Luke 6:36). There are rewards as well for those who "acknowledge" or "receive" others who deserve to be accepted, including Jesus himself: "He who receives you receives me, and he who receives me receives him who sent me. He who receives a prophet because he is a prophet shall receive a prophet's reward, and he who receives a righteous man shall receive a righteous man's reward. And whoever gives to one of these little ones even a cup of cold water because he is a disciple, truly, I say to you, he shall not lose his reward" (Matt 10:41–42).

Thus, although at least some Jews had, by the first century AD, lost their confidence that God responded to human actions in this manner, many Jews had not. Among them, the Essenes and the Christians remained strongly influenced by messianism and apocalypticism, both of which reflected the belief that God would ultimately reward good behavior and punish bad by giving people, on the Day of Judgment, exactly what they deserved. The Essenes expected two Messiahs, one of whom would lead them to victory over the forces of Darkness and, as Geza Vermes explains, "bring into being the Kingdom of God."[1274] The Christians believed that, as the Messiah, Jesus would sooner or later return, help bring God's Kingdom to earth, and not only provide the remnant who followed him—i.e., the Christians—with a transformed society, but also give everyone his or her just deserts: "For the Son of man is to come with his angels in the glory of his Father, and then he will repay every man for what he has done" (Matt 16:27). Thus, like the Essenes, according to Frank M. Cross Jr., "the early Church [also] conceived itself to be precisely an eschatological community"[1275]—that is, a community that expected the present era (characterized by greed and exploitation) to end and a new era (characterized by selflessness and justice) to begin.

This prospect and its accompanying features are precisely what distinguished both the Essenes and the Christian Jews from some of their Jewish predecessors— particularly the psalmists and the Deuteronomist, but not the prophets. Most importantly, they seem to have believed that individuals would no longer be rewarded or punished relatively soon after their good or bad deeds, as some ancient Jewish texts argued. In addition, they no longer expected all of their suffering to be assuaged immediately. Many might be healed, but many more, who had missed the opportunity to benefit from Jesus' program of forgiveness, would remain sick or disabled. And others, trapped in poverty and oppression by the rich and powerful, would remain oppressed—at least for a while.

Instead of hoping and praying for an instantaneous response from God, these Jewish sects now believed that relatively little would change until the end-time, at which moment—understood to be grand, climactic, and transformational—God would intervene and distribute blessings and curses as *all* recipients deserved. The psalmists had asked God to end their suffering as soon as possible; and the Deuteronomist, through Moses, had assured the Israelites that if they obeyed God they would receive immediate rewards: "Therefore you shall keep the statutes and his commandments . . . that it may go well with you" (4:40), by which Moses meant that everything they hoped for—including many children, abundant crops, and their own land—would be given to them quite soon and without any profound changes in either the course of history or the order of the universe (7:12–14; 28:1–14). But neither Jesus nor the Teacher of Righteousness made such promises to their prospective disciples.

Evidently, such ideas had lost their credibility by that time, and groups like the brotherhood at Qumran and the followers of Jesus believed that, although curses might be imposed in the present as they had been imposed in the past—manifested as they were, by the lame and the blind—all blessings would be deferred until the Day of the Lord. The Essenes, as we have seen, thought that the sons of Light, who had lived obedient and virtuous lives would triumph over the sons of Darkness in a cosmic battle, after which they would live happily forever. As Vermes explains: "[F]inally all wickedness would be wiped from the face of the earth and, with the help of the mighty hand of God, goodness and truth would triumph for ever. The world would be renewed; the elect would inherit the 'glory of Adam', 'every blessing and eternal joy in life without end, a crown of glory and a garment of majesty in unending light' (CR IV)." Furthermore, Vermes adds, citing *The Damascus Rule*, "the Community expected the Messianic Age to begin forty years after the death of the Teacher of Righteousness"—in other words, soon enough to affect the lives of many of the members of the current generation.[1276]

Similarly, the Christians would either qualify for entry into the Kingdom of God or not, after which they too would either enjoy the benefits of salvation or suffer the consequences of sin. To be sure, Jesus welcomed repentance and forgave sins—that is, absolved people of their past iniquities—but rewards for being merciful, righteous, and self-sacrificing would not be distributed until his return as the Son of Man: "Truly, I say to you, in the new world, when the Son of man shall sit on his glorious throne, you who have followed me will also sit on twelve thrones, judging the twelve tribes of Israel. And every one who has left houses or brothers or sisters or father or mother or children or lands, for my name's sake, will receive a hundredfold, and inherit eternal life. But many that are first will be last, and the last first" (Matt 19:28–30; Mark 10:29–31; Luke 13:30). Furthermore, like the Essenes, the Christians were told, on at least two occasions, that the end was not far away: "Truly, I say to you, there are some standing here who will not taste death before they see the kingdom of God come with power" (Mark 9:1; Matt 16:28; Luke 9:27). "Truly, I say to you, this generation will not pass away before all these things take place" (Mark 13:30; Matt 24:34).[1277]

Besides tracing the development from prophecy to apocalypticism, scholars also suggest that the latter movement similarly led to Christianity. Anderson says, "The apocalyptic hope for the Kingdom was one of the major influences upon the early Christian community."[1278] Russell argues that, in fact, the work of the apocalyptists "prepared the way for Christianity, not only in its doctrine of the resurrection, but in its belief in the Kingdom of God and of the Messiah who would one day come to reign."[1279] Klaus Koch traces the idea that Christianity grew out of the apocalyptic movement to Ernst Kasemann, who called apocalyptic "the mother of all Christian theology."[1280] Merrill C. Tenney explains: "The Messianic hope and the apocalyptic concept of it which is apparent in Daniel and which is treated at length in later books formed the background for the apostles questioning of Jesus that evoked his well-known Olivet discourse": "[T]hen will appear the sign of the Son of man in heaven, and then all the tribes of the earth will mourn, and they will see the Son of man coming on the clouds of heaven with power and great glory" (Matt 24:30). After this, the evil "will go away into eternal punishment, but the righteous into eternal life" (25:46).[1281]

Sanders says that Jesus derived his apocalyptic ideas from Judaism: "Jesus and his followers probably shared [the] general view of the Jews," which "usually looked forward to a new world in the sense of a new order," establishing peace and justice, as well as safety and security. Specifically, Sanders continues, "By both word and deed [Jesus] proclaimed that the kingdom would come, that Israel would be restored, that the Temple would be rebuilt (or renewed), that he and his disciples would be leading figures in the kingdom and that people previously regarded as 'last' (sinners and toll gatherers) would become the first."[1282] According to Ben Witherington III, like other Jews, both Jesus and Paul "place considerable stress on the ethical prerequisites" for acceptance into the kingdom.[1283] And, like other Jews, they saw themselves as the remnant predicted by the prophets to be saved by God in the final judgment.[1284] Koch says, "So apocalyptic proves to be the bridge which binds together the Old and the New Testaments by means of eschatology and links up the prophets with the community of Jesus."[1285]

According to Edward Schillebeeckx, "[A]pocalypticism is a universal strain in the mental and spiritual outlook of the ancient East," of which "Jewish apocalypse was only one, if perhaps the most explicit variant." Thus, it comes as no surprise that "after AD 70 the literature of apocalypticism became popular reading matter among Christians, who saw this Jewish literature as tending to support and nurture what they had come to believe about Christ."[1286] Arthur E. Zannoni points out: "At the time of Jesus, most religious Jews in Palestine had embraced some form of the eschatological (endtime) hope introduced by the book of Daniel. Many believed that when the Messiah came, he would preside over the end of history and usher in the new creation promised by apocalyptic writers."[1287] Quoting Mark 13:24–26, in reference to Jesus' prediction that the Son of Man would come on clouds of glory as the skies darkened and the stars fell, C. H. Dodd says that Jesus speaks this way because these images were "part of the mental furniture of the period," about which there is nothing original.[1288]

Tyson argues that, like almost all apocalypses, the Christian apocalypse "made its appearance at a time of religiopolitical difficulty." Specifically, it "represent[ed] the religious response to political oppression" and "proclaim[ed] the reality of God to a world which could see no signs of it." Under the circumstances, it was a powerful message: "When Christians were beginning to doubt the meaning of their own lives and the reality of God, an apocalyptist was able to say with conviction: The Lord God Omnipotent reigns!"[1289] According to Koch, however, the early church turned its back on apocalypticism under the influence of Hellenistic metaphysics: "Because of this the symbolic, oriental thought patterns of apocalyptic and its cryptic, eschatological discourses became increasingly incomprehensible." Thus, Koch continues, "the early Fathers of the Church soon put out of court a type of literature which at one time had been of prime importance to Jesus and the first Christians."[1290] As Wayne A. Meeks explains, this futuristic vision made sense to the Jews, including the early Christians, but not to some pagans, especially those who lived west of Palestine: "The point is how natural thought of 'the end' was to the first Christians, and how strange it was to most of their neighbors."[1291]

Chapter Seven

Covenant, Community, and Compassion

IN THE MIDDLE OF the first millennium BC, Israel underwent a profound religious change, as did a few other countries worldwide. During the so-called Axial Age of c. 500 BC, which I discussed briefly in chapter 3, China, India, Greece, and Israel witnessed the birth of religions in which God and morality were redefined. Taoism, Buddhism, Platonism, and Judaism abandoned the belief that the universe was dominated by many gods, some of them representing forces of nature, and embraced the idea that the cosmos was ruled or represented by a single god or spiritual entity who either transcended nature or expressed its essence and unity. They also, in varying degrees, minimized the value of cultic practices, including ritual and sacrifice, and emphasized the importance of morality over ceremony. The idea was that God, in whatever form he could be said to exist, was not amoral; did not require appeasement or abject obedience; and demanded, if anything, knowledge of his ways, conformity to his moral standards, and the practice of love, justice, and nonviolence among his followers.[1292]

Judaism remained unique among these religions insofar as its practitioners retained the belief that God intervenes in the lives of his people by rewarding good behavior and punishing bad. On the one hand, the "gods" of all these faiths were portrayed as sources of wisdom, which human beings acquired only through an act of *metanoia*, a kind of self-transcendence, in which worshipers connected with "god" (e.g., the Tao, the Good, Yahweh) and underwent a spiritual change that left them both wise and willing to act on their newly attained knowledge.[1293] Some religions emphasized the importance of meditation while others emphasized the importance of repentance as a means of acquiring wisdom and undergoing a spiritual transformation.[1294] On the other hand, however, while some of the other major religions of the period believed that people were ultimately—that is, in the afterlife—recompensed for their moral actions, Judaism retained the idea that God rewards and punishes men and women for their good and bad deeds, if not *in this life,* then at least *on the earth* rather than in heaven or in some other undefined celestial sphere.[1295]

G. Ernest Wright points out that, for Jews, God's kingdom would be established on earth: "The central theological theme of the Old Testament is that of the sovereign and redeeming activity of God, who is engaged for his own name's sake in establishing his kingdom over the whole earth." Furthermore, "[i]t is characteristic of the resurrection faith which developed in Judaism . . . that for the most part it was closely related to the fulfillment of God's aims in the earthly creation. The resurrection was usually conceived as taking place in order that the dead might participate in God's new age on earth. There is no thought whatsoever of a salvation *from* the earth to an ethereal existence." Wright adds, unlike "the philosophies and mysticisms of Greece and India," in which "time and history . . . are the source of evil and misery from which man must escape to find the good life," the Jewish Bible "in the most daring fashion asserts . . . the meaningfulness of history and the dynamic working of God within it"—except, of course, during the intertestamental period, when Jews for the first time entertained the idea of escaping both history and mortality.[1296]

In the first century AD, the Jews took two different paths regarding God's role in the everyday life of his people. Many of them—including Essenes and Christians—embraced apocalypticism, the idea that God would eventually intervene in the world not only by destroying evil people but also by eliminating adverse conditions, such as disease, bad weather, and all other sources of human suffering. That is, some Jews, considering the clear evidence that God's system of justice was not working in the way that the Deuteronomist promised, looked to the future for the implementation of God's moral plan. Lawrence H. Schiffman comments: "Although sometimes the righteous appear to suffer in this world, reward is stored up for them in the next. Similarly, although the wicked appear to prosper in this life, their success is only illusory. In the next life they will receive their just punishment."[1297] Other Jews, however—including Zealots and Pharisees—while not denying the idea that God would eventually intervene in the world, believed that any immediate improvement in their lives depended to a large degree on their own actions. As we shall see, the Pharisees, in particular, appear to have minimized the prospect of salvation as it was defined in the apocalyptic works of the intertestamental period.

Considering the wide variety of opinions on this subject, it could be argued that, in the first century AD, Judaism underwent a second major transformation. The most obvious sign of this change was the proliferation of sects in Judea and Galilee, which, as I noted in chapter 6, resulted mainly from the growing fear among Jews that the occupation of ancient Israel by foreign powers was unlikely to end—ever. And this fear was strengthened by the portrait of God in such religious works as the book of Job and Ecclesiastes. As Shaye Cohen explains: "This was the age of sects . . . and of sectarian literature; of apocalypses and of varied speculations about God's control of human events, the nature of evil, and the secrets of the end time; of the growth of the synagogue, of liturgical prayer and scriptural study; [and] of the 'golden age' of diaspora Judaism."[1298] Groups and individuals were clearly searching desperately for answers to their questions about the future. Less obvious, but equally important, is the fact that many of the sects were committed to and actively engaged in the study of the Torah, the ideals of the Covenant Code, and the absolute necessity of establishing a community that offered the kinship relations of village life, the stability of pre-urban society, and the kind of justice that could be established only by institutionalizing the principles of the Covenant.

Edward Schillebeeckx says, "the general trend of Judaism" in the first century AD "was to go for the formation of 'sects', in conformity with the 'holy remnant' concept of the Daniel literature," which resulted in the division of people into groups of "us" and "them": the sons of light and the sons of darkness.[1299] According to Cohen, in the second century AD, after several Jewish sects had simply disappeared, even the Rabbis used the word *heretics* "to designate a wide variety of Jews whose theology or practices [they] found offensive."[1300] Schiffman argues that, although Jews had traditionally debated about their faith, their situation in the intertestamental period was more precarious and uncertain than it had ever been. Compared to "the disagreements and strife" of biblical times, "the sectarianism" beginning in the reign of the Hasmoneans and continuing into the first century AD was "very different": "Matters would revolve around two axes." The first was expressed in the "many differences of opinion" regarding interpretation of the Bible. The second was expressed in widely different views regarding "the exact parameters of assimilation or Hellenization and of separation and pietism."[1301]

Specifically, the problem the Jews of this period faced was that, except for his aid in the Maccabean revolt against the Seleucids in the second century BC, God had not intervened in their lives and for their benefit since the exodus from Egypt and the invasion of Canaan in c. 1200 BC. In the eighth century BC, the domination of Israel by the Assyrians (and, later, by the Babylonians, Persians, Egyptians, Greeks, and Romans) inspired the kinds of doubts raised by Job and Koheleth (and, later, Ezra in 2 Esdras): certainly not doubts about the existence of God but about the existence of the *quid pro quo* system by which he operated and the kind of salvation he was supposed to provide according to the prophets of the eighth through sixth centuries. If, as Jesus said, God "makes his sun rise on the evil and the good, and sends rain on the just and the unjust," then perhaps people's only hope was to "be perfect, as [their] heavenly father is perfect" (Matt 5:45, 48). Anything less would fail to earn God's help, as was the case up to the present time, and, short of that ultimate reward, would fail to create the kind of world that would come to those who established a true community based on the true (i.e., entire) Covenant.

Doing the Will of God

If we ask, again, what Judaism was in the first century AD, we need only look closely at the three sects that could be said to represent both the penultimate phase—the final phase, by most accounts, being the Rabbinic Judaism of the next few centuries—of the evolution of the Jewish faith and the foundation of what it would continue to be for the ensuing millennia. In addition to the similarities we have already found among them, one more looms large: the singular importance of action over mere belief—or, more precisely, the indispensability of action as the fulfillment of belief. In other words, as E. P. Sanders says, the Jews of this period wished "to be properly Jewish," which meant that they wished "to live as God willed."[1302] Essenes, Christians, and Pharisees all seem to have accepted an idea that Walter Brueggemann finds implicit in Moses' mediation between God and Israel in the book of Exodus: the realization that the law, as it came from God, needed to be acted upon, which means that it had to be studied. In short, if the will of God had to be done—completely and effectively—it first had to be discovered and then, of course, articulated and, finally, implemented.

However, what the Jews of the first century AD had begun to realize—and, indeed, what many Jews had understood since the second century BC—was that two issues made these goals problematic. First, because circumstances are constantly changing, God's will had to be interpreted continually—that is, *re*interpreted on an ongoing basis to fit the political, social, and economic realities that are inevitably transformed over time. This fact made it necessary to revise the Mosaic Law, which had, after all, been altered, in small ways and large, over the preceding millennium. Second, because the Jews of the first century AD found themselves still completely under the domination of a foreign power, as they had been for many centuries, many of them came to the conclusion that they had failed to follow the will of God for that long period of time, which is precisely what the prophets claimed by way of explaining why the Jews were suffering. Although Yehezkel Kaufmann argues that the "biblical arraignment" of the Jews for bringing God's punishment on themselves because of their sins "is exaggerated," the charge was "an almost necessary consequence of the biblical postulate that Israel's calamities are caused by its sins."[1303]

The problem faced by the ancient Jews, therefore, was twofold: What did present realities—some old, some new—compel them to change? And what did past errors—all of them tragic, and some irreparable—compel them to do? The desire to return to the laws of the Covenant, expressed in the demand for the highest possible ethical standards and the establishment of Covenant-based communities—subjects we will examine later in this chapter—was an attempt to answer these questions. But it required diligent study, thoughtful interpretation, and cautious enactment. What did the Covenant mean in the first century AD that it didn't mean in earlier centuries? And in what ways and for what reasons did the Jews of earlier centuries so utterly either misconstrue its meaning or fail to live up to its requirements?

To literalists, who assume that the Bible is what it is—that is, unchanging, fixed in meaning—the first question might appear to be not only shocking but irreverent and therefore unacceptable. As recently as 2013, Jay Parini said that he was writing about Jesus "from the viewpoint of someone . . . who regards scripture as continuous revelation." Parini reminds his readers that "the Bible itself declared its openness to interpretation" in the Letter to the Hebrews 4:12: "For the word of God is living and active," an idea that demands from interpreters of the Bible a "living and active reading" that "draws us more fully into the text, into the living Word, which is unstable, always challenging, never set in stone."[1304] As "modern" as this idea sounds, it is, as the passage from Hebrews suggests, nearly two thousand years old. In fact, both the Essenes at Qumran and the Pharisees in Jerusalem seem to have established the need for ongoing interpretation at least a century earlier than the appearance of that epistle.

Indeed, as Walter Brueggemann notes, in Exodus 20—that is, centuries before the work of the Essenes and the Pharisees—although God himself announces the Ten Commandments, it is Moses who translates these general prohibitions into specific laws. This is why Shaye Cohen says that "Greek Jews regularly referred to Moses as their 'lawgiver' . . . , just as rabbinic Jews called Moses 'our master' or 'our teacher.'" In their view, although he was clearly divinely inspired, Moses himself wrote the Torah, which "allows human agency a substantial role in the creation and transmission of the divine message."[1305] "While the text authorizes the person of Moses," Brueggemann explains, "it is a common assumption of scholars that these verses legitimate a continuing *office* or role of Moses in succeeding generations, those who will mediate to Israel the ongoing will and purpose of YHWH." Furthermore, Brueggemann adds, it is evident that, despite God's warning in Deuteronomy 4:2 and 12:32 against adding anything to his commands, that book in itself "*add*[s] to the Sinai Torah in rich and imaginative ways as the commands of the wilderness are repositioned for an agricultural community in the land." Since, even later, Ezra and others are said to have "helped the people to understand the law" by *interpreting* it (Nehemiah 8:2, 7–8), it can be concluded that "the sequence of *Sinai-Deuteronomy-Ezra* form an axis of dynamism that became characteristic of both Judaism and Christianity."[1306]

Cohen also points out that the growing emphasis on the moral and practical necessity to interpret Jewish texts reflected the increasing de-emphasis on the role of priests as intermediaries in the popular understanding of God's will and the growing acceptance of the role of the individual in interpreting and explaining sacred texts: "The major development in the Judaism of the Second Temple and rabbinic periods is the democratization of religion." Indeed, Cohen says, "[d]uring the Second Temple period, the temple was supplemented by the synagogue, a lay institution; the sacrificial cult was supplemented by prayer, a cultic practice open to all; and the priest was supplemented by the scribe, the learned teacher."[1307]

Like Brueggemann, Cohen reminds his readers that Ezra and Nehemiah contributed significantly to this revolutionary change by treating the Torah in revolutionary ways: "explain[ing] its meaning," "making it available to the masses," eliminating "the priest as the intermediary between the people and the sacred traditions," and, thereby, "curbing the power of the priestly magistrates."[1308] Speaking particularly of Ezra's annual public reading of the Torah, Gerhard von Rad says that "its significance," along with that of other changes Ezra introduced, cannot be "overestimate[d]": "Not only did a protracted and complicated process of restoration come to a certain outward finality with Ezra; but also, as is usually the case with major processes of restoration, at the same time something actually new made its appearance. This new thing is actually called Judaism."[1309]

According to Geza Vermes, many of the Jewish sects of the first century "engaged in a process of doctrinal interpretation, and although the emerging syntheses never departed from their biblical foundations, each showed a distinct individuality."[1310] Simply put, as Millar Burrows says, many Jewish groups "had their own way of interpreting the Scriptures."[1311] To Lester L. Grabbe, this interest was typical of the period and particularly strong among the Essenes, the Pharisees, and the Sadducees: "[A]ll gave weight to the written Torah and made use of the scribal skills of study, interpretation,, and composition."[1312] John P. Meier says, "The struggle between Jesus (or early Christians) and the Pharisees over questions of law reflects a wider struggle raging in Israel around the turn of the era over the proper interpretation of the Mosaic Law . . . For the Qumranites, the differences . . . were so great that they felt constrained to cut themselves off from all other Jews, who, in the eyes of Qumran, had gone astray. While divisions did not run so deep among Pharisees, Sadducees, and other Jews, difficulties over the interpretation of the Mosaic Law and the practical consequences thereof (including temple worship) helped give each group its distinctive form."[1313]

Both Essenes and Christians, for example, believed that each of them had been given a new revelation, which compelled them to interpret the Jewish Bible in new ways. Using similar methods of exegesis, according to D. S. Russell, they were inspired to come to new conclusions by the Teacher of Righteousness and Jesus of Nazareth, respectively.[1314] As Dale C. Allison notes, "Millenarianism," of which Christianity and Essenism are good examples, "involves intense commitment and unconditional loyalty" inspired by "leaders who are considered to be set apart from ordinary men and endowed with supernatural power."[1315] Burrows says of the Essenes, "The authority for the interpretation is found in a new revelation given to the leader of the sect, the teacher of righteousness, who is called 'the priest into whose heart God put wisdom to explain all the words of his servants the prophets, through whom God declared all the things that are coming upon his people and his congregation.'"[1316] Clearly, given his frequent references to the prophets and his application of their ideas to first-century Israel, Jesus allowed his followers to treat his message in the same way.

For both Essenes and Christians, says Vermes, "the phrase 'New Covenant'"—suggesting a new relationship between God and his people—"even became part of the idiom of the sect[s]."[1317] According to Russell, the Teacher of Righteousness taught the Essenes "a new interpretation of the Scriptures and bound them together by a 'new covenant' which pledged them to obedience to the Law of God until the dawning of the messianic age." Their new understanding "made clear to them the part they had to play in the fulfillment of God's purpose for their generation."[1318] The Pharisees, without using the phrase "the New Covenant" to describe themselves, nevertheless believed that the Torah and the other works of the Bible required continuous review. All three groups in effect reinterpreted the law because they believed that they alone understood it correctly. As Burrows explains: "The teacher of righteousness claimed, no doubt, as Jesus did, that the new revelation given to him explained and perfected the revelation in the Scriptures."[1319]

Candidates for admission to the Qumran sect had to demonstrate their understanding of the Torah and their commitment to its laws. And members were regularly examined for obedience and conformity. In fact, says Burrows, the Essenes took these requirements so seriously "that a special place was set aside for the purpose of" study and interpretation.[1320] Despite their extreme devotion to Torah studies, however, Burrows suggests that, among the first-century Jewish sects, the Essenes at Qumran were not the most radical: "There is nothing in the Dead Sea Scrolls approaching the radical interpretation of the law given by Jesus, who made everything hang on Deuteronomy 6:5 and Leviticus 19:18. There are sayings of the rabbis, in fact, which come much closer to the teaching of Jesus at this point than anything in the scrolls."[1321] Among the "striking similarities" between Essenes and Christians, Cohen mentions the fact that in both groups "[p]roperty is held in common, violators of the rules are punished, the group is controlled by a board of leaders, lots are used in the selection process, [and] entrants into the group require 'conversion.'" In fact, besides other similarities of "attitude," "doctrine," and "practice," both groups "attempted to create a utopian community."[1322]

Both the Essenes and Christians also justified their ongoing reinterpretation of the Jewish Bible by claiming to have immediate access to God's word and will through the Holy Spirit. Hannah K. Harrington says that to the Essenes, the Holy Spirit offered them not only purification from sin but also "power, both physical and moral." More to the point, they believed that "holiness is also the vehicle for divine revelation": "Like atonement, revelation comes through the Holy Spirit."[1323] References to the Holy Spirit appear in several Qumranite hymns, including Hymn 21: "And I know through the understanding which comes from Thee, that in Thy goodwill towards [ashes Thou hast shed] Thy Holy Spirit [upon me] and thus drawn me near to understanding Thee."[1324] Thus, Harrington adds, "According to the Rule of the Community, the sectarians spent one-third of each night studying the Torah," evidently in the hope that they might receive "a new revelation from God."[1325]

In Acts of the Apostles, Luke attributes every revelation of God's purpose for the Christian-Jewish community to the work of the Holy Spirit. Indeed, according to Howard Clark Kee and his co-writers, "The Spirit is the effective power in enabling the ministry of the community to perform its work." It is "the chief agent of the achievement of God's purpose in this Age."[1326] Thus, while Matthew and Mark use the phrase only five or six times, Luke uses it more than a dozen times in his Gospel and three dozen times in Acts of the Apostles, where the Holy Spirit is said to come to all converts to

Christianity and, indeed, is the sign by which their acceptance by God is demonstrated. Burrows comments, "The statement of the Manual of Discipline that at the end of this age God will cleanse man by sprinkling upon him the spirit of truth recall's John's proclamation that the Messiah will baptize his people with the Holy Spirit."[1327]

By contrast, the Pharisees did not justify their new interpretations of Scripture on the basis of revelations from God. As Meier says, "[T]hey openly admitted that some of their legal views and practices were not to be found as such in the written Mosaic Law, that such practices were instead venerable 'traditions' that had been handed down by the 'fathers' or the 'elders,' and that such practices nevertheless were God's will for all Israel."[1328] Apart from the claim that there was an unwritten (oral) tradition that came from God at the same time as the written tradition, the Pharisees also embraced the idea that none of the traditional laws, written or oral, were sufficient in themselves but had to be adapted to changing conditions. Specifically, Meier continues, "In the face of a perceived threat" from the Hellenizing Seleucids in the second century BC, "the Pharisees emphasized the zealous and detailed study of the Mosaic Law, the careful observance of legal obligations in concrete areas of life such as tithing, purity laws . . . , the keeping of the Sabbath, marriage and divorce, and temple ritual."[1329]

To John Bowker, the Pharisees' focus on holiness, which they shared with other contemporary Jewish sects, mandated this intense concentration on study and interpretation and enabled them to acquire an influence over their fellow Jews that the Essenes and early Christians were unable to match: "If all the people were to achieve holiness as Torah defines it, it was essential that the definitions of Torah should be both intelligible and applicable. That they should be intelligible led to the wide extension of education, and of the synagogue itself, in the Hakamic movement [i.e., as the later Rabbis referred to the Pharisees]; that they should be applicable meant a vigilant and ever-recurring attention to the ways in which the written text of Torah could be brought to bear on situations or circumstances which had not obtained at the time of Moses."[1330] In short, the Pharisees embraced the relatively modern idea that the biblical text, for the delineation and explanation of which they were primarily responsible, had to be reinterpreted continuously because its meaning—its applicability—was assumed to be altered by changing circumstances: new political, social, and economic realities. According to Burrows, the Pharisees "applied and adapted [the law] to changing conditions and enlarged areas of life," which "was done by the development of the oral tradition."[1331]

Significantly, as Russell says, "By teaching and interpreting the Torah, both written and oral, and by applying it to every-day life [the Phasisees] 'democratized religion', making it personal and operative in the experience of the common people."[1332] Thus, like the Essenes at Qumran, the Pharisees dedicated themselves to the study of the Law, which, Schiffman notes, they saw "as a religious value." By means of studying and teaching, they not only "learn[ed] how to fulfill the divine will, but also participate[d] in the ongoing handing down of the tradition." Heirs of the Pharisees, the Rabbis even more strongly emphasized the religious meaning of Torah study because for them, after the destruction of the Temple, "study replaced sacrifice as a form of worship alongside prayer," by which means it eventually became "central to the whole of Jewish life." At this time, Schiffman adds, "when [rabbinic Judaism] became a mass movement seeking to gain the adherence of all Jews, it steadily popularized the idea that Torah study was an act of worship."[1333] As Cohen puts it: "Gradually, . . . Torah study became an end in itself . . . In any case, this idea had a profound influence on the Judaism of the Second Temple and rabbinic periods. Its ultimate expression is the ideal of the sage who meditates on the words of the Lord day and night . . . It is the basis of rabbinic piety."[1334]

Burrows comments, "The rabbis"—following the practice of their predecessors—"also, while claiming no such revelation [as that claimed by the Essenes and the Christians], felt that what they taught was the true meaning of the law, although, more or less consciously, they actually added much that was new."[1335] As Schiffman explains, when the rabbis succeeded the Pharisees in the post-Revolt years, they not only preserved the tradition they inherited from the Pharisees, they rendered it useful and enduring by continuing the practice of examining the Torah in order to make it relevant: "This openness to debate allowed for the development of an interpretation of Judaism for each new generation. The adaptation of Talmudic law and thought to later circumstances was the genius of the rabbis who studied and taught the Torah of Israel. It was the rabbis of the Talmud who ensured that its message would continue to resonate among the Jewish people to the present day."[1336] Lest the innovations represented by the oral law be taken to mean that they departed from mainstream Judaism, however, Meier says that the "basic elements of [the Rabbis'] thinking were something they held in common with almost all Jews."[1337]

It can be argued that, without either an official doctrine or an established authority capable of formulating one, Jews felt free to create their own versions of Judaism and consequently embraced a surprising variety of religious beliefs. R. Travers Herford says that "there was no requirement of doctrinal uniformity." In fact, "[t]here was never any idea of working out a consistent system of theological doctrine."[1338] However, it is clear that the motivation for developing such different ideas was not merely the desire for self-expression and the freedom to speak or write publicly without risk of punishment. A deeper and more pervasive imperative was, as I suggested above, the desire to obey the law as an expression of carrying out *the will of God*.

Brueggemann reminds us that the pervasive practice of interpretation among the various sects of intertestamental Judaism had this goal in mind: "Thus it is clear that while the Ten Commandments provide the absolute, nonnegotiable foundation of covenantal ethics, that nonnegotiable foundation receives, in the tradition, a dynamic afterlife *whereby the will and rule of YHWH, Lord of the covenant, is kept pertinent and germane to every circumstance of this alternative community of covenantal obedience*." In other words, Brueggemann says later, "Israel understood that *Torah must be interpreted* because it is a living command of a living God, and therefore interpretation is witness to the process of Torah itself."[1339]

As I suggested earlier, in the first century AD the ancient Jews found themselves faced with an even more compelling reason for studying the Mosaic Law than the need to keep it up to date. Indeed, the same reason that inspired apocalypticism, messianism, and rebellion also drove the Jews of that time to figure out what God actually wanted from his people. That is, they had begun to realize—increasingly as the centuries passed—that the dire political, social, and economic situation in which they found themselves was a consequence not only of changes beyond their control but also of their failure to carry out God's will. And, in this regard, the other problem that confronted them was the need to determine where they had gone wrong and how, exactly, they could recover their self-determination, reestablish their relationship to God, and regain their collective and individual ability to do what God demanded. In short, it was important not only to *know* the will of God, particularly as his will could be understood in the context of contemporary circumstances. It was also—and perhaps even more—important to *do* the will of God as it had not been done for centuries.

Chief among the concerns of the Jews of the intertestamental period was the fact that they resided in what Anthony J. Saldarini calls "an agrarian society which itself was part of a large agrarian, bureaucratic and partly commercialized aristocratic empire" and which was "marked by a very steep hierarchy and great inequality with control and wealth in the hands of a very few."[1340] Thus, among the factors that encouraged the ancient Jews to reexamine their prospects, William R. Herzog II mentions "the harsh political realities of colonial occupation and the remorseless oppression and exploitation of peasants inherent in the conditions of Roman, Herodian, and temple domination." The temple, Herzog later explains, "became a political power center that used its resources against the very people it was intended to serve."[1341] Putting the situation of first-century Palestine into a larger historical context, John Dominic Crossan says that "peasant resistance tends to develop more and more intensely as agrarian empires become more and more commercialized . . . Such was the status of the Roman Empire at the time of Augustus's peace and prosperity"—clearly two features that characterized the lives of the haves at the time, but not the lives of the have-nots.

Thus, Crossan concludes, "I understand, even at this point in the discussion, why relations between imperial Romans and colonial Jews in and around the Jewish homeland might become both desperate and disastrous."[1342] Burton L. Mack argues, similarly, that the Romans helped bring "to an end the civilizations of the ancient near east that had been in place for three millennia or more." In effect, "their contribution to the well-being of peoples in the Levant was a soulless superimposition of law and order" that led to "an erosion of illustrious traditions" and "a fragmentation of societies."[1343] According to R. David Kaylor, the commercialization of property resulted in devastating changes, including increased wealth and power among the rich and influential; growing impoverishment of small landowners because of high taxes and exploitative lending practices; government expropriation of peasant-owned land; widespread banditry and foreign invasions; and the inevitable and growing opposition between rich and poor.[1344]

Particularly galling to the ancient Jews, says S. G. F. Brandon, was "the basic conflict between the idea of Israel as a theocracy and the fact of Israel as the possession of the emperor of Rome," which was "the setting of politico-religious tension and unrest, exploding often in armed revolt," during the first-century.[1345] According to William K. Klingaman, this was "a place and time of enormous religious ferment, when zealous Jewish nationalists were searching anxiously for the messiah who would lead them out of their bondage to the heathen of Rome" and when everyone and everything "were surging toward the flash point."[1346] As N. T. Wright observes, "They were fed up with their own 'kings' . . . They saw no prospect of any human leader arising from such quarters to do what had to be done, to fight the battle, to overthrow the pagans, to cleanse and restore the Temple, to establish the long-awaited rule of justice and peace."[1347] Clearly, since they found themselves in an intolerable situation, the Jews asked where they had gone astray—what they had done wrong. They concluded that they were suffering because of their sins, as the prophets alleged and as subsequent leaders and writers—including Ezra, Nehemiah, and the authors of 2 Kings, the Psalms of Solomon, 2 Baruch, and both 1 and 2 Esdras—reiterated.[1348]

Yet, as early in their history as the destruction of the first Temple, notes Parini, the loss "was irreparable and seemed to contradict everything God had foretold in the Holy Scriptures about the triumph of Israel over its enemies, forcing a crisis of confidence, even a crisis of faith," out of which "came many of the mournful psalms and lamentations of the Hebrew Bible."[1349] Centuries later, in the time of Jesus, says C. H. Dodd, Galilee was still "a hotbed of Jewish disaffection."[1350] Morton Scott Enslin says that, before Herod's reign Galilee was "a turbulent place, seething with discontent," and continued to be a "hotbed of incipient rebellion, which produced "militant nationalists," who "hated Rome."[1351]

Ben Witherington III comments, "Jewish blood began to boil long before it began to be spilled in large quantities."[1352] Like Herzog, Klingaman calls ancient Palestine a "powder keg."[1353] Thus, according to John Dominic Crossan, "there were constant signs of lower-class resistance to Roman imperial power in the Jewish homeland" from the time of Herod's death at the end of the first century BC to the Jewish Revolt of AD 66.[1354] Judea, too, says Schiffman, was in a "difficult economic and political situation," as was all of the Jewish homeland: "Economic decline proceeded quickly, as did the activities of the growing rebel factions. Anarchy was fast approaching, and soon the nation would be aflame with rebellion and then destruction."[1355] For many, however, the question remained unanswered: What could be done, if anything, to ameliorate these unendurable circumstances?

According to Mack, as passages from 2 Baruch and 2 Esdras remind us, the postwar apocalypses of the late first century AD were "full of laments over Jerusalem as a desolate city, expressions of despair in the face of God's incomprehensible failure to protect it, struggles with guilt for the sins that surely must have been the cause of the disaster, and prayers that cry out for some way to imagine a future for Israel despite the destruction of the city."[1356] Feeling desperate, confused, and yet, hopefully and presumably, fairly treated by the God of Justice, the ancient Jews could only be certain that that they had to change and hope that the God of the Prophets had not finally and irreversibly abandoned them, but, as the prophets argued, had only severely chastised them, as George F. Moore explains: "God's end in punishment was not to make the sinner suffer what he deserved, but through suffering to bring him to penance and amendment. So the prophets had taught both for the nation and the individual, and so Judaism understood."[1357]

No doubt many Jews accepted the responsibility that they and their ancestors had either negligently or deliberately flouted God's will, and many Jews felt (in a state of abject incomprehension) that they had evidently failed to understand exactly what God's expectations were. The former concluded that they could reverse the downward spiral of their lives only by rededicating themselves to obeying the Jewish Law. And the latter concluded that they could achieve the same end only by first determining what the Law required them to do and then, of course, doing it. In either case, following the Law, in the fullest sense of the words, required intensive examination because, in the wake of more than half a millennium of foreign domination, economic decline, and religious confusion, it was obvious that the Law had yet to be obediently and effectively carried out, which occurred either because they had simply failed to live up to its demands or because they had failed to interpret it accurately, understand it completely, and follow it faithfully. As Kugel says, speaking of the tragedy of 526 BC, "there came a moment in history when interpretation of [the ancient] texts suddenly became a great preoccupation in Israel, and a whole new kind of interpreter first emerged"[1358]—particularly one who was less likely to accept traditional meanings and far more likely to work harder, use new methods, and come to revolutionary conclusions.

Thus, on one hand, Schiffman can celebrate the flurry of activity in the area of Bible study and interpretation that characterized the period of Jewish history after the Maccabean revolt as a sign of intellectual vitality and moral rigor : "[T]he second commonwealth period was an era in which Jews engaged in a vibrant religious life based on the study of Holy Scriptures, interpretation of Jewish law, the practice of ritual purity, and messianic aspirations" that characterized the age. Schiffman continues, "Varying interpretations of the biblical tradition were constantly interacting with each other and with Hellenistic notions in the marketplace of ideas." On the other hand, however, it is also important to recognize the dire state of affairs that prompted this intellectual frenzy. As Schiffman later says, this was a "period of decline and unrest": "[T]he difficult economic and political situation in Judea . . . tended to encourage the rise of religious movements."[1359]

The Evolution of Love

As Burrows notes (and as I mentioned earlier), for the Essenes at Qumran, obedience was less a response to the law than "a response to a divine revelation." However, it was "not a revelation of truth to be believed but a revelation of duties to be done." The importance of this knowledge, which had "no saving power in itself," was that it allowed its possessor to avoid judgment: "[I]t is not the immediate vehicle of deliverance," but "the answer to the question, 'What must I do that I may inherit eternal life.'"[1360] For the Pharisees, according to Herford, "[t]he one thing needful . . . was to put the teaching into practice, to lay the whole stress on *doing* the divine will, to make the Torah, which contained the essence of revelation, the one supreme concern for the Jewish community, and for every single member of it." Their goal was simply to "teach . . . practical religion, the doing of right actions for the service of God and . . . man"—that is, "to serve God . . . with greater wisdom, more enlightened conscience, and more devoted will, in the circumstances of their own time."[1361] Furthermore, according to Benjamin Uffenheimer, presumably all Jews understood that words like *mishpat*, *sedek*, and *tsedakah* were "no mere pneumatic, spiritual immaterial concepts. On the contrary, they [were] functional derivatives of concrete ways of behavior: that *mishpat* and *sedakah* [did] not mean 'justice' and 'righteousness' as such, but 'just deeds' or 'righteous deeds.'"[1362]

The point is that the Essenes, like their contemporaries, understood that faith was only a beginning, that knowledge was only a path or a way, and that only *doing*—that is, actually carrying out God's will—satisfied both God's wishes and human needs. As Craig A. Evans says: "The Judaisms of Qumran, the Rabbis, and the community of James [i.e., the early Christians] recognized the authority of the Scripture of Israel and believed that obedience to it was requisite for salvation. It was not enough to know the Law; it was necessary to 'do' it. It was not enough to believe certain things; it was necessary to live them."

To demonstrate precisely which biblical verses might have motivated the Essenes at Qumran, Evans cites five passages from Deuteronomy (27–32) in which the command to "do all the words of this law" clearly indicates that faith must culminate in action. For example, Moses says in 31:12, "Assemble the people, men and women, and little ones and the sojourner within your town, that they may hear and learn to fear the LORD your God and be careful to do all the words of this law." Referring to a passage from *The Damascus Rule* (III), Evans notes the quotation of part of a passage from Leviticus: "You shall therefore keep my statutes and my ordinances, which a person shall do and so have life in them."[1363]

Evidently, the desire to make the laws of the Covenant practical and effective endured into the post-Revolt world of the Pharisees who gathered in Yavneh after the war. Jacob Neusner says that their leader, Yohanan ben Zakkai, laid out a plan for "the social and political life of the Land of Israel." The rabbi's goal was "to provide the people with a source of genuine comfort" without promising, apocalyptically, that their suffering would soon end. Rather, he showed them "how they might extricate themselves from the consequences of their sin" not "through eschatological vision, but through concrete actions in the workaday world." Since they could no longer count on God, they were compelled to obey his will: "Yohanan called on the people to *achieve* a better fortune through their own efforts." Thus, as we have seen, he taught "that sacrifice greater than the Temple's must characterize the life of the community. If one wants to do something for God in a time when the Temple is no more, the offering must be the gift of selfless compassion."[1364]

Evans says that although the Rabbis were "not as emphatic" on this subject as the Essenes, they nevertheless were similarly committed to the principle of doing over knowing, or, rather, the principle that knowing is important only insofar as it leads to doing. Evans quotes Rabbi Eleazar as saying, "When Israel gave precedence to 'we will do' . . . over 'we will listen' . . . , a heavenly voice went forth and exclaimed to them, Who revealed to my children this secret, which is employed by the ministering angels." Then Eleazar refers to Psalm 103: "Bless the Lord, you angels of his: You mighty in strength who *fulfill his word*, who listen to the voice of his word" (v. 20).[1365] Bowker points out that the Pharisees were also driven to give "extreme attention to exegesis" because they assumed that "Torah, if given by God, must be able to be kept." That is, knowledge was necessary because doing was imperative.[1366] Herford says that the Pharisees believed that "the highest duty of man is to *do* the will of God."[1367]

What God *willed or wanted*, according to many first-century Jews, is demonstrated by what all of the members of these sects tried to do in the first century AD. Specifically, their consciousness of individual and collective failure to follow God's will in the past, their keen awareness of the consequences of that failure, their unprecedented commitment to determine to their own satisfaction what God actually wanted them to do, and their unflinching willingness to act on that determination led these ancient Jews to do two things. First, they were committed to embracing the laws of the Covenant as what N. T. Wright calls "the foundations" on which life might be lived obediently and (therefore) perfectly. Second, they were committed to establishing the only means by which the Covenant could be enacted and enforced: that is, a covenant-based community.[1368]

In this way, Essenes, Christian Jews, and Pharisees seem to have assumed that nothing less would satisfy God and that nothing less would provide human beings with citizenship in the Kingdom of God. Robert N. Bellah argues that the tradition passed on in Deuteronomy from the prophets to the Rabbis and which "gave the religion of ancient Israel its fundamental definition" was at its "very core" nothing more or less than "the Covenant": "[W]hat emerged was a new political form, a people in covenant with God," based on the revelation at Mt. Sinai and spelled out, in terms of its "implications," in Deuteronomy. In fact, the agreement between humanity and God clearly indicated that this concept of society was "something new."[1369]

For many scholars, the covenant relationship between God and his people—evolving through several stages, from the pre-exilic to the post-exilic period—is the

The Evolution of Love

central concept in ancient (as well as modern) Judaism. As I explained in chapter 4, the Covenant, based on a contractual agreement, states that God's obligation is to support and guide his people, as God does comprehensively at Mt. Sinai, repeatedly through his prophets, and eternally in his Torah and the other books of the Jewish Bible. Correspondingly, it is his people's obligation to appreciate God's devotion and attention, follow his teaching, and bring to fruition his plan for earthly salvation—that is, prosperity and security: "You shall be careful to do therefore as the Lord your God has commanded you . . . You shall walk in all the way which the Lord your God has commanded you, that you may live, and that it may go well with you, and that you may live long in the land which you shall possess" (Deut 5:32–33; see also 7:12–16; 8:7–10; 11:8–15).

John H. Tullock calls the Sinai experience "Israel's Constitutional Convention": "For Israel, the Ten Commandments were the constitution, the laying down of the basic principles from which a legal system would develop."[1370] Tullock reminds us that the commandments themselves are "apodictic"—that is, "stated as absolutes, . . . they allow for no contradictions."[1371] Brueggemann says that the commandments "provide the absolute, nonnegotiable foundation of covenantal ethics."[1372] Why the Covenant and its laws should be understood in this revolutionary way is explained by Kaufmann: "For the first time morality was represented as a prophetic revelation, an expression of the supreme moral will of God."[1373] As Alan Segal says, however, it was not simply "the divine origin of the law" that was "unusual." Rather, "the Hebrew concept of covenant was unique" because "[i]t conceived of the entire universe as under the sway of one deity." Furthermore, "[t]he law was not simply revealed; it was based upon an actual agreement and guaranteed by an actual oath sworn between the people and that God."[1374]

If Sinai was Israel's constitutional convention, then of course, the Torah was Israel's constitution. Shaye Cohen says that, unlike the Greeks and Romans, who regarded Homer's works as "guide[s] to life," the ancient Jews thought of the Torah as "a text to be absorbed and 'internalized'" because it provided them with a constitutional foundation for the community as a whole. Homer's readers did not see his works "as eternally valid and existentially meaningful." The readers of the Torah, however, believed that "it was the word of God, whose study brought one closer to God, and the observance of whose dictates brought immeasurable rewards." Of all of the books of the Bible, Cohen adds, "[t]he Torah ranked (and ranks) the highest. It was canonized first and placed at the head. It provided the texts for the weekly lections in the synagogue. It was written by Moses, the servant of God and the greatest of the prophets."[1375] And it was indispensable for the creation of the kind of community that the Covenant demanded.

Ultimately, of course, the actions of humanity must eventuate in the creation of what Martin Buber calls "a true community," which in Deuteronomy requires elected leaders and impartial judges (1:13, 17), generosity to the poor (15:7–17), justice for litigants (16:20; 19:15–21), kindness to servants (24:14–15), and charity for "the sojourner, the fatherless, and the widow" (24:17–22). As Buber says, Judaism ultimately and only resides in *communities that realize the will of God*: "The Divine . . . attains its earthly fulness only where, having awakened to an awareness of their universal being, individual beings open themselves to one another, disclose themselves to one another." This is "because the true place of realization is community," which is "that relationship in which the Divine comes to its realization between men."[1376] Kaufmann comments: "The Sinaitic covenant superimposes upon the ancient individual obligation a new, national one. Morality ceases being a private matter. Because the covenant was accepted en masse, by all, all became responsible for its observance." It involved "not only the cult but the structure and rules of society."[1377] As John Barton explains it, "the Commandments . . . see the good life as one lived in a community in an atmosphere of mutual respect and toleration, not encroaching on each other's legitimate spheres."[1378]

God justifies the need for community in two ways. First, his people can retain his support and guidance only if they are as holy as he is: "[B]e holy, for I am holy" (Lev 11:44; see also 19:2; 20:7). Thus, because God "is not partial and takes no bribe," and "executes justice for the fatherless and the widow, and loves the sojourner, giving him food and clothing" (Deut 10:12–22; Lev 19:10–17), so must his followers (cf. Deut 1:17; 24:19).[1379] And, second, they must obey his commandments out of gratitude for his past acts of mercy and compassion: "For I am the Lord who brought you out of the land of Egypt" (Lev 11:45). Thus, he reminds his people that they should love the sojourner because he loved them when they were "sojourners in Egypt." (Deut 10:19; Lev 19:33–34). In sum, he "set his heart in love upon [their] fathers," and they, in turn should simply return that love by extending it to the rest of humanity, especially the most helpless and vulnerable.

To become "a people of God," Buber says, has nothing to do with belief. Rather, it requires "that the attributes of God," which God himself wishes to be realized—that is, "justice and love"—"are to be made effective in [the people's] own life, in the lives of its members with one another; justice realized in the indirect mutual relationships of these individuals; love in their direct mutual relationships rooted in their personal existence." Buber adds in another essay: "Jewish religiosity is built neither on doctrine nor on ethical prescription, but on a fundamental perception that gives meaning to man: that one thing above all is needed. This perception is transformed into a demand (*Forderung*) wherever religiosity is community-forming and religion-founding, wherever it moves from the life of individual man into the life of the community. The founding of the Jewish religion and all its essential revolts are marked by this demand and the struggle for it."[1380]

In this regard, there was no distinction between the apocalyptists and those who were less confident about God's ultimate (or, at least, near-term) transformation of the world. *All* of the groups we have been discussing appear to have been committed to both covenant and community as if their destiny was in their own hands.

For what is true across the board, from Essenes to Zealots and from Christians to Pharisees, these Jewish sects assumed that their single most important responsibility was *to do the will of God*. And this was the case whether they believed that this commitment to action would, as the Essenes and Christian Jews believed, qualify them for membership in the coming Kingdom of God; or, as the Zealots believed, God would come to their aid if they put their lives on the line;[1381] or, as the Pharisees believed, without the certainty of liberation embraced by the other groups, it was the best they could do under the circumstances.

Perfectionism

Shaye Cohen argues that the Jews of the post-exilic period, being more fully conscious of the need to make themselves "a 'holy' people," as the Torah itself demands, not only followed its dictates with renewed dedication but actually added to the "many regulations" that "govern[ed] the daily behavior of the Israelite": "To better achieve this objective, the Jews of the Second Temple period developed new rituals, broadened the application of many of the laws of the Torah, and in general intensified the life of service to God." Among the more important changes, based on the Shema's "metaphorical demand for constant meditation on God's commandments," were daily prayer, "regular Torah study," and both attention to and expansion of "[t]he laws governing the Sabbath, diet, and purity." "The goal of these innovations," Cohen explains, "was threefold: (a) to ensure that every moment of a Jew's life was spent in service to God; (b) to bring the Jew into contact with the sacred; and (c) to democratize religion."[1382]

Furthermore, Cohen adds, these changes were implemented even more stringently among the Jewish sects.[1383] In a state of disillusionment and anxiety, these groups and their members re-examined the sacred texts of their faith in order to discover a way out of their dilemma. In doing so, they developed a variety of solutions to their problem—some of which were based on new interpretations of what it meant to be Jewish, including new ideas not only about the role of God in the lives of humanity but also about the responsibilities of human beings in relation to God's demands and expectations. Clearly, among the solutions were such extreme actions as the many small-scale rebellions and two large-scale revolts against the Romans in the nearly century and a half after the death of Herod the Great. Far less violent but extreme in many ways, as we shall see in the following pages, were the many attempts—by, for example, Christians, Essenes, and Pharisees—not only to create communities that implemented the covenant rules of Exodus, Leviticus, and Deuteronomy, but also to demand from the members of such communities such a high degree of obedience that it can legitimately be called perfectionism.

It is important to recognize that in the passages I cited in chapter 6 all of these groups revealed a strong desire to achieve both goals. First, although the Essenes were far more highly organized and much stricter in their obedience to the laws of Judaism than the early Christians, both movements are notable for their attempt to create a community of kindred spirits.[1384] And it is likely that any Jew who felt the need to enact the will of God on the highest possible level understood that it could not happen without the freedom that exists only in a community with a high degree of self-determination. Clearly, the Zealots carried this idea to its logical extreme in seeking to terminate the Roman occupation. The Essenes went to Qumran to fulfill the same end without the violence that the Zealots were willing to inflict and endure. And, like the Pharisees, various Christian-Jewish groups, including *The Didache* sectarians, created non-separatist communities that maintained the Law of Moses as much as possible under rather difficult circumstances. The massive Jewish support for the revolts of AD 66 and AD 132, with their massive suffering and destruction, demonstrates how strongly this covenantal objective remained in the hearts of first- and second-century Jews.

Second, in the communities these sects created, at least some of the covenantal laws of the Torah were more seriously enforced than they were in the larger society. As Dale C. Allison notes, the millenarian movements in particular were "revivalistic," meaning that, in any age, they typically "deepen the piety of the faithful and stir up religious faith among the indifferent."[1385] Although John P. Meier argues that the "eschatological radicalism" of the Essenes and Christians sometimes "leads to opposite outcomes," sometimes "both appear extremely stringent and demanding on the same issue." Within that limitation, Meier agrees with other scholars that "Jesus and Qumran share an ethical radicalism arising from their intense eschatological expectations."[1386] In many cases, even in the absence of the political power that was necessary to establish Covenant-sanctioned political institutions, these communities managed to enforce some Covenant-sanctioned economic principles and create some Covenant-sanctioned economic institutions—all expressive of the Covenant ideal of distributive economics and, more broadly, in the service of social justice.

As Millar Burrows has noted, both the Essenes and the Christian Jews, particularly, tried and to a large degree succeeded in establishing a sacred community that made every possible effort to live according to their own principles: "More important than the form of organization is what may be called the church, the concept of a spiritual group, the true people of God, distinct from the Jewish nation as such. In the Qumran community's concept of itself can be seen an approach to this, doubtless without a full realization of all its implications; but the Christian church itself did not at once realize the full implications of the church idea." Later, Burrows adds: "Salvation means for the covenanters, as for Paul, not only forgiveness and cleansing from sin but also participation in a spiritual fellowship. One of the Thanksgiving Psalms speaks of 'the eternal assembly,' 'the army of the saints,' and 'communion with the congregation of the sons of heaven.' The prominence of this idea in the New Testament hardly needs to be emphasized."[1387] Edward Schillebeeckx says that the formation of sects "led to more and more groups of separatists, each determined to be 'even holier' and each regarding itself as the sole legitimate heir to the true people of God."[1388] According to Gerd Theissen: "In Palestine every renewal movement wanted to make the better Israel a reality. Each of them had to demote the other Jews to the status of Israelites of the second rank, or even equate them with the Gentiles."[1389]

Like the Essenes at Qumran, the Christian Jews formed a tight-knit community after Jesus' ascension: "All these with one accord devoted themselves to prayer" (1:14). Called "the brethren" by Peter, the disciples cast lots to restore their number to twelve, received the Holy Spirit on the day of the Pentecost, and "attend[ed] the temple together" (1:15, 26; 2:4, 46). In these ways, "all who believed were together," being "of one heart and soul" (2:44; 4:32). Clearly, the Christian Jews recalled that when Jesus was told, in the Gospel of Mark, that his mother and brothers were looking for him, he said to the "crowd . . . sitting about him": "Who are my mother and my brothers . . . Here are my mother and my brothers! *Whoever does the will of God is my brother, and sister, and mother*" (3:31–35; my emphasis; see also Luke 11:27–28). Schillebeeckx explains, "What Jesus lived by was the Jewish passion for searching out God's will in everything."[1390] According to C. H. Dodd, "His aim was to constitute a community worthy of the name of a people of God, a divine commonwealth," which would be based on an absolute ethic determined by the coming of the kingdom of God": "the idea of selfless service as applying not only to the relations of individuals within the community, but also to the function of the community in the world."[1391]

Later, Jesus said that all of his followers were "brethren," who had "one Father, who is in heaven" (Matt 23:8–9). They might also have remembered Jesus' final request to his disciples in the Gospel of John: "This is my commandment, that you love one another as I have loved you" (15:12); or his prayer a few pages later: "I do not pray for these only, but also those who believe in me through their word, *that they may all be one* . . . The glory which thou hast given me I have given to them, that they may be one even as we are one, I in them and thou in me, *that they may become perfectly one*" (17:20–23; my emphasis). As Meier explains, "The historical Jesus was not intent on 'saving souls' in an individualistic sense but on regathering the whole of Israel in preparation for the final coming of God's kingdom." Although he was not interested in establishing, like the Essenes at Qumran, "a faithful remnant separated from the sinful mass of Israelites" (and although the concept of "a saving remnant" was embraced by some later Christians), Jesus' mission "focused on the entire people of God": "The corporate nature of his mission would necessarily raise the question of how the people of Israel . . . was to be ordered or governed in 'the last days.'"[1392]

Theissen says that "socio-political tensions in Palestine" led to "the imminent expectation of the kingdom of God" among "most of the renewal movements within Judaism," which in turn led to "a stricter interpretation of the Torah."[1393] Indeed, the principles embraced by both the Teacher of Righteousness and Jesus of Nazareth were extremely demanding—so much so that both moral leaders did not merely encourage their followers to obey the Mosaic Law, but also demanded that they live up to an ideal of perfection that goes far beyond anything that could be called obedience.[1394] In the

Sermon on the Mount, Jesus indicated exactly what he meant by exceeding the scribes and Pharisees: "You, therefore, must be perfect, as your heavenly Father is perfect" (Matt 5:48).[1395] Later in the Gospel of Matthew, to the young man who assured Jesus that he followed the commandments, Jesus said that obeying the Law of Moses was a beginning, but not enough: "*If you would be perfect*, go, sell what you possess and give it to the poor, and you will have treasure in heaven" (19:21; my emphasis). Jesus said to his disciples that nothing short of absolute selflessness was required of them: "So therefore, whoever of you does not renounce all that he has cannot be my disciple" (Luke 14:33). "If any man would come after me, let him deny himself and take up his cross and follow me" (Matt 16:24; Mark 8:34; Luke 9:23).[1396]

As Geza Vermes argues, "Jesus' religiousness, the piety peculiar to Jesus the religious man, is marked by a tendency to give more than is asked for, to probe deeper than expected, to risk more than is safe."[1397] In fact, as Jesus suggested when he asked his followers to "take up" their crosses, he meant that they should be ready to die: "If any one comes to me and does not hate" not only his entire family, but also "even his own life, he cannot be my disciple. Whoever does not bear his own cross and come after me, cannot be my disciple" (Luke 14:26–27; Matt 10:38). "For whoever would save his life will lose it, and whoever loses his life for my sake will find it. For what will it profit a man, if he gains the whole world and forfeits his life?" (Matt 16:25–26; 8:35–37; Luke 9:24–25; John 12:2). Thus, Jesus was not speaking figuratively when he told his disciples not to "fear those who kill the body but cannot kill the soul; rather fear him who can destroy both soul and body in hell" (Matt 10:28). As he says in the Gospel of John, "If they persecuted me, they will persecute you . . . [T]he hour is coming when whoever kills you will think he is offering service to God" (15:20, 16:2).

What Jesus was requiring of his followers was simply that they should rise to his own level of courage and commitment: "It is enough for the disciple to be like his teacher, and the servant like his master" (Matt 10:25).[1398] After all, this is how Jesus saw his own death in the Gospel of John: "Greater love has no man than this, that a man lay down his life for his friends. You are my friends if you do what I command you" (15:13–14). In requiring that his followers strictly obey every law, exceed all other Jews in righteousness, love everyone, avoid all negative emotions, and willingly accept the possibility of dying for their faith, Jesus was establishing a standard of behavior that E. P. Sanders calls "hothouse ethics," so called because such strict rules "require a special environment and do not do well in the everyday world," a point that Jesus himself fully understood. When, in the Gospel of John, Peter says to him, "Lord, . . . I will lay down my life for you," Jesus replies, "Truly, truly, I say to you, the cock will not crow, till you have denied me three times" (13:37–38). The kind of group that could possibly survive under such a regimen, Sanders continues, would have to be "a small sect that partially withdraws from the world, to which members make long-term commitments"—i.e., like the Essenes at Qumran. They can "take any manner of abuse and do without all but the bare necessities" because they believe "that at the end of this life they will gain the eternal kingdom."[1399]

Sanders's main point is that "[p]erfectionism requires either intense eschatological expectation or a small, disciplined community, or both (as in the sect associated with the Dead Sea Scrolls)." On the one hand, Sanders says that in the Sermon on the Mount Jesus is describing "the perfection of a disciplined community without eschatology." On the other hand, however, Sanders argues that Jesus demanded perfection only from his "disciples,"—i.e., his "immediate followers"—and based his appeal to his audience at large on "eschatological expectation": "In short, Jesus proclaimed the kingdom to all who would hear; he called only a few to a special life of discipleship."[1400] To Peter, who said to Jesus, "What then shall we have" after leaving "everything"—including especially family, home, and occupation—Jesus replied that "every one who has left houses or brothers or sisters or father or mother or children or lands, for my name's sake will receive a hundredfold, and inherit eternal life" (Matt 19:29). Specifically, he seems to have meant by this promise, at least as Matthew explains it, that the disciples alone would "sit on twelve thrones, judging the twelve tribes of Israel," accompanying "the Son of man [sitting] on his glorious throne" in the Kingdom of God (19:28).

Agreeing with Sanders, Gerd Theissen says, "Their *ethical radicalism* makes Jesus' sayings absolutely impracticable as a regulative for every-day behavior."[1401] Indeed, they were appropriate only for the "wandering charismatics" who were Jesus' first disciples and whose responsibility it was to travel all over Palestine, preaching, healing, and converting. Theissen says that Jesus' principal demands—"giving up home, family, possessions and protection"—were laid only on these men, who were distinguished from Jesus' other followers by his "call" and who remained "the decisive authorities at the time of the Didache (in the first half of the second century)." Jesus says to them, "[Y]ou will not have gone through all the towns of Israel before the Son of man comes" (Matt 10:23). Indeed, "[t]he vivid eschatological expectations of these early Christian wandering charismatics went along with their role as outsiders."[1402] After the Christian Jews moved out of Israel, however, and the leadership role of the wandering charismatics was taken over by the sedentary members of local Christian communities, the "radicalism of the Jesus movement" was no longer acceptable: "Rather, within these communities there arose a more moderate patriarchalism of love, oriented on the need for social interactions within the Christian community."[1403]

In *The Community Rule*, the Teacher of Righteousness, like Jesus, insists on perfection as well as obedience. He "admit[s] into the Community of Grace all those who have freely devoted themselves to *the observance of God's precepts*, that they may be joined to the counsel of God and may live *perfectly* before Him." Here, "they may purify their knowledge in *the truth of God's precepts* and order their powers according to *His ways of perfection*" (I; my emphasis; see also CR IX, XI). In the remainder of *The Community Rule*, "walk[ing] perfectly in all His ways" (II, III), members of the community are "reckoned among the perfect" (III) because they have undergone a process of cleansing, purification, expiation, and sanctification, which allows the Essenes to dwell in the "House of Perfection" (VIII). As the writer of *The Community Rule* Hymn emphasizes, however, the process of purification comes entirely from God: "In His hand are the perfection of my way and the uprightness of my heart." "[J]ustification is with God and perfection of way is out of his hand." In short, "without [him] no way is perfect."[1404]

To this end, as God's surrogates, senior members of the community are to "examine [junior members'] spirit and deeds yearly, so that each man may be advanced"—or demoted—"in accordance with his understanding and perfection of way" (V). When those who qualify for inclusion in the Council of the Community "have been confirmed for two years in perfection of way by the authority of the Community, they shall be set apart as holy with the Council" (VIII). At annual assemblies, members of the community "enter . . . ranked one after another according to the perfection of their spirit," including the priests, the Levites, and others, in descending order (II). At the end-time, God will purify, refine, cleanse, and "teach the wisdom of the sons of heaven to the perfect of way" (IV). As Hannah K. Harrington puts it, the Essenes at Qumran believed that "new revelation" would not come about as a result of "mere study and observation of the law." Rather, divine communication could occur only as a consequence of "more holiness." Thus, they "were attempting to live in a state of perfection so that divine holiness could endow them with both revelation and power."[1405]

As far as they were concerned, everything the Essenes at Qumran did was important because their good works, their rituals, and their asceticism—as well as what D. S. Russell calls "their meticulous study and practice of the law"—was not only an expression of their faith but their means of salvation: "They believed that their faithfulness as the representative remnant of Israel would bring about a vicarious expiation for their nation and would help to usher in the new age of which the prophets had spoken."[1406] The Christian Jews who wrote *The Didache* similarly considered their acts of worship and obedience to be salvific. Part of what Aaron Milavec calls their "apocalyptic scenario" is the expectation that "all human creation will come to the fire of testing, and many will fall away and perish, but those who endure in their faith will be saved by the curse itself" (16:5). At this moment, a banner will unfurl in heaven, a trumpet will sound, and the dead will be resurrected (16:6).[1407]

Like the Essenes, Jesus also strongly discouraged any kind of interest in or dependence on wealth or material possessions.[1408] In his most famous statement on the subject, he said: "Do not lay up for yourselves treasures on earth, . . . but lay up for yourselves treasures in heaven . . . For where your treasure is, there will your heart be also" (Matt 6:19–21). However, in addition to avoiding the worst aspects of materialism—that is, selfishness and greed—as the Jewish law required, Jesus encouraged his disciples to avoid these sins altogether by giving away their possessions entirely. That is, the true and final solution to the human dilemma was not merely being generous

The Evolution of Love

and charitable but eliminating every aspect of materialism completely: "No one can serve two masters . . . You cannot serve God and mammon" (Matt 6:24). As Meier explains, "By creating a stark opposition" between these two options, "Jesus personifies Mammon as a false god. He thus confronts every hearer with the primordial choice with which the prophets confronted Israel: the true God or the false idols—which will you worship and obey?" Indeed, Meier continues, "It is precisely Jesus' call to *total dedication* to the kingdom of God."[1409]

Thus, to his disciples who were asked by a needy person for a coat, Jesus advised, "[L]et him have your cloak as well." And "to him who begs from you" or "him who would borrow from you, . . . do not refuse" (Matt 5:40–42). Anything less might be acceptable according to ordinary moral standards, but not necessarily wholehearted—obedient, but imperfect. Indeed, Jesus "astonished" his disciples when he said, "Truly, I say to you, it will be hard for a rich man to enter the kingdom of heaven . . . Again I tell you, it is easier for a camel to go through the eye of a needle than for a rich man to enter the kingdom of God" (Matt 19:23–25; Mark 10:23–25). In Luke, Jesus said—after blessing the poor, the hungry, the sad, and the rejected—"But woe to you that are rich," "you that are full," "you that laugh now," and you who are spoken well of (6:20–26). Clearly, these people would not be welcome in the Kingdom of God. Speaking of such passages, Meier comments, "Rich people are thus in grave spiritual danger; their salvation is nothing short of a miracle possible to God alone."[1410]

Although Meier argues that Jesus did not require *all* of his followers to give up everything, some of them later understood his view of wealth in exactly the same way the Essenes understood the view of the Teacher of Righteousness—that is, as far as the evidence presented in Acts of the Apostles suggests.[1411] As I mentioned earlier and as Geza Vermes explains, the Essenes established a form of "religious communism" that "distinguished them markedly from their Jewish contemporaries" but "bears a strong resemblance to the custom adopted by the primitive Church of Jerusalem."[1412] Like the Essenes, the Christian Jews shared their wealth: They "had all things in common" (Acts 2:44). Indeed, "no one said that any of the things which he possessed was his own" (4:32). Like the young man whom Jesus commanded to sell everything he owned, "they sold their possessions and goods and distributed them to all, as any had need" (2:45). Like the sectaries at Qumran, "There was not a needy person among them, for as many as were possessors of lands or houses sold them, and brought the proceeds of what was sold and laid it at the apostles' feet; and distribution was made to each as any had need" (4:32–35). Vermes adds, "It may be remembered too that in the Fourth Gospel it is said explicitly that the community formed by Jesus and the apostles lived out of a common purse entrusted to the care of Judas (John xii, 6; xiii, 29)."[1413]

Some scholars agree with Meier that the early Christians established a *voluntary* sharing community in which members were urged but not required to contribute all of their wealth to a common fund. According to Joachim Jeremias, regarding the extent to which all of Jesus' followers were required to obey all of his anti-materialist demands, "the evidence of contemporary literature does not allow the 'all' to be pressed too far." For one thing, the "sharing of all things in common . . . was voluntary."[1414] At the other extreme, however, Brian Capper argues against "[t]he critical consensus" that is unwilling to accept the idea that "the earliest Christian community of goods in Acts 2–6 is a historically verifiable aspect of the life of the earliest Jerusalem community."[1415] Morton Scott Enslin refers to the economic system in Jerusalem as "a kind of communism" that was "in strict compliance with the teaching of Jesus," examples of which are "the more primitive form of the beatitudes in Luke (6:20–23)," "the story of Dives and Lazarus" in Luke 16:19–31, and Jesus' advice to "the Rich Young Ruler" in Mark 10:17–31.[1416] And Walter Bauer says that the Roman church, perhaps in imitation of the Jerusalem church, "assessed her members according to each individual's resources and ability to give."[1417]

Whether participation in this kind of program was mandatory or not, however, it survived into the second century, when *The Didache* community also adopted the Sermon on the Mount as its foundational document and created a sharing community.[1418] And Justin Martyr reports that he belonged to the same kind of community: "[W]e who once took pleasure in the means of increasing our wealth and property now bring what we have into a common fund and share with everyone in need."[1419] According to Richard A. Horsley and Neil Asher Silberman, "It is reasonable to assume that at least some of the diaspora assemblies of the Jesus movement, founded by apostles from Jerusalem, were based on a similar principle of sharing."[1420] In the fourth century AD, both St. John Chrysostom and St. Ambrose expressed a strong interest in reviving the economic ideals of the early Christians. And, later, St. Basil of Caesarea implemented these principles in the monastic movement he sponsored.[1421]

It is important to note that both the Essene community and the Christian Jews were guided in their commitment to economic equality by the Covenant Code. Crossan says, "What I see in both cases . . . is a thrust toward establishing sharing community in reaction against commercializing community—an effort made, of course, *to live in covenant with God.*" Furthermore, it was supposed to be a model, "an eschatological ideal" for all of Christendom.[1422] Speaking of the "primitive communism" of the Essenes, Horsley and Silberman argue that "donating all individual wealth and personal possessions to a communal treasury" was a "distinctively Judean practice."[1423] Meeks says that "Christians [who] established the practice of giving to those of the community who were needy " were "doubtless following Jewish models." [1424] After all, according to Maguire, "[t]he distinctive feature of Jewish justice is the stress on redistributive sharing and remedial systemic changes that favor the poor."[1425]

Theodor Gaster reminds us that some of the parallels that can be found in the Dead Sea Scrolls and the New Testament can be found "equally well" not only in the Talmud and the "non-canonical Jewish scriptures," but also in non-Jewish sources in the Near East.[1426] It is not surprising, therefore, to find similarities between the ideas of the Essenes and the Christians, on the one hand, and the Pharisees, on the other.

Nevertheless, it is instructive to recognize the large tract of common ground occupied by the latter group and the two former ones for several reasons. First, the Essenes at Qumran were wiped out in the Jewish Revolt of AD 66. Second, the Christian Jews eventually severed their ties to Judaism. And, third, in the absence of other sectarian groups in post-Revolt Palestine, the Pharisees, as Rabbis, had a stronger influence on the development of Judaism than any other ancient Jewish sect.

As Meier explains: "The burning of the temple in A.D. 70 meant the demolition of the power base of the priestly aristocracy. The capture of Jerusalem likewise entailed the slaughter or imprisonment of large numbers of priestly and lay aristocrats, many of whom were probably Sadducees . . . Qumran was also destroyed by the Romans in 68, and the Essenes as a distinct group disappeared from Judean society. The extremists among the rebels, such as the Zealots and the Sicarii, also perished . . . In short, the only Jewish group to survive intact with significant numbers and the respect of the common people was the Pharisees," who later developed into the Rabbis.[1427] Jacob Neusner comments, "Judaism as it is now known begins with the Pharisees of the two centuries before the destruction of Jerusalem and the Temple in 70 A.D."[1428]

As a result of these historical events, many of the ideas and ideals of the Essenes and Christians became, through the influence of the Pharisees, the core principles of later Judaism. Says Russell, "[T]he Pharisees created a spirit of true piety and devotion which deeply affected the lives of the people and developed a religious individualism which gave a new relevance to the Torah of God." For this and other reasons—such as standing as "a bulwark against the encroachments of Hellenism" and making the religion of the Jews "personal and operative in the experience of the common people"—the Pharisees "did more than any other party to determine the shape of Judaism in the years to come."[1429] Meier comments, "They represented one specific religious and political response to the crisis of Hellenization unleashed by Antiochus IV and his Jewish supporters, a crisis that continued into the reign of the Hasmonean princes and kings."[1430] Of course, the threat of Hellenism extended into the period of Roman domination and the kingship of Herod.

By the first century AD, when the Pharisees were contemporaries of the early Christians and the Qumran brotherhood, their "moral consciousness," in the words of R. Travers Herford, rested not merely on their opposition to Hellenism, but also on their commitment to "[s]uch virtues as kindness, sympathy, pity, [and] brotherly love." Both the Pharisees and the Rabbis, Herford continues, "sought to strengthen the factors which make for unity and peace amongst men—the sense of justice, truth, purity, brotherly love, sympathy, mercy, forbearance, and the rest—in a word, to raise the moral standard amongst their people from age to age."[1431] While acknowledging the differences between the Christians and the Pharisees, Meier says: "No doubt Jesus and the Pharisees would have agreed on many points: God's free election of Israel, his gift of the Law, the need to respond wholeheartedly to the Law's demands in one's everyday life, God's faithful guidance of Israel through history to a future consummation involving the restoration of Israel, a final judgment, the resurrection of the dead, and perhaps some sort of eschatological or messianic figure as God's agent in the end time."[1432]

Besides their embrace of covenantal standards, like the Essenes and Christians, the Pharisees also pursued perfection both in their study of the Torah and in their attempt to live uncompromisingly in accordance with its laws. As John Bowker explains, they were committed to "a vision of holiness—a vision of implementing what God required of his people if they were to *be* his people." This vision, as we have seen, "was shared by many other Jews," and summed up in the biblical formula "Be holy as I am holy." On the question of how to achieve that imitation of God, the Pharisees, like the Qumranites, decided that "holiness require[d] separation from uncleanliness and from anything which the Torah defines as imparting impurity."[1433]

However, unlike the Essenes and like the Christians, the Pharisees chose to live among other Jews because they believed that perfection was achievable by everyone. Consequently, says Bowker, "while others built walls on the shores of the Dead Sea, they built a fence around the Torah"—a scheme of interpretation, instruction, and action that would enable them to set an example and extend their influence to all others.[1434] Neusner explains that the Pharisees intended "to achieve elevation of the life of all of the people . . . to what the Torah had commanded: *You shall be a kingdom of priests and a holy people*. . . . Therefore the complicated and inconvenient purity laws were extended to the life of every Jew in his own home. The Temple altars would be replicated at the tables of all Israel."[1435]

Speaking of the Rabbis, who succeeded the Pharisees after the Revolt of AD 66, Neusner says, "Their religious programs consisted of, first, study of Torah . . . ; second, practice of the commandments of the Torah; and third, performance of good deeds." Indeed, in the wake of the destruction of the Temple in AD 70, speaking to "the surviving Pharisees of Jerusalem," Yohanan ben Zakkai argued that "the old order endures," by which he meant that "[t]he Lord still is served, sin is expiated, and reconciliation is achieved through the new sacrifice, which is deeds of lovingkindness: 'For we have another atonement, which is like sacrifice, and what is it? Deeds of lovingkindness, as it is said, For I desire mercy and not sacrifice' (Hos. 6:6)."[1436] In his study of the Mishnah, Neusner says that the entire document is given over to one dominant theme: "the sanctification of Israel, the people, in its everyday life." This requires "the ordering of all things on earth in conformity with . . . the model and pattern of Heaven, meaning, God's realm."[1437] As Lawrence Schiffman explains: "The Halakah [or Law] seeks to sanctify the Jew's entire life and his relations with God and his fellow man. In it and through it one achieves perfection in both ritual matters and ethical and moral concerns."[1438]

According to Herford, what is new in the Pharisaic attitude toward the law is this: "The one definite innovation which the Pharisees made was to lay the strongest possible emphasis on the doing of the will of God."[1439] And, with this in mind, Herford continues, "their aim was to apply a moral and religious discipline in order to train the people to live as the people of God ought to live." Following "the Halacha"—the law—"was intended to be the means towards the consecration of life, the discipline of the will, the guidance of action."[1440] Gaalyah Cornfeld says, "The early Pharisees, concerned with the practical application of the traditional law in relation to everyday problems, also took an active part in teaching the people."[1441] According to Josephus, "Pharisees generally required a training period of 12 months, and the Essenes likewise imposed a long novitiate."[1442] Bo Reicke says: "During a period of probation, . . . the [Pharisaic] novices had to demonstrate their obedience to the ritual prescriptions governing purity. Then, upon taking an oath, they were received into the association by a scribe—later by three associates (Josephus *Vit*. 10; Tosefta *Dem*. Ii. 3)."[1443]

Their obligation to teach was the justification for the Pharisees' extreme devotion to what Meier calls "the zealous and detailed study and practice of the Mosaic Law, the careful observance of legal obligations in concrete areas of life."[1444] To achieve this end, Herford says, the Pharisees implemented the idea that the laws of the Torah, all of which were 500 to 1,000 years old by the first century AD, had to be adapted to present circumstances in order to be useful to the present generation. This appeared to be the only way of guaranteeing that "God's will [could] be done by a whole people who really mean[t] it, and who [would] put the doing of it before everything else."[1445] That is, God's will could not be done unless it was understood in the context of current obstacles and possibilities—which, again, required yet another kind of perfectionism.

In addition, says Nahum N. Glatzer, like the Essenes at Qumran and the Christian Jews, "in the name of a universal and democratic priesthood of the people," the Pharisees formed "a religious community"—which one might call the only definitive expression of God's will, assuming, of course, that what God wants is a society that is able to operate on the basis of his favorite principles, justice and mercy. It was "not a state but a congregation of faith," which, "[c]onstituted as a community, . . . could survive the fall of the state."[1446] As Herford says later, the concept of "'individual responsibility,' for the Pharisee, included his responsibility as a member of the community." Thus, the Pharisaic teacher emphasized "the solidarity of Israel, the truth that 'no man liveth to himself alone,' and that Jews are members one of another. He taught that everyone, by his own faithful service to God, could thereby also serve his fellow man."[1447]

According to Herford, the morality of the Pharisees was strongly influenced by the Jewish prophets. In fact, "Pharisaism was the direct sequel and necessary completion of the work of the Prophets . . . If there had been no Prophets there would have been no Pharisees. If there had been no Pharisees, the Prophets would have 'perished as though they had never been.'"[1448] Although God, being moral, rewarded good deeds and punished bad ones, Herford argues that the Pharisees were influenced by "persuasion" and not "compulsion" and that their obedience was based on "love" rather than fear, particularly the love of children "doing the will of their Father in heaven."[1449] The Pharisees also "taught that repentance and forgiveness opened the way of escape from the grip of the past" and believed that the best guide to moral probity was God himself: "Man is made in the image and likeness of God; the perfect life of man would be the *Imitatio Dei*." That is, since "the moral nature in man" is "similar" to "the moral nature in God," man should merely follow God's example: "Ye shall be holy, for I am holy." After all, "the forgiveness of God meeting the repentance of man was the natural way in which love went out to meet love."[1450]

One of the few points on which the Pharisees departed from the theological program shared to a large degree by Essenes and Christians was their relative indifference to the entire body of apocalyptic literature. It was not that they doubted either the need for or the prospect of some kind of radical change in the condition of Israel in the intertestamental period. Rather, they believed that change could not come without a strong human commitment to bring it about—of course, short of an organized military effort.[1451] Herford says: "Apocalyptic uses the words of hope but its message is despair, despair of all human means for establishing the kingdom of God on earth, the anxious longing for God to intervene and the distrust of the slow waiting for His purpose to be fulfilled" and "the hasty casting of the responsibility for the future of the world upon God."[1452] The likelihood that this attitude toward apocalypticism grew toward the end of the first century suggests that other Jews came to agree with the Pharisees on this issue. As Russell claims, "Within Judaism the apocalyptic tradition . . . in due course ceased to exist."[1453]

Lawrence M. Wills says that the three Jewish sects shared a devotion to "a new personal penitential religious life," which is represented by Daniel's prayer in chapter 9 of his story: "O Lord, . . . who keepest covenant and steadfast love with those who love him and keep his commandments . . . [W]e do not present our supplications before thee on the ground of our righteousness, but on the ground of thy great mercy" (vv. 4, 18).[1454] But the Pharisees did not respond in the same way to Daniel's apocalyptic vision as the Essenes and Christians did. All three groups believed in some kind of resurrection and afterlife of peace and security, but the Pharisees did not think these things would happen either as the result of a cosmic battle that they would participate in or as the work of a divine messiah who had lived among them and would return to save them.[1455] According to Meier, although "some earlier scholars uncritically" attributed "eschatological messianism" to the Pharisees, more recent "scholars speak much more guardedly about messianic beliefs among the Pharisees and, indeed, in pre-70 Palestinian Judaism in general."[1456] E. P. Sanders says that Jews of the first century generally avoided the subject of eschatology: "In most discussions in the Jewish literature of our period, reward and punishment function within this world; life after death is not a major theme."[1457]

Love

Three of the works we examined in chapter 5 deal with main characters who risk their lives defying tyrants who were enemies of the ancient Jews. Daniel and his three friends refuse to comply with orders from the king of Babylonia. Tobit risks his life to bury Jews who have been killed by the Assyrians. Eleazar defies the Seleucid king, as do the main characters in two other apocryphal works, 1 and 2 Maccabees. In addition, in the book of Esther, living under the Persian King Xerxes, Esther and Mordecai successfully defend themselves against a pogrom initiated by the king's highest-ranking prince, Haman. According to the editors of *The New Oxford Annotated Bible*, the apocryphal book of Judith "is about a [Jewish] saint who risks her life to slay the enemy of her people" (20 AP). As I noted in chapter 3, in defense of his fellow Israelites and calling his act an "atonement," Moses puts his life on the line to save them: "So Moses returned to the Lord and said, 'Alas, this people have sinned a great sin; they have made for themselves gods of gold. But now, if thou wilt forgive their sin—and if not, *blot me, I pray thee, out of thy book which thou hast written*" (Exod 32:30–32; my emphasis).

Of course, these are stories, fictional accounts.[1458] However, it should also be understood that neither Moses nor the fictional heroes of the other works are totally imaginary in the context of ancient Jewish history. By this, I mean that the high-minded principles of Judaism that I have emphasized in this book were not merely expressed in the writings of the ancient Hebrews but often enough enacted by them in real life. Indeed, even if we confine ourselves to the intertestamental period, we see that the Jews of the time showed, persistently and unequivocally, that they were willing to risk their lives in order to preserve and protect their religion. According to D. S. Russell, "The sects of Judaism differed from one another in many respects; but, Sadducees apart, they were bound together by one thing as by nothing else in their fight against the common foe; not devotion to party or even to fatherland, but to the sacred Torah and the holy Covenant of the Lord their God."[1459]

On the one hand, conditions in the Middle East and throughout the empire were uniformly oppressive.[1460] They were bad for everyone except the ruling class. Taxation was excessive, land expropriation was extensive and arbitrary, and lending practices were usurious, all resulting in an increasing separation between rich and poor and a seemingly irremediable sense of hopelessness among peasants and urban workers. Farmers, in particular, lost their land because of high taxes and exorbitant interest rates, which too often forced them to become tenant farmers and day laborers.[1461] Wayne A. Meeks says, "It is generally agreed that the Hellenistic and Roman periods brought increasing social distance between the Haves and the Have-nots."[1462] Rulers were protected from rebellion by their retainers, including priests, soldiers, and civil servants, who were exempt from taxes and other financial burdens and therefore prepared to defend the regime by persuasion, threat of force, and even the claim that the ruling class was authorized to govern by the gods and by the rules of their religion. The old world of independent farmers, village living, and kinship relationships had been supplanted in many areas by urbanization, specialization, and stratification, resulting in challenges to the self-determination, security, and prosperity of ordinary people.[1463]

On the other hand, however, in the view of many scholars, the Jews of Palestine stood out from their contemporaries to the extent that their commitment to their religion compelled them to resist the Romans (as well as their predecessors) in every possible way. According to H. Conzelmann and A. Lindemann, "Judaism in Palestine intermixed less with hellenistic elements than in other areas of the empire."[1464] Robert M. Grant says that Jews were less willing than other ethnic groups in the empire "to amalgamate cults and gods"—that is, to practice the syncretism (the assimilation of elements from other religions) that was "characteristic of the period."[1465] Harold Mattingly argues that the Jews not only resisted the religion of Rome, but also went so far as to reject Roman rule altogether: "The Jews alone [that is, among all the residents of the Roman empire] refused to acquiesce in imperial rule."[1466] W. H. Davies says, "The only province that broke the peace [i.e., the Pax Romana], which began with Augustus and continued to the death of Marcus Aurelius," two hundred years later, "was Judaea."[1467] As Ben Witherington III points out, the Jews rebelled as much against the priestly Jewish families who governed in the name of the Romans as against the Romans themselves: Almost all of the movements in Galilee and Judea "were much more likely to respect local elders, Pharisees, sages, prophets or holy men, or even messianic claimants, than they were such official leaders."[1468]

The first group of Jews who defended their faith at the possible cost to their lives were not the earliest to be conquered, but the first to face the deliberate and comprehensive Hellenization of Israel. Shaye Cohen explains: "Throughout the Persian and Hellenistic periods, the Jews maintained a quiescent attitude toward their rulers. There is no indication of any serious uprising by the Jews against the empires that ruled them. This changed dramatically in the 160s BCE."[1469] As Lester L. Grabbe says, "A change of attitude came when the Jews were no longer allowed to exercise their religion: they would tolerate a lot of things but religious suppression."[1470]

This effort was initiated by the Seleucid king Antiochus Epiphanes, who, in the 160s BC, offered on the altar of the Temple in Jerusalem a pig, dedicated to Zeus. Raymond E. Brown says: "Antiochus proceeded systematically to gain unity among his subjects by having them all share the same Greek culture and religion . . . He punished attempts at resistance by attacking Jerusalem (169 and 167), slaughtering the population, [and] plundering the Temple."[1471] Furthermore, "[a]ll Jewish sacrifices were forbidden; the rite of circumcision was to cease, the Sabbath and feast days were no longer to be observed."[1472] According to R. M. Grant: "The response of the Jewish people was instantaneous. Led by a group of brothers known as the Maccabees . . . , the people revolted, and, after a series of bloody battles, finally recaptured Jerusalem, where in 165 B.C. the temple was cleansed and rededicated."[1473]

Another group of rebels, the Hasidim, reacted to this attempt to Hellenize Israel and to execute violators of the new rules simply by running away. Knowing that these Jews honored the Sabbath by refusing to fight on that day, the Greeks pursued them and found some of them hiding in a cave. "In one terrible case, the Greeks found a few hundred Hasidim" and "built a fire at the entrance, suffocating the Jews inside. Those who tried to escape were slain by the sword." Instead of bowing to Greek idols, other "[p]ious Jews became willing martyrs rather than succumb to this demand."[1474] Russell says of the Hasidim: "Their obvious piety and religious zeal were to be vital factors in the future life of the nation. Their attitude is vividly expressed in the book of Daniel, which in its present form at any rate, was composed in the time of Antiochus by one of the Hasidim."[1475] E. P. Sanders thus notes that the Hasidim not only "wished to resist Hellenization," but were also "willing to fight and die."[1476]

The first of many acts of resistance against the next rulers of ancient Israel, the Romans, occurred in 63 BC, when the Roman general Pompey attacked Jerusalem and, as Grant reports, "captured it on the Sabbath when the Jewish soldiers refused to take up arms." Twenty years later, the Romans appointed Herod, whose "long rule was marked by innumerable murders and harsh repression," as well as continued efforts at Hellenization.[1477] Josephus, the Jewish historian, describes the protest of Jewish teachers and their supporters who tried to cut down a golden eagle, symbol of Rome and its god, which Herod had ordered to be placed on one of the front gates of the Temple in Jerusalem: "The king's captain . . . with a considerable force, arrested about forty of the young men and conducted them to the king . . . Those who had let themselves down from the roof together with the doctors he had burnt alive; the remainder of those arrested he handed over to his executioners."[1478] Russell says, "We read of certain men, worthy successors of the early Maccabees, who entered into a holy covenant to hinder [Herod] even on pain of death, from perpetrating his policy of Hellenization. Even when they were captured and tortured and put to death there were others ready to take their place."[1479]

Abraham Schalit says that Herod's reign enables historians to understand "the religious and social unrest in Judea during the last seventy years of the second Temple, inasmuch as it was the breeding ground for all sorts of messianic and apocalyptic currents," which carried away "the poor and the oppressed who were longing for social justice and the political liberation of the nation." Herod suppressed "with an iron fist" the anger his policies aroused. But soon after his death the rebels "burst all the more forcefully through the constraints which had been set on them, carrying away the poor and the oppressed who were longing for social justice and the political liberation of the nation." [1480] After Herod's death in 4 BC, a man named Judas the Galilean led two revolts, "only to be repressed by a Roman general who crucified two thousand Jews."[1481] And the Jews of Israel continued to fight against the Roman occupation during the first century AD.[1482] According to T. W. Manson, at the time, "Jews were fighting . . . for the life of 'Israel', where 'Israel' is a complex organic whole which includes the monotheistic faith, the cultus in Temple and Synagogue, [and] the law and custom embodied in the Torah," among other things.[1483]

Under the procurators and prefects in Israel, appointed by the Romans, Jews regularly encountered continued insults to these religious practices and ideals. First,

Covenant, Community, and Compassion

says John Dominic Crossan, soon after he assumed his position in AD 26, Pontius Pilate brought soldiers into Jerusalem bearing "imperial images on military standards," which were regarded as desecrations of the holy city by its Jewish residents. "After five days of peaceful demonstration, Pilate called in his troops; however, according to Josephus in the *Jewish War* 2.174, 'the Jews, as by concerted action, flung themselves in a body on the ground and exclaimed that they were ready rather to die than to transgress the law.'"[1484] Next, in AD 36, says R. M. Grant, when a group of Samaritans, who considered themselves Jews, climbed Mt. Gerizim to see some religious objects that Moses had supposedly buried there, Pilate "hastily sent troops which dispersed the prophet's followers by killing many of them."[1485] In AD 40, Crossan says, quoting Josephus again, the Jews of Judea protested against the impending installation of a statue of the emperor Caligula in the Jerusalem Temple: "a 'vast multitude' of men, women, and children confronted Petronius," the governor of Syria, and "told him . . . that to proceed he would first have 'to sacrifice the entire Jewish nation; and they presented themselves, their wives and their children, ready for slaughter.'"[1486]

In the forties, under the Roman rule of Cuspius Fadus, there arose "a self-styled 'prophet' named Theudas, who took his followers to the Jordan, assuring them that like Joshua (4:7) he could make the waters divide." (Theudas, like Judas the Galilean, is mentioned by Gamaliel, the Pharisee, in Acts of the Apostles 5:36–37.) Grant continues, "The procurator sent a detachment of cavalry which defeated Theudas' followers and beheaded him." Finally, Ventidius Cumanus murdered twenty thousand Passover pilgrims who rioted because they had been ridiculed by a Roman soldier. Leading up to the Jewish Revolt of AD 66, Antonius Felix, Cumanus' successor, kept his position for a few years "largely by means of vigorous suppression of revolutionary activities."[1487] In addition to the fact that the Romans utterly defeated the Jews, the Revolt is notable for two unusual incidents. First, six thousand Jews, who took refuge from the battle by gathering in the Temple in Jerusalem, died when the Romans set fire to the building. Second, in the final event of the war, James D. Tabor comments: "We know that 960 Jewish refugees ended up in the Judean desert to the south at the fortress of Masada. It was there that they committed suicide in the spring of A.D. 73 after a prolonged Roman siege."[1488]

Arguing against the idea that the Jews lost both the war and their Temple because they were sinners (the claim of both many Jews and some Christians), Jacob Neusner says that, on the contrary, they "were deeply faithful to the covenant and to the Scriptures." The rebels were "brave and courageous." Furthermore, their goals were fundamentally religious: "That war was waged not for the glory of a king or for the aggrandizement of a people, but in the hope that at its successful conclusion, pagan rule would be extirpated from the holy land. This was the articulated motive. It as a war fought explicitly for the sake and in the name of God."[1489] Craig A. Evans says of "the actions of the Jewish people in this region" under the Romans: "The revolts that took place after the death of Herod the Great (4 BC), after the removal of Archelaus and the Roman census (AD 6), and the riot in Jerusalem that ignited the great revolt (66–70) all point to deep-seated Jewish resentment of the pagan presence in Israel as a whole . . . The actions taken by certain Jewish figures are themselves indicative of the degree of commitment to Israel's biblical heritage and future redemption."[1490] They preferred to die, rather than submit to foreign rule and the challenges it represented to their religious faith.

And what was that faith? That is, what was it, exactly, that these martyrs died for? As we have seen, that question is hard to answer—exactly. Inevitably, Jews died for their own personal beliefs, by which I mean the particular principles and practices that represented for them—individually—the faith they also shared to some degree with millions of other Jews. Indeed, as we have also seen, the religion they shared was, generally, the set of beliefs that most, if not all Jews seem to have embraced by the middle of the first millennium, based on the ideas that appear in Deuteronomy, the works of the prophets, and many of the psalms, as well as reiterated in such later works as the book of Daniel and much of the intertestamental literature, as well as the pronouncements of the Pharisees in the first century AD.

These beliefs included (1) a special relationship with God, derived from a thousand years of devotion to God's covenants with the patriarchs, the Israelites of Moses' time, and King David; (2) a similarly longstanding commitment to the idea of community and a set of laws binding individuals together in inviolable unity; and (3) support for the concept of love as the connecting link between God and humanity and among all human beings, guaranteeing social justice, political equality, and economic fairness. In short, the Jewish religion was based on the traditional Covenant with God, the community it defined and demanded, and the compassion that remained the driving emotion behind both Covenant and community. As Martin Goodman explains: "Among the characteristics shared by the books incorporated into the Bible the most important was the centrality of the covenant . . . The texts are preoccupied with the limits of God's unconditional love for his people." And they assume "that individual Jews have a duty to remain within the national covenant by faithfully observing the injunctions imparted through Moses"—"a moral code which is remarkably consistent across the biblical corpus."[1491]

Rosemary R. Ruether attributes what she understands to be authentic Judaism—the commitment to the aforementioned values—to the prophets: "The search for the 'true Israel' can be traced back to the religious impulse generated by the eighth-century prophets. It was the prophets who translated the Jewish tribal doctrines of election, covenant, and national promise into a religion of ethical demand."[1492] W. O. E. Oesterley and Theodore H. Robinson argue that the Jewish prophets were unsurpassed in this effort: "In this age of ferment in the world of politics, thought and religion, among the saints, philosophers, statesmen and warriors who shine so brightly on the pages of its history, there is no class of men whose influence has been greater or more durable than that of the prophets of Israel. They offered the world a solution of one of man's greatest problems, the correlation of religion and ethics."[1493] A. N. Wilson also emphasizes the ethical core of Judaism, past and present, which he similarly attributes to the prophets: "While other nations were bowing down to images of wood and stone, the Jewish prophets were calling their people to a recognition that the will of God could only be fulfilled by a virtuous and neighborly life; by making provisions for the poor; by establishing a just society in which men and women could live with the dignity of believing that they were the children of God."[1494]

Walter Brueggemann traces this moral revolution to the book of Exodus: "It is evident that the Sinai declaration makes a radically new beginning in ethics in the history of the world that stretches well beyond the Israelite community. Self-disclosure of YHWH stands as an abiding critique of all anticovenantal forms of power, and as a warrant for covenantal forms of power that enhance the human community and that resist reduction of human life to power and wealth."[1495] George Foot Moore adds that this was the beginning of God's self-disclosure but, as Brueggemann notes elsewhere, not the end: "Specific commandments had been given to Adam, Noah, Abraham, and Jacob; to Moses the complete revelation was given once for all. The prophets who came after him repeated, explained, emphasized, applied, what was revealed to Moses; they added nothing to it . . . Nevertheless, theory to the contrary notwithstanding, Judaism had made great progress between the days of the last prophets and the end of the age of the Tannaim [i.e., the Rabbis], and it had made it chiefly through the appropriation and assimilation of the prophetic teaching."[1496]

Israel Finkelstein and Neil Asher Silberman make a similar claim about the book of Deuteronomy. That is, in the final book of the Pentateuch, the "recognition" that Wilson refers to "was not a matter of mere charity, but a consciousness that grew out of a shared perception of nationhood, now strongly enforced by the historical saga of Israel, codified in text . . . The laws of Deuteronomy stand as a new code of individual rights and obligations for the people of Israel. They also served as the foundation for a universal social code and system of community values that endure—even today."[1497] These writers emphasize that the development of these ideals was shaped by adversity: "In specific historical terms, we know that the Bible's epic saga first emerged as a response to the pressures, difficulties, challenges, and hopes faced by the people of the tiny kingdom of Judah in the decades before its destruction and by the even tinier Temple community in Jerusalem in the post-exilic period."[1498] Patrick D. Miller sums up the evolution (and revolution) of Judaism this way: "In such fashion the religion of ancient Israel lives on, transformed, persistent, resilient, asking in its new forms about the faithfulness of those who walk in the way of the Lord and pray to the Creator God."[1499]

Seeing the development of Judaism in the context of the Axial Age, the worldwide religious revolution that occurred in the middle of the first millennium BC, Robert N. Bellah similarly suggests that the Jewish religion, like other Axial Age faiths, was the product of a breakthrough that arose after a breakdown—in this case, represented by "the pressure of Assyria, Babylonia, and Persia on the ancient Israelites." Specifically, "Deuteronomy (and perhaps most of the Pentateuch) comes out of a situation of unparalleled violence in which the northern kingdom had already been destroyed and many of its inhabitants deported, and Judah hung by an uneasy thread in a vassal relation to Assyria." Thus, Bellah continues, "If there was an 'axial breakthrough' in Israel it is here if anywhere that we will find it."[1500] Furthermore, Bellah argues, Deuteronomy, which is "a central, perhaps the central, strand of Israel's faith," was connected to the past through the eighth-through-sixth-century BC prophets and to the future through the first-century AD Rabbis. The "zeal that characterized" the work of the prophets, Bellah says, "was at the center of Deuteronomic faith." And the Deuteronomist "found its ultimate triumph in rabbinic Judaism," for which reason this tradition can be said to have remained "the heart of all subsequent Jewish piety."[1501]

From the point of view of these scholars—and, of course, from the perspective of many others—the religion of the Jews (ancient and modern) is not simply a religion of love, if by the word "love" we mean nothing more than a feeling or an idea. Rather, Judaism is expressed essentially by the implementation of social justice.[1502] In the words of the aforementioned scholars, it derives from God's declaration at Sinai, but it is preserved in "the human community." It is based on the "covenant" and rooted in "neighborly life," but it is fulfilled in "a just society." It was founded on "a new code of individual rights and obligations" and dedicated to the "ideals" of "justice and compassion," but it is embodied in "non-hierarchical and egalitarian social arrangements." And it is always evolving into "new forms" that express what it means to "walk in the way of the Lord." Thus, in Wilson's words, "The Old Testament is the record of an evolving religious consciousness without equal in the literature of the world." This is because what "emerges," is "an inspirational force of ethical and spiritual power" that is manifested in human actions. And these actions result in the establishment of human institutions that represent the highest moral ideals.[1503]

Although this view of Judaism might seem unfamiliar to some readers, it is nevertheless based on the idea that the Jewish faith underwent profound changes in its first millennium. As Alfred Gottschalk explains, Josiah's "religious reform" in the late seventh century BC "stimulated the monumental book of Deuteronomy, with its emphasis on the binding nature of the moral covenantal requirements," which "brought to the apex the synthesis of the prophetic movement" and "changed the matrix of Jewish communal religious life."[1504] From the point of view of Martin Buber, as well as many Old Testament scholars, the high point of this development—represented by the ideas of the Deuteronomist, the prophets, and the psalmists—culminated in two transformations. First, as I noted earlier, the Covenant between God and humanity was transformed from a relationship based on hope (as in Genesis) or fear (as in Exodus and Numbers) into a relationship based on love.

Second, love itself was transformed into a principle of action rather than an expression of emotion. That is, it was explicitly understood to be more than an abstraction, an attitude, or a feeling. Rather, love was understood to be the primary motivator of human behavior at its highest level, the principal basis of human interaction at its most humane, and the main justification for the establishment of a just and compassionate society. In this respect, it was believed to be the fulfillment, the actualization, and the enactment of God's will—without which God's will could not be executed. As Stephen A. Geller says: "[I]n Deuteronomy, loving God has become more than a legal metaphor. It is a total commitment, expressive of the emotion of *kin-ah*, which not only means 'zeal,' but also 'jealousy.'"[1505] Simply put, in the words of Daniel C. Maguire: "Israel's religion was overtly moral, political, and economic. It achieved its unprecedented revolution because it held as sacred ideals like justice, compassion, non-hierarchical and egalitarian social arrangements, the feasibility of eliminating poverty, the preservation of resources, and peace as *attainable only by all of the above*."[1506]

Like Buber, Brueggemann also emphasizes the indispensability of the community in this incarnation of God's principles. He says, for example, that God's will is not enacted by random acts of lovingkindness by individuals: "It is important to recognize that such neighborly *praxis*—that is, doing "justice and righteousness" and judging "the cause of the poor and needy"— "consists not simply in one-on-one, face-to-face neighborly acts, though these are of crucial importance." To put it simply, "the covenantal alternative of Sinai is more than simply a commendation of charity and kindness. Sinai does nothing less than offer a public polity"—that is, *an organized community*—"for the ways in which public power is to be ordered and practiced."[1507] Jon D. Levenson similarly argues that the Torah was intended to "govern a polity." That is, "the Torah and its commandments were not understood as merely personal choices made in response to inward promptings." Instead of seeing itself as "a voluntary organization of disconnected individuals, Israel saw itself as "a body politic, one governed as far as possible by Torah law."[1508]

As I said earlier, Brueggemann traces this fundamental and central tenet of Judaism to the book of Exodus, especially to the laws that Moses presents after God's announcement of the Ten Commandments: "The commands that follow are the *rules of emancipation* by the redeemer God and, at the same time, the *rules for a viable order of life* by the creator God. While there are many parallels and analogues in the ancient Near East to other legal materials in the Old Testament, there is no parallel to this utterance from the holy mountain." Brueggemann emphasizes that the "juxtaposition" of these two kinds of laws, which also reflect the two halves of the Decalogue, "constitute the defining character of Old Testament ethics." Furthermore, because these divine requirements are quite radical, especially in the context of traditional Near Eastern laws, they are often misinterpreted as demands for nothing more than "face-to-face neighborliness without reference to systemic issues in society."[1509]

In fact, Brueggemann concludes that, even if this view of the community is not quite completely expressed in Deuteronomy, "[i]t is clear that the radical ethic of the

[Decalogue] is transposed in the prophetic tradition of Israel into a large scale systemic analysis and demand."[1510] As Buber says, "Through torment and humiliation, [the prophets'] impassioned words storm against the rich, the powerful, the princes" because of their violations of God's commandments.[1511] Furthermore, Brueggemann continues, given that "the prophetic, sapiential, and psalmic traditions are all informed by the covenantal ethic of Sinai in the final form of the text," the obligation of human beings to create "true communities" remained central to Judaism. In the ensuing evolution of the Jewish faith, "that nonnegotiable foundation receives . . . a dynamic afterlife whereby the will and rule of YHWH, Lord of the covenant, is kept pertinent and germane to every circumstance of this alternative community of covenantal obedience."[1512]

These last few words, tying together "covenant" and "community," identify once more the two enduring aspects of the human-divine relationship. As I said in chapter 3, Bernhard W. Anderson argues that the Israelites received special training for establishing a community when they underwent the hardships of the journey through the wilderness: "A powerful centripetal force, the redemptive action of Yahweh, had pulled them toward the center of a common covenant allegiance." By the time they reached Mt. Sinai, they had come "to understand in a deeper way the nature of the community into which they had been called. The peculiar nature of this community is expressed in the covenant relationship between Yahweh and his people, and the laws and institutions by which this relationship was to be expressed." They especially understood that they "were not intended to be a crowd but a *community*, bound to him and to one another by a covenant bond." Thus, "as Israel looked back on the desert experience in the perspective of the covenant faith, it became clear . . . that through these trials Yahweh was uniting and disciplining his people for the historical task that lay ahead of them."[1513]

Anderson says that God's intention was to elicit from his people not "dutiful obedience to a law code, but an inward, personal response." This is so because God's love is manifested not only in his election of Israel as his people, but also in his gifts of mercy and justice—"Yahweh's sovereign deeds of kindness and benevolence." Instead of subservience, as I noted earlier, God's love calls for *imitation*: "Because Yahweh acts in this way, Israel must imitate his manner of dealing with people. This is the basis of the 'humanitarianism' that is evident in the laws found in Deuteronomy 12–26," the new Code of the Covenant. "Thus," says Anderson, "the governing purpose of Deuteronomy is to summon Israel to a renewal of the covenant with Yahweh." And the outcome of this summons was *the human creation of a just and merciful community*: "The righteousness of God demands, negatively, the abolition of anything that defiles the community . . . And, positively, it means imitating God's dealings in order that a spirit of brotherly love and solidarity may pervade the community."[1514]

What all of these writers emphasize is the connection, in ancient Judaism, between *Covenant, compassion, and community*. The Covenant between God and

Covenant, Community, and Compassion

humanity arises because of his compassion, which creates a bond between the two covenantal parties. The bond is based on the understanding that the recipient of God's love is required to respond in kind, for several different reasons: first, out of gratitude; second, out of a corresponding love; and, third, out of the understanding that both gratitude and compassion must be expressed by imitation. That is, if God is compassionate to all of humanity, then every individual must be compassionate to all of humanity. And this compassion must be expressed in an enduring and comprehensive form—a community that embodies and enshrines all of the particular aspects of God's compassion: not only love, but also empathy and justice, and, again, not only these principles acted on by individuals, but established formally and institutionally.

Indeed, without the establishment of community, without the successful effort on the part of humanity to enact God's will, actually and effectively, both God and humanity fail. God's role is to provide the framework for human survival, to lay out the rules by which that survival can be initiated and sustained, and to encourage this achievement not only by teaching human beings because they have to understand what is expected of them, but also by disciplining them when they fail to live up to the high standards that God has established. This is why God himself is so insistent that his expectations are not only high, but also achievable. As James L. Kugel says, God's laws are not merely "divine requirements," but eminently *practical* demands, "constituting in themselves a source of great benefit and well-being"—in fact, "equated with the people's continued life in the land and all its blessings."[1515]

Strikingly, what this means is that God's "reward" is not a supernatural gift of happiness in this life or the next. Rather, the reward is in the doing. That is, if Jews (or, presumably, anyone else) build a society that *institutionalizes* compassion—both mercy and justice—they will be rewarded *by their own actions*. Thus, God's goal for his people is not salvation in any exalted or unusual sense, and it is certainly not eternal life, accompanied by unearthly joy and immeasurable happiness. According to Kugel, "The laws constituted a recipe for well-being, a divinely given guidebook for the right way to live."[1516]

In other words, God's goal for humanity is nothing more or less than living self-sufficiently, securely, and peacefully, with some measure of self-fulfillment and self-satisfaction. Kugel quotes Deuteronomy: "You shall walk in the way which the Lord your God has commanded you, that you may live and that it may go well with you, and that you may live long in the land which you shall possess" (5:30). Josephus thus advises his fellow Jews, regarding God's laws, "[B]y following them you will gain a life of happiness, enjoying an earth that is fruitful and a sea that is untroubled" (*Jewish Antiquities*, 3:87–88). That is, according to Psalm 128, "if you do thus"—that is, if you are one "who fears the Lord, who walks in his ways"—"*You shall eat the fruit of the labor of your hands*; you shall be happy, and it shall be well with you" (vv. 1–2; my emphasis). According to Finkelstein and Silberman, "The power of the biblical saga stems from its being a compelling and coherent narrative expression of the timeless themes of a people's liberation, continuing resistance to oppression, and quest for social equality. It eloquently expresses the deeply rooted sense of shared origins, experiences, and destiny *that every human community needs in order to survive.*"[1517]

In light of this special relationship between God and humanity, with its powerful emphasis on mutual love, it is easy to understand that—at least after the writing of Deuteronomy—Judaism was never merely a *quid pro quo* religion. And this was even more deeply believed to be the case by the second century AD. After all, God was consistently portrayed, from the beginning of the Jewish Bible to the end, as much more than a monarchial figure who merely demanded deference in exchange for protection. Even Adam and Eve were given nothing less than paradise to dwell in—that is, a life of comfort, ease, and security. As Marcus J. Borg explains, the garden has "a symbolic meaning: it means 'garden of delights' (and, by extension, paradise)."[1518] And later recipients of God's graciousness and generosity were provided with ample opportunities to recreate Edens of their own. Describing God's offer to the Israelites of the already developed land of the Canaanites (in chapter 8 of Deuteronomy), Gerhard Von Rad asks, "What is it then but a paradise upon earth?"[1519] To be sure, God's people failed at every attempt to establish a paradise of their own not merely because they disobeyed God and were duly punished for their error but because they failed to understand the terms of their relationship to God and to each other, particularly as this is spelled out in the Torah.

As John Barton explains, the Torah was never intended to be anything more than a list of rules. Rather, it was supposed to be "a system of regulations" whose purpose was not merely to proscribe certain behaviors of the kind forbidden by the laws of the Decalogue, which, after all, are laws "common to almost every human society," including all of Israel's nearest neighbors. Rather, it was a comprehensive definition of "the whole way of life ordained by God for his people." In this respect, unlike the law codes throughout the Near East, it was a unique and precious gift that was, as we are told in a few psalms, "perfect," "sure," "right," and "clear" and should have elicited "delight" and joy because it provided inspiration ("reviving the soul"), enlightenment ("making wise the simple"), and "love" (requiring "meditation all day long"—indeed, "day and night") (1:2; 19:7–8; 119:97–98).[1520] Thus, Martin Buber argues that even as early as the book of Exodus, the covenant relationship between God and humanity was understood to be "all-embracing" because it was "founded as an everlasting bond." Given "the mutual character of this relationship, the Covenant was "no legal agreement, but a surrender to the divine power and grace."[1521]

Speaking of Deuteronomy, von Rad says repeatedly that the book was important in the history of Judaism primarily because it was "a comprehensive revelation of the divine will," in which Israel "never again express[ed] herself so comprehensively and in such detail as to the meaning of the commandments and the unique situation into which Jahweh's revelation of his will put her." Von Rad particularly emphasizes the extraordinary educational and informational feature of the work—its unity, indivisibility, wholeness, and coordination of a wide variety of traditions and "theological thought." This makes Deuteronomy "a summary proclamation of 'the' torah . . . in actual fact the one theological work in the Old Testament which demands a more systematic presentation of its content" and which results in nothing less than "a totality of teaching." This combination of unity and clarity allows the work to be "understood," albeit with intensive study and extensive elucidation, which are possible because "Jahweh's offer" was "made intelligible and easy to understand." By such means, the will of God, demanding not only understanding bur also action, was "easy to fulfill."[1522]

In short, like Barton, von Rad sees the Torah, especially Deuteronomy, as a statement of faith rather than a book of rules, which was never supposed to be fulfilled by an act of submission that was carried out in order to elicit rewards or avoid punishments: "Jahweh wants obedience, admittedly, but he also wants men who understand his commandments and ordinances, that is, men who assent inwardly as well. The obedience which Jahweh wants is the obedience of men who have come of age." Providing "an inner motivation for the keeping of the commandments," Deuteronomy "reduc[es] all the profusion of the commandments to the one fundamental commandment, to love God (Deut. vi. 4), and . . . [emphasizes] the inner, the spiritual, meaning of the commandments." To the Deuteronomist, God is understood to be deserving of humanity's love because of his love of humanity. And, as I noted earlier, the Deuteronomist's "summons to gratitude lets us see the strength of [his] appeal to the inner disposition, in fact to the heart." In short, neither fear nor hope engender submission to God's will. Rather, "love for Jahweh and thankfulness to him will lead Israel into obedience."[1523]

The features that particularly underscore the specialness of Israel's laws include the fact that they were embedded in a narrative and often accompanied by "lengthy explanations and motivations." On the one hand, what Barton calls the "motive clauses" clearly state the "incentives to obey," which are often "related to future outcomes of obedience or disobedience"—that is, *quid pro quo*'s. On the other hand, however, as von Rad similarly argues, the incentives included reminders that God's past blessings should encourage obedience out of "gratitude to God" instead of expectations of future rewards and punishments: God "has done for you these great and awesome things that your own eyes have seen . . . You shall love the LORD your God, therefore, and keep his charge, his decrees, his ordinances, and his commandments always" (Deut 10:21; 11:1). Such appeals, Barton adds, are "more common than [the} concern for future consequences," and remained strong even after the age of miracles, the direct contact between God and humanity, and the mediation of prophets had ended—that is, in the Second Temple period and especially in the early Common Era, when faith in God's help either by saving acts, direct commands, or any other kind of divine intervention seemed increasingly unlikely.[1524]

Besides making "appeals either to future consequences or past benefits," the Jews of the late Second Temple period were inclined "to argue that the laws are good in themselves"—so much so that their readers "can readily grasp the point of them" as well as understand their intrinsic value. For example, the laws that forbid taking one's neighbor's cloak or millstone as collateral for a loan or failing to pay an employee at the end of a workday, says Barton, "appeal to shared human experience, and [have] the effect of making the law . . . a kind of natural moral principle." As Moses explains in Deuteronomy,: the observance of these laws "will show your wisdom and discernment to the peoples, who, when they hear all these statutes, will say, 'Surely this great nation is a wise and discerning people!'" (4:7–8). In this respect, Barton comments, these laws are not "simply commands that must be obeyed because they come from God," as if he were a suzerain interested only in domination and control, but because they represent "one side of a partnership between God and his people."[1525]

That is, the laws are not just constraints but guidelines. Indeed, they are not just demands but offers of support and encouragement. Thus, God says to Joshua: "Only be strong and very courageous, being careful to do according to all the law which Moses my servant commanded you; turn not from it to the right hand or to the left, that you may have good success wherever you go. This book of the law shall not depart out of your mouth, but you shall meditate on it day and night, that you may be careful to do according to all that is written in it; for then you will make your way prosperous, and then you shall have good success" (1:7–8).

Accompanied by incentives, such as motives and explanations, the laws of the Torah also "sometimes contain narratives"—particularly regarding situations that are "ethically challenging," such as intentional and unintentional homicide—which invite intellectual engagement. According to Barton, "We are drawn into the situation envisaged, not presented with a set of rules," but with descriptions of events. In such cases, "we find the legislators speaking to the community and encouraging them to imagine typical situations, on the basis of which they will form good judgements in analogous cases . . . The use of a standard credits a human agent not just with the ability to comply with instructions but with the capacity to engage in practical deliberation." In addition to "appealing to the reader's heart and mind," these laws are not so much "a code to be enforced," but "a statement of general legal principles," which are necessary "for shaping the judicial task and the community life." Like the later legal deliberations of the Rabbis, these laws "are to some degree dialogical in form, inviting the reader into a moral discussion rather than closing off the debate from the start."[1526]

What all of this means is that God and Israel were not bound together by a conventional treaty, rooted in legal demands and contingent on both participants' obedience to its requirements. Rather, they were in a special relationship, bound by a pledge of mutual love, which, as von Rad explains, expressed itself in *tsedakah*—righteousness. On God's part, this was expressed in his choice of Israel out of all the nations and in his offer of what von Rad calls "the orders of life which alone made men's life together possible": not "an absolute ethical norm," but "a kindly gift"—the Covenant Code—"rendering life orderly." Thus, "Israel did not envisage herself as related to a world of ideal values, but to events coming from Yahweh"—that is, "a constantly forthcoming [*tsedakah*] which flowed over upon her." These "events" were nothing other than "the commandments," which Israel "extolled" because "they were 'righteous,' which means that in revealing them Jahweh had given proof of his loyalty to his community relationship with Israel." From this point of view, "[t]here is no terror here, and no sighing, as if they were a burden, but only thankfulness and praise."[1527]

For all of these reasons, as Bruce C. Birch and his fellow writers explain, the obvious similarities between the Jewish Covenant and Near Eastern treaties are less relevant than is often suggested: "It must be stressed that *covenant is a metaphor*, [and] as such it does not fully describe the relationship between God and people. The covenant is much too personally and relationally construed for treaty or agreement language to do it justice." No mere suzerain, "God creates, blesses, gives laws, judges, grieves, saves, elects, promises, makes covenants, provides council, protects, confers responsibility to human beings, and holds them accountable." As a "relational God," he "is present and active in the world, enters into a relationship of integrity with the world, and does so in such a way that both world and God are affected by that interaction."[1528] James Muilenburg says: "There is elsewhere no living, personal, voluntary relationship in which the two parties are dynamically involved. In Israel choice and decision, loyalty and fidelity, obligation and accountability, and mutuality of response are writ large over the whole account."[1529]

In this context, the law itself must be understood "in basically positive terms as that which promotes life." This makes it "a gracious gift," which is "given for the sake of a well-ordered community." It is therefore indispensable for the "stability and well-being [of] all." In Deuteronomy, "the material shows that the concern is not to 'lay down the law' or 'obey because God says so'; these texts seek to persuade, to inculcate, to instill, and to impress upon both mind and heart. God gives Israel reasons to obey that are linked to a fullness of life and the good order of God's creation. Like Barton, Birch et al. argue: "To obey the law is eminently reasonable; any right-thinking person could hardly do otherwise. To obey the law is to trust that God knows what is best for individual and community. Obedience is in *Israel's* own best interest."[1530] Thus, as Birch and his fellow writers indicate, "Yahweh must be obeyed." However, "[a]long with this rather *simplistic theological claim*, . . . there is also an implied *ethic of considerable rigor*, namely, that prosperity in the land has as a precondition the practice of a just and humane social ethic that attentively shares well-being with all inhabitants . . . Fidelity toward the neighbor in socioeconomic matters is understood as an enactment of fidelity toward God." These are the "values" that "promote and protect the well-being of the *community*."[1531]

Chapter Eight

The Hidden Revolution

IN DEUTERONOMY, THE PROPHETS, and the Psalms, it is clear that God is not making demands whose purpose is merely to test humanity's faith or devotion, like his command, in Genesis, that Abraham sacrifice Isaac; in Exodus, that the Israelites refrain from worshiping other gods; in Leviticus, that the Jews demonstrate their piety by following a long list of cultic rules; or, in Numbers, that God's people never question his demands. In the most important biblical works of the mid-first millennium BC, God is not interested in demonstrating his power or his superiority, nor is he seeking submission and obedience. Instead, he wants human beings to live securely and with some degree of happiness and personal fulfillment. In pursuit of this objective, Lawrence H. Schiffman says, "He desires only that His creatures observe His Torah, the instrument by which He reveals the divine will to His people."[1532] As Walter Brueggemann explains, following God's laws in the Torah—which, as I noted in chapter 7, he calls "the *rules of emancipation*" and "the *rules for a viable order of life*"—"is the prerequisite and the guarantee of a life of well-being and prosperity."[1533]

This is not to say that, in the major Jewish documents of the mid-first millennium, the *quid pro quo* system that dominates the earlier books of the Pentateuch disappeared or that God was no longer motivated by a concern for his international reputation. Clearly, God continued to use both carrots and sticks to encourage his people to "do the right thing." What changed was the nature of "the right thing," which slowly but surely evolved into ethical acts—not *instead* of ceremonial acts but in obvious preference to them—that were, from God's perspective, important on their own terms, invaluable to the project of building a community by following God's own ways, and indispensable to the well-being of the people themselves. All of this evolved because God began to be portrayed as a God of love, whose primary concern was not spreading his name as a powerful deity throughout the world but extending his loving arms to embrace his children, the object of his fatherly affection, in order to support them in their endeavor to survive securely and safely, if not necessarily prosperously and powerfully.

The Hidden Revolution

To be sure, God continued to show some interest in his reputation, as he did when his petitioners asked him to act "for [his] name's sake" (1 Sam 13:22; 1 Kgs 8:41; 2 Chr 6:32; and a half-dozen or more psalms) and when he promised Isaiah to act for his "name's sake" (48:9; 66:5). In Ezekiel, God says that he refrained from punishing Israel for her infidelity because he "acted for the sake of [his] name, that it should not be profaned in the sight of the nations among whom they dwelt, in whose sight [he] made [him]self known to them in bringing them out of Egypt" (20:9, 14). God tells Ezekiel that by way of forgiving his people for their more recent iniquities: "It is not for your sake that I am about to act, but for the sake of my holy name, which you have profaned among the nations to which you came. And I will vindicate the holiness of my great name . . . ; and the nations will know that I am the LORD" (36:22–23). Even in Deuteronomy, God sends the Israelites to a place at which they will "make his name dwell" (12:10–11, 14:23), but this act of self-assertion hardly matches the obsessive concern he displays in Numbers (14:13–16) and especially in Exodus, when Moses twice convinces God to repent of his intention to punish the Jews on the grounds that it would compromise his reputation throughout the world (14:13–16; 32:11–12; see also 9:13–16).

As I suggested in the last chapter, however, this evolution of God from king to father (and even husband) and the addition of mercy (and even compassion) to his repertoire was not the final change in the Jewish view of God and humanity in the ancient world. To the extent that the Pharisees exerted a growing influence on the beliefs and practices of the Jews after the Revolt of AD 66 (and the Rabbis not only inherited this power but also later became the officialguardians and proponents of the faith), yet another change occurred in the early centuries of the Common Era. According to Ellis Rivkin, "the Pharisees had carried through one of the most stunning revolutions in the history of humankind—a revolution they never acknowledged and of which they left no record other than their transmutation of Judaism."[1534] This idea may strike many readers as surprising partly because the Pharisees are described in the New Testament as legalistic, casuistic, and preoccupied with the ceremonial aspects of religion. In response to this view of the Pharisees, Stephen M. Wylen comments: "The Pharisees were hardly limited by their sectarian interests. They had a vision for all Israel, a vision so powerful that it generated the religion of Rabbinic Judaism which has survived through good times and bad."[1535]

Rivkin argues that the change that occurred in the first century AD and after was "a hidden revolution," which came about primarily because the Pharisees, without what Rivkin calls Pentateuchal authority—i.e., God's stated support—introduced a number of innovations, some of which were similar to Greek practices and institutions. First, they assumed the position of unofficial religious experts, like the Greek philosopher-sages. Second, they established the kind of "teacher-disciple relationship" that was popular among the Greeks. Third, they developed "the concept of unwritten laws," which was common among Greeks and Romans. And fourth, along with a number of other Hellenistic innovations, they created "law-making institutions," similar to the Roman Senate.[1536] More important, however, the Pharisees initiated several other changes not only in religious practices but also in religious ideas, particularly in the areas of theology and morality, the convergence of which at this time made the revolution even more profound.

All of these mutations are at least partly attributable to the failed revolt and the destruction of the Second Temple in AD 66–73. As I noted earlier, these events resulted not only in the loss of the leading Jewish institution, but also a decline in the authority of the priests, thousands of deaths, and widespread despair in the face of what appeared to many Jews to be God's abandonment of his people. However, according to Rivkin and other scholars, the Pharisees redefined both God's nature and humanity's responsibilities in view of the crisis that, by all accounts, threatened to destroy Judaism itself. Thus, it is widely believed that the Pharisees saved the Jewish religion. And it is important to understand their effort because the innovations they made served as the foundation of modern Judaism.

Rivkin explains: "The authoritative corpus of Jewish Oral Law, the Mishnah, testifies to their enduring impact on the development of normative Judaism. Indeed, all the varied forms of Judaism flourishing today are historically interconnected with the Pharisees; for only the Judaism of the Pharisees survived antiquity."[1537] As John P. Meier says: "[T]he Pharisees were no doubt a major influence on and contributor to the new form of Judaism emerging at Yavneh," the town in which the Pharisees "founded a type of academy ... The rabbis were their spiritual heirs and successors."[1538]

The Disappearance of God

To get an idea of how innovative the Pharisees and Rabbis were, it is useful to begin with their unprecedented view of God's role in the universe. Jacob Neusner says that God is understood throughout the Mishnah, the first major work of the Rabbis, finished in c. AD 200, as the source, but not the enforcer of the laws under which human beings must live: "Indeed, even when proving the essential unity of being, the philosophers of Judaism do not appeal to God, or the idea of One God, to explain that unity, let alone to demonstrate it . . . Like eighteenth century Deists, the Mishnah's philosophers focus upon the government by laws, to be discovered by intelligent use of intellect, that God has set forth in the Torah." Instead of presenting God as an active force in the world, "the authorship of the Mishnah, unlike the diverse scriptural writers, simply did not portray God as a personality." He is the "giver of the Torah" but not actively present "in the everyday and the here and now." Neusner concludes by describing the Mishnah's view of God as "the ground of all being, giver and guarantor of the Torah—and a monumental irrelevance."[1539]

As James L. Kugel argues, "Jews of various allegiances," including both Christians and Pharisees, concluded after the failed Revolt of AD 66, that God was "a kind of *Deus absconditus*," who "seemed to be content to control things from a distance" and under whose rule "the initiative in the divine-human encounter ha[d] *passed from God to human beings*."[1540] It is not that *any* Jews, including either the Pharisees or the Rabbis, publicly announced that God no longer intervened in human life as an administrator of the moral program of the Torah. It is simply that one central tenet of traditional Judaism—the idea that God rewards good deeds and punishes bad—lost its dominance while another traditional concept—the idea of human agency—gained ascendancy.

According to John T. Pawlikowski, "Another important dimension of the Jewish covenantal tradition... is its sense *of the human person as co-creator*,"[1541] an idea that even reaches back to the book of Genesis, when God says to Adam and Eve, "Be fruitful and multiply, and fill the earth and subdue it; and have dominion over... every living thing that moves upon the earth" (1:28). As Bruce C. Birch and his fellow writers argue: "The future shape of this beautiful world is placed directly in human hands. God engages mankind in a risky enterprise on behalf of the creation..., and God will relate to these appointed stewards with integrity in the ongoing divine commitment to the world."[1542]

To Richard Elliott Friedman, the entire Bible is characterized by "the continuing diminishing apparent presence of Yahweh among humans from the beginning of the book to the end, the phenomenon of *Deus absconditus* or, in the book's own terms, *Yahweh hammastir panaw*." Friedmann summarizes this gradual change by referring to a step-by-step process in which God moves from a more or less total involvement in the lives of Adam and Eve, an almost as intimate engagement with Noah, and a lifelong presence in the adventures of Abraham and his progeny. In each relationship, God relinquishes more and more control, so much so, says Friedman, that Joseph must repeatedly "protest to all that it is Yahweh and not himself operating"—most shockingly when he tells his brothers that their self-serving efforts to rid themselves of Joseph were actually part of God's benevolent plan to save Jacob and his family from starvation. Friedman adds, "This phenomenon of the divine deposit of power in a human's apparent control, itself an important stage in the developing metamorphosis of the divine and human roles, reaches a new level in the accounts of Moses."[1543]

The principal change that led to this understanding of the Jewish Bible, discernible at first in several later psalms, according to Kugel, is that *God's search for humanity*—best symbolized by his second visit to the Garden of Eden, when he asks of Adam and Eve, "Where are you?"—was eventually supplanted by *humanity's search for God*, represented not only by the psalmists' question "How long?" but also by the experiential fact that although he might be present and accessible in the sense that he could hear, understand, and sympathize with the psalmists' pleas, God was no longer tangibly or demonstrably prepared to respond to or intervene in the day-to-day lives of suffering men and women. As Friedman explains, "The narrative from Genesis to Esther has come the full cycle from a stage on which God is alone to one on which

The Evolution of Love

humans are on their own. Though no longer in control of miraculous powers, humans have arrived at complete responsibility for their fortunes."[1544]

Kugel says: "It is difficult not to contrast all this"—by which he means not only the yearnings expressed in the psalms, but surely, as well, the questions raised by Job, Koheleth, and Ezra (in 2 Esdras)—"with relations between God and man in an earlier day, when he was said to buttonhole Moses or Jeremiah or Jonah. Then it was indeed 'God in search of man,' a God who calls out from the middle of a burning bush, or who picks up Ezekiel from over here and drops him down over there. But after a while, all this stopped happening . . . The balance had somehow shifted." In earlier times, it was God asking his prophets "Where are you?" and his prophets answering "*Hineni*": "Here am I." "[N]ow," Kugel continues, "it was the human who was searching, reaching out to a remote and hard-to-imagine deity through prayers of praise."[1545]

Two major developments in ancient Judaism contributed to this and other related changes in Jewish theology and morality. Perhaps the most obvious is God's transformation from personal friend and advisor (that is, as El, the tribal God of the patriarchs—"beheld" by Jacob [Gen 48:3], Moses [Exod 24:10–11], and Amos [9:1])—to the almost invisible, though quite audible God of Exodus (that is, as Yahweh, whose presence is potentially life-threatening [33:20]), to the "still small voice" heard by Elijah and emanating from a God who remains unseen by the prophet, who has "wrapped his face in a mantle" (1 Kgs 19:12–13). Instead of appearing to Elijah unsolicited, as he does to the patriarchs, or making his presence undeniable to Moses and the Israelites by means of even more spectacular sights and sounds than the earthquake, wind, and fire seen and heard by Elijah as God "pass[es] by" (19:11–12), God first sends Elijah an angel and then sends him his "word," both evidently evoked by Elijah's request to God "that he might die" and his pious residency in a cave at "Horeb the mount of God." Here, God does not ask Elijah "Where are you," as if he is seeking him out, but "What are you doing here?" since Elijah has desperately, though indirectly, requested the meeting (19: 4–9).[1546]

Kugel argues that, as we have seen repeatedly, "the basic model of God's interaction with human beings came to be reconfigured": "After a time, he no longer stepped across the curtain separating ordinary from extraordinary reality. Now he was not seen at all—at first because any sort of visual sighting was held to be lethal, and later because it was difficult to conceive of. God's voice was still heard, but he himself was an increasingly immense being, filling the heavens, and then finally (moving ahead to post-biblical times), he was just axiomatically everywhere all at once."[1547] Indeed, says Friedman, God became not so much a matter of actual experience as a mere object of belief: "The Hebrew Bible thus tells the story of humankind's movement from a supernaturally charged world of a cracking cosmos, splitting seas, divine voices, and talking animals to the world that we know, a world in which the immanence of God is an enigma, a matter of faith."[1548]

Referring to 2 Esdras as expressive to some degree of the post-biblical mood, Kugel reminds us that "the challenging questions" Ezra raises with the angel Uriel "are hardly unique" to that work. Indeed, in the apocalyptic writings of the intertestamental period, the main characters, instead of being sought out by God on earth, must ascend to heaven in order to discover God's plans. "The reason is that underlying both the heavenly ascents and angel interviews is (among other things) a basic unease with the 'messiness of history,' *a feeling that God may have abandoned his people.*

If this was the problem, then the solution must be somewhere 'up there,' in the secrets of heaven that only a few privileged humans have been allowed to glimpse, or 'down here,' where an angel has consented to answer the questions of a virtuous sage."[1549] The point can be made most clearly by examining, one by one, what G. E. Wright refers to as the ways God typically "ma[d]e himself and his will known upon the earth," most of which were lost—at least for some time—by the middle of the first millennium BC: e.g., miracles, including signs and wonders; revelations, including dreams and visions; and messages delivered by intermediaries, including angels and prophets.[1550]

Gerhard von Rad sees the first sign of God's disappearance in what might be called "the end of miracles," which occurred long after God's "promise to the patriarchs" in Genesis. This promise was followed by the great triad of miracles described in Exodus: the exodus itself, including "the miraculous deliverance at the Red Sea," the appearance of God at Sinai, and "the bestowal of the land of Canaan." The final miracle was "Jahweh's covenant with David," which brought to an end the "saving events brought about by Jahweh for Israel's benefit . . . Beyond them, Israel knew of no further event capable of producing traditions—things of the kind no longer occurred. And Israel on her part no longer expected the saving facts to continue." The age of miracles thus came to an end in the early years of the monarchy, which created a "tremendous vacuum" that was soon filled by the prophets. At this point, von Rad concludes, and as Deuteronomy indicates in its numerous references to Israel's glorious past, "nothing essentially new had come into being in the interval, that is, approximately between 950 and 650 B.C." For Israel, "[t]he consciousness of being herself involved at the centre of a history created by Jahweh had vanished."[1551]

At the same time, says von Rad, without any announcement on their part but clearly evidenced in their writing, especially after Deuteronomy, the ancient Jews seem to have undergone a second change in consciousness, which amounted to a "spiritual transformation"—indeed, "an emancipation of the spirit." On the positive side, Israel "found her way to real historical writing," which the Jews learned to do as, also uniquely in the ancient world, the Greeks did as well. Not only did the ancient Jews write no more accounts that featured the kind of miracles that figure most prominently and indispensably in the early history of Israel but also—increasingly in the centuries after Deuteronomy—they also wrote fewer and fewer accounts of the smaller, less spectacular interventions of God in the lives of people like the patriarchs, the judges, and the prophets.

The Evolution of Love

Von Rad cites as extraordinary the "masterly" ordering of "complex material into a clear sequence of scenes" and the "brilliant" description of characters. Thus, the Jews learned how to acknowledge the involvement of God in the affairs of ancient Israel without mentioning "any outwardly perceptible influence of Jahweh on the history." Indeed, the "intervention of Jahweh" could be alluded to, as it is by Joseph (in Genesis), but "it no longer needed to break from the outside into the normal evolution of events upon earth to make itself felt."

On the negative side, however—lest this change be seen as reflecting nothing more than a new interest in the art of story-telling—von Rad is quick to explain that it "did not arise by chance." The problem was that Israel "no longer experienced Jahweh's working mainly in the sacral form of miracles." Thus, "these story-tellers [had] no need of wonders or the appearance of charismatic leaders" because they began to understand that "events develop[ed] apparently in complete accord with their own inherent nature." For some time, no doubt, the writers retained the idea that, although he no longer intervened spectacularly in the lives of ordinary people, God was nevertheless "the cause of all things." Eventually, however, the sheer absence of evidence of his involvement of any kind in worldly events meant that history could be narrated without any reference at all to his actions. Von Rad explains that "reality—Nature and History—became secularized." There was no "break in the terrestrial chain of cause and effect." As a result, "figures in the stories now move[d] in a completely demythologized and secular world." At some point, "something quite new became the centre of interest, namely man."[1552]

This change of consciousness is also reflected in the fact that at some point, God stops speaking to just *anyone*—as I said earlier, to relatively minor characters in the Jewish saga, as well as the patriarchs—but speaks only to Moses, partly because the people tell their leader that they fear death if they hear God's words and (evidently) partly because, as Friedman explains, they have arrived at "a stage of mediated divine communication": "You speak with us, and we will listen, but let not God speak with us, lest we die" (Exod 20:19). Friedman continues: "Yahweh himself carves the Decalogue, but Moses carries it to the people. The community of descendants of Adam, Noah, Abraham, Isaac, and Jacob are never to experience direct divine speech again. Rather, the divine message is always thereafter to be mediated through the voice, appearance, and personality of a human agent. In a word, prophecy."[1553]

Henceforth, at least for the period of time from Elijah to the last prophet in the fifth century BC, God spoke only through his chosen earthly representatives. As God says in Numbers, "If there is a prophet among you, I the LORD make myself known to him in a vision, I speak with him in a dream" (12:6). As Martin Goodman, says, however, like all other mediated contacts with God, the only remaining means "of discovering the divine will had fallen out of use before the end of the Second Temple." Indeed, Goodman continues, "there are numerous traditions from the end of the Second Temple period that prophecy had ceased some centuries earlier.[1554]

Referring to what has often been called "the end of prophecy," Shaye Cohen explains: "By the time the Jews returned from Babylonia in the Persian period, classical prophecy of the sort perfected by the prophets of the eighth to early sixth centuries was on the wane. The Jews recognized that God no longer spoke to them in the same way as in the past."[1555] In a chapter entitled "The End of Prophecy," Kugel says that "nothing" in the way of traditional prophecy followed Haggai, Zechariah, and Malachi. "Indeed," Kugel adds, "the book of Zechariah itself reports that 'prophet' had become something of a dirty word, referring in later times to liars and charlatans," so much so that God is quoted as saying that he "will rid the land of prophets."

Thus, the author of 1 Maccabees laments, "There was great distress in Israel, such as had not existed since the time when prophets ceased to exist among them" (9:27). And the author of 2 Baruch says that "the prophets," who "in former times" served as "righteous helpers" to "our fathers," have now "gone to sleep" (85: 1–3).[1556] According to Stephen A. Geller, despite the fact that "the independent, fearless brand of prophecy provided the stimulus for the growth of biblical religion," which grew out of earlier forms of Judaism, "prophecy itself eventually became effectively outlawed by later biblical religion."[1557]

Again, part of the reason for the termination of prophetic mediation between God and humanity is the concept of God as transcendent and therefore less accessible than he was earlier assumed to be. Like many other scholars, Geller says that the Judaism of this period "is a religion that implies divine transcendence." Furthermore, "[d]irect divine contact with the world is strongly denied . . . Rather, God remains in heaven."[1558] According to Kugel: "Perhaps the most striking element [in the encounter between God and humanity] is the great distance that now seems to separate God from even those human beings who are held to be closest to him, His prophets . . . He is often conceived to speak indirectly through an angelic intermediary." What Kugel means is that the newer prophets, particularly the later apocalyptists, were not directly inspired by God himself, but by angels, who communicated on God's behalf. And their message was less about repentance and forgiveness than about spectacular visions and grandiose changes in reality, predictions of the future "glimmering with secret meanings that only the initiates can understand."[1559] Indeed, as Cohen says, their message was often incomprehensible: "Unlike the prophet, the apocalyptic seer speaks neither publicly nor clearly. Even after the angel has spoken to the seer and explained the meaning of his vision, the message remains obscure; only the wise will understand it. What was mysterious before the revelation is only slightly less mysterious after it."[1560]

This aspect of apocalypticism is, of course, less an expression of realistic expectations than a desperate cry for help in a time of growing anguish, confusion, and disappointment. And this change represents the second development that redefined the way ancient Jews understood the human condition. According to William A. Irwin: "The Exile was the Great Divide in Hebrew history. It was at once the most terrible and the most transforming experience that befell ancient Israel. From this point onward all streams run in different and generally in deeper channels."[1561] As Yehezkel Kaufmann explains, "The fall of Jerusalem is the great watershed of the history of Israelite religion. The life of the people of Israel came to an end; the history of Judaism began . . . With the fall and the exile, . . . the simple faith of the people in the working of the divine in their life, in the indwelling of God's presence among them, was shattered. YHWH had turned his back upon them. The land of Israel was no longer the arena of his mighty acts."[1562] Goodman notes that many Jews believed that "they needed to return to the path of piety for God again to look after his chastened people." However, Goodman adds, "Presumably not all Jews were equally sanguine about the future under the care of the Jewish God."[1563]

Indeed, Cohen says, expressions of confusion and uncertainty were evoked less by God's "transcendence and remoteness" than "by the incomprehensibility of his actions."[1564] What is remarkable about Kaufmann's comment is that "the fall of Jerusalem" to which he refers is the destruction of this city in the sixth century BC, not the similar event that occurred in AD 70. On this subject, Kugel asks, "How could one possibly believe that Israel was the favorite of the world's one, true deity, the universal God, when that God did not seem to be doing anything to restore Israel to its former glory?" And the later conquest of the Near East by Alexander the Great in the fourth century BC "must have made it seem as if the whole idea of Israel's God controlling their fate had been a mistake from the start."[1565] In short, as James Muilenburg explains, Israel lost its land and, to some degree, its national identity since the year 586 B.C. marked "the destruction of the temple," "the cessation of the cult," the end of rule by David's heirs, and the exile "of substantial elements of the population"—all of which meant that "[t]he nation as the bearer of the people's history was gone."[1566]

The so-called "end of prophecy" was also underscored by the attempt on the part of many Jews in the intertestamental period to preserve and thereby elevate certain written works of the past to canonical status by including them in a sacred text, whose sanctity was assumed to be a consequence of their inspiration by God himself. Thus, on the one hand, Ellis Rivkin says, "the belief that God would always make known His will to prophets" came to an end. On the other hand, however, this idea "gave way to the belief that God had made his will known once and for all time in a book of eternal teachings and immutable laws . . . The God whose demands were bespoken by living prophets was displaced by the God whose demands were to be read and reread by the Aaronide priests whom God had invested with authority over the Law unto all generations. The hearing ear gave way to the reading eye."[1567] That is, according to Friedman: "In the apparent absence of the acts of God, there is the Word of God. The Hebrew Bible becomes a book about itself."[1568]

Von Rad argues that this change did not take place overnight. Although "the source material" does not mention the fact, it must be the case that even as early as the Assyrian invasion in the eighth century some people in Judea "gathered together the comprehensive literary legacy of the Northern Kingdom and made it their own."

Hosea's prophecy was substantially redacted, "stories about Elijah and Elisha" were collected, and historical records of the northern kings "must have been brought to Jerusalem." In other words, von Rad says, Jews who cared about these now-treasured oral and written materials "must have had all of Israel's old traditions at their disposal" and must also have believed they had the right to interpret" this inheritance—hence initiating "the interpretive period" of Jewish history, which Deuteronomy initiated and authorized. These Jews were, after all, "the people of God . . . , and in consequence the legacy of the history of the North belonged to them," which was both a claim of ownership and an acknowledgment of responsibility. Indeed, with the cessation of saving events and the absence of prophets who could remind the people of Israel of their obligations, "Josiah had the will of God in his hands in the form of a book, and that meant taking a decisive step towards the formation of a normative canon."[1569]

As Kugel explains, "There may have been prophets around, but now God spoke principally through the written word. His voice was heard—constantly—from the pages of the Torah and other books."[1570] Geller says, "Contemporary prophecy was demoted and all but abolished in favor of written documents that contained past revelation, so that biblical religion became a completely textual religion, requiring a body of approved interpreters, the scribes."[1571] According to Cohen, "Instead of consulting prophets, people eager to hear the word of the Lord would study the collected words of those who had once spoken with God."[1572] Kaufmann comments: "The goal of the religious ferment that arose in the age of the fall was to found the life of the nation on the basis of *the word of God*." Earlier, of course, the Jews had relied on other "manifestations of God's presence . . . With land, temple, and king gone, [however,] only one contact with the holy was left: *the divine word* . . . The sacred literary legacy of the past was collected and sifted; the age of compilation and canonization began."[1573]

Those who returned to Israel from Babylonia in the second half of the sixth century BC were a special group, chosen as they had been at the time of the exile, Kugel says, from among "the country's political and intellectual leaders." Upon their arrival in their homeland, they were "eager, in one sense or another to go back to what had been before—not just to the land itself, but to everything that living on that land had come to represent in their minds." Their return was "an attempt to resurrect the past," which required that they consult the sacred documents that somehow or other they had misunderstood or misconstrued and needed to re-examine—ardently and comprehensively—in order to save themselves from their past disasters and present dilemma. Where had they gone astray? How could they recover their past relationship with God? "It was Israel's own library of ancient texts that seemed to hold the answers to such questions—records of centuries of historical events as well as the weighty pronouncements of ancient prophets and sages." Kugel explains, "The past, in other words, was to determine what was to be in the future, and saying what had been was thus potentially an act of great political significance."[1574]

The Evolution of Love

As Marc Zvi Bettler says, "Once the biblical canon was fixed, there could be no additions to it or subtractions from it." After all, "books in the biblical canon . . . came to be thought of as divinely inspired." These books gained "canonical status," Brettler adds, because of "the "community's views of their centrality, authority, and inspiration."[1575] "Deuteronomic religion," Geller says, "all but abolishes future prophetic revelation, lest new divine communications compete with the single authoritative written revelation at Horeb/Sinai." Geller explains: "Deuteronomic religion introduced a new text-centeredness by insisting on the unchangeability of the written form of the Torah ('instruction') given to Moses on Horeb (Sinai). More than any other Torah book, Deuteronomy emphasizes the *sefer* or written document. Nothing may be added or taken away (Deut. 4:2; 13:1). This is the beginning of the notion of an immutable canon, an approach to sacred texts quite at variance with the liberal attitude toward textual transmission of most ancient cultures."[1576] Compiled from ancient scrolls, embodying divergent and at times mutually contradictory matter," Kaufmann says, the Torah "is a monument to the diffidence of an age which dared not alter a jot or tittle of, much less add anything to, the ancient revelation. Upon this book the Restoration community made a new covenant, pledging themselves to obey all its commands."[1577]

The movement to create a Bible by choosing a few books over many others also suggests that, as time passed, people increasingly felt that the age of God-inspired writing was over—in other words, that some of what had been written was worthy of special recognition, particularly because it was an expression of God's will, but that God had stopped communicating altogether. Michael E. Stone explains: "The writing down of the Torah also produced a retrospective view of religious authority; the Torah, the embodiment of divine norms, had been revealed in the past. The prophets who had provided an on-going channel for transmission of divine commands and of the summons to divine norms ceased."[1578]

Thus, says Cohen, the Jews of the intertestamental age "collected and treasured the works of the ancients because they knew that God spoke more directly and clearly to their ancestors than to themselves." He adds later, "Both the Jews and the Greeks of the Hellenistic period realized that they were living in a post-classical age, and that the greatest expressions of their national literatures had already been written."[1579] Particularly in the period after the Revolt of AD 66, it was clear that Judaism had profoundly changed: "Prophets were replaced by apocalyptic seers, healers, and magic men; priests were replaced by scribes and lay scholars; the temple was replaced by sects; and sacrifices were replaced by prayer and Torah study . . . The Jews were living in an age of silver but were seeking gold."[1580]

By the time the final choices for inclusion in the Jewish Bible were made—a task assumed by the Pharisees and later the Rabbis in the late first or early second century AD—they reflected the belief that God had not inspired a written work since the composition of the book of Daniel in the second century BC. Furthermore, although the fundamental values of Judaism were restated in such works as the book of Jubilees,

Ecclesiasticus, and the Psalms of Solomon, many intertestamental writings might have been excluded because they were either too strongly influenced by Hellenism or, in the case of the apocalyptic works, expressive of ideas unacceptable to the Rabbis.

Says Cohen of the Jews in general, "They no longer tried to write a Torah, or a work of classical prophecy, or (with one or two exceptions) a history in the style of Judges or Kings; these were genres that belonged to a bygone era . . . The Jews sensed that . . . they lacked the religious authority, perhaps authenticity, of their forebears. For the most part, they no longer wrote works in the biblical style and (at least the writers in Hebrew) seldom put their own names on their work."[1581] After all, Kaufmann explains, "Prophecy had been nurtured by the simple faith in the indwelling God in Israel's life and history. Now that the feeling of God's nearness had been undermined, the spirit of prophecy began to die."[1582]

Given the growing impression among ancient Jews that God was no longer inclined to communicate his commandments and concerns directly; was unlikely to intervene spontaneously in the day-to-day lives of human beings; and was, to some degree, beyond human understanding, the development of a definitive written statement of God's will may well have seemed imperative. After all, if neither God's words nor his actions were forthcoming, some alternative source of wisdom and guidance, if available, would be invaluable. Kaufmann says: "The return from Babylon, the building of the Second Temple, and the crystallization of the Torah book all served to express the yearning to heal the breach between God and people opened by the fall. The temple symbolized God's presence in Israel in the past; *the Torah symbolized Israel's commitment to live by the divine word in the present.*"[1583]

Kugel similarly traces the elevation of the Torah to almost divine status to the time of the Jews' return from exile and to their "renewed dedication to God's will": "It is in this context that one should locate the seeds of the very idea of a Bible, a great, multifarious corpus of divinely given instruction. All those texts saved from the ancient past came, slowly but steadily, to be united behind a single purpose: to tell people what God wanted them to know and believe *and do*." On one hand, "[t]he laws of the Decalogue, according to some scholars, may have begun as the simple code of conduct among scattered tribes, binding them to their distant suzerain and imposing on them minimal standards of decency in dealing with one another." On the other hand, however, these very laws, which were both modified and added to, were eventually considered to be "*divinely* given" because they were "promulgated in . . . God's name." Following them, Kugel says, meant not merely being a good citizen but being a servant of God. And violations of such laws were not just crimes, but sins.[1584]

Thus, as Kugel notes, speaking of Psalm 119 and its persistent repetition of the psalmist's need to examine God's commandments, "perhaps this was . . . a reflection of a new sort of piety, 'seeking Torah as a substitute for seeking God.'"[1585] Cohen says, referring to Ezra 7:10, "Ezra seeks not God but the Torah of God." Later, in the postbiblical era, Cohen adds: "With the canonization of the Torah, Jews no longer seek

The Evolution of Love

God directly. *They seek God through the Torah."*[1586] James Muilenburg similarly comments: "A book became the medium of a divine revelation," which "was not the living voice of" a prophet. Rather, it was the book of Deuteronomy, which "set itself up as the criterion for orthodoxy" and initiated "the movement which was to make of Judaism the people of the Book."[1587]

According to Geller, the transcendence of God—his unwillingness to intervene in human affairs—"place[s] great stress on the word."[1588] Robert N. Bellah similarly argues that the new conception of God as "utterly transcendent" generated the need to discover his will in his word—that is, the Torah and nowhere else. After all, God had made it clear not only that he "demands love and righteousness from his people" but also that he had given them everything they needed to know in order to live up to his expectations: "*God is in the Word, and if the people hear the Word and keep it*"—that is, *do whatever he asks them to do*—"they are in right relation to God." Indeed, Bellah says, quoting Geller, "the text"—the Covenant—"is raised to the level of God Himself, in a sense *is* God."[1589] And everything else is left to his people, who received the "gift of ethical freedom." They were "ruled by divine law, not the arbitrary rule of the state," and were given the means to become "responsible individuals."[1590]

Like Kugel, Cohen refers to Psalm 119 as an expression of "a new type of piety whose origins are not clear." As we noted in the last chapter, the quest for knowledge was associated with the desire to *understand* the will of God in order to *fulfill* the will of God. As Cohen notes, these pursuits may have originated in "the Deuteronomic ordinance that the Torah be read publicly at the central shrine (Deut. 31:10–13)," after which they were sustained by Josephus and Philo, who claimed that Moses "ordained the regular study of [God's] statutes." And then they were carried out frequently and fervently by the Rabbis, who insisted that "sections of the Torah" be read in the synagogue publicly, weekly, and sequentially. Cohen concludes, as I noted earlier, that "this idea had a profound influence on the Judaism of the Second Temple and rabbinic periods. Its ultimate expression is the ideal of the sage who meditates on the words of the Lord day and night . . . It is the basis of rabbinic piety." Thus, having begun as a way of pleasing God—that is, "as a means to an end," study of the Torah among the Rabbis "became an end in itself."[1591]

The elevation of the Torah to, in James Parkes's words, the "Incarnation" of God's will[1592] was not the only response made by the Jews to the distressing circumstances in which they lived in the intertestamental period. Other options that were embraced were, as we noted in chapter 6, (1) the belief in an afterlife in which rewards and punishments would be justly distributed, (2) the expectation that life on earth would be completely transformed, and (3) the assumption that this reassertion of God's rule would be led by a messiah who would defeat the forces of darkness and, with God's help, reestablish the reign of justice, which seemed to have been absent from everyday life for several centuries. By this time, according to Raymond E. Brown, "[t]he idea of an afterlife had . . . developed clearly among some Jews, and that opened the possibility of eternal happiness replacing an existence marked by suffering and torture. In this period we move from prophetic books with apocalyptic traits to full-fledged apocalypses."[1593]

"Most of these books"—that is, apocalypses—says Merrill C. Tenney, "were written in the period of unsettled national life and struggle between the return from the exile and the destruction of Jerusalem. They reflect the restlessness and the dissatisfied spirit of the Jews, who were still dreaming of an independent commonwealth. Their themes indicate the Jewish reaction to the oppression, uncertainty, and hope that characterized the entire period."[1594] The question raised by the long-lasting suffering of the Jews, as we learn particularly from Job, Ecclesiastes, and many of the psalms, was related to God's purpose and power: Why does God accept injustice?

As we have seen, it was this question about God's moral governance of the universe that influenced the slow but growing development of both apocalypticism and messianism in the wake of the destruction of the First Temple in the sixth century BC and which culminated in the intertestamental period. According to Bart D. Ehrman, the claim of the prophets that Israel of the eighth through six centuries BC "continued to suffer military and political setbacks because it had disobeyed God" lost its appeal when "Jewish thinkers eventually became dissatisfied with this answer" simply "because it could not explain historical realities"—particularly the "fact" that "it was not only the sinners who suffered, but people who were righteous as well."[1595] That is, the idea that God is just because he rewards good deeds and punishes bad—at least in this life—was no longer acceptable to many people.

As Edward Schillebeeckx puts it: "Whatever one may think of apocalypticism, the experience at the bottom of it is existential and realistic, even 'modern': if God is the source of all life, then why so much cruelty, inequality, pain and suffering, unhappiness, misfortune and woe, why so much discord in our nature and our human history?" Apocalypticism, Schillebeeckx continues, "looked for a solution" both from God and in the future. And this was the same solution embraced by revolutionaries and messianists: "An ardent longing then ensues; a life liberated and redeemed is about to begin. In such situations of *malaise* fantasy intensifies, Utopian pictures of a totally new world loom ahead: visions of a realm of peace, righteousness, happiness, and love such as never was seen."[1596] Wylen says, "Apocalypticism can be rationally understood as a way of maintaining hope and finding meaning in a situation of powerlessness and unbearable oppression."[1597] According to Muilenburg, as a concept which "sees more deeply into the tragic perplexities of history," apocalypticism was "prophecy transformed by a greater emphasis on transcendence, persistent pessimism concerning any resolution of the divine will within history, and a more passionate and intense faith in the coming of the divine kingdom."[1598]

The rise of apocalypticism in the intertestamental period was not only a symptom of the kind of extreme suffering that derives from political domination and economic oppression. It was also a response to extreme disillusionment, which, in this case, derived from the Jews' reluctant acknowledgement that God's rewards and punishments would be delayed. This means that they were forced to abandon an idea that was universally popular in the ancient world and remains a doctrine that many people continue to embrace in the modern world: the concept of *quid pro quo*. Baruch A. Levine argues that this idea, which, as we have seen, appears so prominently in Deuteronomy, "accords with ancient Near Eastern conventions": "Well-being. peace, and prosperity—in short, all the blessings individuals and nations seeks from divine powers—are made contingent on obedience to codes of law, treaties, oaths, and royal decrees, while divine wrath is the misfortune of the disobedient." As in the Holiness Code in Leviticus, as well as in Deuteronomy, Levine notes parenthetically, "much more space is normally allotted to elaborating horrendous punishments than is devoted to spelling out rewards, testifying to the sad truth that fear of punishment is more real than even the prospect of success!"[1599]

According to Ramsay MacMullen, "For both the Christian and the non-Christian" in the ancient world, "the only thing believed in was some supernatural power to bestow benefits." That is, it was common for people to assume that their lives could be improved by the gods if they made sacrifices or performed rituals. "From divinity," MacMullen adds later, "all good might be received: foreknowledge, safety in risky doings, good crops, and . . . good health." Worshipers "only made offerings . . . in order to gain favor from powerful beings," without feeling "the least uneasiness about the self-interested nature of worship." In other words, "[i]n the world we are studying, there was nothing to be ashamed of in needing and asking favors from heaven."[1600]

However, the very existence of apocalyptic literature indicates that this concept was not utterly rejected, especially by Jews in the Common Era. Rather, what was doubted by many and denied by some was the idea that rewards and punishments follow immediately or at least soon after the performance of acts that are expected to evoke God's favor or disfavor. Now, it was understood that the *quid* of God's approval or disapproval would be delayed until some time after the *quo* of humanity's obedience or disobedience. As Kugel explains, "From such a viewpoint, only some huge, momentous event, a Big Bang that would change everything, could redeem Israel's traditional belief in God's special concern for its fate." Significantly, the book of Jubilees and "other apocalyptic writings sought to reaffirm God's control of events by focusing on the *longue duree*: divine time was dealt out in chunks of centuries, so that the little ups and downs of any given period could only mislead people by having them fail to notice the larger, divinely created patterns." Kugel adds: "In short, the problem of the 'messiness of history' was basically solved by kicking the can down the road. However inexplicable Israel's current situation may have appeared to the Judean remnant, its ultimate resolution had been planned out long in advance and revealed in such works as the biblical book of Daniel or extrabiblical compositions like *1 Enoch*, *Jubilees*, and *4 Ezra* [or *2 Esdras*]."[1601]

There can be little doubt that the Pharisees, like many Jews, put their faith in all of these ways of solving the problems of "suffering," "torture," "unsettled national life and struggle," "restlessness," dissatisfaction, "oppression," "uncertainty," "cruelty," "inequality," and so on. The difficulty was, as these descriptions indicate, that these solutions represented, in Tenney's words, hopes and dreams, and, in Schillebeeckx's words, "fantasy," "Utopian pictures," and "visions"—in short, expectations that, at least from a later perspective, had little prospect of fulfillment. Nevertheless, according to Wylen, "the doctrine of bodily resurrection," the underlying assumption of Jewish apocalypticism and messianism, was one of the "doctrines which became central to later Judaism." Wylen explains: "The Pharisees taught that sometime in the future everyone who ever lived will return to bodily life on earth. Each person will rise from the grave. Then God will judge every human being according to his or her earthly deeds."[1602]

John P. Meier says that the Pharisees shared many of the beliefs held by other Jews: "With almost all other Palestinian Jews the Pharisees shared in what we might call 'mainstream' or 'common' Judaism."[1603] Thus, according to E. P. Sanders, "like most other first-century Jews," except the Sadducees, the Pharisees "also believed in some form of existence after death."[1604] Indeed, says Charles Guignebert, "[t]hey shared the general hope of a resurrection and looked for the imminent advent of the Kingdom of God." Furthermore, "[t]hey shared the illusions of the Jewish nationalist movement; that is to say, they believed in the survival of the Jewish State and in its triumphant return to power at some future date. As a rule they linked up this improbable event more or less closely with the great Messianic drama."[1605]

Meier adds that the Pharisees believed these changes for the better would occur because of their submission to God's will: "Fidelity to God and his Law carried a sure reward. Those Israelites who proved faithful to the Law would be raised from the dead on the last day, acquitted at the final judgment, and given a share, along with all the just, in the world to come."[1606] Not surprisingly, some scholars have argued that it was this optimism, this faith in the future of the Jewish people, that encouraged a large number of Jews to respect the Pharisees, laud their wisdom, and sometimes even embrace their strict application of ethical values and cultic practices. Rivkin says, "The Pharisees were powerful because they had revealed the road to life eternal."[1607]

However, many scholars have expressed serious doubts about whether the Pharisees and Rabbis took the concepts of apocalypticism and messianism as seriously as some scholars once believed. Thus, although "the Mishna excludes from a share in the world to come anyone who says that there is no resurrection of the dead," Meier argues that this claim—and its suggestion that the Pharisees were fully committed to the idea of apocalypticism—is questionable: "This single item of doctrine . . . is a meager fragment that seems to hang almost alone in midair." The problem, Meier explains, is that the written sources are otherwise "all but silent" on the Pharisees' belief in "eschatological and/or apocalyptic events." The contrary view was based on the assumption, no longer held "by many critics today," that apocalyptic works like the Psalms of Solomon and the book of Jubilees "were Pharisaic in authorship."[1608] G. Ernest Wright says that the Pharisees "still looked forward to a future in which God would inaugurate his reign on earth, and this hope indeed took the strongly historical form of a restored realm under a new king of David's line as Messiah." However, like Meier, Wright suggests that these ideas were not as important to the Pharisees as scholars once believed: "Yet these beliefs were peripheral. Their chief interest like that of the wisdom literature was in individual ethics."[1609]

Other scholars insist that, particularly compared to other Jewish groups, the Pharisaic interest in apocalypticism was quite limited. To be sure, on the one hand, as Kee and his co-writers argue, "Such expectations as the victorious coming of God's kingdom, the coming of the Messiah, and the resurrection of the dead, assumed an important place in Pharisaic thought," at least for a period of time.[1610] On the other hand, however, these writers continue, "compared with such a sect as the Essenes, most Pharisees were restrained in their attitude toward eschatological expectation."[1611] As Gaalyah Cornfeld explains, "[I]t is clear that the Essenes were closer to the Jewish-Christians in terms of messianic expectations and eschatological fulfilment." Specifically, although "they too believed in the eventual coming of the messiah," the Pharisees rejected "the extreme hopes of the visionaries and criticized those who 'hasten his coming': They believed that the Kingdom would come when the people obeyed in spirit and in truth the Law and the Word of the Prophets."[1612]

Samuel Umen reminds us that the Pharisees not only excluded both apocryphal and apocalyptic works from the Hebrew canon, but also "forbade the reading of them" and "branded them as 'Outside Books.'" In support of this claim, Umen says that in the Mishnah (Sanh. X.I.) Rabbi Akiba is quoted as "includ[ing] amongst those who had no part in the world to come 'him who reads the 'external books'"—i.e., those excluded from the Bible. The Pharisees opposed the apocryphal works, Umen argues, because "[t]hey [that is, the Pharisees] aimed to make the Halacha"—the Law—"the central feature of Judaism." And they rejected the apocalyptic works because their faith "came to them from a way of life which the Torah gave them, from ideals which the prophets held up before them," not "from the symbols, visions, and empty promises of the Apocryphal and Apocalyptic readings."[1613] According to Schillebeeckx, the Pharisees were "keenly opposed to apocalypticism." They turned to it briefly after the Revolt of AD 66 but, under the influence of the Rabbis in the second century, "attacked this literature once again."[1614]

Although the Rabbis continued to accept and even promote the concept of resurrection, they seem to have lost interest, eventually, in the related ideas of apocalypticism and messianism, particularly after the failed rebellion of Simon Bar Kochba in AD 132.[1615] According to Alan J. Avery-Peck, "Especially the failed revolts" conducted by the Jews against the Romans compelled "Judaism's earliest Rabbinic leadership" to reject "the idea that God is immediately present and ready to respond to the needs of a suffering nation." They found the idea unacceptable because it was not only "unworkable" but "dangerous" since the rebellion "had significantly worsened the community's political, economic, and ritual circumstance."[1616] As Alan Segal says, "The destruction of Jerusalem was exactly what the apocalyptists had predicted." However, "the final consummation, of which the destruction of the Temple was just the first stage, did not arrive. Nor did the destruction bring about a new world order in which the righteous were saved. The result was a partial disconfirmation of apocalyptic beliefs"—and, no doubt, a partial disconfirmation of the concept that God intervenes on his people's behalf.[1617]

Although it was not the last nail in the coffin of both apocalypticism and "active Jewish nationalism," the Bar Kochba revolt may well have been understood by many Jews in the same way that Lee Levine sees it: "[I]t is also possible that the leadership of this revolt was so intoxicated by religious dreams of national restoration that any kind of rational reading of the international political and military map was beyond its capacity."[1618] From this point on, the Rabbis evidently remained skeptical about both the imminence and grandiosity of the end-time as promised in the apocalyptic literature. As Cohen says: "With the defeat of Bar Kosba [the original name of Bar Kochba], who may have had messianic pretensions . . . , the belief that eschatological deliverance was imminent was replaced by more realistic expectations. The Messiah would come, the wicked Roman empire would be destroyed and the righteous would be vindicated—all this would surely happen, but it would happen later rather than sooner."[1619]

Two passages in the Talmud illustrate this point. In one, when Rabbi Akiba, in reference to Bar Kochba, shouts "This is the King Messiah!" Rabbi Yohanan ben Torta replies, "Akiba, grass will grow in your cheeks, and [the Messiah] will not have come!"[1620] In the second passage, Rabbi Yohanan ben Zakkai says, "If a plant is in your hand [ready to be planted]," and you are told that the Messiah has come, "go and plant the planting and after that go out to receive him." Commenting on this passage, Segal explains that, "though one must not give up hope that the messiah will come, it would be foolhardy to give credence to anyone fomenting rebellion or heresy." That is, "[g]iven the Roman forces, messianism and apocalypticism were dangerous to the community in the late second century and thereafter." [1621]

Even before the failed revolt of Bar Kochba, however, the Rabbis exhibited little interest in either reading apocalypses written by others or writing their own. Cohen comments: "One of the major distinctions between the theology of the rabbis and the theology of the Second Temple period is their complete lack of interest in either apocalyptic literature or eschatological speculations."[1622] And this attitude appears to have been adopted early on. According to Craig A. Evans: "In Rabbinic Judaism, eschatology and messianism have receded. This is not to say that they have no place; indeed they do. But the heart of the Judaism of the framers of the Mishnah and its complementary supplement the Tosefta concerns faithful obedience to Torah, its careful study, and the preservation of tradition felt to be edifying and in keeping with God's will." Evans adds that the Rabbis' messianism was "cautious and reserved," largely because of the cumulative effect on their expectations of the "bitter lessons" from the failed "wars and insurrections of 115 C.E., 66–74 C.E., and 4 B.C.E.," as well as the Bar Kochba revolt: "Yes, Messiah will someday make his appearance 'in the world to come,' but not any day soon. For now, one's duty is to obey the Law, to practice charity, and to make disciples."[1623]

As James Charlesworth comments, "Under the influence of the School of Hillel and the fear of further rebellion (as well as the attempt to define itself over against Christianity), post-70 Judaism—especially after 135—attempted to eliminate the apocalyptic elements from its traditions." Thus, just as Cornfeld distinguishes the Pharisees from the Essenes, Charlesworth distinguishes the Rabbis from the Christians: "When Rabbinic Judaism decided largely to eliminate the apocalyptic perspectives and, at the same time, ecclesiastical Christianity embraced them, the two movements took different forks on the road to self-definition."[1624]

E. P. Sanders says that "Rabbinic literature" simply excludes "apocalyptic visions," for which reason, among others, he "doubt[s] that very many Jews"—at least in the period between the Roman invasion of 63 BC and the Jewish Revolt of 66 AD—"spent much *time* contemplating the other world."[1625] Thus, Sanders adds later, although "it is probable that most Jews expected death not to be the end," "the future" was not only "not a major topic of [their] literature" at this time, but also a subject that they seem to have "conceived . . . quite vaguely."[1626]

In the face of the doubts and uncertainties that appear to have dominated the period, according to Cohen, "the rabbis of the second century seem thoroughly unconcerned." Cohen says that they "believed in a world to come, resurrection of the dead, messianic deliverance, [and] corporate and individual reward and punishment." However, "except for one chapter and an occasional paragraph, the Mishnah is not interested in these topics." Indeed, even though Cohen identifies the "resurrection of the dead" and the "divine supervision of human affairs" as two out of the "three core ideas of rabbinic Judaism, . . . the Mishnah does not elevate any of these ideas to the status of dogmas, and does not compose any creeds that would demonstrate how essential these beliefs are to the self-definition of Judaism."[1627]

The Rabbis' view of all end-time theories derives partly from their deep suspicion of thoughts and actions that have not been motivated by Torah study and piety but by what the thinker or actor believes to be divine inspiration. Segal says that the Rabbis suspected "all sources of authority dependent on charismatic or miraculous claims, whether they be outside the rabbinic movement or even . . . within it."[1628] This attitude applied not only to writers of apocalypses and self-proclaimed messiahs, both of whom claimed to be inspired by God, but also to so-called holy men—"charismatic miracle workers and faith healers"—of which there were many in the intertestamental period.

According to Avery-Peck, "Strikingly, the Rabbinic Judaism that emerges in the first centuries CE largely rejects the model of prophet and charismatic leader prominent in Judaic writings." The Rabbis believed that "the intellectual pursuit of the true meaning of the Torah" was "the key to reinvigorating Judaism" after the destruction of the Temple. Simply put, they assumed that, outside of Torah study and true piety, the claim to having "special access to God" was highly questionable, if not unbelievable. The Rabbis did not condemn the ability of holy men "to produce miracles." They merely "Rabbinized" these men by claiming that they were "exemplary models of holiness and piety," as the Rabbis considered themselves to be, and that their powers derived from the same beliefs and practices that empowered the Rabbis: "knowledge of the proper interpretation of Torah."[1629]

The Restoration of God

To be sure, the doubts about divine inspiration and the establishment of a biblical canon were obviously signs of the times—that is, indications that God's ongoing involvement with his people had been greatly reduced, if not terminated. At the same time, however, setting up strict standards for judging both the spiritual claims of human beings and the sanctity of religious texts was also an indication that the Jews (and especially the Pharisees and the Rabbis, who took up both projects with great determination) were struggling to escape from the desperate situation in which they found themselves. If they understood that God no longer communicated directly with his people (as he had in Genesis and Exodus), that he no longer gave them advice through his prophets (as he had in the writings of Isaiah and Jeremiah and others), and that he no longer intervened in their lives by administering rewards and punishments (as the rise of apocalyptic and messianic hopes and dreams implied), they also understood that there were nevertheless things they could do to maintain their relationship with him.

What aided this effort was in fact the elevation of the Torah to a level it had never attained before. That is, the attempt to replace God's direct communication to his people through intermediaries like Moses, Samuel, Elijah, and the later prophets with the written record of their collective expression of God's will actually succeeded. And what had begun as a desperate and defensive attempt to "save the appearances"—to preserve some real, important, and useful contact with God—turned out to be a salvific act. According to Kugel, the transformation of the ancient Jewish texts into objects worthy of deep respect—indeed, reverence—and constant study would have surprised their authors as well as earliest readers: "There is little in the biblical texts themselves to suggest that they were intended to be read in this fashion." Indeed, the prophets themselves "did not really write much of the material the Bible attributed to them." Nevertheless, their works and all those of the other writers of the Bible were, at least by the first century AD–thanks partly to such intertestamental works as Ecclesiasticus, 1 Baruch, and the book of Jubilees—understood to be not only "the word of God," but also the means by which Judaism itself could be saved.[1630]

Thus, as Kugel says, although the Torah began as nothing more than "a collection of narratives and laws," it became something more: "In the early second century BCE,

Ben Sira described it as nothing less than the embodiment of divine wisdom—the set of principles by which God governs the world—so that if you wished to know what God wanted of you, or to explain His ways with the world, you needed to go no further than this book." According to Kugel, Deuteronomy, like Psalm 119, reveals a "striking transformation of the connection between the people and their God, one that would be," as we have seen, "repeatedly ratcheted upward until, toward the end of the Second Temple period, God's aspect as divine lawgiver would be unsurpassed," and his Law would become "a, perhaps *the*, meeting place between God and humans."[1631]

In this respect, the laws of God were not so much arbitrary requirements, obedience to which was a sign of submission—like building altars or undergoing circumcision or making sacrifices in the Temple. Kugel says, these were "laws that gave the Pentateuch its special character" among Jews of the intertestamental period. "They saw in the Pentateuch a great divine guidebook, its laws constituting God's detailed set of do's and don'ts for every human life"—again, not as a token of awe-filled and self-effacing obedience but as an expression of heartfelt and self-enhancing love and gratitude.[1632] Even though the Jews eventually lost both their Temple and their land—at least the city of Jerusalem—Kaufmann adds, "*the Torah book was a self-contained, in itself adequate, embodiment of the religion of YHWH. Of itself the Torah was a fountainhead of sanctity, an eternal expression of the will of God,*" as well as "the seed of an ultimate liberation of the religion of Israel from ethnic and territorial limitations."[1633]

Kugel adds, "God no longer speaks principally to humans through the intermediation of His prophets, but via the words of His book, which had become a detailed guide for living. Indeed, keeping God's laws in all their particulars . . . became the central act of Jewish religiosity."[1634] Andre LaCocque comments: "[D]uring the period of the Second Temple, the Torah underwent a progressive secularization due, paradoxically, to the fact that it was becoming more absolute. This process put increased emphasis on the intrinsic value of the Law, whereas originally its authority was mediated and guaranteed by the authority of God, who had given it. This means that it became possible, at least in theory, to obey the Torah without believing in YHWH; in any event without necessarily making the connection between the Law and the Legislator."[1635]

On one hand, as I noted earlier in this chapter, many of the works of the past had been preserved for centuries, no doubt because they "were considered precious and worthy of preservation." On the other hand, however, "[e]ventually they came to be perceived as bits of timeless ethical instruction, or evidence of the divine plan for history or of the prophet's own foreknowledge of much later times." During the intertestamental period "the great literary heritage of the past was truly becoming Scripture,"[1636] and it was believed to be far more than an expression of the national history and religious beliefs of an obscure group of people. In fact, it was regarded as a collection of transcendent truths that were eternally relevant and universally applicable. In this respect, even if God was not available, at least his extraordinary message was—and that was an exceptionally valuable possession.

The Hidden Revolution

Besides dedicating themselves to discovering God's will by studying these sacred works, which he had inspired in the first millennium of his reign, the ancient Jews also realized that they could maintain their relationship with God in three additional ways. First, under the influence of the Pharisees, they committed themselves to becoming "a nation of priests" by living in absolute purity. As Stephen M. Wylen explains, "The Pharisees wanted the whole world to be God's temple,"[1637] and wanted every individual to understand that he or she—potentially, at least—could participate equally in the faith. Second, they developed new methods of worship that were highly personalized and spiritualized. Alan F. Segal says that the Rabbis, in particular, transformed Judaism "from a national ideology into a Hellenistic spiritual community," in which "personal piety replaced the old corporate concept of the good of the state."[1638] Third, they enthusiastically accepted the responsibility of following the program of compassion and community outlined in the Covenant Code. In other words, they would "be holy, for [God] is holy" (Lev 11:45), they would worship out of love rather than fear, and they would become God's partner by fulfilling his will.[1639]

Samuel Umen traces the democritization of Judaism to the prophets, who, "for the first time in the history of human thought, gave expression to the fundamental ethical truth that God is present in every human heart, and that, by virtue of this, it is in every man's power to enjoy communion with Him without any mediatorship whatever, the only condition being that he who would converse with God must live a life of purity and righteousness and walk humbly with God." Umen continues, "This conception of religion marks a new era in the religious development of Israel, for through it religion became dissociated from the confines of nation and country: it ceased to be part and parcel of the political-social order into which a man was born, and became preeminently the concern of the individual."[1640]

As I noted in chapter 7, Shaye Cohen says that, in pursuit of the goal of making Israel a "holy" people (Exod 19:6; Lev 19:2), "the Jews of the Second Temple period developed new rituals, broadened the application of many of the laws of the Torah, and in general intensified the life of service to God."[1641] These and other changes reflected a general development in which the Jewish religion was both democratized and personalized, a process that reached its highest point after the Roman victory over the Jewish rebels in the first-century AD, at which time Judaism clearly underwent its final transformation. Because the Temple had been destroyed, worship took place in synagogues, and Temple sacrifice was replaced by prayer and Torah study. The synagogues were independent organizations, ruled by local authorities and free to establish their own religious practices.[1642] Religious leadership was assumed by scribes, who were educated laypersons instead of state-authorized officials. And worship, no longer mediated by priests and dominated by Temple standards, became more individualized. Piety was entirely the responsibility of every Jew; it could be practiced anywhere; and the fate of the community rested on the shoulders of everyone.[1643]

According to Michael E. Stone, although the interpretation of the Bible had been in the hands of the Temple priests, the scribes—and, indeed, every other group or sect—were able to engage in the interpretive act when the Bible became both widely available in written form and on its way to canonization. "In biblical times," Stone says, "the weight of teaching and administration of divine law had been largely the task of the priests... The written crystallization of the sacred tradition and the position accorded the written documents changed this situation, even before the concept of 'canon' had fully evolved. Competition developed in society for the role of true exponent of sacred documents."

As we noted in chapter 7, every sect believed it had the right to interpret the scriptures in its own way. Stone comments, "Every group within the Jewish religious spectrum in the Second Temple period based itself on one or another particular claim to the unique, true interpretation of sacred writings." Authority thus moved from a single official conservative body, the priests, to many groups who had no official standing and who represented a wide variety of social and religious ideas, including Essenes and Pharisees. These were "new elites" who henceforth competed for authority and who inherited or assumed "the power" to explain to the people what God said and inspired. "All of these developments," Stone concludes, "signify a change in the centre of power which was entrusted with the task of preserving, teaching, and interpreting the divine norms to which the people were to aspire."[1644]

As Cohen explains, "[t]hese developments... show that during the Second Temple period Judaism was democratized. It was much more concerned with the piety and fate of the individual Jew than the religion of preexilic Israel had been with the individual Israelite." This process "reached its apogee in the piety of various sectarian groups in Second Temple times and of the rabbis after 70 CE." As we also noted in chapter 7, many Jews as well as the Pharisees—that is, for example, the Essenes and the Christians—devoted themselves to one form of perfectionism or another. Furthermore, both "the democratization of religion and the sanctification of life outside the temple... fairly characterize nonsectarian and nonrabbinic... Judaism as well, in both the land of Israel and the diaspora."[1645] Yet, again, it was the Pharisees who led the way, as D. S. Russell argues: "By teaching and interpreting the Torah, both written and oral, and by applying it to every-day life they 'democratized religion', making it personal and operative in the experience of the common people."[1646]

Solomon Zeitlin says that, given their "democratic attitude," the Pharisees fought against "caste distinctions among the people" and tried to liberalize Sabbath restrictions. Furthermore, "when the Pharisees became a force in Judea, they endeavored to make the Jewish religion not only a state religion but an individual religion, by encouraging Israelites to participate in the religious ceremonies as well as the priests."[1647] R. Travers Herford explains: "For the Torah was not the concern of the priests alone," even before the destruction of the Temple in AD 70. "It was for each individual Jew... to take its meaning to heart as it might concern him, and each one must learn that he was responsible for obedience to the Torah in his own case."[1648] Kugel says, "In postexilic times, the 'religion of laws' came to focus increasingly on each person carrying out such duties" as were defined in Deuteronomy and other sacred texts.[1649]

For the Pharisees, Cohen says, the collective and individual quest for spiritual perfection was "marked by the contemplation of scripture and the observance of the commandments."[1650] According to John P. Meier, even the Gospels portray the Pharisees as "a group that expressed itself both in the precise enunciation of rules and in the punctilious observance of them."[1651] Indeed, as much as the Pharisees insisted on the importance of studying the Bible—so much so that they acquired a reputation in some quarters for being literalists and legalists—they developed what eventually became, under the Rabbis, the most liberal approach to biblical interpretation imaginable.

Unlike the Sadducees, who actually *were* literalists in this regard, the Pharisees embraced the idea that, along with the Written Torah, God also gave his people the Oral Torah, which was, over time, revealed by the Jewish elders, especially in the intertestamental period, and formed what came to be known as "the traditions of the fathers." The Oral Torah served the purpose of allowing, first, the elders, and, later, the Pharisees themselves to keep Judaism up to date by enabling them to revise laws in order to make them useful and relevant, as the situation—political, social, and economic—required. Meier comments, "In my view, what made the Pharisees distinctive was that they openly admitted that some of their legal views and practices were not to be found as such in the written Mosaic Law, that such practices were instead venerable 'traditions' that had been handed down by the 'fathers' or 'elders,' and that such practices nevertheless were God's will for all Israel." This idea "was developed in the second and subsequent centuries A.D. into the rabbinic doctrine of the dual Torah."[1652]

Describing "the liberalizing tendencies of the Pharisees," Solomon Zeitlin says, "For the Pharisees, the Law was always plastic; and they were acutely aware of the need to modify the Jewish law in order to enable the Law to accord with the requirements of an ever-changing life."[1653] According to Joseph B. Tyson, the Pharisees thus "attempted to make [the] Torah applicable to their own and succeeding generations." Indeed, "[t]hey would, on occasion, ignore the letter of the law which they felt went against the more basic revelation of God."[1654] As Charles Guignebert explains, "They regarded all such additions as an integral part of the heritage of Israel, accepting them as issuing from the ancestral tradition which they undertook to express in the language of the *Torah* and to bring under its authority." In short, against the clear and apparently unequivocal command in Deuteronomy that *nothing* in the ancient laws could be changed (4:2), the Pharisees were able to keep their religion alive by adapting the Law of Moses to changing circumstances. In this way, "they displayed a deep and instinctive sense of continuity in change, that is to say of true evolution, by which alone religions are vital and enduring."[1655]

The Rabbis carried this interpretive freedom one step further in their composition of the Mishnah. First, in this work, they seldom referred to the Torah to justify any of their legal decisions. Cohen comments, "With few exceptions, [the Mishnah] does not attach its legal rulings to Scripture."[1656] Second, as Jacob Neusner notes, none of the Rabbis cited in the Mishnah consult God directly for that purpose: "[N]o one ever prays to have God supply a decision in a particular case."[1657] As both the Mishnah and the Talmud reveal, the Rabbis continued this tradition by asserting their right to reinterpret all of the existing laws in light of present realities, rational discussion and debate, and their own majority opinion. The Rabbis apparently believed that they had the right—and responsibility—to revise the Laws of Moses as they saw fit.

Specifically, the Rabbis found two ways to leave biblical interpretation permanently open-ended and therefore unsettled. First, they tolerated interpretive pluralism, which means that they chose to leave many issues unresolved, in which cases they preserved not the group's decision, because sometimes there was none, but all of its members' opinions.[1658] As Daniel Boyarin puts it, it is characteristic of the Babylonian Talmud that "disagreement itself . . . is exemplary of the divine mind. Instead of conducing to an ideal of *homonoia*, the Babylonian Talmud leads to an ideal of *polynoia*, the many-mindedness, as it were, of God. This difference is embodied in the famous Talmudic statement that a heavenly oracle declared, with respect to the contradictory opinions of the two Houses, of Hillel and Shammai, that 'these *and* these are the words of the Living God.'"[1659] As a result, Ellis Rivkin explains, the "two schools . . . were allowed to teach publicly their divergent views on what the *halakha* should be."[1660] Sanders says, "Most of the early passages are *debates*, not rules, and one would have to probe behind each debate to see what the Pharisees agreed on."[1661]

Second, the Rabbis assumed that to be understood correctly the Bible and its laws had to be interpreted anew—forever. That is, the Torah is interpretable from different perspectives diachronically as well as synchronically. After all, Rivkin says, the Pharisees believed in "the authority of the scholar class to reaffirm, modify, and alter the law" without ever reaching a final conclusion.[1662] And the Rabbis believed, as Boyarin explains, that "God himself falls into language, and thus into linguistic indeterminacy," which promises a "culture of endless study and argumentation"—again, forever. Boyarin calls this "a theological principle of the undecidability of the divine language," and it was practiced at "the rabbinic Yeshiva with its culture of endless study and argumentation." In other words, "[t]he dialectic can go on forever without resolution."[1663]

Thus, Kurt Schubert comments, "The relation of the Pharisees to the Law"—and the same point is equally applicable to the Rabbis—"has been aptly described as eternal discussion about the Eternal."[1664] Citing Jacques Derrida, Geoffrey Hartman, and Erich Auerbach on the subject, David Jasper says, "With the rabbis we are reminded that the Bible resists closure and conclusion, its endless writing demanding an endless exercise of reading and rereading, writing and rewriting."[1665] Thus, Neusner argues that the word *Torah* "refers to a process, not only to a particular document." And the Rabbis were part of this process insofar as they simply received the Torah from their predecessors, going back to Moses, and then passed it on to their successors. They saw their interpretive task as "a stage in the sedimentary and incremental process by which the Torah continued to come down from Sinai."[1666]

Perhaps the most famous illustration of this point is a story in the Talmud in which Rabbi Eliezer, in a legal dispute with his rabbinical colleagues, "trie[s] to support his position," as Boyarin says, "using the 'normal rabbinic modes of rational argument.'"[1667] Frustrated by his inability to convince the other Rabbis of the validity of his opinion, Eliezer performs three miracles. His goal is evidently to demonstrate that God himself supports his position. He says before the first miracle, "If the law is as I have argued, may this carob tree argue for me." However, after the carob tree "uprooted itself and moved a hundred cubits from its place," the other Rabbis respond, "From a tree no proof can be brought," meaning that God's intervention is irrelevant.

After two more miracles fail to change the minds of the other Rabbis, Eliezer says, "If I am right, may the heavens prove it," to which a heavenly voice responds, addressing the Rabbi's opponents: "What have you against Eliezer? The law is always with him." To this, Rabbi Joshua says, quoting Deuteronomy 30:12, "It [that is, the Law] is not in heaven." According to the biblical passage that Rabbi Joshua alludes to, God says: "For this commandment which I command you this day is not too hard for you, neither is it far off. *It is not in heaven*, that you should say, 'Who will go up for us to heaven, and bring it to us, that we may hear it and do it?'" (Deut 30:11–12).

As if the point needed further clarification, the writer adds two more incidents. The first underscores the idea that the Word of God—that is, the written Torah—takes precedence over contemporary revelation. To the question "What did [Rabbi Joshua] mean by this?" Rabbi Jeremiah says, "The Torah was given to us at Sinai. *We do not attend to this heavenly voice.* For it is already written in the Torah at Mt. Sinai that, 'By the majority you are to decide (Exod 23:2 [my emphasis])."" Thus, as Martin Goodman notes, in reference to what he calls this "striking story in the Babylonian Talmud," "supernatural revelation as a solution to legal conundrums is especially ruled out."[1668]

Indeed, the second incident demonstrates that, despite the clear and unequivocal assertion that revelation—presumably, whether through theophany or miracle or any other kind of divine intervention—cannot contradict the Law presented at Sinai, God supports Eliezer's opponents. Here, Rabbi Nathan later meets Elijah and asks him "what God did in that hour"—that is, when Rabbi Eliezer was rebuked by Rabbis Joshua and Jeremiah. Elijah answers that God "laughed and said, 'My children have defeated me' (Baba Mezia 59b)," which, Segal says, "exposes even God's amusement" and "gives evidence of strongly held rabbinic values."[1669] Again, according to Deuteronomy 30:14, God says that "the word is very near you." Indeed, although it is neither "in heaven" nor "beyond the sea," it is "in your mouth and in your heart, so that you can do it."

Boyarin says that the story clarifies the Rabbis' attitude toward "miracles and heavenly oracles," including faith healers and messianists, which we discussed above: "I would read in this story an explicit rejection of any notion of divine inspiration or prophecy." In addition, Boyarin sees two other themes in the Talmudic tale. First, it implicitly indicates that rabbinical decisions were always to be determined by "the will of the majority" based on "rational argument." That is, "Only the majority decision of the Rabbis has power and authority, and only their decision is relevant."[1670] Second, the story also clearly provides an example of "the end of prophecy," which we also noted earlier.

On the first point, Segal comments: "[T]he rabbinic movement, in putting the interpretation of the law in the hands of an educated class open to anyone, set the stage for rule" by a council like the Athenian *boule*. "This was not the same as democracy, but the oligarchical class had an open membership. Technically, the rulings of the Pharisees and the Rabbis came from God. But in practice, the rulings were made by the majority." Thus, Segal adds, "the rabbis offered a limited democratization, oligarchical rule by an educated professional class of legal experts."[1671] On the second point, Boyarin says. "In the Talmudic narration of rabbinic history, . . . living oral contact, both with an authoritative tradition as represented by Rabbi Eliezer and directly with the divine voice itself, has been broken once and for all." Indeed, Boyarin adds: "Not even God, not even the angels can compete with the Rabbis and their Torah."[1672]

Although it might seem that this approach to the Bible would make the Law appear to be transitory (that is, because it can be changed at any time) and therefore trivial, it was actually intended to make the Law both relevant and practical. Besides democratizing worship and sanctifying every aspect of human behavior, Cohen says, the conscientious effort of the Pharisees to make sure that the Law was clear, precise, and accessible was intended "to bring the Jew into contact with the sacred."[1673] In other words, the goal was to bring God "down" to humanity by bringing humanity "up" to God.[1674]

According to Karen Armstrong, democratization was enhanced and extended by the Pharisaic doctrine that "the whole of Israel was called to be a nation of priests" and that God himself was—*therefore and thereby*—accessible to each individual. Every home was the new Temple, every moral action could become a means of atonement; and the Torah was "the new Holy of Holies"—that is the Inner Sanctum of the Temple, in which the Torah was stored. In this way, Armstrong says, despite the reigning concept of God as transcendent, the Rabbis, following the Pharisees, "made him intimately present within mankind and the smallest details of life." They "did not construct any formal doctrines about God. Instead, they experienced him as an almost tangible presence." Being accessible to individuals commensurate with their capacity to receive him—that is, commensurate with their *ascent*, their achievement of sanctification—God "was *an essentially subjective experience*."[1675]

What aided this attempt by the Pharisees to maintain a personal relationship to God—again, in spite of his transcendence—was the ongoing understanding of God in anthropomorphic terms. This is particularly true of the concept of God as a father, who, according to traditional Jewish theology, not only "created" his children but also loves them and guides them. Benjamin Uffenheimer argues that biblical passages in which God is referred to as Israel's "father" (e.g., Deut 32:6; Pss 68:6, 103:13; Isa 64:8; Jer 3:4) and Israel is referred to as God's "first-born" (Exod 4:22; Isa 43:6), God's "children" (Jer 3:14), and God's "son" (Mal 3:17) helped the "myth of divine kingship" undergo a "process of interiorization." This development was "enhanced by images and symbols"—particularly, the identification of God and his people as bridegroom and bride in Jeremiah and as husband and unfaithful wife in Hosea (chs. 1–3). The point is that "the anthropomorphic description of God in such passages represents "the core of the biblical concept of God," who can "command people to follow Him" only because he is "a paradigmatic personality." That is, "[o]nly because He is a 'man'"—at least, insofar as he possesses *some* human qualities—"can it be said that man was created 'in His image and likeness'" and that humanity is compelled to act in *Imitatio Dei*.[1676]

Geza Vermes has argued that this Latin phrase—meaning, the imitation of God—is an important concept in the writings of the Rabbis: "Rabbinic thought is rich in interpretation of this theme that the lover and worshipper of God models himself on him." Reading the verse "This is my God, and I will praise him," in Exodus 15:2, the second-century sage Abba Shaul understood it to be a demand for imitation: "O be like Him! As he is merciful and gracious, you also must be merciful and gracious" (Mekhita on Exod 15:2). Vermes also refers to a similar rabbinical explanation of Deuteronomy 10:12—"that you may walk in His ways"—as well as two other passages, Exodus 34:6 and Joel 3:5. According to "an anonymous exegete," God requires not only mercy and graciousness but also righteousness and devotion (*Sifre* on Deut 11:22). The third example is by a third-century sage, Rabbi Hama, son of Rabbi Hanina: "As [God] clothes the naked . . . (Gen. 3.21) so you too must clothe the naked. The Holy One . . . visited the sick . . . (Gen. 18.1), so you too must visit the sick. The Holy One . . . comforted the mourners . . . (Gen. 25.11), so you too must comfort the mourners. The Holy One . . . buried the dead . . . (Deut. 34.6), so you too must bury the dead" (*b.Sot.*14a).[1677]

The most elaborate description of God's paternal relationship to Israel, his child, appears in Hosea, chapter 11. Here, according to the editors of *The Oxford Annotated Bible*, God, "as a loving and patient father, must now chastise his disobedient and willful son," the northern kingdom of Israel, nicknamed Ephraim, Israel's (that is, Jacob's) grandson; however, "compassion restrains his anger" (1097–1098). God says that, although the people of Israel have been disobedient, "it was I who taught [them] to walk, I took them up in my arms; but they did not know that I healed them. *I led them with cords of compassion, with the bands of love*" (vv. 3–4; my emphasis). And although Ephraim will be punished, God will not condemn them utterly: "How can I give you up, O Ephraim! How can I hand you over, O Israel! . . . My heart recoils within me, *my compassion grows warm and tender. I will not execute my fierce anger, I will not again destroy Ephraim.*"

God then acknowledges, at least implicitly, that such disobedience as he has witnessed would compel an ordinary father to give up on his sinful children. But God is not ordinary: "[F]or I am God and not man, the Holy One in your midst, and I will not come to destroy" (vv. 8–9; my emphasis). Hosea concludes his prophecy with the hope that God's people will return to his ways through knowledge and understanding: "Whoever is wise, *let him understand these things*; whoever is discerning, *let him know them*; for the ways of the Lord are right, and the upright walk in them" (14:9; my emphasis).

In this way, as Rivkin argues, "the heavenly Father was ever present. One could talk to him, plead with him, cry out to him, pray to him—person to Person . . . It was the establishment of this personal relationship, *an inner experience*, that accounts for the manifest power of Pharisaism to live on."[1678] Cohen says, "[F]or the broader reaches of the population, the worship of God through prayer and Torah study brought a measure of sanctity and communion with God that the Torah never envisioned."[1679] According to Kugel, this process was accompanied by "the gradual emergence of the *nefesh* (or *ruah*, or *neshamah*) as a person's inner, divinely given presence in the late- and post-biblical self." And the belief in this spiritual self evidently enabled the praying individual to experience "an *internal recognition* of what is not obvious to the eyes."[1680] In short, says Frederick J. Cwiekowski: "The theological underpinnings of the Pharisaic interpretation was a deeper awareness of the intimacy between God and each human person."[1681] Putting it in slightly different terms, Werner H. Schmidt says that the very idea of monotheism—that is, the belief in God's absolute sovereignty—requires total recognition and concentration: "The unity of God must be matched by the undivided, unreserved turning of *the whole person* to God."[1682]

It should be remembered, of course, that these changes in the ancient Jewish understanding of the relationship between God and humanity did not necessarily originate with the Pharisees. Herford traces some of them to the return of the Jewish exiles from Babylonia, particularly among "the more highly developed members of the community," whose "awakened mind" or "enlightened conscience" enabled them to gain "a real perception of God through the inward vision of the soul." As many psalms clearly indicate, insofar as prayer became more personalized and individualized, it also became "the intercourse of the spirit between God and man."[1683] Von Rad comments, "Compared with actual legal piety, . . . these psalms breathe a surprisingly ingenuous piety." That is, they express "the divine spirit of inspiration." Similarly, by "reducing all the profusion of the commandments to the one fundamental commandment, to love God," Deuteronomy concerns itself "with the inner, the spiritual meaning." In this respect, "[t]he so-called Wisdom Psalms . . . only play variations upon the theme which Deuteronomy and the Deuteronomist had already struck up: men are to keep these words in their hearts and they are to be present to them in every situation in life."[1684]

For this reason, von Rad says, both the prayers of the psalmists and the commandments in Deuteronomy were considered by the ancient Jews to be gifts, not burdens. "Two expressions keep recurring in [the] psalms—this revelation of the will of Jahweh is the subject of ceaseless meditation and ceaseless joy." Similarly, "Israel understood the revelation of the commandment as a saving event of the first rank." Consequently, they were called "righteous," meaning that in giving them to his people God was providing evidence of his "loyalty" to Israel, as Moses suggests in Deuteronomy 4:6–8. Indeed, says von Rad, the gift of the commandments prompted the recitation of the prayers, especially those of thanksgiving. In such psalms, Israel not only "addressed Jahweh in a wholly personal way" but did so without fear: "There is no terror here and no sighing, as if [the commandments] were a burden, but only thankfulness and praise."[1685] In Psalm 19, for example, the psalmist says that the law revives the soul, makes the simple wise, rejoices the heart, and enlightens the eyes. It is, therefore "[m]ore to be desired than gold (vv. 7–10; see also Ps 119).

Herford says that the Rabbis continued to emphasize this "spiritual conception" of God and insisted upon "the nearness of God," whose "close personal relations with human beings" were a manifestation of his fatherhood—not merely his immanence, however, but his accessibility and compassion.[1686] Indeed, according to Walter Brueggemann, the Jewish God is notable particularly for his frequent display of "pathos"—that is, "the capacity to feel, notice, and care in ways that put YHWH at risk in solidarity, thus a readiness for suffering along with another in vulnerability and weakness. It is the wonder of the Old Testament that it can feature these dimensions of YHWH alongside the characterization of strength and authority." Furthermore, "YHWH's sovereign power and YHWH's compassionate engagement are not in tension, but are taken together in Israel's life and praise and prayer."[1687]

This view is understandable if we read the Jewish prophets through the eyes of Abraham Heschel, for whom the Jewish God—especially as he appears in the works of Isaiah, Amos, and Hosea—is clearly anything but a stern, monarchial, and judgmental deity, whose primary concern is to keep his subjects in line by punishing and rewarding them. Heschel says: "To the prophet . . . God does not reveal himself in an abstract absoluteness, but in a personal and intimate relation to the world. He does not simply command and expect obedience. He is also moved and affected by what happens in the world, and reacts accordingly. Events and human actions arouse in Him joy or sorrow, pleasure or wrath. He is not conceived of judging the world in detachment. He reacts in an intimate and subjective manner." To the prophets, each human being is therefore not a mere "creature" but "a consort, a partner, a factor in the life of God." And, on his part, God is not a mere administrator of rules but "a God of compassion, a God of concern and involvement, and it is in such concern that the divine and the human meet . . . His relationship to His partner is one of benevolence and affection."[1688]

Although it reached its culmination under the Rabbis in the second and third centuries AD, the process by which Judaism became democratized, personalized, and

The Evolution of Love

spiritualized may be said to have begun with the prophets, as Heschel's discussion suggests. The change was slow and steady, and, given the social and economic conditions in ancient Israel, not very surprising. After all, countries around the world that had developed into urban agricultural societies—namely, Greece, Persia, India, and China—underwent a similar transformation in the middle of the first millennium BC. All of these changes in ancient Israel were the result of the same problems that drove Plato, Zoroaster, Buddha, and Lao-Tse to come up with solutions. The solutions offered by the moral teachers of ancient Israel were also a result of the progressive decline of the priesthood, which occurred mainly because of the destruction of the first Temple in 586 BC, the replacement of the Zadokite priests with the Hasmoneans in the second century BC, and the destruction of the second Temple in AD 70, which permanently ended the mediatory role of the priests in the management of worship services, the control of the cultic practices of the ancient Jews, and the interpretation of the laws, both ceremonial and moral.

However, the other important way that Judaism changed—that is, its abandonment of the belief that God rewards virtue and punishes vice—is more complicated. Like the others, this change appears in the psalms, the prophets and Deuteronomy, but it proceeds neither slowly nor steadily. Indeed, it can be said that it was never entirely left anything behind. Thus, although Koheleth in Ecclesiastes repudiates the *quid pro quo* theory completely, the author of Job stops well short of total rejection, and the apocalyptists as late as the first century AD simply postpone God's implementation of rewards and punishments to some time in the future. Even the major Jewish works of the mid-first millennium—by the psalmists, the prophets, and the Deuteronomist—offer two theories of God's role in the universe simultaneously. The psalmists both ask God to reward them for their good works and lament that his response to their request is often unexplainably delayed. The Deuteronomist claims that God offers grandiose rewards and threatens terrifying punishments but also says that God would rather be imitated than merely obeyed.

In distinguishing the God of Judaism from the gods of other religions, Heschel argues that because of the "variety of relations between God and man," the God of the prophets plays different roles requiring different responses to human behavior: not only the role of Judge (or mediator of "the interplay between deed and retribution"), but also the roles of Teacher (to uninformed students), Father (to potentially wayward children), Disciplinarian (to the careless and negligent), Counselor (to sinners who are encouraged to repent), Shepherd (to lost sheep), and even Husband (to a sometimes unfaithful wife). In other words, because God and human beings participate in what Heschel calls "multifarious modes of approach and encounter," God is not limited to either/or reactions. For this reason, "[s]in does not inevitably bring about punishment." As the psalmist says, "So great is His love toward those who fear Him" that God "does not deal with us according to our sins" (103:10–11). To be sure, the inescapable display of his disappointment and approval as well as his pleasure and pain means that God can sometimes appear to be unpredictable and therefore (in Heschel's words) mysterious, obscure, and impenetrable. However, he is "not an inscrutable, blind, and hostile power," Heschel says, "to which man must submit in resignation, but a God of justice and mercy, to whom man is called upon to return, and by returning he may effect a change in what is decreed."[1689]

Yet again, he may not. Thus, in the first century AD, although many Jews defined the divine-human relationship as personal, they did not necessarily see it as supportive, at least in the strictest and oldest sense. That is, they doubted the claims that Moses makes in Deuteronomy pertaining to God's imminent imposition of rewards and punishments. At the very least, the idea that God rewards and punishes in the manner described in earlier Jewish texts had been supplanted in the minds of many Jews by the hope or expectation that God's justice would be enforced only at the end-time. Furthermore, among some Jews, even the idea that God would eventually hold people accountable for their actions seems to have faded away. As I noted earlier, apocalypticism arose in the intertestamental period, first, as a response to the growing realization that people were not rewarded and punished at the present time and, second, as an expression of hope that rewards and punishments would arrive in the future. And, as I also noted, both D. S. Russell and Lester L. Grabbe claim that apocalypticism died a slow death after the destruction of the Temple in AD 70.[1690] The question is, what kind of understanding of God's moral program survived? To what extent did Jews continue to believe that God could be counted on to intervene in the lives of his people?

On the one hand, it may be that some Jews who were disillusioned with that aspect of God's activity solaced themselves with the understanding that although some of God's ways were incomprehensible, he was nevertheless not only real but indispensable. After all, even if he failed to recompense everyone for good and bad deeds, God had created the universe, had provided humanity with a clear and consistent moral code, and now intervened in the lives of human beings by inspiring (at least through his ethical standards, if not the work of the Holy Spirit) the kinds of moral actions displayed by Moses, Joshua, Gideon, Deborah, Samuel, Elijah, Josiah, Ezra, Daniel, and Judah Maccabee. On the other hand, however, the Jewish religious leaders of the post-AD 70 period, first the Pharisees and then the Rabbis, were not necessarily influenced in their interpretation of the divine-human relationship by earlier precedents, including thosethat emphasized the moral system presented by Moses in Deuteronomy. Thus, their response to the plight of the Jews in the first century might not have been driven entirely by disillusionment.

In this context, it is not surprising that both the Pharisees and the Rabbis were less inclined than some of their predecessors and contemporaries to accept any traditional Jewish belief without considering not only how it fit into contemporary life but also whether it made sense in relation to the actual experiences of people, individually and collectively. Indeed, by the first century AD, the divine-human relationship had undergone so many changes over the preceding millennium that the Jews in the early centuries of the Common Era could not escape the need to redefine it for themselves. Having developed what can only be described as a totally paradoxical view of God—as both immanent and transcendent, as both accessible and disengaged, and as both personal and irrelevant, the Jews of the time could not avoid questioning the Deuteronomic concept of rewards and punishments. Clearly, God was no longer thought of as either the tribal god of Genesis or the warrior god of Exodus. Nor was his relationship to the Jews of the first or second century AD even remotely understandable in terms of the God who appears in the later books of the Pentateuch—at least, in his role as moral administrator of the universe.

Living at the end the first millennium of Judaism and the beginning of the second, the Pharisees and Rabbis could look back on God's steady transformation over the years and see not only the radical changes he underwent but also, just as importantly, the persistence with which he retained all of his past identities. It was possible to see a progression, but it was important to recognize that the worship of a tribal god, a belief in his power to help or hurt, and a willingness to blindly obey his demands was still pervasive in the ancient world and even remained an ongoing religious view among some Jews in the Common Era. Nevertheless, if we simply base our understanding of the divine-human relationship on what we perceive to be the major changes in the morality of ancient Judaism, it is easy discern a fairly clear development over time, as I suggested in earlier chapters.

The major stepping-stones are (1) the first four books of the Pentateuch; (2) the writings of the mid-first millennium BC, including Deuteronomy; and (3) the intertestamental and later works, preceded by Job and Ecclesiastes and culminating in the Mishnah and the Talmud. The first revolution in Jewish morality may be said to have occurred in Exodus, with God's presentation of moral guidelines, which clearly did not exist before. The second revolution was represented by Deuteronomy, with its substitution of love as a motive for obedience rather than fear.[1691] And the third revolution was defined by the realization that God was no longer an active agent in the administration of rewards and punishments. Rather, he was seen as the creator of a vast universe in which human beings were offered the opportunity to participate in his creation—not as recipients of favors, dependent for their success and survival on his approval and affirmation, but as co-creators, bringing to fruition, to fulfillment, to actualization his original intentions. Negatively, some Jews believed that God either could not or would not actively help or harm his people. Positively, some Jews—notably, the Rabbis—seem to have believed that God's detachment was a consequence of his desire to have humanity participate fully and responsibly in his acts of creation by doing his will, *God's gift of love*, and enacting his laws, *humanity's gift of love in return*.[1692]

To be sure, it was not that the Rabbis publicly announced this concept and insisted that all Jews understand it and accept it. Rather, although it seems to have become a tacit article of faith by the end of the intertestamental period, it was first likely to have been only tentatively accepted by the Pharisees and later more fully embraced by the Rabbis. Specifically, it developed as a result not only of the growing disillusionment with messianism and apocalypticism—i.e., the growing conviction that God was neither going to reward or punish humanity in this lifetime nor even going to do so at any time in the future—but also of the evolution of ideas about God and humanity that evidently reached a new level of clarity and influence in the early centuries of the Common Era. In this context, it would have been logical for God to regard the self-serving motivation of the *quid pro quo* system as irrelevant and for his people to regard it as inappropriate—that is, as out of character for both God and humanity.

As we have seen, by the time of the Jewish Revolt of AD 66, many Jews—especially the Pharisees and later the Rabbis—had come to understand God as something other than a demanding tyrant, a detached arbiter, or even a mere dispenser of justice. Evolving through a series of redefinitions and reconceptualizations, God was seen as a loving father and an intimate partner, whose goal was not to enforce obedience, but to offer humanity an opportunity to thrive and flourish. At the same time, many Jews had come to see themselves and others not simply as servants under the rule of an arbitrary master, victims of irrational natural forces, or slaves of their own uncontrollable passions, but as morally competent human beings, capable of self-determination as well as self-control. As von Rad puts it, "The obedience which Jahweh wants is the obedience of men who have come of age."[1693] In this regard, they were therefore capable of learning and growing and thereby becoming responsible citizens as well as partners with God himself in using the ideals of their religion to create self-sustaining and viable communities in which God's goals for humanity matched humanity's goals for itself.

The point is that the two-dimensional pictures of both God and humanity, which appear in the earlier books of the Pentateuch and which resulted in a two-dimensional moral system—obey or not, thrive or perish—faded into the background. They were evidently dimmed and diminished by an increased awareness of the facts of life, a deeper understanding of the limitations of human nature, and centuries of exposure to the complexity of things. As Muilenburg explains, "A theodicy which saw life in terms of rewards and punishments only could not cope with the realities of national tragedy; indeed, it was the simple moral logic of the Deuteronomists and their like that made the blow of 586"—the destruction of the first Temple—"and the succeeding years all the more intolerable."[1694] Furthermore, the old *quid pro quo* system was found wanting because it did not fit—apply to or connect with—a world in which God and his creatures were engaged in a relationship that was profoundly different, in terms of its mutual requirements, interdependencies, and expectations, from the relationship between Abraham and El or between Moses and Yahweh.

One of the most important influences on the transformation of the divine-human relationship was the realization that God is omniscient. Being aware of everyone's motivation—being able to see into everyone's heart—he cannot be fooled by empty gestures, self-interested actions, or false promises. As Rivkin says: "His eye peered into the innermost recesses of the individual's soul and discerned every flutter of good and evil. From this all-seeing God no individual could hide his innermost thoughts and feelings."[1695] Thus, most of the prophets and some of the psalmists believed that obedience was unacceptable unless it was accompanied by "intention." And the intention motivating an act could not be to get rewards and avoid punishments: "Although an obedient act gives merit to the actor," says Tyson, "the Jew is frequently warned against obeying for the purpose of being rewarded." Thus, Tyson concludes: "Man must make every effort to do what God requires and to do it out of love for God. He must do it not for reward, but because it is God's will."[1696] As von Rad explains, "Jahweh wants obedience, admittedly; but he also wants men who understand his commandments and ordinances, that is, men who assent inwardly as well."[1697]

Wylen says that the Pharisees regarded this inward assent as indispensable: "To Pharisees, especially of the school of Hillel, the inner turning of the heart is of utmost importance." Thus, they believed that it was necessary to obey the law, but "the mere observance did not fulfill the divine will. The law had to be fulfilled with *kavannah*— 'intention,' 'directedness,' 'will.'"[1698] To Herford, the Rabbis as well as the Pharisees regarded prayer without *kavannah*, "devout intention," as "no prayer" at all.[1699] One of the earliest sages referred to by the Pharisees is Antigonus of Sokho, who is famous for saying, "Do not be like servants who serve the master on condition of receiving a reward."[1700] From this point of view, the goal on both sides of the covenant agreement is to maintain the relationship, not to negotiate its terms; to clarify mutual obligations, not to exchange favors; and to fulfill promises, not to earn either recognition or recompense. Rivkin comments, "To obey God when the rewards are immediately to hand is, after all, only a form of expediency; to obey him when there is no evidence that he cares is to meet the true test of inner faith."[1701]

Commenting on the Rabbis, Samuel Umen says that although they "never tired of urging the belief in reward and punishment," they nevertheless "displayed a constant tendency to disregard it as a motive for action." Indeed, he says, "It is a sentiment running through the Rabbinic literature of almost every age." Besides quoting the famous statement by Antigonus, referred to in the preceding paragraph, Umen quotes two other rabbinical passages. First: "Thus the words in Deut. 11, 13, 'To love the Lord your God,' are explained to mean: 'Say not, I will study the Torah with the purpose of being called sage or Rabbi, or to acquire fortune, or to be rewarded for it in the world to come; but do it for the sake of thy love to God, though the glory will come in the end" (Sifre, 84a). Second: "The words in Ps. 112, 1, 'Blessed is the man who delighteth greatly in God's commandments,' are interpreted to mean that he is blessed who delighteth in God's commandments, but not in the reward promised for his commandments' (Abodah Zarah, 19a)." After referring to several other passages touching on the Rabbis' reasons for obeying God's laws, Umen concludes, "These reasons, namely, the motive of love, the privilege of bearing witness to God's relationship to the world, the attainment of holiness in which the Law educated Israel, as well as the other spiritual motives which I have already pointed out . . . were the true sources of Israel's enthusiasm for the Law."[1702]

E. P. Sanders discusses several aspects of the "inner faith" to which Rivkin refers not only in the prayers of the Pharisees and in the philosophical considerations of the Rabbis but also in the acts of Temple attendance and sacrifice, which can easily be suspected of being merely routine and external. "I think it safe to say," says Sanders, "that everyone knew that those who went up to the temple," which required either a long wait outside or a ritual bath—both for purposes of purification—"should have 'clean hands and a pure heart' (Ps. 24.4), and they saw a connection between inner and outer purity." That is, purification was not merely a ritual act but "a standard metaphor in Judaism for the elimination of evil or unworthy thoughts and desires, and we may assume that many pilgrims took the opportunity to purify their hearts as well as their bodies. While the festivals themselves were joyous, the period of preparation beforehand was a time for self-examination." Citing passages from Leviticus (23:27–32; 26:40–42) and Ecclesiasticus (7:9; 34:18) as well as Philo, Sanders argues that to many Jews sacrifice was the final step in a series of acts that reflected "the interiorization of religion" and which "provide[d] the occasion for repentance and confession of sin"—that is, not merely for appeasement or solicitation. Not surprisingly, as I noted in chapter 2, according to Sanders, rabbinic literature also "offers a rich harvest of passages on the importance of inward intention and of repentance."[1703]

All of these manifestations of the democratization, personalization, and interiorization of ancient Judaism can be understood in relation to what Kugel calls "standing up close" to God. While the Israelites in Exodus wished to be close to God but could experience him only "at a distance," they "began to conceive of a different sort of 'standing up close,' and the change proved revolutionary." Here, the point was, as I noted in chapter 7, not merely to "serve" God by engaging in acts of appeasement, but to imitate him by carrying out his laws—that is, doing his will and by this means achieving "a state of closeness, even familiarity." Unlike the Temple, which was by now destroyed and which, even when it existed, was "far from most people's experience," the laws of God "are ever-present, governing a person's everyday life and that of his neighbors and his village." Kugel explains, however, that it is not the Bible itself that became sacred but the opportunity it offered to God's people to join him in "the imperative that Scripture's very existence embodies (and the changed apprehension that underlies that imperative), the basic divine commandment reflected in Deuteronomy's exhortation 'to serve the Lord your God with all you heart and all your soul.'" When that vision was clarified and embraced, it was "the moment when Israel first stood before God as His familiar servants, eager to carry out His will."[1704]

Von Rad explains this new concept of the relationship between God and humanity by focusing on the idea that righteousness, *tsedakah*, is "the standard not only for man's relationship to God, but also for his relationship to his fellows." In this view, God himself—especially insofar as he is understood to be a father, a teacher, and a mentor—is righteous and wishes all of humanity to be righteous. Righteousness, von Rad emphasizes, is not to be understood as a forensic term, requiring obedience to "an absolute ideal ethical norm" or a body of laws. Rather, it is a commitment to a relationship. That is, "ancient Israel did not in fact measure a line of conduct or an act by an ideal norm, but by the specific relationship in which the partner had at the time to prove himself true." God commits himself to his relationship with Israel by performing "saving acts" and providing his people with guidelines that enable them to survive and even flourish. Israel commits itself to its relationship with God by showing its gratitude for God's support and guidance, which are represented by the Covenant as a historical record and a body of laws. To put it another way, God's righteousness—represented by his justice and mercy—empowers humanity. And humanity's righteousness—its justice and mercy—is its thank-you gift to God.[1705]

Of course, humanity's righteousness is, as the prophets insisted, not to be understood as submissive acts, intended to appease, or magical acts intended to manipulate. Unlike circumcision, shrine making, and Temple sacrifices, Israel's *tsedakah* was to be represented, like God's, in acts of justice and mercy, in honoring the Covenant, and in following its commandments. As I said earlier, this does not mean individual acts of lovingkindness, since, as von Rad says, righteousness "can be described without more ado as the highest value in life," which is not manifested in good deeds, but is something "upon which all life rests *when it is properly ordered*." That is, the Covenant is not merely a set of random guidelines for positive one-on-one human interactions but the foundation for the establishment of a just and merciful society: "Jahweh . . . issued the orders of life which alone *made men's life together possible*. His commandments were not indeed any absolute 'law,' but a kindly gift rendering life orderly" and which required not only "kindness" and "faithfulness" but also "compassion to the poor or the suffering"—systemically and institutionally. This is the sense in which obedience is a joyful act, and the implementation of God's will is simultaneously a gift to God and a gift to oneself—and, indeed, to all of humanity.[1706]

In this context, it is possible to interpret the system of rewards and punishments, as both the Pharisees and the Rabbis seem to have done, differently from the way it appears elsewhere in ancient Judaism—not as a method by which God as an active agent in the universe encourages people to behave properly, but as a product of the natural connection between the way people behave and the consequences of their behavior, a logical sequence in which actions, both good and bad, elicit, as they do in the book of Proverbs, predictable and inevitable results. To be sure, on the one hand, Moses says that God will hold his people accountable for their behavior, and the Rabbis of the second century AD believed that God would actually impose His rewards and punishments in the afterlife. On the other hand, however, the kinds of human actions that both God and the Rabbis demanded can be understood to be self-rewarding, just as failing to perform them can be understood to be self-punishing. Indeed, Brueggemann finds this idea most strongly argued in the works of two of the major prophets:

"Thus the Jeremiah tradition, not unlike the Isaiah tradition, can match sweeping rhetoric concerning YHWH's intention with human agency that is concrete about geopolitical reality. Prophetic rhetoric presents hope as human practice in the service of divine intention."[1707]

As one of the major aspects of the divine-human relationship, the concept of human agency can be understood in relation to two other concepts: first, that humanity is made in the image of God; and second, that humanity is (therefore) expected to imitate God. As Bruce C. Birch and his fellow writers argue, God creates human beings as co-creators: "God is not in heaven alone, but is engaged in a relationship of mutuality and chooses to share the creative process with others. Human beings are thus created in the image of one who creates in a way that shares power with others . . . As image of God, human beings function to mirror God to the world to be as God would be to the nonhuman, to be an extension of God's own dominion." Referring to God's orders to Adam and Eve in Genesis 1:28, Birch et al. conclude: "This responsibility assigned to the human has not simply to do with maintenance and preservation . . . God creates not a static state of affairs but a highly dynamic world in which the future lies open to various possibilities, and human beings are given a key role to play in developing them."[1708]

This concept was embraced by the prophets because the actions in question—that is, those required by the laws of the Covenant—are, in and of themselves, capable of both creating and sustaining an ideal society. That is, if people follow the Covenant Code by implementing its system of distributive justice, its egalitarian social rules, and its non-monarchial political system, they will have created the kind of community in which justice is enshrined, stability is assured, and peace is achieved—not, of course, because God gave them these things as a reward for obedience but because the present dilemma in first-century Israel (including foreign domination and economic injustice) was a consequence of either ignoring the laws of the Covenant or simply failing to obey them, and its transformation would be the result of implementing them. As Brueggemann says (and as I noted earlier), what remained undamaged and unchanged even in the final stages of ancient Judaism was faith in "the process of *divine intentionality* enacted through *human effort.*"[1709]

Thus, what remained undamaged and unchanged, as well, was the Covenant itself, made new, most importantly because it was seen as the missing link between past and present. In short, although Jewish theology and morality changed over time, the covenant concept remained constant, not so much in its laws, which were deliberately altered to meet new conditions, but in its principles. As Susan Niditch explains, the Covenant Code "deals with matters of economic justice." It "envisions a kind of modified utopia in which all have some access to the riches of the community." It is *achievable*, however, only if it is understood to be dependent not on "each person's morality" but on "the tenor of a society"—that is, the establishment of a "community" based on the principles of the Covenant Code.[1710] Although the Code had been forgotten or ignored or neglected, it was now being revived for the simple reason that its neglect had brought disaster, just as its resurrection would bring redemption.[1711] S. N. Eisenstadt says that along with "the monotheistic concept of God," which the Jews of the late Second Temple period adopted, they also re-embraced the covenant concept of God: "[T]he ideology of the covenant was reinforced. It emphasized access of all members of the community to the sacred and thus in a sense caused a return to some of the original premises of the confederacy but in a new, non-tribal setting."[1712]

The New Covenant

If all of this sounds vaguely familiar, it is because this understanding of the human condition is similar to the one presented in Wisdom literature, including the book of Proverbs. It is not unreasonable to suggest, after all, that, just as the proverbs, like all the works in the Wisdom tradition, were based on lessons learned from everyday experience, so too were the laws of the Covenant Code. As Franz Mussner says, "the Decalogue in its final form grew from the developing structure of the kinship ethos of the tribes of Israel." That is, the Code, insofar as it was "designed to serve as a protection for the community," preserved the ancient rules of tribal life that were intended to serve the same purpose. In particular, "'[t]he Decalogue enumerates the crimes which are so grave that they compromise and endanger the community itself'"—*and always have*. In this respect, the laws of the Covenant were "not strict 'statements of revelation,' but rather"—as I noted in chapter 3—"statements of the 'natural moral law.'" Thus, the laws of the Covenant "are correctly understood as the essence of moral consciousness not only of Israel but of all humanity."[1713]

John Barton raises this point when he too compares the idea of morality in the Wisdom literature to the idea of morality in Deuteronomy. In the former, he says "we find fewer references to God as the giver of laws or moral norms, and more interest in presenting morality as a matter of fitting one's life to the orders and patterns observable in the world that is God's creation"—i.e., the natural order. "This has some affinities with what the western tradition of moral philosophy called natural law." As different as Deuteronomy is in some respects from the Wisdom books, however, it too instructs its readers to follow the laws of God because they are practical and, in this way, encourages its readers to align themselves with the way things are. Thus, says Barton, "[T]he law is to be kept because it is inherently good—the kind of law that anyone in his senses would be only too pleased to have the chance of keeping." In this view, "[T]he God who gives such a law is both good and reasonable." As Psalm 119 and Deuteronomy 4:8 imply, "God is not a tyrant, but knows what is best for his people, and this in itself is an incentive to do as he commands."[1714]

As Barton explains later, God's laws are not only reasonable but universal: "[T]he same law that Moses received existed already before the creation of the world, and served as the pattern or even as the tool God used when he made the world. As the pattern of God's intentions—the guiding principle of his own conduct as well as the conduct of Israel—it is rather more like what we might call natural law in many ways. God has made the world in such a way that it exhibits a moral order; and this has the corollary, drawn explicitly in later Judaism, but already essentially present in the OT, that God himself is in some sense bound by his own laws." That is, the Jewish law was pre-existent because it was universal. Indeed, "the moral principles on which the OT books are agreed" are not unusual or exotic. Rather, they are "mostly commonplaces for anyone brought up in traditional western morality." Furthermore, since the principles "are of a fairly high order of generality," Barton says, the "practical moral conduct" they generate "is inextricably linked with what we would probably call 'spirituality': it is a matter of a style of life, not just of particular rulings on 'moral issues.'"[1715]

Birch and his fellow writers go so far as to suggest that this is the best way to understand the theodicy of the ancient Jews from the prophets onward. That is, it is not that God responds spontaneously to every human act by determining whether the act is deserving of either praise or condemnation and then providing the appropriate reward or punishment. Rather, every act that bears on either the establishment or the maintenance of the covenant community—that is, *every act that affects the fate of humanity positively or negatively*—elicits its own consequences: "God does not introduce these effects; they grow out of the actions themselves . . . Yet, God is not removed from this process" because he "sees to the moral order that God built into the creation." The "benefits" (or "negative effects," as the case may be) "grow out of the deed." In short, "obedience will lead to a fuller life, more in tune with God's intention in creation." And disobedience will lead to a less satisfying life, inconsistent with God's will.[1716] Gary Anderson says, "The connection between deed and consequence is part of the natural order of creation."[1717] According to von Rad, "Like a stone thrown into water, every act initiates a movement for good or evil: a process gets underway which, especially in the case of a crime, only comes to rest when retribution has overtaken the perpetrator."[1718]

In this cosmic scheme, every good deed is not an act of self-interest in which the actor solicits a favorable response from God. That is, even the highest of all benevolent actions, almsgiving, is not performed for the sake of a reward. Rather, according to Birch et al., given "the God-Israel relationship in which obedience is *already* an integral component," obedience "entails more than obeying the laws given at Sinai." It "is a way of exhibiting trust in the God who speaks the word in any time or place."[1719] From what might be called a covenantal perspective, all acts of lovingkindness are self-rewarding if only because they benefit the entire community, which means all of its members, including oneself. That is, obedience—at least insofar as it is practiced by those who are able and willing to be generous—sustains, nurtures, and protects not only the needy but virtually everyone. And as a contribution to collective survival, almsgiving is less an act of generosity than it is an act of faith—and even of reason and logic. Thus, as Anderson explains, charity "is not just a good deed but a declaration of belief about the world and the God who created it." More specifically, "it is about giving testimony to the love of God inscribed in the moral order." That is, "[t]he

The Evolution of Love

connection between deed and consequence is part of the natural order of creation," which God himself designed.[1720]

In this context, God is worthy of obedience not because he is powerful and not because he rewards and punishes, but because he is wise and, as the God of justice and mercy, exemplary in both his laws and his actions. In this role, he does not demand subservience but provides guidance. He does not threaten because he is strong but leads because he is both compassionate and knowledgeable. And his most important message is not "Do as I say," but "Do as I do": "You shall be holy; for I the Lord your God am holy." As Barton explains, "To do good, . . . is to imitate God, to do the things that he would do if he were a human being." John Rogerson says that the writers of the Old Testament were "aware of the limitations of 'natural' social organizations, and that [these writers] confronted ancient Israel with moral obligations that were based upon Israel's belief in God's graciousness and *the need to reflect that graciousness in the organization of daily life.*"[1721] "Thus," Barton concludes, "'natural' and 'revealed' law are regarded as one and the same thing. But this is not a matter of mere theory or of definition. It is a conclusion won through a hard struggle with the facts of the nation's experience, a struggle duly recorded by the OT writers" and perhaps finally understood by the Pharisees and the Rabbis.[1722]

Indeed, Shaye Cohen raises the question as to whether the Jewish Law was believed to be eminently practical because it derived from God or believed to be derived from God because it was eminently practical: "The Bible clearly enjoyed (and still enjoys) a measure of authority unlike that of other canonical works, and that authority is connected with the Tanak's status as the revealed or inspired word of God. But what is the nature of the connection between the Tanak's special authority and its special status? Which is the cause and which the effect?" On the one hand, although many Jews, past and present, have assumed that the Torah as well as the Prophets and the Writings "were inspired or revealed by God," Cohen says that "not all Jews accepted this theological definition, which, in any case, is not attested before the first century C.E." On the other hand, however, Cohen says that the Bible came to be seen as "*existentially meaningful and eternally valid.*" That is, he proposes "the 'existential' definition of canonicity" (as Mussner does, in so many words), but also "concede[s] that it too was not necessarily accepted by all the Jews of antiquity." Cohen resolves this conflict by noting that many Jewish (and pagan) writings "claimed to be the repository of divine revelation" and yet were not included in the official Jewish Bible. His point is that these works were ignored because of their irrelevancy. Those that were included "enjoy[ed] special status" at the time because of their practicality: "The canonical books of the Tanak possess existential value for the Jewish community. *They transcend the period of their origins and respond to the community's needs by shaping its identity and endowing its existence with meaning and purpose* . . . They contain laws that are still binding and must be obeyed; prophecies that present *eternal verities which speak, even generations after they were first delivered, to the present and the future.*"[1723]

The Hidden Revolution

What this means, as we have seen, is that the post-biblical Jewish view of the human condition rested not on the theology and morality of traditional Judaism but on the actual experience of the Jews, who—since they had, in fact, once lived in the kind of society the Covenant Code seeks to establish—saw precisely what they needed and what they could do without. Norman Gottwald argues that "pre-conquest Israel was, for a period of two hundred years an egalitarian society," which "provided the 'leading edge' in bringing Israelite Yahwism into being, which then in turn sustained egalitarian social relations."[1724] By AD 200, when the Mishnah was completed, the Jews of Israel had endured many centuries of oppression, both internal and external, and yet continued to embrace the ideals of the Covenant. Thus, even if the Code had actually been created by God, it was not only a religious document, but also a treatise that reflected a profound understanding of how humanity succeeds or fails, based on a sense of history and an idea of how things work—one might say—according to the natural order.[1725]

It is important to recognize these features of the Covenant—its reasonableness, its practicality, its historical significance, and its adaptability—in order to understand why it was adopted by the Pharisees and the Rabbis, who not only obviously embraced it as the foundation of their religious faith but also understood it to be indispensable for their very survival. The Covenant, after all, in the wake of the destruction of the Temple, the loss of Jerusalem, the disappearance of the priesthood, and the demise of traditional views of God and morality, remained the one thing—whether viewed as a code of laws, a body of principles, or an expression of hope—that could enable the ancient Jews to recover from their terrible losses, rededicate themselves to God, implement his will, and thereby—independent of his involvement or cooperation or even encouragement—preserve their heritage, restore their community, and preserve their faith.

It was also the very thing that saved their relationship to God as well as to each other.[1726] The Covenant allowed them to honor not only the commandment to love one another, but also the commandment to love God by actually joining him in his work and becoming co-equal partners with him in the process of creating a viable and rational and compassionate community. In this respect, the Pharisees and the Rabbis seem to have continued to believe that the natural order, as God designed it, rewarded and punished obedience to the Covenant, at least in the sense that social success or failure was a direct consequence of humanity's willingness to obey its laws and its commitment to establishing a community based on its principles.

The logic of this idea is (and was) irrefutable, but not because God directly responds to human desires and efforts. The fact is, as the Pharisees and Rabbis evidently believed, if you fail to create a good community, you are left with a bad one. Like the natural laws in the Wisdom literature, however, the natural laws that apply to communities do not require God's further involvement because—as the proverbs say repeatedly—actions bring about their own rewards and punishments. This is particularly true of actions (according to Deuteronomy, though not the book of Proverbs) that derive from either the presence or absence of compassion and result in either (1) the creation of a community that preserves and sustains its original motivation and fulfills its *raison d'etre* or (2) the perpetuation of the status quo—in the case of ancient Israel, domination and exploitation.

Although it sounds revolutionary, this idea was not entirely new. "Like the prophets themselves," says Bernhard Anderson, "the Deuteronomic Torah does not pretend to lead Israel forward to new heights of religious development . . . This is a program of reform, not innovation."[1727] Indeed, understood in the context of experience—that is, interpreted within the limits of the humanly possible—many of its promises are modest, and their fulfillment depends entirely on human action. The latter insight, however, evolved over time, and when it was embraced by the Pharisees and Rabbis it was, in fact, revolutionary.

As Stephen A. Geller argues (and as Mussner suggests, when he traces the Jewish Covenant to its pre-monarchial origins), "In its final form [biblical religion] marks an attempt to restore pre-exilic Judah, reinterpreted as a religious community of Israel, by restructuring old institutions and formulating new theological ideas projected back into a Mosaic age that was now viewed as uniquely authoritative."[1728] Of course, this veneration of the past and the desire to return to a former life or historical period is hardly unusual. John Dominic Crossan says that, typically, people "go . . . either to future or past to find that ideal or utopian world whose existence profoundly subverts present normalcies and fundamentally criticizes present actualities." That is, when the present is intolerable, negating it "goes either backward or forward in time to locate that perfect otherworld alternative."[1729] Apocalyptists looked to the future, while many Jews looked backward, not to the Garden of Eden or to the dawn of creation, before sin, but to an actual period in their own history—idealized, to be sure—but fundamentally real, genuinely memorable, and theoretically, at least, achievable.

To be sure, throughout their history, the Jews found high points in their collective past that continued to inspire them, especially the liberation from Egypt and the theophany at Mt. Sinai. Anderson says that Deuteronomy "recall[s] the people back to the original faith of the Mosaic period."[1730] According to T. J. Meek, quoting W. F. Albright, the fifth book of the Pentateuch "may indeed have been 'a conscious effort to recapture both the letter and the spirit of Mosaism which, the Deuteronomists believed, had been neglected or forgotten by the Israelites of the Monarchy.'" However, Meek adds, the Jews also looked back to the Jewish world after Mt. Sinai and before the monarchy: "More or less unconsciously the prophets read back into the past"—that is, "the olden time with its simple nomadic life"—"what they wanted for their own time, bolstering up their own ideas of what ought to be with the sanctity and authority that always belong to the past." And, in reference to Deuteronomy, Meek says that it "represents a similar effort on the part of the Hebrews."[1731] Thus, when the Jews of the first century AD were looking for a way out of their present dilemma, it was easy enough for them to come to the same conclusions that Jews had come to repeatedly. Richard A. Horsley says that they had "a utopian ideal over against which later subjection to kings and foreign empires was measured and found contrary to the will of God."[1732]

Horsley particularly emphasizes the fact that the Covenant, although written down centuries after it was operative, was nevertheless both in effect for a long enough time and sufficiently successful to remain in the collective memory of Jews long after they ceased to be independent: "Not only did the Israelites, under the leadership of Yahweh, . . . establish their independence as a peasantry free of any ruling class, they also formed a covenant with Yahweh and each other to maintain that freedom."[1733] Horsley says that in the twelfth and thirteenth centuries, after the exodus and before the establishment of the monarchy, Jews lived in small villages with neither large buildings, of the type we find in urban agricultural societies that traced their roots to the third millennium BC, nor luxury goods, of the kind we find in the possession of the ruling class in such societies. Rather, "these people lived a simple hand-to-mouth existence," "grew barely enough food to survive," had "little social stratification," and remained "basically self-sufficient." Like pre-urban peasant societies everywhere, they had engaged in no trade, and lived communally, burdened only by the uncertainties of nature (flood and famine) and the dangers of foreign invasion and depredation.[1734]

Speaking generally of neolithic societies, Gordon Childe notes the absence of specialization "apart from a division of labour between the sexes," each household making its own utensils and tools and preparing its own food, and entire villages surviving self-sufficiently. "The potential self-sufficiency of the territorial community and the absence of specialization within it may be taken as the differentiae of neolithic barbarism to distinguish it from civilization and the higher barbarisms of the Metal Ages. A corollary therefore is that a neolithic economy offers no material inducement to the peasant to produce more than he needs to support himself and his family and provide for the next harvest. If each household does that, the community can survive without a surplus."[1735]

Evidently looking backward, to social models that were actually implemented in the distant past, instead of to the future, to social models that were promised but never became realities, the Jewish writings of the Axial Age—unlike most of the proverbs—focus emphatically on two ideas: first, God's origination of the moral system that derived from pre-monarchial times and, second, *the role of the community in its implementation*.[1736] Indeed, according to the Rabbis, as well as to Deuteronomy and the prophets, individual happiness is possible only *within* a community and as a consequence of the establishment of compassion as its organizing principle. The source of this moral system is the Covenant itself, and the means by which it is enforced is the community, which is also a product of the Covenant. In short, this concept might be understood to be a marriage of two traditions, Wisdom and covenantal, the principal feature of which is that, while it is divinely inspired and articulated, it is also totally now in the hands of humanity, to do or not to do, to implement or to ignore, to save mankind in the only way it can be saved or to allow it to perish by its own hand.[1737]

In this regard, if we assess the theology and morality of the Jews at the end of the ancient period, we find some continuity and some discontinuity. As for the Jewish concept of God in the post-biblical period, one can only say that it was profoundly changed, as it had been throughout the previous history of the Jews. Quite obviously, as I noted earlier, the God of the Pharisees and the Rabbis appears to be quite different from the God of Abraham, the God of Moses, and the Gods of Job, Daniel, and *Sirach*, all of whom differed from each other. Fundamentally, he is a God who no longer speaks to, appears before, or acts on behalf of humanity. Indeed, as "co-creator," God is responsible for the creation of the universe and the Covenant Code, but he no longer intervenes in any conspicuous way in the lives of human beings. And while the sages of the early centuries of our era seem to have retained at least a modest belief in God's promise to reward and punish everyone in the afterlife as well as change the human condition for the better—despite the fact that this prophecy remained unfulfilled during all of their lifetimes—they also seem to have maintained a respectful silence regarding God's involvement in the present world. As Cohen says, "Not a single tractate of the Mishnah is devoted to a theological topic."[1738]

There is little question that Jewish morality—at least insofar as it was embodied in the Covenant Code and expressed not only in the major works of the mid-first millennium BC, but also in the intertestamental literature—remained unchanged. It was then, as it is now, in the words of John T. Pawlikowski, rooted in three basic principles: (1) "the sense of peoplehood," that is, the idea that salvation is a promise made not just to individuals but to all of "humankind"; (2) the ideal of "authentic freedom," that is, the understanding that "liberation will not be fully realized in a society until it has been transformed from political/religious ideals into concrete sociocultural structures"; and (3) "the sense of the human person as co-creator," that is, the idea that humanity is "responsible for history and for the world God created." All of this, says Pawlikowski, rests on the Torah and the Covenant.[1739]

Jacob Neusner says, similarly, referring to the ideas expressed in the Mishnah, (1) "In this Judaism the manipulation and application of power . . . invariably flow through institutions, on earth and in heaven, of a quite concrete and material character"; and (2) "The will of man, expressed through the deed of man, is the active power in the world."[1740] It is clear, however, that, to the extent that the Jews of the post-biblical period gradually adopted Pawlikowski's third principle and Neusner's second as an important feature of Jewish morality—the concept of human agency—it must be admitted that Jewish morality underwent a transformation as significant as the one that affected Jewish theology. Indeed, the change in the latter—the Jewish concept of God's role in the universe and expectations for humanity—necessitated the change in the former—the Jewish concept of humanity's role on earth and responsibility to God.

If this is, in fact, the understanding of God and humanity at which ancient Judaism arrived, then it must be acknowledged that the Jewish religion had not only *evolved* over the millennium and a half of its existence, but had by the early years of the Common Era *undergone a complete transformation*. That is, if the Jews of the first or second century AD actually embraced the idea, as Pawlikowski says, that "the human person" is the "co-creator" of history, and, as Neusner says, the human will is "the active power in the world," then it is important to understand that they had moved as far away from their earliest religious views—short of atheism—as possible. The most obvious point is that the concept of human agency—the idea that if God's will is not carried out by human action it will not be carried out at all—*totally* undermines the idea that God himself is the *active* power in the universe and that the fate of humanity is in his hands. It also supplants the idea that God maintains and administers a program of rewards and punishments that provides the indispensable foundation for moral behavior—at least in this life.

If we return to the Talmudic story of Rabbi Eliezer, which signals a number of changes in Jewish theology, as I noted, we can discover yet another theme, which in this case signifies a change in Jewish morality as well. The story indicates that, although the Torah came to be seen as a meeting place between God and his people, it also imposed on humanity the task of interpretation—that is, the burden of finishing God's work by translating it, even redefining it, in order to understand it from a contemporary perspective. In this respect, the work of the Rabbis is an example of the necessity of human agency as a means of fulfilling God's will.

As Daniel Boyarin explains: "Authority is transferred to another sense of Oral Torah, the endless work of human invention in front of the text, the authority of which is now guaranteed by divine voices that can only confess their submission to the rabbinic power, as it were," especially when God laughingly says twice, "My sons have defeated me." Boyarin quotes William A. Graham: "The power of the holy word is realized only through the human word of the seer, prophet or spiritual master"—a function, in Boyarin's view, now taken over by the Rabbis. This "holy word" is not realized "through a manuscript," which, though "exalted" as scripture, is nevertheless "worthless, or at least worth little, without a human teacher to transmit both it and the traditions of learning and interpretation associated with it."[1741] To Adin Steinsaltz, the Talmud story refers not only to humanity's role in interpreting the Law but to humanity's larger role in "the creative process," illustrating that because "man was created in God's image" he "is able to create independently" and, indeed, become "a creator."[1742]

This new faith—or, indeed, new *Covenant*—acknowledges that God's will must be done, but not as a favor to God, in exchange for which he offers either success or salvation. Rather, his will must be done because it is the best (or only) path to survival. The motivation for doing the will of God is not, in this regard, either fear or hope, but knowledge—especially practical knowledge, which is capable of generating real and enduring change. And God's will is not merely a set of rules requiring deference

The Evolution of Love

and obedience but a set of guidelines requiring understanding—especially the kind of understanding that can, if followed by action, redound to the great benefit of its users.

This new Covenant can be understood in relation to the traditional Jewish emphasis on the so-called Two Commandments, which Jesus calls the first and second commandments in Mark 12:28–31 and "the great commandments" in Matthew (22:35–39).[1743] The first of the two is based on the Shema: the commandment to love God (Deut 6:4–5). The second is derived from the Holiness Code: the commandment to love humanity (Lev 19:18). E. P. Sanders argues that these commandments were generally understood to be the heart of the original Covenant, particularly insofar as they summarize the two kinds of love expressed in the Decalogue.[1744] That is, "it was widely recognized that love of God and love of humanity were the two main aspects of the law." Sanders adds, "The division of the law into two parts, sometimes called 'two tables' (one governing human relations with God and the other relationships among humans), was widely recognized in the first century, and it will enhance our understanding of Judaism if we consider the two tables more fully and note the terminology in the Greek-writing authors."

Philo and Josephus seem to have used the words *eusebia* and *dikaiosyne*, or piety and justice, "as words that encapsulated the two parts of the law"—that is, the two tablets on which the Decalogue was originally written.[1745] Gregory E. Sterling points out that Philo thus provided a summary of the Jewish law "that is broadly similar to the controversy story about the great commandment in the Gospels": There are "two main headings of the innumerable individual rules and teachings: our obligation to God through piety and holiness and our obligation to humanity through love of humanity and justice; each of these is divided into many subcategories that are all praiseworthy."[1746]

What is especially interesting about this interpretation of the Two Commandments is that the first of the two, derived from the Shema—which, Sanders says, "urges Israel to hear and love the Lord who had just spoken, to bear the commandments always in mind, and to do them"[1747]—clearly expresses *by itself* a concern for both piety and justice. This is because the laws referred to in the Shema, especially the laws of the Decalogue but also the entire array of subordinate laws, pertain to both loving God through cultic actions and loving humanity through ethical actions. Discussing the book of Deuteronomy, especially the Shema, James Muilenburg argues, "It is Israel's responsibility both in the practices of the cult and in acts of humanitarianism to live as a holy people." Furthermore, Muilenburg adds, although "the second command of the gospel"—i.e., to love humanity—"appears in Lev. 19:18 and not here, yet it really appears everywhere in Deuteronomy also. For the writers would certainly agree that this was the motivation of all the ethical requirements laid upon Israel."[1748]

Throughout Deuteronomy, the commandment to love God is often accompanied by the commandment to follow God's laws, which, in and of themselves, represent the worship of God through both ceremonial and moral actions. Edward Schillebeeckx cites a number of passages in Deuteronomy which repeat these two main messages of the Shema. Moses says that "the faithful God keeps covenant with *those who love him and keep his commandments*" (7:9; my emphasis) and restates the formula in 10:12–13; 11:1, 22; 19:9; and 26:17. In other words, as Schillebeeckx says, "[I]t seems that 'to love Yahweh' and 'to keep his commandments' were originally synonymous" and that, by implication, to do one was not only to do the other, but to do the other was also to be both pious and just.[1749] The obvious question is this: What purpose was served by adding to the double commandment of the Shema the commandment from Leviticus that appears to duplicate the commitment to ethical behavior, which is expressed in many of the commandments referred to in Deuteronomy?

One possibility is that the addition of Leviticus 19:18 to Deuteronomy 6:5 was either an attempt to prioritize morality over piety or a means of making sure that morality was sufficiently emphasized. There was, after all, a strong tradition in Judaism, grounded especially in the work of the prophets, that the *principal*, if not the *only*, way to love God was to love humanity (e.g., Hosea 6:6 and Micah 6:6–8).[1750] Furthermore, Sanders says, although "the Bible considers intentional transgression against God" to be more serious than transgression against humanity—and "punishable by death" or "extirpation"—"[m]any rabbis . . . reversed the order of severity."[1751]

Even earlier, however, as Sanders notes, Judaism was unique among ancient religions because it was not, as pagan religions tended to be, exclusively concerned with cultic matters: "As a religion it was not strange because it included sacrifices"—which were, after all, the central focus of religions "[i]n Rome, Greece, Egypt, Mesopotamia and most other parts of the ancient world"—"but because it included ethical, family and civil law," all of which came "under the heading, 'Divine Law.'"[1752] In this context, it is not so surprising that most of the prophets and many of the Rabbis—the latter especially after the destruction of the Second Temple—regarded violations of the moral law as more important than violations of the cultic law and therefore required both repentance and restitution for the former and only repentance for the latter.[1753]

To the Greek Jews, in particular, says Schillebeeckx—influenced not by Greek religion, but by Greek philosophy[1754]—"[t]he love of neighbor" was not understood to be "a second main commandment here, but an epitome of them all." Schillebeeckx continues, "Eventually, Greek Jews [like Philo] . . . in the Greek combination of *eusebia* and *dikaiosune* replaced the latter with *philanthropia*[1755] and, as Sanders notes, *koinonia*—that is, not justice or fairness generally, but love of humanity and fellowship.[1756] This is the spirit in which Jesus says in the Gospel of John, "A new commandment I give to you, that you love one another" (13:34).[1757] Even in the Gospel of Mark, the scribe, whose statement Jesus affirms, follows his articulation of the Two Commandments with the assertion—after the fashion of the Jewish prophets—that they are "much more than all whole burnt offerings and sacrifices" (12:33). Schillebeeckx suggests that the passage is "critical of the cult: love and ethics are much more than all the cultic requirements of the Torah—the very thesis of the Greco-Jewish literature between the Testaments, at the same time associated with the ancient prophetic critique of the cult."[1758]

David Flusser reminds us that Jesus' use of the Two Commandments "stemmed from attitudes [in Judaism] already established before his time." Speaking of the intertestamental period, he says, "Revolution broke through at three points," two of which we discussed earlier: "the radical interpretation of the commandment of mutual love" and "the call for a new morality." Indeed, the commandment to love humanity was—at least "[i]n those circles where the new Jewish sensitivity was then especially well developed"—"regarded as a precondition to reconciliation with God." Indeed, it "was esteemed by Jesus and the Jews in general as a chief commandment of the law."[1759] As C. H. Dodd explains: "In the first century, some of the most advanced of Jewish of Jewish teachers . . . were attempting to bring out [Judaism's] central or overruling intention by giving prominence to one or another 'great commandment' upon which the rest might be supposed to hang. Jesus was aware of these attempts and in sympathy with them." Thus, "in discussing the question he found himself in friendly agreement With some teachers of the Law that there are two 'great commandments.'"[1760]

According to Schillebeeckx, the meaning of the word *neighbor* changed in the late Second Temple period and came to mean not so much a "social peer" but "the poor and the lowly, less important and socially inferior fellow-countryman needing protection"—i.e., someone "entitled to help." In this way, the Two Commandments came to represent the commitment to social justice embodied in the Covenant Code. That is, love of neighbor, "extended to all one's fellows within the nation," was understood to mean "beyond all law and justice, . . . a brotherly, protective, loving attitude" that required "an inward disposition of love and kindness."[1761]

This point is illustrated by the assertion of Pharisees and Rabbis that the Golden Rule and its variants epitomized the entire body of covenantal laws, including Hillel's famous dictum, "What is hateful to you, do not do to your neighbor: *that is the whole Torah, while the rest is commentary thereof.*"[1762] Thus, Flusser says, like the commandment to love one's neighbor, the Golden Rule "was regarded as the summation of the entire [Jewish] law." It was obviously so in Ecclesiasticus, in the second century BC, when Ben Sira advised Jews to practice forgiveness and mercy (26:30), and in the thinking of Rabbi Hanina, one generation after Jesus, when he claimed that this commandment was "a saying upon which the whole world hangs" (*Abot de R. Nathan*, 53). Jesus similarly says in Matthew that the Two Commandments are statements on which "depend all the law and the prophets" (22:40). And he says of the Golden Rule that it *is*, evidently by itself, "the law and the prophets" (7:12).[1763]

According to Sanders, "The conclusion"—that is, Jesus' claim that the Golden Rule actually *represents* the Torah as well as the prophetic writings—"shows that [it] is meant to epitomize the whole law, though in terms of contents it summarizes only the second table," i.e., the love of humanity. In this context—that is, given the persistent emphasis on this concept in the broadest and deepest sense, especially by the first century AD—it is not difficult to imagine the step from "Love God and love humanity" to "Love God *only (or at least most completely and sincerely) by loving humanity.*" Thus, Sanders comments, "Love of God and of neighbour were seen as inseparable; so Jews taught one another and, when they had the chance, others who would listen."[1764]

All of this suggests that in the post-biblical period, as Gary A. Anderson argues, "the second table" of the Decalogue not only came to represent the sum total of humanity's obligation to God but also came to be represented by the *positive* commandment that Jesus added to his list of mostly *negative* commandments: i.e., not only the proscriptions against murder, adultery, theft, and "bearing false witness," but also the commandment to "love your neighbor as yourself," which is expressed at the highest level by almsgiving. That is, moral perfection can be achieved only by "sell[ing] what you possess and giv[ing] it to the poor" (Matt 19:18–21). Anderson explains that only this act turns "what takes place [merely] between human beings" into something that takes place "between human beings and God." In fact, almsgiving is the "good deed" that would allow "the young man" who asks Jesus about attaining "eternal life" to acquire "treasure in heaven." "For to Jewish and Christian thought, charity to the poor was not simply a kind thing to do. It was *avodah*, a privileged means of serving God."[1765]

Referring to a passage from the Mishnah, Anderson says that, by this time in the evolution of Judaism, "[t]o give alms to a poor person was just like bringing a gift to the temple." That is, "[j]ust as the altar was a direct conduit of sacrificial donations to heaven, so, too, was the role of the poor person who receives another's coins." In other words, particularly because the other commandments could be performed merely by exercising self-restraint, "Jesus was looking for an additional command that would allow the man's true love for God to surface. And almsgiving was just such a commandment." In giving away *everything*, Jesus' interlocutor would have been imitating Jesus, who, in immediately preceding and succeeding biblical passages, indicates that he too is willing to make a spectacular sacrifice: "Just as the crucifixion constitutes the highest form of sacrifice Jesus would make, so for the distribution of all one's goods to the poor."[1766]

According to Proverb 19, "Whoever is kind to the poor lends to the Lord, and will be repaid in full" (v. 17). Echoed by both St. Basil and St. John Chrysostom, Anderson says, the idea was deeply grounded in Jewish writings of the intertestamental period, which stated again and again: "It is not merely the poor but God himself who receives these 'trifling things.' God, as it were, resides (becomes incarnate) among the destitute."[1767] Lest it be assumed that this concept circulated in isolation merely as an encouragement for almsgiving as one among many other good deeds, Anderson argues that the Hebrew word *mitzvah*, which originally meant "commandment," came to mean almsgiving: "In postbiblical texts, . . . the term undergoes a radical transformation. It develops the secondary meaning of 'charity' . . . Charity toward the poor had become *the commandment that towered above all others*. One rabbinic text puts it succinctly: *Giving alms is equal to keeping all the commandments in the Torah.*"

Anderson adds later, "The Tosephta's position is hardly unique. The declaration that almsgiving is equal to all the other commandments is a motif found in every corner of rabbinic literature."[1768]

It must be remembered that the laws of the Covenant—particularly the *moral* laws—were treated reverently at least partly, as I said earlier, because they were based on political, social, and economic principles that had been tried and tested and therefore seemed to be both rational and practical. Similarly, according to Alan F. Segal, the ideals expressed in the Pharisees' Oral Tradition "were derived from experience, reason, and precedent." The Pharisees "essentially tailored a primitive code of the tenth through the fifth centuries B.C.E."—i.e., the Covenant—"by operating as if the Torah's ostensible meaning was but a pathway to the more relevant contemporary meaning."[1769] Thus, it could be said (and was, no doubt, believed by many Jews) that the Law of the Torah (both oral and written) was, in the words of another scholar, "the perfect expression of what man himself would choose, if he had perfect knowledge."[1770]

What must be understood, from this point of view, is that the only thing to fear is not God's punishment for disobedience but the negative consequences of *failing to act in accordance with his will*. And the only thing to hope for is not God's reward for obedience but the positive—and inevitable—consequences of following his advice. According to the Mishnah, "The sword comes upon the world because of the delaying of justice and the perverting of justice."[1771] Under these circumstances, prophecy might as well end, as it did, for the simple reason that sufficient wisdom is contained in the work of the prophets and other Jewish writings of the mid-first millennium. And humanity might as well rely on a book—the Torah, as well as others—that contains that wisdom, as the Pharisees and Rabbis did.

As Samuel Umen puts it: "The Rabbis refer to the author of the Torah and its commandments as the God who because of his mercy and great love gave the people of Israel these commandments which should help them to lead a noble and pure life." Of course, what is indispensable is not merely the presentation of God's will in the Prophets, Deuteronomy, and the Psalms but the opportunity to enact it. Unfortunately, until that opportunity arises, the will of God will be unfulfilled, and he will be insufficiently loved and honored. Here, the assumption is not that God is acting out of self-interest—say, for glory or recognition or even gratitude. According to Umen, the Rabbis "realized that God has no profit in these laws and no other purpose than to further the welfare of His creatures."[1772]

Despite the ongoing failure of the Jews (or anyone else) to enact the laws of the Covenant, the ideals of the Jewish faith embodied therein remained intact in the early years of the Common Era. As Neusner argues, despite its inattention to moral issues, the Mishnah is a work in which the Covenant Code—at least in general principles—is fully represented. After all, the book describes an ideal society founded on distributive economics and social justice. According to John Dominic Crossan, "What the *Mishnah* proposed was a radical egalitarianism, but restricted to certain people in a certain place. It was interpreted as holding them to a certain rest, a stasis, a steady-state situation in which nobody could become richer or poorer."[1773]

Bo Reicke explains that the Pharisees, whose successors wrote the Mishnah, expressed their "fundamental theory" in both "a system of ritual observances" and an "optimistic and idealistic social politics intended to realize the covenant demands." Their goal was to allow all Jews to "realize the ideal of the covenant people." Reicke adds, "They did not take political ideas as their models, however, but rather the Mosaic ideal of the covenant community." And this, according to the Mishnah and other writings of the period, they understood to be entirely the responsibility of humanity: "God predetermines, in every detail, Israel's destiny or 'Heiligeschichte'; but the people must contribute to its own satisfaction and perfection through precise fulfillment of the law."[1774] Thus, Stephen M. Wylen comments: "From the point of view of the Mishnah, the essential covenantal relationship between God and Israel was unaffected by the destruction of the Temple. The communion of the Jews with their God continues as before."[1775]

On the one hand, the idealism or utopianism of the Mishnah appears to be, in Cohen's words, an attempt on the part of the Rabbis to "escape from the imperfect world around them."[1776] On the other hand, however, this ideal world is "utopian"—a point that Neusner makes repeatedly[1777]—not merely because it was or is completely imaginary. As Niditch says, "In many instances, the texts [of the Bible] reveal conceptions of *the way the world should work.*"[1778] Furthermore, says Crossan, "The *Mishnah's* vision is not impossible, however ideal, theoretical, or utopian it may seem. Maybe it would not work, but at least it could be tried."[1779] It has been unattainable, Neusner suggests, because, under the circumstances (which have, of course, prevailed for most of the last two thousand years), the Jews were unable to gain the degree of independence that would have allowed them to create the kind of society that they continued to both remember and hope for.

Particularly, under the rule of the Romans, the Jews had little opportunity to implement their program and the ideals on which it was based. Neusner explains: "The system of the initial Judaism"—that is, the faith of the Pharisees and the Rabbis—"while influential for nearly two millennia, never actually dictated how people would do things at all." The Roman government "accorded to holy Israel in the holy land . . . limited rights of self-government that were mainly focused upon matters of no interest to the provincial authorities (e.g., issues of personal status, transactions of petty value, ritual and cultic questions that meant nothing to anybody who mattered)."[1780] Nevertheless, Neusner says that, because Jewish laws are "universally applicable," they could "be kept by Jews living in every civilization," of course, as long as they retain enough freedom of self-determination to exercise some degree of self-governance. "Wherever Jews might go, they could serve God through prayer, study of Torah, practice of the commandments, and acts of lovingkindness . . . The Jews thus formed a commonwealth within an empire, a religious nation within other nations."

The Evolution of Love

Despite Neusner's optimism in this regard, however, insofar as the Jews were, to use Neusner's words, "living in conformity with the laws of alien governments," they could hardly be expected to follow "their own Torah"—in the deepest sense. Without the power to establish a society that conforms *meaningfully* to the highest divine commandments, which may well be the most practical rules for survival, Jews and the rest of the citizens of the world are condemned to live, in Neusner's words, without the benefits of "a commonwealth founded on religious belief, a holy community, membership in which [is] defined by obedience to laws believed given at Sinai."[1781] Since no such place exists on earth, an achievement of this kind lies, for now, beyond the grasp of a yearning, hoping, waiting humanity. It would be wrong to assume that we have caught up with God.

Endnotes

1. Segal, *Rebecca's Children*, 1.
2. Meek discusses what he takes to be the earliest form of the Jewish religion, which included worship of El and other gods, as well as spirits, ancestor worship, ritual and magic, and worship of clan gods (*Hebrew Origins*, 84–93). "It is clear from the Old Testament, then," he says, "that the early Hebrew religion was a very primitive one and many of its elements remained long in the popular religion despite the efforts of priests and prophets to eradicate them. The religion was polydaemonistic and polytheistic" (91).
3. According to Frankfort, the Egyptians worshiped more than eighty gods, some of whom were less than beneficent and helpful to humanity (*Ancient Egyptian Religion*, 4, 25). The Sumerian gods were equally unreliable (26). For a more detailed explanation, see Wilson, "Egypt," 76–77.
4. Segal, *Rebecca's Children*, 2.
5. Fox, *Unauthorized Version*, 64–66.
6. For a brief overview of this subject, see Friedman, "Hiding of the Face," 210–11.
7. Gottschalk, "Prophetic Thinking," 51.
8. Geller, "Religion of the Bible," 2039. Geller adds, "Yet there is an underlying unity in the varying traditions: the development of the characteristically biblical notion of faith in God." Yet again, this faith "is a much more complex idea than it is commonly held to be" (2040).
9. Meek, *Hebrew Origins*, 56.
10. Wright, *Evolution of God*, 101. Specifically, Wright says later, "more and more scholars [are] acknowledging 'a gradual evolution of a complex Yahwistic religion from a polytheistic past.' Increasingly, 'the perception of a gradual emergence of monotheism combines with an understanding that stresses Israel's intellectual continuity with the ancient world'" (124–25). Wright is quoting from Robert Karl Gnuse's *No Other Gods*.
11. Barton, "Old Testament Theology," 94.
12. Smith, *Early History of God*, 195. Furthermore, "the accuracy" of the historical information in the Bible "is complicated by centuries of textual transmission and interpretation" (27).
13. Barton, "Approaches to Ethics," 116. Barton finds unity in diversity, but it is at such a high level of generality that it is indistinguishable from conventional western morality ("Old Testament Theology," 126–27).
14. Kugel, *How to Read*, 5, 667.
15. Barton, *Ethics*, 6.
16. Levenson, *Hebrew Bible*, 55. Levenson says that the attempt to translate the Hebrew Bible into a single idea "has produced a bewildering array of candidates." He describes such claims by Walther Eichrodt, Georg Fohrer, and G. Ernest Wright (54).
17. Friedman says that the writers referred to as J (for Yahweh) and E (for Elohim) described God anthropomorphically, unlike P (the priestly writer), who is less inclined to use anthropomorphisms. In the sections of Genesis and the early part of Exodus written by J and E, "God walks in the garden of Eden, God personally makes Adam's and Eve's clothes, personally closes Noah's

ark, smells Noah's sacrifice, wrestles with Jacob, and speaks to Moses out of a burning bush" (*Who Wrote the Bible?*, 191).

18. Frankfort, *Ancient Egyptian Religion*, 81, 124.

19. White, *Ancient Egypt*, 22.

20. According to Israel Finkelstein and Neil Asher Silberman, "[T]he traditions of ancient Israel gradually crystallized, spanning roughly six hundred years—from about 1000 to 400 BCE" (*Bible Unearthed*, 4–5).

21. "So important is this story of the liberation of the Israelites from bondage that the biblical books of Exodus, Leviticus, Numbers, and Deuteronomy—a full four-fifths of the central scriptures of Israel—are devoted to the momentous events experienced by a single generation in slightly more than forty years" (Finkelstein and Silberman, *Bible Unearthed*, 48).

22. Wright, *Evolution of God*, 102. On this subject, Wright cites Richard Elliott Friedman, *The Bible with Sources Revealed* (HarperSanFarncisco, 2003).

23. Anderson, *Understanding the Old Testament*, 2. Tyson briefly discusses Israel's "deep interest in history" in *Study of Early Christianity*, 96–97.

24. Bellah, *Religion in Human Evolution*, 285. Bellah adds: "Of course the Israelite monarchy was a latecomer—monarchy in Mesopotamia and Egypt was thousands of years old by the time of Saul, David, and Solomon. Still, that the premonarchical period—remembered, elaborated, or invented—should have had such a prominent role in Israel (the first seven books of the Bible are concerned with it) requires an explanation." On the Egyptian concept of the universe as "static" and unchanging, see Frankfort, *Ancient Egyptian Religion*, 49. The result of this view was that the Egyptian had no sense of history. That is, "the incidents of history, like all singular and isolated events, lacked real significance for the Egyptian" (139). This explains, as well, why theology, morality, and art changed very little over three millennia of Egyptian history.

25. Kaufmann, *Religion of Israel*, 132. Childe says that Zoroaster "believed himself called . . . to purify Iranian religion from polytheism, devil-worship, magic, and ritualism." As a result, "the old tribal gods (the *devas* of the Vedic Aryans) become in his hymns evil spirits, the commercial sacrifice is condemned, the will of one god sustains the cosmic order" (*What Happened in History*, 211).

26. Meek, *Hebrew Origins*, 56–57. Meek says that Jewish law, as it appears in the Hebrew Bible, is not only far less organized than Roman law of the fifth century BC, but less organized than the laws of Hammurabi, which significantly antedate the Jewish law (54–56).

27. Stone, "Eschatology, Remythologization," 247.

28. Brown, *Introduction*, 329.

29. Akenson, *Saint Saul*, 49.

30. Davies, *Invitation*, 27–31.

31. Miller, *Religion of Ancient Israel*, 47.

32. Moore, *Judaism*, 1:110–11. Thoma says, "Throughout the history of the Jewish people, the preservation of unity proved extremely difficult and was never fully achieved." Furthermore, "unity never referred exclusively to doctrine. Different opinions were accepted as more or less a matter of course, even of enrichment" (*Christian Theology of Judaism*, 41).

33. Tabor, *Jesus Dynasty*, 115.

34. Miller, *Religion of Ancient Israel*, 46. Miller adds, "Further, the distinction between what goes on in public worship and what happens of a religious nature outside the public and formal sphere, what is commonly called 'popular religion,' has been widely recognized as apropos of Israelite religion."

35. Stegemann and Stegemann, *Jesus Movement*, 137.

36. White, *From Jesus to Christianity*, 16. Segal agrees: The period between 600 BC and AD 70 produced "an enormous variety of Jewish communities, adapted to the plethora of new and different social, political, and economic environments brought about by the dispersion of Jews

throughout the ancient world. In each place where Jews sought to dwell, the meaning of the covenant seemed different" (*Rebecca's Children*, 12). See also Meyer, *Aims of Jesus*, 230–31.

37. Joyce, "Individual and the Community," 82, 92. Joyce adds, "If we are to appreciate the full richness of this diversity, we should resist the tendency to think of the OT as one book, and view it rather as the library of a nation, reflecting that nation's varied experiences of God over many generations" (89).

38. Segal, *Rebecca's Children*, 45. Armstrong says that "in the diaspora Jewish spirituality tended to be less exclusive and more open to Hellenistic ideas" (*Bible*, 47).

39. Russell, *Between the Testaments*, 48–49.

40. Meier, *Marginal Jew*, 1:93. See also 336. "Some of the most potent elements . . . in Jewish society of the first century stood outside the official establishment. There were various sects with their own peculiar doctrines and practices" (Dodd, *Founder of Christianity*, 18).

41. Charlesworth, "Foreground of Christian Origins," 72, 78. On this subject, see also Fredriksen, *From Jesus to Christ*, 62; Bowker, *Jesus and the Pharisees*, 15–16; and Riches, *Jesus and the Transformation*, 83.

42. Anderson, *Understanding the Old Testament*, 2. Bellah says that "there is little ground for asserting a strong ethnic identity in the premonarchical period" (*Religion in Human Evolution*, 286). Following the lead of Alexander Joffe, Bellah argues that the ancient Israelites might actually have been Canaanites (287).

43. Kaufmann, *Religion of Israel*, 218.

44. Meek, *Hebrew Origins*, 42–43. Meek adds later, "The Hebrews by their own confession were a mixed people and of composite origin," including according to various biblical passages, Aramean, Hittite, Canaanite-Amorite, and even Egyptian. "Hence the Hebrews from the beginning were open to all sorts of foreign influences" (185–87).

45. Meek, *Hebrew Origins*, 185. Meek says, "The most original of peoples appropriates most, drinking deeply from the common heritage of mankind." This is why the "the Hebrew people . . . so far outdistanced their contemporaries in real cultural development" (185).

46. Bellah, *Religion in Human Evolution*, 289. Bellah says later that this external influence continued: "What we have seen so far is the emergence in Israel, or at least in Judah, of a classic Near Eastern monarchy, with all its attendant ideology. Israel has moved from being a tribal society to being an archaic society with an early state. As secondary states, Israel and Judah did not need to invent archaic culture from scratch—they could take much of it over from the surrounding high cultures" (298–99). Irwin comments, "The Hebrews, then, had august guides, and the stimulus of a great and ancient culture so all-comprehending as to constitute their native air" ("Literature of the Old Testament," 176).

47. Tenney, *New Testament Survey*, 82.

48. Geller, "Religion of the Bible," 2021. Geller identifies the Deuteronomic, Priestly, and Wisdom religions as the main sources of ancient Judaism.

49. Irwin, "Literature of the Old Testament," 176.

50. Muilenburg, "History of the Religion," 296.

51. Von Rad, *Old Testament Theology*, 1:115–18. Von Rad says earlier, "There were up and down the land many traditions which little by little combined into ever larger complexes of tradition. Theologically, these accumulations were in a state of constant flux" (112).

52. Fox, *Unauthorized Version*, 95.

53. On this subject, see Collins, *Short Introduction*, 29–30.

54. For a brief discussion of the history of this discovery, see Friedman, *Who Wrote the Bible?*, 17–29. Friedman displays the sections of the story of the Flood (Gen 6:5—8:22) written respectively by J and E on 54–59; and sections of the story of the Heresy at Peor (Num 1–16) written by P and J on 202–3. In the first example, J and E are represented by alternating passages. In the second example, J wrote vv. 1–5, and P wrote vv. 6–16.

55. Armstrong, *Bible*, 4.

56. Ramsay, *Westminster Guide*, 5.

57. Collins mentions this doublet in *Short Introduction*, 52.

58. Friedman, *Who Wrote the Bible?*, 236, 197. Friedman says: "The point, apparently, is to develop the idea that forgiveness cannot be had just because one is sorry . . . Rather, in P, God is *just*. He has established a set of rules by which one can acquire forgiveness, and the rules must be followed."

59. Ramsay, *Westminster Guide*, 1. Speaking of a similar problem in the New Testament—i.e., "the difficulty of understanding what the Bible means"—Ramsay says that the result has been a proliferation of sects: "Christians in the United States are split into more than three hundred denominations, in part because they cannot agree in their interpretations of scripture."

60. Simpson, "Growth of the Hexateuch," 185. Simpson discusses these issues in detail on 186–88.

61. Saldarini, *Pharisees, Scribes and Sadducees*, 248–49.

62. Smith, *Early History of God*, xxii–xxiii, 15. Simpson credits Hermann Gunkel, in a book published in 1901, with a "brilliant and penetrating analysis" of Genesis that emphasizes (1) the diverse sources of the text, (2) their "adaptation" over time, and (3) the interweaving of legends into the document, all of which resulted in "the fact that the tradition in its final form was complex in the extreme—the product of centuries of assimilation and development of material drawn from many sources" ("Growth of the Hexateuch," 191). Goodman mentions two exacerbating problems. First, Israel was not only surrounded by other countries but also invaded by other countries, each of which "had left its mark on the Jews by the time that Josephus was writing his history at the end of the first century C.E." Second, many parts of the Bible were "the product of several generations of writers who reworked or added to a text inherited from earlier generations" (*History of Judaism*, 21, 26–27).

63. Wright, *Evolution of God*, 191.

64. Grant, *Historical Introduction*, 13. Grant later explains his method of reading the Bible as a deliberate attempt "to safeguard [his] interpretation from an excessive degree of subjectivity" and to "thereby reach conclusions which can be more generally accepted" (18).

65. Levenson, *Hebrew Bible*, 104.

66. Segal, *Rebecca's Children*, 45.

67. Cohen, *From the Maccabees*, 185.

68. Wright, *Evolution of God*, 191.

69. Heschel, *Prophets: Volume II*, 51. Barton says: "In every age interpreters ask different questions, and so different aspects of the text's meaning emerge. The task of interpretation . . . is never finished even in principle" ("Introduction," 1). On this subject, see also Allison, *Jesus of Nazareth*, 75–77.

70. Bellah, *Religion in Human Evolution*, 283. Anderson says: "To open the Bible is to enter a world that is strange to the modern mind. This ancient literature, written thousands of years ago, in a faraway place, may seem obsolete in a streamlined age when men demand to have the latest in everything. Its idioms of speech, reflecting the life and thought of the ancient Near East, are so different from the West's scientific and philosophical ways of thinking that, it may seem, 'never the twain shall meet'" (*Understanding the Old Testament*, vii). "Because of the tension between the biblical outlook and the modern world view, the interpreter is constantly pushed toward the realm of apologetics—the intellectual defense of the validity of biblical truth." Speaking of the New Testament, which was, of course, written after the Bible that Anderson is referring to, Brown comments, similarly, "From the viewpoint of culture and context, the authors and their audiences had a worldview very different from ours: different background, different knowledge, different suppositions about reality" (*Introduction*, 36). Talking about the New Testament, Brown says, "From the viewpoint of language, even the most competent English translation cannot render

Endnotes

all the nuances of the original Greek." Anderson thus calls the world of the Bible "enigmatic" (*Understanding the Old Testament*, vii).

71. Barton, *Ethics*, 1, 7. Barton says that "establishing the relevance of Old Testament ethics to life today is an uphill task." Nevertheless, he adds that "in many areas of ethical enquiry the Old Testament has much to teach us" (2). Smith says that certainty about many aspects of the Jewish Bible is hard to come by because "the texts have been written so much after the fact or have undergone such long redactional histories." That is, "The fundamental difficulty lies in the nature of textual evidence" (*Early History of God*, xxii-xxiii). See also 15, 27.

72. Muilenburg, "History of the Religion," 293.

73. Collins, *Short Introduction*, 14. Collins says, "The responsible use of the Bible must begin by acknowledging that these books were not written with our modern situations in mind, and are informed by the assumptions of an ancient culture remote from our own."

74. Sanders, *Judaism*, 190.

75. Wright, *Evolution of God*, 193, 191.

76. Gorringe, "Political Readings of Scripture," 69-70.

77. According to Borg: "What we bring to our reading of a text or document affects how we read it. All of us, whether we use reading glasses or not, read through lenses." Specifically, "We are aware that how people think is pervasively shaped by the time and place in which they live, as well as by social and economic class" (*Reading the Bible Again*, 3, 14).

78. Smith, *Early History of God*, 15.

79. Barton, "Historical Critical Approaches," 15.

80. Meier, *Marginal Jew*, 1:5. Meier continues: "The solution to this dilemma is neither to pretend to an absolute objectivity that is not be had nor to wallow in total relativism. The solution is to admit honestly one's own standpoint, to try to exclude its influence in making scholarly judgments by adhering to certain commonly held criteria, and to invite the correction of other scholars when one's vigilance inevitably slips" (5-6).

81. Segal, *Rebecca's Children*, 45.

82. Rogerson, "Outline of the History," 18. Rogerson says that, although scholars have at times through the centuries "tried to face up to the problems raised by apparent contradictions between the Bible and philosophical and scientific accounts of the world," the post-1750 approach was revolutionary insofar as "critical investigation was prepared to be critical of the doctrinal positions of churches" (17).

83. Meier, *Marginal Jew*, 1:3. Provan makes a similar point: "It is certainly sometimes the impression of the reader of such interpreters that he or she is finding out considerably more about the interpreter than about the Old Testament" ("Historical Books," 206). Olson says, "Some biblical statements are like intergroup Rorschach ink blots, in that the content they elicit comes not from the text but from the writer" (*Faith and Prejudice*, 38). Olson provides examples of varied responses to biblical passages on 39-40.

84. Kugel, *How to Read*, 676.

85. On this subject, Rogerson says, "[T]he OT does not contain the history of ancient Israel. It contains historical and story-like traditions whose primary purpose is to express the faith of the authors of the OT that God had been involved in the events of Israelite history" ("Old Testament History," 56).

86. Segal, *Rebecca's Children*, 26. Segal adds: "Hellenistic thought was accepting of foreign religions. The rule seems to have been toleration of Jewish presence combined with genteel discrimination against nonclassical cultures" (27).

87. Parini, *Jesus*, 139. Parini reminds his readers that, although "3,000 manuscripts of the Greek New Testament have been preserved, . . . no original manuscripts exist for the gospels, the letters of Paul, or any other material that appears in the New Testament," with no complete versions from before the fourth century. Consequently, "[o]ne can only guess what the earlier versions must have looked like, or how scrupulous those who copied these texts might have been."

88. Meier, *Marginal Jew*, 3:640–41.

89. Armstrong, *Bible*, 76–77.

90. Spong, *Liberating the Gospels*, 5–6, 30–31, 54.

91. Meier, *Marginal Jew*, 1:65. Vermes says, "St. John Chrysostom compared the Jewish synagogue to a brothel," and St. Jerome called Jewish prayers "the grunting of a pig and the braying of donkeys" (*Jesus in His Jewish Context*, 38).

92. Smith, *Early History of God*, 15.

93. Kugel, *Great Shift*, 168.

94. Muilenburg, "History of the Religion," 297.

95. Sanders explains: "The idea that suffering was God's punishment or chastisement was very common in our period [i.e., the first century AD], as well as before and afterwards, and with all this went the view that justice had been done when a person had suffered. Further punishment would be unjust, but God was righteous. The punishment for sin was not damnation, but suffering and, at worst, death" (*Judaism*, 273). Sanders adds: "The chastisement was not in proportion to the sin . . . Those who trespassed were corrected 'little by little', punished with 'great care and indulgence' (Wisd. Sol., 12.2, 20). God corrects transgressors only temporarily and 'not in anger' (Bibl. Antiq. 19.9) . . . The righteous, to be sure, do suffer, but they accept it as chastisement (*Psalms of Solomon* 3.3f; 8:26; 10.1f.)" (275).

96. Fredriksen, *From Jesus to Christ*, 107. Lieu says: "Already in the first century 'the Jews' are becoming the archetypal enemies of Christ and of Christians: as Jesus's death becomes paradigmatic for believers so too does the role of the Jews within it, as is well illustrated by 1 Thessalonians 2. 14–16" (*Image and Reality*, 281).

97. Fredriksen, *From Jesus to Christ*, 103.

98. Carroll, *Constantine's Sword*, 134.

99. Wright, *Simply Jesus*, 187.

100. Lieu says that "the constructed 'identity' of Judaism, which has continued to form part of the 'knowledge' of many in both church and academy, is at best a distorted reflection of the reality of both past and present" (*Image and Reality*, 1). Lieu later adds, "Continuing a process already found in the New Testament, the role of the Romans is submerged, while that of the Jews loses any element of contingency or specificity by being set within a continuous tradition of disobedience or of murder of the prophets" (281).

101. As Jaher says, "Christian doctrine, while by no means the only source of anti-Semitism, has exerted a primary influence since the early days of Christianity." Rooted in the New Testament, in which "Jews were linked with Satan and the Antichrist," Christianity is "inherently and intensely anti-Semitic" (*Scapegoat*, 1–2, 9, 23). For a brief discussion of anti-Judaism and anti-Semitism in the New Testament, see Sanders, *Jews in Luke–Acts*, xv–xvii.

102. On the popular modern view that the Bible is not infallible, see Schillebeeckx, *Jesus*, 57–62.

103. Pelikan, *Jesus through the Centuries*, 182. Pelikan provides an overview of eighteenth-century theology in chapter 15.

104. Sperling, "Judaism and Modern Biblical Research," 23. On this subject, see Ruether, *Faith and Fratricide*, 218–19.

105. Levenson, *Hebrew Bible*, 10–12. The Wellhausen quotations are from *Prolegomena to the History of Ancient Israel*. The original 1878 version was entitled *Geschichte Israels* (*History of Israel*). The Hegel quotation is from *Der Geist des Christentums und sein Schicksal*, written in 1798–99. Levenson later quotes Hegel again, from the same book: "In the nineteenth century, no less a thinker than Hegel could describe Judaism as 'a direct slavery, an obedience without joy, without pleasure or love . . . the most senseless bondage,' 'bondage to external demands'" (149).

106. Levenson, *Hebrew Bible*, 162n15.

107. Frei, "Literal Reading' of Biblical Narrative," 74.

Endnotes

108. Blenkinsopp, "Tanakh and the New Testament," 104; my emphasis.

109. Blenkinsopp, "Tanakh and the New Testament," 110. On this subject, see Sanders, *Judaism*, 277.

110. Wright, *Simply Christian*, 88–89. Earlier, Wright says, "It is fundamental to the Christian worldview in its truest form that what happened in Jesus of Nazareth was the very climax of the long story of Israel" (71). Childs makes a similar point in *Myth and Reality*, 98, 105, 106.

111. Wellhausen, *Prolegomena*, 1 (quoted in Blenkinsopp, "Tanakh and the New Testament," 104–5.

112. Sperling, "Judaism and Modern Biblical Research," 23.

113. Blenkinsopp, "Tanakh and the New Testament," 105. Sperling says that "[t]he most important modern higher criticism is based . . . chiefly on that of Wellhausen." Indeed, "It was Wellhausen's synthesis . . . which proved to be the most persuasive and influential" ("Judaism and Modern Biblical Research," 22.

114. Levenson, *Hebrew Bible*, 92.

115. Riches, *Jesus and the Transformation*, 67.

116. Klein, *Anti-Judaism*, 15–16, 38.

117. Schmidt says that Kant also embraced the idea that Christianity owed nothing at all to Judaism since there was no connection between them: Kant "turned the distinction of the two Testaments into a complete break between Judaism and Christianity. Though the Jewish faith 'immediately preceded' the founding of the Christian Church, it 'stands in no essential connection whatever, that is, in no unity of concepts' with this ecclesiastical faith . . . 'General church history, if it is to constitute a system,' can only begin with the origin of Christianity, 'which, completely forsaking the Judaism from which it sprang,' is 'grounded upon a wholly new principle' . . . The new faith is not in continuity with the old" (*Old Testament Introduction*, 340).

118. Eichrodt, *Theology of the Old Testament* (Phila.: Westminster, 1967), II, 315; quoted in Blenkinsopp, "Tanakh and the New Testament," 117n36. On Eichrodt, Levenson says, "His willingness to accept traditional Christian slurs at face value both contributed to and was influenced by his apparent inability to read the rabbinic sources. In this, he resembled Wellhausen, who confessed his lack of knowledge of Jewish literature, especially the Talmud, and his consequent dependence of Greek sources, but did not allow this handicap to prevent him from presenting a very negative picture of Judaism throughout his career" (*Hebrew Bible*, 20–21). See also 16, 19, 40.

119. Maguire, *Moral Core*, 55.

120. Carroll makes the same point in *Constantine's Sword*, 110.

121. Fredriksen, *From Jesus to Christ*, 94.

122. "In the Old Testament we frequently meet with the idea of the nation of Israel as the bride of God. God is the divine lover who has chosen Israel for himself" (Barclay, *Jesus*, 255).

123. Moule, *Birth*, 40–41.

124. See, for example, Isa 5:18–22; Jer 13:27; Ezek 34:2.

125. According to Barclay, the allegation that the Jews of Jesus' generation were "adulterous" is understandable in the context of the description of God as the Bridegroom and of Israel as His Bride: "It is this idea that is responsible for another New Testament phrase. More than once the generation to which Jesus spoke is called 'an evil and adulterous generation' (Matt. 12.39; 16.4; Mark 8.38; NEB 'wicked and godless'). The word 'adulterous' is not there to be taken in the sense of physical and fleshly sin, but in the sense of spiritual infidelity" (*Jesus*, 256). It means "unfaithful to God."

126. Sanders, *Judaism*, 445, 428. Sanders cites Joachim Jeremias, O. Betz, and Matthew Black as scholars who have made such allegations about the Pharisees. Sanders discusses four of "Jeremias' errors" in his evaluation of the Pharisees on 461–64.

127. In Matthew, the word appears in quotations from Micah (2:6) and Jeremiah (18:1–3), and it is used by Jesus in 8:10, 10:23, and 19:28; by the narrator in 15:31; and by others in 9:33

and 27:42. Jesus also refers to "the lost sheep of the house of Israel" in 10:6 and 15:24. In Luke, the word "Israel" occurs several times in the first two chapters, including in Mary's "Magnificat" (1:54), and several times thereafter.

128. Kee, *Medicine, Miracle and Magic*, 76.

129. Ehrman, *Jesus: Apocalyptic Prophet*, 127.

130. Commenting on "the anti-Jewish tone of the New Testament," Sandmel says, "The progressive shift of blame from the Romans to the Jews in the developing Christian literature, both within the New Testament and beyond it, is a result of the need to appease the Romans" (*Jewish Understanding*, 204).

131. Ruether, *Faith and Fratricide*, 88.

132. Bammel, "*Ex illa itaque*," 24.

133. Lieu, *Image and Reality*, 3. Lieu says, "Each of the other Gospels reveals something of the same tensions expressed in different ways."

134. Ruether, *Faith and Fratricide*, 88. As Kung notes, "Strikingly, the Pharisees are not mentioned in the reports of the trial" (*Judaism*, 333). Smith says, "It is noteworthy that neither Mark nor Luke attributes to the Pharisees any role in the passion story" (*Jesus the Magician*, 155).

135. On this conversation, see Ehrman, *Jesus: Apocalyptic Prophet*, 95. Ehrman points out that Nicodemus misunderstands Jesus because Jesus uses a word that had two meanings in Greek but only one in Aramaic: "From a historical point of view, the problem with this passage . . . is that the confusion created by the word Jesus uses makes sense in Greek, the language of the Fourth Gospel, but it cannot be replicated in Aramaic, the language spoken by Jesus himself."

136. Saldarini, *Pharisees, Scribes and Sadducees*, 188n27. Saldarini adds: "Raymond Brown, *The Community of the Beloved Disciple*, . . . points out that for the author of John and his community, late in the first century, after separation from the synagogue, Jews refers to all Jews. They are seen as the heirs of the Jewish authorities who opposed Jesus in his lifetime. Both the Jews of John's time and the Jewish authorities of Jesus' time are bitterly attacked."

137. Sanders attributes Luke's hostility to Jews, especially in Acts, to his anger with Jewish Christians, who stood in the way of the Gentile mission. Luke "carried his annoyance with Jewish Christians back to Jews generally" (*Schismatics, Sectarians, Dissidents, Deviants*, 186).

138. Sanders notes "the general tendency in early Christianity to blame 'the Jews' for all Christianity's difficulties." Sanders continues, "One sees this tendency, as a matter of fact, particularly well in the speeches in Acts addressed to Jewish audiences" (*Jews in Luke–Acts*, 182–83).

139. The only indication that Jews are in the audience is Peter's direct address to "Men of Israel." Earlier, Luke said, "Now there were dwelling in Jerusalem Jews, devout men from every nation under heaven" (2:5).

140. According to May and Metzger, "Amos 5:25–27 is quoted [in Acts 7:42–43] to suggest that the Hebrews had always been idolators" (*Oxford Annotated Bible*, 1326).

141. Sanders says, "Chapters 8–11 then shift the story line of Acts from the Jewish mission to the Gentile mission, at the beginning of which the attitude towards the Jewish people is completely reversed from that in chs. 3–5, for in 12.3 'the Jews' favour persecution of the Christians" (*Jews in Luke–Acts*, 40).

142. Enslin, *Christian Beginnings*, 92–93. Enslin cites both Paul's experience in Pisidian Antioch in Acts 13 and Jesus' invitation to read at a synagogue service in Luke 4:16–21.

143. Later, in Corinth, Paul reasserts his decision to abandon the Jewish Mission and reaffirms his commitment to the Gentile Mission: "Your blood be upon your heads!" he says to the Jews. "From now on I will go to the Gentiles" (18:6).

144. May and Metzger explain that forty lashes was a Jewish punishment, while a beating with rods was a Roman punishment (*Oxford Annotated Bible*, 1405).

145. Sanders, *Jews in Luke–Acts*, 63, 317. Elsewhere, Sanders says, "The witness of the speeches in Acts is, therefore, that the Jews generally are irredeemably resistant to God's will and his offer of salvation, and that they are the murderers of Jesus" (54).

Endnotes

146. Ruether says, "The Church read back into Jewish history a record of apostate Israel as rejecting and killing the prophets, in order then to read this pattern forward again to make the death of Jesus the predicted and culminating act of this history of apostasy" (*Faith and Fratricide*, 91).

147. Moule, "How the New Testament," 100–101.

148. Latourette, *History of Christianity*, 52.

149. Latourette, *History of Christianity*, 56. Latourette says that Stephen was "[s]toned by the orthodox Jews for views [that outraged] their complacent assumption that they were a people peculiarly chosen by God to the exclusion of others" (67).

150. Latourette, *History of Christianity*, 57.

151. Latourette, *History of Christianity*, 56–57. So extreme is Latourette's position in some instances that he even suggests that his readers should refrain from seriously studying Judaism: "[A] complete knowledge of Judaism . . . might make difficult a real understanding of Christianity" (19).

152. Richardson, "Israel-Idea in the Passion Narratives," 4, 10.

153. Bammel, "*Ex illa itaque*," 25. Bammel cites T. Mommsen: "It may be taken as settled that Jesus was sentenced by a Jewish people's court in accordance with the rules prevailing, and that Pontius Pilate the procurator . . . entered into the trial merely on the basis of his right to confirm capital sentences" (35n138).

154. Klein, *Anti-Judaism*, 92. Klein provides an overview of scholarly opinion in chapter 5 of her book, 92–126.

155. Catchpole, "Historicity of the Sanhedrin Trial," 54, 65.

156. Moule, *Birth*, 96.

157. Vogt, "Augustus and Tiberias," 8.

158. O'Neill, "Charge of Blasphemy," 77. Klingaman says, "Had Jesus claimed only to be the Messiah (which he never did), the Sanhedrin would have had a difficult time convicting him of blasphemy. But Jesus refused to deny that he felt a special kinship with God and—far more important—his assumption of the privileges reserved exclusively to God, such as the forgiveness of sins, which . . . condemned him as a blasphemer in the eyes of the High Priest and a majority of the Sanhedrin" (*First Century*, 199).

159. Goulder, "Jesus, the Man of Universal Destiny," 57–58.

160. Vogt, "Augustus and Tiberias," 8; and Reicke, "Galilee and Judea," 35.

161. Hoehner, "Why Did Pilate Send Jesus?" 89–90.

162. Klein, *Anti-Judaism*, 93, 102, and 124.

163. Reicke, "Galilee and Judea," 32–35.

164. Klingaman, *First Century*, 189–92.

165. Blinzler, "Jesus and His Disciples," 84.

166. Moule, *Birth*, 105–10. At the end of the chapter, Moule reiterates this point: "What [persecution] can be identified is mainly Jewish rather than imperial" (124). Moule cites an essay by Bo Reicke, written in 1953, in which Reicke identifies three phases of Jewish persecution of Christians: (1) in the thirties by Jewish authorities and the "Zionist" diaspora; (2) in the forties by Herod Agrippa I, on behalf of "legalistic Jews"; and in the fifties by the Zealots (106n2).

167. Wright and Fuller, *Book of the Acts*, 257, 259. The first half of the book, on the Jewish Bible, was written by G. Ernest Wright.

168. Lieu, *Image and Reality*, 4.

169. Levenson, *Hebrew Bible*, 40.

170. Ruether discusses these events in *Faith and Fratricide*, 184–225.

171. Gager, *Origins of Anti-Semitism*, 31. Gager cites two major studies of anti-Semitism and anti-Judaism: Klein, *Anti-Judaism in Christian Theology*; and Sanders, *Paul and Palestinian Judaism* (*Origins of Anti-Semitism*, 32).

172. Gager, *Origins of Anti-Semitism*, 14. For an overview of scholarly anti-Judaism on this subject, see Klein, *Anti-Judaism*, esp. chapter 3, "Law and Legalistic Piety," 39–66.

Endnotes

173. Johnson, *Jesus: A Biography*, 169; my emphasis.

174. Johnson, *Jesus: A Biography*, 38, 83.

175. Quoted in Bornkamm, *Jesus of Nazareth*, 37. On Bultmann, Dibelius, and Bornkamm, see Klein, *Anti-Judaism*, 27–30, 54, 56.

176. Bultmann, *Primitive Christianity*, 66–67; Bultmann's emphasis. Bultmann discusses "The Jewish Ethic of Obedience" in *Jesus and the Word*, 65–72.

177. Johnson, *Jesus: A Biography*, 107. In the words of Blenkinsopp, quoting Martin Noth, Jewish law turned into "an 'absolute entity' (absolute Grosse) in the later period; that Jews came to worship 'dead ordinances and statutes' is seen to be typical of an ever-recurring tendency to inauthentic faith" ("Tanakh and the New Testament," 118).

178. Harnack, *What Is Christianity?*, 50–51.

179. Bultmann, *Primitive Christianity*, 62–63.

180. Bornkamm, *Jesus of Nazareth*, 40.

181. Bultmann, *Primitive Christianity*, 65, 68.

182. Bultmann, *Primitive Christianity*, 62.

183. Riches, *Jesus and the Transformation*, 113.

184. Bultmann, *Primitive Christianity*, 66. Bultmann continues, "It was almost impossible to know the rules, let alone put them into practice."

185. Bornkamm, *Jesus of Nazareth*, 100.

186. Harnack, *What Is Christianity?*, 47. Harnack acknowledges that the Pharisees said the same things that Jesus said. The problem is that, unlike Jesus, they failed to express his ideals with sufficient "strength" and "vigour." Thus, "where will you find any message about God and the good that was ever so pure and so full of strength . . . as we hear and read of in the Gospels?" (47–48).

187. Bultmann, *Primitive Christianity*, 62.

188. Bornkamm, *Jesus of Nazareth*, 40.

189. Bultmann, *Primitive Christianity*, 65.

190. Guignebert, *Jewish World*, 71. On LaGrange, see Klein, *Anti-Judaism*, 36–37, 65.

191. Klein, *Anti-Judaism*, 62–64. Klein says, "Scarcely any of the authors mentioned [including Wellhausen and Schurer] refers to Jewish sources or seems to be acquainted with them except in quotations from the very early Christian writers—for example, the Fathers of the Church—or in such an anti-Semitic work as *Das entdeckte Judentum* (1699) by J. A. Eisenmenger. The descriptions in the Gospels, attributable to the conflict of the early Church with Judaism, are regarded as objective descriptions of the Jewish view of life and religion."

192. Levine, *Misunderstood Jew*, 125.

193. Wright, *What Saint Paul Really Said*, 108. According to Gager, "The alleged separatism of Jews in the Greco-Roman world has served as the most frequent explanation of pagan antipathy to Judaism . . . This view is mistaken in every respect" (*Origins of Anti-Semitism*, 31).

194. Freyne, *Galilee, Jesus*, 100. Bruce agrees: "The Pharisaic concern for ceremonial purity involved not only strict separation from Gentiles, who were beyond the pale of the law altogether, and from Samaritans, whose interpretation of the laws of purity differed from that current among the Jews, but even a considerable degree of aloofness from those of their fellow Jews who were not so particular about the laws of purity and tithing as the Pharisees themselves were. Chief among these were the ordinary artisans and peasants, who could not devote much time to the study and practice of these laws" (*New Testament History*, 81).

195. Freyne, *Galilee, Jesus*, 99–102, 210–11, 161.

196. Harnack, *What Is Christianity?*, 103.

197. Freyne, *Galilee, Jesus*, 102.

198. Freyne, *Galilee, Jesus*, 121; my emphasis; 118.

199. Herzog, *Jesus, Justice*, 154–55.

200. Herzog, *Jesus, Justice*, 171. On this subject, see also Horsley, *Covenant Economics*, 161–62.

Endnotes

201. Chilton, *Rabbi Jesus*, 117, 121. In the middle of this discussion, Chilton dials back on his charges: "Although the Gospels portray the Pharisees as the stock villains in the drama of Jesus' life, they were decent (if somewhat pompous) men, with a considered understanding of religion, grounded within the authority of the Torah and reasoned debate in the community" (118).

202. Nolan, *Jesus before Christianity*, 116–17. Nolan quotes Segundo, who says that the "oppression" of "the Jewish multitudes . . . depended much less on the Roman Empire and much more on the theology ruling in the groups of scribes and Pharisees. They, and not the Empire, imposed intolerable burdens on the weak" (118). For Nolan, not even the Zealots were free of guilt because their struggle "had nothing whatsoever to do with genuine liberation. They were fighting for Jewish nationalism, Jewish racialism, Jewish superiority and Jewish religious prejudice" (119).

203. Riches, *Jesus and the Transformation*, 67–68.

204. Riches, *Jesus and the Transformation*, 117. Of course, Riches's point is that Jesus rejects these separatist ideas: "Jesus' teaching in these very critical areas thus shows clearly the way in which he understands the will of God as the will of a loving and forgiving father rather than of a God who will have dealings only with the pure and righteous and who will exact retribution from the impure and the wicked . . . His love is to all men, just and unjust alike" (135).

205. Bruce, *New Testament History*, 81. Theissen makes the same point in *Early Palestinian Christianity*, 85.

206. Harnack, *What Is Christianity?*, 91. Later, Harnack mocks the Pharisees' "elevated 'practice of virtue' . . . and its routine observance in 'righteousness'" (92). On the Pharisees' preoccupation with purity, see Kaylor, *Jesus the Prophet*, 131.

207. Marty, *Christian World*, 8–9. Marty says that although "some . . . have wondered whether Jesus himself was a Pharisee or had been Pharisee-trained, . . . he was also a Pharisee with a difference."

208. McKenzie, *New Testament without Illusion*, 179. In his chapter on the Pharisees, McKenzie also mentions their inhumanity and their hypocrisy (173–84).

209. Christie-Murray, *History of Heresy*, 19.

210. Riches, *Jesus and the Transformation*, 114.

211. Christie-Murray, *History of Heresy*, 19. Rivkin explains, "To obey God when the rewards are immediately to hand is, after all, only a form of expediency; to obey him when there is no evidence that he cares is to meet the true test of inner faith" (*Hidden Revolution*, 300.

212. Bultmann, *Jesus and the Word*, 71.

213. Bultmann, *Theology*, 1:11; my emphasis.

214. Bultmann, *Primitive Christianity*, 69; my emphasis.

215. Riches, *Jesus and the Transformation*, 69–70, 73. Riches discusses this point in detail, especially as it applies to the book of Daniel, on 74–77. Bultmann says: "[A] belief in retribution after death was gradually developed . . . God allowed the wicked to prosper in this life in order to punish them in the next, whereas the righteous paid for their sins in this life in order to receive a full reward for their righteousness in the next" (*Primitive Christianity*, 70). Bornkamm discusses the contrast between Jewish and Christian concepts of rewards in *Jesus of Nazareth*, 137–43.

216. Bultmann, *Theology*, 1:11–12. See also Bultmann, *Primitive Christianity*, 69.

217. Jeremias, *Jerusalem*, 250.

218. Latourette, *History of Christianity*, 50.

219. Quoted in Klein, *Anti-Judaism*, 44.

220. Bornkamm, *Jesus of Nazareth*, 140.

221. Harnack, *What Is Christianity?*, 51. According to Moule, this is the aspect of Judaism that Paul vehemently attacked (*Birth*, 142, 173).

222. Bultmann, *Jesus and the Word*, 70.

223. Fuller, *Book of the Acts*, 229–30.

224. Latourette, *History of Christianity*, 50. Latourette says that "this portrait of the Pharisees

Endnotes

was a caricature." Nevertheless, Latourette continues, Jesus "deliberately" emphasized "the contrast as sharply as possible." His message "was that one could not acquire merit with God by piling up good deeds" (51, 72–73).

225. Bultmann, *Primitive Christianity*, 70–71.

226. Quoted in Klein, *Anti-Judaism*, 45.

227. Sanders, "Jesus, Ancient Judaism," 49; and *Jesus and Judaism*, 18. Sanders examines the argument that Jesus opposed Judaism because of its moral shallowness by such scholars as Bousset, Bultmann, Bornkamm, Dibelius, Kasemann, Fuchs, and Kummel in *Jesus and Judaism*, 26–37.

228. Sanders, *Judaism*, 400.

229. Meier, *Marginal Jew*, 3:346.

230. Harnack, *What Is Christianity?*, 51–52.

231. Bornkamm, *Jesus of Nazareth*, 40. Herzog refers to Jerome Neyrey's outline of the contrasting views of Jesus and the Pharisees in *Jesus, Justice*, 177.

232. Dihle, "Greco-Roman Background," 17; Braun, "Qumran Community," 74. On the superiority of Jesus' ethics to those of his fellow Jews, see also Lace, "What the New Testament Is About," 152; and Cook, *Introduction to the Bible*, 109, 123.

233. Dodd, *Founder of Christianity*, 73–74.

234. Stark, *Rise of Christianity*, 86–87, 212.

235. Johnson, *Jesus: A Biography*, 83.

236. Fuller, *Book of the Acts*, 271–72. Riches says that, to Jesus, "God is not a God of battles, a warrior destroying his enemies," as the Jews believed, "but a Father who forgives and commands his children to forgive" (*Jesus and the Transformation*, 104). On the same view of the Jewish concept of God, see Conzelmann and Lindemann, *Interpreting the New Testament*, 130.

237. Brown, *Introduction*, 222. Brown says of Matthew 27:24–25 (in which "all the people" say, "His blood be on us and on our children!") that, "tragically, the Matthean passage has been used to support horrendous antiJudaism that must be repudiated" (202n71).

238. Freyne, *Galilee, Jesus*, 5–6.

239. Levine, *Misunderstood Jew*, 9.

240. Crossan, *Birth of Christianity*, 340. Senior says that labeling "the Old Testament as a religion of justice and the New Testament as a religion of love and mercy" is a "too-common stereotype" (*Jesus: A Gospel Portrait*, 94).

241. Witherington, *What Have They Done*, 201.

242. Friedman, *Who Wrote the Bible?*, 240.

243. Davies, *Invitation*, 28.

244. Ruether, *Faith and Fratricide*, 12–13, 229.

245. Hagner, *Jewish Reclamation of Jesus*, 191.

246. Levine, *Misunderstood Jew*, 19, 119.

247. Carroll, *Constantine's Sword*, 117.

248. Bultmann, *Primitive Christianity*, 79.

249. Riches, *Jesus and the Transformation*, 18.

250. Riches, *Jesus and the Transformation*, 360n12. On Bousset's ideas and influence, see also Klein, *Anti-Judaism*, 33–35.

251. Tabor, *Jesus Dynasty*, 110.

252. Fredriksen, *From Jesus to Christ*, xxvi.

253. According to Klein, the anti-Judaism that seems to have dominated German criticism and also appeared, though more sporadically, elsewhere in the works of continental scholars was "different among Anglo-American authors." That is, most of the stereotypes popularized by Germans were relatively absent in the scholarship of British and American writers (*Anti-Judaism in Christian Theology*, 143). Klein's chapter 7 is devoted to a survey of these scholars (43–56). Klein says that American scholar George F. Moore "observed [in 1921] that Christian interest in Jewish

Endnotes

literature had always been apologetic or polemical rather than historical." Specifically, Moore said that the mostly German scholars he quoted had "an inadequate, one-sided selection of Jewish sources, an *a priori* biased attitude towards those sources, and [he] objected to their continual use of a method of comparison which tended to depreciate everything Jewish and to upvalue everything Christian at the expense of the former" (1, 3).

254. Meier, *Marginal Jew*, 1:15n7. Earlier, Meier calls Bornkamm's *Jesus of Nazareth* "somewhat dated." He continues: "[R]ecent work on early Judaism leads one to detect in Bornkamm's portrait of Jesus of Nazareth some of the features of those two great Martins of Germany, Luther and Heidegger. The more recent and extensive *Jesus and Judaism* by E. P. Sanders (1985) avoids many of the pitfalls of Bornkamm's *Jesus*" (3).

255. Akenson, *Saint Saul*, 52–53.

256. Hengel, *Four Gospels*, 33 and n135. Ironically, despite his evident desire to see Judaism without the common German bias, Hengel has no difficulty seeing both the Sadducees and the Pharisees in the worst possible light. As Fredriksen notes, Hengel has said, "In the temple, the Sadducean priestly nobility were exploiting the pious visitors; as the predominant spiritual movement in Palestine, Pharisaism, with its subtle casuistry and its esoteric arrogance, was not especially attractive either" (*From Jesus to Christ*, 103).

257. Yoder, *Politics of Jesus*, 114.

258. Levenson, *Hebrew Bible*, 42.

259. Blenkinsopp, "Tanakh and the New Testament," 106, 118n41. The second half of this quotation comes from Blenkinsopp's *Prophecy and Canon* (20) and is quoted by Levenson (42).

260. Fredriksen, *From Jesus to Christ*, 104.

261. Blenkinsopp, "Tanakh and the New Testament," 105. The quotation is from Wellhausen's *Prolegomena to the History of Ancient Israel*.

262. Gager, *Origins of Anti-Semitism*, 32–33.

263. Brown, *Introduction*, 578.

264. Carroll, *Constantine's Sword*, 73.

265. Levenson, *Hebrew Bible*, 45.

266. Saldarini, *Pharisees, Scribes and Sadducees*, 7. Saldarini continues, "Though many recent studies have clarified aspects of Judaism in the second Temple period, the Pharisees, scribes and Sadducees remain obscure because of the paucity of evidence and the biases of the sources."

267. Charlesworth, *Jesus within Judaism*, 47. Charlesworth is quoting Schurer's *History of the Jewish People in the Time of Jesus Christ* (Edinburgh, 1898), 2:115.

268. Klein, *Anti-Judaism*, 36.

269. Freyne, *Galilee, Jesus*, 2.

270. Carroll, *Constantine's Sword*, 517; and Vermes, *Changing Faces of Jesus*, 285.

271. Klein, *Anti-Judaism*, 11–13.

272. Vermes, *Jesus in His Jewish Context*, 55, 58. Vermes briefly summarizes the views of Wellhausen. Ferdinand Weber, and Gerhard Kittel on 58–60.

273. Freyne, *Galilee, Jesus*, 268.

274. Freyne, *Galilee*, 270, 272. Freyne's only mistake is to have stated that in not recognizing Jesus' divinity and attributing his powers to demonic forces, the Jews "are cutting themselves off from God *irrevocably*" (85; my emphasis). Freyne later says, "Thus the rejection of Jesus by Jerusalem and Jerusalem's rejection by God are two poles of the axis around which the narratives revolve" (269). These accusations are quite irresponsible.

275. Latourette, *History of Christianity*, 60.

276. Meier, *Marginal Jew*, 1:15–16n7. Meier explains that some scholars use the term "late Judaism" pejoratively "to describe a religion that saw God as a distant and almost impersonal Sovereign, a religion of fear" (16). Judaism at this point in its history was "late" because it was doomed, quite soon, to extinction. Thoma says that the term "late Judaism" (or *Spaetjudenten*) "was conceived of

Endnotes

at a time when Christian biblical religious scholarship and exegesis were stamped by apologetics, ignorance of and animosity toward Jews" (*Christian Theology of Judaism*, 38).

277. Wright, *What Saint Paul Really Said*, 16.

278. Mussner, *Tractate on the Jews*, 161.

279. Paget, "Quests for the Historical Jesus," 141. Kugel attributes these changes in the view of the Bible to (1) "the rapidly spreading knowledge of the Hebrew language among Christians" and (2) "the nascent Protestant Reformation" (*How to Read*, 25).

280. Kugel, *How to Read*, 29. Kugel examines the role of Spinoza, the principles of Deism, and the influence of the Enlightenment on biblical studies on 30–38.

281. Blenkinsopp, "Tanakh and the New Testament," 100. Gabler said, "Biblical theology is historical in character and sets forth what the sacred writers thought about divine matters; dogmatic theology, on the contrary, is dogmatic in character, and teaches what a particular theologian philosophically and rationally decides about divine matters, in accordance with his character, time, age, place, sect or school, and other similar influences." In short, the former is objective, and the latter is subjective (quoted in Levenson, *Hebrew Bible*, 35).

282. Powell, *Jesus as a Figure*, 16. Powell notes that Reimarus "feared retribution for his controversial views during his lifetime" and that both David Friedrich Strauss and Ernst Renan, two Bible scholars who followed in Reimarus's footsteps, were dismissed from their university professorships.

283. Powell attributes this way of framing the interpretational issues to Martin Kähler, author of *The So-Called Historical Jesus and the Historic, Biblical Christ*, published in 1892 (Powell, *Jesus as a Figure in History*, 4).

284. Tyson, *Study of Early Christianity*, 341.

285. Riches, *Jesus and the Transformation*, 3–4. Schweitzer provides an overview of Remairus's reassessment of Jesus' relation to Judaism in *Quest*, 16–24. Paget says that this revision of Jesus' relationship to Judaism was initiated by Sebastian Munster in 1537, who claims "that the world out of which Jesus emerged was best understood as Jewish, and that, therefore, the use of rabbinical works and other Judaica was a desideratum of any commentary on the gospels" ("Quests for the Historical Jesus," 140–41).

286. Meyer, *Aims of Jesus*, 30. See also Paget, "Quests for the historical Jesus," 142.

287. Fredriksen notes that, since Schweitzer was highly critical of studies of Jesus written in the nineteenth century, his book was followed by half a century of relative silence on the subject of the historical Jesus: "Scholars of the first half of our century, stoically acknowledging the nonhistorical interests of the gospel writers and the distance in time, language, and outlook between them and Jesus, embraced a radical skepticism. Consoled by the rigor of their intellectual consistency, they abandoned all hope (at least consciously) of retrieving the Jesus of history." In the second half of the century, however, Fredriksen continues, "academic attention has refocused on the gospels" and has arrived at "something like a consensus . . . on the public career of Jesus" (*From Jesus to Christ*, 96–97).

288. Bokenkotter, *Concise History*, 17.

289. Smith, *Jesus the Magician*, 3. Robert Morgan comments: "The Early Christians . . . worked backwards *from* the answer *to* the question and said that Jesus died because it was God's will. Then they retold the story complete with this theological explanation . . . This does not disprove the historical accuracy of what they relate, but it does cast a shadow of doubt over it" ("Concluding Unscientific Postscript," 39).

290. Segal, *Rebecca's Children*, xvi.

291. Carroll, *Constantine's Sword*, 232.

292. Sanders, *Jews in Luke/Acts*, xv–xvi. Langmuir says that "most Europeans . . . had been brought up on the New Testament account on Jesus' life and death." Thus, "they associated their history with Christianity . . . and they attributed Jesus' death to 'the Jews,' whom they thought different and inferior" (*History, Religion*, 320).

Endnotes

293. Herford, *Pharisees*, 11–14.
294. Herford, *Pharisees*, 11–14.
295. Herford, *Pharisees*, 238, 214; my emphasis.
296. Meier, *Marginal Jew*, 3:345–46, n4. "Worse still," Meier adds, "uncritical acceptance of ancient anti-Jewish polemic was sometimes mixed with modern anti-Semitism" (346).
297. In his introduction to a recent edition of Herford's book, Glatzer says that Julius Wellhausen and others, including Harnack and Schurer, "overstressed the ritualistic and legal aspects of pharisaic religious thought, ignoring in the main its piety, loving concern, and humaneness" (*Pharisees*, 1). Robert R. Wilson says this view was "eventually rejected by biblical scholars" ("[P]rophetic books," 216). See also, in the same volume, Reif, "Aspects of the Jewish Contribution," 145–46. Friedman devotes an entire chapter to Wellhausen's errors in *Who Wrote the Bible?*, 161–73. See also Brueggemann, *Old Testament Theology*, 8–9; and Blenkinsopp, "Pentateuch," 181–83. Collins summarizes both sides in the debate on the place in the order of composition of the Priestly tradition in *Short Introduction*, 91–93.
298. Thoma, *Christian Theology of Judaism*, 38. Meier says that the portrait of Judaism as "a religion of legalism and fear will no longer be taken seriously by most scholars." He cites Thomas Sheehan for using the term "late Judaism" (meaning "almost dead") in his book *The First Coming* as recently as 1986 (*Marginal Jew*, 1:16).
299. Reif, "Aspects of the Jewish Contribution," 156n9.
300. Schweitzer, *Quest*, 255.
301. Levenson, *Hebrew Bible*, 15. Levenson provides an extensive critique of Eichrodt, von Rad, and other followers of Wellhausen on 16–27. Of Eichrodt, he says, "He accepted New Testament caricatures, stereotypes, and outright perversions of Judaism in the same manner as would the most unlettered fundamentalist" (17).
302. Brueggemann, *Old Testament Theology*, 8–9.
303. Frerich, "Introduction: The Jewish School," 3.
304. Kaufmann, *Religion of Israel*, 1–2. Kaufmann criticizes the Wellhausen hypothesis in depth on 153–57 and 175–79.
305. McConnell, "Introduction," 5.
306. Neusner, *Judaism in the Beginning*, 49–50.
307. Cwiekowski, *Beginnings of the Church*, 30. Cwiekowski discusses the Pharisees' "flexibility . . . in applying the Torah to new situations" and emphasis on "religious individualism" (31).
308. Hill, *Hellenists and Hebrews*, 35. Hill refers to Martin Goodman, E. P. Sanders, Jacob Neusner, Morton Smith, and Robert A. Wild on this point (n43).
309. Smith, *Jesus the Magician*, 156–57. Herford says, "There was nothing to compel anyone to accept [the Pharisaic position], and no one would accept it unless he took his religion very seriously. If he did accept it, he did so because he desired to serve God" (*Pharisees*, 119). Smith's phrase "Jamnian Judaism" refers to the brand of Judaism that developed under the auspices of the Pharisees who met in Jamnia after the destruction of Jerusalem in the Jewish Revolt of AD 66–73.
310. Saldarini, *Pharisees, Scribes and Sadducees*, 210–11. Saldarini makes this point on 120, 122, 132–33, 214, 277, and 281.
311. Jeremias, *Jerusalem*, 259, 263–64.
312. Sanders, *Historical Figure of Jesus*, 44–45. Sanders adds that "the basic character of Judaism meant that lay people could challenge the priesthood and could claim to be the best interpreters of the law" (46). See also Sanders, *Jesus and Judaism*, 196–97.
313. Sanders, *Judaism*, 392–93. Sanders adds: "Thus in place of Josephus' statements that the Pharisees were indirectly powerful, I propose that, after the reign of Salome [in the first century BC], they were in moderate but ineffective opposition, and that those who spoke out too loudly, or acted rashly, were executed or killed during the futile uprisings" (395).
314. Kaylor, *Jesus the Prophet*, 36. See also Moore, *Judaism*, 2:77.

315. Fredriksen, *From Jesus to Christ*, 106. Fredriksen continues: "If they had disagreed with Jesus . . . they might have refused to eat with him or otherwise avoided his company; or they might have disputed with him. But there is little else they could have done." Neusner says that the Pharisees "had no real hold either on the government or on the masses of the people." In their effort to influence others, they "were much like any other Hellenistic philosophical school or sect" (*Judaism in the Beginning*, 52–53).

316. Mack, *Lost Gospel*, 60.

317. Meier, *Marginal Jew*, 3:335. Sanders, citing Jacob Neusner, also claims that the Pharisees did not control all of the synagogues: "I think that we cannot safely generalize about who dominated how many synagogues, but we may doubt the general view that the Pharisees ran all of them" (*Judaism*, 398).

318. White, *From Jesus to Christianity*, 314.

319. On this point, see Enslin, *Christian Beginnings*, 116; Meier, *Marginal Jew*, 3:315–16, 335; Moore, *Judaism*, 1:282; and Sanders, *Jesus and Judaism*, 181.

320. Sanders, *Jesus and the Judaism*, 15–16.

321. Meier, *Marginal Jew*, 3:297.

322. Thoma, *Christian Theology of Judaism*, 66.

323. Sanders, *Judaism*, 402.

324. Carroll, *Constantine's Sword*, 110; my emphasis.

325. Quoted in Grant, *Jesus: An Historian's Review*, 112; my emphasis. Cohn goes on to say that the Pharisees were lenient, temperate, and spiritual. Thoma says that the Pharisees "gained esteem among the inhabitants of Jerusalem and Judea, first as opponents of the rebellion and later as representatives of as orderly a defense as possible against the Roman aggressors" (*Christian Theology of Judaism*, 66).

326. Maccoby, *Mythmaker*, 6. Quoting Josephus, Goodman says that "the Pharisees [were] affectionate to each other" and also "show[ed] respect and deference to their elders" (*History of Judaism*, 119).

327. Klingaman, *First Century*, 7–8. Saldarini agrees: "The Pharisees cultivated harmonious relations with all, had great respect for their traditions and elders and consequently had a large following for their attractive way of life." In other words, despite their lack of power, "they stressed social relations to build up their own group and win it favor and influence with others" (*Pharisees, Scribes and Pharisees*, 122).

328. Sanders, *Judaism*, 402–3, 404, 446. Thus, Sanders concludes: "The summaries of Josephus are exaggerated: [the Pharisees] did not really govern indirectly; the priesthood did not dance to their tune. Nevertheless, some truth lies behind the summaries" (403). See also 449–50.

329. Brown, *Introduction*, 79. Brown says in a footnote, "In part, the overly negative picture may stem from English connotation; the Greek *hypoktrites* means 'unscrupulous, casuistic,' but not 'insincere'" (n19).

330. Segal, *Rebecca's Children*, 127. Herford says that the view of the Pharisees as hypocritical is "inadequate and superficial" (*Pharisees*, 11). He explains his view in more detail on 116–17.

331. Wylen, *Jews in the Time*, 143. On this point, see also Maguire, *Moral Core*, 132–33; and Moyise, *Jesus and Scripture*, 84.

332. Senior, *Jesus: A Gospel Portrait*, 40.

333. Guignebert, *Jewish World*, 165. However, Klein says that negative portrayals of Pharisaism like Schurer's have been "taken as authoritative even up to the present time. From 1902 till 1976, there has been no perceptible difference in the judgement—or, more precisely in the condemnation—of Pharisaism" (*Anti-Judaism*, 87).

334. Grant, *Jesus: An Historian's Review*, 112.

335. Enslin, *Christian Beginnings*, 116.

336. Winter, "Sadducess and Pharisees," 53. Winter says, "In the Gospels the Pharisees are represented as the most bitter opponents of Jesus. This is a biased view" (51).

Endnotes

337. Craveri, *Life of Jesus*, 132–33.

338. Sanders, *Judaism*, 445–46. Sanders explores this subject thoroughly on 428–29. He concludes: "It is not true that Pharisees would not come into contact with others. They took part in civic life and associated with other members of society . . . Not only did Pharisees not achieve apartheid, they seem not to have wished for it: there is not a word about social isolation in any of the ancient literature. Josephus' silence on this point is especially striking . . . There is no hint that they avoided contact with others. We can dismiss this kind of creative scholarship and its results." See also 450.

339. Sanders, *Jesus and Judaism*, 181, 188.

340. Sanders, *Judaism*, 265. Sanders provides a detailed explanation of the Pharisees' attitude toward purity laws on 438–40. Later, he accuses both Joachim Jeremias and Jacob Neusner of accusing the Pharisees of the kinds of over-the-top religious practices engaged in by the Essenes at Qumran: "They describe the wrong group: the only true Israel, communal meals, meals eaten in purity, sacred food, closed societies, unwillingness to mingle with others because of fear of impurity, exclusion of everyone else from the realm of the sacred, hatred of other Jews, expulsion of people who transgress food and purity laws from the commonwealth of Israel. These characteristics are found in the Dead Sea Scrolls and in Josephus' description of the Essenes. They are not found in any source that might conceivably come from or reflect the Pharisees" (422). Sanders also notes that Neusner did not go as far as Jeremias in these accusations (422–23). Later, Sanders adds: "In this long tradition of scholarship, at least on the Christian side, the two laws that the people would not obey, tithing and eating food in purity, are regarded as externalistic, ritualistic, snobbish, elitist, self-righteous rules. The Pharisees excluded those who would not keep such rules from Jewish religion and society. This view, which is standard in the handbooks (with some variations), offers a completely unrealistic picture" (460).

341. Theissen, *Early Palestinian Christianity*, 82–83.

342. Saldarini, *Pharisees, Scribes and Sadducees*, 290. In a footnote, Saldarini adds, "See Mary Douglas, *Purity [and Danger]* and *[Natural] Symbols* for purity rules as boundary setting mechanisms and for the necessity of such boundaries in groups which do not control society and must protect themselves from assimilation" (n27). Saldarini discusses this subject in greater detail in 215. Although Sanders grants that the Jews embraced exclusivism, like Saldarini, he says that their motive was not snobbery but self-preservation—that is, the desire to protect Judaism from outside influences (*Judaism*, 266). See also 71–72, 75.

343. Meier, *Marginal Jew*, 3:315–16.

344. Moyise, *Jesus and Scripture*, 22.

345. Zeitlin, *Jesus and the Judaism*, 15–16. Zeitlin continues: "Nor is there any Pharisaic opposition to the *am ha-aretz* (literally 'people of the land') for their lack of learning or education" (16).

346. Sanders, *Judaism*, 401.

347. Sanders, *Jesus and Judaism*, 180.

348. Thus, despite the generally negative picture of them in the Gospels, Flusser notes, the Pharisees display some degree of integrity, for example in Acts 5:17–42 and 22:30—23:10. Flusser discusses these passages and other examples in *Sage from Galilee*, 48–49).

349. Moore, *Judaism*, II-III, 193.

350. Parkes, *Conflict of the Church*, 35; and Senior, *Jesus: A Gospel Portrait*, 41.

351. Perkins, *Reading the New Testament*, 35. Perkins adds, "Thus, the Pharisees, not the high priests, were the ancestors of rabbinic Judaism and, through the rabbinic traditions, of the various forms of Judaism that we know today." See also Perrin and Duling, *New Testament: An Introduction*, 265.

352. Mussner, *Tractate on the Jews*, 161–63. Craveri says of the Pharisees: "They represented real Judaism, and not merely 'extreme and sterile conservatism.' Deeply religious and sincerely patriotic, they considered the Temple the religious and national center of Israel, and their concern with total compliance with the precepts of the Torah as standards of day-to-day behavior was

dictated by nothing but the desire to preserve their national customs and traditions unchanged." Craveri acknowledges, however, that, in pursuit of these goals, the Pharisees can be accused of "intransigent rigidity against the danger of foreign infiltration and contamination" (*Life of Jesus*, 133).

353. Segal, *Rebecca's Children*, 123.

354. Grant, *Jesus: An Historian's Review*, 112. Despite his clearly high regard for the Pharisees, Grant nevertheless believes that the conflict between them and Jesus was real to some degree: "For the constant references in the Gospels to strife between the Pharisees and scribes, on the one hand, and Jesus on the other, leave no doubt that such strife, even if the Gospels exaggerated it, had genuinely existed" (117). Grant discusses the Pharisees' hypocrisy on 119.

355. Hagner, *Jewish Reclamation of Jesus*, 172, 189.

356. Gonzalez, *Story of Christianity*, 10.

357. Klingaman, *First Century*, 7. Sanders argues that "observation of the biblical purity laws was not a special concern of the Pharisees" (*Jesus and Judaism*, 183). Sanders examines this issue on 183–88.

358. Ruether, *Faith and Fratricide*, 53. Ruether continues: "Through the device of the oral Torah, the Pharisees were able to free Israel from the letter of the past and to find an open way into new futures, while simultaneously making it their intention to preserve every jot and tittle of that past itself."

359. Guignebert, *Jewish World*, 166. Senior says that "the Pharisees, unlike the Sadducees, were open to new development in Jewish thought. For them, the great network of oral commentary that had grown up around the law in the rabbinic schools of Israel was not a subversion of the law but an insurance that it was living and active" (*Jesus: A Gospel Portrait*, 41).

360. Thompson, *Jesus Debate*, 159.

361. Ruether, *Faith and Fratricide*, 54. On this point, see also Tyson, *Study of Early Christianity*, 98–99. Tyson says that the Pharisees were aware of the dangers of literalism, casuistry, and formalism, all of which they conscientiously tried to avoid.

362. Saldarini, *Pharisees, Scribes and Sadducees*, 95. See also 126, 282.

363. Segal, *Rebecca's Children*, 170.

364. Guignebert, *Jewish World*, 166. On the Pharisees' opposition to legalism, see 71–72. On the Pharisees' emphasis on both *kavannah* and *teshubah*, see Herford, *Pharisees*, 161–62, 165–66.

365. Thompson, *Jesus Debate*, 160.

366. White, *From Jesus to Christianity*, 79.

367. Sanders, *Judaism*, 446–47. Sanders is quite emphatic about the intimate connection between the Pharisees and the Rabbis. He says of the former, "After the destruction of Jerusalem, they led the reconstruction of Judaism, giving up their party name, becoming more catholic, and taking the title 'rabbis', 'teachers'" (412). Sanders adds: "There are substantial continuities between the two, such as the emphasis on non-biblical traditions. It is also important that the rabbis of the late first century and the second century regarded themselves as heirs of the Pharisees" (413). Speaking of the Shema and the Eighteen Benedictions, Sanders says, "These prayers focus on repentance, forgiveness, thanksgiving for the election, and the hope of redemption. It is difficult to pray them every day and not to be reminded of the basic theological themes of Judaism: love, mercy and repentance. Further, they inculcate the feeling of the presence of God" (448).

368. Jeremias, *Jerusalem*, 266–67.

369. Grant, *Jesus: An Historian's Review*, 112–13.

370. Saldarini, *Pharisees, Scribes and Sadducees*, 281–82, 286–87.

371. Sanders, *Judaism*, 262, 416, 421, 457.

372. Lee, *Galilean Jewishness of Jesus*, 13. Flusser says that Jesus and the Pharisees were "basically rooted in universal non-sectarian Judaism." Therefore, considering Jesus' ties to mainstream Judaism. "[i]t would not be wrong to describe Jesus as a Pharisee in the *broad* sense." However, he "did not identify himself with them" (*Sage from Galilee*, 47). On this point, see also Schiffman, *From Text to Tradition*, 151.

Endnotes

373. Guignebert, *Jewish World*, 165.

374. Gonzalez, *Story of Christianity*, 10. Ehrman comments: "[I]t should not be imagined that Jesus opposed the Pharisaic interpretations because they stood so far apart on most issues. In fact, they were extremely close. Hence the emotional rhetoric" (*Lost Christianities*, 160).

375. Vermes, *Jesus the Jew*, 35.

376. Bainton, *Early Christianity*, 14. Bainton adds, however, that Jesus would not have approved of the Pharisees' "keeping of the law, whose meticulous enactments served neither God nor man" (14–15).

377. Guignebert, *Jewish World*, 166. Like Bainton, however, Guignebert faults the Pharisees for "their strict legalism" and "labored casuistry" (165).

378. Meier, *Marginal Jew*, 3:338. Meier lists other similarities, as well as some dissimilarities, between Jesus and the Pharisees.

379. Craveri, *Life of Jesus*, 132.

380. Guignebert, *Jewish World*, 73.

381. Wilken, *First Thousand Years*, 9. Brown says that the process began with "memories of what Jesus did and said" and was, as Wilken argues, "influenced by the life-experience" of the particular Christian community to which the Gospel was addressed and finally "shaped . . . from the second stage into a written Gospel" by the evangelist (*Introduction*, 363).

382. Boyarin, *Jewish Gospels*, 22.

383. Armstrong, *History of God*, 81. Armstrong says that, like the Pharisees, Jesus "believed that charity and loving-kindness were the most important of the *mitzvot*." In addition, like them, "he was devoted to the Torah and was said to have preached a more stringent observance than many of his contemporaries." According to Armstrong, Jesus "also taught a version of Hillel's Golden Rule, when he argued that the whole of the law could be summed up in the maxim: do unto others as you would have them do unto you."

384. Wilken, *First Thousand Years*, 10, 18, 20. For a comprehensive examination of Jesus' Judaism, see Sanders, *Jesus and Judaism*, 1–58; and my *Great Betrayal*, 94–152. In my chapter on this subject, I cite, in support of this argument, John P. Meier, Hans Conzelmann and Andreas Lindemann, Bart D. Ehrman, Raymond E. Brown, James D. Tabor, Bruce Chilton, John Dominic Crossan, F. E. Peters, R. David Kaylor, Paula Fredriksen, William C. Placher, and many others.

385. Klein, *Anti-Judaism*, 67, 90. Klein argues that the "separation" between Christians and Pharisees occurred much later than the Gospel accounts suggest: "Many New Testament scholars would admit that the break must be seen as coming much later, six decades after the death of Jesus, at the time of the definitive redaction of Matthew" (76).

386. Senior, *Jesus: A Gospel Portrait*, 41–42. Despite his belief that historical circumstances affected the Gospel treatment of the Pharisees, Senior says that the Gospel picture of this group is at least true to some extent: "Jesus himself undoubtedly had fundamental differences with the Pharisees over interpretation of the law and even more basic differences about the nature of religious fidelity. It is likely too that the Pharisees' zeal for the law could lead to an excess of legalism and to a concern for externals bordering on hypocrisy. Thus the gospels' indictment of the Pharisees cannot be completely overturned" What concerns Senior most of all is the danger that "the gospel critique of the Pharisees [could] become an excuse for antisemitism and anti-Judaism" (41).

387. On this point, see Gonzalez, *Story of Christianity*, 10.

388. Cwiekowski, *Beginnings of the Church*, 73.

389. Borg, *Reading the Bible Again*, 186.

390. Theissen, *Early Palestinian Christianity*, 1, 17–18, 22, 118. For a comprehensive study of the first generation of early Christians, see Fredriksen, *When Christians Were Jews*. The author says repeatedly of the early Christians, "[M]embers of this movement were traditionally observant Jews" (e.g., 185).

391. Cwiekowski, *Beginnings of the Church*, 30, 74, 75.

Endnotes

392. Sanders, *Jews in Luke–Acts*, 239.

393. Tenney comments: "Jesus quoted with equal readiness from the Law, from the Psalms, and from the Prophets (Luke 24:44), the three divisions of the Hebrew Bible, and argued from them as the basis of revelational authority (John 10:34–36) concerning His own person. Throughout the Acts and Epistles the apostolic writers show by their frequent quotations their familiarity with the Old Testament, whether they used the Hebrew text or the Greek Septuagint" (*New Testament Survey*, 102).

394. Herford says: "[I]t does not appear that [Jesus] ever looked on himself as being other than a Jew. Certainly his first followers continued their observance of Jewish usage after he was gone, with as much or as little strictness as before" (*Pharisees*, 212).

395. Brown, *Introduction*, 288, 232.

396. Cwiekowski, *Beginnings of the Church*, 79–80.

397. Not only did Paul comply with these requirements, but he also continued to identify himself as a Jew (21:39; 22:3) and finished his ambitious proselytizing career in Rome preaching to Jews, as he had done almost exclusively during his long series of visits to synagogues throughout the Diaspora. Tenney adds: "As late as A.D. 56 the church in Jerusalem still had in its ranks men who made vows in the temple (21:23–26) and who adhered closely to its legal observance. Only with the development of the Gentile church did its connection with Christianity cease" (*New Testament Survey*, 92).

398. Brown, *Introduction*, 289n25.

399. Bultmann, *Theology*, 1:56.

400. Levine, *Misunderstood Jew*, 84.

401. Carroll, *Constantine's Sword*, 562.

402. Vermes, *Changing Faces of Jesus*, 282.

403. Quoted in Levine, *Misunderstood Jew*, 84.

404. Hengel, *Four Gospels*, 85.

405. Attridge, "Christianity from the Destruction," 153.

406. Crossan says: "As Christian Jewish communities are steadily more alienated from their fellow Jews, so the 'enemies' of Jesus expand to fit those new situations. By the time of John in the 90s, those enemies are 'the Jews'—that is, all those other Jews except us few right ones" (*Birth of Christianity*, 525).

407. Fredriksen, *From Jesus to Christ*, 211.

408. On this subject, see Meier, *Marginal Jew*, 3:298–99.

409. Klingaman, *First Century*, 370–71. Klein quotes John Reumann: "After A.D. 70 when the temple was destroyed, there were no more priests; it was the Pharisees and rabbis who constituted, and hence were identified with, the Jewish opposition to Christianity. The long tirade in Matthew 23 against 'Scribes and Pharisees' doubtless reflects the changed situation" (*Anti-Judaism*, 148–49). The quotation comes from *Jesus in the Church's Gospel*.

410. Although it is generally asserted that the non-Pharisaic sects lost their power after the Revolt of AD 66, Saldarini reminds his readers that sects did not simply disappear: "The absence of sects in rabbinic literature does not prove that there were none. Even after it did gain control in the mid and late Talmudic period, various sect-like movements and protests against Talmudic control emerged" (*Pharisees, Scribes and Sadducees*, 8n11). On this point, see also Goodman, *History of Judaism*, 242–43.

411. Stegemann and Stegemann, *Jesus Movement*, 245. Horsley says that the destruction of the Temple and of some portions of the city of Jerusalem "became a turning point" for the Jews: "In reaction against the apocalyptic spirit and revolutionary impulse, sobered Pharisaic sages laid the foundation not only of a reconstructed Jewish society, but also of what became Rabbinic Judaism" (*Bandits, Prophets, and Messiahs*, xxiii).

412. Spong, *Liberating the Gospels*, 46.

Endnotes

413. Robinson, *Gospel of Jesus*, 18.

414. Stegemann and Stegemann, *Jesus Movement*, 243. White notes that the power to expel anyone who confessed Jesus "from the Jewish community" existed only in the years after the destruction of Jerusalem, not before (*From Jesus to Christianity*, 314).

415. Klingaman, *First Century*, 371. Klingaman mentions the expulsion of Christians from synagogues in AD 85 by Gamaliel II (372). Senior explains: "One result of Jewish effort to rebuild was a lessening of tolerance for fringe groups within Judaism. The leadership of the Pharisees gradually imposed a tighter orthodoxy on Jewish life, based on strict fidelity to the law. Christian critique of the law and the church's openness to Gentile converts put the early community on a collision course with Judaism" (*Jesus: A Gospel Portrait*, 42).

416. Davies, *Invitation*, 456–57.

417. Thompson, *Jesus Debate*, 158. For more detailed discussions of this separation, see Ruether, *Faith and Fratricide*, 79–80; and Stegemann and Stegemann, *Jesus Movement*, 221–23, 243–46. Ruether makes three important points. First, dissidents were flogged but never executed by synagogue leaders. Second, as early as the mid-80s, Pharisees added a curse on all sectarians to be read at synagogue services, which "made it impossible for a Christian to actually lead a synagogue service." And, third, although "Christian preachers" were by this means barred from synagogue attendance, ordinary participants were not (*Faith and Fratricide*, 87, 115).

418. Meier, *Marginal Jew*, 3:339.

419. Carroll, *Constantine's Sword*, 562.

420. Gager, *Kingdom and Community*, 26. Gager is quoting Jacob Neusner.

421. Spong, *Liberating the Gospels*, 48.

422. Lieu, *Image and Reality*, 253.

423. Smith, *Jesus the Magician*, 153.

424. Bultmann, *Jesus and the Word*, 25.

425. LaCocque, *Jesus the Central Jew*, 100.

426. Sanders, *Judaism*, 325.

427. White says that the "separation between the Jesus movement and rabbinic Judaism . . . proceeded at a different pace in different localities depending on the local makeup of emerging Christian groups" (*From Jesus to Christianity*, 294).

428. Ruether, *Faith and Fratricide*, 75.

429. Mussner, *Tractate on the Jews*, 174.

430. Carroll, *Constantine's Sword*, 129.

431. Cwiekowski, *Beginnings of the Church*, 30.

432. On this subject, see Tenney, *New Testament Survey*, 82; and Tyson, *Study of Early Christianity*, 236, 239.

433. Vermes, "Introduction," xvii–xviii. Of course, the "later ages" began after the fall of Jerusalem.

434. Clark, *Christianity and Roman Society*, 25–26. Clark says that this contemporary understanding of the Pharisees is "a good example of how changes in scholarship have affected interpretation."

435. Schillebeeckx, *Jesus: An Experiment*, 235. Schillebeeckx says earlier, "The conflict over the Law is therefore a traditional controversy within Judaism and so pre-dates Christianity" (232).

436. Meier, *Marginal Jew*, 3:338.

437. Meier, *Marginal Jew*, 3:644. Meier discusses points of difference between Jesus and the Pharisees on 642–45.

438. Gager, *Origins of Anti-Semitism*, 136.

439. Akenson, *Saint Saul*, 251. Basser says: "[I]n both style and structure the teachings of Jesus recorded in Matthew's Gospel reflect the methods and oral corpus of his Jewish culture . . . John presents Jesus giving a classic argument in the standard style and form of Rabbinic reasoning" ("Gospel and Talmud," 291).

Endnotes

440. Sanders, *Schismatics, Sectarians, Dissidents, Deviants*, 18. Meier also mentions the "nasty clashes" between the "the House of Hillel and the House of Shammai" (*Marginal Jew*, 3:338.) Says Gager, "[O]nce we imagine [Jesus' attacks on the Pharisees] in their original pre-gospel form, we will almost certainly find ourselves in the presence of debates and arguments within rather than outside Judaism" (*Origins of Anti-Semitism*, 28–29).

441. Crossan, *Birth of Christianity*, 583. Referring to arguments between various Jewish sects, Crossan says earlier, "No matter what those groups said about one another or did against one another, . . . theirs was an intra-Jewish debate . . . [T]he confrontation was never an attack on Judaism from outside but an attack on other Jews from inside" (xxxiii).

442. Saldarini, *Pharisees, Scribes and Sadducees*, 214.

443. Mussner, *Tractate on the Jews*, 163.

444. Zeitlin, *Jesus and the Judaism*, 15.

445. Ehrman, *Lost Christianities*, 160.

446. Akenson, *Saint Saul*, 245.

447. Meier, *Marginal Jew*, 3:329.

448. Flusser, *Sage from Galilee*, 44.

449. Meier, *Marginal Jew*, 3:338–39.

450. Thoma, *Christian Theology of Judaism*, 66.

451. Gager, *Origins of Anti-Semitism*, 136; my emphasis.

452. Guignebert, *Jewish World*, 165.

453. First, McKenzie says, "The best explanation of the hostility toward Jesus and Christians which the New Testament attributes to the Pharisees is that the Pharisees were hostile to Jesus and the Christians." Thus, he argues that Matthew did not have to "falsify his sources in order to compose" his "great invective against the Pharisees in Matthew 23." Second, however, McKenzie says elsewhere, "If one argues that the hostility which the gospels show between Jesus and the Pharisees reflects rather the experience of the early church than the experience of Jesus, it is difficult to refute this claim." In addition, "we cannot be sure that all of [Matthew's charges] go back to the words of Jesus, or that early controversies between Christians and Jews, or even between Pharisaic Jewish Christians and Gentiles may not have exaggerated some of the charges" (*New Testament without Illusion*, 173–84). On the one hand, Nolan attributes the Pharisees' "uniformly negative image" to "the prominence of the Pharisees 'when the gospels were being written'"—i.e., in the last half of the first century. On the other hand, however, he says that the criticism of the Pharisees "cannot be completely overturned" because "the Pharisees' zeal for the law could lead to an excess of legalism and to a concern for externals bordering on hypocrisy" (*Jesus before Christianity*, 41). Nolan says in an endnote: "The early Church no doubt exaggerated Jesus' opposition to the Pharisees because of its conflict with them . . . Nevertheless Jesus' indignation about hypocrisy as such can hardly have been invented by the early Church" (177n5).

454. Schiffman, *From Text to Tradition*, 151–52. The emphases in this and other quotations in this paragraph are mine. According to Bultmann: "From this time"—that is, *after* the Crucifixion—"come the disputes over interpretation of the Law . . . [T]he disputes between Jesus and his opponents were now recounted and written down as models, and were naturally told in such a way as to correspond *to the interests of the church.* Doubtless, then, without critical scrutiny *some words were attributed to Jesus which had originated in the community*, in controversy with opponents or in the interests of closer organization of the church" (*Jesus and the Word*, 125; my emphasis).

455. Sanders, *Schismatics, Sectarians, Dissidents, Deviants*, 17.

456. Grant, *Jesus: An Historian's Review*, 114, 120–21.

457. Parkes, *Conflict of the Church*, 44–45. Charlesworth argues, "The harsh portraits of the Pharisees reflect *not so much* Jesus' time as the clashes between the Christians and the Pharisees after 70 C.E." (*Jesus within Judaism*, 46; my emphasis). According to White, the Gospel portrait "of the Pharisees in the time of Jesus is *colored by* . . . post-70 developments and the growing

Endnotes

tension between emergent Christianity and rabbinic Judaism" (*From Jesus to Christianity*, 228; my emphasis).

458. Meier, *Marginal Jew*, 3:644.

459. Lieu, *Image and Reality*, 3.

460. Saldarini, *Pharisees, Scribes and Sadducees*, 144, 156, 292.

461. Saldarini, *Pharisees, Scribes and Sadducees*, 146, 156, 164, 165, 175, 181, 195, 197.

462. Saldarini, *Pharisees, Scribes and Sadducees*, 156, 172–73, 196, 283, 291, 293.

463. Carroll, *Constantine's Sword*, 562–63, 110; my emphasis. Akenson comments: "[T]he historical Yeshua of Nazareth was not in a root-and-branch war with the Pharisees" (*Saint Saul*, 251).

464. Craveri, *Life of Jesus*, 133.

465. Ruether, *Faith and Fratricide*, 58.

466. Lee, *Galilean Jewishness of Jesus*, 71–72.

467. Lieu, *Image and Reality*, 253.

468. Guignebert, *Jewish World*, 165.

469. Sanders, *Jesus and Judaism*, 292.

470. Brown, *Introduction*, 79.

471. Schiffman, *From Text to Tradition*, 153.

472. Meier, *Marginal Jew*, 3:300–301, 643. Meier adds: "While Luke may at times sound more irenic in his Gospel and Acts, it is Luke's theological program (i.e., continuity in salvation history) rather than reliable history from the pre-70 period that we are probably hearing" (301).

473. Stegemann and Stegemann, *Jesus Movement*, 223.

474. Thompson, *Jesus Debate*, 158.

475. Meier, *Marginal Jew*, 3:335. Johnson says, "Matthew's Gospel was written in the context of conflict and conversation with the form of Judaism that developed out of the religious aspirations of the Pharisees and the textual interpretations of the scribes into what is known as classical or rabbinic Judaism after the destruction of the temple in 70 C.E." (*Living Jesus*, 151).

476. Parkes, *Conflict of the Church*, 42, 44.

477. Perrin and Duling, *New Testament: An Introduction*, 265.

478. Tabor, *Jesus Dynasty*, 59, 222.

479. Vermes, *Changing Faces of Jesus*, 231, 180. On the retrojection of conflicts in the Diaspora, see also Ruether, *Faith and Fratricide*, 75.

480. Sanders, *Schismatics, Sectarians, Dissidents, Deviants*, 155. See also Hengel, *Four Gospels*, 195, 199; Meeks, *Origins of Christian Morality*, 202; and White, *From Jesus to Christianity*, 243.

481. Sanders, *Schismatics, Sectarians, Dissidents, Deviants*, 17.

482. Brown, *Introduction*, 339, 345.

483. Kee et al., *Understanding the New Testament*, 329.

484. White, *From Jesus to Christianity*, 314.

485. Smith, *Jesus the Magician*, 157.

486. Hengel, *Four Gospels*, 201. Hengel adds: "The lack of understanding, indeed the hatred, had intensified in a pernicious way *on both sides* in the 'family dispute.'"

487. Pagels, *Origin of Satan*, 98. Pagels continues: "Writing from within a Jewish community, perhaps in Palestine, John is anguished that after a series of clashes with Jewish leaders, he and his fellow Christians have been forcibly expelled from the synagogue and denied participation in common worship."

488. Meier, *Marginal Jew*, 3:340.

489. More than thirty-five years ago, McKenzie said that "some historians, Gentile as well as Jewish, have asserted that the Gospel presentation [of the Pharisees] is largely the product of anti-Jewish prejudice" (*New Testament without Illusion*, 173).

490. Vermes, *Changing Faces of Jesus*, 10–11.

491. Tabor, *Jesus Dynasty*, 239. Toynbee says, "Christianity . . . eventually broke right out of its original Jewish framework, to become a separate religion—though the integrally Jewish opening

chapter of the history of Christianity was longer and more important than the 'pagano-Christian' tradition presents it as having been" ("Mediterranean World's Age of Agony," 37).

492. Stark, *Rise of Christianity*, 138. Stark quotes Harnack: "The synagogues of the Diaspora . . . formed the most important presupposition for the rise and growth of Christian communities throughout the empire." Stark says elsewhere that "Jews continued as a significant source of Christian converts until at least as late as the fourth century and that Jewish Christianity was still significant in the fifth century" (49).

493. Stegemann and Stegemann, *Jesus Movement*, 340, 353.

494. Lieu claims that there are "many examples of Christian knowledge of Jewish practice and particularly exegesis, which cannot be explained as merely an inheritance from the past . . . Contemporary, and not just 'Old Testament', Judaism continued in the second century to be part of the immediate religious, literary and social world of early Christianity" (*Image and Reality*, 12).

495. Stark, *Rise of Christianity*, 65. On the influence of the response to Marcion, see Placher, *History of Christian Theology*, 51–52; and Meeks, *Origins of Christian Morality*, 209.

496. Wilken, *First Thousand Years*, 37.

497. According to Lieu, "Chrysostom's sermons *Against the Jews* . . . imply that at least some ordinary members of the church [in Antioch] saw nothing out of order in attending the synagogue services, joining in other Jewish festivities, regarding the synagogue as a sacred place, appropriate for the taking of oaths, and respecting the supernatural powers of the teachers" (*Image and Reality*, 24). Markus says, "In John Chrysostom's sermons preached in Antioch in 387 we can catch a note of the hysterical denigration, now turned by a Christian against Jews, which in an earlier age had been a feature of some of the more obscene accusations made by pagans against Christians" (*Christianity*, 23).

498. Levine, *Misunderstood Jew*, 84. Boyarin comments, "For centuries after Jesus' death, there were people who also insisted that in order to be saved they must eat only kosher, keep the Sabbath as other Jews do, and circumcise their sons" (*Jewish Gospels*, 10). For an overview of early Jewish Christianity, see Tyson, *Study of Early Christianity*, 312–16.

499. Brown says, "No NT writer knew that what he wrote would be included in a collection of twenty-seven books and read as an enduring message centuries or even millennia later. Indeed, given their strong emphases on certain issues, some writers might not have been happy about having works of a different cast set alongside their own with similar authority" (*Introduction*, 42).

500. Carroll, *Constantine's Sword*, 134, 91.

501. As Spong describes it, this loss was more than symbolic: "The expelled Christians soon faded into increasingly Hellenized and gentile circles. In a generation of both association and intermarriage, the Jewish Christians ceased even to think of themselves as Jews, while those who claimed the Jewish identity moved sharply to the right in quest of survival and became more and more firmly entrenched in their tradition. The common ground between Jews and Christians, once so powerful, became nonexistent" (*Liberating the Gospels*, 53).

502. According to Meeks, not all Christians followed Paul's acknowledgement that Christianity derived from Judaism: "While Paul did have a keen sense for the reality and the problematic character of Israel, the same was not always true of other Christian interpreters of Israel's scriptures . . . It was by no means a foregone conclusion, then, that the early Christians would preserve the sense of rootedness in Israel's history that is an indispensable ingredient in the narrative they would ultimately produce" (*Origins of Christian Morality*, 207).

503. Spong, *Liberating the Gospels*, 54.

504. Cwiekowski, *Beginnings of the Church*, 205. Thoma disagrees with "[p]ractically everyone these days" who "attempts to prove that there is no anti-Jewishness in the New Testament." On the contrary, says Thoma, "[t]he New Testament contains accusations and theses which at times are hostile toward certain groups of Jews or toward all of them. Some passages even call in doubt the very essence of Jewish faith and Jewish law." Thoma rejects the claim "that such statements and ideas are merely inner-Jewish disputes or prophetic scoldings" (*Christian Theology of Judaism*, 17).

Endnotes

505. Crossan, *Birth of Christianity*, 583.
506. Meeks, *Origins of Christian Morality*, 206.
507. Ruether, *Faith and Fratricide*, 56–57.
508. Pagels, *Origin of Satan*, 14.
509. Schillebeeckx, *Jesus: An Experiment*, 32.
510. Speaking of the post-biblical Christian tradition, Parkes says: "The Christian theologian did not set out deliberately to blacken the character of his Jewish opponent, nor did he deliberately misrepresent his history . . . His mistake was due to his belief in the verbal inspiration of the Scriptures which he read on the basis of the two separate communities." Modern scholars, Parkes says, must therefore avoid "bas[ing] their conceptions of Judaism exclusively on the gospel narratives" (*Conflict of the Church*, 374, 29).
511. MacCulloch, *Silence: A Christian History*, 208. See also Langmuir, *History, Religion*, 320.
512. Borg and Crossan, *Last Week*, xi. Herzog says, "Crossan is surely right to connect his concern for interpreting the trial of Jesus to the problem of anti-Semitism" (*Jesus, Justice*, 245).
513. Marty, *Christian World*, 13.
514. Senior, *Jesus: A Gospel Portrait*, 138.
515. Freyne, *Jesus, a Jewish Galilean*, 166. Freyne adds, "This is a gross distortion of the historical facts" (166–67). Chilton says that this misrepresentation "produced the myth of Jewish 'blood guilt,' and the countless cruelties of Christian anti-Semitism" (*Rabbi Jesus*, 264n6).
516. Pagels, *Origin of Satan*, 15, 105.
517. Conzelmann and Lindemann, *Interpreting the New Testament*, 328. On the Gospels generally, these writers say: "Form criticism established that the Gospels are presentations that already have their own theological character and, therefore cannot be viewed as trustworthy historical witnesses." In other words, the Gospels "are not the result of attempts to reconstruct the vita of Jesus. Rather they intend to awaken faith and to strengthen already existing faith. In this they obviously do not distinguish between authentic Jesus tradition and secondary formation by the [Christian] community" (288).
518. Crossan, *Historical Jesus*, 391.
519. Charlesworth, *Jesus within Judaism*, 1.
520. Smith, *Jesus the Magician*, 39.
521. Nineham provides several reasons for doubting the authenticity of Mark's description of Jesus' trial in *Gospel of Mark*, 400–412.
522. McKenzie, *New Testament without Illusion*, 191.
523. Smith, *Jesus the Magician*, 38. Peters similarly finds the facts behind the narratives inaccessible: "That there was an arrest, trial and execution is beyond reasonable doubt. Equally clearly, the Romans executed the sentence; it could hardly be otherwise. But the instigators, the connivers and the issues themselves are hopelessly buried under the sentiments of the Christian editors" (*Harvest of Hellenism*, 486–87).
524. Bornkamm, *Jesus of Nazareth*, 163.
525. Meier lists the arrest of Jesus, the immediate convening of the Sanhedrin, the holding of a formal trial with witnesses, the finding of guilt, the delivery of the prisoner to Pilate, the trial before Pilate, and the execution of Jesus (*Marginal Jew*, 1:389, 396).
526. Tyson, *Study of Early Christianity*, 378.
527. Thompson, *Jesus Debate*, 207.
528. McKenzie, *New Testament without Illusion*, 191. Fredriksen explains, "The [Jewish] trial as it is reported violates the traditions of Jewish legal procedure as set out in the late second-century text *mishnah Sanhedrin*": "The court could not convene at night, nor on a major feast day" (*From Jesus to Christ*, 117). Bornkamm makes the same point (*Jesus of Nazareth*, 163). See also Borg, *Jesus: Uncovering the Life*, 263; and Smith, *Jesus the Magician*, 38.
529. Chilton, *Rabbi Jesus*, 268n8.

Endnotes

530. Ehrman, *Jesus: Apocalyptic Prophet*, 220–21. Fredriksen says, "And what Jesus says, or what his examiners take him to imply, does not constitute blasphemy" (*From Jesus to Christ*, 117). See also Conzelmann and Lindemann, *Interpreting the New Testament*, 331.

531. Bornkamm, *Jesus of Nazareth*, 163. Bornkamm adds, "Moreover, in the case of blasphemy, the Jewish authorities would certainly have had the right to have Jesus executed, for instance to have him stoned . . . But Jesus is not stoned, but handed over by the High Court to the Procurator Pontius Pilate, and is crucified by him" (163–64).

532. Crossan, *Historical Jesus*, 390. Borg and Crossan, emphasizing that, since "no follower of Jesus was with him subsequent to his arrest," the trial "may represent a post-Easter construction and not history remembered" (*Last Week*, 128).

533. Herzog, *Jesus, Justice*, 240–41. Like Crossan, Herzog states that Jesus "was a poor, insignificant peasant, and his judges deemed him unworthy of such attention" as a real trial would have provided.

534. Sanders, *Jesus and Judaism*, 300. Parkes says: "The actual facts of the arrest and trial are exceedingly difficult to establish. Since the disciples are all recorded to have forsaken Him and fled, there is no certain basis for the narratives which follow the scene in the garden of Gethsemane" (*Conflict of the Church*, 45).

535. It should be noted that the Roman government in Palestine, unlike Roman rulers in other provincial areas in the Empire, actually dealt with many rebellions, large and small, over the 136 years between Herod's death and the Revolt of AD 132. Levenson discusses six rebel "messiahs" and eight rebel "kings" who threatened the political establishment in Palestine and other cities and whose rebellions, armed or not, were met almost invariably by military suppression. See Levenson, "Messianic Movements," 532–34.

536. Wright, *Simply Jesus*, 69, 30. See also Sanders, *Judaism*, 388.

537. Borg and Crossan, *Last Week*, 19–20. Theissen notes that "only three [of the eighteen high priests] ruled for more than two years." Caiaphas, under Pilate, served from AD 18 to AD 36 (*Early Palestinian Christianity*, 70).

538. "The Temple authorities did not represent the Jews. Rather than representing the Jewish people, they were, as local collaborators with imperial authority, the oppressors of the vast majority of the Jewish people" (Borg and Crossan, *Last Week*, 128). Nevertheless, as Parkes says, "[W]hile the authorities were unwilling to risk their precarious autonomy for a teacher whose teaching they did not accept, it is also clear that they did not wish to endanger their own position with the populace who thronged Jerusalem for the feast, by themselves executing some sentence upon Him" (*Conflict of the Church*, 46). See also Sanders, "Life of Jesus," 75.

539. Sanders, *Jesus and Judaism*, 315.

540. Ehrman, *Jesus: Apocalyptic Prophet*, 219–20. Ehrman notes that the Romans were disengaged from ordinary events in the provinces: "They allowed local aristocracies the right to control their own internal affairs" (219). McKenzie says: "There is ample evidence that the high priesthood was a political plum, a source of wealth and power as long as the ruling clique maintained amicable relations with the Romans. This they did; they were not sympathetic to the Zealot movements of rebellion and they supported the Roman suppression of the Zealots. There is hardly any doubt that such a group would move against Jesus if they thought he was a threat to their interests. This he was" (*New Testament without Illusion*, 194).

541. Sanders, *Jesus and Judaism*, 305.

542. Fredriksen, *From Jesus to Christ*, 119. Sanders explains: "If the high priest did not preserve order, the Roman prefect would intervene militarily, and the situation might get out of hand. As long as the Temple guards, acting as the high priest's police, carried out arrests and as long as the high priest was involved in judging cases (though he could not execute anyone), there was relatively little possibility of a direct clash between Jews and Roman troops" (*Historical Figure of Jesus*, 265).

Endnotes

543. Parkes says: "It was not the teaching of Jesus that led to His death. It was the fear of His Messianic claims by the Jewish authorities in Jerusalem, the fear that it would lead the Romans to remove what little privileges they still enjoyed" (*Conflict of the Church*, 45).

544. Saldarini comments: "The concerns by the council are typically political. They feared that all the people would believe in Jesus and thus disrupt civil order, with the consequence that the Romans would destroy their place and nation." Saldarini adds in a footnote, "The links between Roman provincial officials and native aristocracy and the tendency of the aristocracy to cooperate with the Romans to their own benefit and sometimes to the detriment of their own people is brought by Richard P. Saller, *Personal Patronage Under the Early Empire*, . . . for the case of North Africa" (*Pharisees, Scribes and Sadducees*, 194n45).

545. Pagels, *Origin of Satan*, 107. Fredriksen, commenting on John 11:47–50 (*From Jesus to Christ*, 109), and Sanders (*Jesus and Judaism*, 105) make the same point. Sanders says elsewhere, "The high priest wanted [Jesus] dead for the same reason Antipas wanted John [the Baptist] dead: he might cause trouble" (*Historical Figure of Jesus*, 265).

546. Shanks and Witherington, *Brother of Jesus*, 166. Bruce suggests that this is precisely the problem that Paul faced when he encountered opposition from the Jews in the cities of the Diaspora in which he preached. Referring to the complaints against Paul expressed in Acts 17:16–17, Bruce says, "The wording of the charge fits well into the picture of unruly movements within Jewish communities throughout the empire, more or less 'messianic' in character . . . which were deplored and denounced by responsible Jewish leaders who knew the importance of maintaining acceptable relations with the Roman power" (*New Testament History*, 300).

547. Chilton, *Rabbi Jesus*, 101.

548. Smith, *Jesus the Magician*, 38.

549. Meier says, "To be sure, the high-handed and insensitive Pilate ignited a number of dangerous political-religious conflicts" (*Marginal Jew*, 3:296).

550. Koester, *History, Culture, and Religion*, 396.

551. Grant, *Jesus: An Historian's Review*, 162. McKenzie argues that the Pilate who finds Jesus guilty only "under Jewish pressure" does not match the Pilate described by Josephus, who says that Pilate was "ruthless in suppressing even what he suspected was rebellion. According to Josephus it was precisely his ruthlessness which was the reason for his deposition by Tiberius" (*New Testament without Illusion*, 190).

552. Tyson, *Study of Early Christianity*, 377.

553. Pagels, *Origin of Satan*, 10.

554. Vermes, *Changing Faces of Jesus*, 196. Later, Vermes says, "The province was the seat of unrest from the mid-first century B.C. to the great rebellion in A.D. 66–73/74, and together with the neighboring Golan produced the most notorious leaders of the fight against Rome" (241). Grant comments: "The procurator of Judaea had already experienced many difficulties with seemingly seditious Jews, as we have seen. Since it was his duty to maintain law and order in this troublesome frontier province, he was bound to suppress any activity even potentially revolutionary" (*Historical Introduction*, 366).

555. Ehrman, *Jesus: Apocalyptic Prophet*, 221. "The historian Mary Smallwood observes that rounding up and killing troublemakers, especially those who ignited public demonstrations, was a routine measure for Roman forces stationed in Judea" (Pagels, *Origin of Satan*, 14). Smallwood's statement appears in *The Jews under Roman Rule from Pompey to Diocletian* (Leiden: Brill, 1981), 164. After Herod's death, the Roman governor of Syria crucified two thousand rebels. During the Jewish Revolt, the Romans torched the Temple and killed the six thousand Jews who had gone there to avoid the wrath of their enemies.

556. Ehrman, *Jesus: Apocalyptic Prophet*, 221. Ehrman continues: "A governor could . . . free [an offender] on the spot" or "decide that the accused was likely to cause more trouble and have him executed." Immediately, Sanders says, "It is also clear from Josephus that whoever was in power . . . could execute or free whom he wished without a formal trial" (*Jesus and Judaism*,

Endnotes

317). Meier says, "The Roman prefect... had ultimate life-and-death power over everyone in the province who was not a Roman citizen" (*Marginal Jew*, 3:296).

557. White, *From Jesus to Christianity*, 105. "Recent historical studies have shown that the Jewish authorities could have had, at best, a subsidiary relation to the death of Jesus" (Ruether, *Faith and Fratricide*, 87). Tyson says, "Jewish complicity in the execution is questionable and at best secondary" (*Study of Early Christianity*, 395).

558. Senior, *Jesus: A Gospel Portrait*, 137.

559. Sanders, *Jesus and Judaism*, 317. Sanders adds, "He was executed by Pilate at the behest of the Jewish leadership, including at least the chief priests" (318). Earlier, Sanders says, "And why do the Gospels also have the Jewish leadership play any role at all? The Romans were not slow to act when sedition threatened, nor, were this a large demonstration [i.e., at Jesus' entry into Jerusalem], would they have needed a Jewish 'trial' in order to urge them on" (306).

560. Chilton, *Rabbi Jesus*, xxi. Nolan says: "The most certain and well-attested fact about Jesus of Nazareth is that he was tried, sentenced and executed by the Roman procurator Pontius Pilate on a charge of high treason... Jesus was found guilty of being involved in some such conspiracy and, moreover, of claiming to be the rightful king of the Jews" (*Jesus before Christianity*, 113).

561. Borg and Crossan, *Last Week*, 146–47.

562. Moltmann, *Crucified God*, 136. Moltmann rather thoroughly examines the question of whether Jesus was arrested for religious or political reasons on 128–45. Moltmann refers to Oscar Cullmann, who speculates that Jesus was in fact first arrested by "Roman cohorts" and appeared before the High Priest only to assure Pilate that "the Jewish authorities and the Jewish people would not rise against him" because of his execution of Jesus (136).

563. Koester, *History, Culture, and Religion*, 396.

564. Tabor, *Jesus Dynasty*, 120. Markus says, "Jesus had been suspect in the eyes of the Jewish authorities in Jerusalem and, on their denunciation, executed by the Roman government as a political agitator" (*Christianity*, 19).

565. Wylen, *Jews in the Time*, 126.

566. Conzelmann and Lindemann, *Interpreting the New Testament*, 333. Kaylor, after devoting an entire chapter to the subject, comes to the same conclusion: "[T]here is nothing historically implausible in Jesus' execution by the Romans on the charge of political crimes" (*Jesus the Prophet*, 68).

567. Manschreck, *History of Christianity*, 22.

568. Wright, *Simply Jesus*, 7, 11–12, 69, 80, 85–86.

569. Lieu, *Image and Reality*, 253.

570. Cook, *Introduction to the Bible*, 146. Cook continues, "This condemnation of the Jews is carried on in Acts, which culminates in Paul's speech at Rome: the Jews had rejected Jesus, God's salvation is now sent unto the Gentiles."

571. Senior, *Jesus: A Gospel Portrait*, 137.

572. Carroll, *Constantine's Sword*, 563. Carroll continues: "Christians accounted for the rejection they were experiencing by a version of that rejection—'his own people received him not'—central to the experience of Jesus, not just in his Passion but throughout his life."

573. Wylen, *Jews in the Time*, 126.

574. Wylen, *Jews in the Time*, 126. On "shifting the blame," see also Spong, *Liberating the Gospels*, 274. Referring to Matthew 27:25 and John 19:15, Brown says, "Obviously here both Gospels... are reflecting apologetic theology rather than history—they are having the audience of the trial give voice to a late 1st-century Christian interpretation of salvation history. The tragedy of Jesus' death is compounded as it is seen through the veil of hostility between the Church and the Synagogue in the 80s or 90s" (*Gospel According to John*, 895).

575. Smith, *Jesus the Magician*, 38–39. On this point, see Jaher, *Scapegoat*: "Transferring guilt from Pilate to the Jews absolved Christ of having aspired to the secular kingship of Israel and thus of having conspired against the *imperium*" (21).

Endnotes

576. Ruether, *Faith and Fratricide*, 88–89.

577. Sheehan, *First Coming*, 87. Sheehan cites similar views by Raymond E. Brown and Edward Schillebeeckx on 252.

578. Brown, *Introduction*, 167.

579. Grant, *Jesus: An Historian's Review*, 163. De Ste. Croix says that, regarding the death of Jesus, the Jews are incriminated and the Romans exculpated in the speeches of Acts of the Apostles because of Luke's "propagandistic purpose": Christians are portrayed "as the victims of Jewish vindictiveness," and Romans "either maintain a benevolent neutrality or intervene in favor of the Christians." Contrary to the claims of Peter, Paul, and Steven, "Jesus had been tried and sentenced as a political criminal by the Roman governor of Judaea, Pontius Pliate." He was charged with being "a Resistance leader" ("Christianity's Encounter," 345).

580. Chilton, *Rabbi Jesus*, 264. Nineham adds yet another reason for the shift in blame: "The experience of the Church, especially after A. D. 70, was that while the Jews increasingly refused to accept Christ's claims, the Romans were sometimes surprisingly friendly and Gentiles in general seemed much more inclined to believe" (quoted in Klein, *Anti-Judaism*, 151.)

581. Perrin and Duling, *New Testament*, 300.

582. Stegemann and Stegemann, *Jesus Movement*, 211. These writers argue that Jesus "was condemned and crucified by the Roman procurator Pontius Pilate as a 'bandit.' Apparently, because of the nearness of the festival, this quick trial was also supposed to serve as a deterrent and forestall potential disturbances."

583. Sanders, *Judaism*, 49.

584. Moore, *Judaism*, II-III, 16–17. Moore adds: "[I]t is practiced in all parts of Africa, but not by all races or tribes. In Asia it is confined to the Semites, except for peoples that have embraced Mohammedanism; and in Europe to Jews and Moslems." Levine says, "Egyptians, Ethiopians, Arabs and Phoenicians also circumcised young males" ("Judaism from the Destruction," 144).

585. Segal, *Rebecca's Children*, 124, 127.

586. Wright, *Evolution of God*, 162.

587. On this point, see Olivelle, *Upanishads*, xxv.

588. Wilson, "Egypt," 41.

589. Anderson, *Understanding the Old Testament*, 67. See also 6–7. Wright comments, "The difficulties of Israel in her promised land and her involvement in the wars between the nations in a corridor between Asia and Africa where lay the two centers of power presented a tragic picture" (*Book of the Acts*, 95). See also 70–71.

590. Brueggemann, *Old Testament Theology*, 6.

591. Moore, *Judaism*, 2.20–21.

592. Wright and Fuller, *Book of the Acts*, 70. This explanation simply answered the question "How had it happened?"

593. Armstrong, *Great Transformation*, 47.

594. Moore, *Judaism*, 1:22. Moore notes that the idea appears in Isa 40–41 and Zech 8:20–23; 14:16–21. He adds, "The Jews were the only people in their world who conceived the idea of a universal religion." See also *Judaism*, 2:371–74.

595. On this subject, van Leeuwen says: "It is now apparent, not only that we are unjustified in regarding Israel's 'particularism' as something set over against her 'universalism' and even opposed to it, but that in so doing we obscure and pervert the obvious meaning of the Old Testament. It is in her 'particular' function and calling—and precisely there—that Israel is truly 'universal'. If God had called this 'particular' people into being, it can only be because of the 'universal' purpose which he has in view" (*Christianity and World History*, 97–98).

596. Kaufmann says, "In marked contrast to the repudiation of Greek popular religion by the higher religion of Greece's philosophers, or Buddhism's independence of and aloofness toward the religion of the masses, biblical religion neither disdains not detaches itself from the

popular legends" (*Religion of Israel*, 132). "Unlike the faiths of Akhenaton, or Buddha, or early Christianity, Israelite religion was from the first a national religion, the expression of a national culture" (298).

597. On this point, see Moore: "[I]t is necessary to bear in mind the twofold character of nationality and universality which had been inseparably impressed upon [Judaism] by its history" (*Judaism*, 1:219).

598. Anderson, *Understanding the Old Testament*, 2. Anderson says, as I noted earlier: "The most distinctive feature of the Jewish people is their sense of history."

599. Collins, *Short Introduction*, 88, 89.

600. Finkelstein and Silberman, *Bible Unearthed*, 285.

601. Brueggemann says that "the particulars of the new obedience in Isaiah, Jeremiah, and Ezekiel vary greatly." Furthermore, "[t]he matter is not different in the Book of the Twelve" (*Old Testament Theology*, 233).

602. Collins, *Short Introduction*, 29–30. Schmidt discusses the problem of "doublets," all of them reflecting two versions of the same story by the writers known as J, E and P, in *Old Testament Introduction*, 84–86). Schmidt compares the two versions of the flood on 104. On this subject, see Oesterley and Robinson, *Introduction to the Books*, 29–32.

603. Irwin, "Literature of the Old Testament," 177.

604. Miles, *God: A Biography*, 13.

605. Kaufmann, *Religion of Israel*, 208.

606. Anderson, *Understanding the Old Testament*, 20. See also 179. On some specific borrowings from Sumerian, Babylonian, and Hurrian sources, see 24–25, 172–73. On borrowings from Canaanite sources, see 164–65, 180.

607. Armstrong, *Great Transformation*, 46–47. Kaufmann says that "Israel is thus depicted as an ethnic mixture of Hebrew, Aramaic, Canaanite, and Egyptian elements" (*Religion of Israel*, 218). He calls the patriarchs "historical personages wrapped in legend" (219).

608. Anderson, *Understanding the Old Testament*, 180. See also McKenzie, *Old Testament without Illusions*, 66–67, 74; and Collins, *Short Introduction*, 46.

609. Although Redford believes that the story of Joseph achieves a "literary standard" that "[n]o piece of prose elsewhere in the Bible can equal," reading it "as history is quite wrongheaded," as is also the case regarding "the Sojourn and Exodus narrative" (*Egypt, Canaan, and Israel*, 422, 429).

610. Brueggemann, *Old Testament Theology*, 10.

611. Von Rad, *Old Testament Theology*, 1:109.

612. Finkelstein and Silberman, *Bible Unearthed*, 3. On Israelites in Egypt and their conquest of Canaan, see 58–64 and 76–83. For a different view of the stories of the patriarchs, see Tullock, *Old Testament Story*, 45. Rogerson refers to Martin Noth's treatment of "the material about the patriarchs and the Exodus as traditions expressing Israel's belief about its past rather than as data that could be used to reconstruct that past historically." Questions have also been raised, Rogerson adds, about the history of the Jews up to and including the monarchies of David and Solomon ("Old Testament History," 49–50).

613. Cornfeld argues, "There is still no direct evidence from Egyptian sources on the vital story of the Bondage and Exodus, or of Moses, his encounters with Pharaoh, and the plagues" (*Archeology of the Bible*, 34). Miles says: "Despite the lack of any historical record outside the Bible, most historians do not believe that the story of the Exodus is a total fabrication. But were it an event of the size that the Bible reports [that is, a crowd of more than two million people], the likelihood of its leaving no record outside the Bible would be small" (*God: A Biography*, 104).

614. Armstrong claims, "The general scholarly consensus is that the story of the exodus from Egypt is not historical" (*Great Transformation*, 46). Armstrong also challenges the historical accuracy of the biblical account of Joshua's conquest of Canaan. However, May and Metzger argue,

"Although Egyptian records make no reference to this border incident"—that is, the exodus—"there can be no doubt that Israel's faith rests on an actual historical occurrence" (*Oxford Annotated Bible*, 67).

615. Brueggemann, *Old Testament Theology*, 6–7. "A specific subset of this general liturgic-mythic practice that pertains especially to the Old Testament is the *Canaanite religion* evidenced by the ancient library at Ugarit (Ras Shamra) that details the liturgic-mythic practice of Israel's closest neighbors." On borrowings from Ras Shamra, see Cook, *Introduction to the Bible*, 24–25, 156. Irwin also comments on the Canaanite influence of Israelite religion ("Literature of the Old Testament," 177), as does Muilenburg in "History of the Religion" on 296 of the same volume.

616. Goodman, *History of Judaism*, 18. Goodman adds, "Such extreme skepticism is probably unwarranted."

617. Bellah, *Religion in Human Evolution*, 284. Bellah attributes the most radical view to Niels Peter Lemche, *Prelude to Israel's Past*. Bellah says, "The transition from tribal to monarchical society as described in Judges through 1 Kings seems to me in outline plausible, though in detail often dubious."

618. Friedman, *Who Wrote the Bible?*, 191.

619. Brueggemann, *Old Testament Theology*, 129. Brueggemann says that the Jewish God is thereby "capable of rage and anger, capable of newness and forgiveness, and deeply moved by pain and alienation." On God's pathos, see 137–40.

620. Miles, *God: A Biography*, 20–21. Smith describes Israel's gods in the years 1500–1200 BC—such as Yahweh, Baal, and El—in *Early History of God*, 39, 41–42. One of Smith's main theses is that during the monarchy Judaism experienced the convergence of these gods, whose features were eventually absorbed by Yahweh: "In general, the oldest stages of Israel's religious literature exhibit some limited signs of Yahweh having assimilated the imagery of the primary deities" (57). On this subject, see also 33–35, 184, 198.

621. Wright argues that, in the earliest stories of Genesis, God is neither transcendent nor omniscient. First, "God was a hands-on deity," who "personally 'planted' the Garden of Eden, and he 'made garments of skins' for Adam and Eve 'and clothed them. Second, Adam and Eve hide from him when they hear him walking through the garden, which "may sound like a naïve strategy to deploy against the omniscient God we know today, but apparently he wasn't omniscient back then." Indeed, Wright says that, at this point, "Yahweh is . . . remarkably like all those 'primitive' gods of hunter-gatherer societies and chiefdoms: strikingly human—with supernatural power, to be sure, but not with infinite power" (*Evolution of God*, 103).

622. Thus, Miles suggests that God "enters time and is changed by experience. Were it not so, he could not be surprised; and he is endlessly and often most unpleasantly surprised. God is constant; he is not immutable" (*God: A Biography*, 12).

623. Isaac does the same thing with his wife Rebekah when he visits Gerar many years later (26:1–11). Tullock comments, "While the biblical narratives present Abraham as a man of God, they certainly do not present him as a plaster saint" (*Old Testament Story*, 46). Indeed, Tullock says later, "The biblical narrative did not gloss over the weaknesses of the ancestors, neither with Abraham nor with Jacob" (52).

624. Anderson comments: "Abraham's act was tantamount to surrendering the promise, even though it brought him great material advantage . . . Abraham, despite his rash deed, was sent away from Egypt a rich man" (*Understanding the Old Testament*, 181).

625. Niditch, *Ancient Israelite Religion*, 40.

626. May and Metzger, *Oxford Annotated Bible*, 25. Miles says that driving Hagar into the wilderness—i.e., the desert—is, "in effect, to her likely death" (*God: A Biography*, 51).

627. Anderson says that "Jacob shrewdly tricked his twin brother out of his birthright . . . and later tricked him out of their father's final blessing." From a modern perspective, these events sound unforgivable, and it is hard to believe that Jacob's blessing would be considered authentic.

However, Anderson comments, "[A]ccording to the ancient belief, words spoken in blessing (or curse) were efficacious. They had the power to produce the intended result. And, like an arrow in flight, they could not be retracted" (*Introduction to the Old Testament*, 183–84). Anderson refers to Jacob's actions as "shady dealings" (185).

628. McKenzie, *Old Testament without Illusion*, 181, 194. Collins calls Jacob "the trickster" (*Short Introduction*, 51).

629. Miles comments: "In these words, for which there is no parallel in anything Abraham has ever said, Jacob is spelling out the conditions under which he will *not* accept his grandfather's and his father's God as his own . . . And note how humble Jacob's demands are—food, clothing, and safe conduct—and how humble, correspondingly is his offer of a stone pillar as 'abode' and tithe, a mere tithe, to the being who has just promised, grandly: 'Your descendants shall be as the dust of the earth'" (*God: A Biography*, 69–70).

630. Tullock distinguishes between Joseph's experiences and those of his ancestors: "First of all, [Joseph's] have about them certain of the characteristics of wisdom stories in the Near East: (1) the theme of the stories is that goodness is always rewarded and evil is always punished, which is a major theme of the Book of Proverbs; (2) the theme of the oppressed, righteous man who overcomes all obstacles and comes out on top, particularly because he possesses the wisdom to interpret dreams, is like that found in the stories concerning Daniel. A second difference in these stories is in how God communicates with Joseph. Here there are no divine messengers—no epiphanies. Instead, God guides Joseph through the events and circumstances of life. A third major difference is in the background reflected by the Joseph stories. It is an Egyptian background." Tullock adds that a final difference lies in the fact that Joseph's saga is "a more unified single story," without the repetitions and interruptions that characterize the more fragmented stories of Abraham and Jacob (*Old Testament Story*, 54).

631. Anderson says that this story might have been "influenced by the Egyptian 'Story of Two Brothers'" (*Understanding the Old Testament*, 185; see note 28).

632. Anderson, *Understanding the Old Testament*, 186. Collins, however, says that "Joseph is credited with centralizing wealth in the hands of the pharaoh and bringing the people into a state of slavery (47:20). Even as Joseph saved his family from famine, he set the stage for their future oppression" (*Short Introduction*, 53).

633. Von Rad, *Old Testament Theology*, 1:175.

634. Kaufmann, however, argues that Abraham was, in fact, a moral exemplar: "Although the Bible does not portray Abraham as a fighter for YHWH, it does depict him as a God-fearing and moral man. He pursues peace (Gen 13:8 f.), is generous (14:21 ff.), hospitable (18:1 ff.), and intercedes on behalf of the Sodomites (vss. 23 ff.). He charges his descendants to observe 'the way of YHWH' to do righteousness and justice (v. 19)" (*Religion of Israel*, 222–23).

635. Wright and Fuller, *Book of the Acts*, 59, 61; my emphasis.

636. Von Rad, *Old Testament Theology*, 1:163.

637. May and Metzger call the passage "[a]n ancient song, probably once sung in praise of Lamech," which "is here quoted to illustrate the development of wickedness to measureless blood revenge" (*Oxford Annotated Bible*, 6).

638. May and Metzger say, "The curse implies that Canaan's subjugation to Israel was the result of Canaanite sexual perversions" (*Oxford Annotated Bible*, 12).

639. Anderson says that this legend "circulated independently as an explanatory story of the origin of diverse peoples and languages" (*Understanding the Old Testament*, 177).

640. A similar event occurs in the book of Judges involving the horrible treatment of a visitor's concubine by both the townsmen and the visitor himself after the host, protecting his guest, says to the townsmen, "Behold, here are my virgin daughter and [my guest's] concubine . . . Ravish them and do with them what seems good to you" (19:22–30).

641. May and Metzger, *Oxford Annotated Bible*, 37.

Endnotes

642. Tullock says, "Why this story is here is not clear" (*Old Testament Story*, 55).

643. Collins comments, "Trickery and deception appear as a theme throughout the narratives [in Genesis], particularly in the narratives about Jacob and in the story of Judah and Tamar." Collins adds later, "There is no suggestion that Judah should be punished for his action, but the passage (Gen 38:26) is unique in Genesis for its explicit admission that a patriarch was in the wrong" (*Short Introduction*, 44, 52).

644. Kaufmann says that Genesis contains "embarrassing material," including "stories and expressions certainly offensive to later religious tastes," which "means that already in early times the sources were quasi-canonical, so that later one hesitated to alter them" (*Religion of Israel*, 209–19).

645. Although the story of Joseph "says nothing of appearances or discourses of God" of the kind we see earlier, Schmidt says, he appears to be both magnanimous and thoroughly under God's guidance and protection (*Old Testament Introduction*, 73).

646. Referring to these incidents, von Rad says that "the reader completely loses sight of God and his action in the jungle of unedifying manifestations of human nature," which add up to what would, in another context, appear to be "a fairly trivial piece of entertainment" (*Old Testament Theology*, 1:171).

647. Collins, *Short Introduction*, 51. Von Rad comments: "This era in the saving history lacks the divine will for justice which was revealed to Israel in the commandments, as it also lacks the revelation of his holiness . . . In the main, God's way of dealing with the ancestors of the race is by unobtrusive guidance" (*Old Testament Theology*, 1:175).

648. Wright and Fuller, *Book of the Acts*, 65.

649. Miles, *God: A Biography*, 112. Brueggemann notes that "Abraham is guaranteed a prominent place in history and a secure land in time to come" (*Old Testament Theology*, 200). Although God's covenant with Moses is conditional on Israel's obedience, His covenant with David returns to the patriarchal arrangement, as Psalm 89 indicates: "Forever I will keep my steadfast love for him, and my covenant with him will stand firm. I will establish his line forever, and his throne as long as the heavens endure" (vv. 28–29). But see also Psalm 103: "But the steadfast love of the Lord is from everlasting to everlasting *upon those who fear him, and . . . do his commandments*" (vv. 17–18; my emphasis).

650. Wright and Fuller, *Book of the Acts*, 72, 88.

651. Borg, *Reading the Bible Again*, 92. Borg comments: "The theme of promise and fulfillment provides the overarching structure and narrative flow of the Pentateuch" (89).

652. Anderson comments, "Apparently the covenant partner, by passing through the bloody corridor, invoked upon himself the curse of becoming like the divided animals if he violated the covenant obligation." Anderson also cites Jer 34:18 for a reference to this interpretation (*Understanding the Old Testament*, 28).

653. In the first scene, Jacob dreams of God and, upon waking up, sets up the pillar without God's commandment. As in the later passage, he calls the pillar "God's house," or Bethel. In the last of the three passages, Jacob also pours "a drink offering" on the pillar. Armstrong says that when Jacob uses a stone as a pillar and pours a libation over it he is "consecrat[ing] this holy ground in the traditional pagan manner of the country . . . Standing stones were a common feature of Canaanite fertility cults, which . . . flourished at Beth-El until the eighth century BCE" (*History of God*, 16–17). Jacob also "offered sacrifices to the God of his father Isaac" at Beer-sheba, which, May and Metzger remind us, is "associated with Isaac (26.23–25; 28:10)" (*Oxford Annotated Bible*, 59). Collins says that this manner of worship was challenged in Deuteronomy 12, when God called for a centralization of worship and a demolition of altars (*Short Introduction*, 47).

654. May and Metzger explain: "The worshippers had to undergo ceremonial purification, which involved changing garments and ablutions (Ex.19.10; Jos.7.13) and to renounce foreign gods . . . The earrings and other magical amulets belonged to foreign idolatry" (*Oxford Annotated Bible*, 44).

655. Collins, *Short Introduction*, 47.

656. Levenson discusses Genesis 15:6 at length in *Hebrew Bible*, 59–60.

657. Wright and Fuller, *Book of the Acts*, 93. Cook says, "The general meaning of the word is that of the harmony or conformity of a thing to its nature: it is 'what is right' and as it should be . . . *Its ethical or other value depended upon current standards or ideals*" (*Introduction to the Bible*, 140; my emphasis). Earlier, Cook associates the term with "integrity" (84).

658. Wright and Fuller, *Book of the Acts*, 68.

659. Armstrong, *History of God*, 17–18. Von Rad says: "Jahweh indicated to Abraham his plan for history (Gen xv. 5): and Abraham believed it to be something real, and 'made himself secure' in it. That was his faith" (*Old Testament Theology*, 1:171).

660. Wright and Fuller, *Book of the Acts*, 68.

661. Kaufmann, *Religion of Israel*, 200. "The whole political background of the Torah's narratives, laws, and songs points to the preconquest period." Kaufmann's point is that, although the Torah was not compiled until the middle of the first millennium, its stories date to a much earlier time. According to Wright, "the God of Israel was first apprehended as *King* and *Lord*, who rescued a people, formed them into a nation, and bound them to him in a relationship of *servants* to a ruler" ("Faith of Israel," 355).

662. Kaufmann, *Religion of Israel*, 159–60.

663. Brueggemann, *Old Testament Theology*, 128. Brueggemann summarizes other theories also (128–29).

664. Miles, *God: A Biography*, 111.

665. Miles, *God: A Biography*, 111–12. Miles mentions some of the tribal customs honored by the patriarchs on these pages.

666. Wright and Fuller, *Book of the Acts*, 72, 23. "The Abrahamic covenant is one of promise, and it looks forward to its fulfillment" (72).

667. Kaufmann, *Religion of Israel*, 223.

668. Anderson, *Understanding the Old Testament*, 28. Other scholars trace El to Canaan, as does Wright (*Evolution of God*, 110). Tullock discusses a variety of gods named "El" in *Old Testament Story*, 46–48. Later, he explains that "Elohim" is a generic term, meaning any god, unlike "Yahweh," which was the name of the Jewish God. "Thus there were many *elohims* but only one YHWH" (62–63). Smith says, "The original God of Israel was El. This reconstruction may be inferred from two pieces of information. First, the name of Israel is not a Yahwistic name with the divine element of Yahweh, but an El name . . . Second, Genesis 49:24–25 presents a series of El epithets separate from the mention of Yahweh in verse 18" (*Early History of God*, 32).

669. Armstrong, *History of God*, 15. Indeed, Armstrong continues, all of the patriarchs are shown to be "living on familiar terms with their god. El gives them friendly advice, like any sheik or chieftain: he guides their wanderings, tells them whom to marry and speaks to them in dreams." Armstrong identifies El as "the high god of Canaan," who "introduces himself to Abraham as El Shaddai (El of the Mountain)" (14). In his fourth meeting with Abraham, God calls himself "El Shaddai," God Almighty (Gen 17:1). On this point, see May and Metzger, *Oxford Annotated Bible*, 19n1. For a lengthy discussion of "family religion" in the ancient world, see Miller, *Religion of Ancient Israel*, 62–76. On the personal god, see 63, 75–76; Bellah, *Religion in Human Evolution*, 288–89; and Geller, "Religion of the Bible," 2022.

670. Anderson, *Understanding the Old Testament*, 30. According to Brueggemann, "This capacity of YHWH for empathy, solidarity, and mercy with Israel in its need is especially apparent in Israel's lament psalms," as well as in his responses to the patriarchs (*Old Testament Theology*, 154–55). Brueggemann cites Gen 18:22–33; Exod 32;11–14; Jer 12:5–6, as well as Psalms 18, 34, and 40.

671. Anderson, *Understanding the Old Testament*, 29. On angels and personal gods, see also Cook, *Introduction to the Bible*, 97–99.

Endnotes

672. Jacobsen, "Mesopotamia," 220–21. For a fuller explanation of the Mesopotamian personal god, see 218–22.

673. Anderson, *Understanding the Old Testament*, 186–87.

674. Brueggemann cites, among other passages that emphasize this view of God, Job 38–41, Psalm 145, and Isaiah 40:18–23. "The God who speaks in [Job] shows how the splendor of creation and the wonder of creation override and completely dispose of every human management of the world" (*Old Testament Theology*, 160–63). Of course, if God is in complete control, then human beings are not responsible. However, as Collins says, although "[i]n much of the Hebrew Bible the Lord is responsible for everything, good and bad, . . . this in no way lessens human responsibility" (*Short Introduction*, 60).

675. Cook, *Introduction to the Bible*, 114.

676. Kugel, *Great Shift*, 182. Kugel adds that this situation changed very little even after God's presentation of the Decalogue and many ancillary laws at Sinai: "Who in the period of the Judges . . . ever mentions those laws? . . . King David lived after their time, yet he seems to have gone about his life without ever referring to the laws of Sinai or showing any awareness of them" (182–83).

677. Collins, *Short Introduction*, 68. According to Philo, Collins adds, the patriarchs "followed the unwritten law with perfect ease."

678. Wright and Fuller, *Book of the Acts*, 54. To be sure, many scholars would disagree. Ramsay, for example, says that the phrase simply means "that human beings are intended for a unique relationship to their Creator, able to respond to God and to take responsibility" (*Westminster Guide*, 25). This is, however, more of an inference than an interpretation. Mussner discusses this subject at length in *Tractate on the Jews*, 59–62).

679. Wright, "Faith of Israel," 368. Wright's lengthy discussion is worth reading (366–69).

680. Wright, "Faith of Israel," 369.

681. Brueggemann, *Old Testament Theology*, 336, 232; my emphasis. Brueggemann also notes the "specificity" of both Jeremiah and Ezekiel on 232–33.

682. Muilenburg, "History of the Religion," 299.

683. Brueggemann, *Old Testament Theology*, 317–18.

684. Brueggemann discusses this passage extensively in *Old Testament Theology*, 61–62: "The words of verses 6–7 provide in summary form the essential characteristics of YHWH as the Lord of the covenant."

685. Miles, *God: A Biography*, 107.

686. Cook, *Introduction to the Bible*, 93–95. Wright says that Yahweh at this point in the Bible is "more interested in destroying" than in creating. Like other gods in the Near East, "Yahweh was not yet a *cosmic* creator" (*Evolution of God*, 103).

687. Cook, *Introduction to the Bible*, 135.

688. Armstrong, *Great Transformation*, 40. Miles comments: "As a common noun in Hebrew[,] . . . ba'al means 'owner,' 'master,' or 'lord' in that sense: the "lord of the manor." As a proper name, the same word refers to a deity, Baal, who is the master of the universe but who, notably, has acquired his mastery by military force" (*God: A Biography*, 97).

689. Armstrong, *History of God*, 21. Collins says: "The idea that gods are warriors was a common one in the ancient Near East. A major reason why the early Israelites worshiped YHWH was that they believed that he was a powerful warrior who could help them defeat their enemies" (*Short Introduction*, 62).

690. Friedman says that "the first version of the creation story always refers to the creator as *God*—thirty-five times. The second version always refers to him by name, *Yahweh* God—eleven times" (*Who Wrote the Bible?* 51).

691. Brueggemann, *Old Testament Theology*, 155. Brueggemann cites two passages in which "Yahweh is portrayed as *decisive warrior* and as *sustaining nursemaid*" or as God of War and gentle shepherd: Deut 1:29–31 and Isa 40:10–11 (156).

692. Anderson, *Understanding the Old Testament*, 40. Miller discusses Yahweh at length in *The Religion of Ancient Israel*, 23–29. On the "convergence" of El and Yahweh, see Bellah, *Religion in Human Evolution*, 295; and Smith, *Early History of God*, 33–35, 56, 57, 184, 198.

693. Miles, *God: A Biography*, 63, 66, 64.

694. Kaufmann argues that while the development of monotheism is accompanied by the development of morality, it is also accompanied by the development of violence: "Precisely because of its exclusiveness monotheism can be ruthless." This is because enemies of the nation are understood to be enemies of God: "God's glory, name, and sacra become the highest values; and offense against them is the supreme crime which justifies any punishment" (*Religion of Israel*, 75).

695. This aspect of the Exodus story is rather strange. God predicts in Genesis that the descendants of Abraham "will be sojourners in a land that is not theirs and will be slaves there, and they will be oppressed for four hundred years" (15:13). However, God does not say when the slavery will begin and why his people will be so badly treated. May and Metzger argue that "[a]n inserted tradition explains the delay in the fulfillment of the promise" of land to Abraham's heirs (*Oxford Annotated Bible*, 18). The narrator of Exodus says that the bondage in Egypt did not begin until the pharaoh whom Joseph worked for had died: "Now there arose a new king over Egypt, who did not know Joseph." The new pharaoh decides to "set taskmasters over them" in order to control them because they are "too many and too mighty" (1:8–11). "And God heard their groaning, and God remembered his covenant with Abraham, with Isaac, and with Jacob" (2:23–24; 6:5). The obvious questions are: (1) When were the Israelites enslaved? (2) Why were they enslaved? And (3) why did God wait so long to liberate them?

696. Kugel comments: "God could have freed the Israelites in any manner He chose. He could have instantaneously transported them back to their ancestral homeland, or struck Pharaoh dead as soon as he refused to let them go, or brought about their freedom in some other, immediate fashion. Instead, He took the slow route" (*Bible as It Was*, 316–19).

697. No reason is given for this event, which is never framed as a theft. That is, "each woman shall *ask* her neighbor" for silver and gold (3:22; 11:2; 12:35; my emphasis). Twice the narrator says that asking worked because "the Lord had given the people favor in the sight of the Egyptians, so that they let them have what they asked" (12:36; 11:3). According to May and Metzger, "The 'spoliation of the Egyptians' . . . is explained as evidence of the favor which Moses and the Israelites had gained in Egypt" (May and Metzger, *Oxford Annotated Bible*, 80). Tullock argues, however, that the Israelites' "Egyptian neighbors also were anxious for the Israelites to leave, even giving them jewelry and clothing" (*Old Testament Story*, 71). Levenson says that David Daube connects the Egyptians' gifts to the former Hebrew slaves to God's command in Deuteronomy 15:12–14 that liberated slaves or servants should not leave their masters empty-handed (*Hebrew Bible*, 150–51.).

698. McKenzie, like many scholars, believes that these horrific acts never took place: "The Bible reader may in this respect be comforted by the general agreement of biblical historians that the atrocities of Jericho and Ai and Hazor are unhistorical" (*Old Testament without Illusion*, 85).

699. It must be noted, however, that the people later say to Moses, "You speak to us, and we will hear; but let not God speak to us, lest we die" (20:19). In Deuteronomy, Moses says of the Sinai event: "Then the Lord spoke to you out of the midst of the fire; you heard the sound of the words, but saw no form; there was only a voice. And he declared to you his covenant . . . And the Lord commanded me at the time to teach you statutes and ordinances" (4:12–14). "The Lord spoke with you face to face at the mountain, out of the midst of fire, while I stood between the Lord and you at that time, to declare to you the word of the Lord; for you were afraid because of the fire, and you did not go up into the mountain" (5:4–5). It might be the case that the Israelites heard the sound of God's voice but did not hear the words because they were too far away. Thus, Moses later told them what Yahweh said. On the other hand, Deuteronomy 4:35–36 suggests that the Israelites actually heard the words as well as the voice of Yahweh, which is why, as Moses says,

it is surprising that they survived the experience (4:33). Kaufmann says: "God descended upon the mountain before all the people, let them all hear his voice, and committed them to things . . . At Sinai, God speaks with Moses; the people hear God's voice only that they may believe in Moses and his mission (Ex. 19:9)" (*Religion of Israel*, 212). See also Kugel, *Bible as It Was*, 377; and von Rad, *Old Testament Theology*, 1:220.

700. After Yahweh delivers the Ten Commandments, the details of the scene are repeated: "Now when all the people perceived the thunderings and the lightnings and the sound of the trumpet and the mountain smoking, the people were afraid and trembled; and they stood afar off" (20:18). Anderson argues that "the traditional storm imagery . . . is used to describe the awesome holiness of God and the majesty of his coming to visit his people." He continues: "It is significant that Israel adopted religious metaphors not from the quiet rhythms and beauties of nature, but from the violent storm that shakes the earth, overwhelming man with an awareness of the transcendence and holiness of God and a sense of the frailty and precariousness of human life" (*Understanding the Old Testament*, 59).

701. Brueggemann comments: "The characterization of the coming of God expressed in a way that is characteristic in Israel is of a loud, disturbing intrusion that is immensely disruptive." The theophany is described as dangerous and dramatic. As for the requisite preparations for God's arrival, Brueggemann adds, "The rhetoric of the paragraph effects a priestly agenda, otherwise lined out in the traditions of the book of Leviticus in which the approach to the presence of YHWH must be done with punctilious attentiveness" (*Old Testament Theology*, 44–45). Later, Brueggemann says, "As the tradition reports, this is a one-time disclosure that has brought Moses and Israel into dangerous contact with what is most revolutionary in YHWH's rule of the world" (50).

702. Kugel, *Bible as It Was*, 318. Kugel examines Yahweh's motives on 316–19.

703. May and Metzger, *Oxford Annotated Bible*, 72.

704. Ramsay says: "What our writers want us to know [regarding the plagues] is not some catalog of catastrophes in nature. The truth lies not so much in the signs themselves as in what the signs point to: 'You shall know that I am the Lord your God' (6:7). In every way they can think of, the writers seek to remind us of the power of the redeeming God. 'Who is the Lord that I should heed him and let Israel go?' (5:2), the pharaoh demands. All is told in order that we, like pharaoh, will learn the answer" (*Westminster Guide*, 44). Brueggemann comments: "This is a God who is preoccupied with 'getting glory' for YHWH's own self . . . In sum, God is for God's self and will be glorified. It is Israel's primal task to give YHWH glory, to enhance YHWH in the eyes of the world and in the eyes of the other gods" (*Old Testament Theology*, 35).

705. The plague is later attributed to Yahweh (32:35), but there is no indication that Yahweh ordered Moses to implement the trial in the first place. On the other hand, Yahweh says to Moses, after the latter has conducted the ordeal, "'[I]n the day when I visit, I will visit their sin upon them.' And the Lord sent a plague upon the people, because they made the calf which Aaron made" (32:34–35).

706. Brueggemann refers to this event as an example of "the dialogic work of biblical theology" (*Old Testament Theology*, 29). For an extensive analysis of Moses' first encounter with Yahweh, see 29–33.

707. Kugel, *Bible as It Was*, 313. Ehrman discusses the divinization of Moses in *How Jesus Became God*, 80–82.

708. Brueggemann, *Old Testament Theology*, 39. Later, Brueggemann says: "What is surprising is Moses' role in the ensuing tradition. In Exodus 32:10, YHWH bids Moses to leave him alone in anger, for YHWH is not free to be recklessly angry in the presence of Moses. By his very presence Moses is a curb on YHWH's ferocious self-regard, so that Moses promptly emerges in the narrative as a definitive force in the life of Israel's covenant" (58).

709. May and Metzger comment: "By sending his angel or alter ego (32.34), the Lord will not forsake his people, despite their sin. He will not, however, accompany the sinful people himself, lest his holiness consume them" (*Oxford Annotated Bible*, 111).

Endnotes

710. According to May and Metzger, "*The tent* was portable, like Arabic tent-shrines (26.7–14 n.). Unlike the priestly tabernacle which was centrally located (25.8; Num.2.2), the tent was pitched *far off from the camp*. Originally, the tent was perhaps both a place of tribal assembly and an oracle place, both ideas being implied in the term *meeting*. However, it was chiefly a tent of revelation to Moses" (*Oxford Annotated Bible*, 111).

711. Kugel, *Bible as It Was*, 428. Wright notes that this passage reappears ("at least in part") in 2 Chr 30:9; Neh 9:17, 31; Joel 2:13; Jonah 4:2; and Ps 86:15 ("Faith of Israel," 364).

712. Wright, "Faith of Israel," 428–31.

713. May and Metzger explain that "to inquire of God" means "seeks a verdict by oracle (Jg.4.4–5)." After Jethro's changes, Moses alone appears to deal exclusively with cases involving Yahweh's judgment: "Moses was to deal with cases without legal precedent which required a special oracle (compare Dt.17.8–13); ordinary cases were to be handled by lay leaders (Num.11.16–22) or appointed judges (Dt.16.18–20)" (*Oxford Annotated Bible*, 91).

714. Borg, *Reading the Bible Again*, 95, 100.

715. Von Rad, *Old Testament Theology*, 1:290–91. Von Rad cites Exod 4:17; 9:23; 10:13; 14:16; and 17:9–10 (290n13).

716. Segal, *Rebecca's Children*, 138.

717. Brueggemann, *Old Testament Theology*, 26–27. For a brief description of the oppression of the Israelites in Egypt, see Epstein, *Judaism: A Historical Presentation*, 15.

718. McKenzie, *Old Testament without Illusion*, 90.

719. Brueggemann, *Old Testament Theology*, 200–201.

720. Tullock, *Old Testament Story*, 71.

721. Anderson, *Understanding the Old Testament*, 50–51.

722. Friedman, *Who Wrote the Bible?*, 82–83. Friedman adds that when the Yahwists from Egypt arrived in Israel and "met Israelite tribes who worshiped the God El, . . . the two groups accepted the belief that Yahweh and El were the same God" (82).

723. Collins, *Short Introduction*, 57. Collins concludes that Exodus "is not an exercise in historiography, even by ancient standards." Von Rad comments, "Critical historical scholarship regards it as impossible that the whole of Israel was present at Sinai, or that Israel crossed the Red Sea and achieved the Conquest *en bloc*—it holds the picture of Moses and his leadership drawn in the tradition of the Book of Exodus to be as unhistorical as the function which the Deuteronomistic book of Judges ascribes to the 'judges'" (*Old Testament Theology*, 1:106–7; see also 5).

724. Muilenburg, "History of the Religion," 298.

725. Meek, *Hebrew Origins*, 96–97. Meek says: If the people Moses liberated were not Israelites, Moses would have to have persuaded them that "there was a god in the desert interested in them, who would deliver them, and with whom they might enter into a covenant." The tribe of Dan, Meek notes, "lost faith in its own god" and eventually accepted a new one. "Here, we have a tribe adopting a deity hitherto unknown to it, adopting him in sheer desperation for want of any other god." However, as I indicated, Meek finds that the weight of the evidence supports the other side of the argument.

726. Meek, *Hebrew Origins*, 29–31. Meek provides a substantial amount of textual evidence for his conclusions and claims that he is in agreement with "the opinion of practically all scholars today" (31 n. 97). Meek's succeeding discussion of the Egyptian experience on 31–36 is comprehensive.

727. Levenson, *Hebrew Bible*, 157.

728. Schmidt, *Old Testament Introduction*, 76–77.

729. Ramsay, *Westminster Guide*, 45.

730. Von Rad, *Old Testament Theology*, 1:133.

731. According to May and Metzger, although the Israelites "could behold the glory which signified [his] presence," they "could not see God" himself (*Oxford Annotated Bible*, 87–88).

Endnotes

732. Muilenburg, "History of the Religion," 301.

733. May and Metzger, *Oxford Annotated Bible*, 180. The editors state that the Israelites seem to have remained in Kadesh waiting for the sinful adult males, cursed by Yahweh, to die off.

734. Tullock, *Old Testament Story*, 74.

735. Levenson, *Hebrew Bible*, 137. Levenson says that it was "roundly condemned in the Hebrew Bible."

736. McKenzie, *Old Testament without Illusion*, 89.

737. Anderson, *Understanding the Old Testament*, 55. Anderson adds: "These narratives in Exodus 32–34 are marked by a sober realism. They show that Israel could not claim to be *better* than other nations, either morally or religiously, for the people displayed the same weakness and strength that are found in the life of any people. If there was any difference, it lay in the extraordinary experience that had formed them into a community and the destiny to which they were called in the service of God" (64).

738. Miles says that the mood of the Bible is frequently "one of irritability, denunciation, and angry complaint." To be sure, the complaints originate with God's people. However, as Miles says, God "complains endlessly about their complaining." Particularly "in the Book of Numbers, as Israel complains about Moses, Moses complains about Israel, God complains about Israel, Israel complains about God, God complains about Moses, and Moses complains about God" (*God: A Biography*, 133).

739. We learn in Deuteronomy that the Israelite soldiers decided not to fight because the majority report was so frightening that it "made [their] hearts melt" (1:28). Furthermore, Moses was told by Yawheh himself to warn the repentant soldiers that He would not be supporting them. Moses now refers to them as "presumptuous." After the losing battle, the returning soldiers "wept before the Lord; but the Lord did not hearken to [their] voice" (1:42–43, 45).

740. Miles, *God: A Biography*, 136. Miles explains that Baal was not only a god of war, like Yahweh, he was also "a fertility god whose cult involves ritual copulation" (137).

741. Anderson, *Understanding the Old Testament*, 68.

742. The evidence that Moses does not know that some Israelites will settle in the area of Shittim is that he later initially rejects the request of "the sons of Reuben and the sons of Gad" to raise their cattle there. Moses asks them, "Why will you discourage the heart of the people of Israel from going over into the land which the Lord has given them?" Also, he reminds them of God's anger when the Israelite spies returned from the surveillance of Canaan and offered "an evil report" that similarly discouraged the Israelites from continuing their journey to Canaan (32:1–10). In Deuteronomy, Moses says, "And the Lord said to me, 'Do not harass Moab or contend with them in battle, for I will not give you any of their land for a possession, because I have given Ar to the sons of Lot for a possession" (2:9).

743. Brueggemann, *Old Testament Theology*, 26.

744. As Anderson notes, thanks to Yahweh, "daily sustenance was providentially provided" (*Understanding the Old Testament*, 55).

745. Brueggemann, *Old Testament Theology*, 169.

746. Miles, *God: A Biography*, 133–34.

747. Tullock, *Old Testament Story*, 66–67. Tullock makes the same point about Moses' miracles later in Exodus (74).

748. Wright and Fuller, *Book of the Acts*, 79. May and Metzger agree: "*The sea*, known in Hebrew as the 'sea of reeds,' was not the Red Sea itself but a shallow body of water farther north . . . The divine victory was rooted in a natural phenomenon: during a storm the shallow waters were driven back by *a strong east wind* (v. 21), making it possible for the Israelites to cross on foot. Egyptian chariots, however, were mired in the mud and engulfed by the returning waters" (*Oxford Annotated Bible*, 84–85).

749. Anderson, *Understanding the Old Testament*, 49.

Endnotes

750. Miles comments, "A determination on [Yahweh's] part to impress the Egyptians was indeed a motive repeatedly mentioned in the Book of Exodus," a point Moses makes in Exodus 14:11–18 (*God: A Biography*, 135).

751. Anderson, *Understanding the Old Testament*, 49.

752. Moses prays to Yahweh to stop killing the people after they register their first complaint and Yahweh's "anger was kindled" (11:2). He appears to be horrified at Yahweh's infliction of leprosy on his sister Miriam and tries to convince him to rescind his decision (12:13). As we have seen, when the Israelites object to the task of fighting the inhabitants of Canaan, Moses appeals to Yahweh's honor and integrity in order to prevent him from killing all of them (14:13–19). In response to Yahweh's next threat to kill everyone except Moses and Aaron, after the Israelites complain about God's execution of Korah and the other Levites, the two mediators fall on their faces again and stop Yahweh's plague from spreading by carrying a censer "to the congregation, and mak[ing] atonement for them" (16:44–46). Finally, after the Israelites object again to the lack of water and remind Moses of the kind of food they were accustomed to eating in Egypt, Moses prays to Yahweh to forgive them by withdrawing the "fiery serpents" whose bite is fatal for "many people of Israel," particularly since they repented: "We have sinned, for we have spoken against the Lord and against you; pray to the Lord that he take away the serpents from us" (21:5–8).

753. Brueggemann says, "In general YHWH seeks to meet Moses' resistances and objections; but most spectacularly in the fifth Mosaic objection, YHWH concedes the point to Moses and makes an alternative arrangement" (*Old Testament Theology*, 39).

754. Von Rad, *Old Testament Theology*, 1:293.

755. As we noted earlier, Moses says the same thing to Yahweh in Exodus after the creation of the Golden Calf. First, he says to the people, "You have sinned a great sin. And now I will go up to the Lord; perhaps I can make atonement for your sin." Then, to Yahweh, Moses says, after acknowledging what the Israelites did, "But now, if thou wilt forgive their sin—and if not, blot me, I pray thee, out of thy book which thou hast written" (32:30–32).

756. Friedman, *Who Wrote the Bible?*, 201.

757. This interpretation is offered by both Cohn-Sherbok, *Hebrew Bible*, 35; and Friedman, "Hiding of the Face," 217.

758. Ramsay combines the first and third options: "[I]nstead of simply commanding a rock to bring forth water, he struck it with his staff, as if he rather than God were doing the miracle" (*Westminster Guide*, 58). May and Metzger argue that Moses "failed to interpret the giving of water as a sign from the Lord" (*Oxford Annotated Bible*, 190), but they fail to indicate which specific part of the incident indicates this.

759. Friedman, *Who Wrote the Bible?*, 200–201.

760. May and Metzger add later: "Deuteronomy is a sermon which interprets Israel's covenant responsibilities . . . The making of the covenant (Ex. ch. 24) was not just a past ceremony involving another generation but it is a contemporary covenant . . . The language may reflect a liturgy in which the covenant was periodically recalled and renewed (26.16–19; 31.10–11)" (*Oxford Annotated Bible*, 221).

761. Collins, *Short Introduction*, 70.

762. Kaufmann, *Religion of Israel*, 175; see also 290. The word *commandments* appears more than forty times in this book, more than twice as many times as it appears in the earlier books of the Pentateuch combined. Figuratively (and more accurately), of course, the command to place the words of God "between [one's] eyes" and "on the doorposts of [one's] house" means to be guided by God's directives and to make one's dwelling place reflective of his principles.

763. Indeed, Miles goes on to explain some fundamental differences between Deuteronomy and the other books in the Pentateuch (*God: A Biography*, 139).

764. Ramsay, *Westminster Guide*, 65.

765. Schmidt, *Old Testament Introduction*, 120.

Endnotes

766. Kugel adds that "Deut. 6:4 epitomized all laws concerning relations between man and God" (*Bible as It Was*, 458).

767. Miles, *God: A Biography*, 142–43. Miles continues: "Leaving aside the difference, if any, between straining to keep a covenant and fearing to break one, has Israel done either? Obviously not." Furthermore, he says, for the Hebrew word for *heart* in the Jewish Bible, "we must understand the mind and the imagination" (144).

768. Collins, *Short Introduction*, 87–88.

769. Anderson, *Understanding the Old Testament*, 70.

770. Anderson, *Understanding the Old Testament*, 316.

771. Muilenburg, "History of the Religion," 325–26.

772. For an explanation of the connection between the Jewish Covenant and treaties between rulers (or suzerains) and their subjects (or vassals), see Wright and Fuller, *Book of the Acts*, 86–91.

773. Collins, *Short Introduction*, 91. Collins continues, "The saying attributed to Jesus in the Gospels (Matt 22:34–40; Mark 12:28–31; Luke 10:25–28) on the twofold greatest commandment, sums up at least one strand of Deuteronomic theology."

774. Kugel, *Bible as It Was*, 506.

775. Anderson, *Understanding the Old Testament*, 315.

776. Miles, *God: A Biography*, 147.

777. Van Leeuwen, *Christianity in World History*, 94–95. Mussner says that the "individual statements" of the Decalogue "are of an ancient age and have their origin in the kinship ethos of the tribes of Israel; they are designed to serve as a protection for the community" (*Tractate on the Jews*, 95). According to Goodman, "Pentateuchal law betrays traces of earlier assumptions of social structures based on tribal groups and extended families" (*History of Judaism*, 78).

778. Goodman, *History of Judaism*, 96. Von Rad says that "even after her settlement, in contrast to other peoples who also adopted the settled life after formerly being nomads, Israel hallowed and cherished the traditions of her early days" (*Old Testament Theology*, 1:15). According to Kaufmann: "The laws of the Covenant Code are for the most part entirely in accord with the nomadic stage of Israel's prehistory, as reflected in the patriarchal narratives . . . We may assume that these laws had their origin in the ancient legal traditions that the Israelite tribes shared with the other tribes and peoples of that sphere of culture" (*Religion of Israel*, 170–71). Collins says, "In general, the laws of Exodus stand in the legal tradition of the ancient Near East" (*Short Introduction*, 71).

779. Wright and Fuller, *Book of the Acts*, 89. Wright says later: "Legal obligation was always qualified, therefore, by a relationship involving love and affection, whereas sin became all the more a felt reality because it was a form of infidelity" (97).

780. Anderson, *Understanding the Old Testament*, 317. Van Leeuwen distinguishes between the Jewish law and the Code of Hammurabi, which, though authorized by a god, is entirely secular: It "is not at all religious in character." But "[a]ll the ordinances of the Torah . . . are the commandment of the Lord" (*Christianity in World History*, 95). Bellah makes a similar distinction: "We must not, however, overlook the sea change in the Israelite usage [of the Covenant]: Assyrian covenants were between ruler and subject; Israelite covenants were between God and human beings" (*Religion in Human Evolution*, 308). Bellah also distinguishes between "vassal" and "grant" covenants. The covenants with Abraham and David, he says, were of the latter type. The Deuteronomic covenant was of the former type (306–8).

781. Mussner, *Tractate on the Jews*, 67. Speaking of the command in Leviticus "You shall love your neighbor as yourself," Kaufmann comments, "What is meant by this is not a mere state of mind, but its actualization in deeds of generosity and kindness" (*Religion of Israel*, 320). And if that point was not clear in Leviticus, it certainly is in Deuteronomy.

782. Armstrong, *History of God*, 20.

783. Borg, *Reading the Bible Again*, 139. Referring to the laws of the Covenant Code, Borg says that they "reflect Israel's origin in Egypt as a radically oppressed and marginalized people." The

purpose of these laws "was to prevent the emergence of a permanently impoverished class within Israel" (100).

784. Ramsay, *Westminster Guide*, 29. See also Wright and Fuller, *Book of the Acts*, 94–95.

785. Armstrong, *History of God*, 52.

786. Anderson, *Understanding the Old Testament*, 315. Collins says, "The central theme in Deuteronomy is the covenant" (*Short Introduction*, 31).

787. Soares, *Social Institutions*, 31. Meek says that "a spirit of kindness and humanity" can be found in "the Hebrew Code" that is not nearly so prominent" in the Code of Hammurabi (*Hebrew Origins*, 76).

788. de Vaux, *Ancient Israel*, 144.

789. Ramsay, *Westminster Guide*, 63–65. Ramsay says that this theme is underscored by Deuteronomy's change in the rationale for honoring the Sabbath, which requires the Israelites to "liberate themselves; their families; their slaves, both Hebrew and alien; and even their livestock, at least for one day each week." This freedom from work is required because "the people of Israel" need to remember their liberation from Egypt and to recall, week after week, that they "are to treat others as those who have themselves experienced oppression and know its horror (10:1; 15:15; 24:18)." Collins makes the same point regarding both the Sabbath laws and the Deuteronomic laws generally (*Short Introduction*, 87). Von Rad says that Deuteronomy, influenced by the prophets, "drafted a kind of constitution" (*Old Testament Theology*, 1:99). Epstein makes the same point in *Judaism: A Historical Presentation*, 96; as does Wright, "Faith of Israel," 355.

790. Kaufmann, *Religion of Israel*, 233–34. Kaufmann says later, "In the conception of the entire people receiving as a man the moral-legal covenant at the mouth of God, the unique essence of the Israelite idea of morality found its ultimate expression: it is the absolute command of God, revealed and imposed on mankind by him" (328).

791. Kaufmann, *Religion of Israel*, 329. Earlier, Kaufmann says that this book was "the first attempt to make the Torah the law of the land." Furthermore, the idea of the Torah "as the basis of national life took its first great step toward realization. This is its lasting historical significance" (*Religion of Israel*, 290).

792. Wright and Fuller, *Book of the Acts*, 96–97.

793. Anderson, *Understanding the Old Testament*, 70, 56.

794. Armstrong, *Bible*, 81.

795. Some might argue that the Jewish creed is stated in the famous prayer in Deuteronomy: "Hear, O Israel: The Lord our God is one, and you shall love the Lord your God with all your heart, and with all your soul, and with all your might" (6:4–5). Wright calls this prayer a summary of the Covenant: "God is one, not many. Therefore, the people must not have a divided loyalty; the focus of the religious attention must be single. And they must love God with heart and soul and might" (*Book of the Acts*, 101). However, the Shema has never been formally approved as a credal statement.

796. Smith, *Early History of God*, 182, 198–99. The Jews in ancient Israel eventually recognized Yahweh as the "sole legitimate god in Israel," but acknowledged "the existence of other national gods" (Kaufmann, *Religion of Israel*, 8). Brueggemann says, regarding Exod 20:3 ("You shall have no other gods before me"): "In such a preclusion, of course, the existence, reality, and attractiveness of other gods are acknowledged . . . It is, along with Deuteronomy 6:4 when rendered as 'only YHWH,' a declaration for YHWH in the context of polytheism" (*Old Testament Theology*, 122–23. See also 75 (where Brueggemann discusses similar views throughout the Near East), and 134. See also Collins, *Short Introduction*, 68–69, 88.

797. Keck says: "The Bible talks about God as if he were a man. From beginning to end, from one stratum of tradition to another, it uses anthropomorphisms." Thus, God "planted a garden," "he becomes angry," and "he has eyes, nostrils, mouth, ears, face, arms, hands—even a posterior!" (*Taking the Bible Seriously*, 73.) Although most scholars regard the anthropomorphic picture of

Endnotes

God or the gods as an archaic (or primitive) feature, Wright objects: "[T]his language is not a luxury or primitivism which later stages of the faith outgrew... The relationship of God to people and of people to God can be depicted in no other way, when the covenant as the framework of understanding is central to the faith" (*Book of the Acts*, 92–93).

798. Armstrong says that "until the sixth century Israel's religion was not in fact very different from that of the other local peoples" (*Great Transformation*, 48). According to Soares: "The religion of the Hebrews in the nomadic stage was very simple. There was the recognition of the tribal God, Jehovah, from whom protection and benefit were expected. There were certain animal sacrifices offered by the Clan-Father, and certain ceremonials to be observed at stated periods of the year and of human life. And there was a body of custom, consisting largely of taboos, which regulated the relation of the people with the Deity" (*Social Institutions*, 20).

799. de Vaux, *Ancient Israel*, 21.

800. Wright and Fuller, *Book of the Acts*, 23, 89.

801. Collins, *Short Introduction*, 71.

802. Kaufmann says: "The Covenant Code is to be considered rather an early formulation and crystallization of the common Near Eastern law of which Hammurabi's laws are a more advanced development" (*Religion of Israel*, 170). See also 233–34.

803. Bellah, *Religion in Human Evolution*, 301. Bellah says that this change occurred in Israel and Judah in the eighth century. On the class conflict associated with urbanization, as early as the third millennium BC, see Childe, *What Happened in History*, 98–99, 116, 123, 127, and 205.

804. "The fundamental unity of Eastern law is of greater importance than the variations to be found between regions and epochs. It is the expression of a common civilization, in which the application of the same juridical principles has produced a similar customary law" (de Vaux, *Ancient Israel*, 146). de Vaux says that the Covenant Code that appears in Exodus "is a law for a community of shepherds and peasants." The evidence suggests that this Code dates "from the early days of the settlement in Canaan, before the organization of the State. It is the law of the tribal confederation" (143).

805. Uffenheimer, "Myth and Reality," 153–55.

806. Robinson, "History of Israel," 284. Robinson explains the process by which farmers lost their land and became victims of "plutocracy," as well as the "judicial corruption" that also contributed to the economic decline of Israel and the "internal disunion" that contributed to its vulnerability to foreign domination (284–85).

807. Muilenburg, "History of the Religion," 324.

808. The quotations in this and the following five paragraphs, when not otherwise identified, are from von Rad's discussion of Deuteronomy in *Old Testament Theology*, 1:219–31. Von Rad says of the Jews' self-condemnation: "Israel had rejected Jahweh and his commandments. For that reason judgment had overtaken Israel and Judah" (82). Von Rad returns to a discussion of Deuteronomy in the second volume of his book (2:393–95).

809. Gerhard von Rad, *Old Testament Theology*, 1:219–31.

810. Kaufmann, *Religion of Israel*, 203. Kaufmann concludes, "There is, then, no doubt, that the Torah literature was crystallized at the latest by the beginning of the monarchy" (204).

811. "The editor of the Book of Judges characterizes the twelfth and eleventh centuries as a time when there was no king in Israel and every man did that which was right in his own eyes (21:25). Israel in possession of the land is now faced with the problem of settling down to a new mode of life" (Wright and Fuller, *Book of the Acts*, 111).

812. Finkelstein and Silberman, *Bible Unearthed*, 107–10.

813. Horsley and Silberman, *Message and the Kingdom*, 13, 27).

814. Wright and Fuller, *Book of the Acts*, 85. Wright adds later: "[T]here was in Israel a deep and radical interest in the poor and the weak, and the whole effort of the economic life was to provide for their welfare. The weakness and the poverty of some should never be the occasion for profit on the part of the strong" (108). "Israel's God is the protector of the legally defenseless"

Endnotes

(May and Metzger, *Oxford Annotated Bible*, 96). Again, however, this attitude was characteristic of tribal society and not unique to Israel. On this point, see Soares, *Social Institutions*, 70–71.

815. Soares says, "It is not implied that the whole land should lie fallow at the same time, but that each field should have its regular sabbatic [*sic*] rest" (81).

816. de Vaux, *Ancient Israel*, 21. Examples can be found in Ruth 2:20 and Jeremiah 32:6–7. The story of Ruth indicates that the paternal uncle was first in line to become the *go-el*, followed by "his son, then other relations" (22).

817. Soares, *Social Institutions*, 95. Niditch adds: "In a world without security in which families may exist at a bare subsistence level, generations of kin are a source of political and economic protection and survival. The care for kin (the closer the kin, the greater the obligation to care) is integral to Israelite worldview" (*Ancient Israelite Religion*, 74).

818. de Vaux, *Ancient Israel*, 10–11.

819. de Vaux, *Ancient Israel*, 10.

820. Niditch, *Ancient Israelite Religion*, 17. Niditch cites John Holladay, "The Kingdoms of Israel and Judah," in Levy's *The Archeology of Society in the Holy Land*; and Carol Meyers, "Kinship and Kingship," in Coogan's *The Oxford History of the Biblical World*.

821. de Vaux, *Ancient Israel*, 166. de Vaux adds: "The peasant was deeply attached to the piece of ground he had inherited from his father . . . Public feeling and custom took care that this patrimony was not alienated, or that at least it should not pass out of the family. It is probable that when land was inherited it was not shared like other property but passed to the eldest son or remained undivided."

822. Niditch, *Ancient Israelite Religion*, 13–14.

823. de Vaux, *Ancient Israel*, 173. L. Kohler comments: "[T]he eighth century . . . shows a marked shift in economic circumstances and the beginning of a distinct stratification of Hebrew society. Beside the possessors of property we find those who have no possessions; beside independent citizens we find dependents. At this point the legal assembly fails" because "fear of those who have economic power and who can do real harm in the narrow common life of the village makes men subservient and lacking in independence" (quoted in Schmidt, *Old Testament Introduction*, 38.

824. de Vaux, *Ancient Israel*, 170.

825. de Vaux explains: "In credit operations the pledge is a surety, an object in the possession of the debtor which he hands over to the creditor as guarantee for his debt. The garment . . . was not a real pledge, proportionate in value to the credit, but a symbolic instrument, a probative pledge, which seems to have been generally true of movable pledges in Israel" (*Ancient Israel*, 171).

826. In Deuteronomy, Moses announces that God does not merely demand that "a widow's garment in pledge" be returned. Rather it must not be taken in the first place (24:17).

827. Soares, *Social Institutions*, 55.

828. Soares, *Social Institutions*, 49–50.

829. Soares, *Social Institutions*, 50–51.

830. Soares, *Social Institutions*, 138.

831. May and Metzger comment, "This law reflects a developed society in which responsibility for legal administration was delegated to appointed officials in every town" (*Oxford Annotated Bible*, 236).

832. Moore, *Judaism*, II-III, 182.

833. de Vaux, *Ancient Israel*, 157.

834. Moore comments: "At the opening of the court a solemn charge was given to the witnesses, cautioning them against testifying to anything that is their own inference, or that they know only at second hand, however trustworthy they believe the informant to be. They are bidden remember that where only property is at stake errors can be redressed, but that when a man's life is involved his blood and that of his (potential) posterity sticks to the author of his death to the

Endnotes

last human generation; but are urged not to be deterred by this reflection from giving testimony" (*Judaism*, II-III, 185).

835. Soares, *Social Institutions*, 139–40.

836. de Vaux says that there was neither a public prosecutor nor a defense attorney in these cases. "[E]ach party pressed or defended his own case" (*Ancient Israel*, 156).

837. According to May and Metzger, the words *before the Lord* mean that "[t]he case must come to the supreme tribunal" (*Oxford Annotated Bible*, 240).

838. One safeguard against false witnesses was the requirement that two witnesses were required for any conviction: "A single witness shall not prevail against a man for any crime or for any wrong in connection with any offense that he has committed; only on the evidence of two witnesses, or of three witnesses, shall a charge be sustained" (Deut 20:15). Elsewhere, this requirement is operative only in death penalty cases (Deut 17:6; Num 35:30).

839. Kaufmann, *Religion of Israel*, 319–20.

840. Wright, "Faith of Israel," 383.

841. Schmidt, *Old Testament Introduction*, 113.

842. de Vaux, *Ancient Israel*, 149–50. However, as de Vaux later notes, the death penalty could also be applied for sins against God and against parents (158).

843. de Vaux, *Ancient Israel*, 148–49.

844. Wright, "Faith of Israel," 382.

845. de Vaux, *Ancient Israel*, 149.

846. de Vaux, *Ancient Israel*, 150, 151. Soares explains: "As regards legislation, it is particularly to be noted that there was no idea of a legislative authority in ancient times. Law was not thought of as the result of enactment, but as the time-honored custom of the tribe or nation. It was God who gave laws" (*Social Institutions*, 118).

847. Kaufmann, *Religion of Israel*, 256.

848. Wright and Fuller, *Book of the Acts*, 116, 130. Wright says, "Private property could not be claimed by a royal court simply because the court desired it."

849. Weinfeld, "Protest against Imperialism," 178.

850. de Vaux, *Ancient Israel*, 73.

851. Wright and Fuller, *Book of the Acts*, 121.

852. Von Rad, *Old Testament Theology*, 1:59. Von Rad says earlier, "In spite of the inadequacy of our information, we can well imagine that the rural population, which was tied to the patriarchal way of life, did not by any means accept without protest the great innovation of the imposition of the kingdom." This is because "the monarchy . . . brought in its train a considerable curtailment of the rights of the free landed peasantry, as well as considerable economic burdens" (58).

853. de Vaux says: "The king had of course an extensive administrative authority; he organized his kingdom, appointed his officials, and made decrees, but he did not enact law. It is remarkable that the two 'laws of the king' ([1 Sam] 8: 11–18; Dt 17: 14–20) make no allusion to any power of the king to lay down laws. On the contrary, the first warns the people against arbitrary acts, and the second orders him to have a copy of the divine law and obey it to the last detail" (*Ancient Israel*, 1:150).

854. According to May and Metzger, 1 Samuel consists of an Early Source and a Late Source. The Late Source, "compiled in the latter days of the monarchy (750–650 B.C.)," claims that "the choosing of a king" in tenth-century Israel "was really a mistake." The Early Source portrays "the establishment of the kingship . . . as a divinely ordained blessing and the salvation of the nation" (*Oxford Annotated Bible*, 330).

855. Crossan says that these abuses were typical for kings in the region: "All of that was but the normalcy of royal privilege in the ancient Near East" (*Birth of Christianity*, 198.).

856. Provan discusses the conflicting views of monarchy in chapters 8 and 9 of 1 Samuel in "Historical Books of the Old Testament," 207–8.

857. Anderson, *Understanding the Old Testament*, 196.

858. Wright and Fuller, *Book of the Acts*, 121, 135.

859. de Vaux, *Ancient Israel*, 150.

860. Maguire, *Moral Core*, 54–55.

861. Schmidt, *Old Testament Introduction*, 191.

862. Cornfeld, *Archeology of the Bible*, 139. Bellah argues that Second Isaiah opposed monarchy. Regarding his prophecy, Bellah quotes Mark Smith: "This work modifies the old royal theology in many respects. First, the Judean king vanishes from the picture . . . Second, Israel itself, instead of the Judean king, becomes the new servant who is to mediate blessing" (*Religion in Human Evolution*, 319).

863. Von Rad, *Old Testament Theology*, 1:99.

864. Von Rad says that, "as a general principle, the prophets never disputed the legitimacy and necessity of, for example, the kingdom, or the priests, or the judicial office of the elders. Indeed, they took these authorities, as organs of the will of Jahweh, much more seriously than the bearers of those offices were able to do at that time" (*Old Testament Theology*, 1:99.)

865. Heschel, *Prophets: An Introduction*, 159. Objecting to the idea that the prophets were social conservatives because they merely embraced "a traditional morality" and failed to offer "practical suggestions for change in the structure of society," Gorringe says: "To this charge we have to reply that social reformers such as William Cobbett or William Morris also thought they were appealing to a traditional morality, idealized in much the same way as Amos or Micah's may have been. Both contributed far more in terms of ethical critique of injustice, through the education of desire, than through proposing alternative structures. The prophets of Israel are the great teachers of such ethical critique, now widely recognized as an essential part of a radical agenda" ("Political Readings of Scripture," 77).

866. Ramsay, *Westminster Guide*, 183. Uffenheimer comments, "This vast literature bears witness to [the prophets'] relentless struggle for justice, righteousness, and social equality, on the one hand, and to their quest for the goal and meaning of the history of Israel and its relations to the nations, on the other" ("Myth and Reality," 162). In the same volume, Weinfeld argues that the struggle for justice in the writings of the prophets is accompanied by a strong and persistent protest against imperialism ("Protest against Imperialism," 169–74).

867. "The eighth-century prophets were the first of a series of remarkable religious leaders who appeared over the known world, including Buddha, Zoroaster, and Confucius" (Tullock, *Old Testament Story*, 181).

868. Armstrong, *Great Transformation*, 162.

869. Von Rad, *Old Testament Theology*, 1:97–98.

870. Kaufmann, *Religion of Israel*, 340, 347. Kaufmann continues: "Amos, Isaiah, Micah, and Hosea accuse the wealthy and aristocratic class of dispossessing and impoverishing the masses, of living wantonly and luxuriously. This sort of social decay was new in Israel." Specifically, Kaufmann mentions royal expropriations, war-profiteering, and slavery, as well as "famine, drought, plague, war, and captivity . . . Not all, but some of the prophets repudiate the power state, military culture, and the trust in fortifications and armies. A kingdom founded on righteousness is their political ideal" (345).

871. Von Rad, *Old Testament Theology*, 1:64–65.

872. May and Metzger, *Oxford Annotated Bible*, 1107.

873. Newsome, *Hebrew Prophets*, 18.

874. Muilenburg, "History of the Religion," 318.

875. Collins, *Short Introduction*, 156.

876. Ramsay, *Westminster Guide*, 234–36. Oesterley and Robinson state that several of the early prophets (Isaiah, Amos, and Hosea) "insisted on such doctrines as the supremacy of Yahweh, the demand for morality and the futility of sacrifice as a substitute for righteousness" (*Introduction to the Books*, 260).

877. Muilenburg, "History of the Religion," 318–19.

Endnotes

878. Ramsay, *Westminster Guide*, 25. On this subject, see Crossan, *Birth of Christianity*, 200.

879. Heschel, *Prophets: An Introduction*, 35.

880. Referring to this passage, Ramsay says: "Human life is cheap. There is no justice in the courts for the poor. The needy may be sold into slavery for a trifling debt" (*Westminster Guide*, 237). Schmidt comments: "When we describe Amos as a prophet of social justice, we put our finger on the principal but not the only theme of his arraignment. There is also an attack on false security or even arrogance (6:1f., 8, 13; 8:7)—a motif that will reappear especially in Isaiah—and a criticism of the cult" (*Old Testament Introduction*, 199).

881. Tullock comments: "Chapter 4 [of Amos] was directed to the women of Samaria. Amos compared them to the fat, sleek cows of the pastures of Bashan. They, like their husbands, were greedy drunkards concerned only with their own desires" (*Old Testament Story*, 186).

882. Soares, *Social Institutions*, 219.

883. Newsome, *Hebrew Prophets*, 37.

884. Collins, *Short Introduction*, 160. Hosea sees "the love of God" not as an expression of "the loyalty of a vassal," but "on the analogy of the love between husband and wife or father and son." The point is that obedience is not merely "the observance of laws," but "more fundamentally requires an underlying attitude of faithfulness, loyalty, and 'knowledge of God'" (161).

885. Newsome, *Hebrew Prophets*, 37. Newsome notes that Hosea refers to Israel's historical record, especially regarding its time in Egypt and the wilderness, "in such a manner as to remind the people that they were chosen as God's own."

886. Tullock, *Old Testament Story*, 195.

887. Anderson comments: Hosea "condemned the institution of the monarchy, seeing in it a symptom of a harlotrous spirit. Saul's hometown of Gibeah and his coronation at Gilgal were evidences of Israel's determination to reject Yahweh as king (8:4; 9:15; 10:3, 9). The consequences of Israel's betrayal of the covenant were to be seen in the regicides (7:3–7), the feverish foreign policy aimed at courting Egypt or Assyria (7:11), and the foolish reliance upon arms and fortifications (8:14)" (*Understanding the Old Testament*, 248).

888. Newsome, *Hebrew Prophets*, 37.

889. Heschel, *Prophets: An Introduction*, 40. According to 2 Kings 15:8–26, Shallum killed Zechariah, Menahem killed Shallum, and Pekah killed Menahem's son and heir, Pekahiah.

890. Quoting this line, Schmidt says, "Hosea of all the prophets is probably the severest critic of the monarchy as such" (*Old Testament Introduction*, 207).

891. Collins says that, in demanding that the inhabitants of Judah "wash themselves," God does not intend "to substitute one ritual for another. The washing is metaphorical"—that is, not ceremonial (*Short Introduction*, 169).

892. Newsome, *Hebrew Prophets*, 60, 63. As Soares notes, "[T]he prosperity which was so marked in the north had also its parallel in Judah. And again, the lion's share of the benefits went into the hands of the military aristocracy, while the poor were little advantaged. Oppression, fraud, and the injustice of the courts gave the wealth of the kingdom to the privileged classes" (*Social Institutions*, 234–35).

893. Soares, *Social Institutions*, 238. Newsome comments: "The basic causes of this waywardness will be familiar to every reader of Amos, Hosea, and Micah: people, especially the upper classes, have become greedy and they have allowed their love of material wealth to lead to the suppression of the rights of the weak and defenseless" (*Hebrew Prophets*, 63).

894. Collins says that "Isaiah comes close to Amos's concern for social justice" in the Song of the Vineyard (5:1–7). "The choice of the vineyard may be determined by the kind of offenses that Isaiah was condemning: those who joined house to house and field to field. The story of Naboth's vineyard (1 Kings 20) comes to mind" (*Short Introduction*, 169).

895. Kaufmann comments: "The thought pervades Isaiah that moral evil originates in idolatrous pride and love of power." In Assyria and Israel, "wealth and idolatry go hand in hand" (*Religion of Israel*, 387).

Endnotes

896. Thus, Heschel says, "The prophets consistently singled out the leaders, the kings, the princes, the false prophets, and the priests as the ones responsible for the sins of the community" (*Prophets: An Introduction*, 203). Tullock reminds us that Isaiah's relationship to the kings of Judah was complicated by the fact that he was an official adviser to both Ahaz and his son Hezekiah. Thus, "he seemed to have access to the royal court that few people enjoyed" (*Old Testament Story*, 204–5).

897. Newsome, *Hebrew Prophets*, 70. For a detailed discussion of this subject, see 70–79.

898. Newsome, *Hebrew Prophets*, 66.

899. Newsome, *Hebrew Prophets*, 51. Newsome continues, "The expropriation may have taken place by quite legal means, but its effect upon its poor victims was nonetheless devastating."

900. Schmidt comments on this passage: "When Micah criticizes the economy based on large estates and the greed of the upper classes for houses and property, he seems to be giving concrete form to the tenth commandment (Exod 20:17): 'Woe to those who devise wickedness . . . They covet fields, and seize them'" (*Old Testament Introduction*, 223).

901. Ramsay says: "The rich were getting richer, but they were doing so at the expense of the poor . . . Divine law had attempted to prevent the accumulation of wealth in the hands of a few. Property was supposed to stay in the family that had originally owned it . . . But shrewd capitalists had learned how to get around the law. Social and economic justice was perverted" (*Westminster Guide*, 248).

902. Newsome, *Hebrew Prophets*, 48–49.

903. Muilenburg, "History of the Religion," 323.

904. Schmidt says: "In general, Micah laments the oppressive actions of society, and especially their violations of justice" (*Old Testament Introduction*, 223).

905. Soares explains that Micah's vision of the good life was based on the assumption that "urban development" was the source of Judah's problems and that "nothing but a return to the simplicity of the earlier days would insure purity." Soares adds, "Solomon had turned the course of Israel's life from the simplicity of agriculture to the more highly organized commercialism of the city, with all the luxury, extravagance, and consequent extortion and heartlessness that characterize it" (*Social Institutions*, 245).

906. Heschel notes, "Utterances denoting the wrath of God, the intent and threat of destruction, are found more frequently in Jeremiah than in any other prophet" (*Prophets: An Introduction*, 106).

907. Newsome says, "The main focus of attention [in chs. 26–29] is the conflict between the prophet and the religious establishment of his day" (*Hebrew Prophets*, 118). On this subject, see also Schmidt, *Old Testament Introduction*, 241, 242–43.

908. Soares warns against distinguishing too severely between idolatry and immorality. The worship of idols, he contends, is based on an "unethical conception of deity": "The lofty idea of a God of righteousness gave place to that of the familiar deity represented by the image, who could be fed with sacrifices, pleased with incense, cajoled by flattery. Instead of the God of ethical demands, Jerusalem had gods who could serve her ends. The question of idolatry, therefore, was not merely ecclesiastical . . . Gods who could be bought were the allies of the aristocracy, of the privileged classes" (*Social Institutions*, 251).

909. Collins comments, "Jeremiah certainly shared basic values of the Deuteronomic reform—opposition to the worship of deities other than YHWH and to social injustice" (*Short Introduction*, 178). Tullock argues that, to Jeremiah, "the people's only hope was a return to the great moral principles of the Sinai Covenant" (*Old Testament Story*, 237).

910. Heschel says, "There could hardly be a greater incompatibility than that between Jeremiah and King Jehoiakim, whose chief interest was to enlarge his palace, apparently using forced labor to do so" (*Prophets: An Introduction*, 133).

911. Ramsay says: "Jeremiah's whole life seemed to him to be one of conflict. The book's editor has brought together several stories of Jeremiah's verbal battles with Jerusalem's leaders," particularly in chapters 21 and 22 (*Westminster Guide*, 205).

Endnotes

912. Schmidt, *Old Testament Introduction*, 243. Schmidt adds, "Once again, inner compulsion and subjective intention, character and behavior, inability and unwillingness, are interwoven."

913. Heschel notes a dozen references to the heart, which is, in this prophecy, invariably depraved (*Prophets: An Introduction*, 128). There are nearly sixty references, all told, to the heart in the prophecy of Jeremiah.

914. Although I referred to this idea in Jeremiah as "anomalous," it occurs as well in Ezekiel and Isaiah. On Ezekiel's view of human depravity, Schmidt says, "Since the indictment emphasizes the deep-seated guilt of Israel, the promise of salvation cannot be based on the behavior and character of the people; instead, the prophet expects new life from a new creative act of God" (*Old Testament Introduction*, 255)—i.e., the same act of God in Jeremiah: "A new heart I will give you" (36:26; cf. Jer 24:7). On Isaiah's view, see 43:25: "I am He who blots out your transgressions for my own sake, and I will not remember your sins" (see also 48:9). Schmidt also connects Jeremiah's idea to Hosea 5:4.

915. Again, Soares resists viewing idolatry as a non-moral issue: "Ezekiel knew that the loyal worship of Jehovah, conceived as righteous, loving, infinitely concerned about the good character of his people, produced a certain type of life, while the debased worship of Jehovah under the form of an idol, which could be fed and censed and carried in procession, produced an entirely different type of life; and the worship of gods whose rites were cruel and sensual produced a worse life still. Therefore the demands of religion and morality were one" (*Social Institutions*, 266).

916. Ezekiel in fact refers to the Covenant by name as often as Isaiah does and almost as often as Jeremiah does: 16:8, 59–62; 17:13–15; 20:37; 34:25; 37:26; 44:7.

917. Newsome, *Hebrew Prophets*, 134.

918. Tullock says that Ezekiel held "the leaders of the land" accountable: "the upper classes, the priests, and the prophets," who "were like voracious animals, seizing by force things that were not theirs. The priests had become so materially minded that spiritual things were meaningless to them. The rulers had become thieves, while the prophets had become purveyors of false oracles." The people "were extortioners and robbers" (*Old Testament Story*, 272).

919. The prophet uses the word "created" (40:26; 41:20; 42:5; 43:1, 7; 45:8, 12, 18; 48:7, 54:16) to refer to God's actions far more than any other writer in the entire Jewish Bible. God refers to himself as incomparable or "besides whom there is no other" (40:18, 25; 41:4; 42:8; 43:12; 44:6, 8; 45:5–6, 14, 18, 21–22; 46:5, 9; 47:8) with similar frequency.

920. Second Isaiah quite often uses the words "formed" (43:1, 10, 21; 44:2, 10, 21, 24; 45:18; 49:5; 54:17), "chosen," and "servant" (41:8–9; 42:1, 19; 43:10, 20; 44:1–2, 21; 45:4; 49:5–6; 52:13; 53:11).

921. Newsome, *Hebrew Prophets*, 172.

922. Newsome, *Hebrew Prophets*, 173.

923. Schmidt, *Old Testament Introduction*, 228.

924. Tullock, *Old Testament Story*, 234.

925. LaCocque, *Jesus the Central Jew*, 81.

926. Wright, "Faith of Israel," 384. Wright says that "it was under the influence of the prophetic proclamation that Pss. 50 and 51 do imply a spiritualization of the term 'sacrifice'" (381).

927. Kaufmann, *Religion of Israel*, 340, 365.

928. Heschel, *Prophets: An Introduction*, 195. Crossan comments, "[N]otice that while there is no problem in finding biblical prophetic statements in which God rejects worship in the absence of justice, there is not a single biblical statement in which God rejects justice in the absence of worship" (*Birth of Christianity*, 205).

929. Here, according to May and Metzger, Amos satirizes "Israel's love of manifold public rites at the chief sanctuaries" (*Oxford Annotated Bible*, 1110–11).

930. "Using all the phrases that priests have used to indicate God's acceptance of sacrifices and ceremonies, Amos depicts God as repulsed by the sight, sound, and even smell of their worship" (Ramsay, *Westminster Guide*, 238).

Endnotes

931. Tullock says that 5:24 "sums up the major theme of the preaching of Amos—that a righteous God demanded righteous living to accompany sincere worship. Right living involved giving every man his due" (*Old Testament Story*, 188). Heschel warns against interpreting such passages as a complete rejection of cultic activities: "Of course, the prophets did not condemn the practice of sacrifice in itself . . . They did, however, claim that deeds of injustice vitiate both sacrifice and prayer" (*Prophets: An Introduction*, 196).

932. Collins, *Short Introduction*, 158. Collins continues: "The service of God is about justice. It is not about offerings at all."

933. In Hosea 3:18-20, as Newsome notes (*Hebrew Prophets*, 40-42), Hosea adds to *mishpat* and *tsedakkah* two other Covenant concepts: *chesed* (steadfast love) and *rachamim* (mercy).

934. Ramsay says that, despite Isaiah's description of God's objection to ceremonial practices, Isaiah was not anti-cult: "Isaiah is not really opposed to prayer and worship; his own call to ministry occurred in the Temple (6:1–8)" (*Westminster Guide*, 187).

935. Ramsay refers to Bernhard Anderson's proposal "that into this one verse Micah has packed a summary of the messages of the greatest eighth-century prophets. There is Amos's demand for justice (Amos 5:24), Hosea's emphasis on steadfast love (Hos. 2:19), and Isaiah's humble reliance on the Lord (Isa. 30:15)" (*Westminster Guide*, 249).

936. Meyer, *Aims of Jesus*, 223.

937. Kaufmann, *Religion of Israel*, 103, 160.

938. Wright and Fuller, *Book of the Acts*, 154. LaCocque notes that Jesus similarly "introduced a hierarchy, within which the ethical is recognized as the supreme criterion, thus expressing an implicit criticism against a 'formalism' that confuses the essential with the accessory" (*Jesus the Central Jew*, 81).

939. Crossan, *Birth of Christianity*, 186.

940. Umen, *Pharisaism and Jesus*, 41-42, 37.

941. Umen, *Pharisaism and Jesus*, 197-98; my emphasis.

942. Soares, *Social Institutions*, 223-24, 229, 231; my emphasis.

943. Bellah, *Religion in Human Evolution*, 304. Bellah adds, "The prophets, the earliest exponents of the Yahweh-alone position, claimed that they were more truly 'called' by Yahweh than were the kings." Later, Bellah says that, when "the ten tribes of Israel revolted" against Rehoboam, it can be seen "as an effort to return to the lighter rule of Saul, closer to the old tribal ideal of independence." This event and the choice of Jeroboam as king "testify to the continued ambivalence in the tradition about the institution of kingship" (293–94).

944. Crossan, *Birth of Christianity*, 202, 201.

945. Irwin, "Literature of the Old Testament," 180.

946. Miles says, Isaiah insists on both "the Lord's immediate, intimate access to the experienced sorrow of Israel (making him, implicitly, every Judean's personal God)" and "the Lord's cosmic, world-creating power" (*God: A Biography*, 235). Heschel says, similarly, that God not only "rules the world in the majesty of His might and wisdom," but also responds to human actions with "the most intimate and profound concern" (*Prophets: Volume II*, 4).

947. Sanders rejects "the frequent contrast between Grace and Works, and the claim that Christianity is a religion of grace and Judaism is a religion of works" ("Jesus, Ancient Judaism," 51). Witherington calls the charge "simply false" (*What Have They Done*, 201).

948. Cornfeld says, "The prophets should be considered conservative reformers, who wished to restore an earlier form of society, rather than as revolutionaries" (*Archeology of the Bible*, 140). Miles puts it even more simply: "The Lord's underlying question in all the prophets is . . . *Can we begin again?*" (*God: A Biography*, 228).

949. Bellah, *Religion in Human Evolution*, 302.

950. Wilson, "Prophetic Books," 215.

Endnotes

951. Moore says that "in the current Christian representations of Judaism neither the character of this teaching nor the central significance of the doctrine of repentance in the Jewish conception of the religious life and of the way of salvation is adequately recognized" *(Judaism*, 1:507).

952. Anderson, *Understanding the Old Testament*, 458.

953. Enslin makes the same point: "Keeping the law was synonymous with morality and religion." That is, Jews "sought to keep [the law] with no ulterior motive." The individual "did it because he loved God and wished to do his will" (*Christian Beginnings*, 99).

954. Moore, *Judaism*, II-III, 214; 1:503. Heschel says: "The divine reaction to human conduct does not operate automatically. Man's deeds do not necessitate but only occasion divine pathos... There is no nexus of causality, but only one of contingence between human and divine attitudes, between human character and divine pathos" (*Prophets: Volume II*, 5).

955. Kaufmann, *Religion of Israel*, 284.

956. Kaufmann, *Religion of Israel*, 285. Cornfeld says of the Book of Jonah, "It is a parable which illustrates the power of repentance and divine mercy for all living creatures" (*Archeology of the Bible*, 190).

957. Moore, *Judaism*, 1:507, 510.

958. Segal says: "The Jewish so-called doctrine of works is often represented as a scoreboard religion. One simply totals up one's virtues against one's sins, and if the sum is negative, the result is damnation. But this is a misrepresentation, for repentance overrides any arithmetical calculations of reward and sin" (*Rebecca's Children*, 169).

959. Miles says that "punishment has not been used as a discipline at any earlier point in the Bible," except in 2 Samuel 7 (*God: A Biography*, 206).

960. Moore, *Judaism*, II-III, 319.

961. Moore discusses God's action "for His name's sake" in *Judaism*, II-III, 101–3.

962. Kaufmann, *Religion of Israel*, 439.

963. Heschel says that "God's pathos... has never been accorded proper recognition in the history of biblical theology" (*Prophets: Volume II*, 2). Miles asks, referring to the Jews' "loss of the land of Israel": "And what is the effect upon God of this epochal defeat of his covenant partner? In brief, it is poignant but powerfully engaging agitation. God—a god of parts, as we have already seen—draws on his own inner tensions in prophecy with a focused and creative resourcefulness" (*God: A Biography*, 196–97).

964. Miles, *God: A Biography*, 202.

965. Anderson, *Understanding the Old Testament*, 251, 253. Speaking of God's approach to chastisement in Second Isaiah, Anderson adds, "As iron is tempered by fire and shaped on the anvil, so Yahweh re-creates his people through sufferings so that they may be a more effective instrument of his sovereign purpose in history" (418).

966. Heschel, *Prophets: Volume II*, 10.

967. May and Metzger comment, "With a formula taken from the Exodus narrative (*found grace* [favor], Ex.33.12–17; compare Jer.23.7–8) and the emphatic historical-theological implications of *everlasting love* and *faithfulness*, God promises the joyful restoration of all Israel" (*Oxford Annotated Bible*, 953).

968. Newsome says: *Chesed* "is a term used frequently in the Old Testament to refer to God's covenant love, the enduring, persistent commitment which Yahweh has for Israel and which is exercised in good times and in bad. Hosea's continued reference to this term demonstrates his concern that Israel reciprocate this same loving loyalty to Yahweh" (*Hebrew Prophets*, 40).

969. Heschel, *Prophets: An Introduction*, 135.

970. In this way, May and Metzger interpret "he does not eat upon the mountains" in 18:6 (*Oxford Annotated Bible*, 1019).

971. Soares, *Social Institutions*, 266.

972. Soares (*Social Institutions*, 60) says that this emphasis on knowledge of God led to the ancient Jewish emphasis on education: "As the great religious leaders sought to lift religion from

ritualism to spiritual fellowship with God, and to lift morality above conventional customs, they sought to make education more definite. Thus the prophets in the great exhortation to Israel . . . laid special emphasis on the parental training of children." As Moses says in Deuteronomy, "Only take heed, and keep your soul diligently, lest you forget the things which your eyes have seen, and lest they depart from your heart all the days of your life: make them known to your children and your children's children" (4:9; see also 6:6–7; 11:19; 32:46).

973. Heschel, *Prophets: An Introduction*, 59. Heschel says that the Hebrew verb "to know" suggests "more than the possession of abstract concepts. Knowledge compasses inner appropriation, feeling, a reception into the soul" (57). Newsome also discusses *daath elohim*, as well as four other Hebrew terms that connect Hosea's concept of the relationship between God and the Israelites to the Covenant (*Hebrew Prophets*, 40–42). See also Miles, *God: A Biography*, 237; Schmidt, *Old Testament Introduction*, 131–32; and Anderson, *Understanding the Old Testament*, 235.

974. Mussner, *Tractate on the Jews*, 94, 65.

975. Anderson, *Understanding the Old Testament*, 249. Anderson says that Hosea links *chesed* and *daath elohim*. That is, "love" is inseparable from "knowledge of God" (248–49).

976. Newsome, *Hebrew Prophets*, 136.

977. Notably, Ezekiel suggests that there are two ways of acquiring new hearts and minds. First, in 18:30–31, God urges people to renew themselves. Second, in a later passage, he says that, at the end-time, he will accomplish this change himself: "A new heart I will give you, and a new spirit I will put within you" (36:26). Kaufmann says that these acts are related—that the acquisition of new hearts and spirits begins with people's self-initiated change: "Thus man must strive to attain the new heart before God will bestow it" (*Religion of Israel*, 442). However, it seems rather that God's end-time gift will be unconditional, accompanied as it will be by other end-time changes, including the ingathering of the Jews and the return of all Jews to their newly fertile and famine-free homeland (Ezek 36:24–25, 28–30). That is, this new heart and mind will not be a result of people's repentance. Indeed, repentance will occur *after* the end-time event, when the Jews will recall "their evil ways" and experience self-loathing (Ezek 36:31–32). God makes it clear that, in the latter case, he will not be responding to his people's remorse. He will be acting "for the sake of [his] holy name" (36:22–23).

978. Moore, *Judaism*, 1:503; my emphasis.

979. Anderson emphasizes both points. On the one hand, he says, "One of the greatest defects of Deuteronomic theology was that it oversimplified the ways of God in history": "Obey God and all will go well; disobey him and hardship will come." On the other hand, however, the Deuteronomist made two changes in the traditional *quid pro quo* doctrine. First, he added "the belief that obedience or disobedience could be measured by a code of rules." Second, and more important, he portrayed the relationship between God and humanity as personal and emotional rather than impersonal and transactional: "Now, in defense of Deuteronomy we must say that it was not the intention of the Mosaic address to encourage a bargain-counter religion. For this address is concerned primarily with man's personal relationship to Yahweh, rather than with personal profit gained by obeying religious rules" (*Understanding the Old Testament*, 320).

980. Mussner lists four distinctive qualities of the Jewish God. He is trustworthy, nonmanipulable, exclusive, and always-present (*Tractate on the Jews*, 54–55). Mussner's use of the word *exclusive* is the same as its use by Kaufmann, who says, "It is conceded on all hands that by the age of literary prophecy Israelite religion was militantly exclusive" (*Religion of Israel*, 62). The Jews worshiped Yahweh exclusively, "with no other gods before him."

981. On this point, see Kaufmann: "There is no avoiding the conclusion that paganism ascribed to the gods what it knew to be evil acts . . . They, no less than all beings, are fated to live under subjection to sin, as they are fated to need food and drink. Although they are the guardians of justice and morality, other forces which are equally rooted in their nature may at times gain the upper hand . . . The sinning god is thus another characteristic manifestation of the pagan idea" (*Religion of Israel*, 39).

Endnotes

982. Kaufmann says: "In the work of the literary prophets, Israelite religion reached a new height. They were the first to conceive of the doctrine of the primacy of morality, the idea that the essence of God's demand of man is not cultic, but moral. This doctrine regards human goodness as the realization of the will of God on earth" (*Religion of Israel*, 345.).

983. McKenzie comments on this special feature of Yahweh: "The ancient world had no gods of the oppressed. I am aware that gods in Mesopotamia and Egypt . . . are called defenders of the poor and needy. We know that these gods . . . were owned and managed by the landowning aristocracy for whom they worked . . . No one ever doubted that Yahweh was the God of the oppressed as no other god was; the history of the religion of Israel showed that he resisted the ownership and landowning aristocracy" (*Old Testament without Illusion*, 93).

984. Umen, *Pharisaism and Jesus*, 6.

985. Miller, *Religion of Ancient Israel*, 26–27. Miller considers the divine council in the Jewish Bible to be the Jewish version of a change in worship that occurred in Mesopotamia in the first millennium: "[T]here was a centralization or integration of one single deity to whom all other beings are subordinate." Marduk and Ashur are other examples (26).

986. May and Metzger offer *mighty lords* as an alternative to *gods* in both passages (*Oxford Annotated Bible*, 699). Armstrong similarly explains the term as a reference to a "streamlined" form of the council of gods, which was later understood to be God's "divine household" or "the warriors in his divine army" (*Great Transformation*, 73–74).

987. Armstrong, *Great Transformation*, 73–75. See also 56. Kaufmann argues strongly against the view that Jews at any time worshiped gods other than Yahweh and that they worshiped Yahweh with the understanding that he was not the only God, but the highest of the gods (*Religion of Israel*, 127–48).

988. Mussner, *Tractate on the Jews*, 52–53. Armstrong comments: "When people cried, 'Who is like Yahweh among the other gods?' they were obviously not denying the existence of other deities, but declaring that their patronal god was more effective than the other 'sons of El,' the national gods of their neighbors. None could rival Yahweh's faithfulness" (*Great Transformation*, 74).

989. Armstrong, *Great Transformation*, 55. See also 56. Armstrong says that Yahweh's specialization as a god of war meant to some of his worshippers that "[h]e had no expertise in agriculture or fertility," which was why "so many Israelites, as a matter of course, performed the ancient rituals of Baal and Anat to ensure a good harvest," Baal being "the power that fertilized the land" (74).

990. God is reported to have said to David, "Sit at my right hand, till I make your enemies your footstool" (110:1). And God is reported to have said to the psalmist, "His enemies I will clothe with shame, but upon himself his crown will shed its luster" (132:18).

991. Moore, *Judaism*, II-III, 103. Moore connects the passage in Leviticus with the passage in Matthew, in 169n4.)

992. The writers of Psalms 5 and 75 also condemn (besides "wickedness") boastfulness, deception, and insolence. What is particularly striking is the difference between these sins and those typically named by the prophets, such as the oppression and exploitation of the weak and helpless.

993. May and Metzger explain that a *Horn* is a "symbol of strength and power" (*Oxford Annotated Bible*, 713).

994. Miles, *God: A Biography*, 272.

995. On this point, see Anderson, *Understanding the Old Testament*, 496.

996. Cornfeld says, "In sum, wisdom in Israel was part of a much wider and older tradition which extended throughout the Near East" (*Archeology of the Bible*, 208).

997. Soares, *Social Institutions*, 277. Soares notes that the Jewish philosopher Philo was a conspicuous product of this meeting of cultures in the intellectual capital of Egypt in the first century AD.

998. Anderson, *Understanding the Old Testament*, 488. Anderson says that "most scholars regard the second collection [10:1—22:16] as the oldest portion of the book of Proverbs" and that many more "belong to the tradition of Solomon" (495–96).

Endnotes

999. Kaufmann, *Religion of Israel*, 326.

1000. Anderson, *Understanding the Old Testament*, 490. Anderson continues, "Indeed, there are no explicit allusions to Israelite history or to outstanding Israelite personalities, with the single exception of Solomon."

1001. On this point, see Schmidt, *Old Testament Introduction*, 321.

1002. Kaufmann, *Religion of Israel*, 326, 317. Barton makes the same point in "Approaches to Ethics," 120–21, 129.

1003. Kaufmann, *Religion of Israel*, 491. As Miles says, the "impersonal tradition of secular wisdom" was presented "by a completely unexpected alternative to the prophets—namely, Lady Wisdom" (*God: A Biography*, 290). Kaufmann says, "The personification of wisdom in the early chapters has its pagan counterpart in the embodiments of wisdom in deities as Thoth, Ea, etc." (*Religion of Israel*, 323n11).

1004. Anderson, *Understanding the Old Testament*, 495.

1005. To Anderson, Proverbs "consists of practical advice to the young on how they may attain a successful and good life" (*Understanding the Old Testament*, 488).

1006. Alter, "Poetic and Wisdom Books," 233.

1007. McKenzie, *Old Testament without Illusion*, 145, 147, 149. In other words, to Cornfeld, Proverbs is "a text-book of instructional materials for the young to inculcate practical wisdom and cultivate personal morality" (*Archeology of the Bible*, 215).

1008. Anderson, *Understanding the Old Testament*, 497.

1009. Miles, *God: A Biography*, 294.

1010. Von Rad, *Old Testament Theology*, 1:435–36.

1011. Schmidt, *Old Testament Introduction*, 323. Schmidt provides a comprehensive list of themes in Proverbs on 327.

1012. Anderson, *Understanding the Old Testament*, 497.

1013. These are the words of Wilson, in "Egypt," 91. See also White, *Ancient Egypt*, 35–36.

1014. Childe, *What Happened in History*, 137–38.

1015. White, *Ancient Egypt*, 38–39.

1016. Frankfort, *Ancient Egyptian Religion*, 118.

1017. Von Rad, *Old Testament Theology*, 1:385–86, 436. Von Rad explains, the "retribution is not a new action which comes upon the person concerned from somewhere else; it is rather a last ripple of the act itself"—as if the initiatory act were "a stone thrown into water"—"which attaches to its agent almost as if something material" (384–85).

1018. Von Rad, *Old Testament Theology*, 1:386, 417. Von Rad adds: "The collection in chs. xxv–xxix reckons as the oldest: it is also the most 'worldly.' Compared with it, the collection in chs. x–xxii.16 says much more about Jahweh, and his will and action" (437n40).

1019. Brueggemann, *Old Testament Theology*, 46, 48. Brueggemann cites Proverbs 17:5 and Moshe Weinfeld's *Deuteronomy and the Deuteronomic School* on this point (48). Frankfort argues that the Wisdom literature in Egypt has also been mistakenly called secular. First, he says that "the contrast between the secular and the religious is hard to draw in ancient culture." Second, he discusses the connection between the Wisdom tradition and the religious concept of Maat: "The Egyptians recognized a divine order, established at the time of creation . . . Maat is this order," and Wisdom operates within its framework, which reflects a "deep religious conviction" (*Ancient Egyptian Religion*, 60–64).

1020. Soares, *Social Institutions*, 289.

1021. Wright comments: "The righteous and the wicked are evaluated according to a given standard, which can only be the revealed law of Yahweh. Thus the wisdom ethic in Israel cannot be conceived as unrelated to revelation; in the contrary, it rests squarely upon the peculiarly Israelite understanding of what constitutes good and evil" ("Faith of Israel," 382).

1022. Frankfort, *Ancient Egyptian Religion*, 119.

Endnotes

1023. Soares, *Social Institutions*, 288.

1024. Ramsay, *Westminster Guide*, 162.

1025. Kaufmann notes that this "doctrine of retribution [in the book of Proverbs] resembles that of general Eastern wisdom." He adds, "The dogma of individual retribution (found in chaps. 10–22) is no sign of lateness; the idea is found throughout the wisdom of ancient Egypt and Mesopotamia" (*Religion of Israel*, 323 and n11).

1026. On the contrary, Anderson believes that it is *the fear of God* that provides a common ground for prophecy and the proverbs. However, the passage he quotes from Jeremiah proves the opposite: "I am Yahweh who practices kindness, justice, and righteousness in the earth; for in these things I delight, says Yahweh" (*Understanding the Old Testament*, 498). The point is that God in the work of the prophets is consistently concerned with love and the other covenant values. The writers of proverbs seem to be preoccupied with fear and obedience.

1027. McKenzie, *Old Testament without Illusion*, 150.

1028. Miles, *God: A Biography*, 290. Miles comments, "God is marginal as a picture frame is marginal. He is not often in the picture, but the picture requires him" (291).

1029. Anderson, *Understanding the Old Testament*, 462.

1030. On this point, see Kaufmann, who claims that *all* of the psalms are pre-exilic (*Religion of Israel*, 311). Cornfeld contends that most of the psalms are pre-exilic and traces the oldest of these to the twelfth century BC, when some psalms were influenced by Canaanite poetry (*Archeology of the Bible*, 197–200). Anderson says that all of Book II (Psalms 42–72) is pre-exilic (*Understanding the Old Testament*, 466). Collins argues that both the order and the content of the book of Psalms were "still fluid in the first century B.C.E. and can only have been settled finally after that time" (*Short Introduction*, 238).

1031. Von Rad cites Rainer Maria Rilke as someone who turned to the psalms for solace. He quotes Rilke as saying that he "spent the night in solitude . . . and finally . . . read the Psalms, one of the few books in which one is completely at home, however preoccupied and unsettled and troubled one may be" (*Old Testament Theology*, 1:399n33).

1032. Armstrong, *Great Transformation*, xix, 197.

1033. Muilenburg, "History of the Religion," 331.

1034. Miles, *God: A Biography*, 292–93.

1035. Alter, "Poetic and Wisdom Books," 232.

1036. Brueggemann, *Old Testament Theology*, 109. In his discussion of wisdom literature, Brueggemann says, "the great threat to life in sapiential teaching is an arrogant autonomy that is sure to be destructive." In the book of Job, "YHWH makes clear that the almighty has no interest in or patience with the detailed moral calculations of conventional wisdom" (235). See also 307, 315.

1037. Levine, "Bearing False Witness," 502.

1038. Conzelmann and Lindemann, *Interpreting the New Testament*, 316.

1039. Anderson, *Understanding the Old Testament*, 471.

1040. Anderson, *Understanding the Old Testament*, 475. As Wright notes, "The existence of God was never doubted in Israel; but this powerful, direct, energetic, and pervasive activity of God was and has always been the chief source of men's difficulty with biblical faith" ("Faith of Israel," 362).

1041. Muilenburg, "History of the Religion," 337–38.

1042. Miles notes that this idea virtually *begins* in the psalms. For the first time, God is off-stage, and his people are wondering when he will arrive to save them from their dilemma. "He has promised a new creation on 'the day of the Lord.' But when will the day of the Lord come?" (*God: A Biography*, 253). Citing Amos 5:15 ("It may be that Yahweh, the God of hosts, will be gracious to the remnant of Joseph"), Anderson says that forgiveness and salvation depend on both "the unpredictable response of the people" and "the *incalculable* grace of God" (*Understanding the Old Testament*, 240; my emphasis).

Endnotes

1043. Ramsay, *Westminster Guide*, 161. Ramsay cites Psalms 119, 37, and 41.

1044. On punishment as chastisement, see Moore, who says, "Retribution . . . was not vindictive, or was so only in the case of the irreclaimably bad who persisted in provoking their doom" (*Judaism*, II-III, 252.

1045. The idea in this passage is related to the prophets' emphasis on the need for a heartfelt and whole-hearted commitment to the Law. The concept of human dependence on God's help in this regard is suggested in the following verses in Jeremiah: "I will give them one heart and one way, that they may fear me for ever . . . I will put the fear of me in their hearts" (32:39–40). God also says in Jeremiah, "I will write it upon their hearts . . . [and] they shall all know me" (31:33–34). This idea occurs also in Deuteronomy 10: "And now, Israel, what does the Lord thy God require of you, but to revere the Lord your God, to walk in all his ways, to love him, to serve the Lord your God with all your heart and with all your soul; to keep the commandments and statutes of the Lord, which I command you this day for your good" (vv. 12–13).

1046. The connection between the question "How long, O Lord" and the hope that God's steadfast love and/or righteousness will express themselves in some kind of consolation also appears in Psalms 13, 35, 40, 42, 44, 62, 63, 69, 77, 88, and 89.

1047. The KJV translation is "Surely every man walketh in a vain show: surely they are disquieted in vain: he heapeth up riches, and knoweth not who shall gather them."

1048. Moore, *Judaism*, II-III, 214, 154; 1:514. Moore notes later that no one in the New Testament needs to explain repentance because the Gospel writers, Jesus, and his followers "assume that their hearers know well enough what repentance is, and how the forgiveness of sins depends upon it . . . It is to be observed, further, that the conceptions of the necessity, nature, and effects of repentance entertained by John or by Jesus and his disciples differ in no respect from those of their countrymen to whom they addressed their appeal; and naturally, since they were derived from the same source, the liturgy and the homilies of the synagogue" (519).

1049. It is worth noting that, as May and Metzger say, "Although v. 8 makes it clear that the psalmist's problem is one of illness, the main emphasis is upon moral, rather than merely physical, health." This point comes out more strongly when the psalmist confesses "that his nature has been sinful even from the moment of conception" (*Oxford Annotated Bible*, 694): "Behold, I was brought forth in iniquity, and in sin did my mother conceive me" (v. 5).

1050. Muilenburg, "History of the Religion," 338. Crediting Claus Westermann with this insight, Brueggemann refers to several psalms that "move from lament to hymn." He adds that, although some psalms remain unanswered and Job "receives a harsh answer," showing "that the pattern can be broken," this "only attests to the normative reality of the pattern" (*Old Testament Theology*, 240).

1051. Collins, *Short Introduction*, 241.

1052. Brueggemann, *Old Testament Theology*, 110. Brueggemann adds: "Perhaps that is because Israel has nowhere else to go. But perhaps it is also because Israel's most elemental conviction concerns YHWH's compassion, a conviction from which Israel is not dissuaded even by divine silence and indifference."

1053. Von Rad, *Old Testament Theology*, 1:401–3.

1054. Van Leeuwen, *Christianity in World History*, 96.

1055. Russell points out that the legalism that the Jews are often accused of "was not the only things which Torah religion fostered. It encouraged in many *a deep personal piety* which found expression in *good works* and in service to others" (*Between the Testaments*, 83). Maguire says, "Because of its overarching concern for the poor, biblical justice is not quibbling legalism. It is largehearted and magnanimous" (*Moral Core*, 132).

1056. Von Rad, *Old Testament Theology*, 1:400–401.

1057. It is interesting to note that Matthew and Luke identify these two different groups in their respective Beatitudes. Matthew says that the "blessed" are, among others, those who seek righteousness and those who make peace, as well as those who are meek, merciful, and pure in heart (5:5–9). Luke says that the blessed are the poor and the hungry (6:20–21). Both say that the blessed also include the mournful and the persecuted.

1058. Von Rad, *Old Testament Theology*, 1:400–401.

1059. Maguire, *Moral Core*, 133. Moore also emphasizes the importance of "distributive justice, which gives to each his due, along with "public justice, the function of the community in defining and enforcing the duties and the rights of individuals and classes," and "rectitude, or integrity of personal character" (*Judaism*, II-III, 180.) Moore says elsewhere, "It is needless to multiply quotations here from many places in all parts of the Scripture commanding or commending beneficence to the poor. The same theme runs through the uncanonical literature" (165).

1060. Crossan, *Birth of Christianity*, 186.

1061. Moore, *Judaism*, II-III, 180. Brueggemann quotes Walter Harrelson on the subject of the support for human rights in ancient Jewish sources, such as "the Torah of Zion, the wisdom teaching of Israel, and the affirmation that the creator God has set curbs and limits on human brutality and exploitation": "[T]he Bible has much to say about human rights. It is possible to see in the basic understandings of human rights, reflected in, for example, the United Nations Universal Declaration of Human Rights, a large measure of the biblical understanding of human obligation under God" (*Old Testament Theology*, 255).

1062. Miles says, "Enemies are referred to in perhaps one third of all the Psalms, and the attack that they have launched against the Psalmist, the attack that prompts his prayer, is far more often than not an accusation of wrongdoing," as opposed to a threat to the person or power of the psalmist (*God: A Biography*, 274). As opposed to the victories celebrated in such Psalms as 144, "[a] different spirit . . . shapes the group of thirty or forty Psalms that make no reference to war or to any national enemy, past or present" (275–76).

1063. Guignebert, *Jewish World*, 66.

1064. Wright says that Psalm 29 "was certainly a hymn to the Canaanite god Baal before it was borrowed by Israel and adapted for worship in the Jerusalem temple" (*Book of the Acts*, 185). Cornfeld says, "It is generally admitted that Psalms 29 and 68 derive from a Canaanite background, and in their present form they come from the earliest period of Israel's history—the 12th–10th centuries B.C." (*Archeology of the Bible*, 199). Cornfeld also cites Psalms 18, 45, and 89 as tenth-century "Canaanizing psalms." These psalms notably emphasize God's earth-shattering aid in war (18:7–19, 33–45; 89:5–13), his rewards for obedience (18:20–25; 89:30–34), and his appointment of David as a warrior king (45:2–5; 89:19–29).

1065. I do not mean to suggest that it is therefore easy to determine when any psalm was written. According to Oesterley and Robinson, "The nature of the content of most of the psalms makes the assigning of dates precarious . . . The matter is also complicated by the fact that so many psalms have been subjected to revision; such revision may sometimes make a psalm appear to be of later date than it is in its origin" (*Introduction to the Books*, 187). Furthermore, Schmidt says that "it is hardly possible to determine the historical locus of the psalms, because they translate their concrete occasion in general, more or less formulaic language" (*Old Testament Introduction*, 303).

1066. Miles, *God: A Biography*, 286. Indeed, Miles goes so far as to suggest that the Jews embraced the ideas (1) of "the law as a good in itself" and (2) of "morality as an end rather than a means, as a good in itself rather than an instrument to achieve some other good" (285). Miles adds, "And after the failure of prophecy, which is to say the failure of God to restore Israel to autonomy and even hegemony as he had said he would, the Jews were faced with the choice of Torah as good in itself or no Torah at all. They chose the former and celebrated their choice in the Psalms" (287).

1067. Miles, *God: A Biography*, 243–44, 277. Armstrong says that the term *chesed*, "often translated as 'love,' was originally a tribal term, denoting the loyalty of a kinship relationship

Endnotes

that demanded generous and altruistic behavior toward one's family group . . . Many of the early covenants of the Middle East used these kinship terms, and it is likely that this ethos informed the covenant that bound together the different ethnic groups of the new Israel" (*Great Transformation*, 47).

1068. Wright and Fuller, *Book of the Acts*, 183–84, 190.

1069. Muilenburg, "History of the Religion," 336. On the subject of "anthropopathy," See Heschel, *Prophets: Volume II*, 48–58.

1070. Collins, *Short Introduction*, 244.

1071. Miles, *God: A Biography*, 276, 278, 282.

1072. Herford, *Pharisees*, 102–3.

1073. Childs, *Myth and Reality*, 98. Moore says, "The two aspects of God's character which are here displayed [in Exod 33:19, 34:6f., Deut 5:9f., Jer 32:17–19], his mercy and his justice, are the essential moral attributes on which religion in Jewish conception is founded" (*Judaism*, 1:386–87).

1074. Herford, *Pharisees*, 125.

1075. Guignebert, *Jewish World*, 93–94. For passages in which God is called "father" in Jewish Scriptures, see Moore, *Judaism*, II-III, 201–11.

1076. According to Muilenburg, "Amos is the first to refer to the 'day of Yahweh.' On this 'day' Yahweh well reveal himself decisively. He will engage in battle and will come forth in triumph as victor over his foes" ("History of the Religion," 318).

1077. Oesterley and Robinson, *Introduction to the Books*, 175. Claims for this date of publication appear in most discussions of the book.

1078. Cohn-Sherbok, *Hebrew Bible*, 180.

1079. Alter, *Wisdom Books*, 3, 18n3. Alter mentions especially Job's "rhythmic effects, virtuosic wordplay and soundplay" (3). Borg calls the book of Job "a document whose magnificent language, provocative content, and stunning climax make it one of the most remarkable books in the Bible" (*Reading the Bible Again*, 170).

1080. Oesterley and Robinson, *Introduction to the Books*, 171.

1081. Cornfeld, *Archeology of the Bible*, 209.

1082. Wright and Fuller, *Book of the Acts*, 195.

1083. Fohrer, *Introduction*, 324–25.

1084. Armstrong, *History of God*, 65.

1085. Gruner, "Job: Introduction," 1500.

1086. Wright, among others, says that 'the prose introduction and conclusion in the present book are probably not by the same hand as the poetic section" (*Book of the Acts*, 196).

1087. On this point, see Tullock: "Chapter 28, a discourse on wisdom, and the Elihu speeches (Chapters 32–37) add little to the overall arguments of the book and thus seem not to have been part of the original work" (*Old Testament Story*, 319). Tullock adds, on Elihu's speeches: They "reveal a brash young man who possesses more wind than wisdom. The speeches are ignored by the previous characters in the drama and by the Lord" (327). For a similar critique, see Alter, *Wisdom Books*, 133n2.

1088. Ramsay, *Westminster Guide*, 142.

1089. Wright and Fuller, *Book of the Acts*, 196.

1090. Oesterley and Robinson, *Introduction to the Books*, 178. See also 173. Cornfeld refers to "the many obscurities in the book of Job" (*Archeology of the Bible*, 211). Kaufmann and Ramsay, however, claim that the Elihu chapters belong in the original text (*Religion of Israel*, 336–37; and *Westminster Guide*, 149).

1091. Von Rad, *Old Testament Theology*, 1:409. Von Rad adds later, "Because of the abundance of the themes which Job strikes up, and the rapid way in which he changes from one to the other, it is far from easy to see what the real point at issue for Job is in this struggle or why he accepted it" (413).

Endnotes

1092. Alter, *Wisdom Tradition*, xv. Alter repeats this point on 3, emphasizing that "it dissents from a consensus view of biblical writers."

1093. Ramsay, *Westminster Guide*, 150.

1094. Wright and Fuller, *Book of the Acts*, 195, 202.

1095. Gruber, "Job: Introduction," 1500.

1096. Brueggemann, *Old Testament Theology*, 235.

1097. Kidner, *Wisdom of Proverbs*, 56.

1098. Kidner, *Wisdom of Proverbs*, 61.

1099. Oesterley and Robinson, *Introduction to the Books*, 177–78.

1100. Miles, *God: A Biography*, 313.

1101. May and Metzger say that the quoted passage indicates that Job's "[s]elf-righteousness leads man to condemn God" (*Oxford Annotated Bible*, 653).

1102. Gruber, "Job: Introduction," 1499. Commenting on God's first speech to Job, Gruber says, "God will not give a straight answer to his demand for a hearing . . . If the reader is looking for God to explain why bad things happen to good people and how justice reigns in the cosmos, neither God nor the book of Job as a whole provides an answer" (1555). On two possible interpretations of God's response to Job, Gruber says, "Unfortunately, it is difficult to decide between these (and still other) interpretive possibilities, especially because the speeches are indirect and ambiguous."

1103. Miles, *God: A Biography*, 310.

1104. Wright, *Evolution of God*, 21.

1105. Alter, *Wisdom Books*, 10.

1106. Anderson, *Understanding the Old Testament*, 517, 512–13.

1107. Alter, *Wisdom Books*, 176n2.

1108. Gruber, "Job: Introduction," 1517n12b. Gruber says later, "Job anticipated in 9:13 the argument that the Lord's power over the mythical sea-monsters proves that God is indeed in charge of the universe and that cosmic anarchy cannot explain Job's unjust suffering" (1560).

1109. In his commentary on this passage, Gruber calls Job's view of God as supremely powerful "a central theme" ("Job: Introduction," 1520).

1110. Job earlier says, "God has cast me into the mire, and I have become like dust and ashes" (30:19).

1111. Kidner notes that as "brusque" as God's "direct rebukes" in his final speeches are, they "are not concerned with [Job's] sins of the past." Thus, although "there is nothing soothing or explanatory in these chapters," they culminate in Job's return to normality (*Wisdom of Proverbs*, 71).

1112. Contra Oesterley and Robinson, who say, "Yahweh replies to Job's challenge, giving a picture of His majesty and power, which reduces Job to humble submission" (*Introduction to the Books*, 171). These writers add, however—more correctly, I think—that Job "has seen God for himself, and in that vision all his doubts and questionings sink into the background."

1113. Kaufmann, *Religion of Israel*, 337. To Fohrer, Job receives "assurance of fellowship with God, beside which all else pales into insignificance" (*Introduction*, 334).

1114. Von Rad, *Old Testament Theology*, 1:416–17.

1115. According to Wright, Eliphaz "is represented as the kindest and wisest of the three; Zophar "is the most violent and hot-headed of the three," and Bildad is somewhere in between (*Book of the Acts*, 198–99).

1116. Oesterley and Robinson go into more detail on Job's friends, whom they regard as "delicately distinguished from one another." "Eliphaz, the eldest is kindly, pious, even mystical . . . Bildad is less sympathetic, but has the weight of ancient authority behind him; Zophar, the youngest, needs neither divine revelation nor tradition, for he himself knows all that needs to be known, and feels that he states the truth with absolute and serene dogmatism" (*Introduction to the Books*, 168).

Endnotes

1117. KIdner, *Wisdom of Proverbs*, 61. Anderson says that, "as Job stubbornly insists on his innocence, the friends become vehement in their accusation" (*Understanding the Old Testament*, 514). See also Alter, *Wisdom Books*, 17n13.

1118. Von Rad, *Old Testament Theology*, 1:409. Von Rad discusses a series of gradual changes in Job, including his increasing "terror and abhorrence," his growing anger with and criticism of God, his desire to confront God one on one, and his "Insistence . . . on his own righteousness," all of which is exacerbated and "sharpened" by Job's growing sense of God's remoteness and unresponsiveness (413–15).

1119. Oesterley and Robinson, *Introduction to the Books*, 168–69, 178.

1120. Wright and Fuller, *Book of the Acts*, 201.

1121. Anderson, *Understanding the Old Testament*, 514.

1122. Kidner, *Wisdom of Proverbs*, 67.

1123. Tullock is referring in this passage to Job 27:7 (*Old Testament Story*, 325).

1124. Kaufmann, *Religion of Israel*, 335.

1125. Ramsay, *Westminster Guide*, 148.

1126. Wright and Fuller, *Book of the Acts*, 198.

1127. Anderson, *Understanding the Old Testament*, 315.

1128. Anderson, *Understanding the Old Testament*, 316. Wright calls Job's statement a "climax," expanding on Job's earlier claim: "[B]ehold, my witness is in heaven, and he that vouches for me is on high" (16:19).

1129. May and Metzger contend that this passage reflects the idea "that has dominated the speeches of Job": that is, "his intense desire to see God" (*Oxford Annotated Bible*, 643).

1130. Kidner, *Wisdom of Proverbs*, 68–69. Kidner argues that in all these passages the witness or vindicator is God: "[T]here can be little doubt that when he speaks of [this figure] . . . it is to God himself, not some unidentified third party, that he is looking" (68).

1131. Oesterley and Robinson, *Introduction to the Books*, 168. May and Metzger explain that what Job offers is figuratively his signature, but literally his *taw*, "the last letter of the Hebrew alphabet"—i.e., his last word (*Oxford Annotated Bible*, 643).

1132. Wright and Fuller, *Book of the Acts*, 201.

1133. Alter, *Wisdom Books*, 83–84n25. Alter continues, "The redeemer is someone, usually a family member, who will come forth and bear witness on his behalf, and the use of 'stand up' [or 'upon'] in the second verset has precisely that courtroom connotation." Gruber translates *stand up* or *upon* as *testify* (*Jewish Study Bible*, 1529). Both Gruber and Cornfeld argue that the redeemer is not God but, in Cornfeld's words, "a member of the divine court who acts as legal advocate and defender of accused men before the great god who sits in judgment" (*Archeology of the Bible*, 213).

1134. Borg, *Reading the Bible Again*, 178.

1135. Fohrer, *Introduction*, 333. Fohrer adds, "[T]he demonstration of innocence [i.e., in 31:5–40] conforms to an apodictic series of rules of conduct and behavior together with an oath before the court." Fohrer also notes parallels between Job 3:3–11, 6:15–21, and 6:23; and Jer 20:14–18, 15:18, and 15:21, respectively (330). Alter says of Job 31:5, "This line ["Have I walked"] initiates a whole series that employs the Hebrew form that indicates swearing an oath" (*Wisdom Books*, 127n5). Oesterley and Robinson call the passage "an oath of purgation" (*Introduction to the Books*, 168, 170)—that is, it bears some resemblance to a medieval ecclesiastical practice in which the accused is afforded an opportunity to defend his or her innocence before supporting witnesses.

1136. Von Rad cites Job 29:14—"I clothed myself in righteousness"—and comments, "These identical words could stand in one of the psalms of the innocent sufferers, the only difference being that Job insists on his [righteousness] in a very much more impassioned way" (*Old Testament Theology*, 1:414).

1137. May and Metzger note that in chapter 10 Job "appeals to the love of an artist for his handiwork," echoing Ps 139:14–18 (*Oxford Annotated Bible*, 622).

Endnotes

1138. Fohrer, *Introduction*, 332.

1139. Kidner, *Wisdom of Proverbs*, 111. Collins argues that the story of Job "may be said to represent a crisis in the wisdom tradition, arising from the realization that some of the most hallowed assumptions are proved false by experience" (*Short Introduction*, 262). Oesterley and Robinson say of Ecclesiastes that "its paucity of ideas shows that the religious spirit, so characteristic of the writers in Israel, had practically exhausted itself" (*Introduction to the Books*, 215).

1140. On this point, see Ramsay, *Westminster Guide*, 170. Kidner says, "The audacity of Job in the face of the anomalies of life is matched and even outmatched here—for now the question is whether life itself has any point" (*Wisdom of Proverbs*, 90). Thus, Wright comments, "The author of Ecclesiastes is far more skeptical than is the author of the poetical portions of Job" (*Book of the Acts*, 205).

1141. Anderson, *Understanding the Old Testament*, 501. "Among the passages that are held to come from orthodox editors," Anderson says, "are 2:26; 3:17; 5:19; 7:18b, 26b; 8:11–13; 11:9b; 12:1." On interpolations, see also Schmidt, *Old Testament Introduction*, 329. Oesterley and Robinson go into much more detail in *Introduction to the Books*, 209–12.

1142. This sentence is quoted in Kidner, *Wisdom of Proverbs*, 105.

1143. Alter, *Wisdom Books*, 342. Collins says, "Attempts to find a literary structure in the book have not been very successful." However, Collins adds that the book can be divided into two thematic halves (*Short Introduction*, 263). Machinist finds a modest structure in the book but describes it as a "leisurely, self-conscious, ruminative process" ("Ecclesiastes: Introduction," 1604).

1144. Alter, *Wisdom Books*, 340.

1145. Anderson, *Understanding the Old Testament*, 504.

1146. Kidner says: "The beguiling rhythm in 3:1–8, of a time for this and a time for that, rocks us awake, in the end, rather than asleep, with the question, 'What gain has the worker from his toil?' (3:9)—for it is evident that we spend our days shuttling back and forth in a pattern that we can neither choose nor fully grasp, busy now with one thing, now with its opposite" (*Wisdom of Proverbs*, 98). Tullock argues that this passage shows "history moving in circles, having no purpose or goal" (*Old Testament Story*, 329). See also Cohn-Sherbok, *Hebrew Bible*, 201; and Machinist, "Ecclesiastes: Introduction," 1609–10.

1147. "Quite in tune with this pessimistic attitude," say Oesterley and Robinson, "is the theory of determinism, which runs through the book; man is a helpless being, everything is fixed, and there is nothing he can do to shape or alter the events of life" (*Introduction to the Books*, 213).

1148. On God's total control of everything, see Kidner, *Wisdom of Proverbs*, 95, 97; Anderson, *Understanding the Old Testament*, 506; and Miles, *God: A Biography*, 352.

1149. Ramsay, *Westminster Guide*, 170. Miles comments, "The notion of reward as in any way the consequence of human action—whether as covenant reward or simply as the reward of diligence—is seriously undercut by the quasi-Platonic notion of total divine foreknowledge of an endlessly recurring cycle of events" (*God: A Biography*, 351). See also 353; and Brueggemann, *Old Testament Theology*, 185, 186.

1150. Schmidt says: "Not to have been born is better . . . [is] a judgment that is understandable as a heartfelt cry from an individual in great distress . . . but as a statement of principle it is unknown elsewhere in the OT" (*Old Testament Introduction*, 331). Ramsay, too, notes that Koheleth, unlike Job, who cries out "in agony," speaks "in a far more detached, abstract, philosophical fashion" (*Westminster Guide*, 170). Alter makes the same point in *Wisdom Books*, 358.

1151. Wright says that these pleasures may be trivial, but they are not "irresponsible": "Man's lot is simply to enjoy the simple things of life which he has before him" (*Book of the Acts*, 204). As Oesterley and Robinson argue, this advice from Koheleth simply urges people to make the best of what must be acknowledged to be a bad bargain: "[H]e is the truly wise man who acts under every circumstances in such a way as to secure a maximum of the material good to be got out of life" (*Introduction to the Books*, 212–13).

1152. Schmidt, *Old Testament Introduction*, 330.

1153. Alter notes that Koheleth offers a series of admonitions, which he refers to as "prudential advice," in 10:8, 10; and 11:6 (*Wisdom Books*, 383–85).

1154. Kidner, *Wisdom of Proverbs*, 123.

1155. Alter, *Wisdom Books*, 358n1, 381–82. See also 10:16.

1156. Alter, *Wisdom Books*, 341; my emphasis.

1157. Alter, *Wisdom Books*, 356; my emphasis.

1158. Wright and Fuller, Book *of the Acts*, 204.

1159. On this point, for example, see Tullock, *Old Testament Story*, 329, 331. Any reference to Ecclesiastes as fatalistic (Cohn-Sherbok) or deterministic (Oesterley and Robinson) suggests a similar interpretation of Koheleth's view of God's role in the universe.

1160. Von Rad, *Old Testament Theology*, 1:453–59.

1161. Von Rad, *Old Testament Theology*, 1:453.

1162. Pfeiffer, "Literature and Religion of the Apocrypha," 398.

1163. Levine, "Judaism from the Destruction," 131.

1164. Pfeiffer, "Literature and Religion of the Apocrypha," 399.

1165. Anderson, *Understanding the Old Testament*, 538.

1166. Fohrer, *Introduction*, 775n2. Russell says of "the message of the Jewish apocalyptic writers": "It pointed men away from this evil and troubled world to the great unfolding purpose of Almighty God who held the history and the destiny of the world in the hollow of his hand" (*Between the Testaments*, 94).

1167. Grabbe, *First-Century Judaism*, 73.

1168. Anderson, *Understanding the Old Testament*, 537. Russell explains that apocalypticism took root in the time of persecution under Antiochus IV . . . and thrived in the atmosphere of oppression, torture, and threat of death which prevailed in Palestine throughout that monarch's reign" (*Between the Testaments*, 95).

1169. Fohrer, *Introduction*, 775–76. Brown adds: "Our oldest illustration of biblical apocalyptic, and one indicative of its beginnings, may be dated to the Babylonian exile. That catastrophe, following the capture of Jerusalem, destruction of the Temple, and fall of the monarchy, began to call into question the possibility of salvation within history . . . To this day catastrophic times continue to revive the apocalyptic spirit among some Christians (and some Jews), as they come to believe that the times are so bad that God must soon intervene" (776, 778).

1170. The idea of a day of judgment appears most prominently in the works of the prophets. On the influence of the prophets on the apocalyptists, see Russell, *Between the Testaments*, 103–6.

1171. Anderson, *Understanding the Old Testament*, 537. Anderson adds, "God's activity in history was for the purpose of shocking his people into an awareness of their unfaithfulness to the covenant and bringing about a 'return' or repentance" (538).

1172. Russell, *Between the Testaments*, 97.

1173. Wright, *Simply Jesus*, 50–51.

1174. Parkes, *Conflict of the Church*, 22.

1175. Feldman, "Palestinian and Diaspora Judaism," 16.

1176. Russell, *Between the Testaments*, 97–98.

1177. Anderson, *Understanding the Old Testament*, 553.

1178. Witherington, *Jesus, Paul*, 244, 253. Grabbe comments on the tie between prophecy and apocalypse in *First-Century Judaism*, 77. Stone discusses the connection between God's transcendence (and remoteness) and the rise of apocalypticism in the late Second Temple period in "Eschatology, Remythologization," 246–49.

1179. Crossan, *Birth of Christianity*, 262–63. Crossan says earlier that writings concerning the so-called end-time, or eschatologies, presume "that there is something fundamentally wrong with the way of the world—not something that could easily be fixed, changed, or improved, but something so profoundly and radically wrong that only something profoundly and radically opposite could remedy it"—i.e., "something divine, transcendental, supernatural" (259-60). See also 282-83.

1180. Grabbe, *First-Century Judaism*, 84. Anderson says that the "Day of Yahweh" referred to the time at which "Yahweh would vindicate Israel by humbling her foes and raising her to a position of prestige and blessing in the world" (*Understanding the Old Testament*, 537).

1181. Sanders, *Jesus and Judaism*, 335-36. Pelikan says that in "Jewish apocalypticism, the fervid expectation that the victory of the God of Israel over the enemies of Israel, so long promised and so often delayed, was now at last to break" (*Jesus through the Centuries*, 24).

1182. Russell, *Between the Testaments*, 73. Russell particularly emphasizes the "*deep personal piety*," manifested in "good works and in service to others" encouraged by the later writers in this genre (83).

1183. On this subject in later apocalyptic works, Russell says: "In Baruch, for example, the promise is given to the Jewish people that they will see their triumph over their enemies and [that] God will restore them to their own land (2.30-35, etc.). Tobit declares that the time will come when Jerusalem will be rebuilt and the Temple will be restored to its former glory and even beyond; the tribes will assemble once again in Jerusalem and the heathen will worship the Lord as their God (13.1ff.; 14.4-7)" (84).

1184. On this point, see Anderson, *Understanding the Old Testament*, 93, 95, 103-4. On the influence of Zoroastrianism on late post-exilic apocalypticism, see 107.

1185. Anderson, *Understanding the Old Testament*, 539.

1186. Russell, *Between the Testaments*, 110-11. Russell also argues that apocalypses from this period tended to redefine the afterlife as other-worldly and universal rather than this-worldly and nationalistic (121).

1187. Cohen, *From the Maccabees*, 189. Cohen adds that the righteous would be rewarded and the wicked would be punished. But since present suffering was not intended to be a learning experience, repentance was not an option.

1188. Ramsay, *Westminster Guide*, 219.

1189. Weinfeld, "Protest against Imperialism," 182.

1190. Thoma, *Christian Theology of Judaism*, 75.

1191. Quotations from the intertestamental works quoted in this section are from Metzger and Murphy, *New Oxford Annotated Bible*.

1192. Russell, *Between the Testaments*, 79. "Like other short stories in the Old Testament, and in the Apocrypha, Tobit inculcates the principles of Judaism both by example and by precept" (Pfeiffer, "Literature and Religion of the Apocrypha," 402).

1193. Ramsay, *Westminster Guide*, 277.

1194. Herford, *Pharisees*, 191.

1195. How is it, Ezra queries, "that you have gotten for yourself one people, and to this people, whom you have loved, you have given the law that is approved by all. And now, O Lord, why have you handed the one over to the many, and dishonored the one root beyond the others, and scattered your only one among the many." In fact, the others "opposed your promises," while we "believed your covenants" (5:27-29; see also 3:32-33). Later, Ezra says to God: "[Y]ou said that it was for us that you created the world." You regarded the other nations as "nothing," but now they "domineer over us and devour us. But we your people, whom you called your firstborn, only begotten, zealous for you, and most dear, have been given into their hands. If the world has indeed been created for us, why do we not possess our world as an inheritance?" (6:55-59). Furthermore, "If you really hate your people, they should be punished at your own hands" (5:30).

1196. Ezra's essential concern is that, if everyone is sinful, then goodness appears to be unattainable, in which case punishment seems excessive or even completely unwarranted. "But what are mortals, that you are angry with them; or what is a corruptible race, that you are so bitter against it. For in truth there is no one among those who have been born who has not acted wickedly; among those who have existed there is no one who has not done wrong" (8:34-36).

Endnotes

1197. As Pfeiffer notes, Uriel makes this point in 4:1–21 and restates it in 5:21–40 ("Literature and Religion of the Apocrypha," 398).

1198. "Since God alone created the world and Adam (3:4–6), whence comes the evil impulse (4:4)? The author reverently refrained from giving the obvious answer—namely that the evil impulse was created in Adam by God" (Pfeiffer, "Literature and Religion of the Apocrypha," 400).

1199. Pfeiffer, "Literature and Religion of the Apocrypha," 400.

1200. The point is made by Metzger and Murphy, *New Oxford Annotated Bible*, 928 AP. The editors also mention Isaiah 44:6 and 60:21.

1201. Metzger and Murphy state that the first and last two chapters of 2 Esdras are later additions. On Uriel's subordinate role in the work, the editors add, "The answers given by the angel are more conventional responses to the questions than they are definitive teachings of the author of 2 Esdras" (*New Oxford Annotated Bible*, 300 AP).

1202. Pfeiffer, "Literature and Religion of the Apocrypha," 410.

1203. Pfeiffer, "Literature and Religion of the Apocrypha," 410. "Notably vivid," Pfeiffer says, "are Sirach's sketches of family life . . . and his reflections about social intercourse with friends (good and bad), dinner parties, conversation," and "sins of the tongue."

1204. This is why "[t]hose who hate reproof walk in the sinner's steps" (21:6). The author urges fathers to treat their sons in the same fashion: "He who loves his son will whip him often, so that he may rejoice at the way he turns out" (30:1).

1205. "The literary genre is generally described as protreptic, a form of didactic exhortation." The Greek influence is "indicated by the mention of the four cardinal virtues in 8.7 and the philosophical treatment of the knowledge of God in 13.1–9. There is also a wide range of Greek vocabulary in the work" (Metzger and Murphy, *New Oxford Annotated Bible*, 57 AP).

1206. Ramsay, *Westminster Guide*, 279.

1207. Russell, *Between the Testaments*, 80–81.

1208. Metzger and Murphy explain, "God chastens Israel in *mercy* and for their own good" (*New Oxford Annotated Bible*, 73 AP). Of course, Ezra in 2 *Esdras* would argue that God has punished the Jews and ignored the sins of the Gentiles.

1209. It should be noted that both "the life of wisdom" and "the law" have special meanings for a Jewish writer of the period. The word *wisdom* refers to the literary tradition that includes Proverbs and *Sirach*. The word *law* refers to the Torah.

1210. Barnstone translates "rational judgment" as "prudence" (*Other Bible*, 155). The word "piety" is added to the four virtues in 5:24. Metzger and Murphy comment, "In Xenophon's Memorabilia, and sometimes in Philo, piety or religion is the fourth virtue" (*New Oxford Annotated Bible*, 347 AP).

1211. Barnstone, *Other Bible*, 153.

1212. Feldman, "Palestinian and Diaspora Judaism," 12. Epstein says that the specific source of this information in the Jerusalem Talmud is Sanhedrin, x, 5 (*Judaism: A Historical Presentation*, 119n2). There are various definitions of the word *sect* and therefore differences of opinion as to whether the Pharisees, for example, constituted a sect. Jeremias defines the word broadly and describes the Pharisees as "men living according to the religious precepts laid down by Pharisaic scribes." They "formed *closed communities*" because they were "*members of religious associations*" (*Jerusalem*, 247). See also 251.

1213. Grabbe, *First-Century Judaism*, 53.

1214. Kugel, *Great Shift*, 332.

1215. Levine, "Judaism from the Destruction," 147.

1216. Levine, "Judaism from the Destruction," 147. Meier says that the Essenes and Christian Jews "were one expression of a larger phenomenon in Palestine at the turn of the era: Jewish eschatological groups with radical lifestyles, fervent hopes for Israel's future, and tense or hostile relations with the priestly establishment in Jerusalem" (*Marginal Jew*, 3:532).

Endnotes

1217. Glatzer, "Foreword," 7. As Wright explains, "The apocalyptic literature begins in the Old Testament with the Book of Daniel and blossoms into full flower in the 'pseudepigraphic' literature such as the Book of Enoch, IV Esdras, and the Testaments of the Twelve Patriarchs" (*Book of the Acts*, 232).

1218. Saldarini, *Pharisees, Scribes and Sadducees*, 210

1219. Saldarini, *Pharisees, Scribes and Sadducees*, 60, 210, 278. Saldarini adds later: "In bureaucratic empires and states, such as the Jewish state, religious functionaries and groups tend to emerge as partially independent political power centers. Especially in times of turmoil and change such as the period after Alexander's death, they . . . can be expected to compete for power" (94). "The Hellenistic institution of voluntary associations very probably prompted the formations of the voluntary Jewish groups, the Pharisees, Sadducees and Essenes" (68).

1220. The claim that the residents at Qumran were Essenes is almost always made at least somewhat tentatively because the evidence is not entirely convincing. For an in-depth discussion of the controversy, see Burrows, *Dead Sea Scrolls*, 279–93.

1221. Vermes, *Dead Sea Scrolls*, 16. Burrows discusses apocalypticism at Qumran in *Dead Sea Scrolls*, 260–62.

1222. Vermes, *Dead Sea Scrolls*, 14.

1223. Vermes, *Dead Sea Scrolls*, 19–25. On this subject, see *The Community Rule* (V and VI) and *The War Rule* (II).

1224. Gaster, *Dead Sea Scriptures*, 7. "They hold that by virtue of their 'enlightenment' they are members not only of the consecrated earthly brotherhood but *eo ipso* also of the Eternal Communion."

1225. Burrows says that the Essenes at Qumran based their authority to reinterpret the work of the prophets on the "new revelation given to the leader of the sect, . . . who is called 'the priest into whose heart God put wisdom to explain all the words of his servants the prophets'" (*Dead Sea Scrolls*, 247). See also 271.

1226. Vermes, *Dead Sea Scrolls*, 39. Evidently, the members regularly recited *The Community Rule* Hymn, which concludes with an emphatic confession of man's lowliness (XI). See also Hymns 1, 5, 7, 15, 18–20, and 25, which repeat almost exactly the sentiments in *The Community Rule* Hymn.

1227. Harrington, "Halakah and Religion of Qumran," 79.

1228. Burrows, *Dead Sea Scrolls*, 243–44. Burrows continues: "So important was the study and interpretation of the law for the community that a special place was set aside for the purpose, and at every hour during the day and night it was required that members of the group be present and engaged in this pursuit . . . The Manual of Discipline [i.e., *The Community Rule*] emphasizes also the necessity of sincere, wholehearted devotion" (250–51).

1229. Gaster, *Dead Sea Scriptures*, 9. Gaster returns to the mystical (and deeply spiritual) element in the Hymns of the Essenes on 120–21.

1230. Kugler, "Rewriting Rubrics," 90.

1231. VanderKam, "Apocalyptic Tradition," 134.

1232. Vermes, *Dead Sea Scrolls*, 35–37. *The Damascus Rule* also points to "the Law of Moses" as a guidebook for Essenes, "for in it all things are strictly defined" (XVI).

1233. Harrington, "Halakah and Religion of Qumran," 85. For specific examples of strictness, see 76–86.

1234. Vermes, *Dead Sea Scrolls*, 29–30. See CR VI.

1235. Kippenberg, "Christianity in the Depolitization," 265.

1236. Vermes, *Dead Sea Scrolls*, 288–89. Gaster quotes Philo as saying of the Essenes, "They do not lay up treasures of gold and silver, nor acquire real estate out of a desire for revenues, but provide themselves only with the bare necessities of life." Josephus says that "they despise riches," and Pliny says that "they live without money" (*Dead Sea Scriptures*, 249n7). Grabbe provides a

Endnotes

longer quotation from Pliny's *Natural History* (5.73): The Dead Sea community "has no women and has renounced all sexual desire, has no money, and has only palm-trees for company" (*First-Century Judaism*, 47).

1237. Vermes, *Dead Sea Scrolls*, 46.

1238. Gaster, *Dead Sea Scriptures*, 13. Later, Gaster says that "the Brotherhood at Qumran... organized itself into what may fairly be described as a 'church'" (37). Kugler similarly argues that "the group constituted itself as a temple community" and "arrogate[d] to itself priestly roles, requirements and practices... The group conceived of itself as having the atoning function reserved to the priesthood..., and it claimed for itself the holy status of priests" ("Rewriting Rubrics," 91).

1239. Vermes, *Dead Sea Scrolls*, 39. Stressing the unworthiness of humanity, the community also claimed to offer a level of knowledge of divine things available nowhere else. This being a gift of God, Vermes says, "the sect taught that even correct observance of the Rule was an act of divine grace." Thus, the recipients of God's generosity "were indebted to God for their knowledge, the infinitely valuable gift of *gnosis*, and also for the divine succour which permits a man with an inborn tendency to evil to cling faithfully and unceasingly to truth and justice" (41).

1240. Burrows comments: "Many expressions containing the Hebrew word for 'eternity' are used in the Manual of Discipline [*The Community Rule*] to indicate the destinies of the wicked and the righteous. The wicked are eternally cursed," and the "righteous are promised eternal peace, eternal light, eternal truth, eternal glory" (*Dead Sea Scrolls*, 270).

1241. Burrows, *Dead Sea Scrolls*, 272.

1242. Burrows, *Dead Sea Scrolls*, 262–63.

1243. Wright and Fuller, *Book of the Acts*, 238.

1244. Burrows, *Dead Sea Scrolls*, 336. The only other reference to God's division of human beings into two different groups is unclear: "The nature of all the children of men is ruled by these (two spirits), and during their life all the hosts of men have a portion of their divisions and walk in (both) their ways. And the whole reward for their deeds shall be, for everlasting ages, according to whether each man's portion in their two divisions is great or small" (CR IV). In Burrows's version of this passage, the word *portion* is translated *inheritance* (375).

1245. Meier discusses the differences between the two groups in *Marginal Jew*, 3:523–28.

1246. Wright says: "If there was any link between the Qumran movement and the early Church, that link must have been John the Baptist... [I]t is becoming increasingly probable that he was in some sense a 'breakaway' from Qumran. Luke's statement that he 'was in the wilderness till the day of his manifestation to Israel' (Luke 1:80) suggests that he was actually brought up as a boy in the community." Wright also emphasizes John's connection with the Jordan River, his practice of baptism, and "[h]is teaching about the Coming Age" as other indications of his tie to the Essenes at Qumran (*Book of the Acts*, 240, 242).

1247. Meier, *Marginal Jew*, 3:498–500.

1248. Kugel, *Great Shift*, 334.

1249. Gaster cites the use of these terms by both groups in *Dead Sea Scriptures*, 13–14. However, Gaster warns against carrying these similarities too far since some of the common ideas and practices also characterize not only other Jewish sects, but also other religious groups in the Near East (20–22).

1250. On his point, see Dodd, *Founder of Christianity*, 89.

1251. Meier, *Marginal Jew*, 3:502. Meier discusses these issues in more detail (and also indicates some differences) on 503–9.

1252. Gaster, *Dead Sea Scriptures*, 39–40. Vermes cites the similarities in the common meals of both groups and in the instructional purpose of both *The Community Rule* and *The Didache*, an early Christian manual (*Dead Sea Scrolls*, 47, 71).

1253. On these points, see Wright and Fuller, *Book of the Acts*, 238–40.

1254. Wright and Fuller, *Book of the Acts*, 239. On the role of the twelve, see CR VIII.

Endnotes

1255. Burrows, *Dead Sea Scrolls*, 332.

1256. Evans, "Qumran's Messiah," 143n32.

1257. Gaster, *Dead Sea Scriptures*, 333.

1258. Anderson, *Understanding the Old Testament*, 555.

1259. Sanders, "Life of Jesus," 70. For a discussion of specific instances, see 70–73. Theissen says, compared to the Essenes at Qumran, "[t]he local Christian communities were more open to the world around. They kept at less of a distance from other Jews than did the Essenes" (*Early Palestinian Christianity*, 22).

1260. Parkes notes that, although Jesus "attacked the scribes and Pharisees" for various reasons, he did not, at the same time, abrogate the Jewish law: "[H]e did not by a single word suggest that he rejected the Torah itself" (*Conflict of the Church*, 37, 41).

1261. Sanders, "Life of Jesus," 56.

1262. After summarizing Jesus' missionary activities, Meier says "that Jesus the eschatological prophet did not intend to create an elite group or esoteric sect within or apart from Israel." Rather, he wanted to announce to "the whole of God's people, the whole of Israel, . . . the coming kingdom of God" (*Marginal Jew*, 3:289). On Jesus' lack of interest in starting a new religion, see also Chilton, *Rabbi Jesus*, xxi; Lee, *Galilean Jewishness of Jesus*, 56; Parini, *Jesus*, xiii, 5, 152; Wilson, *Jesus: A Life*, x, 186; Enslin, *Christian Beginnings*, 166; Witherington, *Jesus Quest*, 39; Borg, *Meeting Jesus Again*, 22; and Cwiekowski, *Beginnings of the Church*, 6–7. Many other scholars claim that Jesus remained a Jew for his entire life, including Fredriksen, *From Jesus to Christ*, 98–100; Sanders, *Historical Figure of Jesus*, 203–4; Pelikan, *Jesus through the Centuries*, 11–13, 19; Bainton, *Early Christianity*, 9; and Robinson, *Gospel of Jesus*, 55.

1263. Collins, *Short Introduction*, 91.

1264. The Christian parallel occurs in the Gospel of Matthew: "If your brother sins against you, go and tell him his fault, between you and him alone. If he listens to you, you have gained your brother. But if he does not listen, take one or two others along with you, that every word may be confirmed, by the evidence of two or three witnesses. If he refuses to listen to them, tell it to the church; and if he refuses to listen even to the church, let him be to you as a Gentile and a tax collector" (18:15–17).

1265. Perrin, *Rediscovering the Teaching*, 90.

1266. This claim is made by Tyson, in *Study of Early Christianity*, 246. Tyson gives the date of composition as mid-second century; Ehrman suggests AD 100 or 120 (*Lost Scriptures*, 212); and Milavec argues for a mid-first-century date of origin (*Didache*, xiv).

1267. Ehrman, *Lost Scriptures*, 211. Milavec notes that "[s]imilar passages can be found in Deut 11:26–28; Prov 2:1–22; 4:18–19; Sib. Or., 8:399" (*Didache*, 46). Milavec says that "the Didache unfolds the training program calculated to irreversibly alter the habits of perception and standards of judgment of novices coming out of a pagan lifestyle." That is, it is intended "to form and transform the lives of gentiles" (39).

1268. Milavec also provides other Jewish sources for the concept of "loving God and loving neighbor." Although Tyson says that the *Didache* reveals only "a residue of Jewish Christianity" (*Study of Early Christianity*, 246), Crossan calls the manual "profoundly Jewish." He adds, "That general Jewish tradition is then taken over into Christian Jewish texts in the first common-era century" (*Birth of Christianity*, 396).

1269. Tyson, *Study of Early Christianity*, 246.

1270. Milavec, *Didache*, 88.

1271. Crossan, *Birth of Christianity*, 369.

1272. Milavec, *Didache*, 47. The quotation is from the 1964–68 edition of the *Dictionary*, edited by Gerhard Kittel and Gerhard Friedrich (3:135).

1273. Crossan, *Birth of Christianity*, 401–2.

1274. Vermes, *Dead Sea Scrolls*, 49. For a thorough discussion of this subject, see Evans, "Qumran's Messiah," 135–49; and Russell, *Between the Testaments*, 119–42.

Endnotes

1275. Quoted in VanderKam, "Apocalyptic Tradition," 113.

1276. Vermes, *Dead Sea Scrolls*, 48. "At first," Vermes says, "this figure must have been a real one, but with the passage of time it doubtless came merely to symbolize the forty years of wandering in the wilderness."

1277. Speaking of the *Didache*, Ehrman says, "The book concludes with a kind of 'apocalyptic discourse,' an exhortation to be prepared for the imminent end of the world, to be brought by the Lord coming on the wings of the sky" (*Lost Scriptures*, 212).

1278. Anderson, *Understanding the Old Testament*, 554.

1279. Russell, *Between the Testaments*, 85. Later, Russell adds that these writers "serve[d] as a bridge" from the Old Testament to the New, especially in the "belief concerning the resurrection from the dead" (145).

1280. Koch, "Apocalyptic and Eschatology," 57.

1281. Tenney, *New Testament Survey*, 89.

1282. Sanders, "Life of Jesus," 57, 80. Sanders says that "the best evidence" for his claims are "(1) the sayings that the disciples will judge the 12 tribes, (2) the disciples' debates about who will be greatest, (3) Jesus' promise to drink wine with his followers in the kingdom (Mark 14:25) and (4) the material that shows that he expected a renewed or new Temple"—all of which "converges on . . . the future establishment of God as a new order on earth" (57).

1283. Witherington, *Jesus, Paul*, 66. See also 225. On the Old Testament sources of the Beatitudes, see 134–35. Pelikan comments: "From contemporary Jewish sources we know that the proclamation of Jesus himself about the kingdom of God, as well as such proclamations of his followers about him, resounded with the accents of Jewish apocalypticism, the fervid expectation that the victory of the God of Israel over the enemies of Israel, so long promised, and so often delayed, was now at last to break" *(Jesus through the Centuries*, 23–24). See also Meeks, *Origins of Christian Morality*, 17.

1284. Vermes makes this point about the Essenes at Qumran: "It was the Teacher of Righteousness . . . who discovered that the end of time was at hand, and that all the prophecies alluding to the final age referred to the Community of the Covenant and either had been, or were about to be, fulfilled" (*Dead Sea Scrolls*, 37).

1285. Koch, "Apocalypse and Eschatology," 61.

1286. Schillebeeckx, *Jesus*, 119.

1287. Zannoni, *Jesus of the Gospels*, 154. Zannoni adds, "Some Jews also believed that a glorious Messianic Reign on earth would come as a temporal preamble to eternal life and the new creation."

1288. Dodd, *Founder of Christianity*, 46. On Jesus' adoption of what he calls "Jewish restoration eschatology," see Sanders, *Jesus and Judaism*, 335–36.

1289. Tyson, *Study of Early Christianity*, 254.

1290. Koch, "Apocalyptic and Eschatology," 60.

1291. Meeks, *Origins of Christian Morality*, 174–75.

1292. Armstrong explains: "What mattered was not what you believed but how you behaved. Religion was about doing things that changed you at a profound level." Instead of encouraging "ritual and animal sacrifice," the new religious leaders "still valued ritual, but gave it a new ethical significance and put morality at the heart of the spiritual life" (*Great Transformation*, xviii).

1293. Brown says that John the Baptist uses the Greek word *metanoia*, meaning *repentance*, in Luke 3:3. As Brown explains, "Literally the Greek verb *metanoein* (*meta* = "across, over"; *noein* = "to think") means "to change one's mind, way of thinking, outlook"; for sinners changing one's mind involves repentance" (*Introduction*, 285).

1294. Armstrong says: "In one way or another, their programs were designed to eradicate the egotism that is largely responsible for our violence, and promoted the empathic spirituality of the Golden Rule." In this way people were "introduced" to the experience of "*ecstasis*, a 'stepping out'

Endnotes

from their habitual, self-bound consciousness that enabled them to apprehend a reality that they called 'God,' *nibbana*, brahman, atman or the Way" (*Great Transformation*, 467).

1295. Bellah says, for example, that Buddhism retained the idea of Karma, which is "the belief that actions have consequences for happiness or suffering in this and future lives." However, this idea was based on the assumption not that some supreme power actively rewards and punishes but that the moral order is more or less built into the nature of things—that is, it operates automatically, as it does in the Wisdom tradition, but not in Deuteronomy. See *Religion in Human Evolution*, 532.

1296. Wright, "Faith of Israel," 370–71.

1297. Schiffman, *From Text to Tradition*, 243.

1298. Cohen, *From the Maccabees*, 5. Cohen later argues that the sects disagreed less on theology than on laws—that is, less on beliefs than on practices (53).

1299. Schillebeeckx, *Jesus*, 144.

1300. Cohen, "Judaism to the Mishnah," 215. In their urgent attempt to "follow *God's* will," says Sanders, the sects often disagreed: "Although often there was a good deal of tolerance, every disagreement was potentially serious, since to some it might reveal that certain others rejected the will of God" (*Judaism*, 4).

1301. Schiffman, *From Text to Tradition*, 103–4. Cohen comments: "The relationship of Jews and Judaism to gentiles and gentile culture is a complex topic that consists of three distinct but interrelated themes: political (to what extent should the Jews submit to foreign domination?), cultural (to what extent should the Jews absorb gentile ideas and practices?), and social (to what extent should Jews mingle and interact with gentiles?)" (*From the Maccabees*, 19).

1302. Sanders, *Judaism*, 3.

1303. Kaufmann, *Religion of Israel*, 135. Speaking of an earlier period, Kaufmann says, "The evaluation of this age as idolatrous is part of the historiosophic idealism of the Bible, according to which every national distress is the result of apostacy" (260). Later, Kaufmann adds, "It was a punishment, first for the sin of adultery, and second for moral sin; both were violations of the covenant which entailed . . . political collapse and exile" (401).

1304. Schillebeeckx, *Jesus*, ix, 141–42.

1305. Cohen, *From the Maccabees*, 194.

1306. Brueggemann, *Old Testament Theology*, 207–9. Thus, Brueggemann concludes, "It is clear that such interpretation is a primary mark and responsibility of the community that continues to engage the enduring liveliness of the God of the covenant" (210). He returns to this subject on 367–68.

1307. Cohen, *From the Maccabees*, 97.

1308. Cohen, *From the Maccabees*, 132–33. See also 154. "Since the word of God no longer was revealed through the prophets, as in the old days, the Jews turned to the exegesis of holy writ. Through interpretation, the eternal verities of the texts could be discovered and made relevant to the contemporary situation. Torah study became a fixed part of the liturgy, and a class of learned sages arose whose claim to prominence was based on their erudition and expertise in scriptural interpretation" (128).

1309. Von Rad, *Old Testament Theology*, 1:89.

1310. Vermes, *Dead Sea Scrolls*, 34.

1311. Burrows, *Dead Sea Scrolls*, 271.

1312. Grabbe, *First-Century Judaism*, 112–13.

1313. Meier, *Marginal Jew*, 1:315. According to Hannah Harrington, quoting Joseph Baumgarten, the Dead Sea Scrolls emphasize that revelation is . . ."a continuing process involving a constant search for new illuminations" ("Halakah and Religion of Qumran," 88).

1314. Russell, *Between the Testaments*, 56.

1315. Allison, *Jesus of Nazareth*, 89.

1316. Burrows, *Dead Sea Scrolls*, 247.

1317. Vermes, *Dead Sea Scrolls*, 34–35. Wright says, "Like the early Christians, [the Essenes at Qumran] believed themselves to be members of the New Covenant" (*Book of the Acts*, 238). Wright argues, however, that these Jewish groups interpreted the phrase differently: Although both "speak of the New Covenant," it was for the Essenes "a covenant of law and promise, rather than the covenant of an already inaugurated redemption" (239).

1318. Russell, *Between the Testaments*, 55, 56.

1319. Burrows, *Dead Sea Scrolls*, 331. Meier says that this sect "appealed to ongoing revelation and prophetic inspiration" (*Marginal Jew*, 3:315).

1320. Burrows, *Dead Sea Scrolls*, 250.

1321. Burrows, *Dead Sea Scrolls*, 331.

1322. Cohen, *From the Maccabees*, 112, 160. Cohen says that although there were disagreements among Jews from the monarchy onward, sectarianism did not emerge until the late Second Temple period (131). Besides the Rechabites, Cohen mentions as sects or proto-sects "the members of the exile" in the time of Ezra and the covenant signatories mentioned in Nehemiah 10 (134–36), the "chosen" referred to in Third Isaiah (136–37), the Zealots (157–59), the Samaritans (162–64), and the Theraputae in Egypt (164).

1323. Harrington, "Halakah and Religion of Qumran," 88.

1324. Vermes, *Dead Sea Scrolls*, 192. For other examples, see 173, 182, 189, 193, 197, and 199.

1325. Harrington, "Halakah and Religion of Qumran," 89. Russell makes exactly the same point in *Between the Testaments*, 56.

1326. Kee et al., *Understanding the New Testament*, 306.

1327. Burrows, *Dead Sea Scrolls*, 329.

1328. Meier, *Marginal Jew*, 3:315.

1329. Meier, *Marginal Jew*, 3:330.

1330. Bowker, *Jesus and the Pharisees*, 16. Bowker later argues that the name *Pharisee* can be understood to mean interpreter as well as separatist. The name is connected "with exegesis" because "the root letters, *prsh*, also bear the meaning 'interpret' or 'interpretation'" (19). On this point, see also Grant, *Historical Introduction*, 57.

1331. Burrows, *Dead Sea Scrolls*, 277. On this subject, see also Cohen, *From the Maccabees*, 194–200.

1332. Russell, *Between the Testaments*, 51. For this reason, according to Zannoni, the Pharisees disagreed among themselves; "[T]he movement encompassed a wide range of viewpoints and, more important, . . . heated internal disputes were quite common" (*Jesus of the Gospels*, 29).

1333. Schiffman, *From Text to Tradition*, 243, 263.

1334. Cohen, *From the Maccabees*, 64. Cohen adds, "At public services, the Torah was not only read, it was also explained and interpreted."

1335. Burrows, *Dead Sea Scrolls*, 331.

1336. Schiffman, *From Text to Tradition*, 269.

1337. Meier, *Marginal Jew*, 3:329. Flusser says, "Fundamentally, the Pharisaic philosophy of life was in line with non-sectarian universal Judaism" (*Sage from Galilee*, 44). Sanders agrees: "Pharisees shared common Judaism, not only the general spirit of zeal for God and his law, but also obedience to his commandments in everyday life. They did not invent common Judaism, nor did other people share it because of the Pharisees' influence" (*Judaism*, 450–51).

1338. Herford, *Pharisees*, 147–48.

1339. Brueggemann, *Old Testament Theology*, 51, 209; my emphasis in the first sentence quoted. Brueggemann adds: "It is recognized in this mode of Judaism that the text is open, suggestive, invitational, and requires extrapolation in order that [the] ancient text is heard as fresh summons, exhortation, and consolation" (368).

1340. Saldarini, *Pharisees, Scribes and Sadducees*, 35–36.

Endnotes

1341. Herzog, *Jesus, Justice*, 66, 109–10.

1342. Crossan, *Birth of Christianity*, 209.

1343. Mack, *Lost Gospel*, 65. Sean Freyne comments, "Those who were less well off in terms of the primary resource of land were motivated by loyalty to ancestral values and maintenance of their subsistence situation for themselves and their families," rather than the alien commercial values introduced by the Romans, principally the "burning desire to exploit resources to their full economic potential" (*Galilee, Jesus*, 158). Freyne discusses the hazards of village life on 153–59 and the problem of poverty generally on 160–61. On the dire poverty in both rural and urban Palestine, see also Stark, *Rise of Christianity*, 149–62.

1344. Kaylor, *Jesus the Prophet*, 27–31.

1345. Brandon, *Trial of Jesus*, 41. Zeitlin says: "There was a deeper basis for the growing antagonism between Jew and Roman, an antagonism rooted in different and conflicting ideologies. It was conflict between Rome and Jerusalem, between the Jewish conception of the state and the Roman conception of the state" (*Who Crucified Jesus?*, 54).

1346. Klingaman, *First Century*, 168.

1347. Wright, *Simply Jesus*, 41.

1348. See, for example, Ezra (9:10); Nehemiah (1:4–11; 9:36–37); 2 Kings (17:7); the Psalms of Solomon (2:7–9; 8:13); 2 Baruch (1:17–19; 2:2–3); 1 Esdras (1:23; 8:75–76, 86–87); and 2 Esdras (1:24–25).

1349. Parini, *Jesus*, 9–10.

1350. Dodd, *Founder of Christianity*, 16.

1351. Enslin, *Christian Beginnings*, 41–42.

1352. Witherington, *What Have They Done*, 209.

1353. Klingaman, *First Century*, 49; and Herzog, *Jesus, Justice*, 105. Horsley and Silberman refer to the "many popular demonstrations and riots" in first-century Israel (*Message and the Kingdom*, 80). Markus calls it "a perpetually troubled region" (*Christianity*, 8).

1354. Crossan, *Birth of Christianity*, 210.

1355. Schiffman, *From Text to Tradition*, 149. See also Brandon, *Trial of Jesus*, 210; and Klingaman, *First Century*, 168.

1356. Mack, *Who Wrote the Bible?*, 149. Speaking of this period, Schalit says: "In these circumstances, large sections of the people became embittered. This bitterness is reflected in IV Esdras [2 *Esdras*], whose author is perplexed at the grim punishment visited upon Israel and at the inexplicable success of Rome, who stands in his eyes, for wickedness" ("Palestine," 75).

1357. Moore, *Judaism*, II-III, 252.

1358. Kugel, *How to Read*, 8.

1359. Schiffman, *From Text to Tradition*, 137–38, 149.

1360. Burrows, *Dead Sea Scrolls*, 251, 259.

1361. Herford, *Pharisees*, 137, 111–12. See also 126, 143, 185, 194–96.

1362. Uffenheimer, "Myth and Reality," 159. Uffenheimer adds: "Last but not least, *davar* means 'word,' but the compound *devar YHVH* is not only the 'word of God'; it is a concrete force of creative and destructive power: By the word God created the world (Gen 1:3, etc.; Ps 33:6).

1363. Evans, "Comparing Judaisms," 168–69, 171.

1364. Neusner, *From Politics to Piety*, 150–52. Although Neusner warns against assuming that the Rabbis accurately and completely preserved the beliefs and practices of the Pharisees (3, 43, 121), he also makes it clear in this book that, besides establishing the foundations of modern Judaism, the Rabbis can count among their "achievements" the "preservation of the pre-70 Pharisaic tradition and development of the legal corpus which guided Judaism thenceforward" (97; see also 99, 122, 124, and 135).

1365. Evans, "Comparing Judaisms," 170; my emphasis.

1366. Bowker, *Jesus and the Pharisees*, 17.

Endnotes

1367. Herford, *Pharisees*, 126.

1368. Wright, *Simply Jesus*, 212.

1369. Bellah, *Religion in Human Evolution*, 306, 312.

1370. Tullock, *Old Testament Story*, 75, 77. Ramsay says that Deuteronomy might have been "prepared in secret by plotters"—enemies of King Manasseh—"waiting for the moment when the law of God could again be taught to God's people." In this regard, as I said in chapter 3, it might be the case that the document "was drafted to be a written constitution by which the revolutionary party hoped to establish a constitutional monarchy" (*Westminster Guide*, 63). As I noted in chapter 4, Horsley and Silberman also refer to the Covenant as a constitution (*Message and the Kingdom*, 27). Wright says that God gave the Jews "the law as the constitution of the society, which to keep meant life and peace within the nation" ("Faith of Israel," 355).

1371. Tullock, *Old Testament Story*, 79. On the differences between *apodictic* and *casuistic* laws, see Schmidt, *Old Testament Introduction*, 110–11, 114–17; and Collins, *Short Introduction*, 66–67.

1372. Brueggemann, *Old Testament Theology*, 51.

1373. Kaufmann, *Religion of Israel*, 233–34.

1374. Segal, *Rebecca's Children*, 4–5. Segal adds, "Nowhere else in the ancient Near East was there so systematic an appropriation of the concept of lawful, contractual obligation to express the relationship between a whole people and their god and consequently to define morality within society" (5).

1375. Cohen, *From the Maccabees*, 193–94. Sanders says that the Bible was read aloud weekly in the synagogue by the first century AD (*Judaism*, 198).

1376. Buber, *On Judaism*, 110. Joyce says, "The reader of the Old Testament cannot help being struck by the importance attached in ancient Israel to the social group or community." Indeed, Joyce continues, "[I]n ancient Israel the community, whether the immediate family, the extended family, the tribe or the nation itself, was of enormous importance, and . . . there was a close link between the worshipping life of Israel and this strong sense of community" ("Individual and the Community," 77–78).

1377. Kaufmann, *Religion of Israel*, 234. Schmidt says: "While older laws are addressed to the individual, Deuteronomy addresses itself to the people of God as a whole, both in sections using 'you' in the singular and those using the plural. Is this once again due to the influence of the prophets, who seldom address the individual but regularly address the people as a whole (Hos 2:2ff.; Amos 3:2; etc.)? In any case, the oneness of the people corresponds to the oneness of God: Yahweh confronts 'all Israel' (Deut 5:1; etc.)" (*Old Testament Introduction*, 132–33).

1378. Barton, *Ethics*, 11.

1379. As Buber explains, God is realized "through imitation, an *imitatio Dei*." That is, "God is man's goal, the primal being whose image he ought to strive to become, 'for God created man to be His image' (Genesis 1:27)" ("Jewish Religiosity," 83–84). Thus, "The more man realizes God in the world, the greater His reality."

1380. Buber, "Silent Question," 207; "Jewish Religiosity," 87.

1381. Cohen comments, "Many of the revolutionaries [in the first century AD] believed that the messiah would soon come to redeem Israel and that all the Jews had to do was to get the ball rolling; God and the angelic hosts would do the rest" (*From the Maccabees*, 25). Insofar as they were represented by Yohanan ben Zakkai, Cohen says, the Rabbis were opposed to this messianic expectation: Yohanan "is alleged to have left Jerusalem during the siege [of AD 66] and to have hailed Vespasian as a man destined to destroy the temple and become emperor" (24; see also 26).

1382. Cohen, *From the Maccabees*, 65. Cohen says: "The democratization of religion had as its goal the sanctification of daily life . . . The new regiment of study, prayer, ritual, and ethics was incumbent not upon some priestly or monastic elite but upon the entire community" (97; see also 165).

Endnotes

1383. *From the Maccabees*, 65.

1384. Meier says that "the Qumran community was a highly organized hierarchical society with preference given to priests and Levites ... By comparison, Jesus' movement shows a very low level of organization during his public ministry" (*Marginal Jew*, 3:530).

1385. Allison, *Jesus of Nazareth*, 86.

1386. Allison, *Jesus of Nazareth*, 502. Evans says of "the Judaisms of Qumran, the Rabbis, and the Jacobean community"—that is, the Christian Jews addressed in the Epistle of James—"we have an important cross section of Torah-observant Jewry from late antiquity" ("Comparing Judaisms," 164). Summing up his comparison of the three sects, Evans adds: "[O]ne cannot help but be struck by the extent of systemic agreement. Piety, practice, authority, heritage, sense of the rule of God—in all of these things we find significant overlap" (182). Theissen comments: "Opposition to the existing structure of government can be understood only in the light of radical theocratic intentions. All the opposition movements wanted to realize the rule of God consistently or hoped that it would be realized in miraculous fashion. All put forward an explicitly imminent eschatology" (*Early Palestinian Christianity*, 62).

1387. Burrows, *Dead Sea Scrolls*, 332.

1388. Schillebeeckx, *Jesus: An Experiment*, 144. Schillebeeckx adds: "The notion of the 'Holy Remnant' was in its hey-day. Despite an irreligious 'we are the holy remnant' mentality this movement—in the constellation of that time a fairly 'conservative' one—was none the less motivated by a genuinely Jewish and religious impulse, and in particular a zealous commitment to the one and only God, Yahweh, to Jerusalem and to its Temple" (118). On the "separation" of the Pharisees, see Schiffman, *From Text to Tradition*, 104; and Burrows, *Dead Sea Scrolls*, 277.

1389. Theissen, *Early Palestinian Christianity*, 85.

1390. Schillebeeckx, *Jesus: An Experiment*, 218.

1391. Dodd, *Founder of Christianity*, 84, 86, 87.

1392. Meier, *Marginal Jew*, 3:229.

1393. Theissen, *Early Palestinian Christianity*, 77. "Discussion of the true Torah and its interpretation," Theissen adds, "points to a crisis of identity within Judaism."

1394. For parallels in "matters of ethics and piety" between the Essenes at Qumran and the Christian Jews addressed in the Epistle of James, see Evans, "Comparing Judaisms," 165–66.

1395. Vermes asks, speaking of Jesus, "[W]hat in the last resort was the principle that he adopted, and himself embodied, in his endeavours to live to perfection as a son of God? The reply must be ... the *imitatio dei*, the imitation of God." Vermes quotes Leviticus 19:2 and its echoes in Matthew 5:48 and Luke 6:36 (*Jesus in His Jewish Context*, 47–48).

1396. Dodd comments: "Considered as regulations for the conduct of daily life these maxims are utopian. They were not intended as such regulations. Yet they were meant to be taken seriously ... It is no time for the nicely calculated less and more of 'practical' morality. It is time for total commitment. There is no limit to what is demanded of the children of God" (*Founder of Christianity*, 66–67). Flusser says, "In those days it was obviously very difficult for people to rise up to the heights of Jesus' commandment" (*Sage from Galilee*, 61).

1397. Vermes, *Jesus in His Jewish Context*, 49.

1398. On Jesus' "intensification of norms" and parallels among other Jewish sects at the time, see Theissen, *Early Palestinian Christianity*, 78–87.

1399. Sanders, "Life of Jesus," 65, 67.

1400. Sanders, "Life of Jesus," 66. Sanders questions the attribution of these ideas to Jesus. First, "The legal perfection required in Matthew 5:17–20 is counter to the theme that Jesus was not overly strict with regard to the law." Second, "The ascetic tone is quite different from Jesus' reputation as one who ate and drank, and who associated with toll gatherers and sinners (Matthew 11:19)." Sanders mentions Qumran as an example of "a small disciplined community" on 67–68.

1401. Crossan is quoting Theissen's *Social Reality and the Early Christians* (1982) in *Birth of Christianity*, 278. Elsewhere, Theissen comments: "The intensification of the commandments against killing and against adultery makes impossible demands on every man: aggressive dispositions and erotic fascination cannot be made subject to human wills. Anyone who is asking that is asking for the impossible" (*Early Palestinian Christianity*, 106).

1402. Theissen, *Early Palestinian Christianity*, 8–15.

1403. Theissen, *Early Palestinian Christianity*, 115. Theissen identifies the "social interactions" as "the problems of the common life of masters and slaves, men and women, parents and children"—all of them addressed in the Pauline and deutero-Pauline epistles. Later, Theissen comments: "Christianity became more and more the social cement of the totalitarian state of late antiquity. The vision of love and reconciliation faded" (119).

1404. Vermes, *Dead Sea Scrolls*, 92–94.

1405. Harrington, "Halakah and Religion of Qumran," 89.

1406. Russell, *Between the Testaments*, 56.

1407. Milavec, *Didache*, 81. I have used Ehrman's translation of 16:5 in *Lost Scriptures*, 217.

1408. Horsley and Silberman comment, "At precisely the same time and in the same small province of Judea, another group [i.e., the Jerusalem Christians] who condemned the evils of Roman society and opposed the present priestly leadership of the Temple had organized themselves into a community in which admission to full membership entailed handing over all individual earnings and private property" (*Message and the Kingdom*, 102).

1409. Meier, *Marginal Jew*, 3:518. "In typical apocalyptic style, Jesus stresses that two competing forces, the divine and the demonic, are struggling to control human hearts" (517).

1410. Meier, *Marginal Jew*, 3:520. Meier continues, "[T]he historical Jesus did take a strong stance against excessive concern about or trust in money and property."

1411. Thus, on the one hand, Meier says, Jesus' "peremptory call to his disciples to follow him physically on his itinerant ministry naturally tended to detach them from their work, homes, and property for an indefinite future." On the other hand, however, Meier adds, "Jesus did not demand that all those who adhered to him in a spiritual sense, all those who in some way believed in him or accepted his message, had to forsake their livelihoods and homes or had to sell all they had and give it to the poor" (*Marginal Jew*, 3:520). Of course, it must be said that not all Essenes joined the Qumran community, just as not all Christian Jews became *full-fledged* members of the Jerusalem church insofar as it was a sharing community. Meier explores the issue in more detail on 512–15.

1412. Vermes, *Dead Sea Scrolls*, 30. Burrows says: "A spirit of love and unity was cultivated in both [communities], though their attitudes toward those outside their own number were conspicuously different. The fellowship of the members found radical expression in the Jerusalem church, as in the community of Qumran, in the sharing of property" (*Dead Sea Scrolls*, 333).

1413. Vermes, *Dead Sea Scrolls*, 30.

1414. Jeremias, *Jerusalem*, 126–30. Bainton, says: "With regard to property the Church never espoused a thoroughgoing communism of production and consumption. There was a sharing of goods and a drastic philanthropy for the benefit not only of fellow Christians but also of the heathen, especially in times of calamity" (*Early Christianity*, 56). Conzelmann and Lindemann argue that "nothing is said of a general and compulsory, mandated commonality of property" (*Interpreting the New Testament*, 345). The authors add: "In principle, such communistic communities were feasible in the Judaism of that time, as the Qumran community shows. However, this does not yet constitute evidence of a similar tendency in the Christian church. On the contrary, it is possible that the original account was given an idealistic coloration in dependence upon such models." According to Meeks and Maguire, although the Christian Jews in Jerusalem did not require everyone to give up everything and deposit it in a common fund, they nevertheless expressed an ideal that remained important to the Jesus movement for many years. Maguire calls Luke's description of the economic system established by the Christian Jews in Acts of the Apostles "more symbol than fact," but an ideal that was "pressed relentlessly" by both Jews and Christians (*Moral Core*, 135). See also Meeks, *Origins of Christian Morality*, 129; and the first letter of John: "[W]hoso hath

Endnotes

this world's goods, and seeth his brother have need, and shutteth up his bowels of compassion from him, how dwelleth the love of God in him? My little children, let us not love in word, neither in tongue: but in deed and in truth" (3:17–18).

1415. Capper, "Palestinian Cultural Context," 323–56.

1416. Enslin, *Christian Beginnings*, 160. Regarding Jesus' claim that a wealthy man cannot get into the kingdom of God, Enslin says, "Attempts have been made to tone down this clear word . . . , but the evangelists give no support to this attempt to side-step an unpleasant teaching."

1417. Bauer, *Orthodoxy and Heresy*, 124.

1418. After warning initiates to "[a]bstain from fleshly passions" and stating the demands for generosity that also appear in the Sermon on the Mount, *The Didache* establishes the rules typical of the contemporary sharing communities at Qumran and in Jerusalem: "How fortunate is the one who gives according to the commandment, for he is without fault. For if anyone receives because he is in need, he is without fault. But the one who receives without a need will have to testify why he received what he did, and for what purpose . . . Do not be one who reaches out your hands to receive but draws them back from giving. If you acquire something with your hands, give it as a ransom for you sins. Do not doubt whether to give, nor grumble while giving. For you should recognize the good paymaster of the reward. Do not shun a person in need, but share all things with your brother and do not say that anything is your own. For if you are partners in what is immortal, how much more in what is mortal?" (*Didache*, 1:5, 4:5–8, in Ehrman, *Lost Scriptures*, 212–13).

1419. Justin Martyr, *1 Apol.* 14:2–3. Everyone in need was cared for, including orphans, widows, sojourners, the sick, and prisoners (67:5–6).

1420. Horsley and Silberman, *Message and the Kingdom*, 142,

1421. On Chrysostom, see Maguire, *Moral Core*, 154, 156. On Ambrose, see Lovejoy, "Communism of St. Ambrose," 296–307.

1422. Crossan, *Birth of Christianity*, 472; my emphasis.

1423. Horsley and Silberman, *Message and the Kingdom*, 104.

1424. Meeks, *Origins of Christian Morality*, 106. See also MacMullen, *Christianizing the Roman Empire*, 54.

1425. Maguire, *Moral Core*, 133.

1426. Gaster, *Dead Sea Scriptures*, 20. Burrows makes a similar point in *Dead Sea Scrolls*, 339.

1427. Meier, *Marginal Jew*, 3:298–99. Meier adds that the Pharisees "mutate[d] into the early rabbinic movement." As Schiffman says, "Pharisaism would become Rabbinic Judaism, the basis for all subsequent Jewish life and civilization" (*From Text to Tradition*, 107).

1428. Neusner, *From Politics to Piety*, 11.

1429. Russell, *Between the Testaments*, 50–51.

1430. Meier, *Marginal Jew*, 3:330. The battle was difficult, however, given the extent to which, as Neusner says, "Judaism . . . had behind it a long period of thoroughgoing Hellenization—Hellenization modified, but not thrown off, by the revival of nationalism" and other conservative influences (*From Politics to Piety*, 10).

1431. Herford, *Pharisees*, 143, 111.

1432. Meier, *Marginal Jew*, 3:338.

1433. Bowker, *Jesus and the Pharisees*, 15–16.

1434. Bowker, *Jesus and the Pharisees*, 15–16.

1435. Neusner, *From Politics to Piety*, 146. Neusner continues, "At first only a small minority of the Jewish people obeyed the law as taught by the Pharisaic party,=." However, after the conclusion of the Revolt of AD 66, the Roman government gave the Pharisees an "opportunity to reenter the political arena" by "reconstitut[ing] limited self-government among the Jewish people through loyal and nonseditious agents" (146–48). Under these circumstances, Pharisaic influence (which, Bowker notes, was already "strong") expanded (*Jesus and the Pharisees*, 23).

1436. Neusner, *From Politics to Piety*, 98.

1437. Neusner, *Mishnah: Social Perspectives*, x.
1438. Schiffman, *From Text to Tradition*, 243.
1439. Herford, *Pharisees*, 144, 143.
1440. Herford, *Pharisees*, 185.
1441. Cornfeld, *Archeology of the Bible*, 246.
1442. Neusner, *From Politics to Piety*, 47.
1443. Reicke, *New Testament Era*, 159.
1444. Meier, *Marginal Jew*, 3:330.
1445. Herford, *Pharisees*, 144.
1446. Glatzer, "Foreword" to *Pharisees*, 4. Tenney says, "They were the separatists, or Puritans of Judaism, who withdrew from all evil associations and who sought to give complete obedience to every precept of the oral and written law" (*New Testament Survey*, 110).
1447. Herford, *Pharisees*, 118, 184.
1448. Herford, *Pharisees*, 138. Herford adds: "The Prophets (including, of course, Moses) gave the moral lead which made the religion of Israel a new thing, and not a mere development of Canaanite nature-worship. The Pentateuch contains various more or less definite expressions of the moral teaching of the Prophets, in the form of divine commands" (139).
1449. Herford, *Pharisees*, 142. "There was, at least in the loftier minds, a real perception of God through the inward vision of the soul, and not merely a blind subjection to the letter of a command" (139). Herford discusses the Jewish concept of God as Father on 151–52. Perrin says, less grandly, "The Pharisees strove to maintain a balance between man's duty to strive to earn pardon and his inability to attain it except as a gracious gift from God (*Rediscovering the Teaching*, 91).
1450. Herford, *Pharisees*, 165, 140, 167. Herford discusses repentance—*teshubah*—as "one of the great words of the Pharisaic theology" on 167–68. Vermes says, "Rabbinic thought is rich in interpretation of this theme that the lover and worshipper of God models himself on him" (*Jesus in His Jewish Context*, 47). Vermes provides examples on 47–48.
1451. Wright says, "The Pharisees were uninterested in it, for their hopes for the future . . . took a purely historical, this-worldly form" (*Book of the Acts*, 231).
1452. Herford, *Pharisees*, 191. Furthermore, Herford says, "The Pharisees recognised the fact that prophecy had come to an end, and drew their own conclusion from that fact" (180).
1453. Russell, *Between the Testaments*, 72. Grabbe says, "The apocalypticists," among other groups, "disappeared after 70, not always straight away but with time" (*First-Century Judaism*, 118).
1454. Wills, "Daniel: Introduction," 1659–60.
1455. Citing Daniel 12:1–13, Wills says, "Whether bodily resurrection or some form of spiritual resurrection is intended is not stated. This is the only certain biblical reference to this doctrine, a doctrine that became central in Christian theology and remained a strong current in Judaism as well. It was a tenet of belief for the Pharisees" (1665).
1456. Meier, *Marginal Jew*, 3:382n148. In support of this point, Meier cites works by James H. Charlesworth, John J. Collins, and Albert I. Baumgarten.
1457. Sanders, *Judaism*, 272.
1458. On this point, see Pfeiffer, "Literature and Religion of the Apocrypha," 401, 403–4.
1459. Russell, *Between the Testaments*, 57.
1460. Thus, Leon Epsztein comments: "Thanks to the discoveries of the last two centuries, it is possible to demonstrate from the texts the existence of a general aspiration towards justice extending over the various regions of the ancient Near East . . . The quest for justice which appears in Israel has analogies to that which appeared among its neighbors" (quoted in Crossan, *Birth of Christianity*, 184).
1461. On this subject, see Horsley, *Covenant Economics*, 6–12.

Endnotes

1462. Meeks, *Origins of Christian Morality*, 43. Herzog comments, "There was no mutually beneficial reciprocity between rulers and ruled" (*Jesus, Justice*, 98). Borg refers to the kind of society maintained by the Romans as a preindustrial agricultural "*imperial* domination system" (*Jesus: Uncovering the Life*, 85).

1463. On this subject, see Peters, *Harvest of Hellenism*, 526.

1464. Conzelmann and Lindemann, *Interpreting the New Testament*, 118.

1465. Grant, *Historical Introduction*, 249.

1466. Mattingly, *Roman Imperial Civilisation*, 63.

1467. Davies, *Invitation*, 15.

1468. Witherington, *Jesus Quest*, 23. See also Brandon, *Trial of Jesus*, 34.

1469. Cohen, *From the Maccabees*, 2. As Cohen notes, "[T]he Jews of both the diaspora and the land of Israel lived almost exclusively under foreign domination" from the Babylonian invasion in 586-87 BC to "the establishment of the modern state of Israel" (19). However, "[t]hey seldom rebelled, even when provoked" (21).

1470. Grabbe, *First-Century Judaism*, 69. "This began a tradition of resistance to foreign rule which then continued as a powerful current through the next three centuries." Unfortunately, Cohen notes, "Several times in antiquity, the Jews tried to make their dream into reality, but only once with any degree of success" (*From the Maccabees*, 49; see also 99). According to Goodman, the Maccabees were "the only known case of the adherents of an eastern religion opposing by force the encroachment of Greek culture in their native land" (*History of Judaism*, 95).

1471. Brown, *Introduction*, 57.

1472. Russell, *Between the Testaments*, 28.

1473. Grant, *Historical Introduction*, 255.

1474. Wylen, *Jews in the Time*, 52. Speaking generally about Second Temple Judaism, Wylen says, "Jews were prepared to lay down their lives rather than serve idols. They opposed syncretism—that is, they refused to identify Jewish worship with other peoples' worship of their gods." According to Wylen, Jews at this time began to recite the Shema twice daily: "Hear, O Israel, the Lord is our God, the Lord is One" (82).

1475. Russell, *Between the Testaments*, 29.

1476. Sanders, *Judaism*, 18.

1477. Grant, *Historical Introduction*, 268-69.

1478. Quoted in Borg and Crossan, *Last Week*, 43. Josephus' account is in *Jewish Antiquities*, 17.149-67.

1479. Russell, *Between the Testaments*, 37.

1480. Schalit, "Herod and His Successors," 37. Schalit says later: "This angry violence of the tyrant greatly embittered the people of Judea and intensified the hatred they felt for him. Herod reacted to this with pitiless severity. Secret police infiltrated everywhere and sought out enemies of the regime throughout the whole country. Suspects were arrested and taken to such fortresses as Hyrcania where they disappeared for ever" (40).

1481. Grant, *Historical Introduction*, 268-69.

1482. Borg comments: "The two hundred years from the imposition of Roman rule in 63 BCE until the last major Jewish revolt in 132-35 CE were marked by periodic outbursts of armed resistance. These outbreaks would not have happened if there were not a significant number of Jews sufficiently desperate and resentful to take up arms against Rome and its client rulers. The path of violence was never far beneath the surface" (*Jesus: Uncovering the Life*, 227). In *Last Week*, Borg and Crossan say that the first century AD "witnessed thousands of such executions" as the crucifixion of Jesus (190).

1483. Quoted in Russell, *Between the Testaments*, 41.

1484. Crossan, *Birth of Christianity*, 284. Crossan comments: "Within the first four hundred years of foreign control, under the Persian empire and its Greek replacements, there was only a single revolt, at the very end of that period. But within the first two hundred years of Roman control there were three major revolts" (177).

1485. Grant, *Historical Introduction*, 271.

1486. Crossan, *Birth of Christianity*, 284–85. Peters explains that Caligula thought of himself as a god, the brother of Jupiter, and meant for his statue to be worshiped in religious shrines throughout the empire. "The governor held off and fortunately Gaius [Caligula] died before he could force the issue further" (*Harvest of Hellenism*, 510).

1487. Grant, *Historical Introduction*, 269–72.

1488. Tabor, *Jesus Dynasty*, 300.

1489. Neusner, *Judaism in the Beginning*, 20. Neusner adds: "The Jerusalemites fought with amazing courage, despite unbelievable odds. Since they lost, later generations looked for their sin, for none could believe that the omnipotent God would permit his Temple to be destroyed for no reason."

1490. Evans, "Context, family and formation," 13. On this point, see also Brown, *Harvest of Hellenism*, 516.

1491. Goodman, *History of Judaism*, 34, 38.

1492. Ruether, *Faith and Fratricide*, 40.

1493. Oesterley and Robinson, *Introduction to the Books*, 222. The authors add, "[T]he fact remains that, but for them, as far as our records of humanity can teach us, the two lines of human development would have remained apart, and the gulf between them would have steadily widened."

1494. Wilson, *Jesus: A Life*, 8–9.

1495. Brueggemann, *Old Testament Theology*, 50.

1496. Moore, *Judaism*, 1:122–23.

1497. Finkelstein and Silberman, *Bible Unearthed*, 285, 287. Schmidt says, "Deuteronomy seeks to use the unity of the people of God as the basis for conclusions regarding the social life of human beings." That is, "[t]he relationship between the brethren to one another likewise yields social consequences" (*Old Testament Introduction*, 134).

1498. Finkelstein and Silberman, *Bible Unearthed*, 318.

1499. Miller, *Religion of Ancient Israel*, 209).

1500. Bellah, *Religion in Human Evolution*, 282, 308, 313. Bellah explains: "By the eighth century the ferocity of the Assyrian conquest, involving wholesale destruction and deportation, roused both fear and desperate desire to resist in all the Levantine states" (306).

1501. Bellah, *Religion in Human Evolution*, 305–7, 315, 313. What Bellah calls "[t]he enormous creativity of Israelite religion" in the works of both the early prophets and the Pentateuch "must be seen, then, as in part responses to the Assyrian challenge" (307).

1502. As Ramsay says, "Deuteronomy . . . over and over called for that social justice which prophets such as Amos and Micah and Isaiah had proclaimed as the essence of the will of God" (*Westminster Guide*, 63). Fox says of Deuteronomy, "It is an old and compelling view that the most distinctive themes connect with the prophets whom scripture locates in the northern kingdom" (*Unauthorized Version*, 66).

1503. Wilson, *Jesus: A Life*, 8–9. Horsley says: "Israelite society thus required ways to apply and implement the principles of Israel's Covenant with Yahweh that aimed to protect people's inalienable right to their ancestral lands." The Covenant also "protected the economic rights of all to an adequate living" (*Covenant Economics*, 44).

1504. Gottschalk, "Prophetic Thinking in the Nonprophetic Society," 51.

1505. Geller, "Religion of the Bible," 2033.

1506. Maguire, *Moral Core*, 54.

1507. Brueggemann, *Old Testament Theology*, 381.

1508. Levenson, *Love of God*, 182.

1509. Levenson, *Love of God*, 45, 47. Brueggemann explains in greater detail: "'The God who will be unrivaled in Israel is the God who wills and orders a viable and sustainable community' (Exodus 20:12). This cryptic set of commands sets rigorous limits on exploitative abuse of the neighbor, and guarantees that the neighbor who cannot defend life or property is defended and guaranteed by divine sanction . . . This neighborly ethic is, of course, decisive of Old Testament faith. We may see it worked out in some detail in the particular commands of Deuteronomy 21–24 in which rules are provided for the protection of the vulnerable and the economically needy" (*Old Testament Theology*, 46).

1510. Brueggemann, *Old Testament Theology*, 46–47.

1511. Buber, *On Judaism*, 119. Earlier, Buber says that the later prophets "repudiated the 'abomination' of the sacrificial cult, demanding true service of God," by which he means the establishment of "justice" (*On Judaism*, 89).

1512. Brueggemann, *Old Testament Theology*, 49, 51.

1513. Anderson, *Understanding the Old Testament*, 56, 58, 70. Anderson quotes Deuteronomy 8:2–3: "You shall remember all the way which Yahweh your God has led you these forty years in the wilderness, that he might humble you, testing you to know what was in your heart, whether you would keep his commandments or not." This is where the Israelites learned that "man does not live by bread alone, but that man lives by everything that proceeds out of the mouth of Yahweh."

1514. Anderson, *Understanding the Old Testament*, 317–18. Muilenburg says, similarly, along with the liberation from Egypt, "the covenant itself with its tremendous demands of monolatry, imageless worship, and *the elemental commands for the cohesion and purity of the social solidarity* . . . stand as the pillars which uphold the faith" ("History of the Religion," 305; my emphasis).

1515. Kugel, *Bible as It Was*, 522.

1516. Kugel, *Bible as It Was*, 523.

1517. Finkelstein and Silberman, *Bible Unearthed*, 318; my emphasis.

1518. Borg, *Reading the Bible Again*, 70. Borg adds, "Living in a semi-arid climate, the ancient Hebrew pictured paradise as a green and bountiful garden filled with streams of flowing water."

1519. Von Rad, *Old Testament Theology*, 1:224.

1520. Barton, *History of the Bible*, 72–73.

1521. Buber, *Writings of Martin Buber*, 164.

1522. Von Rad, *Old Testament Theology*, 1:219–26, 230.

1523. Von Rad, *Old Testament Theology*, 1:198–99, 201, 225. Bruce C. Birch and his fellow writers comment: "The prominence of stipulations—the Deuteronomist's law code—might give the impression that the Deuteronomist represents a religion of overly refined and arid legalism. Such could not be further from the case," as the command to "love the LORD your God with all your heart" (6:5–7) suggests. The covenant relationship represents a religion of the heart and family, quite simply, a person's entire being" (*Theological Introduction*, 298–99).

1524. Barton, *History of the Bible*, 79–80. According to Birch et al., "Obedience is seen not as a response to the law as law, but as a response to the story of all that God has done" (*Theological Introduction*, 162). After all, Levenson says, God's "unprovoked love for the vassal . . . was manifested in the benefits the LORD conveyed on Israel before entering into the covenant of Sinai with them." In this way, God "holds a perpetual claim upon the specific people he has liberated," whose "service . . . is the condign response to the generosity of the liberator. It is their response of love to his antecedent love for them" (*Love of God*, 61). On the subject of gratitude, see also xiv–xv, 1.

1525. Barton, *History of the Bible*, 81.

1526. Birch et al., *Theological Introduction*, 81–84. In other words, according to Birch et al., "those who wrote Deuteronomy understood Israelites to be capable of living in a covenant relationship" (299). Thus, "[t]he statutes are more witnesses to the will of God than prescriptions with statutory force. The hortatory rhetoric in particular suggests that these statutes constitute but one source for a more fundamental agenda" (145). For this reason, "the people commit themselves more to God than to specific laws" (148). "It is important to keep in mind that 'obedience' has to do with a certain quality of life that is rooted in an elemental relationship of love, loyalty, and gratitude" (204).

1527. Von Rad, *Old Testament Theology*, 1:374–75, 196. See also 381.

1528. Birch et al., *Theological Introduction*, 153, 35–36.

1529. Muilenburg, "History of the Religion," 300.

1530. Birch et al., *Theological Introduction*, 45, 127, 161. "This motivation is important because . . . it makes clear that obedience of the law is not a means to right relationship with God. As the introduction to the Decalogue shows (Exod 20:2), these statutes are given to those already redeemed" (162).

1531. Birch et al., *Theological Introduction*, 186–87, 128. On "the affective dimension" of covenantal love, see Levenson, *Love of God*, 22–27. Levenson concludes that "in part because covenant is based on a more primal relationship" than is often assumed, which is "one of kin, and draws on its idiom, the affective dimension of the language is no mere metaphor" (29).

1532. Schiffman, *From Text to Tradition*, 241.

1533. Brueggemann, *Old Testament Theology*, 45, 48. Brueggemann says that God's demands in the Covenant Code "reflect a simple face-to-face agricultural community that must manage concrete realistic disputes and contested claims" (52).

1534. Rivkin, *Hidden Revolution*, 15.

1535. Wylen, *Jews in the Time*, 144.

1536. Rivkin, *Hidden Revolution*, 242–43.

1537. Rivkin, *Hidden Revolution*, 27.

1538. Meier, *Marginal Jew*, 3:299.

1539. Neusner, *Mishnah: Social Perspectives*, 79–81. Neusner says that in the Mishnah God is "extrinsic to the world-order" (79).

1540. Kugler, *Great Shift*, 336–37; my emphasis. Redford sums up the post-Revolt mood this way: "One might almost say that 'God was dead'" (*Egypt, Canaan, and Israel*, 471).

1541. Pawlikowski, "Jewish Covenant," 117; my emphasis.

1542. Birch et al., *Theological Introduction*, 37. In these early chapters of the Bible, Birch et al. say, God appears "as sole Creator of a good and purposeful world [and] the . . . human creatures in a cocreative role" (40).

1543. Friedman, "Hiding of the Face," 215–16.

1544. Friedman, "Hiding of the Face," 219.

1545. Kugel, *Great Shift*, 289. Kugel says that even in the most pessimistic sounding psalms "it is God's presence, rather than existence that is being denied . . . Only toward the end of biblical times did faith in God's very existence begin to emerge as a central item; those who did not perceive God's presence on their own were now urged to believe, in any case, to 'have faith'" (347n1).

1546. Friedman comments: "One by one the apparent signs of Yahweh's immanence in the world are disappearing. In a fascinating juxtaposition, the portrayal of the last of the disappearing signs, Elijah at Carmel, is followed by the portrayal of Elijah at Horeb. Again, we see a lone prophet on Horeb/Sinai, but Elijah's experience there is a reversal of that of Moses." God asks Elijah twice why he is there and sends him in search of Elisha. "At precisely the narrative juncture at which divine appearances, cloud and glory, angels, and public miracles cease, comes this account of the deity's refusal to appear as before. Yahweh never again speaks to a king or to the people" ("Hiding of the Face," 218).

1547. Kugel, *Great Shift*, 188–89. Kugel reviews the changes I discussed in the preceding paragraph on 164–68.

1548. Friedman, "Hiding of the Face," 220.

1549. Kugel, *Great Shift*, 297.

1550. Wright, "Faith of Israel," 367.

Endnotes

1551. Von Rad, *Old Testament Theology*, 1:69–70. Friedman argues that, given the number of editors and redactors who worked on the Bible over its centuries of composition and compilation, the so-called decline of miracles had to have been a consequence of their current (and, collectively, steadily changing) understanding of God rather than an increasing inattention to the steady flow of supernatural events: "That is, it cannot be simply explained as the result of early authors portraying theophanies and miracles more frequently than later authors. Apparently, no matter when an author lived he or she would picture the most distant times as ages of miracle, and more recent times as less so" ("Hiding of the Face," 220).

1552. Von Rad, *Old Testament Theology*, 1:48–56.

1553. Friedman, "Hiding of the Face," 217.

1554. Goodman, *History of Judaism*, 75, 211–12.

1555. Cohen, *From the Maccabees,* 127. Von Rad says that "in the early years of the post-exilic period, prophecy has already come to its end—from then on it apparently disintegrated as an order in its own right" (*Old Testament Theology*, 1:100).

1556. Kugel, *Great Shift*, 231. Kugel also cites two passages from the rabbinical writings claiming that "prophecy simply had ceased to exist" (232).

1557. Geller, "Religion of the Bible," 2025.

1558. Geller, "Religion of the Bible," 2032.

1559. Kugel, *Great Shift*, 253–54. Cohen makes the same point in *From the Maccabees*, 188. Cohen also notes not only that Zechariah predicts the future end of prophecy but that he himself receives God's message through an angelic intermediary on whom he depends for interpretations of "fantastic and unreal visions" (191).

1560. Kugel, *Great Shift*, 188.

1561. Irwin, "Literature of the Old Testament," 182.

1562. Kaufmann, *Religion of Israel*, 447–48. Redford says, "The events of 586, considered at the time as but a stage in the annihilation of the independent states of the southern Levant, were to prove a major watershed in the history of the Hebrews" (*Egypt, Canaan, and Israel*, 470).

1563. Goodman, *History of Judaism*, 242.

1564. Cohen, *From the Maccabees,* 82.

1565. Kugel, *Great Shift*, 244.

1566. Muilenburg, "History of the Religion," 330.

1567. Rivkin, "Revealing and Concealing God," 155.

1568. Friedman, "Hiding of the Face," 221.

1569. Von Rad, *Old Testament Theology*, 1:71–72.

1570. Kugel, *Great Shift*, 316. Stern says: "In the earlier books of the Bible, the root [i.e., the Hebrew *d-r-sh*, from which the word *midrash* is derived] is used to refer to the act of seeking out God's will (e.g., Gen. 25.22; Exod. 18.15), particularly through consulting a figure like Moses or a prophet or another type of oracular authority. By the end of the biblical period, the locus for that search appears to have settled on the text of the Torah where, it was now believed God's will for the present moment was to be found" ("Midrash and Jewish Interpretation," 1863).

1571. Geller, "Religion of the Bible," 2031.

1572. Cohen, *From the Maccabees*, 168.

1573. Kaufmann, *Religion of Israel*, 447; my emphasis.

1574. Kugel, *How to Read*, 9–10. Kugel adds: "It is difficult to overstate the importance of this change. From now on, the books in Israel's sacred library would have a new role: these books may have been written long ago, but they were not just about things that happened in the past. Carefully analyzed, the words of these ancient texts might reveal a message about how people ought to arrange their affairs now and in the future" (10).

1575. Brettler, "Canonization of the Bible," 2073, 2075. Brettler notes, however, that "although we may speak of 'the' canon forming in the first century CE, there was a certain amount of flexibility or variability around the fringes." The status of several works continued to be debated in various Jewish communities.

1576. Geller, "Religion of the Bible," 2033, 2029.

1577. Kaufmann, *Religion of Israel*, 448. For quite a different view of Jewish Scripture, see Rivkin, who argues that just as the age of prophecy ended, so did the idea that the Law was unchangeable: "[T]he God of the immutable written Law gave way to the God of the open-ended oral Law" ("Revealing and Concealing God," 156). Rivkin explains his point on 156–61.

1578. Stone, "Eschatology, Demythologization," 244.

1579. Cohen, *From the Maccabees*, 184, 171. "In Jeremiah's time, Torah, counsel, and the word of God were sought from living people; in Ben Sira's time, they were sought through the study of books" (179).

1580. Cohen, *From the Maccabees*, 204.

1581. Cohen, *From the Maccabees*, 184, 186. More specifically, Cohen adds, "[T]he sense that they could not compete with their past, because their ancestors were giants but they themselves were but dwarfs, impelled them to express their literary creativity in new forms: apocalypses, testaments, romances, histories, poems, hymns, oracles, translations," etc. (204).

1582. Kaufmann, *Religion of Israel*, 448.

1583. Kaufmann, *Religion of Israel*, 448.

1584. Kugel, *How to Read*, 683–84.

1585. Kugel, *Great Shift*, 197.

1586. Cohen, *From the Maccabees*, 196; my emphasis.

1587. Muilenburg, "History of the Religion," 326. Muilenburg adds later, "'Moses' addressed Israel with such an emotional appeal and urgency seldom equaled elsewhere in the Bible. Deuteronomy, which contains the 'Book of the Covenant,' became sacred par excellence. It was the first book to become authoritative, and the movement toward canonicity finds in it its *fons et origo*" (332).

1588. Geller, "Religion of the Bible," 2032.

1589. Bellah, *Religion in Human Evolution*, 321, 314; my emphasis. Bellah says later, "A God who is finally outside society and the world provides the point of reference from which all existing presuppositions can be questioned, a basic criterion for the axial transition" (322).

1590. Bellah, *Religion in Human Evolution*, 322–23. Bellah says that this was "an idea of God unique in the world and with enormous historical implications" (321). Elman comments, "Scripture, according to the Rabbis, is the abiding evidence of God's presence and continued love for His people." However, the Rabbis reserved the right to interpret Scripture, believing that "a reasoned argument has the force of a scriptural decree (*b. Pes.* 21b, *Ketub.* 22a, *B. K.* 46b, *Hul.* 114b, *Nid.* 25a)" ("Classical Rabbinic Interpretation," 1861–62).

1591. Cohen, *From the Maccabees*, 63–64.

1592. Parkes, *Conflict of the Church*, 35–36.

1593. Brown, *Introduction*, 777. Brown says that the style and content of later apocalyptic writings can be traced to Ezekiel, whose visions are characterized by "extravagant imagery" and whose "idealistic anticipation of the New Israel virtually go[es] beyond history and overlap[s] into apocalyptic style and anticipation" (776). On this point, see also Anderson, *Understanding the Old Testament*, 538.

1594. Tenney, *New Testament Survey*, 105. Tenney adds: "Apocalyptic literature was usually produced in a period of persecution, when men's hopes turned to future deliverance. It was intended to encourage the believers to persist in their allegiance to God, and its imagery discouraged hostile readers from attempting to fathom its meaning (107).

1595. Ehrman, *Jesus: Apocalyptic Prophet*, 120.

1596. Schillebeeckx, *Jesus: An Experiment*, 124. See also 119–20.

1597. Wylen, *Jews in the Time*, 116. Redford says that apocalypse "offer[s]" nothing more than "the promise of a brighter day ahead, a forlorn and desperate hope" (*Egypt, Canaan, and Israel*, 471).

Endnotes

1598. Muilenburg, "History of the Religion," 332. Muilenburg adds, "Apocalyptic actually represented a deepening of Israel's prophetic consciousness in the light of the destruction of the nation and the somber years of suffering and tragedy which followed" (340).

1599. Levine, "Epilogue to the Holiness Code," 9–10.

1600. MacMullen, *Christianizing the Roman Empire*, 4, 13, 14.

1601. Kugel, *Great Shift*, 244, 246.

1602. Wylen, *Jews in the Time*, 58–59. Segal says that although "in general Hebrew concepts of resurrection tend toward this model," 2 Maccabees and 1 Enoch describe the afterlife as an ascent "to the eternally constant, deathless heaven where the most deserving and righteous go" (*Rebecca's Children*, 63).

1603. Meier, *Marginal Jew*, 3:329.

1604. Sanders, *Historical Figure of Jesus*, 44. Zeitlin says that the Pharisees "believed in reward and punishment in the future world, and in resurrection" (*Who Crucified Jesus?*, 86). And Reicke argues similarly that the Pharisees "taught survival of the soul, resurrection of the dead," and both "a last judgment" and "a world to come" (*New Testament Era*, 160).

1605. Guignebert, *Jewish World*, 167.

1606. Meier, *Marginal Jew*, 3:330.

1607. Rivkin, *Hidden Revolution*, 253. I. Zeitlin says, "This certainly helps us to understand why the Pharisees were popular and the Sadducees were not: the latter undermined the people's hope for salvation" (*Jesus and the Judaism*, 13). See also S. Zeitlin, *Who Killed Jesus?*, 21. Meier, on the other hand, says that the Pharisees were popular and influential because of "their exact knowledge of the Mosaic Law" (*Marginal Jew*, 3:297).

1608. Meier, *Marginal Jew*, 3:323–24.

1609. Wright and Fuller, *Book of the Acts*, 236.

1610. Kee et al., *Understanding the New Testament*, 40. Kee et al. go on to discuss the Pharisees' theory of two ages, during the second of which "a new order of existence would characterize human life."

1611. Kee et al., *Understanding the New Testament*, 40. Within the first, or present, age, "the one certain path was that of obedience to the Torah through which the powers of temptation and sin could be overthrown and overcome."

1612. Cornfeld, *Archeology of the Bible*, 265. Schubert notes that Hillel, the most famous Pharisee, is quoted in the Mishnah as saying, "He who has acquired for himself words of the Torah has acquired life in the coming world." However, Schubert adds, "When this straightforward call of Hillel's to study and observe the Law is compared to the brightly coloured visions of the apocalyptists . . . an acute difference is immediately apparent . . . For Hillel, life, based on the Torah, was to be lived in the present era and in the present world; the apocalyptists, in contrast, sought to transcend the present era and the present world" ("Jewish Religious Parties," 90).

1613. Umen, *Pharisaism and Jesus*, 103–4, 107.

1614. Schillebeeckx, *Jesus: An Experiment*, 119. Glatzer says: The apocalyptic works of the period "were composed against the background of national calamity and disappointment at the failure of the Messianic hopes to materialize." However, "the prophetic faith" that the apocalyptists tried to retain "was not required by these men"—that is, the Pharisees—"who were inspired by anxiety and whose 'hope was never far from despair.'" Rather, "[t]he ancient faith was maintained and strengthened by the Pharisees and the rabbis, who overcame the mood of catastrophe and concentrated on the will of God" ("Foreword," 7). Goodman says, "There are no good reasons to believe" that "speculation" about the future, "however common it may have been, played a dominant role in the religious life of many Jews in the late Second Temple period" (*History of Judaism*, 214). "It seems that most Jews . . . were willing to remain vague about their doctrine in this area" (218).

1615. Cohen explains: "Modern scholars have highlighted the social and economic stress engendered by the war of 66–74 C.E. In the wake of that war, the Romans confiscated a great deal of land, leasing or giving it to their supporters and soldiers. The process created a large number of landless poor in Judea, and this group seems to have provided Bar Kokhba the bulk of his support ... Bar Kokhba was seen by some of his followers as the anointed redeemer who would inaugurate the end by destroying the Romans and rebuilding the temple" (*From the Maccabees*, 25–26).

1616. Avery-Peck, "Galilean Charismatic, Rabbinic Piety," 62, 150.

1617. Segal, *Rebecca's Children*, 129. Stroumsa says that messianism was neutralized in both Judaism and Christianity, especially in the second century AD: "Parallel to the de-eschatologization of Christian thought, which sought to come to terms with the postponement of Christ's Second Coming (Parousia), the Rabbis seem to have succeeded to a great extent in de-activating messianic impulses after the loss of all aspects of Jewish national life in Palestine" ("Old Wine and New Bottles," 257).

1618. Levine, "Judaism from the Destruction," 147. Levine adds: "For 300 years, ... nationalist aspirations had been a significant factor in Jewish history, often finding expression in revolts or attacks on Gentile neighbors. With the end of the Bar-Kochba revolt, a new period in Jewish history began in which active Jewish nationalist aspirations were in abeyance."

1619. Cohen, "Judaism to the Mishnah," 198.

1620. Avery-Peck quotes this passage (from *Lamentations Rabbah* 2:4) and comments: "The central point is that the Rabbis rejected such messianic figures and looked down on anyone who would imagine that the Messiah was destined soon to arrive" ("Galilean Charismatic, Rabbinic Piety," 163).

1621. Segal, *Rebecca's Children*, 136, 130. However, despite such disappointments, Segal says that apocalypticism did not die out completely: "Much apocalyptic writing took a new, more comforting tone. Like literary prophecy, ... the message of apocalypticism turned to foreseeing the eventual reward of the righteous." On this point, see also Cornfeld, *Archeology of the Bible*, 265.

1622. Cohen, *From the Maccabees*, 212. Epstein comments: "Like their spiritual fathers, the Prophets, [the Rabbis] were essentially practical men concerned primarily with conduct. As such, they were on the whole little interested in arid speculations that had no bearing on human behavior" (*Judaism*, 133).

1623. Evans, "Comparing Judaisms," 181.

1624. Charlesworth, "Christians and Jews," 312. According to Koch, "[s]oon after" a three-century flirtation with what many Jews and Christian considered to be a fantasy, apocalypticism "experienced a violent rejection on the part of Jewish and Christian theologians" ("Apocalyptic and Eschatology," 65). The three centuries Koch is referring to are 200 BC to AD 100.

1625. Sanders, *Judaism*, 8, 9.

1626. Sanders, *Judaism*, 298. Again: "[I]t was not just the Pharisees, but most Jews, perhaps all but the Sadducees, who thought that there was an afterlife, though often they have conceived it vary vaguely" (301). Still later, Sanders notes, "The rabbis tried to discourage speculation about what was in the heavenly places." However, he wonders, first, whether this implies that such speculation was common and, second, if it was, whether it was taken "seriously" (303).

1627. Cohen, *From the Maccabees*, 212.

1628. Segal, *Rebecca's Children*, 135.

1629. Avery-Peck, "The Galilean Charismatic, Rabbinic Piety," 149–51, 164.

1630. Kugel, *How to Read*, 667–68.

1631. Kugel, *Great Shift*, 312, 185–86. Referring to the gigantic scroll in Zechariah's prophecy that lodges in the houses of otherwise undetected criminals, Kugel comments, "It is no longer God Himself, but His written word, that enacts justice (247).

1632. Kugel, *How to Read*, 6.

1633. Kaufmann, *Religion of Israel*, 448; my emphasis.

1634. Kugel, *Great Shift*, 337.

1635. LaCocque, "Torah—Nomos," 87–88.

1636. Kugel, *How to Read*, 669–71.

1637. Wylen, *Jews in the Time*, 144. Wylen adds: "The Pharisees took literally the words of Exodus 19:5-6, 'You shall be to Me a kingdom of priests, a holy nation.' The Pharisees tried to realize this vision as if they were priests."

1638. Segal, *Rebecca's Children*, 137. Segal says that the change began earlier—presumably under the Pharisees. Indeed, he adds, "[m]ost varieties of Judaism were influenced by Hellenistic spirituality" (138).

1639. Evans discusses "the rabbinic understanding of the covenant" and cites several references to the Covenant in rabbinical works in "Comparing Judaisms," 175–78.

1640. Umen, *Pharisaism and Jesus*, 43, 46.

1641. Cohen, *From the Maccabees*, 65.

1642. Sanders says that members of synagogues were unlikely to pray the same prayers and pray them in the same way: "If Jews were in a synagogue at a time for prayer, . . . they may all have prayed, but not necessarily precisely the same prayer, and probably not in unison . . . In a synagogue of long standing, to be sure, certain routines would have been established, but our scanty evidence is against congregational participation in unison" (*Judaism*, 207–8). Sanders adds later that "there was no standard worship service in the synagogues" (261).

1643. Cohen says later: "The democratization of religion had as its goal the sanctification of daily life. Every act and every moment was to be in the service of God. The new regimen of study, prayer, ritual, and ethics was incumbent not upon some priestly or monastic elite but upon the entire community" (*From the Maccabees*, 97). See also 154.

1644. Stone, "Eschatology, Remythologization," 243–44.

1645. Cohen, *From the Maccabees*, 66.

1646. Russell, *Between the Testaments*, 51.

1647. Zeitlin, *Who Crucified Jesus?*, 25–39.

1648. Herford, *Pharisees*, 56–57.

1649. Kugel, *Great Shift*, 320. See also 336.

1650. Cohen, *From the Maccabees*, 65.

1651. Meier, *Marginal Jew*, 3:315. Meier comments, "The precise opinions about relatively minor points of legal observation found in the Pharisees-Sadducees disputes in rabbinic literature support this picture," as does Josephus' opinion (314).

1652. Meier, *Marginal Jew*, 3:315, 320.

1653. Zeitlin, *Who Crucified Jesus?*, 28–29. Zeitlin provides three examples of Pharisaic liberalization and concludes, "The liberal interpretation of the Pentateuchal law was crucially vital to the Jews of Judea" (29–31).

1654. Tyson, *Study of Early Christianity*, 98.

1655. Guignebert, *Jewish World*, 166–67. White says that "the Pharisees represent a 'populist' orientation toward piety, in contrast to the 'elitist' orientation associated with the Sadducees and the priests. Their scholastic debates," though often characterized as legalistic, actually represent "broader or liberalizing trends in theology." The Pharisees "sought greater flexibility rather than rigidity . . . [and] criticized the tendency of other Jews . . . to restrict the sense of religious piety to matters associated only with the Temple and sacrifice" (*From Jesus to Christianity*, 79–80).

1656. Cohen, "Judaism to the Mishnah," 222. The "rabbis debate numerous points of law but seldom cite the biblical authority that would substantiate their positions."

1657. Neusner, *Mishnah: Social Perspectives*, 211.

1658. Thus, Steinsaltz says, "The Talmud contains an immense number of rulings on various subjects and an even greater number of debates and controversies." That is, "it records discourses and debates and contains not only definitive conclusions but also the alternative solutions proposed and rejected" (*Essential Talmud*, 246–47, 57).

1659. Boyarin, *Border Lines*, 162. Boyarin adds that this idea occurs only in "the latest layers of classical rabbinic literature, in the Talmuds themselves." That is, it is "only in the final stage, represented by the redactional level of the Babylonian Talmud . . . that we find the multiplicity of interpretations as well as the multiplicity of halakhic views thematized as the very essence of Torah, as its very quintessence as representative of the divine mind on earth" (162, 183). Kurt Schubert mentions, as an example, the unresolved rabbinical disagreement over whether non-Jews had to convert to Judaism to be saved. Joshua ben Hananiah said in the Mishnah that "righteous non-Jews would have a place in the world to come, without conversion, but "several passages in the rabbinical literature" state that "gentiles . . . must be converted to Judaism for their salvation." Schubert concludes, "This variety of opinions is characteristic of Pharisaism" ("Jewish Religious Parties," 92).

1660. Rivkin, *Hidden Revolution*, 258. Rivkin adds, "This contrasted with the past procedure which had limited discussion and debate to the *Bet Din ha-Gadol*. Once the *halakha* was determined by that body, it was exclusively the *halakha*. Now, however, for the first time, two renditions of the *halakha* were allowed."

1661. Sander, *Judaism*, 414.

1662. Rivkin, *Hidden Revolution*, 259. On this subject, see Steinsaltz, *Essential Talmud*, 272–75.

1663. Boyarin, *Border Lines*, 189, 185, 179.

1664. Schubert, "Jewish Religious Parties," 90.

1665. Jasper, "Literary Readings of the Bible," 30.

1666. Neusner, *Talmud: A Close Encounter*, 178, 147. Von Rad argues that this willingness to treat the Torah as changeable predates the Pharisees and Rabbis: "Israel regarded the will of Jahweh as extremely flexible, ever and again adapting itself to each situation where there had been religious, political or economic change." That is, "Jahweh's will for justice positively never stood above time for Israel, for every generation was summoned anew to hearken to it as valid for itself and to make it out for itself." Thus, von Rad makes the same point that Neusner makes: "[T]he commandments were not a law, but an event, with which Jahweh specifically confronted every generation in its own *hic er nunc*, and to which it had to take up its position. The grandest example in the whole field of such fresh interpretation is Deuteronomy" (*Old Testament Theology*, 1:199).

1667. Boyarin, *Border Lines*, 169. Steinsaltz says of this story: "It is the description of the controversy between the great R. Eliezer and most of his disciples, headed by R. Joshua, on questions of ritual purity and pollution. The dispute was aroused by a seemingly marginal question, namely, whether a pottery utensil could be defined as a broken vessel, one that is unpollutable" (*Essential Talmud*, 217).

1668. Goodman, *History of Judaism*, 277.

1669. Segal, *Rebecca's Children*, 135. The passage in Exodus (23:2) referred to in the Talmudic story says, "You shall not follow a multitude to do evil; nor shall you bear witness in a suit, turn aside after a multitude, so as to pervert justice."

1670. Boyarin, *Border Lines*, 169, 171, 172. Boyarin adds in an endnote: "I am not claiming that the Rabbis were more rational than their opponents among the Jewish leaders. Their own modes of authorizing themselves, namely divination through the reading of Torah . . . are hardly, from our perspective, less magical than divination via carob trees . . . The point is that their own divination was thematized as Oral Torah, but not the divinatory methods of opponents or dissenters" (314n74).

1671. Segal, *Rebecca's Children*, 135, 136.

1672. Boyarin, *Border Lines*, 171.

1673. Cohen, *From the Maccabees*, 65.

1674. Parkes says that the Torah "contained far more than mere 'precept' or laws, although even the precepts, by being Divine ordinances, *brought men to God* in the performance of them" (*Conflict of the Church*, 36; my emphasis).

1675. Armstrong, *History of God*, 72–74; my emphasis. Elman reminds us that, like the Pharisees, "[t]he Rabbis also aimed to define legal requirements more exactly. The resulting explanations were primarily concerned with interpreting biblical passages in terms that were more understandable or palatable to their contemporaries" ("Classical Rabbinic Interpretation," 1849).

1676. Uffenheimer, "Myth and Reality," 151–52.

1677. Vermes, *Jesus in His Jewish Context*, 47–48, and notes 61–62.

1678. Rivkin, *Hidden Revolution*, 310; my emphasis. Von Rad says, similarly, that Israel "offered praise to [God], and asked him questions, and complained to him about all her sufferings, for Jahweh had not chosen his people as a mere dumb object of his will in history, but for converse with him" (*Old Testament Theology*, 1:355).

1679. Cohen, *From the Maccabees*, 66.

1680. Kugel, *Great Shift*, 306, 335. This inner, spiritual self, usually translated as *soul*, might well have been influenced by Platonism, especially the idea that it actually had access to God in a way that the ordinary self did not. Wylen says, "Eventually Jews and Christians adopted the Greek belief in the eternal soul and added it to their belief in bodily resurrection" (*Jews in the Time*, 61).

1681. Cwiekowski, *Beginnings of the Church*, 31. Cwiekowski adds: "This insight is behind the religious individualism (though always within the context of the community) which is characteristic of Pharisaic piety" and which suggests that there may be "stronger resemblances between Jesus and the Pharisaic movement than between Jesus and either the Sadducees or the Essenes."

1682. Brueggemann, *Old Testament Introduction*, 131–32.

1683. Herford, *Pharisees*, 148, 161. Brueggemann discusses God's "empathy, solidarity, and mercy with Israel" in the psalms in *Old Testament Theology*, 154–56.

1684. Von Rad, *Old Testament Theology*, 1:101, 200–201.

1685. Von Rad, *Old Testament Theology*, 1:193, 196, 200, 355. Von Rad says later, "People loved to solemnize Jahweh's commandments as ... beneficent" (375). Again: "[F]rom the earliest times onward Israel celebrated Jahweh as the one who bestowed on his people the all-embracing gift of his righteousness." It was "bestowed on Israel [as] ... a saving gift." Although it appeared early, however, von Rad notes that "the references which mention human righteousness in relation to Jahweh are only infrequently found in the earlier literature, while appearing extensively in the exilic and post-exilic texts" (376).

1686. Herford, *Pharisees*, 151–54.

1687. Brueggemann, *Old Testament Theology*, 137–38, 155.

1688. Heschel, *Prophets: Volume II*, 3–4, 9–10.

1689. Heschel, *Prophets: Volume II*, 7–8, 17–21.

1690. See note 1443.

1691. Von Rad says: "Deuteronomy, like the earlier codes, gives a variety of substantiations of the commandments which Jahweh promulgated. But it shows a new feature too; it also gives an inner motivation for the keeping of the commandments: love for Jahweh and thankfulness to him will lead Israel into obedience" (*Old Testament Theology*, 1:199).

1692. "These two area of relationship," says von Rad, "of men with one another and of men with God, seem to some extent independent," but in ancient Judaism they were "bound together ... in a continuing 'primitive pansacrality'" (*Old Testament Theology*, 1:374). Isidore Epstein says of the concept of co-creation: "[F]or the fulfilment of divine purpose human cooperation is necessary. Developing the Biblical idea of man as co-worker with God, the Talmud conceives man as having been chosen by God as *shuttaf* 'partner' for the fulfilment of creation." Epstein argues, however, that this idea did not arise because of disillusionment or despair: "It is a genuine historical tradition, based on the conviction that this is God's world chosen by Him to become the scene of a divine order wherein goodness and truth are to reign supreme" (*Judaism*, 138–39).

1693. Von Rad, *Old Testament Theology*, 1:198.

1694. Muilenburg, "History of the Religion," 326.

1695. Rifkin, *Hidden Revolution*, 296.

1696. Tyson, *Study of Early Christianity*, 97–101.

Endnotes

1697. Von Rad, *Old Testament Theology*, 1:198.

1698. Wylen, *Jews in the Time*, 94.

1699. Herford, *Pharisees*, 162.

1700. Quoted in Neusner, *Talmud: A Close Encounter*, 19. The quotation of Antigonus is from Aboth 1:3.

1701. Rivkin, *Hidden Revolution*, 300.

1702. Umen, *Pharisaism and Jesus*, 78–80.

1703. Sanders, *Judaism*, 252–56. Sanders adds that the Jews who "feasted on a shared sacrifice" might not have believed that they were communing with God, but "they at least knew that they were participating in a very personal way in the divine service." Furthermore, "[t]he other strictly theological ideas" that were associated with the entire Temple experience—"inner purification, atonement, thanksgiving and petition—need very little comment. These were all a part of standard Jewish belief" (256).

1704. Kugel, *How to Read*, 683–87. Kugel adds, "What Scripture is, and always has been, in Judaism is the beginning of a manual entitled *To serve God*, a manual whose trajectory has always led from the prophet to the interpreter and from the divine to the merely human" (685).

1705. Von Rad, *Old Testament Theology*, 1:370–76.

1706. Von Rad, *Old Testament Theology*, 1:370, 374; my emphasis. This is why "[t]he commandments were regarded as perfectly capable of being fulfilled, and indeed as easy to fulfill" (378).

1707. Brueggemann, *Old Testament Theology*, 358. Brueggemann says: "[T]he Isaiah tradition does not foster much direct 'supernaturalism.' The most remarkable feature of hope for Israel . . . is that this hoped-for newness will be enacted through human agency" (354). In Jeremiah, "the 'supernaturalist' rhetoric of YHWH's future is grounded in concrete historical reality. This is evident first in the more-or-less historical narrative of chapters 37–44 that witness to real human agents in the historical process" (357).

1708. Birch et al., *Theological Introduction*, 43–44. On the emphasis of this concept in Exodus, see 120–22,

1709. Brueggemann, *Old Testament Theology*, 355.

1710. Niditch, *Ancient Israelite Religion*, 80–82. Niditch adds: "It is in the light of this image of community justice that Deuteronomy's strong message about blessing and cursing make sense." And the key question is "What kind of society are you?" (82). Like Brueggemann, Niditch points out that the idea of the Covenant is as strongly presented in the works of the prophets as in Deuteronomy (92–97). On the pervasiveness of the concept in ancient Jewish literature, see 71.

1711. Schmidt says, "The descent into idolatry and the loss or 'forgetting' of past history are two errors against which Deuteronomy issues warnings, because these errors rob the Yahwistic faith of its very essence" (*Old Testament Introduction*, 132).

1712. Eisenstadt, "Secondary Breakthrough," 230. On the relationship between the Covenant and monotheism, Benjamin Uffenheimer says that the former is the source of the latter: "[T]he covenant between the nation and its God is the kernel of this belief [i.e., in monotheism] and its formative basis" ("Myth and Reality," 162). Later, Uffenheimer adds, "The very heart of biblical monotheism is the idea of the primeval covenant between Israel and its Divine King, who revealed himself as lawgiver, warrior, loving father, bridegroom, and husband as well." The "political implication" of this myth "is the establishment of the kingdom of God based on the repudiation of any human domination over men" (164).

1713. Mussner, *Tractate on the Jews*, 95–96. Mussner is quoting N. Lohfink, *Bibelauslegung im Wandel* (1967).

1714. Barton, "Approaches to Ethics," 120–21, 123.

1715. Barton, "Approaches to Ethics," 128–29. It might also be argued that the Jewish Covenant had a special appeal because of its derivation from kinship values. As Levenson says, the

Endnotes

Covenant "borrows much of its character and force from something more primal: namely, from family relations." After quoting Frank Cross Moore, on the subject, Levenson says that Covenant "makes the outsider a member of the family" (*Love of God*, 22–23).

1716. Birch et al., *Theological Introduction*, 159, 162.

1717. Anderson, *Charity*, 119.

1718. Von Rad, *Old Testament Theology*, 1:384–85.

1719. Birch et al., *Theological Introduction*, 148.

1720. Anderson, *Charity*, 4, 32, 119. On this concept of faith, *emunah*, see Buber, *Writings of Martin Buber*, 267.

1721. Rogerson, "World-View of the Old Testament," 75; my emphasis.

1722. Barton, "Approaches to Ethics," 129.

1723. Cohen, *From the Maccabees*, 172–74, 183; my emphasis.

1724. Gottwald's idea is reported by Gorringe in "Political Readings of Scripture," 71.

1725. Rogerson discusses ancient Israel's tribalism and egalitarianism in "World-View of the Old Testament," 72–75. He argues that the ancient Jews created their own version of communal society, meaning that their version did not entirely match other tribal organizations: "In fact what is important in what the OT says about social relationships is the way in which it takes what ought *ideally* to be functions of family groups—supporting family members especially in times of difficulty—and extends these obligations to the whole people" (74). Jacobsen says that ancient Mesopotamia similarly went through a stage of "primitive democracy" ("Mesopotamia," 142, 148, 162, 196).

1726. On the continuing importance of the Covenant to Jews generally, including the Essenes and the early Christians, see Horsley, *Covenant Economics*, 92–93, 100–108. Horsley says, "The covenant was still very much alive in Jesus' time, or at least some of is mechanisms were still widely observed" (113).

1727. Anderson, *Understanding the Old Testament*, 313.

1728. Geller, "Religion of the Bible," 2031.

1729. Crossan, *Birth of Christianity*, 266.

1730. Anderson, *Understanding the Old Testament*, 313.

1731. Meek, *Hebrew Origins*, 220–21. As I indicated earlier, both Ruether and Brueggemann trace the Deuteronomic and prophetic ideals of the Covenant to pre-monarchial times (*Faith and Fratricide*, 40; and *Old Testament Theology*, 50).

1732. Horsley, *Bandits, Prophets & Messiahs*, 6.

1733. Horsley, *Bandits, Prophets & Messiahs*, 5. Kaylor says, "Traditions rooted in the distant past formed the attitudes of common people and provided standards for social justice and economic equality." More specifically, tracing these standards to the Covenant laws that predated the monarchial period, Kaylor adds: "The ideal of social equality remained, especially in the northern kingdom of Israel, even after the development of the monarchy. The accounts of such early prophets as Elijah and Elisha show strong challenges to monarchy from the point of view of the older, more egalitarian ways. They assert the power and authority of God over the land, its fertility, and its just use (see especially 1 Kings 17:1—19:21; 21:1–29)." Kaylor concludes: "The importance of these traditions for the present purpose does not depend on whether Sabbath year and Jubilee were observed regularly or at all. The point is that they provided a basis for prophetic appeals for covenant justice in a time of crisis" (*Jesus the Prophet*, 31, 32, 34).

1734. Horsley, *Covenant Economics*, 34–35. In *Message and the Kingdom*, Horsley and Silberman say, "The laws . . . enabled the People of Israel to maintain a stable system of social relations, economic welfare, and local autonomy" (27). According to Crossan, the covenant laws protected their beneficiaries from "indebtedness, enslavement, and dispossession" (*Birth of Christianity*, 188). See also de Vaux, *Ancient Israel*, 1:72–73.

1735. Childe, *What Happened in History*, 60.

Endnotes

1736. Horsley warns against romanticizing peasant life under these circumstances (*Covenant Economics*, 36). Clearly, the communal basis of this kind of social organization was not an expression of idealism and freely chosen but a natural extension of kinship and a consequence of more or less universal laws of social development. Furthermore, this kind of living was fragile, vulnerable as it was to disruption by powerful neighbors. There is also a question as to whether all or most of the covenant laws were actually enforced, although Herzog argues that most of the laws were observed (*Jesus, Justice*, 107).

1737. On the influence of the Wisdom tradition on the heightened regard for the covenantal tradition, Kugel says, "The special role of wisdom writings and the wisdom mentality—in its ascendancy after the return from the Babylonian exile—deserves to be singled out. It is really the wisdom mind-set that made so many ancient texts into Scripture. Like wisdom writings, all of Israel's ancient library now became a series of eternally valid lessons, the wisdom of the ages" (*How to Read*, 671).

1738. Cohen, *From the Maccabees*, 212. Referring to the major theological issues, including "corporate and individual reward and punishment," Cohen adds: "[E]xcept for one chapter and an occasional paragraph, the Mishnah is not interested in these topics. The Talmudim show a markedly greater interest in theology, but no rabbinic work sets forth the dogmas or essential beliefs of Judaism."

1739. Pawlikowski, "Jewish Covenant," 114–17.

1740. Neusner, *Mishnah: Social Perspectives*, 209, 265.

1741. Boyarin, *Border Lines*, 171, 172. "What we find represented, then, at this latest layer of Talmudic storytelling about Yavneh is a history of transformation not from a time of dissensus to a time of consensus . . . but rather a canonization of dissensus, unending dissensus as the very essence of the Torah as given at Sinai" (170–71). Later, Boyarin says, "I want in the end to assert that the notion that God himself suffers a fall into language, and thus into linguistic indeterminacy, may be the most powerful and creative, perhaps even unique, theological notion of rabbinic Judaism" (178).

1742. Steinsaltz, *Essential Talmud*, 217–18.

1743. As I noted in chapter 2, White says that seeing the two commandments as a summary of the entire Torah "was a typically Pharisaic way of thinking" (*From Jesus to Christianity*, 79). Indeed, as Vermes notes, it was also characteristic of Jews in an earlier period: "There was a general tendency among Jews in the early post-exilic centuries to discover a small number of all-inclusive precepts" (*Jesus in His Jewish Context*, 41). Vermes says that "[t]he fullest illustration of this trend comes from Rabbi Simlai, a third-century AD sage," who provides several examples of this practice of reducing the 613 laws of the Torah to many fewer commandments, from eleven by David to six by Isaiah, three by Micah, two by Third Isaiah, and one by Amos.

1744. In Mark, Jesus says, "There is no other commandment greater than these" (12:31). And in Matthew, he says, "On these two commandments depend all the law and the prophets" (22:40).

1745. Sanders, *Judaism*, 257, 193.

1746. Sterling, "Philo of Alexandria," 299, 304.

1747. Sanders, *Judaism*, 257.

1748. Muilenburg, "History of the Religion," 325.

1749. Schillebeeckx, *Jesus: An Experiment*, 249–50.

1750. May and Metzger claim that the dialogue between Jesus and the Jewish scribe in Mark. 12:28 "indicate[s] that Jewish religion in Jesus' day linked" the passages from Numbers and Deuteronomy (*Oxford Annotated Bible*, 1231–32). Thus, according to Carroll, Jesus "was never more Jewish than in this proclamation" of love (*Constantine's Sword*, 118).

1751. Sanders, *Judaism*, 192–93.

1752. Sanders, *Judaism*, 49–50. "Voluntary offences against a fellow human require inward conviction of the sin, a confession, restoration of what was taken, an added fifth, and a sacrifice, which shows that the sin was also against God" (192).

1753. Eisenstadt says that the increasingly transcendental concept of God "led to the development of universalization and rationalization of the religious orientations and a strong emphasis on the ethical dimension of the religious experience" ("Axial Age Breakthrough," 128).

1754. In another essay in the same text, Eisenstadt says that one of three new orientations in the Second Temple period "was a more contemplative, ethical, or philosophical one which emerged out of the encounter with Hellenism and/or developed in relation to the literature of Wisdom." Later, Eisenstadt says again, "One tendency . . . was the philosophical ethical one," which was "strongly influenced by the Hellenistic environment" ("Secondary Breakthrough," 230, 233).

1755. Schillebeeckx, *Jesus: An Experiment*, 249, 250.

1756. Sanders, *Judaism*, 193.

1757. Quoting this passage, Schillebeeckx comments, "The Johannine gospel, being more in line with the Wisdom tradition, even regards the love of neighbor as summing up the Christian way of life" (*Jesus: An Experiment*, 254).

1758. Schillebeeckx, *Jesus: An Experiment*, 253. Theissen says that "the encounter with Hellenistic education and its philosophical coloring created a desire to derive the manifold variety of the law from a few basic principles: love of God and of one's neighbor . . . or the 'golden rule'" (*Early Palestinian Christianity*, 77).

1759. Flusser, *Sage from Galilee*, 55, 57–59.

1760. Dodd, *Founder of Christianity*, 63.

1761. Schillebeeckx, *Jesus: An Experiment*, 250. Schillebeeckx notes that this meaning of the word is adopted by Luke in 18:22–30, but not by Mark and Matthew (255).

1762. This passage, from *Shabbat* 31a, in the Babylonian Talmud, is quoted in Sanders, *Judaism*, 258. Sanders also quotes Pe'ah 4.10, in the Tosefta: "Charity and deeds of loving-kindness are equal to all the commandments [*mitsvot*] in the Torah" (259).

1763. Flusser, *Sage from Galilee*, 59–62.

1764. Sanders, *Judaism*, 257, 260. Sanders adds: "Did Jews in general think that the 'whole law' was fulfilled by loving God and loving neighbour? Did they know that one implied the other, that to love God meant to obey his commandments, including the command to love other people? We may confidently say that this is what their teachers taught."

1765. Anderson, *Charity*, 158–59, 18. "Acts of charity to the poor," Anderson says elsewhere, are a privileged way of participating in the love of God"—that is, "in the grace he has to offer" (175).

1766. Anderson, *Charity*, 158–59. Anderson notes that, according to both Jesus (Luke 6:36) and Rabbi Tanhuma (Gen. Rab. 33.3), almsgiving, as mercy, was also an imitation of God: "Almsgiving, it would stand to reason, became an effective petition when it was joined to prayer because it *mirrored* a defining characteristic of God" (144). After quoting Ecclesiasticus 35:1–2, Anderson adds, "What Ben Sira teaches us is that the acts of charity toward the poor became the equivalent of temple sacrifice even while the temple was standing" (21). On this point, see also 143, 158.

1767. Anderson, *Charity*, 30–31.

1768. Anderson, *Charity*, 16–17, 156; my emphasis. The source of the statement is Tosefta *Peah* 4:19. Anderson says elsewhere that "speakers in rabbinic times could use the word *commandment* . . . either to speak of one of the 613 commandments that Moses received at Mt. Sinai or to highlight the significance of the most important of all commandments—almsgiving" (105, my emphasis). Even much earlier, however, "Tobit 4:9–10 and Ben Sira 29:10–11 declare that it is charity alone that can find a treasury in heaven" (133).

1769. Segal, *Rebecca's Children*, 122–23.

1770. Guignebert, *Jewish World*, 164. Guignebert is quoting K. Lake, *Landmarks in the History of Early Christianity* (London, 1920).

1771. This passage is quoted by Zeitlin in *Jesus and the Judaism*, 12.

Endnotes

1772. Umen, *Pharisaism and Jesus*, 77.

1773. Crossan, *Birth of Christianity*, 580.

1774. Reicke, *New Testament Era*, 157, 160, 159.

1775. Wylen, *Jews in the Time*, 109.

1776. Cohen, *From the Maccabees*, 210.

1777. Neusner calls the system described as imaginary by the Rabbis in the Mishnah "utopian," "made up," and "mythical" (*Mishnah: Social Perspectives*, 200–202; see also 245–47).

1778. Niditch, *Ancient Israelite Religion*, 71. Niditch explains: "If one explores passages such as Exodus 20, Exodus 21–23, Joshua 24, large sections of Deuteronomy, and key concepts lying behind the oracles of the biblical prophets, one begins to understand the pervasiveness of the notion of covenant as a means of describing God's relationship with Israel. Implicitly one begins to discover *what a wide range of biblical writers considered to be proper ethical behavior*" (71; my emphasis).

1779. Crosan, *Birth of Christianity*, 580.

1780. Neusner, *Mishnah: Social Perspectives*, 266–67. Neusner adds, "Nor in the realities of Jews' limited self-administration in the third and fourth centuries, down to ca. 400, do we find actual examples of the passion, responsibility, and proportion and balance of a concrete system of political life, such as the document's authorship has made up for itself."

1781. Neusner, *Way of Torah*, 6. After lamenting the failure of the church to retain and implement the ideals expressed by Jesus in the Sermon on the Mount, Theissen expresses similar sentiments: "The necessity for inward and outward peace, coupled with the urgency of social change, perhaps requires of us more of a radical change in attitudes than we realize. What has failed to function so far may one day prove to be functional, and what has been counted as an ethical luxury may prove to be mankind's chance of survival" (*Early Palestinian Christianity*, 119). Likewise, Crossan laments the failure of modern civilization to act upon such values, which have been affirmed by moral leaders throughout the world: "Lest you imagine, by the way, that I am inventing some unique theology for a unique Jesus, let me assure you that I find ethical eschatology"—that is, "the ethical radicalism" of Jesus' sayings—"in the nonviolent resistance to structural evil put forward by such diverse people as the Jain Mahatma Gandhi, the Catholic Dorothy Day, and the Protestant Martin Luther King, Jr. If enough people lived like *they* did—lived in nonviolent protest against systemic evil, against the normalcies of this world's discrimination, exploitation, and oppression—the result would be a new world we could hardly imagine" (*Birth of Christianity*, 279).

Bibliography

Akenson, Donald H. *Saint Saul: A Skeleton Key to the Historical Jesus*. New York: Oxford University Press, 2000.
Albright, William F. "The Old Testament World." In *The Interpreter's Bible*, edited by George Arthur Buttrick, 233–71. New York: Abingdon, 1952.
Allison, Dale C., Jr. *Jesus of Nazareth: Millenarian Prophet*. Minneapolis: Fortress, 1998.
Alter, Robert. "The Poetic and Wisdom Books." In *The Cambridge Companion to Biblical Interpretation*, edited by John Barton, 226–40. Cambridge: Cambridge University Press, 1999.
———. *The Wisdom Books: Job, Proverbs, and Ecclesiastes*. New York: Norton, 2010.
Anderson, Bernhard W. *Understanding the Old Testament*. 2nd ed. Englewood Cliffs, NJ: Prentice-Hall, 1966.
Anderson, Gary A. *Charity: The Place of the Poor in the Biblical Tradition*. New Haven: Yale University Press, 2013.
Armstrong, Karen. *The Bible: A Biography*. New York: Atlantic Monthly, 2007.
———. *The Great Transformation: The Beginning of Our Religious Traditions*. New York: Anchor, 2006.
———. *The History of God: The 4,000-Year Quest of Judaism, Christianity and Islam*. New York: Ballantine, 1994.
Attridge, Harold W. "Christianity from the Destruction of Jerusalem to Constantine's Adoption of the New Religion: 70–135 C.E." In *Christianity and Rabbinic Judaism: A Parallel History of Their Origins and Early Development*, edited by Hershel Shanks, 151–94. Washington, DC: Biblical Archeological Society, 1992.
Avery-Peck, Alan J. "Galilean Charismatic, Rabbinic Piety: The Holy Man in Talmudic Literature." In *The Historical Jesus in Context*, by Amy-Jill Levine et al., 149–65. Princeton Readings in Religions. Princeton, NJ: Princeton University Press, 2006.
Bainton, Roland H. *Early Christianity*. An Anvil Original 49. Princeton: Van Nostrand, 1960.
Bammel, Ernst. "'Ex illa itaque die consilium fecerunt . . . .'" In *The Trial of Jesus: Cambridge Studies in Honour of C. F. D. Moule*, edited by Ernst Bammel, 11–40. Studies in Biblical Theology (Series Two) 13. London: SCM, 1971.
Bammel, Ernst, ed. *The Trial of Jesus: Cambridge Studies in Honour of C. F. D. Moule*. Studies in Biblical Theology (Series Two) 13. London: SCM, 1971.
Barclay, William. *Jesus as They Saw Him: New Testament Interpretations*. 1962. Reprint, Grand Rapids: Eerdmans, 1978.
Barnstone, Willis, ed. *The Other Bible: Jewish Pseudepigrapha, Christian Apocrypha, Gnostic Scriptures, Kabbalah, Dead Sea Scrolls*. San Francisco: HarperSanFrancisco, 1984.

Bibliography

Barton, John. "Approaches to Ethics in the Old Testament." In *Beginning Old Testament Study*, edited by John Rogerson, 114–32. London: SPCK, 1998.

———. *Beginning Old Testament Study*. Edited by John Rogerson. London: SPCK, 1998.

———. *Ethics and the Old Testament*. London: SCM, 1998.

———. "Historical Critical Approaches." In *The Cambridge Companion to Biblical Interpretation*, edited by John Barton, 7–20. Cambridge: Cambridge University Press, 1999.

———. *A History of the Bible: The Story of the World's Most Influential Book*. New York: Viking, 2019.

———. "Introduction." In *The Cambridge Companion to Biblical Interpretation*, edited by John Barton, 1–6. Cambridge: Cambridge University Press, 1999.

———. "Old Testament Theology." In *Beginning Old Testament Study*, edited by John Rogerson et al., 94–113.

Barton, John, ed. *The Cambridge Companion to Biblical Interpretation*. Cambridge: Cambridge University Press, 1999.

Basser, Herbert W. "Gospel and Talmud." In *The Historical Jesus in Context*, by Amy-Jill Levine et al., 285–95. Princeton Readings in Religions. Princeton, NJ: Princeton University Press, 2006.

Bauckham, Richard. *Palestinian Setting*. Vol. 4 of *The Book of Acts in Its First Century Setting* Grand Rapids: Eerdmans, 1995.

Bauer, Walther. *Orthodoxy and Heresy in Earliest Christianity*. 2nd ed. Mifflintown, PA: Sigler, 1996.

Bellah, Robert N. *Religion in Human Evolution: From the Paleolithic to the Axial Age*. Cambridge: Belknap, 2011.

Berlin, Adele, and Marc Zvi Brettler, eds. *The Jewish Study Bible*. New York: Oxford University Press, 2004.

Birch, Bruce C., et al. *A Theological Introduction to the Old Testament*. 2nd ed. Nashville: Abingdon, 2005.

Blenkinsopp, Joseph. "The Pentateuch." In *The Cambridge Companion to Biblical Interpretation*, edited by John Barton, 181–97. Cambridge: Cambridge University Press, 1999.

———. "Tanakh and the New Testament: A Christian Perspective." In *Biblical Studies: Meeting Ground of Jews and Christians*, edited by Lawrence Boadt et al., 96–119. Studies in Judaism and Christianity: Exploration of Issues in the Contemporary Dialogue between Christians and Jesus. New York: Paulist, 1980.

Blinzler, Josef. "Jesus and His Disciples." In *Jesus on His Time*, edited by Hans Jürgen Schultz, 84–95. Philadelphia: Fortress, 1980.

———. "The Jewish Punishment of Stoning in the New Testament Period." In *The Trial of Jesus: Cambridge Studies in Honour of C. F. D. Moule*, edited by Ernst Bammel, 147–61. Studies in Biblical Theology (Series Two) 13. London: SCM, 1971.

Boadt, Lawrence, ed. *Biblical Studies: Meeting Ground of Jews and Christians*. Studies in Judaism and Christianity: Exploration of Issues in the Contemporary Dialogue between Christians and Jesus. New York: Paulist, 1980.

Bockmuehl, Markus, ed. *The Cambridge Companion to Jesus*. Cambridge Companions to Religion. Cambridge: Cambridge University Press, 2002.

Bokenkotter, Thomas. *A Concise History of the Catholic Church*. Garden City, NY: Doubleday, 1977.

Bibliography

Borg, Marcus J. *Jesus: Uncovering the Life, Teachings, and Relevance of a Religious Revolutionary.* San Francisco: HarperSanFrancisco, 2006.

———. *Reading the Bible Again for the First Time: Taking the Bible Seriously But Not Literally.* San Francisco: HarperSanFrancisco, 2002,

Borg, Marcus J., and John Dominic Crossan. *The Last Week: What the Gospels Really Teach about Jesus's Final Days in Jerusalem.* San Francisco: HarperSanFrancisco, 2007.

Bornkamm, Gunther. *Jesus of Nazareth.* Minneapolis: Fortress, 1995.

Bowker, John. *Jesus and the Pharisees.* London: Cambridge University Press, 1973.

Boyarin, Daniel. *The Jewish Gospels: The Story of the Jewish Christ.* New York: New Press, 2012.

———. *Border Lines: The Partition of Judeo-Christianity.* Philadelphia: University of Pennsylvania Press, 2010.

Brandon, S. G. F. *The Trial of Jesus.* London: Batsford, 1968.

Braun, Herbert. "The Qumran Community." In *Jesus in His Time*, edited by Hans Jürgen Schultz, 66–74. Philadelphia: Fortress, 1980.

Brettler, Marc Zvi. "The Canonization of the Bible." In *The Jewish Study Bible*, edited by Adele Berlin and Marc Zvi Brettler, 2072–76. New York: Oxford University Press, 2004.

Brown, Raymond E. *The Churches the Apostles Left Behind.* New York: Paulist, 1984.

———. *The Gospel According to John, XIII–XXI.* Anchor Bible 29A. Garden City, NY: Doubleday, 1970.

———. *An Introduction to the New Testament.* New York: Doubleday, 1997.

Bruce, F. F. *New Testament History.* New York: Doubleday, 1980.

Brueggemann, Walter. *Old Testament Theology: An Introduction.* Library of Bible Theology. Nashville: Abingdon, 2008.

Buber, Martin. "Jewish Religiousity." In *On Judaism*, edited by Nahm N. Glatzer, 79–94. New York: Schocken, 1996.

———. *On Judaism.* Edited by Nahum N. Glatzer. New York: Schocken, 1996.

———. "The Silent Question." In *On Judaism*, edited by Nahum N. Glatzer, 202–13. New York: Schocken, 1996.

———. *The Writings of Martin Buber.* Edited by Will Herberg. Cleveland: Meridian, 1967.

Bultmann, Rudolf. *Jesus and the Word.* New York: Scribner's, 1958.

———. *Primitive Christianity: In Its Contemporary Setting.* New York: Meridian, 1960.

———. *Theology of the New Testament.* Vol. 1. New York: Scribner's, 1951.

Burrows, Millar. *The Dead Sea Scrolls.* New York: Viking, 1968.

Buttrick, George Arthur, ed. *The Interpreter's Bible.* New York: Abingdon, 1952.

Capper, Brian. "The Palestinian Cultural Context of Earliest Christian Community of Goods." In *The Book of Acts in Its First Century Setting: Palestinian Setting*, edited by Richard Bauckham, 4:323–56. Grand Rapids: Eerdmans, 1995.

Carroll, James. *Constantine's Sword: The Church and the Jews.* Boston: Houghton Mifflin, 2002.

Catchpole, D. R. "The Problem of the Historicity of the Sanhedrin Trial." In *The Trial of Jesus: Cambridge Studies in Honour of C. F. D. Moule*, edited by Ernst Bammel, 47–65. Studies in Biblical Theology (Series Two) 13. London: SCM, 1971.

Charlesworth, James H. "Christians and Jews in the First Six Centuries." In *Christianity and Rabbinic Judaism: A Parallel History of Their Origins and Early Development*, edited by Hershel Shanks, 305–25. Washington, DC: Biblical Archeological Society, 1992.

Bibliography

———. "The Foreground of Christian Origins and the Commencement of Jesus Research." In *Jesus' Jewishness: Exploring the Place of Jesus within Early Judaism*, edited by James H. Charlesworth, 65–83. New York: Crossroad, 1996.

———. *Jesus within Judaism: New Light from Archeological Discoveries*. New York: Doubleday, 1988.

Charlesworth, James H., ed. *Jesus' Jewishness: Exploring the Place of Jesus within Early Judaism*. New York: Crossroad, 1996.

Childe, Gordon. *What Happened in History*. Hammondsworth, UK: Penguin, 1954.

Childs, Brevard S. *Myth and Reality in the Old Testament*. London: SCM, 1968.

Chilton, Bruce. *Rabbi Jesus*. New York: Doubleday, 2000.

Chilton, Bruce, and Jacob Neusner. *The Brother of Jesus*. Louisville: Westminster John Knox, 2001.

———. *Judaism in the New Testament: Practices and Beliefs*. London: Routledge, 1995.

Christie-Murray, David. *A History of Heresy*. New York: Oxford University Press, 1991.

Clark, Gillian. *Christianity and Roman Society*. Cambridge: Cambridge University Press, 2006.

Cohen, Shaye J. D. *From the Maccabees to the Mishnah*. Louisville: Westminster John Knox, 2006. 2nd ed.

———. "Judaism to the Mishnah: 135–220 C.E." In *Christianity and Rabbinic Judaism: A Parallel History of Their Origins and Early Development*, edited by Hershel Shanks, 195–223. Washington, DC: Biblical Archeological Society, 1992.

Cohn, Haim. *The Trial and Death of Jesus*. Old Saybrook, CT: Konecky & Konecky, 1963.

Cohn-Sherbok, Dan. *The Hebrew Bible*. London: Cassell, 1996.

Collins, John J. "Introduction." In *Religion in the Dead Sea Scrolls*, edited by John J. Collins and Robert A. Kugler, 1–8. Grand Rapids, MI: Eerdmans, 2000.

———. *A Short Introduction to the Hebrew Bible*. Minneapolis: Fortress, 2007.

Collins, John J., and Robert A. Kugler, eds. *Religion in the Dead Sea Scrolls*. Grand Rapids, MI: Eerdmans, 2000.

Conzelmann, H., and A. Lindemann. *Interpreting the New Testament: An Introduction to the Principles and Methods of N.T. Exegesis*. Peabody, MA: Hendrickson, 1999.

Coogan, Michael. *The Oxford History of the Biblical World*. Oxford: Oxford University Press, 2001.

Cook, Stanley. *An Introduction to the Bible*. Hammondsworth, UK: Penguin, 1950.

Cornfeld, Gaalyah. *Archeology of the Bible: Book by Book*. New York: Harper & Row, 1976.

Craveri, Marcello. *The Life of Jesus*. New York: Grove, 1967.

Crossan, John Dominic. *The Birth of Christianity: Discovering What Happened in the Years Immediately after the Execution of Jesus*. San Francisco: HarperSanFrancisco, 1999.

———. *The Historical Jesus: The Life of a Mediterranean Jewish Peasant*. San Francisco: HarperSanFrancisco, 1992.

Cwiekowski, Frederick J. *The Beginnings of the Church*. New York: Paulist, 1988.

Davies, W. H. *Invitation to the New Testament: A Guide to Its Main Witnesses*. Garden City, NY: Doubleday, 1969.

de Ste. Croix, G. E. M. "Christianity's Encounter with the Roman Imperial Government." In *The Crucible of Christianity: Judaism, Hellenism and the Historical Background to the Christian Faith*, edited by Arnold Toynbee, 331–51. New York: World, 1969.

de Vaux, Roland. *Ancient Israel*. Vol. 1, *Social Institutions*. New York: McGraw-Hill, 1965.

Dihle, Albrecht. "The Greco-Roman Background." In *Jesus on His Time*, edited by Hans Jürgen Schultz, 10–18. Philadelphia: Fortress, 1980.

Bibliography

Dodd, C. H. *The Founder of Christianity*. Bristol: Shoreline, 1993.

Edelheit, Joseph, ed. *The Life of the Covenant: The Challenge of Contemporary Judaism: Essays in Honor of Herman E. Schaalman*. Chicago: Spertus College of Judaica Press, 1986.

Ehrman, Bart D. *How Jesus Became God: The Exaltation of a Jewish Preacher from Galilee*. New York: HarperCollins, 2014.

———. *Jesus: Apocalyptic Prophet of the New Millennium*. New York: Oxford University Press, 1999.

———. *Lost Christianities: The Battles for Scripture and the Faiths We Never Knew*. New York: Oxford University Press, 2003.

———. *Lost Scriptures: Books That Did Not Make It into the New Testament*. New York: Oxford University Press, 2003.

Eisenstadt, S. N. "The Axial Age Breakthrough in Ancient Israel." In *The Origins and Diversity of Axial Age Civilizations*, edited by S. N. Eisenstadt, 127–34. Albany: State University of New York Press, 1986.

———. "The Secondary Breakthrough in Ancient Israelite Civilization." In *The Origins and Diversity of Axial Age Civilizations*, edited by S. N. Eisenstadt, 227–51. Albany: State University of New York Press, 1986.

Eisenstadt, S. N., ed. *The Origins and Diversity of Axial Age Civilizations*. Albany: State University of New York Press, 1986.

Elman, Yaakov. "Classical Rabbinic Interpretation." In *The Jewish Study Bible*, edited by Adele Berlin and Marc Zvi Brettler, 1844–63. New York: Oxford University Press, 2004.

Enslin, Morton Scott. *Christian Beginnings: Parts I and II*. New York: Harper, 1956.

Epstein, Isidore. *Judaism: A Historical Presentation*. Hammondsworth, UK: Penguin, 1977.

Evans, Craig A. "Comparing Judaisms: Qumranic, Rabbinic, and Jacobean Judaisms Compared." In *The Brother of Jesus*, edited by Bruce Chilton and Jacob Neusner, 161–83. Louisville: Westminster John Knox, 2001.

———. "Context, Family and Formation." In *The Cambridge Companion to Jesus*, edited by Markus Bockmuehl, 11–24. Cambridge Companions to Religion. Cambridge: Cambridge University Press, 2002.

———. "Qumran's Messiah: How Important Is He?" In *Religion in the Dead Sea Scrolls*, edited by John J. Collins and Robert A. Kugler, 135–49. Grand Rapids, MI: Eerdmans, 2000.

Feldman, Louis H. "Palestinian and Diaspora Judaism in the First Century." In *Christianity and Rabbinic Judaism: A Parallel History of Their Origins and Early Development*, edited by Hershel Shanks, 1–40. Washington, DC: Biblical Archeological Society, 1992.

Finkelstein, Israel, and Neil Asher Silberman. *The Bible Unearthed: Archeology's New Vision of Ancient Israel and the Origin of Its Sacred Texts*. New York: Touchstone, 2002.

Flusser, David, with R. Steven Notley. *The Sage from Galilee: Rediscovering Jesus' Genius*. 1968. Reprint, Grand Rapids, MI: Eerdmans, 2001.

Fohrer, Georg. *Introduction to the Old Testament*. Translated by David E. Green. 1961. Reprint, Nashville: Abingdon, 1968.

Fox, Robin Lane. *The Unauthorized Version: Truth and Fiction in the Bible*. New York: Knopf, 1992.

Frankfort, Henri. *Ancient Egyptian Religion*. New York: Harper, 1961.

Frankfort, H., et al., eds. *Before Philosophy: The Intellectual Adventure of Ancient Man*. Baltimore: Penguin, 1966.

Fredriksen, Paula. *From Jesus to Christ: The Origins of the New Testament Images of Jesus*. New Haven: Yale University Press, 2000.

Bibliography

———. *When Christians Were Jews: The First Generation*. New Haven, CT: Yale University Press, 2018.

Fredriksen, Paula, and Adele Reinhartz, eds. *Jesus, Judaism, and Christian Anti-Judaism: Reading the New Testament after the Holocaust*. Louisville: Westminster John Knox, 2002.

Frei, Hans W. "The 'Literal Reading' of Biblical Narrative in the Christian Tradition: Does It Stretch or Will It Break?" In *The Bible and the Narrative Tradition*, edited by Frank McConnell, 36–77. New York: Oxford University Press, 1986.

Frerichs, Ernest S. "Introduction: The Jewish School of Biblical Studies." In *Judaic Perspectives on Ancient Israel*, edited by Jacob Neusner et al., 1–8. Philadelphia: Fortress, 1987.

Freyne, Sean. *Galilee, Jesus and the Gospels: Literary Approaches and Historical Investigations*. Philadelphia: Fortress, 1988.

———. *Jesus, A Jewish Galilean: A New Reading of the Jesus-Story*. London: T. & T. Clark, 2004.

Friedman, Richard Elliott. "The Hiding of the Face: An Essay on the Literary Unity of Biblical Narrative." In *Judaic Perspectives on Ancient Israel*, edited by Jacob Neusner et al., 207–24. Philadelphia: Fortress, 1987.

———. *Who Wrote the Bible?* New York: Harper & Row, 1989.

Gager, John G. *Kingdom and Community: The Social World of Christianity*. Englewood Cliffs, NJ: Prentice-Hall, 1975.

———. *The Origins of Anti-Semitism: Attitudes Toward Judaism in Pagan and Christian Antiquity*. New York: Oxford University Press, 1985.

Gaster, Theodor H. *The Dead Sea Scriptures: In English Translation*. Garden City, NY: Anchor, 1976.

Geller, Stephen A. "The Religion of the Bible." In *The Jewish Study Bible*, edited by Adele Berlin and Marc Zvi Brettler, 2021–40. New York: Oxford University Press, 2004.

Glatzer, Nahum N. "Foreword." In *The Pharisees*, edited by R. Travors Herford, 1–9. Boston: Beacon, 1962.

Gonzalez, Justo L. *The Story of Christianity*. Vol. 1, *The Early Church to the Dawn of the Reformation*. San Francisco: HarperSanFrancisco, 1984.

Goodman, Martin. *A History of Judaism*. Princeton: Princeton University Press, 2018.

Gorringe, Tim. "Political Readings of Scripture." In *The Cambridge Companion to Biblical Interpretation*, edited by John Barton, 67–80. Cambridge: Cambridge University Press, 1999.

Gottschalk, Alfred. "Prophetic Thinking in the Nonprophetic Society." In *The Life of the Covenant: The Challenge of Contemporary Judaism: Essays in Honor of Herman E. Schaalman*, edited by Joseph Edelheit, 51–60. Chicago: Spertus College of Judaica Press, 1986.

Goulder, Michael. "Jesus, the Man of Universal Destiny." In *The Myth of God Incarnate*, edited by John Hick, 64–86. London: SCM, 1977.

Grabbe, Lester L. *An Introduction to First-Century Judaism*. Edinburgh: T. & T. Clark, 1996.

Grant, Michael. *Jesus: An Historian's Review of the Gospels*. New York: Scribner's, 1977.

Grant, Robert M. *A Historical Introduction to the New Testament*. New York: Harper & Row, 1963.

Gruber, Mayer. "Job: Introduction." In *The Jewish Study Bible*, edited by Adele Berlin and Marc Zvi Brettler, 1499–505. New York: Oxford University Press, 2004.

Guignebert, Charles. *The Jewish World in the Time of Jesus*. New York: University Books, 1959.

Bibliography

Hagner, Donald A. *The Jewish Reclamation of Jesus: An Analysis and Critique of the Modern Jewish Study of Jesus.* Eugene, OR: Wipf & Stock, 1997.

Hamilton, Edith. *Witness to the Truth: Christ and His Interpreters.* New York: Norton, 1957.

Harnack, Adolf. *What Is Christianity?* New York: Harper & Row, 1957.

Harrington, Hannah K. "The Halakah and Religion of Qumran." In *Religion in the Dead Sea Scrolls*, edited by John J. Collins and Robert A. Kugler, 74–89. Grand Rapids, MI: Eerdmans, 2000.

Hengel, Martin. *The Four Gospels and the One Gospel of Jesus Christ.* Harrisburg, PA: Trinity, 2000.

Herford, R. Travers. *The Pharisees.* Boston: Beacon, 1962.

Heschel, Abraham J. *The Prophets: An Introduction.* New York: Harper & Row, 1969.

———. *The Prophets: Volume II.* New York: Harper & Row, 1975.

Herzog, William H., II. *Jesus, Justice, and the Reign of God: A Ministry of Liberation.* Louisville: Westminster John Knox, 2000.

Hick, John, ed. *The Myth of God Incarnate.* London: SCM, 1977.

Hill, Craig C. *Hellenists and Hebrews: Reappraising Division within the Earliest Church.* Minneapolis: Fortress, 1992.

Hoehner, Harold W. "Why Did Pilate Hand Jesus Over to Pilate?" In *The Trial of Jesus: Cambridge Studies in Honour of C. F. D. Moule*, edited by Ernst Bammel, 84–90. Studies in Biblical Theology (Series Two) 13. London: SCM, 1971.

Horsley, Richard A. *Covenant Economics: A Biblical Vision of Justice for All.* Louisville: Westminster John Knox, 2009.

Horsley, Richard A., with John S. Hanson. *Bandits, Prophets & Messiahs: Popular Movements in the Time of Jesus.* Harrisburg, PA: Trinity, 1999.

Horsley, Richard A., and Neil Asher Silberman. *The Message and the Kingdom: How Jesus and Paul Ignited a Revolution and Transformed the Ancient World.* New York: Penguin Putnam, 1997.

Irwin, William A. "The Literature of the Old Testament." In *The Interpreter's Bible*, edited by George Arthur Buttrick, 175–84. New York: Abingdon, 1952.

Jacobsen, Thorkild. "Mesopotamia." In *Before Philosophy: The Intellectual Adventure of Ancient Man*, edited by H. Frankfort et al., 137–236. Baltimore: Penguin, 1966.

Jaher, Frederic Cople. *A Scapegoat in the Wilderness: The Origins and Rise of Anti-Semitism in America.* Cambridge: Harvard University Press, 1994.

Jasper, David. "Literary Readings of the Bible." In *The Cambridge Companion to Biblical Interpretation*, edited by John Barton, 22–34. Cambridge: Cambridge University Press, 1999.

Jeremias, Joachim. *Jerusalem in the Time of Jesus: An Investigation into the Economic and Social Conditions during the New Testament Period.* Philadelphia: Fortress, 1987.

Johnson, Luke Timothy. *Living Jesus: Learning the Heart of the Gospel.* San Francisco: HarperSanFrancisco, 1999.

Johnson, Paul. *Jesus: A Biography from a Believer.* New York: Viking, 2010.

Joyce, Paul. "The Individual and the Community." In *Beginning Old Testament Study*, edited by John Rogerson et al., 77–93.

Kaufmann, Yehezkel. *The Religion of Israel: From Its Beginnings to the Babylonian Exile.* Translated and abridged by Moshe Greenberg. New York: Schocken, 1972.

Kaylor, R. David. *Jesus the Prophet: His Vision of the Kingdom on Earth.* Louisville: Westminster John Knox, 1994.

Bibliography

Keck, Leander E. *Taking the Bible Seriously*. Nashville: Abingdon, 1979.

Kee, Howard Clark. *Medicine, Miracle and Magic in New Testament Times*. New York: Cambridge University Press, 1988.

Kee, Howard Clark, et al. *Understanding the New Testament*. Englewood Cliffs, NJ: Prentice-Hall, 1965.

Kidner, Derek. *An Introduction to Wisdom Literature: The Wisdom of Proverbs, Job & Ecclesiastes*. Leicester, England: InterVarsity, 1985.

Kippenberg, H. B. "The Role of Christianity in the Depolitization of the Roman Empire." In *The Origins and Diversity of Axial Age Civilizations*, edited by S. N. Eisenstadt, 261–79. Albany: State University of New York Press, 1986.

Klein, Charlotte. *Anti-Judaism in Christian Theology*. Philadelphia: Fortress, 1978.

Klingaman, William K. *The First Century: Emperors, Gods, and Everyman*. New York: Harper, 1991.

Koch, Klaus. "Apocalyptic and Eschatology." In *Jesus on His Time*, edited by Hans Jürgen Schultz, 57–65. Philadelphia: Fortress, 1980.

Koester, Helmut. *History, Culture, and Religion of the Hellenistic Age*. New York: de Gruyter, 1987.

Kugel, James L. *The Bible as It Was*. Cambridge: Belknap, 2001.

———. *The Great Shift: Encountering God in Biblical Times*. Boston: Mariner, 2018.

———. *How to Read the Bible: A Guide to Scripture, Then and Now*. New York: Free Press, 2008.

Kugler, Robert A. "Rewriting Rubrics: Sacrifice and the Religion of Qumran." In *Religion in the Dead Sea Scrolls*, edited by John J. Collins and Robert A. Kugler, 90–112. Grand Rapids, MI: Eerdmans, 2000.

Kung, Hans. *Judaism: Between Yesterday and Tomorrow*. New York: Crossroad, 1992.

Lace, O. Jesse. "What the New Testament Is About." In *Understanding the New Testament*, edited by O. Jesse Lace, 145–63. New York: Cambridge University Press, 1965.

Lace, O. Jesse, ed. *Understanding the New Testament*. New York: Cambridge University Press, 1965.

LaCocque, Andre. *Jesus the Central Jew: His Time and His People*. Atlanta: SBL, 2015.

———. "Torah—Nomos." In *The Life of the Covenant: The Challenge of Contemporary Judaism: Essays in Honor of Herman E. Schaalman*, edited by Joseph Edelheit, 85–96. Chicago: Spertus College of Judaica Press, 1986.

Langmuir, Gavin I. *History, Religion, and Antisemitism*. Berkeley: University of California Press, 1990.

Latourette, Kenneth Scott. *A History of Christianity*. Vol. 1, *Beginnings to 1500*. San Francisco: HarperSanFrancisco, 1975.

Lee, Bernard J. *The Galilean Jewishness of Jesus: Retrieving the Jewish Origins of Christianity*. New York: Paulist, 1988.

Levenson, David B. "Messianic Movements." In *The Jewish Annotated New Testament*, edited by Amy-Jill Levine and Marc Zvi Brettler, 530–35. New York: Oxford University Press, 2011.

Levenson, Jon D. *The Hebrew Bible, the Old Testament, and Historical Criticism*. Louisville: Westminster John Knox, 1993.

———. *The Love of God: Divine Gift, Human Gratitude, and Mutual Faithfulness in Judaism*. Princeton: Princeton University Press, 2016.

Bibliography

Levine, Amy-Jill. "Bearing False Witness: Common Errors Made about Early Judaism." In *The Jewish Annotated New Testament*, edited by Amy-Jill Levine and Marc Zvi Brettler, 501–4. New York: Oxford University Press, 2011.

———. *The Misunderstood Jew: The Church and the Scandal of the Jewish Jesus*. San Francisco: HarperSanFrancisco, 2006.

Levine, Amy-Jill, and Marc Zvi Brettler. *The Jewish Annotated New Testament*. New York: Oxford University Press, 2011.

Levine, Amy-Jill, et al. *The Historical Jesus in Context*. Princeton Readings in Religions. Princeton, NJ: Princeton University Press, 2006.

Levine, Baruch A. "The Epilogue to the Holiness Code: A Priestly Statement on the Destiny of Israel." In *Judaic Perspectives on Ancient Israel*, edited by Jacob Neusner et al., 9–34. Philadelphia: Fortress, 1987.

Levine, Lee I. E. "Judaism from the Destruction of Jerusalem to the End of the Second Jewish Revolt: 70–135 C.E." In *Christianity and Rabbinic Judaism: A Parallel History of Their Origins and Early Development*, edited by Hershel Shanks, 125–50. Washington, DC: Biblical Archeological Society, 1992.

Levy, Thomas, ed. *The Archeology of Society in the Holy Land*. London: Cassell, 1998.

Liebman, Sheldon W. *The Great Betrayal: Christians and Jews in the First Four Centuries*. Eugene, OR: Wipf & Stock, 2018.

Lieu, Judith M. *Image and Reality: The Jews in the World of the Christians in the Second Century*. London: T. & T. Clark, 2003.

Lovejoy, A. O. "The Communism of St. Ambrose." In *Essays in the History of Ideas*, 296–307. New York: Braziller, 1955.

———. *Essays in the History of Ideas*. New York: Braziller, 1955.

Maccoby, Hyam. *The Mythmaker: Pail and the Invention of Christianity*. New York: Barnes & Noble, 1998.

MacCulloch, Diarmaid. *Silence: A Christian History*. New York: Viking, 2013.

Machinist, Peter. "Ecclesiastes: Introduction." In *The Jewish Study Bible*, edited by Adele Berlin and Marc Zvi Brettler, 1603–22. New York: Oxford University Press, 2004.

Mack, Burton L. *The Lost Gospel: The Book of Q & Christian Origins*. San Francisco: HarperSanFrancisco, 1994.

———. *Who Wrote the New Testament? The Making of the Christian Myth*. San Francisco: HarperSanFrancisco, 1995.

MacMullen, Ramsay. *Christianizing the Roman Empire (A.D. 100–400)*. New Haven: Yale University Press, 1984.

Maguire, Daniel C. *The Moral Core of Judaism and Christianity: Reclaiming the Revolution*. Minneapolis: Fortress, 1993.

Manschreck, Clyde L. *A History of Christianity in the World: From Persecution to Uncertainty*. Englewood Cliffs, NJ: Prentice-Hall, 1974.

Markus, R. A. *Christianity in the Roman World*. New York: Scribner's, 1974.

Marty, Martin. *The Christian World: A Global History*. New York: Modern Library, 2009.

Mattingly, Harold. *Roman Imperial Civilisation*. New York: Norton, 1971.

May, Herbert G., and Bruce M. Metzger, eds. *The Oxford Annotated Bible*. New York: Oxford University Press, 1962.

McConnell, Frank. "Introduction." In *The Bible and the Narrative Tradition*, edited by Frank McConnell, 3–18. New York: Oxford University Press, 1986.

Bibliography

McConnell, Frank, ed. *The Bible and the Narrative Tradition*. New York: Oxford University Press, 1986.

McKenzie, John L. *The New Testament without Illusion*. New York: Crossroad, 1982.

———. *The Old Testament Without Illusion*. Chicago: More, 1979.

Meek, Theophile James. *Hebrew Origins*. New York: Harper, 1960.

Meeks, Wayne A. *The Origins of Christian Morality: The First Two Centuries*. New Haven: Yale University Press, 1993.

Meier, John P. *A Marginal Jew*. Vol. 1, *Rethinking the Historical Jesus*. New York: Doubleday, 1991.

———. *A Marginal Jew*. Vol. 3, *Rethinking the Historical Jesus*. New York: Doubleday, 2001.

Metzger, Bruce M., and Roland E. Murphy. *The New Annotated Oxford Bible*. New York: Oxford University Press, 1994.

Meyer, Ben F. *The Aims of Jesus*. San Jose: Pickwick, 2002.

Milavec, Aaron. *The Didache: Text, Translation, Analysis, and Commentary*. Collegeville, MN: Liturgical, 2003.

Miles, Jack. *God: A Biography*. New York: Vintage, 1996.

Miller, Patrick D. *The Religion of Ancient Israel*. Louisville: Westminster John Knox, 2000.

Moltmann, Jürgen. *The Crucified God: The Cross of Christ as the Foundation and Criticism of Christian Theology*. Minneapolis: Fortress, 1993.

Moore, George Foot. *Judaism in the First Centuries of the Christian Era: The Age of the Tannaim*. 3 vols. Cambridge: Harvard University Press, 1958.

Morgan, Robert. "A Concluding Unscientific Postscript to Historical Research on the Trial of Jesus." In *The Trial of Jesus: Cambridge Studies in Honour of C. F. D. Moule*, edited by Ernst Bammel, 133–46. Studies in Biblical Theology (Series Two) 13. London: SCM, 1971.

Moule, C. F. D. *The Birth of the New Testament*. New York: Harper & Row, 1962.

———. "How the New Testament Came into Being." In *Understanding the New Testament*, edited by O. Jesse Lace, 64–120. New York: Cambridge University Press, 1965.

Moyise, Steve. *Jesus and Scripture: Studying the New Testament Use of the Old Testament*. Grand Rapids, MI: Baker Academics, 2011.

Muilenburg, James. "The History of the Religion of Israel." In *The Interpreter's Bible*, edited by George Arthur Buttrick, 292–348. New York: Abingdon, 1952.

Mussner, Franz. *Tractate on the Jews: The Significance of Judaism for Christian Faith*. Philadelphia: Fortress, 1984.

Neusner, Jacob. *From Politics to Piety: The Emergence of Pharisaic Judaism*. Englewood Cliffs, NJ: Prentice-Hall, 1973.

———. *Judaism in the Beginning of Christianity*. Philadelphia: Fortress, 1984.

———. *The Mishnah: Social Perspectives*. Boston: Brill, 2002.

———. *The Talmud: A Close Encounter*. Eugene, OR: Wipf & Stock, 2004.

———. *The Way of Torah: An Introduction to Judaism*. Encino, CA: Dickenson, 1974.

Neusner, Jacob, et al., eds. *Judaic Perspectives on Ancient Israel*. Philadelphia: Fortress, 1987.

Newsome, James D., Jr. *The Hebrew Prophets*. Atlanta: John Knox, 1984.

Niditch, Susan. *Ancient Israelite Religion*. New York: Oxford University Press, 1997.

Nineham, Dennis. *The Gospel of Mark*. Baltimore: Penguin, 1967.

Nolan, Albert. *Jesus before Christianity*. Maryknoll, NY: Orbis, 1998.

Oesterley, W. O. E., and Theodore H. Robinson. *An Introduction to the Books of the Old Testament*. New York: Meridian, 1960.

Bibliography

Olivelle, Patrick. "Introduction." In *Upanishads*, xxiii–lvi. Oxford World Classics. Oxford: Oxford University Press, 1996.

Olson, Bernhard E. *Faith and Prejudice: Intergroup Problems in Protestant Curricula*. New Haven: Yale University Press, 1963.

O'Neill, J. C. "The Charge of Blasphemy at Jesus' Trial Before the Sanhedrin." In *The Trial of Jesus: Cambridge Studies in Honour of C. F. D. Moule*, edited by Ernst Bammel, 72–77. Studies in Biblical Theology (Series Two) 13. London: SCM, 1971.

Pagels, Elaine. *The Origin of Satan*. New York: Vintage, 1996.

Paget, James Carleton. "Quests for the Historical Jesus." In *The Cambridge Companion to Jesus*, edited by Markus Bockmuehl, 138–55. Cambridge Companions to Religion. Cambridge: Cambridge University Press, 2002.

Parini, Jay. *Jesus: The Human Face of God*. Boston: New Harvest, 2013.

Parkes, James W. *The Conflict of the Church and the Synagogue: A Study in the Origins of Anti-Semitism*. New York: Hermon, 1974.

Pawlikowski, John T. "The Jewish Covenant: Its Continuing Challenge for Christian Faith." In *The Life of the Covenant: The Challenge of Contemporary Judaism: Essays in Honor of Herman E. Schaalman*, edited by Joseph Edelheit, 114–17. Chicago: Spertus College of Judaica Press, 1986.

Pelikan, Jaroslav. *Jesus through the Centuries: His Place in the History of Culture*. New York: Harper & Row, 1987.

Perkins, Pheme. *Reading the New Testament: An Introduction*. New York: Paulist, 1988.

Perrin, Norman. *Rediscovering the Teachings of Jesus*. New York: Harper & Row, 1967.

Perrin, Norman, and Dennis C. Duling. *The New Testament: An Introduction*. San Diego: Harcourt Brace Jovanovich, 1982.

Peters, F. E. *The Harvest of Hellenism: A History of the Near East from Alexander the Great to the Triumph of Christianity*. New York: Simon & Schuster, 1970.

Pfeiffer, Robert H. "The Literature and Religion of the Apocrypha." In *The Interpreter's Bible*, edited by George Arthur Buttrick, 391–419. New York: Abingdon, 1952.

Placher, William C. *A History of Christian Theology: An Introduction*. Philadelphia: Westminster, 1983.

Powell, Mark Allan. *Jesus as a Figure in History*. Louisville: Westminster John Knox, 1998.

Provan, Iain. "The Historical Books of the Old Testament." In *The Cambridge Companion to Biblical Interpretation*, edited by John Barton, 198–211. Cambridge: Cambridge University Press, 1999.

Ramsay, William M. *The Westminster Guide to the Books of the Bible*. Louisville: Westminster John Knox, 1994.

Redford, Donald B. *Egypt, Canaan, and Israel in Ancient Times*. Princeton, NJ: Princeton University Press, 1992.

Reicke, Bo. "Galilee and Judea." In *Jesus on His Time*, edited by Hans Jürgen Schultz, 28–35. Philadelphia: Fortress, 1980.

———. *The New Testament Era: The World of the Bible from 500 B.C. to A.D. 100*. Translated by David E. Green. Philadelphia: Fortress, 1968.

Reif, Stefan C. "Aspects of the Jewish Contribution to Biblical Interpretation." In *The Cambridge Companion to Biblical Interpretation*, edited by John Barton, 143–59. Cambridge: Cambridge University Press, 1999.

Richardson, Alan. *The Gospel According to Saint John: A Commentary*. New York: Collier, 1962.

Bibliography

Richardson, Peter. "The Israel-Idea in the Passion Narratives." In *The Trial of Jesus: Cambridge Studies in Honour of C. F. D. Moule*, edited by Ernst Bammel, 2–10. Studies in Biblical Theology (Series Two) 13. London: SCM, 1971.

Riches, John. *Jesus and the Transformation of Judaism*. New York: Seabury, 1982.

Rivkin, Ellis. *A Hidden Revolution*. Nashville: Abingdon, 1978.

———. "The Revealing and Concealing God of Israel and Humankind." In *The Life of the Covenant: The Challenge of Contemporary Judaism: Essays in Honor of Herman E. Schaalman*, edited by Joseph Edelheit, 155–71. Chicago: Spertus College of Judaica Press, 1986.

Robinson, James M. *The Gospel of Jesus: A Historical Search for the Original Good News*. San Francisco: HarperSanFrancisco, 2006.

Robinson, Theodore H. "The History of Israel." In *The Interpreter's Bible*, edited by George Arthur Buttrick, 272–91. New York: Abingdon, 1952.

Rogerson, John. "Old Testament History and the History of Israel." In *Beginning Old Testament Study*, edited by John Rogerson et al., 49–57.

———. "An Outline of the History of Old Testament Study." In *Beginning Old Testament Study*, edited by John Rogerson et al., 6–24.

———. "The World-View of the Old Testament." In *Beginning Old Testament Study*, edited by John Rogerson et al., 58–76.

Ruether, Rosemary R. *Faith and Fratricide: The Theological Roots of Anti-Semitism*. Eugene, OR: Wipf & Stock, 1997.

Russell, D. S. *Between the Testaments*. Philadelphia: Fortress, 1968.

Saldarini, Anthony J. *Pharisees, Scribes and Sadducees in Palestinian Society: A Sociological Approach*. Grand Rapids, MI: Eerdmans, 2001.

Sanders, E. P. *The Historical Figure of Jesus*. London: Penguin, 1995.

———. *Jesus and Judaism*. Philadelphia: Fortress, 1985.

———. "Jesus, Ancient Judaism, and Modern Christianity: The Quest Continues." In *Jesus, Judaism, and Christian Anti-Judaism: Reading the New Testament after the Holocaust*, edited by Paula Fredriksen and Adele Reinhartz, 31–55. Louisville: Westminster John Knox, 2002.

———. *Judaism: Practice and Belief, 63 BCE–66 CE*. London: SCM, 1994.

———. "The Life of Jesus." In *Christianity and Rabbinic Judaism: A Parallel History of Their Origins and Early Development*, edited by Hershel Shanks, 41–84. Washington, DC: Biblical Archeological Society, 1992.

Sanders, Jack T. *The Jews in Luke–Acts*. London: SCM, 1987.

———. *Schismatics, Sectarians, Dissidents, Deviants: The First One Hundred Years of Jewish-Christian Relations*. Valley Forge, PA: Trinity, 1993.

Sandmel, Samuel. *A Jewish Understanding of the New Testament*. New York: Ktav, 1974.

Schalit, Abraham. "Herod and His Successors." In *Jesus on His Time*, edited by Hans Jürgen Schultz, 36–46. Philadelphia: Fortress, 1980.

———. "Palestine under the Seleucids and Romans." In *The Crucible of Christianity: Judaism, Hellenism and the Historical Background to the Christian Faith*, edited by Arnold Toynbee, 47–76. New York: World, 1969.

Schiffman, Lawrence H. *From Text to Tradition: A History of Second Temple and Rabbinic Judaism*. Hoboken, NJ: Ktav, 1991.

Schillebeeckx, Edward. *Jesus: An Experiment in Christology*. New York: Crossroad, 1989.

Schmidt, Werner H. *Old Testament Introduction*. New York: Crossroad, 1990.

Bibliography

Schubert, Kurt. "Jewish Religious Parties and Sects." In *The Crucible of Christianity: Judaism, Hellenism and the Historical Background to the Christian Faith*, edited by Arnold Toynbee, 87–98. New York: World, 1969.

Schultz, Hans Jürgen, ed. *Jesus in His Time*. Philadelphia: Fortress, 1980.

Schweitzer, Albert. *The Quest of the Historical Jesus*. New York: Collier, 1968.

Segal, Alan F. *Rebecca's Children: Judaism and Christianity in the Roman World*. Cambridge: Harvard University Press, 1986.

Senior, Donald. *Jesus: A Gospel Portrait*. New York: Paulist, 1992.

Shanks, Herschel, and Ben Witherington III. *The Brother of Jesus: The Dramatic Story and Meaning of the First Archeological Link to Jesus and His Family*. San Francisco: HarperSanFrancisco, 2003.

Shanks, Hershel, ed. *Christianity and Rabbinic Judaism: A Parallel History of Their Origins and Early Development*. Washington, DC: Biblical Archeological Society, 1992.

Sheehan, Thomas. *The First Coming: How the Kingdom of God Became Christianity*. New York: Dorset, 1986.

Simpson, Cuthbert A. "The Growth of the Hexateuch." In *The Interpreter's Bible*, edited by George Arthur Buttrick, 185–200. New York: Abingdon, 1952.

Smallwood, E. Mary. *The Jews under Roman Rule from Pompey to Diocletian*. Leiden: Brill, 1981.

Smith, Mark S. *The Early History of God: Yahweh and the Other Deities in Ancient Israel*. 2nd ed. Grand Rapids, MI: Eerdmans, 2002.

Smith, Morton. *Jesus the Magician*. New York: Barnes and Noble, 1993.

Soares, Theodore Gerald. *The Social Institutions and Ideals of the Bible*. New York: Abingdon, 1915.

Sperling, S. David. "Judaism and Modern Biblical Research." In *Biblical Studies: Meeting Ground of Jews and Christians*, edited by Lawrence Boadt et al., 19–44. Studies in Judaism and Christianity: Exploration of Issues in the Contemporary Dialogue between Christians and Jesus. New York: Paulist, 1980.

Spong, John Shelby. *Liberating the Gospels: Reading the Bible with Jewish Eyes*. San Francisco: HarperSanFrancisco, 1996.

Stark, Rodney. *The Rise of Christianity*. San Francisco: HarperSanFrancisco, 1997.

Stegemann, Ekkehard W., and Wolfgang Stegemann. *The Jesus Movement: A Social History of Its First Century*. Minneapolis: Fortress, 1999.

Steinsaltz, Adin. *The Essential Talmud*. Translated by Chaya Galai. New York: Basic Books, 1976.

Sterling, Gregory E. "Philo of Alexandria." In *The Historical Jesus in Context*, by Amy-Jill Levine et al., 296–308. Princeton Readings in Religions. Princeton, NJ: Princeton University Press, 2006.

Stern, David. "Midrash and Jewish Interpretation." In *The Jewish Study Bible*, edited by Adele Berlin and Marc Zvi Brettler, 1863–75. New York: Oxford University Press, 2004.

Stone, Michael E. "Eschatology, Remythologization and Cosmic Aporia." In *The Origins and Diversity of Axial Age Civilizations*, edited by S. N. Eisenstadt, 241–51. Albany: State University of New York Press, 1986.

Stroumsa, Gedaliahu. "Old Wine and New Bottles: On Patristic Soteriology and Rabbinic Judaism." In *The Origins and Diversity of Axial Age Civilizations*, edited by S. N. Eisenstadt, 252–60. Albany: State University of New York Press, 1986.

Tabor, James D. *The Jesus Dynasty: The Hidden History of Jesus, His Royal Family, and the Birth of Christianity*. New York: Simon & Schuster, 2006.

Bibliography

Tenney, Merrill C. *New Testament Survey*. Grand Rapids, MI: Eerdmans, 1983.

Theissen, Gerd. *Sociology of Early Palestinian Christianity*. Translated by John Bowden. Philadelphia: Fortress, 1989.

Thoma, Clemens. *A Christian Theology of Judaism*. New York: Paulist, 1980.

Thompson, William M. *The Jesus Debate: A Survey and Synthesis*. New York: Paulist: 1985.

Toynbee, Arnold, ed. *The Crucible of Christianity: Judaism, Hellenism and the Historical Background to the Christian Faith*. New York: World, 1969.

———. "Introduction." In *The Crucible of Christianity: Judaism, Hellenism and the Historical Background to the Christian Faith*, edited by Arnold Toynbee, 9–17. New York: World, 1969.

———. "The Mediterranean World's Age of Agony." In *The Crucible of Christianity: Judaism, Hellenism and the Historical Background to the Christian Faith*, edited by Arnold Toynbee, 19–46. New York: World, 1969.

Tullock, John H. *The Old Testament Story*. Upper Saddle River, NJ: Prentice Hall, 1999.

Tyson, Joseph B. *A Study of Early Christianity*. New York: Macmillan, 1973.

Uffenheimer, Benjamin. "Myth and Reality in Ancient Israel." In *The Origins and Diversity of Axial Age Civilizations*, edited by S. N. Eisenstadt, 135–68. Albany: State University of New York Press, 1986.

Umen, Samuel. *Pharisaism and Jesus*. New York: Philosophical Library, 1963.

VanderKam, James C. "Apocalyptic Tradition in the Dead Sea Scrolls and the Religion of Qumran." In *Religion in the Dead Sea Scrolls*, edited by John J. Collins and Robert A. Kugler, 113–34. Grand Rapids, MI: Eerdmans, 2000.

Van Leeuwen, Arend Theodoor. *Christianity in World History: The Meeting of the Faiths of East and West*. New York: Scribner's, 1964.

Vermes, Geza. *The Changing Faces of Jesus*. New York: Penguin, 2002.

———. *The Dead Sea Scrolls in English*. Hammondsworth, UK: Penguin, 1973.

———. *Jesus in His Jewish Context*. London: SCM, 2003.

———. *Jesus the Jew: A Historian's Reading of the Gospels*. Philadelphia: Fortress, 1981.

———. "Introduction." In *Christianity and Rabbinic Judaism: A Parallel History of Their Origins and Early Development*, edited by Hershel Shanks, xvii–xxii. Washington, DC: Biblical Archeological Society, 1992.

Vogt, Joseph. "Augustus and Tiberius." In *Jesus on His Time*, edited by Hans Jürgen Schultz, 1–9. Philadelphia: Fortress, 1980.

Von Rad, Gerhard. *Old Testament Theology*. Translated by D. M. G. Stalker. 2 vols. New York: Harper & Row, 1962, 1965.

Weinfeld, Moshe. "Protest against Imperialism in Ancient Israelite Prophecy." In *The Origins and Diversity of Axial Age Civilizations*, edited by S. N. Eisenstadt, 169–82. Albany: State University of New York Press, 1986..

Werner, Martin. *The Formation of Christian Dogma: A Historical Study of Its Problem*. Translated by S. G. F. Btandon. Boston: Beacon, 1965.

White, J. E. Manchip. *Ancient Egypt: Its Culture and History*. New York: Dover, 1970.

White, L. Michael. *From Jesus to Christianity*. San Francisco: HarperSanFrancisco, 2004.

Wilken, Robert L. *The Christians as the Romans Saw Them*. New Haven: Yale University Press, 1984.

———. *The First Thousand Years: A Global History of Christianity*. New Haven: Yale University Press, 2012.

Wills, Lawrence M. "Daniel: Introduction." In *The Jewish Study Bible*, edited by Adele Berlin and Marc Zvi Brettler, 1640–65. New York: Oxford University Press, 2004.

Bibliography

Wilson, A. N. *Jesus: A Life*. New York: Ballantine, 1993.

Wilson, John A. "Egypt." In *Before Philosophy: The Intellectual Adventure of Ancient Man*, edited by H. Frankfort et al., 39–136. Baltimore: Penguin, 1966.

Wilson, Robert R. "The Prophetic Books." In *The Cambridge Companion to Biblical Interpretation*, edited by John Barton, 212–25. Cambridge: Cambridge University Press, 1999.

Winter, Paul. "Sadducees and Pharisees." In *Jesus on His Time*, edited by Hans Jürgen Schultz, 47–56. Philadelphia: Fortress, 1980.

Witherington, Ben, III. *Jesus, Paul, and the End of the World: A Comparative Study of New Testament Eschatology*. Downers Grove, IL: InterVarsity, 1992.

———. *The Jesus Quest*. Downers Grove, IL: InterVarsity, 1997.

———. *What Have They Done with Jesus?* San Francisco: HarperSanFrancisco, 2006.

Wright, G. Ernest. "The Faith of Israel." In *The Interpreter's Bible*, edited by George Arthur Buttrick, 349–90. New York: Abingdon, 1952.

Wright, G. Ernest, and Reginald H. Fuller. *The Book of the Acts of God: Contemporary Scholarship Interprets the Bible*. Garden City, NY: Doubleday, 1960.

Wright, N. T. *Simply Christian: Why Christianity Makes Sense*. San Francisco: HarperSanFrancisco, 2006.

———. *Simply Jesus: A New Vision of Who He Was, What He Did, and Why He Matters*. San Francisco: HarperSanFrancisco, 2011.

———. *What Saint Paul Really Said: Was Paul of Tarsus the Real Founder of Christianity*. Grand Rapids, MI: Eerdmans, 1997.

Wright, Robert. *The Evolution of God*. New York: Little, Brown, 2009.

Wylen, Stephen M. *The Jews in the Time of Jesus: An Introduction*. New York: Paulist, 1996.

Yoder, John Howard. *The Politics of Jesus*. Grand Rapids, MI: Eerdmans, 1978.

Zannoni, Arthur E. *Jesus of the Gospels: Teacher, Storyteller, Friend, Messiah*. Eugene, OR: Wipf & Stock, 2008.

Zeitlin, Irving M. *Jesus and the Judaism of His Time*. Cambridge: Polity, 1989.

Zeitlin, Solomon. *Who Crucified Jesus?* 5th ed. New York: Bloch, 1964.

www.ingramcontent.com/pod-product-compliance
Lightning Source LLC
Chambersburg PA
CBHW080531300426
44111CB00017B/2675